Mind, Body, Soul and Spirit in Transactional Analysis: an Integral Approach to Relationships

Gordon Law

First published 2006 by IMPACT
5 Bawdsey Avenue Malvern WR14 2EW
www.impact-uk.org

Copyright © Gordon Law 2006

Cover Design by Gordon Law.
Manufactured in Great Britain by Lionel Parker Print Services Ltd., Wellingborough, NN8 3PJ
www.llpsltd.co.uk

British Library Cataloguing-in-Publication Data
A catalogue record for this book is available from the British Library.

ISBN 978-0-9552287-0-4

Contents

v   **Acknowledgements**

vi   **Foreword**

viii   **Preface**

Part One - Themes

1/1   **An integral approach to relationships**

2/5   **Tensions and divides**

3/26   **Beyond the divides**

Part Two - Preamble

4/36   **Basic concepts**

5/43   **ERICA - an overview**

6/58   **A framework for describing relationships**

7/67   **Rationale for using roles, imagos and contact**

Part Three - Model One

8/75   **The Contact Cube**

9/110   **Second order analysis**

10/119   **Working at three levels**

11/139   **Adding formalised roles**

12/165   **Adding situational roles**

Part Four – Model Two

13/**177**   Role sequences

14/**201**   Role imago repertoires

Part Five – Model Three

15/**214**   Role imago templates

16/**227**   Identifying imago images and qualities of contact

17/**232**   ERICA with individual clients

18/**264**   Reflections

Part Six - Synthesis

19/**272**   The transpersonal dimension

20/**281**   The spectrum of consciousness

21/**293**   Witnessing, the self and the Observer self

22/**300**   People have bodies - and shadows

23/**321**   The Observer role

24/**332**   Coda

Appendices

AA/**338**   Structure of the Contact Cube

AB/**342**   Spiral dynamics

AC/**348**   Role Sequences - Examples

R/**359**   References

AI/**373**   Author Index

SI/**377**   Subject Index

Acknowledgements

My thanks to my family, colleagues and friends who supported, encouraged and inspired my efforts over the time it has taken to write this book. I am especially grateful to my wife Cally and children for their forbearance in tolerating the many hours of my "playing on the 'puter" – a task thankfully shortened by Ali and Beth's periodic quick fingered assistance.

I am particularly indebted to Ken Mellor for all he has unwittingly taught me by way of modelling positive roles and for all that I have imbibed meditatively under guidance from him and Elizabeth Mellor over many years.

I have also benefited from the encouragement and support of Nancy Porter-Steele and James Allen, each of whom generously contributed their time and commendations. My thanks go also to Andrew Samuels, John Rowan and Gianpiero Petriglieri for their review comments.

I also wish to acknowledge the collegial discussion of theory and practice I enjoyed with Diane Salters, Valerie Heppel and Robin Hobbes and to thank them, Jenni Hine, Susannah Temple, Anita Mountain, Georgia Lepper and Elizabeth Leiper for their readings of and suggestions on various drafts of my work.

I am particularly grateful to Mary Tweed, Gill Miller and especially, Vaughan Malcolm for their unstinting proof reading labours and to Sue Wells for editorial comment. Indeed, without their help and encouragement the book would have been of considerably lesser quality.

New technology and the advent of self-publishing shed a new light on an authors' task. Without the technical expertise of my computer-genius son Owen, the hardware would have died several times during production. Chris Goodrich's generous support, advice and resolution of software glitches are likewise greatly appreciated.

I also want to thank all those who contributed less directly yet most importantly, often without realising they were doing so. They include my trainers, therapists, colleagues, trainees and, above all, clients who taught me lessons that took me years to understand and appreciate.

My thanks, too, to the following publishers and authors for permission to quote:

From *Spiral Dynamics* by Donald Beck and Christopher Cowan, Copyright © 2000. Used by permission. Blackwell Publishing, www.blackwellpublishing.com

From *TA Today* by Ian Stewart and Vann Joines, Copyright © 1987. Used by permission of the authors.

From *Ken Wilber* by Frank Visser, Copyright © 2003. Reprinted by arrangement with the author, www.worldofkenwilber.com

From *Eye to Eye* by Ken Wilber, Copyright © 1983. Used by permission. All rights reserved.

From *Integral Psychology* by Ken Wilber, Copyright © 2000. Reprinted by arrangement with Shambhala Publications, Inc., Boston, www.shambhala.com

From *A theory of everything* by Ken Wilber, Copyright © 2001. Reprinted by arrangement with Shambhala Publications, Inc., Boston, www.shambhala.com

Forewords

What a pleasure it is to write an introduction to this book – and what a pleasure it has been to read it for it is filled with sparkling ideas and enticing syntheses.

Gordon Law is one of the theoreticians and practitioners currently expanding our understandings of and our approaches to transactional analysis. In an engaging manner, he presents a method of analyzing relationships between people in a way that links roles, imago images, and existential positions, and describes how to exercise conscious choice over them.

To this end, he presents three models that are truly generative: the contact cube, role sequencing, and the role imago template. The contact cube is a way to profile the roles of a single person. Role sequencing is a way to describe interactions between two or more people. The role imago template is a heuristic device to describe the contexts in which significant events occur. These three models facilitate structured observation, enhance capacity for self-awareness, and present a framework for research, while also allowing the exercise of the widely differing preferences in techniques, skills, and purposes that characterize transactional analysis today.

This is a scholarly work but it is also practical. Each chapter begins with a clear statement of the material to be covered, and ends with a list of key points. I especially appreciated the bridges Law makes between health and pathology, theory and research, and the different flavors of transactional analysis, as well as his emphasis on the contractual commitment of clients' researching their own behavior. For those studying at home, he has useful sections on self-supervision.

This is a book filled with sparkling ideas and enticing ways of reconceptualizing current practices. It bridges divides within transactional analysis and between it and other approaches. It encompasses topics which are usually not covered in more traditional works on the subject such as consciousness, altered states, body work, grounding, centering, witnessing and memes. In short, it lifts transactional analysis to a whole new level. Best of all, Law does all this in a clearly practical way.

Whether psychotherapist, counselor, educator, or organizational consultant, you will find this a significant contribution!

James R. Allen, M.D., F.R.C.P.(C.).
Professor of Psychiatry and Behavioral Sciences, University of Oklahoma Health Sciences Center, Oklahoma City, and President, International Transactional Analysis Association, 2005.

This book speaks with the voice of extensive experience, with maturity of perception and with breadth of vision – a wonderful combination indeed.

Gordon Law is clearly a man of powerful, integrative and encompassing intelligence. His book is saturated with these qualities and is a pleasure to read. Throughout, he takes us on a stimulating journey into new realms of human understanding with a clarity and command that is impressive. Some ideas are well established in transactional analysis or elsewhere, some are innovative combinations of these, and some are substantially new. All are presented with a fluency and warmth that makes the reading a pleasure and fosters a desire to keep on going.

In places, the content is easy and I romped along enjoying Gordon's obvious mastery of what he describes. In other places, where the content is complex, even daunting in its complexity, his systematic and simple ways of putting things enable the persistent reader to come to grips with what he presents. The exercises he offers at the end of each chapter are creative aids to this learning. All through, too, he adds richness and profundity to his own ideas by the way he frames and respectfully presents the work of others as it bears on his own.

Gordon's identification of the Observer Role as a dynamic balancing process between, on the one hand, openness, awareness and personal evolution and, on the other, contraction, discounting and stagnation, is particularly intriguing. All of this has strong echoes of Eric Berne's ideas on autonomy and mental health, and takes the reader further than he did. I imagine many people will understand the value of learning to live in the Observer Role. Predictably, not content simply to point out the value of something, Gordon also presents us with a way of learning how to live the dynamic processes outlined.

He presents four 'meditational' techniques for doing this learning. Although not presented as such, each of the four processes is a high-level spiritual practice that has been developed and used in "spiritual contexts" for thousands of years in one form or another. There they were and are used to promote ease of living in everyday life and the profound awakening of each person to body, mind, soul and spirit. So it is of great significance here that this sequence and its integration into Gordon's approach, brings powerful spiritual practices into everyday use, and makes available significant aspects of the advantages of these to people using TA and related personal change technologies. His work will help to expand on this hitherto under developed aspect of TA.

It is while in the Observer Role that people are aware of the full range of options available to them. They can at these times experience great stability in their capacity to make decisions without being pulled back into or actively re-entering more contracted, less helpful patterns of living. In the Observer Role, Gordon convincingly argues, people can progress from each stage of development to the next in ways that integrate where they have been into the much broader wholeness of where they will be in the next stages.

This work will be a great asset to any training program that aims to impart practical ways of understanding and influencing people. It is an example of rigorous thinking, the innovative development of ideas, the skilful presentation of other people's work, and the masterful management of many different concepts and themes in a way that enables the reader to keep an overview as the detail is discussed. It is also an example of how spiritual dimensions can inform and enrich, even encompass, what people learn and understand in other aspects of life.

Ken Mellor, CTA and TSTA
Co-founder of Biame Network and a meditation teacher, master and mentor.

Preface

I have written this book primarily for transactional analysis trainers, researchers, practitioners, and advanced trainees with an interest in learning fresh ideas about relationships and new ways of working with clients. However, you will find that the book is as much about integrative psychotherapy in that it is an integration of transactional analysis, cognitive analytic therapy, cognitive behavioural therapy and transpersonal psychology. There is also wider remit – beyond psychotherapy. Those of you with an interest in the application of transactional analysis in organisations and educational settings will also find the book relevant.

And there is more. I explore the potential of TA theory to incorporate aspects of consciousness alluded to, but not extensively explored in the transactional analysis literature.

Hopefully, the above topics not only will take readers beyond what I perceive as three divides in transactional analysis, but also inform and encourage the interest of a wider readership among the person professions. Partly out of consideration for non-TA readers, the style of writing is "academic", inasmuch as I use the convention of citing references not only to support and illustrate concepts or ideas with which most transactional analysis readers are familiar, but also, to encourage a research-oriented mind set.

Themes

I was introduced to transactional analysis thirty four years ago. I took to it with an enthusiasm that I have maintained ever since. At about the same time I came across meditation as a form of personal and spiritual growth. As I became increasingly immersed in both these disciplines, I found that they were gradually coalescing. The synthesis of these two themes is relationships.

By definition, relationships signify a connection – a connection between mind, body, soul and spirit, between self and others, between one relationship and another, between networks of relationships and between networks of networks. And all this occurs in a context. Contexts vary over time, and according to the commitment of those involved in the relationships. As I perceive it, part of the context is that there is what I regard as divides or divisions within the transactional analysis community that interfere with relationships – both personal and professional.

I see three endemic divides in the international transactional analysis community. There is the divide between health and psychopathology, a divide between theory and research and a divide that represents a combination of and continuation of the first two.

Writing this book signifies my commitment to contributing to bridging these divides by detailing a way of using transactional analysis to understand better and improve relationships with individuals, in groups and in organisations. As a psychotherapist, my primary professional commitment is to my clients; I fulfil this commitment contractually by facilitating their researching their own behaviour. At a more personal level, the book touches on how I have integrated the richness of transactional analysis and meditation to foster my own spiritual growth. Thus there are three themes that run throughout the book – the potency of transactional analysis as an explanatory model of human behaviour, the inevitability of spiritual growth and the ongoing manifestation of these two factors as relationships.

I am also pleased to see that these themes have evolved independently, but are closely allied to John Rowan's views on training of counsellors and psychotherapists. His book:

> "is an attempt to look afresh at the whole question of training, using a very simple but deep framework which I have found valuable. It basically says that there are three

ways of doing therapy, and that any examination of training has to look at all three of them. They are: the instrumental way, where the main emphasis is on treating the client or the patient: the authentic way, where the main emphasis is on meeting the client or the patient; and the transpersonal, where the main emphasis is on linking with the client in a rather intimate way". (Rowan 2005, p. ix)

As you will see, this book reflects all three ways of practising transactional analysis – irrespective of setting. The progression of ideas, concepts and suggestions for practice and /or research follows a rough progression from instrumental, through authentic, and on to transpersonal.

Format

The book is divided into six **Parts.**

The **Forewords** by two eminent exponents of transactional analysis give complementary perspectives and brief commentary on aspects of topics that are likely to be new to some readers.

Part One outlines the basic themes of what I mean by an integral approach to relationships within the context of my perception of divides in transactional analysis. I explain what I see as these divides and offer suggestions for bridging them.

Part Two sketches the basic concepts for understanding the models I have developed, and explains the rationale of the idea that relationships may be regarded as a synthesis of roles, imago images, and the quality of inter-personal contact.

Part Three describes the first model – the Contact Cube – a three dimensional representation of the psychological processes involved in the enactment of social roles.

Part Four describes how the second model – Role Sequences – yields taxonomy of social interaction with equal emphasis on the negative and positive aspects of behaviour.

Part Five explains how the third model - Role Imago Templates - places the other two models within the context of the relationship between client and practitioner. Clients teach the practitioner to understand their (the clients') model of the world, and, in turn, are taught how to research their own behaviour; in doing so, effectively, the divides in transactional analysis are bridged.

Part Six takes transactional analysis beyond a model of intra and inter-personal interaction to encompass realms of transpersonal consciousness and aspects of spirituality. I combine various simple meditational practices with transactional analysis concepts and the models I have developed, demonstrating the efficacy of this amalgamation and its relevance to relationships.

Each **Chapter** starts with a brief statement of the material to be covered, and most Chapters end with a list of **Key Points**. Optional experiential exercises are offered at different stages as **Self Supervision Suggestions**; some of these supplement the argument or concepts I describe, while others carry implications for research-minded readers. Aspects of research are discussed in the **Appendices**, along with comments of a statistical nature. An overview of Spiral Dynamics is included as an invitation to organisational practitioners to explore, research and possibly integrate aspects of the approach with transactional analysis.

The format of the book is such that various sections will hold more appeal for certain readers than will other sections. For example, you may want to skip **Chapter 5**, which is an overview of the entire book. Similarly, if you are not especially interested in the theory of the 'spiritual' aspects of working with clients, you may not wish to take in aspects of **Part Six**. Likewise, **Chapter 11** will probably be of more interest to organisational practitioners than clinicians. **Chapters 13** and **14** are essential for trainers and researchers, recommended for practitioners, but unnecessary for clients. Similarly, the **Appendices** cater for the particular interests of a self-selected readership.

I often draw also upon topics or research findings from disciplines other than transactional analysis. As far as possible I give a brief explanation of the ideas in question; the alternative would have been a volume twice the length of this book. Where my explanations are not sufficiently clear or comprehensive for others who may want to teach them, such readers may find it helpful to consult the original works to appreciate the nuances of my argument.

Many of my ideas are new or "exploratory", or are drawn from disciplines outside TA. Much of the material that comes from existing TA theory and practice has been re-worked. All this has taken time and space – or in this context, pages. Hence the book contains far fewer practical examples than originally intended. I hope that the clarity of my ideas and comprehension thereof by readers, is facilitated by the wide ranging coverage of theoretical material stemming from the theme of integrating transactional analysis and meditational practice in a research-oriented model of relationships.

Chapter 1
An integral approach to relationships

An 'integral approach to relationships' is a view of humankind that describes the whole person in body, mind, soul and spirit. It is an ongoing process that takes account of the inter-personal, cultural and spiritual aspects of social interaction. Transactional analysis says a lot about mind, very little about body and even less about soul and spirit.

In attempting to address this imbalance, I have developed three models of relationships that bridge, and go beyond, what I see as three endemic divides in the international transactional analysis community. There is the divide between health and psychopathology, a divide between theory and research and a divide that represents a combination of and continuation of the first two.

Bridging the divides

The essential requirements of this task are to develop:

- models that are compatible with 'traditional' transactional analysis concepts, values and practice
- models that place equal emphasis on the positive and negative aspects of behaviour
- models that may be used in individual and group work
- models that are relevant to all fields of specialisation in transactional analysis
- a methodology that is easily comprehended by clients, enabling them to research their own behaviour
- models cast in a methodology and language comprehensible to non-TA practitioners and researchers
- models exhibiting sufficient flexibility for accommodating alternative or additional aspects of normal development that are not addressed in the models I will be describing
- models that account for cultural differences
- models that address somatic processes
- models that include a transpersonal or 'spiritual' dimension

The first seven of these points are covered by the three models presented in **Parts One** to **Five**. The last three go beyond the divides and are dealt with in **Part Six**. Strictly speaking, the latter three points, rather than being a fourth specific conceptual model, involve an understanding and (optional) use of a collection of experiential techniques for personal development and spiritual growth.

The rationale of my approach is that relationships may be understood in terms of contact that is describable as the interaction of observable social roles underpinned by inter-personal attitudes. The models offer a framework for understanding and influencing any sequence of interaction, irrespective of setting or transactional analysis specialism. This involves an intersubjective definition of self – self in relation to a context – that encompasses a transpersonal view of human relationships.

ERICA

Primarily for the convenience of using one word instead of an entire phrase, I sometimes refer to *the models and the application or use thereof* as ERICA – an acronym

1

for *existential role imago contact analysis*. This is also a somewhat tongue-in-cheek acknowledgement that the models are an extension or development of Eric Berne's ideas. At the same time "ERICA" is an accurate description of the process involved in using the methods derived from the models. Taking the letters of the acronym in reverse order, what I am presenting is an *analysis* of the *contact* between people that links *imagos* with *roles* to confirm *existential* life positions.

In this context, life positions embody values and beliefs about one's self and others that are used to justify decisions and behaviour. Roles are dispositions to behaviour based on expectations of self, others and the situation. An imago is "an unconscious, stereotypical set, based on a person's fantasies and distortions about a primary relationship experienced within the early familial environment; this set *determines a person's reactions to others*" (Agazarian and Peters, 1981 p. 277: my italics).[1] Contact describes the ways in which people meet their needs. Together, these factors constitute the rudiments of a relationship.

To illustrate, when individuals meet they are said to "make contact", to "exchange strokes."[2] When contact and stroke exchanges confirm expectations, or evoke echoes of some precise, partial, or out of awareness previous pleasing relationship, a "satisfactory" relationship ensues. Impaired contact or unexpected stroke exchanges lead to less than satisfactory relationships. In both cases, relationships become part of mutual expectations, anticipating the next meeting.

ERICA provides clients with tools for researching their own behaviour. For the purpose of analysis, the client recounts (usually, weekly) a series of 'Significant Incidents' and thereby, learns to identify the reciprocal roles and associated qualities of contact played out in each incident. Significant Incidents are defined as such according to whatever the client has experienced during the week as "significant". The aim is to enable clients to exercise conscious choice of roles and imagos, primarily through an awareness of their contact with others.

The models also facilitate the structured observation of psychotherapeutic, counselling, organisational and educational practice of transactional analysis. In addition, they can be used as a formal research tool bridging theory-specific models of *any* interactive process, as well as observational tools for the purposes of training and supervision, enhancing the practitioner's capacity for reflective awareness of the underlying process. For example, Masterson (1981) writes extensively on the intra-psychic dynamics of narcissistic and borderline patients; he describes this process in terms of projections of RORU (rewarding object relations units) and WORU (withdrawing object relations units), making it difficult for non-analytically trained therapists to appreciate and replicate his treatment recommendations. Research based 'translations' of these processes into observable behavioural categories and associated roles would make such insights more widely available. Accordingly, ERICA suggests steps for developing the models as research tools.

The three models presented in **Parts One** to **Five** belie the subtlety of what at first sight may appear to be a mainly cognitive-behavioural approach to social interaction. However, the models describe *relationships* - features of intra- and inter-personal interaction - that are ever present for everyone. Because the models provide a framework for describing interaction at a meta-level, they give ample scope for practitioners to exercise widely differing preferences, techniques and strategies for relating to clients. **Parts One** to **Five**

---

[1] The italicized words are equivalent to Berne's life positions. In **Chapters 6** and **7,** I explain how Berne's definition of a group imago (Berne 1963 p. 244) and life positions, matches Agazarian and Peters' work.
[2] A stroke is a "unit of recognition" (Berne 1961; see also Stewart and Joines, 1987 Chapter 8) I discuss these in more detail in **Chapter 7**.

describe the three models – the 'front end' of ERICA - that rest on the bedrock of a model of the development of consciousness, which is described in **Part Six**.

Implications for research

Because I regard the models and ideas to be presented in this book as "research-oriented" and/or having "implications for research", I want, at the outset, to clarify my use of these phrases. The phrases *do not* mean that this book is a report of ongoing, formalised research undertaken over many years, leading to a neat set of conclusions and suggestions for further research. They *do* mean that the book is an account of the ideas and techniques I have come across or developed in my clinical practice, and have found to be useful to clients.

Moreover, when I use the term "implications", I do so in several senses. Generally I mean that a topic, a concept or even a model, has implications for research. That is, the topic is an interesting and, usually, a new idea that I think warrants further examination. For example, the statement that "a stroke is a unit of recognition", may be regarded as an idea, a concept, or a definition, that has "implications" for research. In other words, does the statement stand up to any sort of empirical enquiry? Likewise, is it merely an idea, an intuitive insight immediately recognisable to everyone, or an assumption that nevertheless, may be a useful assumption under certain circumstances?

Obviously, "implications" can be carried to ludicrous lengths – everything carries implications. However, in the context of a book describing *new* concepts to a professional audience within a culture where a research orientation is not the norm, I think there is merit in examining my assumptions about "implications for research". Principally, these are that *everyone* has something to contribute by way of what is, or maybe, relevant to research whether quantitative or qualitative. Research does not burst fully formed onto the pages of journals; it grows and in some senses never ends. How it grows is what counts. Usually this entails having ideas, trying them out and writing them up in a "research-oriented way" – in a way that invites you to react to, comment on or replicate my ideas, and in doing so, contribute your ideas - in a similarly research-oriented way.

In this respect my agenda is to share my passion for research. For me "research" is merely another word for what as a child, was the experience of curiosity, of wonder, of delight, the near ecstasy of noticing relationships between one thing and another. I grew up on a farm in South Africa and initially, my basic inquisitiveness was about natural phenomena. When I was about six I realised two things about "research" - that the same curiosity was equally relevant to *people*, and that others had views that *differed* from mine. Adolescence brought the first glimmerings of the idea that understanding others was relative to self-understanding. At university I discovered that "helping" others was not only rewarding, but also the basis of a career. By the time I was twenty-six I was working in the United Kingdom as a housemaster in a classifying school for delinquent boys; the task was to assess their needs for "treatment" in reform schools. I learnt a great deal about psychometric testing, but more importantly, began to appreciate the complexities of context – of socio-economic, cultural and political factors, of individual versus group behaviour, the role of observation – and perhaps above all, the significance of relationships.

In many ways not a lot has changed since then. The echoes of my childhood fascination with "what", "where", "when", "why", "how", and "who", remain features of my daily life. Nowadays there is a lot more to this process than there used to be. I have learned to live with my curiosity, mostly quietly, more wondrously, more respectfully, but still enthusiastically. Sharing this curiosity with others and comparing their ideas is an essential part of my interest in research. Additionally, I believe that ongoing testing of ideas, concepts and skills is an integral part of the responsibility for one's continuous professional development. It is primarily for this reason that I have included research-orientated items in virtually all the **Self Supervision Suggestions** at the end of most Chapters. Although each item stems directly from the material presented in the Chapter and thereby reinforces understanding of the **Key Points**, my aim has been to suggest topics that will encourage a research-oriented mind set for trainees. For trainers, the Suggestions stand as ready made examples of transactional analysis ideas that may be used for teaching and fostering a research ethos, in conjunction with standard texts on research (McLeod, 2000, 2003, Loewenthal and Winter, 2006, and particularly, Etherington, 2004). And there will also be other readers who will simply regard this book as a story – the narrative of an everyday person going about the business of being a transactional analysis practitioner in the twenty-first century.

Chapter **2**

Tensions and divides

Virtually all institutions and social movements have divides – internal sources of tension that have become polarised and overspill organisational boundaries.

Dealing with tensions and avoiding divides is part and parcel of the process of organisational formation, growth and development. Sometimes divides exist for years, rumbling on as covert differences beneath the surface of formal procedures and practice but flaring up at stressful times and dying down again. With multi-national organisations or networks, some disputes are localised, having little or no effect elsewhere in the organisation. In other cases, tensions (rather than divides) are not only endemic, ever present, but necessary to balance forces within an organisation; the source of such potential conflict is deliberately built into the structure of the organisation. For example, most social work agencies have a structural split between administrative and social work staff, with procedures controlled by the former that curtail the professional autonomy of the latter. Social workers may grumble about lack of resources, but comply with the bureaucracy of procedural and budgetary constraints in order to provide their clients with a service. Political parties are particularly prone to tensions and divides; exploiting, or even creating them in opposition camps, is an almost a stock-in-trade tactic for party politicians.

Generally speaking the more an organisation is open to public or external professional scrutiny, the greater the need for attention to be paid to internal splits and conflicts. Although professional organisations guard against these by having ethics, professional practice and complaints procedures, stresses are a normal part of organisational growth. Increasing membership, geographical expansion, new divisions or satellite branches of a central body all bring challenges that must be met if tensions are not to proliferate. When this happens, polarised positions become more important than relationships and/or allegiance to common methods of practice, shared values and beliefs. Indeed, the irony is that the stronger the commitment of older or founder members to organisational goals, values and standards of professional practice, the more resistant to change the organisation as a whole becomes.

Divides in transactional analysis

Not everyone would agree that there *are* divides in the transactional analysis community. I believe that there are three divides that are internationally endemic. I outline these briefly and then examine each one in sufficient detail for readers to grasp the gist of my concern.

The first divide refers to the fact that transactional analysis has long had to grapple with the issue of how to apply a theory developed from observations of 'dysfunctional' behaviours, to practise in settings with 'functional' behaviours. Berne created a new theory of psychotherapy. However, in doing so, Berne also created a theory of psychopathology (Barnes 1999, 2004). For many years this was not regarded as a problem by most adherents of transactional analysis – of whom the bulk are clinicians. It was and largely, still is, left to organisational, educational and (more recently) counselling specialists to 'translate' the language of pathology and apply clinically relevant concepts to settings antithetical to such ways of thinking.

Secondly, in all spheres of the study of human endeavour, a balance has to be struck between the simultaneous application of theory to practice, with the need to continuously observe, question, research, validate existing concepts and develop new aspects of theory and practice. Without this process theories fall into disuse, are overtaken by other approaches or become ideology. As I outline below, transactional analysis has been slow off the mark in fostering a tradition of research into its basic tenets that would make it more amenable to investigation and critique by, and/or informed contributions from, non transactional analysts. Instead, the user friendly pop culture argot of transactional analysis is either widely cited without reference or often, with insufficient understanding (Kovel 1976). Although Kovel's comments are easily rebutted (Stewart 1996 pp. 41-50), our use of 1960s West Coast American jargon as a shorthand terminology for major theoretical concepts does not make for a body of knowledge that can be readily assimilated by others within the human sciences.

More recently there are signs that a third divide could be starting to emerge. At present this potential third divide is represented by what I refer to as the diversity/competitive labelling divide. At best, it is a tension that encompasses an integration of transactional analysis theory and practice with concepts, procedures and techniques derived from other approaches. At worst the emergent divide is evidenced either by the existence of rival national associations, or by cracks in the edifices of national associations along the lines of specialisation within transactional analysis. In both cases, individuals assume polarised positions on various issues of principle, practice or procedure. Somewhere between these extremes is the process of espousing allegiance to a particular interpretation or 'model' of transactional analysis and implying, or declaring by fiat, the "truth" of the chosen model. Such stances are often accompanied by the ulterior level implication that other approaches are somehow less worthy, useful, or are simply "not TA".

My perception of these models is that they are as much a reflection of contextual factors along with a particular exponent's personal preferences, values and style of communicating with others, as they are any sort of epistemologically sound attempt to integrate the theory and practice of transactional analysis with a wider spectrum of non-TA models of human interaction.

Inasmuch as I present below an integration of the theory and practice of transactional analysis and several other models/theories of human interaction, according to my own personal preferences, values and style of communicating with others, this book is no different. However, the thrust of my work is to present theoretical concepts derived from observations in a way that will permit others to judge whether they are consistent with existing transactional analysis theory, practice and values and above all, to replicate the observations, undertake the necessary research to validate the concepts I propose and assess their efficacy.

Nevertheless, theories emerge from interpretations of observations and evolve as the context in which they emerged evolves. To remain theories they need new concepts that either challenge previous ideas or take the original theory in a different direction. When this process does not occur, theories become dogmas. In my view, transactional analysis has not yet reached this stage, but it has been a considerable time since totally new concepts have been proposed. This book does not advance a new 'theory'; it builds on existing TA ideas and introduces several new concepts. However, before delving into these, closer examination of each divide will enable us to guard against their perpetuation.

The first divide – health/pathology

The first divide stems from the way in which Berne formulated his ideas, how he described his observations, conveyed these to others, and how others have come to understand and use his insights. This process is ingrained in the current theory and practice of TA, and it would be difficult, if not tedious, to unpick it. My point is that Berne wrote in a highly personalised, phenomenological style:

> "Berne wrote more for the intuitive mind than the rational mind. His style is intuitive and concrete with few definitions in the technical sense and concrete descriptions instead. This is part of the charm of his writing and part of the intuitive appeal of transactional analysis". (Grégoire, 2004 p. 12)

Grégoire continues, to point out that:

> "misunderstandings arose when Berne's intuitive and metaphorical phrases were transplanted into theoretical contexts of a more dialectic type without any "translation" or interpretation". (Grégoire, 2004 p. 12)

In this respect, transactional analysis is not an intellectually robust theory. A robust theory is a statement of ideas derived from observations of phenomena, along with existing knowledge of similar or related topics, which follow certain rules (which I explain below) that are conveyed to others in a way that makes the rules 'transparent'. The rules are universal inasmuch as they apply to all spheres of knowledge. Whether wittingly or not, Berne followed some of the rules, and in this respect, his theories is "scientific" or methodologically sound. The difficulty lies in *how* Berne communicated his ideas to *which* others.

Berne created his own audience – the TA community - a feat which earns universal acclaim within, and to some extent, beyond the audience he created. For example, transactional analysis is accepted as a legitimate, professional and effective form of psychotherapy by the United Kingdom Council for Psychotherapy (UKCP). Likewise, glance at any basic reader on counselling or psychotherapy and you will find references to Berne and TA. But it is the *how* Berne transmitted his message that is the kernel of the three divides. As Grégoire notes:

> "Berne's essential theoretical construct in the theory of ego states is his classification of them into three "classes" (Berne, 1963, p. 177) or "types" (Berne, 1961/75, p. 17, p. 66) which he called Child, Adult, and Parent. For him, each class depends on a structure, the "psychic organs" or "systems of personality" (p. 19) that "organizes" it (pp. 264-269). He considered all three to be positive and necessary resources in the healthy individual (e.g. see Berne, 1964, p. 27 Clarkson & Gilbert, 1988); however, he devoted very few lines to *the positive aspects in comparison to the negative ones*". (Grégoire, 2004, p. 11: my italics)

The under-emphasis on the positive aspects of personality and, by extension, social interaction, permeates transactional analysis theory and literature. True, there are passing references to positive features of human behaviour, but descriptions of the negative far outweigh them. This, together with Berne's intuitive, metaphorical style of writing couched in jargon rather than the language conventionally used by researchers, laid the foundations of a theory that is not readily accessible to informed critique from others beyond the TA community. Despite this, the theory "caught on" during the sixties - perhaps for the reasons cited by Barnes:

> "Berne combines two sides of theory making which is an art that imitators often lack. He is constantly introducing new ideas, and he carefully and rigorously weaves them together into a logical and consistent whole. The theorists who do not do that can be heard criticizing him. One group calls him inconsistent. I think they miss how he is always bringing in new ideas, employing new metaphors. They seem not to grasp that

kind of flexibility, that use of the imagination, which weds artistic creativity with scientific rigor. They even miss the elegance that is always hovering above his theoretical constructions. But, from the other side, the creative theorists can be heard criticizing him for his logical rigor. I think both criticisms miss the playfulness and the pleasure of Berne the scientist and artist at work writing his heart out. Criticism notwithstanding, I think all who read Berne, share the pleasure of theory, its simple words and pithy sayings". (Barnes - personal communication)

Indeed, whether or not transactional analysis would have achieved the popularity it did in the '60s if Berne had written in the conventional style of academic researchers, is a moot point. Yet behind his style of writing there lurked an adherence to scientific method. That is, the genesis of transactional analysis stems in part from observations of ex-servicemen and psychiatric patients. Berne observed certain phenomena exhibited by two groups of individuals. He cross-checked these with his earlier writing on the role of intuition (Berne 1957), drew on existing literature (Weiss, 1950 Federn 1952), and (probably) his own experience of psychoanalysis, and not unreasonably, concluded there was sufficient evidence to postulate the concepts of "psychic organs" and their manifestation as "ego states" (Berne, 1961). However, the fact that he devoted attention to concrete descriptions of negative behaviours in a culture that prized phenomenological inquiry effectively set the tone of theory-building that still persists. Many of the tools used by all TA practitioners were designed, appropriately, to identify negative aspects of behaviour. For example, the discounting matrix was developed to identify and counter behaviour "which involves people minimizing or ignoring some aspect of themselves, others, or the situation" (Schiff et. al. 1975, p. 14; see also, Mellor and Schiff, 1975)[1].

So what is wrong with identifying negative behaviour and offering options for avoiding or correcting it? My answer is that there is nothing wrong with such practice when the recipient acknowledges a problem and expects a response couched in terms of ameliorating negative behaviour. The fact is that not only do 'normal' people dislike being 'pathologised', they dislike being described in terms that signify an *absence* of pathology. It is not unlike going to your doctor with a sore throat and being told you don't have cancer. As Barnes has repeatedly pointed out, any theory of psychotherapy creates a theory of psychopathology (Barnes, 1999, 2000, 2002, 2004). In practical terms, it is not particularly useful for a company director to know that there are not many second degree game players in a team. As Zalcman has noted:

> "we need to include behaviors that are "healthy" or "non problematic" and which are useful in understanding desirable functioning". (Zalcman, 1990 p. 11)

She concludes:

> "concepts and techniques which focus on normal or mentally healthy behavior and change (not just those focusing on problems or pathological development) are needed". (Zalcman, 1990 p. 17)

Likewise, a more recent publication echoes this refrain:

---

[1] It is perhaps relevant to note that Erskine, Trautman and Moursund (1999), present a 'keyhole' diagram that embodies the reverse of the discounting matrix.

"TA .... overly emphasises the psychopathology of the client at the expense of their health". (Tudor and Hobbes, 2002 p. 258)

Zalcman makes no less than seven recommendations for correcting and revising aspects of theory. The models presented in later Chapters fulfil Zalcman's demands.

The second divide – the validity, reliability and effectiveness of transactional analysis

The second divide carries the potential of isolating transactional analysis from the wider community of person professions. As a theory of personality and human interaction, transactional analysis 'works'. It is effective probably as much because practitioners and their clients believe the theory to be 'true' as it has been 'proved' to be valid and reliable.

Here I use the terms "effective", "valid" and "reliable" in a technical sense. Validity addresses the question of whether variables - concepts, measures or categories of behaviour – do, indeed, refer to what, or however, the variable in question is defined and not some other related phenomena. For example, if you were interested in investigating "perseverance" you would have to demonstrate that your definitions, categorisation or use of perseverance differentiate it from similar factors like, say, obsessive behaviour. Reliability means that other people have been able to use your methods, and in all cases, have obtained similar results. To demonstrate effectiveness you would have to publish outcome studies that showed how many people with 'poor perseverance' using the methods, improved in various respects.

Historically, transactional analysis has not been consistently rigorous about demonstrating validity, reliability and effectiveness. In brief,[1] what seems to have happened is that most, if not all, transactional analysis theory was developed over a period of about two decades and enthusiastically (and largely uncritically) accepted by hundreds, if not thousands, of practitioners in most developed countries. After Berne's death in 1971 and the emergence of three 'schools' of TA (Barnes 1978), little or no new theory emerged and it was not until some twenty or so years ago that the by then orthodox concepts and practice began to be extended (see for example, Ware 1983, Joines 1986, Jacobs 1987, 1990, 1991, 1997, Clarkson 1992). In addition, some authors such as Erskine have made significant contributions throughout the entire period (Erskine 1997, pp. "Contents")

The past two decades have seen a change. Not only have some of the original ideas been questioned (Zalcman 1990, Barnes 1999a, 1999b, 1999c, 2000), updated (Hine 1990, Jacobs 1997), or elaborated (Allen and Allen 1991, 1997, Summers and Tudor 2000, Novey 2002, Hargaden and Sills 2002, 2003), new links with other therapies (Joines and Stewart 2002) have provided a welcome interest to what could have become a flagging system. However, with some important exceptions, (Kahler 1972, 1982, 1999, Kaplan, Capace and Clyde, 1982) until recently, (for example, Temple 1999, van Beekum and Krijgsman 2000, Novey 2002, Ohlsson 2002, Boholst 2003), transactional analysis has been short on empirical studies designed to validate the basic tenets of the model. This is not to say that transactional analysis is withering on the vine. New publications continue to appear (Hargaden and Sills 2002, Joines and Stewart 2002, Lister-Ford 2002, Cornell and Hargaden

---

[1] This is not an exhaustive review; the cited references are merely examples from among many others that could have been chosen. In addition, some authors, such as Erskine, have made significant contributions throughout the entire period (see Erskine 1997, for articles published in Transactional Analysis Journals from 1974 to 1997)

2005), and there is a lively interest in the implications of current neurological research (Allen 1999, 2000, Gildebrand 2003).

Transactional analysis is not alone in having to deal with the practice/research divide. The function of observation in the research of social interaction is limited by a lack of observational models or tools that are not theory, setting, or model-specific. In addition, many research projects are not readily accessible to researchers with little or no clinical, organisational or educational and/or model-specific training. Moreover, there is no observational research tool that would enable a researcher to describe the full gamut of relationships in a way that permits comparisons of various theoretical approaches. For example, several therapeutic approaches have developed methods of observation that enable clinicians to describe and evaluate practice (cf. Bennett and Parry 1998, Winter 2003). These, however, require a clinical knowledge of a particular approach, and address theory specific concepts.

Compared to other approaches, transactional analysis lacks a tradition of vigorous, ongoing research. For example, Personal Construct theory (Kelly 1955, Winter 1992) and Cognitive Analytic Therapy (Ryle 1982, 1990, 1995, Leiman 1994, Ryle and Kerr 2002) are solidly founded on empirical research and based on a norm of research-oriented methodology.

To illustrate, the similarity between Berne and Anthony Ryle, the founder of Cognitive Analytic Therapy (CAT), is that both created 'new' approaches to psychotherapy, acquired a following and established professional associations based on training leading to clinical competence.

The salient difference between the two innovators is that Ryle's emphasis on research and measurable outcomes has made it difficult for the establishment to ignore CAT. The model has spread to Europe and, within the United Kingdom, academics, researchers and health officials have come to regard CAT as having contributed positively to the theory and practice of treating dysfunctional clients. To a large extent this growing recognition is based on research publications (Leiman 1994, Ryle 1997, Bennett and Parry 2000, Ryle and Kerr 2002,), but also, I suspect, because CAT uses the language and nomenclature familiar to researchers and practitioners of other therapies.

Readers will judge for themselves the extent to which this book contributes to a research-oriented mind set. In particular, I think there are at least three aspects of transactional analysis theory that warrant updating. The conceptual lacunae are that, in choosing a stimulus response paradigm for analysing interpersonal interaction, (transactional analysis proper), Berne did not extend his primary concern with individuals to a higher level of abstraction that encourages an in depth analysis of group processes, cultural influences or larger scale sociological phenomena.[1] Secondly, Berne under-emphasised the role of power in his account of group processes. I address these issues in **Parts One** to **Five**. A third factor is that transactional analysis was conceived, conceptually, as an alternative to the prevailing tradition, research and practice concerning unconscious processes. **Part Six** is devoted to exploration of these issues.

The potential third divide - diversity/competitive labelling

The following discussion of diversity is bound to be coloured by my perception of local events. Nevertheless, I consider that the examples cited below are a reflection of global trends in transactional analysis.

---

[1] Exceptions to this are Jacobs (1987, 1992, 1995), Drego (1978, 1983, 1999) and Sills (2003).

My perception of the divide of diversity/competitive labelling in transactional analysis is as much a source of hope for the future, as it is an anxiety about what could transpire. To illustrate this dichotomy, I cite a recent theme issue on "Core Concepts" in the *Transactional Analysis Journal* (ITAA 2003) as *evidence* of the divide. I then sketch the *contextual factors* relevant to diversity, briefly comment on two *recent publications* by exponents of two very different models and give an overview of the range of *current models* used by transactional analysts. I then touch upon *"splitting"* - the implications of break-away movements within the TA community - and give a brief *case study* illustrating some of the contextual factors that lead to a perpetuation of the third divide.

Evidence of a third divide in transactional analysis

Judging from articles in the Transactional Analysis Journal of April 2003, with the theme issue of "Core Concepts", there is ample evidence to suggest that there are widely differing views on what does, or should, constitute the theory of transactional analysis. For readers without access to the TAJ, I have replicated abstracts of each of the articles:

> ".. the analogy of a tree planted by Eric Berne is used to provide a perspective on what constitutes the "tree" of transactional analysis. In describing the roots, trunk, and branches of the "tree of transactional analysis", the author calls for care and maintenance so that it can grow with greater synergy and less entropy. Some of the challenges that may effect healthy growth .... - such as the integrative psychotherapy movement, constructivism, objection to the use of energy metaphors, the "psychoanalyticalization" of transactional analysis, and lack of scientific validation – are identified and discussed. The author urges transactional analysis to sustain the healthy growth of transactional analysis for the new millennium by following the legacy of Berne's original creative and scientific spirit, without which there would be no transactional analysis today". (Campos, 2003 p. 115)

Parenthetically, Campos' "branches" of the tree are traditional Bernean, psychodynamic, multimodality integrative, redecision therapy, post modernist reconstructions, and educational/organisational applications of transactional analysis. All but the redecision and the educational/organisational applications are discussed in the article.

Writing from a constructivist perspective, Allen concludes that it is the "utility" or usefulness of transactional analysis he favours, and which has enabled it to survive. In other words, it's up to the individual practitioner to choose between aspects of various approaches and apply a range of techniques according to the client's needs.

> "In the process of considering core competencies in transactional analysis, there are several factors that need to be taken into account: (1) biological underpinnings, (2) epistemology (constructivism, expectancy, and membership of an interpretive community), (3) the appropriate boundaries of social psychiatry, (4) practitioners' styles, and (5) the roles of eclecticism and integration". (Allen, 2003 p. 126)

Wadsworth and DiVincenti advance a more specific argument about ego states as the basis to their objection to the idea of 'core concepts':

> "This article presents the history of and some commentary about the theoretical and political polemic surrounding the attempt to determine a set of transactional analysis core competencies. The authors propose that ego state theory is at the heart of the theoretical debate and political struggle. They elaborate this inconsistency found in the

11

A Compilation of Core Concepts document (Steiner et. al. 1999) and assert that the project to establish a set of transactional analysis core concepts should be transformed into an opportunity to clear up such inconsistencies in the fundamental concept of transactional analysis". (Wadsworth and DiVincenti, 2003 p. 148)

Their views are countered by Oller-Vallejo:

"After describing the controversy about the two models recently known as the three ego states model and the integrated/integrating Adult model, [favoured by Wadsworth and DiVincenti] the author argues for the compatibility of these two views and for the exclusive validity of the three ego states model as the single primary model of ego states in transactional analysis". (Oller-Vallego, 2003 p. 162)

O'Reilly-Knapp and Erskine take a wider view of integrative transactional analysis:

"In integrative transactional analysis, the conceptual constructs, theories, and sub-theories are organized into a theory of motivation, a theory of personality, and a theory of methods. The theory of motivation examines human functioning and the need for stimuli, structure, and relationship. The theory of personality describes internal and external contact, interruptions to contact, life script, and ego function. The theory of method emphasizes the power of a healing relationship. These theories and methods assist clinicians in understanding human beginnings, in normalizing the functions of psychological processes, and in healing through relationships". (O'Reilly-Knapp and Erskine, 2003 p. 168)

Steiner, too, weighs in by presenting his own version of a "stroke-centred transactional analysis".

Loria focuses on the philosophical underpinnings of theory:

"This article explores the knowledge base of transactional analysis, focussing on the epistemological errors that potentially limit the theory's power. Possible remedies are discussed". (Loria, 2003, p. 192)

Clearly, the abstracts are no substitute for the articles but give a flavour of the diversity of views in 2003. Since then new publications continue to appear that follow their authors' predilections. I outline two such works below, as examples of how practitioners legitimately continue to opt for their own models, in relation to the context in which the models were developed.

Contextual factors
In considering the question of 'what is diversity', we need to take account of who is asking and/or answering the question, and which audience is being addressed. On the face of it, discussions of diversity seem to boil down to how we communicate with who we are trying to convince what is, and what is not, transactional analysis. Even if one were able to define a theoretical benchmark, the issue becomes considerably more complex once contextual factors are introduced.

Diversity is an issue with which all commercial organisations, professions, social networks and political movements have to cope. Some do so more successfully than others. For example, at the concrete level of a physical product, the automobile has replaced the horse and carriage; the model T Ford has been diversified to encompass an extensive variety of what are all automobiles. Various models or makes that flourished in the 1920s are no longer produced, having been absorbed by other makers or simply succumbing to market forces and failing to survive. The factors relevant to the dynamics of diversity are multifarious and complex – culture, politics, economics, technological innovation and the spread of knowledge and information in seemingly unrelated fields.

Theories of human behaviour are no less prone to such factors and forces as are consumer products. However, the chronicles of most attempts to diversify a theory of human behaviour have tended to focus on the discussion of theoretical ideas or ideological values, largely ignoring contextual factors such as culture, politics, organisational structures, and perhaps, above all, economics. Much of the current discussion on diversity within the transactional analysis community is devoted to comparison of different theoretical approaches, almost exclusively in relation to psychotherapy (thereby perpetuating the first divide) and mostly in Europe and the United States. Relevant as this theoretical discourse is, I think we ignore organisational, cultural, and economic issues at our peril.

That said, the extent to which economic factors influence views on diversity is difficult, if not impossible, to assess. To my knowledge, no one has ever worked out, on an international scale, the comparative cost of training to become a qualified TA practitioner. Speculatively, I imagine that the career path of a typical modern-day transactional analyst is crafted in the context of what for most people is a career change, or an additional professional qualification. In both cases it takes between four to eight years and, for the vast majority of entrants, this is a major undertaking – not only in terms of acquiring knowledge, skills and personal development, but also by way of having the necessary financial resources.

In the United Kingdom a rough rule of thumb is that it takes about twelve percent of the annual income commanded by someone in a professional occupation such as management, teaching, psychology, nursing, social work and so on. Precise data is not available; my impression is that a similar index would probably apply worldwide.

The other side of the equation is that trainees need trainers. Again, as an example, in the United Kingdom, there is no shortage of Teaching and Supervising Transactional Analysts (TSTAs) and Provisional Teaching and Supervising Transactional Analysts (PTSTAs). A recent count revealed that there are 108 TSTAs and PTSTAs in the UK and 26 training programmes. Two thirds of these are thriving small businesses that enable the owners/trainers to earn a full time living.

In short, trainers have to compete economically to attract new entrants; underlying most discussions of the diversity of theories, is straightforward economic rivalry. Obviously, market forces prevail and the tendency to promote a programme that offers something that others do not is almost inevitable. The extent to which such competition prevails varies enormously from country to country. It also has to be said that some trainers travel widely and promote transactional analysis internationally at little or no personal profit. However, in most cases they cannot do so, unless they have private means or, until they have 'made it' economically as a TA practitioner in their own country.

In theory, all training programmes offer different versions of the same curriculum. Transactional analysts take pride in belonging to an international association yet differences of culture do not figure large in current views of diversity. Embracing ideas from all cultures is an essential component of diversifying any product - or theory of social interaction.

Another major contextual feature of diversity is the standing of each of the four areas of specialisation in transactional analysis, at local level across the globe, in relation to comparable professional groups in each country. To my knowledge, no one has ever been able to give anything more than an overall impression. National TA associations exist cheek by jowl with other professional organisations, and are often bound by legal statutes, licensing laws, codes of ethics and professional practice. For example, in Italy you cannot train as a psychotherapist unless you are a psychiatrist or a psychologist. All these factors make for the need to adopt a multi-level view of diversity.

Finally, three crucial features of diversity are *what* is being diversified, who will *benefit* from diversity and what *resources* are needed for diversification.

The usual sequence of events for diversifying a commercial product begins with the realisation that the demand for an existing product is falling off; sales are down. Reasons may vary but generally fall into three classes – the public no longer want or need the product, (for example, video tapes are being replaced by DVDs), the market is becoming saturated (everyone who wants/needs/can afford a television set, already has one), or sales of competitors' products are increasing. The solution to all three factors is defined as a need to diversify – to offer the same product at a cheaper price, or a considerably improved product, or even a new product.

However, this type of analysis assumes that someone is steering the process. The reality is that it is difficult enough to keep track of these variables in the commercial sector, where more or less measurable indices prevail. With political/professional organisations that do not have a physical product, but are trying to "sell" a service or an ideology to a numerically indeterminate yet potentially dedicated clientele the problem is considerably more complex. Add to this the fact that diversity of theory cannot be defined or controlled in the same way as developing a new or better widget, and the answer has to be that those who will benefit from the diversity/competitive labelling polarity, are none other than those who propagate new theories, peddle them assiduously and 'recruit' a following. Hopefully, the utility and deployment of *aspects of* respective approaches according to client needs together with ongoing research will skew this potential divide in the direction of a healthy tension where respect for alternative approaches encourage the development of an egalitarian, rather than an elitist milieu.

Another contextual consideration is perhaps so obvious it hardly needs mentioning. Berne was a modernist. For him there was an "objective" reality – defined by consensus, but informed by a medical model of 'curing' pathology. Not surprisingly, none of this fits comfortably with a post-modernist point of view where particular narratives (the client's, the practitioner's) are co-created.

Taking account of all the above contextual factors, my guess is that the transactional analysis community does not have the organisational structure or procedures that would enable diversity of theory to be "managed" – even were this possible. Personally, I do not believe that diversity of theory can nor should be managed. What *can,* and should, be managed is the delivery of services and resources that *support* diversity. Salters has suggested – and I agree – that what is needed is an organisational structure on a global scale in which everyone has a stake, and to which all regional bodies would contribute financially (Salters, 2004 – personal communication). This would require a radical revision of current arrangements that hold promise not only of a new fiscal viability but also the honouring of the people, structures and values that have contributed to the current richness and diversity of transactional analysis.

Recent publications

Over the past ten or so years articles in the Transactional Analysis Journal (TAJ) reflect a growing recognition of the need to extend the boundaries of theory and practice of transactional analysis. Many of these articles and new publications are concerned with tweaking existing concepts. For example, the *tour de force* of *Personality Adaptations A new guide to understanding in psychotherapy and counselling* (Joines and Stewart, 2002) is the outcome of a sustained elaboration of work originating in the '70s and '80s (Ware 1983,

Kahler, 1972, 1982, 1999, 2000, Kahler and Capers 1974, Joines 1986, 1988). Essentially, Joines and Stewart do not introduce any *new* theory. They offer a new perspective on redecision work (Goulding and Goulding 1979,) by integrating extensive psychometric research (Kahler 1999) with Ware's idea that there are 'doors' (cognitive, affective and behavioural ways of making contact) to therapy. In brief, Joines and Stewart present six personality adaptations common to everyone. Understanding the adaptations enables counsellors and therapists to identify someone's adaptations rapidly and accurately, maintain rapport and work effectively with the issues that are likely to arise in the process of change. They address the first divide of health/pathology by reframing Ware's labels for psychiatric *disorders* (paranoid, schizoid and so on) as bi-polar *personality adaptations* (such as Brilliant-Sceptic, Creative-Daydreamer). Above all, their work is clear, focused and readily accessible to anyone without extensive knowledge of transactional analysis. The implications of their work demand attention from researchers interested in evaluating and exploring the distribution of personality adaptations in many spheres of activity across cultures. Likewise their work is relevant to treatment planning by therapists and counsellors. And for non-clinicians the significance of their work lies in matching adaptations with all manner of variables relevant to personnel selection, team building and organisational development.

In almost complete contrast, Hargaden and Sills (2002) present a model of what they term "relational" transactional analysis. They integrate four domains of self (the emergent sense of self, the core self, the intersubjective self and the verbal self - see Stern, 1987) with their own version of a structural model of ego states. They weave amendments of Berne's therapeutic operations (Berne, 1966) with a Rogerian version of empathy into a creative tapestry of transferential and counter-transferential transactions to describe a theory of self and the development of the therapeutic relationship. Their methodology relies upon case studies and clinical vignettes. Theirs is a creative and brave attempt to push the theory and practice of transactional analysis in a new direction. Although there are several aspects of their work with which I take issue in later Chapters, both the above pairs of authors successfully bridge the theory/research divide – but in very different ways.

The major difference between these authors is that the view of therapy presented by Joines and Stewart is nearer to Rowan and Jacobs's description of an "instrumental position" than the view of therapy presented by Hargaden and Sills:

> 'In the *instrumental position,* the client is usually regarded as someone who has problems, which need to be put right (by the client, the therapist or by both). Technical ability is regarded as something both possible and desirable. In rational emotive behaviour therapy, in neuro-linguistic programming, and in many cognitive-behavioural approaches, and even in some psychodynamic circles, this is the preferred mode; and the treatment approaches in vogue under managed care and employee assistance programmes often take a similar view. Specific techniques have to be learned and put into practice in time-limited work, for example, which nearly always include identification of a clear focus or problem. The client or patient is there to be cured, at least in this one identifiable respect, and application of the correct techniques aims to achieve this in a high percentage of cases. More and better techniques are the way forward, and to test these objectively is the main goal of research. Working with the unconscious can be just as much part of this approach as not working with the unconscious. It is equally possible for the relationship to be long or short, close or distant, self-disclosing or anonymous, using transference or not, analytic or humanistic, cognitive or emotive or otherwise. The key thing is that there should be an aim. Every form of therapy resorts to this level at some time, and the famed 'Working Alliance' is firmly based on it, but it is basically an I-it relationship rather than an I-thou

relationship, in the terms made famous by Martin Buber (1970). Key words here are 'contract', 'assessment', 'treatment goals', 'empirically validated treatments', 'boundaries', and 'manualisation'". (Rowan and Jacobs 2002, p. 5)

In contrast, Hargaden and Sills describe their approach as "relational". This comes closer to Rowan and Jacobs's second category but, as may be seen from the following quotation, their model probably does not fully meet the criteria they specify:

"In the *authentic[1]* way of being, personal involvement is much more acceptable, with the therapist much more closely identified with the client and more openly concerned to explore the therapeutic relationship. The idea of the wounded healer is often mentioned, as is the idea of personal growth. The schools who most traditionally and obviously favour this approach most are the humanistic ones: person-centered, gestalt, psychodrama, bodywork, focusing, experiential, existential and so on. Yet there is also considerable evidence that, under different names, this same type of relationship is very important to many psychoanalytic therapists and even more, perhaps, to Jungians and post-Jungians. Clarkson (1995) calls it the person-to-person relationship. And it is possible to work in this way whether one believes in the unconscious or not. According to one's theoretical position, to work in this way it is essential to have had some experience of what Ken Wilber (2000) calls the Centaur level of psychospiritual development, or what Wade (1996) calls 'authentic consciousness'. Again, the analytic model may express it quite differently, but concepts of countertransference in more recent usage are significant here and depend upon the openness of the therapist to such intuitive information. Key words here are 'authenticity', 'personhood', 'healing through meeting', 'being in the world', 'intimacy, 'openness', 'the real relationship'". (Rowan and Jacobs 2002, p. 6)

Added to this is Rowan's later comment:

"What they do not emphasise enough, in my view, is the importance of body-mind unity at this level. Instead of the instrumental view, that the body is to be disciplined by the mind, much in the manner of a rider on a horse, the sense is that body and mind are a unity. Philippa Vick (2002) speaks of mind/body holism. This is of course a much more demanding way of working, and the therapist has to have a good deal of self-knowledge to engage in it". (Rowan 2005, p.4)

In particular, although Hargaden and Sills make extensive use of countertransference, they do not seem to demonstrate awareness of "the Centaur level of psychospiritual development" – if only because they do not explicitly acknowledge the use of a bodywork dimension of relating to clients. Indeed, speaking strictly within the bounds of Rowan and Jacobs's categories, *all* transactional analysis falls within the instrumental band, partly because we do not pay particular attention to mind-body unity, but mainly because of the way in which Rowan and Jacobs define self (which is not apparent from the above quotations). Nevertheless, there is enough in Hargaden and Sills' work to warrant the view that their approach is closer to Rowan and Jacobs' "authentic" category than is Joines and Stewart's.

---

[1] Rowan and Jacobs (2002) use the term "authentic". Rowan (2005) uses "authentic" and "relational" interchangeably; I prefer "relational"; "authentic" seems to imply that their third way of relating - transpersonal - and the instrumental way are somehow "inauthentic" in the ordinary sense of the word.

Overview of theoretical models

Sills's keynote address at a recent international TA conference provides a convenient starting point for illustrating some of the difficulties inherent in discussing diversity of theory (Sills 2004). Her presentation is probably all that conference organisers would desire; it gives enough for all to identify with and ends on an up-beat note of "celebrating differences". At the same time it demonstrates that the issues raised by the notion of 'core competences' is still very much alive.

In brief, Sills starts with an overview of research that she regards as a relevant neurological basis of our need for, and strategies we use in, tolerating differences. She links these findings with scripting, games and "our shadow" which "we then project onto others" and states:

> "Those qualities that we cannot tolerate in ourselves we unconsciously and painlessly attribute to our enemies". (Sills 2004, p, 1)

She then contrasts religion with politics. Religion is "intended to bring people together under one set of beliefs – thus excluding others" and politics is "intended to be a space for encapsulating differences, using diplomacy, mediating different priorities and needs and finding compromise" (Sills, 2004 p. 6). She continues to caution against:

> "religionizing transactional analysis instead of allowing the diversity of true politics – in other words, providing space for differences to be discussed and negotiated". (Sills, 2004 p. 1)

Sills proceeds to list six "traditions" or different ways in which transactional analysis is currently practised, comments on her perceptions of their strengths, and ends with her hope that

> "we can both recognize and forgive ourselves for our reluctance and resistance to these differences, and still find ways to rise to the challenge of being with each other in our differences, and ultimately, to celebrate them". (Sills, 2004 p. 6)

I have no quibble with her conclusion, if only on the grounds that a presupposition of celebration is respect for alternative points of view. When this does not prevail celebration goes out of the window and respect becomes competitive labelling - an artful process of appearing not to blemish others, while demonstrating that 'mine's better than yours'.

In contrast, Tudor and Hobbes (2002) give a wider perspective than Sills's, perhaps largely because they are writing within a framework that requires them to include dimensions such as an historical context of the development of transactional analysis, its main theoretical assumptions, various approaches, which clients benefit most, and their perception of the strengths and limitations of TA models. They unashamedly express a preference for a "co-creative" constructivist approach which:

> "shifts the therapeutic emphasis away from the treatment of ego-state structures and toward an exploration of how relational possibilities are co-created on a moment-to-moment basis". (Summers and Tudor, 2000 p.36)

Tudor and Hobbes give a succinct account of the major theoretical orientations in transactional analysis:

- Classical TA (psychodynamic), drawing on Berne's early work. developed most recently by Carlo Moiso and Michele Novellino (see Moiso, 1985) and influenced by object relations theory;
- Classical TA (cognitive-behaviourist), also drawing on Berne's work (for a recent contribution to which see Mothersole, 2001), a tradition which has also been influenced by methods from neurolinguistic programming (see Stewart, 1996);
- Redecision School founded by Mary and Robert Goulding (see Goulding and Goulding, 1979) and influenced by Fritz Perls and Gestalt therapy
- Cathexis School, founded by Jacqui Schiff (see Schiff et al., 1975) and developed from Jacqui and Mo Schiff's experience of working with severely disturbed and psychotic clients;
- Radical or Social Psychiatry (in many ways, the 'lost tradition' of TA), originally promoted by Claude Steiner and others (see Agel, 1971: Wyckoff, 1976), based on theory of alienation and influenced by radical politics (for a more recent summary of which see Steiner, 2000);
- Integrative TA, influenced by Gestalt conceptualisations of the ego and self-psychology (see Erskine and Moursund, 1988; Clarkson, 1992);
- Narrative TA, influenced by field theory, social constructivism and dialogic psychotherapy (see Allen and Allen 1995, 1997; Summers and Tudor, 2000)". (Tudor and Hobbes, 2002, p. 243)

Subsequently, Hargaden and Sills have advanced what they regard as another distinctive approach:

"Relational TA involves bringing largely unconscious intrapsychic processes into the interpersonal/intersubjective realm, in order to be understood and changed via the interpersonal process of relatedness". (Sills, 2004 p. 6)

More recently, the April 2005 issue of the Transactional Analysis Journal with the theme of "Transactional Analysis and Psychoanalysis" endorses the view that there is:

"a thirst within the transactional analysis community to find a voice in the world of depth psychotherapy and, to a certain extent, reflect the struggle to find our voice in the marketplace of psychotherapies". (Hargaden, 2005, p. 106)

Nevertheless, by definition, any classification, *by itself*, excludes others as much as it facilitates discussion of differences. Furthermore, classifications create boundaries, and often the implication seems to be that one has to declare allegiance to a particular territory - or that it is impossible or undesirable to adopt different approaches at different times with different clients.

This is not to say that we should blind ourselves to differences – no more so than we should ignore the differences between cars, trucks, vans or buses. Different types of vehicles exist and are used for different purposes. Cars are ideal for rapid journeys on good roads, but have severe limitations when it comes to moving farm manure; vans enable one to do both in a limited sort of way.

The shortcoming of perspectives on the diversity of theoretical models is that practitioners are prone to develop expertise in using one model at the expense of others; the danger is that theory, rather than client needs, comes to dictate practice.

As I see it, the problem with current discussions about diversity is as much a matter of finding a forum for discussing differences of theory and context, as it is a matter of how we do so and to whom our points of view are addressed. To this end, I outline below an extract from a document written by British transactional analysts as the basis for discussion of "Diversity and Shared Identity" at a two day residential meeting of TA trainers.

> "One could focus on many differences, and three that perhaps stand out are:
> - <u>contracting</u> - quintessential in some approaches (e.g. classical, redecision), 'open ended' in relational TA, non-verbal contracting in body TA, and multi level in the organisational field
> - how the therapist accounts and works with <u>transference</u> - compare for example, what [is said] about entering the symbiosis with [what is said] on co-creation, or contrast .... present-centeredness with the role of the therapist in redecision's early scene work
> - the nature of the <u>therapeutic relationship</u> - variously described as permission giver (classical), facilitator (redecision), new parent (cathexis), participant facilitator (co-creative), intersubjective co-creator of the unconscious relationship (relational) - note also [the] discussion of boundaries in comparing and contrasting organisational consultancy and personal work. .... suggests that the relationship becomes the unifying factor that allows us to move flexibly or integratively between traditions". (Davis, 2004, p. 3)

This type of event represents an example of the kind of ongoing discourse that is needed to grapple with the complexity of the topic. In particular, the three factors cited by Davis – contracting, transference and the relationship between client and practitioner (rather than the exclusive notion of the therapeutic relationship) – seem to me to be a useful framework for exploring the diversity of theory. Above all, it seems clear that the notion of diversity is as much a matter of whose perceptions are under consideration, as it is any sort of consensus about the pros and cons of different approaches.

Splitting
Berne started disseminating his ideas via his early publications, and later, in person to his colleagues by way of the San Francisco Social Psychiatry Seminars. It was from these beginnings and against this background that transactional analysis was 'exported' from the clinical domain to other settings. The formation of the International Transactional Analysis Association in 1965 made provision for three categories of specialisation in the application of TA – clinical, organisational and educational. The rationale is that transactional analysis embodies concepts that are relevant to the dynamics of relationships in all settings – and that qualifications in these areas signify proficiency in the application of transactional analysis, rather than other aspects of competence particular to the setting.

Clinicians do not have to consider the positive aspects of theory; the bread and butter of their everyday work are the investigation and correction of negatives. They stop seeing clients once 'normal' behaviour is established. Ideally, organisational and educational specialists start with the assumption of health and strive to improve growth. They often choose to translate concepts (such as drivers) into more everyday sounding terms ('working styles') that are meaningful and acceptable to their clients. In other words, the very language of transactional analysis is a hurdle that clinicians do not have to clear.[1] But there is more to

---

[1] Some clinicians have been at pains to coin 'new' terms for revisions of psychiatric syndromes – see for example, Joines 1986, Joines and Stewart 2002.

the first divide than an emphasis on the negative; the slant slides transactional analysts into the third divide – in the following way.

Over the years many organisational and educational members of the TA community have come to feel discounted by their clinical colleagues. The fact that they are outnumbered in most national associations often seems to add to the view that their contributions and skills are not always fully recognised as being equal to, but different from, those of psychotherapists. In the United Kingdom a group of eminent practitioners have formed an Institute of Developmental Transactional Analysis (IDTA). Their website carries the following statement:

> "Transactional analysis is a social psychology, a theory of human personality and a systematic approach for growth and personal change of individuals, groups and organisations. International qualifications are available (via the ITAA and EATA – the International and European TA Associations) in four fields – Organisational, Educational, Counselling* and Psychotherapy.
> In the past, the non-therapy applications of TA were known as Special Fields, but the term Developmental TA had now been adopted as this captures the emphasis on development rather than the psychotherapeutic focus on cure.
> * EATA defines the Counselling field as related to 'problem management and personal development ..... in relation to their social, professional and cultural environment' – some work and school based counsellors, coaches, mentors, etc may find that their counselling is related more to developmental TA than to psychotherapy". (see http://www.adinternational.com/idta.htm)

This seems to convey an entirely valid point of view and the very existence of IDTA may be as much a solution to, as it is evidence of, a divide. Indeed, I particularly like the contrast of cure versus growth. The extent to which similar associations are likely to spring up in other countries remains to be seen. The fact that IDTA has an affiliation agreement with EATA and is "working in close co-operation" with the UK national association is an interesting development with several implications. For example, it seems to hold the promise of radical institutional growth and development for the whole transactional analysis community. On the other hand, IDTA may end up being seen as a deviant group intent on excluding anyone without formal qualifications in organisational work and unsympathetic to the aspirations posted on their website. Likewise, it seems clear to me that there are wider issues involved – as illustrated by the following case study.

Case study
The background to this case study is the circumstances leading to a dispute among British trainers about the number of hours of personal therapy a psychotherapist should be required to have completed before being registered in the United Kingdom by the major professional body, the United Kingdom Council for Psychotherapy (UKCP). Without going into the detail of a complex situation, the relevant facts are that UKCP is an 'umbrella' organisation whose Member Organisations (MOs) are training agencies that endorse individuals as competent therapists. UKCP accepts names submitted by MOs and publishes a Register of qualified therapists. The local Institute of Transactional Analysis (ITA) is an MO of the Humanistic and Integrative Section (HIPS) of UKCP and, hence, eligible to nominate individuals for inclusion in the Register.

The dispute arose because the HIPS Training Standards Committee had decided that candidates for inclusion in the Register should have completed forty hours of therapy per year for a minimum of four years. Several trainers objected, pointing to the standards of

European Association for TA (EATA) - which leaves the question of personal therapy to the trainers' discretion. By virtue of its UKCP membership, the ITA Council was obliged to implement the HIPS decision; local requirements were regarded by some as superseding the EATA guidelines.

At a meeting of trainers, several splits started to emerge – trainers versus Council, the relative merits of ITA or EATA standards, and 'psychoanalytic' trainers (who argued for forty hours of individual therapy per year) opposing those who were labelled 'cognitive behavioural' (who, broadly speaking, favoured various versions of "personal therapy of a frequency and nature that the candidate intends to practice, for the duration of training").

Eventually it was suggested that trainers should recruit a facilitator with experience of handling conflict in groups to mediate a consensus among trainers (at the next trainers meeting), that could be forwarded to the ITA Council for further negotiation with HIPS. The suggested facilitator was a psychoanalytically trained group therapist. A vote was taken at the meeting and a trainer was nominated to sound out the facilitator. It was also suggested that the ITA Council should renegotiate the matter with HIPS on the basis of "a minimum of 160 hours over four years".

In between trainers meetings, an organisational member of ITA sent the following e-mail to all trainers.

Dear fellow trainers,

I am writing after considerable hesitation - I have thought about doing so in response to some of the stimulating items in ITA News from ..... over the past year. I have hesitated because I am an organisational member and on the face of it what is being discussed are therapy issues; and also because it feels safer as a minority member to keep my head down. However ITA is my professional organisation, and maybe its time for me to take more responsibility as a member. So I offer these thoughts as a contribution to the thinking, as a perspective I have on the ITA, as a stimulus to colleagues.

I joined the ITA in 1990, and went to my first conference and AGM in 1992. It quickly became apparent to me that there was a split in the membership of the ITA - at that point in time it was about the trainers and the rest of the membership/executive. What I noticed then has been a repeating pattern I have observed subsequently - the dynamic of splitting being the way the organisation's culture deals with issues of power - which manifests as 'I am more OK than you'.

This more recently manifest as the split between the psychotherapy and the other fields - and as a result some of my colleagues from other fields split off and set up another organisation [ITDA]. (Not all - I have not gone along with this split as it seems to me to act out into the split does not heal the issues but perpetuates them). The feelings of powerlessness, not being heard, not having impact, being discounted and so on are very real for those in the 'minority' - and do not go away even if the split is formalised and seemingly welcomed. And the enrichment that diversity offers, and the opportunity for tolerance and for practicing what we preach about OK-ness and accounting, rather than discounting, and for finding solutions that heal, are then lost.

When I work with organisations who have called me in as a consultant because there is conflict between people, I point out that even if this is seemingly resolved, or if some of these people leave, the conflict will most likely reappear between others and in other guises, because there will be things still in the structure which are perpetuating conflict in the culture. (It seems to me that Berne is saying this in the Structure and Dynamics book - dynamic manifestations are maintained by the structure). Therefore to make best use of me as a consultant there needs to be a willingness amongst the people in the organisation to look at what's up in the structure - this might be about boundaries, or about leadership, or about resources, or about the type of organisation, about its vision and mission, and so on - and to be prepared to deal with this, in order to bring about change in the culture. Talking about this and any underlying fears and uncertainties, become part of the contractual process. It takes time. This current split between 'cognitive behavioural' and 'psychoanalytic' ideologies within the therapy field seems to me to be one more split that is a reflection of deeper organisational issues.

These organisational issues have been evident too at other levels - the rifts between ITAA and EATA for example. (Conjecture amongst some transactional analysts is that this goes back to the original leader and euhemerus, and the way the organisation was set up initially). These are all voluntary and membership organisations without paid and consistent leadership, and with a mixture of a bureaucratic and ad hoc structure - and as Sari van Poelje who is an organisational TSTA writes, such organisations expect of their consultant either a mechanic (who will tinker and fine tune the engine, which will inevitably go wrong again) or a wizard who will rapidly perform magic! With this in mind I would hope that any external consultant would have enough information to say 'no' to an invitation to a one-off, such as is being proposed, and to negotiate an extended contract.

Is there enough expertise within the ITA to do this consultancy process for ourselves? Certainly - and Berne provides us with lots of ideas about organisations, and there are a number of people with organisational experience. Inviting an external consultant can further the splitting process, and allow for discounting of the consultancy process - especially if a one-off. On the other hand such a parallel process provides the external consultant with real experience of the process in action. The other advantage of an external is that, if there is a deficit in the functions of leadership (which is almost an inevitable with voluntary posts) then the external person can temporarily carry the leadership functions which can be a useful step in the process.

I would have concern that the consultant being considered is from a psychoanalytic frame, if the presenting issue is about psychoanalytic versus cognitive behavioural approaches. I would urge you to all remember that TA does include a field of organisational consultants, and that there are many outside Britain. It seems to me to be healthy to use our own frameworks to consider ourselves - and Berne and others have provided these. I would propose a consultant from TA who has a lot of experience and qualifications in working with organisations, and is not, nor has been, a member of the ITA. I can understand that as therapists make up the majority of ITA members, and the prompting issue is about therapeutic frameworks, it might help foster a sense of security to identify a TA consultant who is also a TA therapist. One example is [name]. I believe that there are others in Germany, France and Switzerland, many of whom have good English.

However this is unlikely to be a one-off event and a more open-ended contract may be necessary. I can foresee that there may be difficulties in defining the contract in the first place - and that is maybe all that can take place at a trainers meeting (remembering that the getting of the contract is often much of the work!) And structures will need to be built in the ITA to carry forward culture change too, if this is part of the process/outcome.

Overall, as this is a voluntary and membership organisation, with only one paid admin post, I consider an external consultant to be worth paying for. £60 per hour is at the lower end of the spectrum - about £500 per day is what is normally charged in Britain to not-for-profit agencies by consultants who specialise in this area. I understand from TA colleagues on the continent that charges can be higher there. With an appropriate contract this can be money well spent.

I hope that this e-mail invites other ways of thinking about the issues and the ways forward. I really want us to find a way forward as an organisation with a way of working that is truly valuing of diversity and equality - and in these times where there is so much splitting going on in our world, we can maybe provide a model of how to be with difference.

As far as I know, the writer received a mere handful of responses from among a hundred or so trainers, all applauding the writer's stance in speaking out. Along with this, a flurry of e-mails crossed the ether raising doubts about whether or not a vote had *actually* been taken at the trainers meeting and if so, had it been *properly* taken?

In the meantime, the ITA Council had delegated the task of renegotiating the matter to its Training Standards Committee. At the subsequent trainers meeting, it was reported that a settlement had been reached. There was some discussion about what this would mean in practical terms but, by and large, the matter was smoothed over; trainees could go before Exam Boards and become Certified Transactional Analysts, but would not be eligible for inclusion in the UKCP Register unless they had completed a minimum of 160 hours of personal therapy. There was a brief discussion about the need for an external facilitator and it was concluded that the issue had become redundant.

My guess is that the above events are not atypical of TA meetings worldwide – or indeed, of meetings conducted in most other professional circles. From my sixteen years of representing the ITA at the UKCP, I know that psychotherapists, in particular, are often lacking in political sophistication yet capable of building egalitarian social institutions. TA practitioners are well placed for such a task but somehow within our own community we do not always rise to the occasion. At one level this is no "big deal", yet at another level it is. Despite the rubric of "I'm OK – You're OK", we do not yet fully "walk our talk." It seems sad that the vast majority of practitioners are able to do so in relation to clients but often struggle with collegial relationships. My hope is that this book will contribute to bridging such divides.

Suggestions

It is often easier to identify problems than it is to advance 'solutions'. What follows are not solutions – merely suggestions for positive courses of action that add grist to the mill of grinding the divides.

In the first place, I think we need a panoramic view of the situation. The divides in transactional analysis are not going to disappear. This is fortunate rather than unfortunate - inasmuch as it enables the TA community to deal with the polarities involved.

> ".. healing and growth depends not on the avoidance of tension but on the maintenance of it for developmental work to continue. This is not only a feature of individual decision making and development. We can see this timeless archetypal movement in the structure and dynamics of the basic unit of collective life and decision-making: the small group". (Wood and Petriglieri 2005 p. 39)

To this I would add "and organisations or networks" – namely the transactional analysis community. In other words, I would suggest that there are ample resources within the TA community to evoke the "synthesis [that] emerges from the tension" (Wood and Petriglieri 2005 p. 39) to affect or, at least, commence the necessary healing.

Secondly, discussion of diversity is not going to disappear – nor should it. In my view, what would help is a considered examination of how to teach transactional analysis from a *historical* perspective. Virtually everyone agrees that there at least seven different models of transactional analysis theory. Given that the official ITAA approved introductory course is based on topics that were prescribed at least thirty years ago, there is ample room for revision and improvement. For example, it would not be impossible to extend the present twelve hours of the official introductory workshop to include, at least, coverage of 'contemporary approaches and their underlying philosophies'.

Similarly, the basic qualification could be widened to include a mandatory written assignment critiquing transactional analysis theory. In Europe, the present requirements for the written exam include thirteen open book questions of which candidates must answer six as a supplement to an extended case study. My suggestion is that at least one of these six questions should require commentary on a candidate's perception of the strengths and potential shortcomings of transactional analysis theory.

Of equal importance is the question of research. I would urge the transactional analysis community to seriously consider expanding the standards of the Certified Transactional Analysis examination process by stipulating that practitioners must demonstrate knowledge of basic research methodology. Again, this could be done via one of the six written exam questions - although I am sure there are other creative ways of assessing this aspect of professional competence. Personally, I would even go as far as introducing an additional, optional post-CTA category of membership – a Teaching, *Research* and Supervising Transactional Analysis member.

I predict that none of the above, or any other, suggestions will carry much weight without a fundamental change in organisational structure. In theory, this could involve the transfer of existing resources of the ITAA to a global body with world wide representation, resources, power and authority. I raise this as a matter for serious consideration while recognising that the complexities of such a change are a political matter beyond the scope of this book.

Key Points 2

2.1 **Divides** in organisations and social movements are internal sources of tension that have become polarised and overspill organisational boundaries. There are **three divides** in transactional analysis.

2.2 The first divide between **health and psychopathology** concerns the application of a theory developed from observations of 'dysfunctional' behaviours, to practice in settings with 'functional' behaviours. The under-emphasis on the positive aspects of personality and relationships permeates transactional analysis theory and literature.

2.3 The **second divide** requires a **balance** to be struck between the simultaneous application of **theory to practice**, with the need continuously to **research and develop** new aspects of theory and practice. This divide carries the potential of isolating transactional analysis from the wider community of person professions.

2.4 Transactional analysis has not been consistently rigorous about demonstrating validity, reliability and effectiveness, but is not alone in having to deal with the practice/research divide.

2.5 The **third divide** ranges from discussions of the diversity of theoretical concepts to competitive labelling – declaring by fiat the "truth" of a particular model of transactional analysis.

2.6 Recent examples of the "**Core Concepts**", provides ample evidence of widely differing views on what does or should constitute the theory of transactional analysis. These discussions have tended to focus on theoretical ideas or ideological values, largely ignoring **contextual factors** such as culture, politics, organisational structures, and perhaps, above all, economics. They also overlook the fact that Berne's modernist perspective does not fit comfortably with a post-modernist point of view.

2.7 Tudor and Hobbes (2002) and Sills (2004) identify **seven distinct models** of transactional analysis. The shortcoming of perspectives on the diversity of theoretical models is that practitioners are prone to develop expertise in using one model at the expense of others; the danger is that theory rather than client needs comes to dictate practice.

2.8 Examples of **best practice** in developing theoretical and practical models are given by *Joines and Stewart* (2002) and *Hargaden and Sills* (2002. Both pairs of authors successfully bridge the theory/research divide – but in very different ways.

2.9 Another way of examining differences between TA models is that there are three ways of using self:

- the **instrumental** way, where the main emphasis is on treating the client,
- the **relational** way, where the main emphasis is on meeting the client,
- the **transpersonal way**, where the main emphasis is on linking with the client in a spiritual way and stressing the importance of body-mind unity.

2.10 Joines and Stewart's work is mostly *instrumental* and Hargaden and Sills adopt a *relational* use of self.

2.11 A case study and the creation of a separate focus on **"developmental" transactional analysis,** demonstrates how many organisational and educational members of the TA community have come to feel discounted by their clinical colleagues.

2.10 Suggestions for **positive courses of action** include teaching transactional analysis from a *historical* perspective, widening the basic qualification to include a mandatory written assignment critiquing transactional analysis theory, and creating a new category of membership of a Teaching, Research and Supervising Transactional Analyst.

2.11 The prediction that none of the above, or any other, suggestions will carry much weight without a fundamental change in organisational structure is beyond the scope of this book.

Chapter 3

Beyond the divides

This Chapter outlines the basis of my ideas for developing aspects of theory and practice that, in the final part of the book, takes transactional analysis beyond the three divides towards what I have termed an integral or holistic view of a person and their relationships, within the context of their culture and society. **Part Six** describes the whole person by incorporating aspects of human behaviour that transactional analysis does not fully address. Principally these shortcomings exist in three of four main areas that, to my way of thinking, constitute a 'whole' person – body, mind, soul and spirit. As previously noted, transactional analysis says a lot about mind, very little about body and even less about soul and spirit. To be fair, it has to be acknowledged that Berne never set out to address the gamut of knowledge encompassed by these concepts. He produced what he referred to as a "social psychiatry" (Berne, 1964 p. 51) that was far in advance of anything else written in his day.

This book does not advance a new 'theory', but does propose several new concepts. However, before delving into these, and because I extend transactional analysis into the realm of the spiritual or transpersonal, it is essential for readers to be clear about the epistemological basis of my approach.

Epistemology

Epistemology is the branch of philosophy that is concerned with knowledge. It addresses questions such as how do we know what we know, how do we convey what we know to others, and how can, or do, others come to decide whether or not what we convey is valid. What follows is my understanding of a *process* – a clarification of the "certain rules" referred to in **Chapter 2** - rather than definitive *answers* to the questions in the preceding sentence.

Wilber (1983) points out that a 13th century monk, St Bonaventure, used the metaphor of three "eyes" or sources of knowledge. He claimed that we know what we know by using the eye of flesh, the eye of reason and the eye of contemplation. In other words, there are three *sources* of knowledge or *modes* of knowing – sensory, mental and spiritual. As long as we remember that one mode cannot usurp the role of the other two, then, subject to certain qualifications (explained below), all three 'eyes' yield legitimate or 'valid' knowledge in their own domain. Trying to explain the nature of phenomena in one sphere through the eye of another constitutes a *category error*. For example, you cannot explain the meaning of *Hamlet* by recourse to sensibilia – data yielded by using the eye of flesh – by explaining how atoms make molecules, how molecules combine to make cells, how under certain circumstances, cells can give rise to thoughts and so forth. To explain the meaning of *Hamlet* you need recourse to intelligiblia – information derived from the use of the eye of reason.

> "there is no *empirical*-scientific proof for the meaning of *Hamlet*. It is a mental-symbolic production and can thus be understood or apprehended only by a mental act – sensory evidence is almost entirely worthless. *Hamlet* is not composed of electrons, molecules, wood or zinc; it is composed of *units of meaning* – mental data - which disclose themselves not as sensibilia but as intelligiblia". (Wilber 1983, p. 48)

Moreover, in transactional analysis all our fundamental concepts are based on knowledge that is rational and deductive, not empirical and inductive. With inductive reasoning a proposition is generally called a hypothesis. When tested in all sorts of conditions and not disproved, a hypothesis is to that extent confirmed. The difference between an empirical-

26

inductive and rational-deductive approach lies mainly in the difference between measurement and classification. Ego states, for example, are classifications of phenomenological data. Indeed, most psychological concepts are derived from knowledge that is grounded in the eye of reason.

> "It has to be kept in mind that the evidence which the analyst can present differs essentially from that which is required in physical sciences, because the whole nature of psychoanalysis is different...the workings of the unconscious mind, and the response of the psychoanalyst to them, cannot be submitted to measurement .." (Klein, 1961)

By the same logic, to argue for or against the existence of God in terms other than transcendelia – revelations (data) stemming from the eye of contemplation – is a category error. It is this hurdle we have to negotiate if we are going to be able to use transactional analysis at a transpersonal level.

However, in all three domains, avoiding the pitfalls of category errors is not enough for the outcome to be an epistemologically sound process. In each domain, there is another process that takes the form of "if you want to know x, do y, then check with others who know how to do y." As Wilber explains:

> ".. all valid knowledge – in whatever realm – consists of three basic components, which we will call injunction, illumination, and confirmation. ..all *valid knowledge* consists most fundamentally of these basic components:
> 1. *An instrumental or injunctive strand.* This is a set of instructions, simple or complex, internal or external. All have the form: "If you want to know this, do this"
> 2. *An illuminative or apprehensive strand.* This is an alternative *seeing* by the particular eye of knowledge evoked by the injunctive strand. Besides being self-illuminative, it leads to the possibility of:
> 3. *A communal strand.* This is the actual sharing of the illuminative seeing with others who are using the same eye. If the shared-vision is agreed upon by others, this constitutes a communal proof of *true seeing".* (Wilber 1983 pp. 31-32)[1]

Wilber illustrates the operation of the three strands by giving:

> " .. the most difficult example: Freudian psychoanalysis. ... Freud began with an empiric-analytic or merely physiological approach. ....But .. It was the *meaning* of psychological data – their intentionality and interpretation (interpretation of dreams, symptoms etc.) - that Freud most wanted to study. That is, his approach, and his territory, was almost entirely mental-phenomenological, hermeneutical, and historical – the *history* here simply being the history and development of the person's own self-system (past fixations, traumas, repressions, etc.) ... psychoanalysis was a *dialogue* – it demanded *inter-subjective discourse* – the "talking cure".

---

[1] Training in transactional analysis follows these three strands exactly. A trainee will spend between four to five years on the first two and it takes somewhere between four to five hours for a written case study to be marked and for an oral Exam Board to listen to and question the trainee on audio-taped client work.

It is also noted that the consensual nature of the *communal strand* constitutes the basis of reciprocity and intersubjectivity (Hargaden and Fenton, 2005), a point to which we will return in later Chapters.

Further .... Freud's major discovery was not a theory, but an *injunction.* The injunction was free association, which disclosed an object domain (data) hitherto largely ignored (unconscious primary process). ... So important was the free association injunction that to this day, it is called the "basic rule of psychoanalysis". .... By using this injunction, Freud began to collect data on this new object domain, unconscious primary process. And these data could be *checked* by anyone willing to follow the three strands: (1) take up the injunction to free associate; (2) note the resultant apprehension or data; and (3) compare and contrast these data in a community of the similarly adequate". (Wilber 1983, p. 57)

Wilber continues to emphasise that:

".. a mental-phenomenological proposition, to be recognized as sound, must not only account for data, it must do so in a fashion capable of withstanding the fire of unrestrained communication and intersubjective discourse. The circle of subjectivity will eventually but soundly rebuff and dislodge those hypothetical forms that do not mesh with its intersubjective structures. Thus, some of Freud's theories have generally passed the test: .... Others of his theories have not meshed with informed intersubjective consensus and have thus been dropped from the ongoing development of psychological theory". (Wilber 1983, p. 58)

But there is more to the three strands than collecting data and checking this with like minded (trained) colleagues. Wilber explains this as follows:

"We have seen that each of the three general modes of knowing – sensory, mental, and spiritual – has access to direct, immediate, and intuitive apprehensions or data (sensibilia, intelligibilia, and transcendelia). Notice, however that the very data of the *mental mode* – its words and symbols and concepts – simply because they are indeed symbolic, intentional, reflective, and referential can be used to *point* to, or *represent, other* data, from any other realm: sensibilia, intelligibilia, or transcendelia. We can indicate all these epistemological relationships as follows:

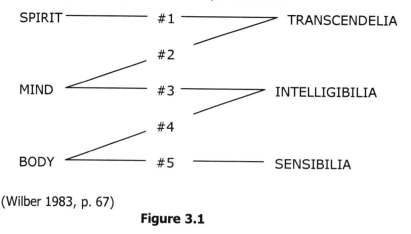

(Wilber 1983, p. 67)

Figure 3.1

Wilber then explains each of these relationships:

"Mode #5 is simple sensorimotor cognition, the eye of flesh, the presymbolic grasp of the presymbolic world (sensibilia)". (Wilber 1983, p. 67)

This is pure experience – without words. For example, I look at my keyboard. To translate this into a "pure experience", I must simply *perceive* without *any labels.* Not everyone finds it easy to do this, but with a little practise, most people get the knack of simply noticing differences. But "differences" is a word, a concept. So, simply notice. An easier task is to listen to music without lyrics – preferably something you have never heard before. If you do not have any musical training and do not 'recognise' particular instruments, you will be left with pure sound. Obviously, these examples are 'artificial' inasmuch as they focus primarily on only one sense modality. Some of the techniques described in **Chapters 19** to **23** are derived from Mode #5 experiences.

The next sentence is a 'minimalist' statement of mode #4. I look at my keyboard on the desk. Wilber explains this as:

> "Mode #4 is empiric-analytic thought; it is mind (intelligibilia) reflecting on and grounding itself in the world of sensibilia". (Wilber 1983, p. 67)

This is kernel of the techniques described in **Chapters 21** to **23**; the exercises *may* lead to mode #5 experiences.

In contrast, knowledge based on mode #3 is the usual way of conceptualising, describing and explaining theoretical ideas. This applies to the three models in **Parts One** to **Five** of this book, as well as the theoretical discourse in **Part Six**. Wilber's description of mode #3 is:

> "Mode #3 is mental-phenomenological thought; it is mind (intelligibilia) reflecting on and grounding itself *in* the world of intelligibilia itself". (Wilber 1983, p. 67)

Mode #2 is a crucial aspect of going beyond a purely interpersonal view of humankind. Berne's statements about Physis, for example, involve this type of thinking/knowledge. Wilber explains mode #2 as:

> "Mode #2 can be called mandalic or paradoxical thinking; it is mind (intelligibilia) attempting to reason about spirit or transcendelia". (Wilber 1983, p. 67)

Finally, the ineffable level of mode #1 is:

> "And mode #1 is *gnosis*, the eye of contemplation, the transsymbolic grasp of the transsymbolic world, spirit's direct knowledge of spirit, the immediate intuition of transcendelia". (Wilber 1983, p. 67)

From these categories, Wilber makes the point that:

> "A theory or hypotheses, then, is an *immediately* apprehended mental datum (or gestalt of data) used to *mediately* [sic?] point to, map, or logically systemize, other *immediately* apprehended data (sensory, mental, spiritual.) But if a theory is a mental map, nonetheless the map may be wrong, and what distinguishes a theory or hypothesis from a merely dogmatic formulation, is its call to experiential or data-based verification. A hypothesis is not just a formulation of present data; it is a formulation of present data in an attempt to create a map that will not be surprised by future data. And the only way to see if a map is surprised by future data is to actually gather future data.

And we have already seen the means for doing so: the three strands of data accumulation and verification – injunction, apprehension and confirmation. With hypotheses, there is simply the *extra step* of *intermediate mapping*: the readjustment (or sometimes total rejection) of the hypothesis or map in light of the newly acquired data. A hypothesis, then, is a tentative map *plus* suggested injunctions". (Wilber 1983, p. 68)

The significance of such considerations is probably not the norm for transactional analysts. The traditional way in which transactional analysis theory and practice has developed is for someone to publish an article – preferably a short article – in the TAJ and then promote the idea by presentations at Conferences. This is by no means unusual in the social sciences. However, as indicated in **Chapter 2**, because transactional analysis lacks a research-oriented culture, alternative new ideas tend not to be replicated, verified or elaborated. For better or for worse, it has taken something like the core competences debate to raise the epistemological status of different approaches.

ERICA and epistemology

There are three reasons why I draw attention to epistemology. The first is that the above "rules" apply to all models of or approaches to transactional analysis. Our inattention to the verification of basic concepts leads to wrangling about various models, rather than taking "the *extra step* of *intermediate mapping*: the readjustment (or sometimes total rejection) of the hypothesis or map in light of the newly acquired data" (Wilber 1983, p.68)

Secondly, in **Part Six**, I suggest that paying attention to consciousness itself as well as its contents is a powerful therapeutic ally largely unengaged by our current repertoire of transactional analysis knowledge and skills.

"Transpersonal experiences may be defined as experiences in which the sense of identity or self extends beyond (trans-) the individual or personal to encompass wider aspects of humankind, life, psyche and cosmos.... Transpersonal therapy is therapy informed by a transpersonal perspective, which recognizes the value and validity of transpersonal experiences and development. The transpersonal model clearly holds consciousness as a central dimension. Traditional Western schools of psychology have held differing positions with regard to consciousness. These range from behaviorism, which ignores it, to psychodynamic and humanistic approaches, which pay more attention to its contents than to consciousness itself. A transpersonal model views "normal" consciousness as a defensively contracted state of reduced awareness". (Walsh and Vaughan 1996, p 16-17)

The final part of this book gives a theory of and rationale for using transactional analysis at a transpersonal level. By incorporating consciousness as will be described, it is possible to expand the perspective of the transactional analysis model from its current intra/interpersonal base to a transpersonal level. I describe techniques for accessing the transpersonal level and discuss the implications of incorporating the development of consciousness within a transactional analysis model of social interaction. All the techniques I introduce address the fact that 'people have bodies'.

As far as I know, few transactional analysts regard the transpersonal dimension (modes #2 and #1) as a significant variable or specifically work with somatic processes (modes #4 and #5). Both modes stem from a model of the development of consciousness (Wilber 1986 pp 267- 291). Although I explain this using the eye of reason (mode #3), ultimately, the techniques (mode #2) target the eye of contemplation to go beyond "a defensively contracted state of reduced awareness" (Walsh and Vaughan 1996, p 17), which is mode#1.

It is also helpful to have a map or system for understanding the nature of consciousness. My preferred map is Wilber's "all quadrants – all levels" approach.

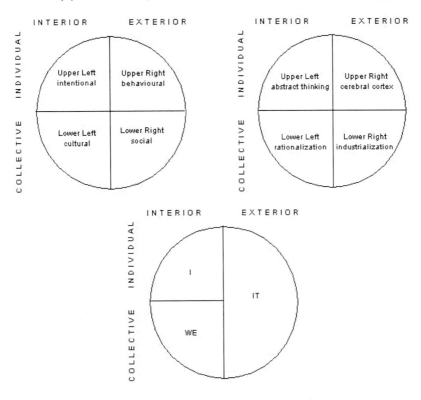

Figure 3.2

Figure 3.2 (derived from Visser, 2003) illustrates how our perception of the world may be seen from different points of view. If we confine ourselves to "objective" reality, we are referring to the right 'exterior' half of each circle. "Subjective" reality on the other hand, is located 'internally' in the left hand halves of the circles. Likewise, the focus of inquiry may be individual or collective. "Reality" is defined by consensus using the language of the three personal pronouns "I", "we" and "it". Thus, in the top right circle for example, if we consider a level of normal developmental such as abstract thought, (upper left quadrant), we can see that the neocortex (upper right quadrant) is a necessary prerequisite for it and those capable thereof will tend to create a rational culture (lower left quadrant), typically within an industrialised society (low right quadrant). Most psychotherapy is concerned with the upper left quadrant and 'traditional' psychiatrists tend to operate mostly in the upper right quadrant. When discussing, say, the relative merits of one drug versus another, or the pros and cons of prescribing medication rather than psychotherapy, psychiatrists will be largely using "it" language. However, the process of their interpersonal communication is a "we" activity. Silent prayer or contemplation at a Quaker meeting focuses on "I" and "we" – as do most theories or models of psychotherapy. Note too, that some of the "we" language

discussion of differences between transactional analysts may involve preferences for the use of "we" or "it" language descriptions of clients or therapeutic procedures.[1]

Wilber's map may even also be extended to accommodate concentric divisions in each of the circles for matter, body, mind, soul and spirit. Intrinsic to the AQAL model is the fact that consciousness develops in an orderly fashion and one may view the entire gamut of human development as a 'spectrum of consciousness' (Wilber 1977). This idea is discussed extensively in **Part Six**.

My third reason for drawing attention to epistemological issues is that this book is an invitation to colleagues to join "the fire of unrestrained communication and intersubjective discourse" that will constitute the third communal strand of verification and, hopefully, contribute to an amelioration of the divides.

Awareness

Awareness is the key to understanding and using ERICA. Awareness simply is. Once you go beyond this statement, you start messing about with awareness. You muddy the waters, you thicken the porridge, you dilute the taste, you snuffle the smell, and you toggle the touch. You start to qualify, to expand, elaborate, focus or constrict your awareness. Even the preceding sentence imperceptibly required you to alter your awareness. It (and virtually every other sentence in this book) is cast in the form of a duality – subject and object – or more likely, subject-predicate-object. I am typing; you are reading. While or as you read, you are thinking whatever it is that you are thinking. However, I'll guarantee that whatever it is that you are/were thinking, is not *all* of which you are/were aware. For example, I am also aware of the music in the background, and, now that I think of it, I am also aware of the low hum-hiss of the computer. And suddenly, I am aware of a surreal kaleidoscoped aural collage of the buzzing bees that swarm in the hollow trunk of the huge, half-dead blue gum tree outside aunt Edie's *stoep* [2] and the swishing sound of *mealiestalks* [2] shivering in the slippery shadow of a departing thunder storm. And sixty years later, I shiver again, aware that the patio door is open.

No one can ever escape being aware – unless they are asleep or dead – and even then, as we shall see, interesting phenomena prevail. In the meantime, do you have to change your awareness, alter your state of consciousness, to know that you are awake, dreaming, or asleep? Is this question different from asking (yourself) does your awareness, your state of consciousness, change when you are awake, dreaming, asleep? I guess you are likely to answer both questions with some or other version of "Of course." But *who* changes your awareness – and *how* does 'it' change? Awareness is a process, not a thing. And awareness comes in at least two varieties – dual and non-dual. Dualistic awareness is what we all know – Wilber's Modes #3 and #4. I (subject) look (predicate) at the keyboard (object). This is how we think, how we perceive the world by categorising or labelling self or

---

[1] Those who espouse the "co-creative" use of ego states or a constructivist model of TA (Summers and Tudor, 2000), are likely to favour "we-language". Cognitive–behavioural exponents allegedly use "it-language". And "psychodynamic" or "relational" modellers would undoubtedly opt for a combined "I-We-language" emphasis. Even more fundamentally, debates about the merits of the structural model versus the functional model of ego states, about ego states as metaphors and so on, are often no more than differences between the various quadrants of the AQAL model.

[2] *Stoep* is an Afrikaans word meaning veranda. *Mealiestalks* are corn stalks. Harvesting (by hand) removes the cobs, leaving the stalks and leaves to dry out before being cut down to make silage. The slightest breeze over a ten acre field results in a hissing, Doppler-effect sound.

non-self. Indeed, Wilber's[1] 'modes' describe a *staged* model of consciousness or awareness. Mode #1 is non-dual awareness; it is no longer self *or* non-self – it is self *and* non-self that is beyond self and non-self. Everyone is capable of attaining non-dual awareness and most people have fleeting glimpses of it from time to time (Maslow's "peak experience", for example). Sustaining it is another matter. How you manage your awareness is how you conduct your life and it usually takes years of disciplined, regular spiritual practice to be able to operate consistently at a non-dual level of awareness.

The distinction between dual and non-dual awareness is an inevitable consequence of a transpersonal dimension of experience. Consider:

> "if we say Reality is ineffable, then we have used the word ineffable to describe it. But if it is truly ineffable, we can not describe it with any word, including ineffable. Similarly, if we say Reality is non-dual, then we have used the word non-dual to distinguish Reality from that which is dual. But if Reality is truly non-dual, then it is not distinct from anything, including the dual. Similar paradoxes arise with concepts like infinite, unconditioned, and Consciousness Without An Object.
>
> These paradoxes and contradictions all arise when we strictly limit concepts to their explicit definitions, then forget this limitation and try to apply them to all of reality. This kind of conception, which is strictly limited to definition in terms of other concepts, creates a closed system. So there is no way for concepts to take us beyond conceptual understanding. This does not mean that there is nothing beyond conceptual understanding. It only means that concepts can not capture all of Reality". (McFarlane 2004)

Clearly, reading the above two paragraphs requires the eye of reason. You will also have used the eye of flesh; you've been trained to read. Reading the paragraphs also requires you to grapple with a paradox; it *may* also have involved your using the eye of contemplation – even though you may not have been "trained" in the use of the eye of contemplation. Certainly, you use sensibilia for most things you 'do' – whether they be deliberately or inadvertently done. You do this without having been "trained". Babies, too, do this, but don't know or, at least, can't tell us, definitively, that they're doing it until they have words to process the experience of the eye of flesh. Once they acquire language, they start to use symbols and concepts. The price tag of language is that our use of concepts tends to outweigh "pure" awareness – that is, the experience of phenomena without categorising whatever it is we are experiencing.

In a clinical setting, I teach ERICA to clients in the *opposite* way to which I have written this book. This is because of my guesses about expectations – both yours and those of my clients. When a client comes to me for individual therapy, I spend most of the first session listening. In three out of four cases, during the second or third session, I will have actively started to engage the client's awareness of somatic processes. By session five most clients will have been offered homework assignments intended to heighten here-and-now awareness.

At an appropriate point in this process of expanding awareness, I start to introduce more abstract concepts (like roles and imagos) to gradually develop a personalised picture of a person's relationships. My experience is that offering clients a way of understanding their

---

[1] Note that "Wilber's 'modes'" do not refer to modes or ways of knowing derived from a model of the development of consciousness that *originated* or was *invented* by Wilber. What Wilber has done with breath-taking clarity is collate, cross reference and distil the essence of hundreds of documented studies, systems and accounts of the development of consciousness tracing back thousands of years.

inter-personal relationships, based on a systematic yet personalised process of heightening awareness, demands no less than a face-to face relationship. **Chapter 15** onwards describes the detail of this process.

Writing a book is a different matter. I do not have a face-to face relationship with you. I don't have the necessary opportunity of obtaining feedback from you on your particular, personal experience of any awareness-raising exercise, and there are limited opportunities for adjusting the nature or sequence of exercises to suit individuals.

For these reasons and, mainly, because the theory behind the models is new, I have chosen to present the models in **Parts One** to **Five** in a step-by-step fashion, so that you will have an understanding of the 'why, wherefore and therefore' issues implicit in the models, before embarking on the optional, experiential exercises scattered throughout **Part Six**. This is the approach that I use in a non-clinical setting and for workshop and conference presentations. Once you have grasped the conceptual basis of the models, you will be able to amend your use thereof to suit your own purposes. **Self Supervision Suggestion 3.8** may help.

Key Points 3

3.1 An **integral** or holistic **view** of a person describes the whole person in body, mind, soul and spirit.

3.2 Because I extend transactional analysis into the realm of the **transpersonal**, it is essential for readers to be clear about the **epistemological basis** of my approach.

3.3 **Epistemology** is the branch of philosophy that is concerned with **knowledge**.

3.4 There are three sources or "eyes" of knowledge or **modes of knowing** – *sensory, mental* and *spiritual.*

3.5 All three 'eyes' yield legitimate or **'valid' knowledge** in their *own domain.*

3.6 One mode or domain cannot usurp the role of the other two.

3.7 Trying to explain the nature of phenomena in one sphere through the eye of another constitutes a **category error.**

3.8 All **valid knowledge** consists of three basic components - *injunction, illumination,* and *confirmation.*

3.9 These basic components specify that "if you want to know X (the *injunction*), do Y (the *illumination*), then check your results with other trained people (the *confirmation*)".

3.10 Data of the **mental mode** can be used to *point* to, or *represent, other* data, from any other realm - sensory, mental, or spiritual.

3.11 A **theory or hypotheses** is an *immediately* apprehended mental datum used to point to, map, or logically systemise other *immediately* apprehended data (sensory, mental, or spiritual).

3.12 A **hypothesis**, then, is **a tentative map** *plus* suggested **injunctions**, namely that the connections between various mode of knowing are confirmed or rejected by other like minded (trained) colleagues.

3.13 The significance of such considerations is not the norm for transactional analysts

3.15 I draw attention to epistemology because:
- the above "rules" apply to all models or approaches to transactional analysis, but we do not take the extra step of **verifying hypotheses** in light of the newly acquired data,
- we do not pay attention to **consciousness itself** as well as its contents. It is also helpful to have a **map** or system for understanding the nature of

consciousness. My preferred map is Wilber's "all quadrants – all levels" approach,

- this book is an **invitation to colleagues to a critique** and verification or otherwise, of the models I present.

3.16 **Awareness** is the key to understanding and using ERICA.

3.17 I teach ERICA to clients **experientially** rather than **conceptually**. Writing a book is a different matter. Once readers have grasped the conceptual basis of the models, they will be able to amend their use thereof to suit their own purposes.

Self Supervision Suggestions 3

3.1 Have you ever had a peak or self-actualising experience? If so, recall the occasion(s) and write a brief description.

3.2 If you have not had a peak experience, what is your understanding of what it would be like to have one? Discuss this with someone who has had peak experience(s).

3.3 Discuss and compare your peak experience(s) with someone else's.

3.4 What is your experience of altered states of consciousness?

3.5 Look around you and simply notice what you see. Can you do this without words or "labels" for what you perceive?

3.6 Touch and feel objects in your immediate reach? Can you do this without words or "labels" for what you feel?

3.7 How long can you maintain **3.5** and **3.6** without any other thoughts, images or distractions intruding upon your consciousness?

3.8 Read the following statement:

Guavas (psidium guajava) are my favoutite fruit. They are native to the Caribbean, Central America and northern South America, but are cultivated in many other sub/tropical parts of the world. Although especially sensitive to frost, they are one of the very few tropical fruit that can be grown to fruitition indoors. They have five-petalled white flowers with numerous stamens. The elliptical leaves are some 5-15 cm long. The round-shaped, edible fruit is 3-10 cm in diameter, has a thin, pale green/yellow rind and white-pink-salmon coloured flesh with many small hard seeds. It is rich in vitamins A, B, and C. They have a strong, characteristic aroma and a distinctive taste.

Consider this information and then answer the following questions:

Would you agree that the above information is sufficient for an understanding of guavas? Is the information accurate? How could you tell? What more would you want/need to know to have an understanding of guavas? How meaningful is the information to you? What would make your understanding more 'meaningful'? How could your understanding of guavas be turned into a direct experience of guavas? List the factors that make a difference between a conceptual understanding and a direct experience of guavas - or elephants, or taorluaths, or models of behaviour.

Chapter 4

Basic concepts

This Chapter provides an introduction to and overview of Existential Role Imago Contact Analysis (ERICA) in relation to salient aspects of transactional analysis. The primary purpose is to set the scene for what follows in later Chapters.

The theory of ERICA is an amalgam of aspects of role theory, group dynamics, personal construct theory, psychoanalytic group therapy, systems theory, cognitive analytic therapy, gestalt, transpersonal psychology, various "energy therapies" and transactional analysis. In practice, the essence of ERICA is that it provides a meta-perspective of people's role expectations of each other and a methodology for understanding, recognising, and reformulating dysfunctional role behaviours.

For readers who have minimal or no knowledge of transactional analysis, this Chapter outlines a brief description and explanation of the essential concepts needed for understanding, appreciating and using ERICA. This is not an overview of the entire theory and practice of transactional analysis; my explanations represent little more than definitions and comments on concepts that are essential to understanding the development of ERICA. These concepts are highly selective and some are either not central to the major theoretical underpinnings of transactional analysis, or address specialised aspects of particular concepts. Those interested in a broader view of transactional analysis may wish to read or consult Ian Stewart and Vann Joines' book *TA Today: A new introduction to transactional analysis* (Stewart and Joines, 1987). This is regarded as the standard introductory transactional analysis text: it covers all the theoretical concepts, is well-referenced and gives brief comments on the development of TA at an international level. Although now 'dated', the book gives an accurate account of all the basic concepts.

TA concepts essential for understanding ERICA

For the totally uninitiated, transactional analysis is "a social psychology developed by Eric Berne, MD (d.1970). Over the past four decades, Eric Berne's theory has evolved to include applications to psychotherapy, counselling, education, and organisational developmental" – according to the official definition given on the website of the International Transactional Analysis Association (ITAA), and in more detail in current issues of the Transactional Analysis Journal (TAJ). While TA started primarily as a theory of intra-psychic structure and function, it has developed beyond that to encompass the development and inter-personal behaviour of individuals, and the structure and dynamics of groups and organisations. TA provides a model for personal growth and change and, by implication, a model for organisational development. TA emphasises values such as an innate drive to health and well-being, responsibility for one's own behaviour balanced by accountability to others, and the belief that everyone has the capacity to think for them selves and make changes. In practice, TA is a contractual way of working with people based on mutually agreed and regularly reviewed goals, and clearly defined responsibilities of all parties.

Ego states, transactions, time structuring and *scripts* represent the cornerstones of TA theory. Stewart and Joines (1987) devote two or more chapters to each of these concepts and for the time being, precise definitions are unnecessary. Suffice it to say that *ego states* are patterns of thinking and feeling and related behaviours that provide a model of individual personality structure. *Transactional analysis proper* describes the interaction or communication between the ego states of two or more people. *Games* (as aspects of time structuring) enable one to identify repetitive, stereotypical patterns of behaviour and *scripts* give a developmental and historical account of how people become and strive to maintain the way they are. Various subsidiary concepts and processes, such as symbiosis (the enmeshed ego states of two people), discounting (unawarely ignoring or minimising the impact of stimuli upon self, others or situations), hungers (similar to needs) and strokes (ways of getting and giving others attention), rackets and the racket system (unproductive and manipulative behaviours and beliefs) and mini-scripts (short sequences of behaviour that reinforce the script proper), may be said to link the four major concepts, completing a thumbnail picture of the theory. Again, definitions are not needed at this stage. What I am outlining is a view of transactional analysis represented by four major concepts and linking subsidiary concepts so that you can locate ERICA within the overall theoretical framework.

Historically the four concepts - ego states, transactions, games and scripts - developed during the sixties and seventies. They stand in an ascending order or level of complexity, emerging within the context of theory and practice of a new method of psychotherapy. However, it soon became apparent that the explanatory power of the theory was such that the concepts were equally useful in describing behaviour in groups other than in a clinical setting. Thus the theory was applied in the fields of management, education, and (later, in Europe) counselling. TA qualifications in these specialisms are on a par with TA qualifications in psychotherapy, but in practice, the majority of TA practitioners work in a clinical setting. Not surprisingly, major contributions to the theory and hence, the bulk of the literature, has come from clinicians.

Four TA concepts are central to ERICA – ego states (Berne 1961), life positions (Berne 1969), Formula G (Berne 1972) and the Drama Triangle (Karpman 1968).

In brief, *ego states* are consistent patterns of thinking and feeling and related behaviours. In TA, there are two models of ego states. To paraphrase Stewart and Joines (1987, p. 36-37), the functional model classifies observed behaviour and the structural model classifies stored memories and strategies; function is observable and structure can only be inferred. In both models, there are three ego states – Parent, Adult and Child. In the functional model, descriptive terms such as "Nurturing Parent", "Adapted Child", are used to indicate behaviours. In the structural model, the content – the memories and strategies - of Parent and Child are archaic. Unlike the Adult, they do not relate to here and now reality and hence communication (transactions) from these ego states will be transferential. For readers wanting a more detailed account of ego states, Stewart and Joines (1987 pp. 11-55) give several Chapters on ego state models, their development, recognition, pathology and so forth. ERICA does not use ego states as a major explanatory concept and extensive knowledge of ego states is unnecessary. However, I draw attention to ego states at this stage as they do feature in later Chapters in discussion of roles based on transference phenomena. Unless otherwise stated, the structural model is used throughout this book.

Life positions (Berne 1969, 1972), Formula G (Berne 1972) and the Drama Triangle (Karpman 1968) are subsidiary aspects of two of the major theoretical concepts, namely, scripts and games.

Berne gave various definitions of script (Berne 1958, 1966, 1972) all of which add up to the idea that children form "an unconscious life plan" (Berne 1966 p. 228) which significantly influences their later life. He later elaborated this definition to read:

> "a life plan made in childhood, reinforced by the parents, justified by subsequent events, and culminating in a chosen alternative". (Berne, 1972 p. 445)

In other words, from their earliest days, children are faced with the task of adapting to the world under the influence of parents and other caretakers, their physical, social and cultural environment. For all species, the purpose of adaptation is survival. For humans, categorisation of perceptions of events, objects, people and assigning meanings thereto, forms the basis for language and communication as crucial aspects of adaptation. However, in their attempts to make sense of the world, children will sometimes make or reach self-limiting conclusions about themselves and how they are supposed to relate to others. Although adaptation is an on going process, early decisions made at a particular developmental level will often hold sway. Berne was not alone in this line of thinking; along with Freud's interest in the drama of Oedipus, selective aspects of the work of Jung (1946), Rank (1910) and Campbell (1949) demonstrated for Berne the way in which life patterns may be seen in terms of a drama with dramatic themes and a beginning, a middle and an end. Adler's notion of a "life goal" (Adler 1963) is not dissimilar to scripts, but Berne's distinctive contribution was that children unconsciously formulate a *specific* life plan, and then often redefine reality to fit into this plan.

Several concepts are central to a full understanding and use of script theory – life course, components of the script, transmission of the script, process-type scripts and life positions. The first three need not concern us here, and the last is fairly straightforward. The term "position" is derived from Melanie Klein's use of the word to describe the attitudes infants adopt in their earliest relationships with others (Klein, 1949). Berne replaced Klein's descriptions of the positions - paranoid, depressive and schizoid – with more colloquial terms signifying an individual's perception of worth or worthlessness; he also added a fourth, healthy position. Using all the possible combinations of the subjects "I" or "You" and the predicates "OK" or "not-OK", Berne arrived at four basic positions – I'm OK-You're OK (the healthy position), I'm OK-You're not-OK (the paranoid position), I'm not-OK – You're OK (the depressive position) and I'm not-OK – You're not-OK (the schizoid position). Several writers (Steiner 1974, Harris 1973, Groder 1977, Barnes 1981, White 1995a, Jacobs 1997) have elaborated and refined Berne's basic conceptualisation of positions; I deal with these differences in later Chapters. For the time being, the salient point is that there is general agreement that *life positions* embody values and beliefs about one self and others that are used to justify decisions and behaviour.

The concept of games is implicit in Berne's definition of script; people distort reality in order to make it fit their script. Such distortions are then "justified by subsequent events". Without over-simplifying a complex process, for our purpose, it will suffice to say that some of these events are referred to as games. A non-technical description of *games* is that people often interact on the basis of saying one thing yet meaning another and when the "hidden message" becomes apparent, both parties are disconcerted and, finally, aggrieved. The essential features of games are that they are repetitive patterns of behaviour that end with one or both the protagonists feeling negatively about each other and, usually, themselves. These feelings are called racket feelings. There are some twenty or so standard games (with numerous variations), which once known are easily spotted. Despite this, even those well informed in such matters will play games. This is because (by definition) games are played "out of awareness" of the current reality of situations. Berne was able to identify games by analysing the interaction between two sets of ego states. Generally speaking, incongruity between overt and covert communication indicates the likelihood of a game. In addition, all games are based on discounting – a particular mode or type of distorting reality. More specific aspects of game theory need not concern us except to note that there are five ways of analysing games. Three of these are based on the recognition of ego states and identification of types of interaction between sets of ego states (these are known as transactions). The remaining two involve the analysis of roles and the use of Berne's "Formula G" (Berne 1972). Formula G reads:

$$C + G = R \rightarrow S \rightarrow X \rightarrow P$$

Formula G gives a sequential account of the stages ("moves") of a game which, when translated, signifies "**C**on plus **G**immick equals **R**esponse leading to **S**witch, leading to **C**rossup, leading to **P**ayoff." I explain the jargon below.

Formula G describes the process of all games whether they last a few seconds as in the example given below, or whether they continue for minutes, hours or even years. All games start with an ulterior message involving a distortion of reality (the Con), followed by an ulterior confirmation (the Gimmick) by the second player of the opening discount. A series of transactions then ensues (the Response) until one or other player switches roles (the Switch – which I will explain shortly). This creates a moment of confusion (the Crossup) which leads to the final "bad feeling" end (the Payoff). In longer lasting games, the Response phase becomes an increasingly complex series of transactions, but the basic formula holds good. An often-quoted example by Berne illustrates the meaning of the terms.

> " ....a patient asked: 'Do you think I'll get better, doctor?' and the sentimental therapist replied 'Of course you will.' At that point the patient revealed her ulterior motive in asking the question. Instead of saying 'Thank you,' as in a straight transaction, she pulled the switch with: 'What makes you think you know everything?' This reply crossed the therapist up and threw him off balance for a moment, which is what the patient wanted to do. Then the game ended, the patient feeling elated at having conned the therapist, and he feeling frustrated; and those were the payoffs.
>
> This game followed Formula G precisely. The con was the original question, and the gimmick was the therapist's sentimentality. When the con hooked into the gimmick, he responded in a way she expected. Then she pulled the switch, causing a crossup, after which each collected a payoff". (Berne, 1972 p.24)

The Switch of roles in Formula G refers to the roles in the **Drama Triangle** (Karpman 1968). Karpman's conceptualisation of this dynamic stems from analysis of dramatic themes in fairy tales and is strikingly original. He identifies three roles – Persecutor, Rescuer and Victim, that seem to be universally present in some or other guise in most if not all forms of fiction – be it folk tales, fairy tales, myths, legends, pantomime or even serious literature and history, from Shakespeare to Schindler. So basic are these themes and roles that any five year old will tell you which character in any story is the "baddie", which is the "goodie" and which is "the one the baddie is going to get." Stories are based on variations of the themes of mystery, suspense, surprise and shock. The drama comes from the audience or the reader not knowing why, when or how someone will do something. Underlying all this is the psychological process of the audience identifying with the roles enacted by particular characters.

Although the Switch and the resultant Crossup in a game are included in Formula G and indeed, represent distinguishing features that differentiate Formula G from Berne's earlier thinking about games, Drama Triangle analysis of games exists in its own right. The idea is simple, if not elegant – spot a Drama Triangle role and wait for one or other person to change to another of the three roles. If the change occurs, you are witnessing (or in) a game. If there is no change of role, then the interaction is either "pastiming" (gossiping) or "racketeering" – as a way of eliciting recognition ("strokes") for racket feelings[1].

Karpman did not define roles as a concept. He merely drew attention to the universality of the three roles by using fairy tales to illustrate how these "subconsciously may provide an

---

[1] "We define racket feelings as a familiar emotion, learned and encouraged in childhood, experienced in many different stress situations, and maladaptive as an adult means of problem solving". (Stewart and Joines 1987, p.209)

attractive stereotyped number of roles, locations, and timetables for an errant life script" (Karpman, 1968 p. 39) He continues to explain that:

> "Only three roles are necessary in drama analysis to depict the emotional reversals that are drama. These action roles ..... are the Persecutor, Rescuer, and Victim, or P, R, and V, in the diagram [below]. Drama begins when these roles are established, or are anticipated by the audience. There is no drama unless there is a switch in the roles. This is indicated by a change in the vector direction along the diagram". (Karpman, 1968 p.39)

Karpman diagrams the roles as shown in **Figure 4.1**

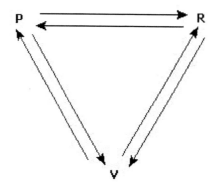

Figure 4.1

The arrows in **Figure 4.1** represents switches from one role in the Triangle to another, For example, person A may start in the Rescuer role; in doing so they define person B as a Victim. If person B accepts the Victim role and person A's attempts to Rescue are inadequate, the likelihood is that person B will switch to the Persecutor role, thereby defining the erstwhile Rescuer as a Victim. It is equally likely, however, that person A is the one who "pulls the switch" – probably because person B refuses to be rescued. Person A thus becomes the Persecutor and B has his/her Victim role confirmed. The game payoff for A is "Well, I always knew you were inadequate and this just proves it!" – accompanied by feelings of anger/frustration/impatience etc. Person B reacts despairingly with "See! It's happened again. No one can help me!"

Merely by noticing non verbal cues such as tone of voice, body posture, gestures, facial expressions and so forth, it is also possible at the start of a game to predict the role to which a person will switch. There is a world of difference, for example, between someone using a soft, yet slightly patronising tone of voice, saying "Why don't you tell me what's been going on? I'm sure we can sort this out" and the person who uses exactly the same words but speaks firmly, if not sternly, in a brusque, no nonsense manner. Even on paper and without taking account of the second person's response to this opening move the prediction is that, in the first case, the switch is likely to be from Rescuer to Victim; in the second it will be from Rescuer to Persecutor.

By way of locating ERICA within the overall framework of TA, ERICA is pitched at a level of abstraction that falls somewhere between games and scripts. In addition, I have identified another concept that I term sets – which are the positive counter-part of games. Theoretically, and in practice, sets fill the gap identified by Zalcman; they represent "concepts and techniques which focus on normal or mentally healthy behavior and change" (Zalcman, 1990) and extend the application of ERICA to non-clinical settings by focusing on patterns of role behaviour that do not involve the pathology implicit in identifying games.

In a nutshell, the models described in this book are based on links between the four concepts I have highlighted – ego states, life positions, Formula G and Drama Triangle roles. Armed with the above minimal knowledge of TA concepts, readers new to TA will be in the same position as those with wider experience or knowledge; from here on all theory is new theory for all. This is not to say that I won't refer to other TA concepts not yet mentioned, but where I do, such mention will not be central to the theory of ERICA and, in any case, will be explained either in footnotes or within the context of the main discussion.

Key points

4.1 Transactional analysis is "a theory of personality and a systematic psychotherapy for personal growth and change".

4.2 **Ego states** provide a model of individual personality structure. **Transactional analysis proper** describes the interaction or communication between the ego states of two or more people. **Games** enable one to identify repetitive, stereotypical patterns of behaviour and **scripts** give a developmental and historical account of how people become and strive to maintain the way they are. **ERICA** is pitched at a level of abstraction that falls somewhere between games and scripts.

4.3 **Scripts** are "a life plan made in childhood, reinforced by the parents, justified by subsequent events, and culminating in a chosen alternative". (Berne, 1972 p. 445)

4.4 **Ego states** are consistent, related patterns of thinking, feeling and corresponding behaviours.

4.5 **Life positions** are a component of scripts that embody values and beliefs about self and others that are used to justify decisions and behaviour.

4.6 **Games** are repetitive patterns of behaviour that end with one or both protagonists feeling negatively about each other and usually, themselves.

4.7 **Formula G** is one of the ways of analysing games: "Con plus Gimmick equals Response leading to Switch, leading to Crossup, leading to Payoff."

4.8 The Switch of roles in Formula G refers to the roles in the **Drama Triangle** (Karpman 1968). "Only three roles are necessary in drama analysis to depict the emotional reversals that are drama. These action roles are the **Persecutor, Rescuer**, and **Victim**". (Karpman, 1968 p.39)

Self-Supervision Suggestions 4

4.1 ERICA suggests that life positions are attitudinal. How would you assess a person's attitude?

4.2 Do you think there is any correlation between attitudes and behaviour?

4.3 Identify someone you know well who would fit each life position.

4.4 Select statements by prominent citizens from a TV news bulletin and assess the underlying life position.

4.5 Recall your favourite childhood fictional story and allocate Drama Triangle roles to the characters.

4.6 Watch a film or TV soap and identify Drama Triangle roles.

4.7 Repeat **4.6** and see if you can spot role switches.

4.8 Repeat **4.6** and see if you can predict role switches before they occur.

4.9 Repeat **4.6** and see if you can identify situations that fit Formula G.

4.10 If you don't have time or access to TV, without intervening, observe people at work or in public places and apply **4.6** to **4.9**.

Chapter **5**

ERICA – an overview

This Chapter gives an overall description of ERICA – both as a series of models and as a way of working with people. The aim is to present the "big picture" – a panoramic view of the models and how they may be used with clients. Each of the models is presented in outline with sufficient detail to make them meaningful. If you prefer a step-by-step presentation of the 'real thing' rather than a broad-brush account of the main features of the models, you will not lose out by proceeding to **Chapter 6**.

Overview

Chapters 6 and 7 give the **rationale** of the models: roles plus imagos, plus contact, leads to a relationship. Relationships are the common feature of all applications of TA theory and hence, ERICA may be used by practitioners of all persuasions, irrespective of setting.

A **role** is a disposition to act based on expectations of self, others and the situation. ERICA differentiates between *formalised, personalised* and *situational* roles. **Formalised** roles refer to the expectations we have of people with whom we have certain types of relations (for example, husband or wife, neighbours, your employer) and people in certain positions in society, organisations and groups (such as doctor, Chief Executive, receptionist and so on). **Personalised** roles are the actual behaviours of people. They are derived from observations of behaviours that are *proactive, reactive responsive* or *inactive.* **Situational** roles are roles that arise from the dynamics of a particular group or situation at a particular time; they represent the enactment of personalised roles by the holders of formalised roles at a particular time in the relationship. **Imagos** are the historical influences on the internalised perceptions people have of each other in a group/situation. **Contact** is a dynamic pattern of experiencing and meeting a need. A **relationship** is a pattern of attachment and interaction between two people.

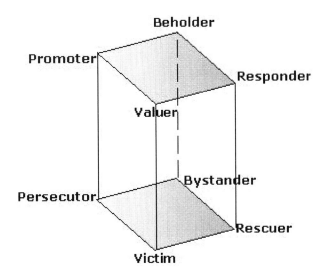

Figure 5.1

Chapters 8 to 12 show how these variables combine to form the first of three models - the **Contact Cube** - a three dimensional role space, representing the behaviours and hence, personalised roles, available to an individual. These are shown in **Figure 5.1.** There are four negative roles - *Persecutor, Rescuer, Victim* and *Bystander* – and four positive roles – *Promoter, Responder, Valuer* and *Beholder*.

The lower, Negative Square roles are based on discounting, not OK-ness, contaminations and exclusions. Adult may be experienced as Real Self, but Executive power is always in either Parent or Child. More usually, Real Self and Executive power are in Parent or Child. Positive Square roles do not entail discounting, contaminations or exclusions and there is always congruence between Real Self and Executive power. Detailed descriptions of each role are given in **Chapter 8**.

By definition, the roles within each Square operate reciprocally. For example, Persecutors initiate interaction by discounting another person, thus defining them as a Victim. If the person complies, they accept the Victim role. They can resist by adopting a Persecutor role, or attempt to ignore the discount by becoming a Bystander.

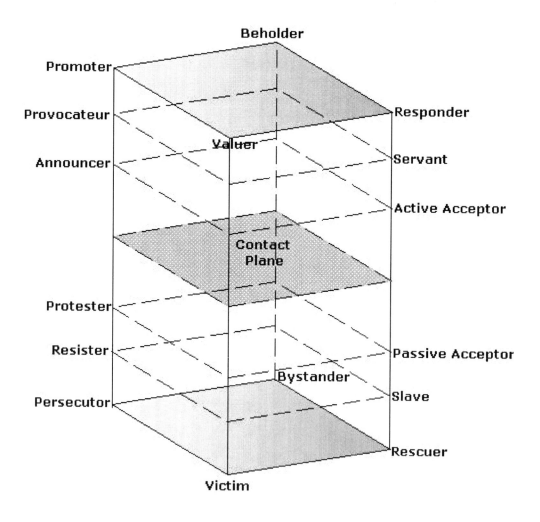

Figure 5.2

Likewise, Victims "attract" Persecutors or Rescuers. Rescuers "need" Victims to fulfil their role expectations. Bystanders always endeavour to remain unengaged. When this fails they move to another role. The same logic applies to mirror image positive roles – except that discounting is absent. The entire process may be monitored by tracking discounts and/or strokes – in terms of who gives, invites, gets, accepts, rejects or ignores positive/negative strokes and/or discounts. All this is standard procedure for a first or second year trainee. However there is more to the Contact Cube than simple role reciprocity.

The *Beholder* and *Bystander* roles are of crucial importance. Both appear to *do* nothing, but their presence is crucial to the maintenance of the other six more active roles. Indeed, changes from Beholder or Bystander (in response to approaches from the other roles) fuel the creation of additional roles. These are located along the vertical sides of the Contact Cube as depicted in **Figure 5.2** – and **Table 5.1** - according to the following descriptions:

Promoter	Provocateur	Announcer	Beholder	Active Acceptor	Servant	Responder	Valuer
Provide Self and /or offer others Perception, Prescription, Practice, Potency Permission & Protection. Potency is always present. Two types of protection – historical & current	**Challenge** others in OK –OK ways; **Use** extensive repertoire for confronting incongruity in others' frame of reference, in ways that invite or require a response	**Ask clearly** for what they want in a straight way **Can be assertive**; but always define them selves & others from OK-OK position.	**Stay neutral** in situations that require action; **have a capacity** to be **involved**, yet postpone engagement. Assimilate information & can self – activate.	**Accept others** as they are; information sought by inquiry in ways that encourages & facilitates others to convey their views	**Involvement and dedication** over & above any contractual agreement for benefit of others. Kindness altruism compassion. May impinge on formalised role relation ships	**Empathic; open & direct** responses to others' needs; communicati on style is contactful; affirm own & others' OK-ness. Often used en-route to other roles	**Openness to Physis** and the potential for healing self others & being healed by others Believe (& will permit) others to affect them **positively**.
Do not identify with others; do things that **are not** needed, wanted, or asked for to make others feel not OK about them-selves. **Compete** for OK-ness on the basis of scarcity ("someone has to be not-OK & it wont be me").	Maintain a position of **semi-independ-ence** & are able to define themselves to limited extent, but eventually accept Victim role **Often rebellious; will** Persecute when can "get away with it"	Vary from being passive aggressive (sulking muttering glowering) in specific situations, to righteous protestation about generalised issues. **May support** legitimate or "alternative" fringe groups	Do nothing when action is required; have a capacity to remain un-involved & avoid engagement. **Don't usually self–activate** but are difficult to engage. Often move to Victim in order to racketeer with others	**Over adapt** to misperceived external cues & approaches **Operate** largely from internal frame of reference & discount self & will comply with others even when this is clearly not in their own interests.	Go to extreme lengths to please others without questioning their motives or authority Discount personal ability &/or existence of any options **Seem unable** to resist complying even when don't want to.	**Over-identify** with others. Discount self others & situations. Feel obligated to take responsibility for others (usually by thinking for them) attempting to make others OK & thus, make them-selves OK.	Believe (& only allow) others to affect them **negatively** Discomfort is shifted to others. Often present do nothing type of passive behaviour. **Invite** others to racketeer with them or to persecute &/or rescue them.
Persecutor	Resister	Protester	Bystander	Passive Acceptor	Slave	Rescuer	Victim

Table 5.1

Bearing in mind that behaviour along the Promoter-Persecutor dimension is proactive, roles along this side of the Cube (Promoter, Provocateur, Announcer, Protester, Resister and Persecutor) represents *degrees* of a quality of contact that is "**compelling**". For example, "Don't think of a blue sky" is a typical Provocateur interjection, that 'compels' a recipient to respond (internally or externally). The characteristic of all the roles on this dimension is that *they elicit a response* from others.

Co-operative contact stems from responsive behaviour enacted via roles along the Responder-Rescuer dimension; it occurs, for example, when one person enacting the Valuer role, discloses feelings of vulnerability, asks for and receives reassurance from a Responder. The same quality prevails when a Rescuer attempts to help a Victim; the defining feature of the roles along the Responder-Rescuer edge of the Cube is *the extent of their co-operation* with others.

The contact between two Valuers has the same '**collaborative**' quality as the contact between two Victims. The former leads to intimacy and the latter to racketeering.

The quality of contact associated with the largely non-verbal behaviours along the Beholder-Bystander dimension is termed **co-existent**. The protagonists maintain their roles by *avoiding contact* and tacitly, *accord the same privilege* to others.

It is suggested that developmentally, each of the above four aspects of the Contact Cube are associated with bi-polar imago images as outlined in **Table 5.2**

Behaviours	Personalised roles enacted at the social level	Existential Imago images	Quality of contact based on attempts that are
Reactive	Valuer	Trust	Collaborative
Inactive	Beholder	Recognition	Co-existent
Responsive	Responder	Attachment	Co-operative
Proactive	Promoter	Growth	Compelling
Reactive	Victim	Mistrust	Collaborative
Inactive	Bystander	Anonymity	Co-existent
Responsive	Rescuer	Detachment	Co-operative
Proactive	Persecutor	Survival	Compelling

Table 5.2

Contact also describes the above qualities as a threshold between the positive roles and the negative roles. As shown in **Figure 5.2**, the four negative personalised roles located at the base of the Contact Cube are separated from the upper four positive roles by the 'Contact Plane'. The point at which contact with another person changes from positive to negative is located on the Contact Plane and is called the '**Critical Point**'. The role associated with such moments is the **Observer role**; the behaviours that are based on learned self-expectations, which engage our capacity to be simultaneously in contact with self and others. The Observer role includes the **Observer self** or capacity for self-reflective awareness without identifying with or occupying any other role. The **Observer role** differs in several respects from other Contact Cube roles and is pivotal to changing from one Square to the other. As I shall explain in **Part Six**, teaching clients to access the Observer role by *grounding, centring* and *witnessing* is the cornerstone of using ERICA.

The Contact Cube not only defines, describes and locates personalised roles structurally but also dynamically. Within each Square there are rules that enable one to predict short and longer term changes of role. The rules are based on the fact that personalised roles are manifested at three levels. Game analysis uses the Karpman Drama Triangle to analyse stereotypical, repetitive patterns of interaction with negative outcomes[1] at two levels – social and psychological (Karpman 1968, 1972, Berne 1972). Barnes (1981) added a third level which is attitudinal or existential. If we confine ourselves to a first order level of analysis using four positive and four negative roles rather than a second order analysis, which uses all sixteen roles, we can specify the roles that are being enacted simultaneously at three levels. Moreover, since we are dealing with either four positive or negative roles, we can also specify the role that is not being used. I explain below how these rules may be elaborated to yield a bi-lateral analysis of Bernean games.

Teaching clients to understand and use Contact Cube roles is a staged process. The starting point is an explanation of strokes and how these may be identified in behavioural terms (the presence or absence of discounting, giving, getting, inviting, accepting, rejecting and ignoring positive/negative strokes). This is then linked with a clear explanation of reciprocal roles. Thereafter, client and therapist jointly chart the roles involved in the client's report of "Significant Incidents". Significant Incidents are defined according to whatever the client has experienced during the week as "significant". Data is systematically accumulated to demonstrate the client's characteristic role preferences over an extended period.

Initially the therapist coaches the client to give a clear, sequential account of one or more **Significant Incidents**. The next stage is for the therapist to help the client identify the roles of the protagonists involved in a Significant Incident. Thereafter the client learns to recognise roles him/herself and eventually, evolves strategies for formulating more satisfactory role responses.

Although at first sight, the Contact Cube may seem complicated, it is not rocket science. I seldom meet clients who are unable to grasp the idea within three or four sessions. Indeed, the Contact Cube is a model that adds little more to existing TA theory – but what is added has implications that are radical. To summarise:

- The Drama Triangle with *roles at three levels* is *expanded to include the Bystander role* and thus, forms the base of the Cube.
- Four mirror image *positive roles* form the top of the Cube. The way in which these are conceptualized and function at three levels is entirely new, fully redressing the hitherto one-sided emphasis on negative aspects of social interaction.
- Equally novel is the notion of the Contact Plane and the emphasis on the four *qualities of contact* associated with the four positive-negative dimensions of behaviour.
- The lynch pin of the Contact Cube is *a learned Observer role* and the capacity of the *Observer self* for self reflective awareness, without identifying with the content of one's awareness. Detailed consideration of this role is postponed until **Part Six**.

The downside of the Contact Cube as it is explained thus far is that it does not take account of formalised or situational roles. Although this is less of a problem for counsellors and therapists than it is for educational or organisational practitioners, ERICA includes significant additions to Berne's description of the dynamics of groups and organisations. In particular, relationships are seen as the variables that link persons and social structures. I examine this in **Chapter 11** by exploring power and influence.

In the Contact Cube, **power** is the ability to influence others. **Influence** is the process whereby one person modifies their behaviour in response to, or as a result of, the behaviour of another person, persons or the situation. There are various sources of power and different

---

[1] In transactional analysis, these are called "games". Other models of therapy have similar concepts. Psychoanalysts talk about "repetition compulsion" and Cognitive Analytic Therapy focuses extensively on "target procedures".

methods of influence. I discuss each of these definitions and categories in their own right and cross-refer to the others. The inter-relationship between sources of power, methods of influence, modes of adaptation, likely outcomes and authority is outlined in **Table 5.3;** detailed discussion of each cell of the Table is given in **Chapter 11**.

Power source	Personal (personalised roles)		Resources domain/relevance/balance/ access/competence			Formalised roles Primary Secondary		
	Choice of role	Con-gruence	Physical	Material	Invisible	Social	Relational	Occupat-ional
Methods of Influence	Persuasion based on use of positive roles Rhetoric based on use of negative roles		Age Gender Ethnicity Presentation Transactions Stroking Force	Exchange Environmental Negotiation Image Contractual		Cultural/social norms, culture, rules & procedures, information, networking access, social mobility, expertise		
Individual adaptation via process of	Leadership, role modelling, mentoring, counselling, therapy supervision, apprenticeship		Socialisation mortification	Reporting, monitoring, appraisal, mediation, arbitration, working to rule, official or wildcat strikes		Legal statutes, education training co-option promotion qualification, ethics complaints and grievance procedures, continuous professional development		
Likely outcomes	Identification		Adaptation/compliance			Internalisation		
Authority	A mode of securing assent among a group of people about behaviour in a particular situation relative to their goals; depends on congruence between power sources and use of appropriate method(s) of influence.							

Table 5.3

In groups and organisations there are various sources of power and methods of influence. In **Table 5.3** the second, third and fourth columns represent sources of power, namely, power derived from the use of personalised roles, from control of or access to resources, and power – and hence, authority - which is associated with various formalised roles or positions. The methods of influence are shown in the cells below the power sources. The next row gives the various ways in which individuals may adapt to the combined use of power and influence. The upshot of this is the three likely outcomes – alienation, adaptation or compliance and internalisation.

Note that the various ways in which all these variables interact, leads to **authority** as a mode of securing assent among a group of people about behaviour in a particular situation, relative to their goals. Authority depends on congruence or otherwise between power sources and the use of appropriate methods of influence. What emerges from this type of analysis is that the variable that connects people and social structures is relationships.

I also offer the suggestion that within an organisation or group, one may hypothesise that there will be congruence between authority and the value memes proposed by Graves (1981) and subsequently extensively researched and refined by Beck and Cowan (1996) and more recently, Cowan and Todorovic (2005). As this is likely to be a new area of exploration for most clinical transactional analysts, I have included the rudiments of this approach in **Appendix B** - along with what I hope will be the provocative suggestion that the direct link between ego states and the Gravesian concept of memes, warrants further research.

Chapter 12 rounds off the Contact Cube by adding *situational roles*. Strictly speaking these are role functions – the outcome of *personalised* roles enacted by individuals in

 IMPACT

Institute for Mentoring, Psychotherapy And Counselling Training

with

Compliments

You can now order and pay for this book online
Go to: www.impact-uk.org, then to "Publications"
and follow the link to Order Online

5 Bawdsey Avenue Malvern WR14 2EW
44 (0)1684 566268 www.impact-uk.org
gordon.law1@btopenworld.com

formalised roles, at a particular time in a group, organisation or social network. I describe situational roles in relation to the intentions behind an intervention, the direction of an intervention (towards an individual, sub-groups, the whole group or the external boundary), the level of energy involved (high, medium, low) and the outcome in terms of diminishing, maintaining, enhancing or eliminating whatever is happening in the group at a particular stage of group development.

Chapters 13 and 14 are devoted to the second of the three models – which I have termed **Role Sequences**. Unlike the other Chapters in this book, clients do not *need* to know about the theory contained in these two Chapters. Furthermore, not all practitioners need to understand the theory; trainers and researchers definitely do.

Role sequences are simply the ways in which we enact personalised roles to confirm our **life position**. Role sequences are defined by outcome – the roles occupied at the end of a sequence of role interactions. There are positive outcome role sequences (PORS), negative outcome roles sequences (NORS), and indeterminate outcome role sequences (IORS). There are also mixed outcome role sequences (MORS), signifying the fact that role sequences are a relational concept; they describe ways in which relationships may be regarded as the ongoing confirmation (or otherwise) of *mutual* OK-ness. Role sequences give operational definitions of all the possible ways in which two people may enact any combination four roles at three levels. This follows logically from consideration of Contact Cube roles. Roles enacted at the social, psychological and existential levels constitute a **role profile**. For example, I may be a social level Victim, a psychological level Persecutor and an existential level Rescuer; the role I am not manifesting is the Bystander. My role profile maybe abbreviated as "vprb", or more simply, vpr.

At any moment I have a choice between twenty four negative and twenty four positive role profiles – representing all the possible combinations of the eight roles. Confining ourselves, for the moment, to negative roles, dyadic interaction involves 24 x 24 or 576 possible modes of interaction. Each of these is called a **reciprocal**.

Relationships may be regarded as a series of constantly changing reciprocals. Fortunately, Berne's use of Formula G seems to have anticipated such complexity. Accordingly, I have amended Berne's analysis of games to include the role profiles of two people (in other words, the reciprocals) for all the six stages of Formula G. The entire process may be conveniently referred to as **the 3Cs** ("the three Cs").

Con		Gimmick		Response		Switch		Crossup		Payoff	
Contact				Communication				Confirmation			
External		Internal		Emergent		Revealed		Options		Closure	
A	B	A	B	A	B	A	B	A	B	A	B
Social		?	?	Social		Psychological		?	?	Existential	
Psychological		?	?	Psychological		Existential		?	?	Social	
Existential ?		?	?	Existential ?		Social ?		?	?	Psychological	
Not Used ?		?	?	Not Used ?		Not Used ?		?	?	Not Used	

Table 5.4

The 3Cs 'formula' is illustrated in **Table 5.4.** The first row gives the standard Bernean stages of Formula G. The next two rows give my revision of Berne's analysis of games. This is largely self-evident. I propose a three stage process – Contact, Communication and Confirmation (with sub-divisions during each stage) - that match a combination of Berne's account of Con and Gimmick, Response and Switch, and the Crossup and Payoff. In the fourth row, the columns "A" and "B" represent person A and person B. Shaded areas represent behaviours that are not directly observable. The lower four rows show the levels of roles and how these change during the various stages of a role sequence. That is, the role occupied at the social level at the start of the role sequence is the role a person moves to (Berne's "switch") at the psychological level and finally is held at the psychological level. Similar dynamic rules apply to the other levels.

Again, I emphasise that none of this is 'new' theory; all the above 'rules' are reported in the literature (Law 1979, Barnes 1981, Hine 1990). The point of the 3Cs 'formula' becomes clear when we consider the negative Square roles in **Table 5.5**

Table 5.5 shows how the existential level roles of the initial reciprocal, (shown in bold) progressively move towards the social level confirmation of the protagonist's life positions, which, in this case, is mutual not OK-ness. Thus the 3Cs 'formula' enables one to predict role sequences associated with any reciprocal. Various statistical considerations enable us to reduce the mind-boggling number of possible combinations to manageable proportions. For example, we can immediately halve the number of interactions if we ignore the order of who "starts" the interaction - person A or person B. In addition, there are practice realities that render the role sequences associated with a large number of reciprocals "unobservable".

Con		Gimmick		Response		Switch		Crossup		Payoff	
Contact				Communication				Confirmation			
External		Internal		Emergent		Revealed		Options		Closure	
A	B-	A	B	A	B	A	B	A	B	A	B
V	*R*	*R?*	*V?*	*V*	*R*	*R*	*P*	***P?***	***V?***	***P***	***V***
R	*P*	*P?*	*R?*	*R*	*P*	***P***	***V***	*V?*	*R?*	*V*	*R*
P	***V***	*V?*	*P?*	***P***	***V***	*V*	*R*	*R?*	*P?*	*R*	*P*
B	*B*	*B*	*B*	*B*	*B*	*B*	*B*	*B*	*B*	*B*	*B*

Table 5.5

To illustrate, consider a situation where two people are both social level Bystanders. Whatever interaction ensues is an internal "skull game"[1] and an observer has no immediate way of discerning psychological or existential level roles. There are also "single entry" and "single exit" interactions where one person attempts to engage a Bystander. Likewise, two people may both have Bystander roles at the psychological level and, hence, they appear to withdraw, rather than 'switching' to other roles.

All in all, it transpires that the 576 reciprocals fall into eight definitive clusters. These may be further simplified into three basic patterns of fully observable, bilateral negative outcome role sequences (NORS) similar to Bernean games, and another two types of interaction that are equivalent to racketeering. Moreover, it would seem that individuals have preferred **repertoires** of role sequences. Clinicians working with borderline clients will be familiar with the patterns of "acting out" behaviours characterised by alternating Victim to Persecutor role switches. ERICA suggests that *everyone* has similar but, obviously, less extreme preferences, signifying ongoing confirmation (or otherwise) of mutual OK-ness. The implication is that confirmation of life positions is an ongoing affair, and calls to question Berne's (untested) claim that everyone has a basic, "fixed" position.

---

[1] Berne's term for this phenomenon is "skull games". (Berne 1970, p. 189)

The same line of reasoning may be applied to positive outcome role sequences (PORS), mixed outcome role sequences (MORS) and indeterminate outcome role sequences (IORS). Certain differences prevail of which the most important is that every NORS (Bernean game) has its PORS counterpart. Berne mentions this *en passant;* he refers to "sets of operations" (Berne 1963, p. 44). I have taken my cue from this and coined the concept of **sets** as an additional way of time structuring. Sets are no less than a way of confirming mutual OK-ness via the use of positive Contact Cube role profiles. In other words, sets describe "normal", everyday social interaction. Apart from the use of positive rather than negative roles, the main difference between sets and Bernean games is that with sets, all *four* levels of a role profile are used. In **Part Six**, I discuss this difference and explore the idea that the role that is avoided in games ("not used" in **Tables 5.4** and **5.5**) exists at the "shadow" level.

Role sequences and role imago repertoires offer both practical and theoretical benefits. Simply by assessing an individual's role profile, one can predict their pattern of social interaction relative to any situation. Likewise, effectively, the methodology of ERICA requires clients to generate volumes of data amenable to empirical research. Theoretically, role sequences redress the imbalance of Berne's Formula G and permit analysis of normal social interaction. Perhaps more importantly, they provide a set of operational definitions that may be used for a practitioner's reflection on their role behaviours in practice, training, and supervision, and the observation and analysis of *any* method or model of interaction.

In **Chapters 15 to 17** I discuss a series of models that are variations of my third model - the **Basic Role Imago Template** (BRIT). These models are concerned primarily with the practical application of the previously discussed models, the Contact Cube and Role Sequences. I have also drawn upon ideas from Cognitive Analytic Therapy (CAT)

The Contact Cube gives the overall framework for understanding the personalised role behaviours of a single person; the unit of analysis is a role profile. Role Sequences add a dynamic, interactive dimension; the units of analysis are reciprocals. A **BRIT** adds a contextual dimension. CAT provides similar concepts, based on a well-researched view of role reciprocity.

A BRIT is a diagram similar to a script matrix that shows a "focal person's" past and present role relations. It is a diagnostic device used to provide a baseline for mapping changes in role relations. The components of a BRIT are shown in **Figure 5.1.**

A person occupies a focal role within the context of their *role set* and their *role networks;* the latter being sub-sets of the former. A role set consists of all the role relations a person has experienced and hence, all those with whom one has had 'significant' role relationships. For example, some of the role relations in my role set are as "father", "neighbour", "work colleague", "friend", "psychotherapist" and so on.

Role sets also embody a time dimension and thus have historical and current dimensions. In **Figure 5.3** the historical role set is represented by the large shaded circle; within this the current role set is shown as the non-shaded circle. The boundary between the two is largely conceptual and in practice, is determined by frequency of contact and the focal person's perception of the significance of the relationship.

Role sets may be further sub-divided into role networks. These may be regarded as being either active (the shaded rectangle in **Figure 5.3)**, or influencing (A to G in **Figure 5.3**). Some influencing networks are operative and transferential (C, D and E) and may be located in the focal person's current network or their historical network (as in K). Other networks merely exist as potential sources of transferential, influencing networks (A, B, F, and G in the current role set and all but K in the historical role set).

An active network is the network or situation experienced by the focal person at any particular time. By definition it is constantly changing and may be regarded as the (changing) network a person "carries around" with them. Thus time and place and the immediate context largely determine the nature of one's active role network. All the roles in a BRIT are formalised roles; they become personalised roles when enacted as a Significant Incident in the active role set.

The distinction between an active role network and a current role set is that "active" refers to whatever particular network or situation a person is in at any moment. Once the situation - say a meeting at work - changes, the erstwhile active role network becomes part of the current role set and the next situation - say, having tea at home - becomes the active role network.

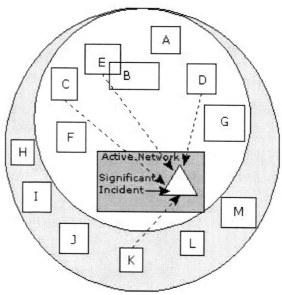

Figure 5.3

A similar dynamic applies to influencing networks. For example, I may be chatting to a group of friends, but am pre-occupied by what may take place the next day at work. Here the actual active role network is "friends" but, to some extent, my behaviour will be coloured by the operative "work" role network. Both networks are in the current role set.

Additionally, role networks sometimes overlap. If I work with someone who is also a personal friend, my "work" and "friends" networks overlap (as in B above). Which of the two networks is active at any time will depend on our topic of conversation.

A refinement of the BRIT is a cRIT or **Contextual Role Imago Template**. Not only does a cRIT provide a baseline for an individual's repertoire of role behaviours relative to a *particular* context, it enables a practitioner, researcher or supervisor to identify the influencing networks extraneous to the interaction of the Significant Incident per se. For example, if a researcher is interested in the role profile of a particular individual in a work setting, he or she can elaborate the person's work network to include tasks, designations or positions of various colleagues.

To illustrate, **Figure 5.4** shows three specific formalised roles in a work network – Chief Executive Officer, Senior Research Officer (SRO), Senior Finance Officer (SFO) and various other individuals in the Finance and Research and Development sub-sets. I also further differentiate between individuals, by using circles to depict females and squares for males and showing the initials of each person. External group boundaries are depicted by the perimeter lines of a network and the major internal boundaries are shown by the solid lines separating the person in the leadership slot (the CEO) from the two categories of membership – Finance and Research and Development staff. The unfilled slot in the Finance team is shown as a circle within a square – indicating a vacant post. Minor internal boundaries are drawn with dashed lines. A cRIT may be enlarged to show other influencing network roles by including arrows between interacting networks.

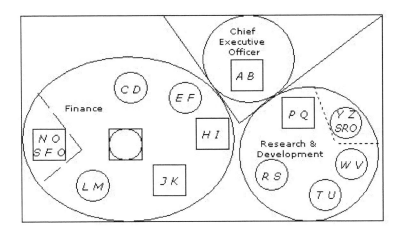

Figure 5.4

Both a BRIT and a cRIT map formalised roles, yielding a static picture of role influences against which the Significant Incident may be seen. cRITs can easily be extended to include personalised roles and hence, actual behaviours; this transforms the cRIT into a **Dynamic Role Imago Template** (a dRIT). The following example of a Significant Incident illustrates this process.

Figure 5.5 is a dRIT that shows the interaction between three people - AB as the CEO, YZ the Senior Research Officer and HI, a member of the Finance Team. These are all formalised roles. The two-way arrows signify the enactment of personalised roles at social, psychological and existential levels, enacted by each person according to the focal person (AB) who defined the role profiles. These are shown below each person's initials. To complete the picture, AB would write a brief 'narration' of the Significant Incident. AB's narration would read: *SI 1: Sat in on a meeting where YZ briefed HI on reasons for the over spend on the new product. HI probably over-anxious and YZ did not seem to acknowledge validity of her perceptions. I did not intervene but will discuss with YZ.*

The role profiles for AB, YZ and HI are a shorthand way of recording a single Significant Incident, in this case, according to AB. If necessary the detail of the interaction could be further analysed using the phases of Contact, Communication and Confirmation. A wider perspective emerges if we continue to map further Significant Incidents over a specified time scale. If AB systematically charted his/her dRITs, and wrote narrations for every appointment over the period of month, a researcher would have a fair picture of AB's self-perceived role imago repertoire.

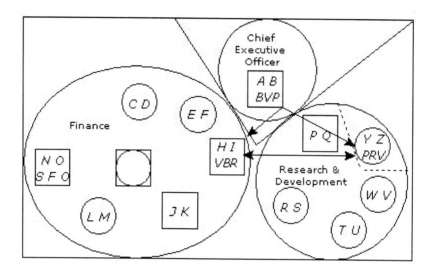

Figure 5.5

A derivative of the dRIT is well suited to group therapy, and in educational or organisational settings. I illustrate how a dRIT may be adapted to provide a Group Role Imago Template (a gRIT). In essence, a gRIT is a diagram showing role interactions in a group setting, compiled *post hoc* by an individual (usually the group facilitator), in relation to a Significant Incident that occurred during a group session. The use of audio-recording obviously aids this process. As with dRITs of sessions with individual clients, gRITs are invaluable props for supervision, teaching and research.

And as if this is not enough, there is an even more creative version of dRITs – a Spontaneous Process Role Imago Template (a spRIT). spRITs are compiled in-situ, with everyone contributing their perceptions of role interactions. Needless to say, spRITs are as much a group-norm building device, as they are a means of teaching clients to define their own individual dRITs. **Chapter 16** summarises the research implications of more explicitly defining indices for imagos and contact.

As implied above, in individual therapy, (**Chapter 17**) clients are taught to research their own behaviour by compiling weekly dRITs over an extended time-scale. This information forms the basis for ownership of their progress towards a preference for a more positive role imago repertoire. Clinically this process does not occur in isolation; it proceeds hand-in-glove with other standard therapeutic operations, such as decontamination, redecision work and so on. However, I have developed a contractual 'seventeen step' programme, with clearly demarcated criteria for progression that facilitates the application of ERICA in both clinical and non-clinical settings.

Chapter 18 reflects on the three models and considers some of the epistemological issues involved in applying the models.

In **Part Six, Chapter 19**, I discuss the rationale for extending the scope of transactional analysis beyond intra- and inter-personal domains, to encompass transpersonal dimensions of experience.

Transactional analysts prize **autonomy**, which, according to Berne, consists of three capacities – awareness, spontaneity and intimacy. Perhaps because of his reaction to psychoanalytic practice (rather than psychoanalytic thinking), I think Berne tends to downplay awareness at the expense of spontaneity and intimacy. He pays little, if any attention to **consciousness**, per se. Likewise, his emphasis on the autonomy of the integrated Adult ego state has probably led subsequent generations of transactional analysts to shy away from unconscious processes. Until recently, the norm is to talk or write about processes or phenomena that are "out of awareness".[1] Along with this, Berne encountered and, in my view, sidestepped the question of **self**. Taking a trans-cultural view of self leads to an examination of the development of consciousness – a factor not explicitly addressed in transactional analysis theory.

In **Chapter 20** I use this omission as a pivot for explaining how Wilber's "**spectrum of consciousness**" (Wilber 1977), provides not only an extensively researched basis for understanding *stages* of human growth and development, but also how various *states* of consciousness (such as awake, sleeping, dreaming), are inherently entwined with our identity and selfhood.

I then discuss **identification** in some detail - the process of how we come to acquire a sense of identity. This, in turn, leads to an examination of **trance** and **dissociation** as particular states of consciousness.

From this, it emerges that Berne's account of ego states parallels Wolinsky (1991), who refers to those aspects of our identity that are not based on here and now information, as "**trance identities**". I show that Wolinsky could just as easily have been writing about ego states, as he does in writing about trance identities. In other words, "trance identities" and "Parent" and "Child" ego states refer to the same, or similar, states of consciousness.

To this proposal I add Wilber's description of **proximate self** ("an inner subject or watcher"), **distal self**, ("since it is objective and "farther away"") that, together, he refers to as **overall self** (Wilber 2000 p. 33).

Finally, I draw attention to another parallel between ego states and Wilber's conceptualisation of self:

> "...during psychological development, *the "I" of one stage becomes a "me" at the next* (original italics). That is what you are identified with (or embedded in) at one stage of development (and what you therefore experience very intimately as an "I") tends to become transcended, or disidentified with, or dis-embedded at the next, so you can see it more objectively, with some distance and detachment". (Wilber, 2000 p. 34)

I cite this as the basis for further exploration of the idea that Wilber's proximate, distal and overall self offers an enriching view of the **development of ego states** (from C_0 to C_1, C_1 to C_2; A_0 to A_1, and so on). Such a view of self legitimates the use of a transpersonal level to explore aspects of spirituality that, at present, lie beyond the 'orthodox' model of transactional analysis. The implications of such a view of self is that transactional analysis can 'take on board' the notion of unconscious processes that go beyond roles at the inter-personal level.

---

[1] Exceptions to this tendency are Moiso (1983), Novellino and Moiso (1990), and more recently, Hargaden and Sills (2000). See too, the April 2005 issue of the Transactional Analysis Journal with the theme issue of Transactional Analysis and Psychoanalysis.

In **Chapter 21** I return to Wilber's reference to 'witnessing'. I note that the concept has received little more than passing reference from a handful of TA writers, and suggest that we all have the capacity to witness or observe our own behaviour without having to dissociate, or to identify with the object of our attention. This is simply our capacity for self-reflective awareness.

> "The moment you step outside of your problem to observe it, you create a larger context for it. Observing or witnessing thus becomes a key activity of therapy". (Wolinsky, 1991 p. 61)

Implicit in this view is a definition of self as *a **process***. Allowing for the fact that self is a concept of enormous complexity, I give a "working" definition of self as the experience, or on going awareness, of one's own presence or existence and one's capacity to define one's self in relation to a context – a unit of consciousness with the capacity for self-activation.

As such, self is both an ontological experience and a relationship. It is one's ongoing existence in relation to whom or whatever one is relating. This is very different to/from the general understanding of self in transactional analysis.

In **Chapter 22** I describe briefly the significance of unconscious processes and the crucial link with developmental stages of consciousness.

The paucity of articles on the body-mind split in the transactional analysis literature probably stems from Berne's emphasis on the 'here-and-now' awareness associated with the integrated Adult. Only in recent times have transactional analysts started to pay attention to the shadow and the significance of unconscious processes. I touch upon these concepts briefly and only in detail sufficient to their relevance to the Observer self and the Observer role.

By way of illustrating this I outline a number of new developments in the field of body and energy therapy. This is a precursor to the need to ensure that clients prone to dissociation know how to stay grounded when learning to access transpersonal realms of awareness.

In **Chapter 23** I turn to the aspect of the self that I call the Observer self and explain how this natural capacity may be exploited to become the Observer role. I describe and comment on three simple yet powerful meditational techniques that, with regular practice, inculcate the self expectations of staying grounded and centred without identifying with the focus of our attention.

Grounding and centring are techniques that can be taught routinely to facilitate witnessing – an extension of one's natural self-reflective awareness. Witnessing represents the beginnings of consciously exploring aspects of consciousness at a transpersonal level where "normal" consciousness no longer has to remain "as a defensively contracted state of reduced awareness" (Walsh and Vaughan 1996, p. 17). Additionally, learning another meditational technique for goal setting enables clients to grapple with the process of manifesting intentions.

ERICA aims to facilitate autonomy and interdependence by teaching clients how to change from negative to positive role profiles. Central to this and, indeed, to ERICA as a troika of related conceptual models is the use of the **Observer self**. Without this clients learn little more than the *difference* between negative and positive roles. I would even go as far as suggesting that no-one can fail to access positive roles once they have learned to use **the Observer role**.

The Observer *role* is an extension of the Observer *self*. Whereas the latter is a state of awareness, the former is a learned set of expectations. These are expectations of self; they are self perceived and self-defined relative to an individual's stage or level of the development of consciousness. By and large they give the individual the conscious ***choice*** between positive and negative roles. Of course, individuals may ***choose*** not to use positive roles. Learning to use the Observer role via dRITs gives the 'technology' for this choice. My experience is that the Observer role provides the motivation. In addition, optionally teaching clients techniques that address somatic processes and transpersonal levels of awareness, lays the foundation for an integral approach to the growth of the whole person.

In the final **Chapter 24** I give a bullet point summary of the models and the main points of the argument covered in **Part Six**.

I close by pointing to the flexibility of using ERICA with clients. That is, the models may be used either together – more or less as described in the book as a whole – or selectively, according to a practitioner's need/interests and the client contract. For example, a mentor/coach practitioner may give a brief outline of strokes and Contact Cube roles and then use dRITs over a period of time in an educational or organisational setting. Or a clinician may work with individual clients using aspects of roles at three levels, exploring qualities of contact, imago and shadow issues and so on. Supervisors may invoke Contact Cube roles as an aid to tracking transference/counter-transference. Clients can become researchers into their own behaviour. Researchers, students and trainees can/will have mountains of data to test an extensive range of hypotheses. And there will be some who wish to do no more than explore the implications of the ideas and techniques covered in **Part Six.**

Chapter 6

A framework for describing relationships

In **Chapter 1**, I suggested that the models to be presented in **Parts Two** to **Five** constitute a framework for describing relationships. This Chapter outlines this framework and explains the terms and definitions I use.

Framework: roles + imagos + contact = relationships

As noted in **Chapter 1**, I refer to this framework as Existential Role Imago Contact Analysis (ERICA). Existential Role Imago Contact Analysis is a dynamic synthesis of four separate ideas – roles, imagos, contact and relationships. Roles describe dispositions to act and/or patterns of observable behaviour based on individuals' expectations of themselves, others and their situation. Imagos are not directly observable, but describe historical influences on the ways in which expectations arise. Contact refers to the quality of our interactions with self, others and the world. Combining these ideas provides a framework for examining relationships.

Relationships are an inescapable fact of life. Storytellers, novelists, poets, playwrights, musicians, librettists and other entertainers extol or decry them; historians, journalists and others of the media spend much of their time directly or indirectly telling others about relationships. People such as parents and teachers continually model relationships for and with children. Even those engaged in vocations or professions from agriculture to astronomy, which are not based on human relationships, have interpersonal relationships. We tend to take relationships for granted, probably because they are so much part of everyday life. Although we all spend most of our time engaged in relationships, they are extraordinarily difficult to describe in ways that may be replicated. Part of the reason for this is that relationships are something we experience all the time.

In investigating and writing about relationships, one immediately encounters the enormous breadth and depth of the topic. Like beauty, relationships may be said to be in the eye of the beholder; they (and accounts thereof) are as simple or complex as one chooses to make them. Consider the following scenario: (For the time being, disregard the numerals in brackets; I explain the significance of these later).

Scenario 6.1

A man goes into a shop and says "May I have a small loaf of bread, please" (1)
The shopkeeper smiles and replies "Certainly. (2) Do you want brown or white?"(1)
"Oh sorry, (4) brown please, medium sliced." (2)
"That'll be fifty seven pence, please." (1)
"Here you are. (2) Fifty- and five – and a two. Right?" (1)
"That's it, right. Thank you. (2) Nice weather we're having, aren't we?" (1)
"Oh yes, much better than last week. (2) Well, thank you, Bye." (1)
"'Bye. (2) Have a nice day." (1)

Now ask yourself, does the scenario describe a relationship? I guess most people would give a qualified "yes". How would you describe the relationship? Again, I guess; your answer could well depend on who you are, what interests you have, what you already know about observing and 'analysing' social situations and maybe, even factors such as how old you are, where you live, what your cultural background is and so forth. Consider too, whether your answers would have been different had the italicised words been omitted and if so, why? If on the other hand, I changed the opening question to 'does the scenario describe roles?' I guess that most people would readily reply 'yes' and even continue to add 'a customer and a shopkeeper'. Moreover, I guess the same reply would have been given if the scenario had been presented without the italicised words. On the other hand, if I asked 'what does the scenario describe?' I am sure the answer would be some or other version of 'a man buying bread'

Consider another scenario – a work place meeting. (Again, disregard the numerals).

Scenario 6.2
"Mr. Chairman, should we not start? It's gone quarter past and we do have a lot to get through." (1)
"We must have Peter's views on the new product. (2) It would be foolhardy to proceed without his know-how." (1)
"I'm fed up to my back teeth with Peter! (4) His time keeping is appalling! Even if he holds all the cards, he shouldn't be allowed to get away with his 'sorry I'm late' number – yet again! (1) Third time this week I've had to sit around waiting for him! (4) I reckon we should get on with it without him!" (1)
The room goes quiet. (3) The Chairman stands up, walks slowly over to the window and says "I share your frustration. (2) We'll give him another three minutes." (1)

This time, ask yourself the question: 'what do the above two scenarios have in common?' Irrespective of your answer, proceed to the next scenario:

Scenario 6.3
Miss Miue is a Hong Kong born, newly qualified English teacher who has just taken up her appointment in a large comprehensive school in a provincial town in England. Her first lesson is with a class of 13 year old students. She enters the room and the students immediately fall silent – apart from a few suppressed sniggers. She is about to introduce herself when she notices the blackboard on which someone has written in large letters:
'A' IS FOR APPLE
'M' IS FOR CAT (1)
"Very good! (2) I'm getting used to English jokes about my name. (4) I shall have to remember this one. (4) Do you know how I'd write my name in my own language?" (1)
She deftly writes the characters on the board.
"See (1) – this is my full name. (4) You can see I use characters that are very different to the English alphabet. (4) Now, (1) let me learn about your names. (4) I'll start with the register and when I call out your name I want you to stand up and tell me what you like your friends to call you." (1)

This time we can widen our enquiry by asking whether there are any rules that would enable us to demonstrate what all three scenarios have in common. Assuming for the moment that such rules exist, we would have to formulate them in our minds and apply them to hundreds of scenarios such as those described above. If the rules stood up we would then probably invite others to apply them to their observations. If they in turn agree that the rules hold 'true' – that is, no one comes up with observations to which the rules may not be applied – then we and others who have used our rules may reasonably conclude that the outcome of the observations are reliable. In addition, there would also be a discussion about the validity of the proposed rules; everyone would have to agree that the rules describe or 'measure' what we say they describe – in this case, a way of describing relationships. Thereafter anyone could apply the rules with reasonable confidence for whatever purpose they have in mind – helping others understand relationships, improving relationships, comparing the prevailing relationships in one group with the relationships in another group and so forth. Anywhere along the line the rules could be amended to accommodate exceptions; subsequent observations may even require that one or more rules be ditched altogether and replaced by a better or more powerful rule. At the end of the day the usefulness of the rules would probably be the overriding factor that would ensure their continued popularity.

My observations of scenarios similar to those described above lead me to hypothesise that relationships are characterised by behaviour that may be categorised as (1) proactive or initialising, (2) responsive, (3) inactive and (4) reactive. These four features of behaviour constitute a particular way of describing human interaction. In this context I use the word "behaviour" as a generic term for thinking, feelings, sensations, beliefs and actions. This is a simple observation rather than a profound philosophical statement. I am using these terms generally, yet not quite loosely. Reactivity is an aspect of our physiology and consciousness[1] and therefore, but sometimes less obviously, behaviour, that precedes the other three factors. Proactive/initialising and responsive are obviously opposites and, in turn, are both the opposite of inactive. More formally, I am suggesting that, at any moment, behaviour may be seen, literally, as the outcome of our capacity for reacting somatically and affectively, in the following senses: of being continuously open to the existence and impact of external and internal stimuli and disclosing our feelings thereon; OR our capacity to initiate action in situations devoid of any action; OR our capacity to respond to action or stimuli external to ourselves; OR our capacity to do neither of the aforementioned.

Notice that I refer to behaviour as the outcome of four "capacities"; whether or not we exercise these capacities is a matter that I will discuss later. However, whenever we do exercise one of these capacities, we may be said to behave in one, and only one, of four ways – proactively, responsively, inactively or reactively. The basic idea is quite straightforward: observe any couple or group of people and sooner or later someone will do or say something to which others will respond OR, apparently, not respond. There may be a lull in the interaction, or someone else will redefine the topic of conversation by making a new (proactive) statement or asking a question that takes the discussion in a completely different direction. On the other hand, someone may react to the first speakers' opening statement by disclosing their feelings, or more generally, giving information about themselves rather than responding specifically to the previous speaker's comments.

In the above scenarios the numerals in brackets refer to whichever of the four categories may be said to apply. For example, in the first two scenarios the opening statements fit the category "proactive or initialising" and are therefore followed by a "1" in brackets. In the third scenario it is an event (the writing on the board) that initiates the teacher's response of "Very good"; this in turn is categorised as response and receives a "2

Interesting and promising as the four categories seem at first sight, they have limitations as a method of describing relationships. Even if the categories were refined or

---

1 It also seems legitimate to describe these four factors as aspects of consciousness, while quite clearly stating that there are additional features of consciousness – for example, self-reflective awareness – that would be needed to negotiate the philosophical quagmire of defining consciousness. Here the word "consciousness" connotes cognitive, affective, physiological and linguistic processes that make up our experience of self. I mention consciousness at this stage because I believe the four factors described above are "bottom line" variables that differentiate consciousness from non-consciousness. I will be writing mostly about behaviour, but at times, will focus specifically on consciousness *per se*.

elaborated, four shortcomings of the approach remain. The first is that, by definition, they are not mutually exclusive; reactivity underpins the remaining three factors. Secondly they are 'culture bound'; they may well hold true for most versions of the English language, but are unlikely to apply to all languages. Thirdly, a sophisticated system for analysing conversations already exists among sociologists (Jayyusi 1984, Jefferson 1989, Sacks 1992a, 1992b, Silverman 1997, 1998, Lepper 2000) and, even within TA, there are well established communication rules (Berne 1964, 1966, Mellor and Sigmund 1975) that map interaction independently of language. Perhaps more importantly, I was not entirely satisfied that the above categories themselves as 'stand-alone' measures are, or could be, all that useful for describing relationships.

This is not to say that the categories do not tell us anything about social interaction; as you will see, they form the basis for mapping social roles.

When individuals meet, they are said to "make contact", to "exchange strokes[1]". When contact and stroke exchanges confirm expectations a "satisfactory" relationship ensues. Impaired contact or unexpected stroke exchanges lead to less than satisfactory relationships; the relationship then becomes part of mutual expectations, anticipating the next meeting.

The person in an organisation who "makes good relationships" with colleagues or customers, does so as much by their management of expectations, imagos and contact - and hence, their relationships – as by their use of formalised roles and adherence to organisational procedures. Generally speaking, successful or "good" therapy or counselling facilitates improved interpersonal relationships. "Good" teachers are defined as such by their students as much according to their ability to make relationships, as their breadth of knowledge and expertise in imparting it. No one except the perverse is going to argue that relationships are not important. The thesis of the first **Part** of this book is that roles, imagos and contact are concepts that give us a 'handle' for influencing relationships.

Overview of roles and role theory

"Role" and "roles" seem to be words that everyone understands. The *Shorter Oxford English Dictionary* gives:

> "A part played by a character, which one assumes, undertakes or has to play. Chiefly fig. with ref. to the part played by a person in society or life". (SOED p. 1842)

Broadly speaking, roles are used in two ways in the social sciences – as a unit in society (Linton 1936) and as another term for social interaction (Mead 1934). Linton links roles with status which he defines as "a collection of rights and duties" whereas a role is "the dynamic aspect of a status" (Linton 1936 p. 113-4). In other words, to put rights and duties into effect is to perform a role – a view that has important implications for organisational transactional analysis practitioners.

On the other hand, Mead developed a theory which links personality development and communication; to be able to communicate (role playing) is to be able to "take the role of the other" towards one's own vocalisations and behaviour by taking the role of the other into the self. Here "role" refers to how the self is presented, or to what people who interact expect of each other in any situation. This has implications for the clinical use of transactional analysis.

---

1 A stroke is a "unit of recognition" (Berne 1961; see also Stewart and Joines, 1987 Chapter 8) I discuss these in more detail in **Chapter 7**.

In both ways of conceptualising, roles are "intermediary between 'society' and 'individual' ... in that strategic area where individual behavior becomes social conduct, and where the qualities and inclinations distributed over a population are translated into differential attributes required by or exemplifying the obtaining social norms". (Nadel 1957 p. 20).

Despite Nadel's observation, the above two ways of addressing the concept of role are, nevertheless, different; the use of roles as a concept seems to be relative to a particular point in the writer's frame of reference. Agazarian and Peters (1981), for example, relate aspects of group dynamics (Lewin 1951, Cartwright and Zander 1960) with the traditions of Bion (1959), Foulkes (1965, 1975) and Foulkes and Anthony (1973) and other psychoanalytically oriented group psychotherapists. Their observations on roles are couched in terms of the existence of "visible and invisible" group processes. I address the significance of these views for transactional analysts in **Chapter 12**. Linton's view of roles (Linton 1936) is more sociologically orientated, yet of relevance to practitioners working with a focus on the dynamics within or between organisations; this topic is addressed in **Chapter 11**.

I have attempted to capture both the above aspects of the concept by defining roles at *three* levels. Some roles (for example, doctor, teacher) are legitimated within groups, organisations, a culture or society and carry with them consensually agreed, and often legally prescribed, obligations, rights and duties. In organisations these roles usually emerge from the existence or creation of specific positions and are characterised by a range of expected attitudes and behaviours, together with socially legitimated sanctions and rewards. I refer to these as *formalised* roles and regard them as being similar to Linton's sociological view of a "unit in society" (Linton 1936) and Berne's notion of roles as an aspect of the public structure of a group (Berne 1963). These roles usually vary from one situation to another and are certainly influenced by cultural factors. Broadly speaking there are two main categories of formalised roles – relational (such as husband, wife, friend, neighbour) that describe interpersonal relationships and occupational (manager, teacher, engineer). Arguably there is a third category – recreational or social – that is neither relational nor occupational.

In addition to formalised roles, people also interact on the basis of less formalised roles which by their nature are universal, *personalised* and not overtly linked to or constrained by particular organisational expectations, structures or positions. They are similar to what Berne describes as personas or "The way a member [of a group] chooses to present himself to the group. The way in which he wants to be seen". (Berne 1963, p. 246) This perspective is similar to Mead's social psychology account of roles (Mead 1934) and generally speaking, these roles are outside our awareness. Nevertheless, they are easily discerned if you know what you are looking for; much of this book is devoted to spelling out what is an everyday aspect of social interaction. Personalised roles emerge developmentally as part of the unfolding of consciousness that accompanies normal growth and development. Although relative to situational variables they are nevertheless present in and enacted by all humans; there are indications that initially they are based on genetically encoded reflex phenomena (Basch 1988, Tomkins 1962, 1963) and may even be archetypal.[1] The subsequent and equally universal process of socialisation that prevails within all societies has an ameliorating effect, but, by and large, a finite number of personalised roles evolve and remain with us for the rest of our lifetime. I explain the minutiae of this process in subsequent Chapters; for the present it will suffice to say that personalised roles are based on essentially psychological

---

[1] Recent neurological research indicates that mirror neuron properties in the brain may enable people to resonate with the intentions of others (Rizzolatti, et al, 1998). This may apply to the expectations associated with roles.

processes common to everyone. Furthermore, they cannot be seen and do not exist in isolation. That is, the enactment of a personalised role will occur where or when there is the expectation and often, the probability that it will be reciprocated. I develop this idea in **Chapters 8** to **10**.

I later combine the two aspects of roles to take account of the situations in which roles are enacted. I call these *situational roles.* Strictly speaking, situational roles are role functions that describe the personalised roles enacted by those in a formalised role relative to the major variables present in group situations at a particular time or stage in the life of a group.

There are other aspects of roles such as role conflict, role overload and role strain, which are not explored extensively in this book. Readers interested in these aspects of role theory may wish to consult *Role theory: Concepts and research.* (Biddle and Thomas (Eds.), 1966)

Terms and definitions

Allowing for these factors, the following definitions and summary represents my interpretation of selective features of role theory.

A ***role*** *is a disposition to act based on a set of expectations an individual has of him or her self and others relative to any situation.*

I sometimes use the synonymous terms "role enactment" or "role behaviour" to refer to the ways in which people behave relative to their expectations of self, others and the situation. I use the term "role" as defined above generally to refer both to formalised and personalised roles and make the distinction between the two aspects of the term whenever the context so requires.

A major thrust of this book is the description and classification of types of personalised roles based on an elaboration of Berne's use of the term "group imago" (Berne 1963, p 244), which refers to progressive stages of differentiation in people's perception of their relationships during the life of a group. My use of the word "***imago***", although derived from Berne's use of the term, signifies *the historical influences on internalised perceptions people have of each other in a group* (Berne, 1963 p. 22). The "historical influences" are the individual's *life position* (Berne 1972, pp. 84-89); I explain this concept in more detail in **Chapter 10**.

The idea of ***contact*** as a component of a relationship seems so obvious that it scarcely warrants a definition; it is used in the general sense of 'being in touch', a meeting between two or more people. That said, I am using the term in a specific sense that combines Berne's notion of strokes[1] with the Gestalt emphasis on contact as *"a dynamic pattern of experiencing and meeting a need"* (Erskine, Moursund and Trautmann, 1999 p. 8). It is perhaps as well to point out that Erskine et. al. are writing about "relational needs" and therapeutic relationships – which imply relationships within a particular formalised role relationship. Nevertheless with appropriate qualification their views are applicable to all relationships.

I use Tilney's useful definition of *relationships* as *"a pattern of attachment and interaction between two people"* (Tilney, 1998) with two qualifications. The first is that I sometimes refer to "significant relationships" where significance is defined by whoever (usually a client) is describing a particular relationship. Secondly, I regard relationships as a co-creative process.

---

[1] Berne writes about "hungers"- the needs for physical contact, recognition and confirmation of worth, for stimulation, predictability and leadership. A stroke is a "unit of recognition" (Berne 1961; see also Stewart and Joines, 1987 Chapter 8) I discuss these in more detail in **Chapter 7**

The phrase *role imago* refers to *behaviour arising from expectations of self, others and a situation that leads to a significant relationship, or influences an existing relationship.*

Note too, that all the terms defined above are the constituents of a *process.* Although I refer to the idea that roles plus imagos and contact are the building blocks of relationships, these are purely artificial distinctions made solely for explanatory purposes. And even though I have emphasised that relationships involve a "dynamic synthesis" of roles, imagos and contact, I cannot stress too strongly that each of the components of relationships are themselves descriptions of a process. That is, personalised roles, imagos and contact are not 'things' to be seen in isolation – no more so than are arms, legs and so on, not to be seen solely as body parts. Metaphorically speaking, one approach to understanding bodies is knowledge of anatomy; add physiology and psychology and you come nearer to understanding the whole person. Even then, social and cultural factors will have significant contributions to an integral description of a person. Analogously, describing relationships in terms of roles, imagos and contact carries the dangers of reductionism and reification of a holistic process. By extension, understanding relationships is as much an experiential process as it is a cognitive exercise in grappling with concepts and constructs.

I elaborate on all these definitions in later Chapters and unless otherwise indicated, I use the terms Existential Role Imago Contact Analysis as a phrase referring to both the theoretical base for describing social relations and as a way of working with people.

All the above definitions may be encapsulated in the conceptual framework of roles + imagos + contact = relationships. ERICA uses a model of roles, imagos and contact based on an observer's appraisal of these factors. Usually the client and the observer are the same person; clients are discovering how to identify roles, imagos and contact. This is achieved initially simply by getting clients to describe what they regard as Significant Incidents ("Scenarios" in the following examples). Later they discover how to match their descriptions with the model and to consider other roles they could have adopted. Eventually they are able to recognise roles in situ and are better placed to make choices. Note that the words "discovering" and "discover" refer to a co-creative process.

The following ***Scenarios*** illustrate the diversity of situations to which the framework may be applied and some the methodological issues involved:

Scenario 6.4

Jon is the Marketing Director for a software company that has just launched a state of the art product that has received praiseworthy reviews. He has a meeting scheduled with a Dr. Singh, a "marketing representative" from a Taiwanese company interested in "possible collaboration." Contrary to Jon's expectations Dr. Singh turns out to be a smartly dressed attractive woman in her late twenties. She speaks fluent English with an American accent, is extremely well briefed about the new product, and explains that her company would like to explore the possibility of marketing the product in Asia. Jon realises this would require a substantial re-write of some of the software but recognises that this could be the beginnings of a major contract in a totally unexpected sector of the market. He makes non-committal comments about "ironing out minor teething troubles." Dr. Singh leaves Jon a portfolio detailing her company's standing in far Eastern markets and invites him to call her in a week's time for possible further discussion. Dr Singh has clearly impressed Jon and he spends the next half hour perusing the portfolio before going to see the Managing Director. Jon is excited but worried that he may have given Dr Singh the wrong impression by referring to "teething troubles".

Scenario 6.5

Mary arrives ten minutes late for her weekly therapy group. She is distraught and tearfully explains that on her way to the group she'd had a minor car accident and is now "petrified" about what her husband will say when she gets home. Various group members offer reassurances to no avail. Eventually Mary announces that her insurance cover ran out two weeks earlier and has "just not got round to renewing it". The group members gasp and look expectantly at the therapist; Mary continues sobbing inconsolably.

"Look at me Mary" says the therapist, touching her arm. Mary flinches and starts to wail. She reminds the therapist of his mother who was frequently given to melodrama. "I hear you're upset, Mary. If you're not going to talk to us there's not much we can do. You need to stop that howling and calm down"

Mary resorts to sniffling. The therapist turns to one of the group members and says "OK Tom. You were saying...?"

Tom says "I'm worried about Mary"

"I think that's what is supposed to have happened" says the therapist. "She needs to think about what she wants from us. Now, let's get back to what you were saying..."

Later, on reflecting on the session, the therapist concludes that he could have handled the incident more effectively and sensitively.

Apart from the difference in setting the two *Scenarios* differ in that personalised roles in the first are largely "positive" and "negative" in the second. If you are already familiar with TA you will know that there are negative personalised roles that could be invoked to 'analyse' the therapist's concerns. ERICA extends these to include positive personalised roles that would be relevant to Jon's doubts. I elaborate on the conceptual framework and all the above definitions in later Chapters.

Key Points 6

6.1 ERICA is a synthesis of four separate ideas – **roles, imagos, contact** and **relationships**. *Roles* describe dispositions to act and/or patterns of observable behaviour based on individuals' expectations of themselves, others and their situation. *Imagos* are not directly observable, but describe historical influences on the ways in which expectations arise. *Contact* refers to the quality of our interactions with self, others and the world. Combining these ideas provides a framework for examining *relationships*.

6.2 **Relationships** are characterised by behaviour that may be categorised as (1) *proactive* or initialising, (2) *responsive*, (3) *inactive* and (4) *reactive.*

6.3. **Roles** are used in two ways in the social sciences – as a unit in society and as another term for social interaction.

6.4. In ERICA roles there are **three types of role**. *Formalised* roles usually vary from one situation to another and are influenced by cultural factors. There are two main categories of formalised roles – relational (such as husband, wife, friend, neighbour) that describe interpersonal relationships and occupational (manager, teacher, engineer). *Personalised* roles are actual behaviours that are not overtly linked to or constrained by particular organisational expectations, structures or positions. Generally speaking these roles are outside our awareness. *Situational* roles are role functions that describe the personalised roles enacted by those in a formalised role, relative to the major variables present in group situations at a particular time or stage in the life of a group.

6.5. **Contact** combines Berne's notion of strokes with the Gestalt emphasis on a dynamic pattern of experiencing and meeting a need.

6.6. An **imago** is the internalised perceptions people have of others in a group. They signify the historical influences on existing relationships.

6.7. **Relationships** are defined as *a pattern of attachment and interaction between two people.* I regard relationships as arising or emerging from a co-creative process.

Self Supervision Suggestions 6

6.1 Review the *Scenarios* in this Chapter and see if you agree with the way in which I have divided up the text and assigned categories to each segment.

6.2 If you come up with exactly the same categories as I have chosen, would you agree that this would indicate that the categories are **reliable** – that is, they may be replicated?

6.3 If not, my guess is that you would either want to know why I have assigned a particular number to one or more statements or more likely you would want to have a more refined set of definitions and rules for applying them. If this is the case, what additional or different rules would you wish to apply?

6.4 Are the rules really or truly mutually exclusive and exhaustive?

6.5 If not, how would you qualify one or more rule? Which rule(s) would that be?

Chapter 7

Rationale of using roles, imagos and contact

The previous Chapter described the framework for regarding relationships as a synthesis of roles plus imagos and contact. I also gave specific definitions of the terms to be used throughout the book. There are innumerable ways of describing relationships. This Chapter explains the rationale for choosing roles, imagos and contact as significant variables.

Roles

I have made the distinction between formalised, personalised and situational roles for four reasons. The first is that is that roles are a widely used concept in social psychology and sociology and clarity about the ways in which I use the term will enable readers to make links with other approaches.

Secondly, the use of roles is an accepted aspect of transactional analysis theory and practice – namely, the Drama Triangle roles (Karpman 1968, 1971, Choy 1990, and Le Guernic 2004).

Thirdly, Berne also wrote about roles both formalised (Berne 1963) and personalised (Berne, 1971) without making clear the above distinctions. As we shall see, this oversight contributed in part to the difficulties TA theory encounters when attempting to relate persons to social structures (Massey 1987).

My fourth – and most important - reason for differentiating between formalised, personalised and situational roles is that I have drawn on work by non-TA authors (Ryle 1990, 1995, Polster 1996, Ryle and Kerr 2002, Benjamin 1993, 1994, 1996a. 1996b, 2003) that throws new light on the traditional use of Drama Triangle roles and adds an entirely new dimension to both theory and practice.

As indicated in **Chapter 2**, until recently, TA has been short on empirical studies designed to validate the basic tenets of the model. In particular, concepts like Drama Triangle roles were incorporated in Formula G by Berne and have stood ever since as part and parcel of the standard method of game analysis. In other words, the TA community introjected the concept of roles – swallowed the idea of 'roles' whole - without questioning or examining its validity. For example, in his early work, Berne is quite explicit about roles as a concept; he relates them to organisational structure and differentiates them from personas and personalities:

"The organizational structure provides for each person a role – the way in which he is supposed to be seen; the individual structure allows him to exhibit his persona – the way in which he wants to be seen; the private structure puts him into a slot – the way in which he is seen". (Berne, 1963 p. 38)

Later in the same work Berne gives a more general definition of roles as:

"A pattern of behavior on the part of a member which meets or is designed to meet certain expectations of other members, especially in a game or script". (Berne, 1963 p.249)

As indicated above, Berne later adopted Karpman's (1968) use of the Drama Triangle roles of Persecutor, Rescuer and Victim – without indicating that these roles were in any way different to the above definitions (Berne 1963), of what I have termed formalised roles. Karpman (1968, 1973), Schiff et. al. (1975) and Steiner (1974, 1979) all use the concept of roles without defining what is a role. Barnes (1981) comes closest to giving a conceptual definition. He defines a role as that which "characterizes coherent patterns of behavior" and as "behaviors in which an individual engages in his or her relations with others" (Barnes 1981 p. 25). In contrast, most other TA writers seem to rely on the everyday meaning of the word. For example, Clarkson (1987) and Jacobs (1987) introduce the role of the Bystander in behavioural terms but do not give an account of roles as a concept. Jacobs (1987) and English (1987) discuss various other roles, but with similar lack of conceptual clarity. Choy (1990) and more recently, Le Guernic (2004), make significant contributions by describing 'positive' roles that counter-balance Drama Triangle roles – but again, like other TA authors, do not define roles as a concept.

In contrast, Cognitive Analytic therapists have done the empirical groundwork on roles that has enabled them to formulate a psychological model of roles using sophisticated psychometric measures derived from Kelly's Repertory Grid technique (Kelly 1955, Fransella and Bannister 1977, Fransella and Dalton 1990). In Cognitive Analytic Therapy (CAT) the use of "Self States Sequential Diagrams" or SSSDs is a central feature of the method:

> "Everyone experiences different states ... (which are better regarded as states of being than states of mind).... A state in this approach will be understood in relation to its reciprocal ..... a patient's state will be identified with a role. Roles are defined as combining memory, affect and action organized in relation to the search for, or the experience of, reciprocation....Once the different self states have been identified, transitions between them can be monitored and a Self States Sequential Diagram (SSSD) can be constructed. The SSSD plots the patient's self state, the transitions between them and the procedures generated by each, and allows the events or procedures triggering state shifts to be monitored". (Ryle, 1997 p. 27)

CAT stems largely from the work of Anthony Ryle, a British psychiatrist working mainly in the National Health Service. His work (Ryle, 1992, 1997) with clients who fit the DSMIV diagnostic category of borderline personality disorder (American Psychiatric Association, 1995,) has its roots in Kleinian psychodynamics, much of which Ryle seems to have eschewed in favour of a more cognitive, personal constructivist model (Kelly 1955). CAT now emphasises "procedures" for eliciting responses from others as well as for self-management. Ryle had originally sought to describe and measure psychotherapeutic change (Ryle, 1979). Based on the observation by Horowitz (1979) that "states of mind" could be linked with dominant object relations, defences and moods, more recent developments in CAT have incorporated Vygotsky's ideas about the process of internalisation (Vygotsky, 1937, Toomela, 1996a, 1996b). Hence CAT seems to have arrived at the position of regarding "states of mind" as being the equivalent of roles. Ryle's use of the term "role" harks back to Kelly's notion that individuals constantly 'construe' or actively attempt to give meaning to their world and furthermore,

> "To the extent that one person construes the construction processes of another, he may play a role in a social process involving another". (Kelly 1955, p. 95)

From this Ryle concludes:

"In seeking relationships with another, one plays a role based on the expectation of, wish for, or the attempt to elicit, one particular outcome, namely their acknowledgement and reciprocation". (Ryle and Kerr, 2002, p. 9)

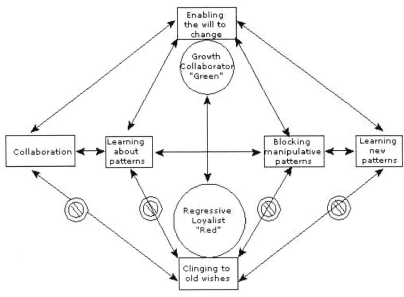

Figure 7.1

In addition to Ryle's work, another approach by Benjamin (1996a, 2003) uses both empirical measures (Benjamin 1994, 1996a) and a model of working with 'nonresponders' (Benjamin 2003) – that is, clients with a long history of not responding to psychotherapy and/or pharmacological treatment. **Figure 7.1** (Benjamin 2003 p. 23) captures the essence of her model.

Benjamin's account of the overall process of therapy is based on her earlier use of a model she calls the Structural Analysis of Social Behaviour (SASB). SASB draws on Bowlby's observation that important early relationships provide children with "internal working models" (Bowlby 1977). Benjamin demonstrates how this internalisation:

"occurs via one or more three "copy processes" (Benjamin 1993, 1994, 1996a, 1996b) These are (1) "Be like him or her" (2) "Act as if he or she is still there and in control," and (3) "Treat yourself as he or she treated you". (Benjamin 2003 p. 9)

SASB provides empirical measures of the "Red" and "Green" variables shown in **Figure 7.1.** Benjamin holds that the therapist's task is to ally him or herself with the 'Green' rather than the 'Red' part of the client's self concept. I comment further on Benjamin's approach in **Part Five**. My present point is that a) there appears to be considerable overlap between SASB and a structural model of ego states and b) the three copy processes are closely allied to Drama Triangle roles. More specifically, it transpires that the three "copy processes" are "contaminations" of the Adult ego state. In other words, the archaic (historical) content of Parent and Child overlap, or interfere with, the here-and-now functioning of the Adult. Hence, when operating the 'copy rules' described by Benjamin, individuals relate to others in a transferential manner.

This has obvious implications for role behaviours, and in **Chapter 19** I explain how the process of reciprocation described by CAT therapists links with Benjamin's work. Reciprocation is also implicit in the TA concepts of imagos and life positions (Berne 1962, 1966, 1972), and, in turn, relationships may be described in terms of attempts to affirm mutual OK-ness. For the present, we may note that the link between CAT and my use of personalised roles (Law 1978a, 1979, 2001) is supported by Gilbert who notes that Polster:

> "holds that a person comprises a "multiplicity of selves" all of which form part of his being in the world. He distinguishes between 'member selves' (the more peripheral aspect of self) and 'essential selves' (core senses of self) in his discussion of different experiences of self that become constellated into clusters. He maintains that people 'animate' these clusters by naming them "my angry self" "my loving self", "my business-like self", and so on. The 'essential selves' form part of the person's enduring core experience of self and when such a sense of 'self' is threatened in relationship, a person is likely to react strongly and protectively (Polster, 1995 pp. 49-52). Polster's position is close to that of Ryle (1992) in his discussion of reciprocal roles and that of Karpman (1968) in his delineation of script drama roles. What Polster adds to the discussion is the concept of 'animating' different facets of ourselves". (Gilbert 2003. pp. 242-243)

Gilbert also points out that:

> "Our internalised network of relationship dynamics will include the 'games' we learnt to play in childhood in imitation of, and in response to, our parents. We have in our internal world a record of all the roles in a particular game and when we move into Victim we will project onto the other protagonist the role of Persecutor or Rescuer, or the reverse may apply. This relates directly to Ryle's concept of internalised reciprocal roles. The reciprocal roles that form part of our internalised experience of relationship networks, subconsciously influence the manner in which we engage with new relationships (Ryle 1992)". (Gilbert, 2003, p. 243)

She continues to suggest that:

> "The 'subselves' [described by Polster] or 'reciprocal selves' [described by Ryle] may well constitute the functional ego states of Transactional Analysis". (Gilbert, 2003, p. 243)

Gilbert's contribution (made at an EATA Conference in 1996) anticipated subsequent discussion regarding the status of a functional model of ego states (Oller-Vallego 2002, Grégoire 2004). Stewart suggests that functional ego states are a "myth" (Stewart, 2001, 2002) and even goes as far as advocating that the functional model of ego states is conceptually so ill founded that it should be "banned".

My conceptualisation of personalised roles builds on Gilbert's points of view. As an alternative to functional ego states, personalised roles are presented as a higher order concept that offers a whole new level of analysis of social interaction. This is a subtle but important change of emphasis.

For over thirty years theorists and practitioners have accepted Berne's concept of ego states along with transactional analysis proper, time structuring and life scripts as the four cornerstones of the transactional analysis model. More correctly in my view, it is the *structural* model of ego states that deserves the status of a cornerstone - inasmuch as ego states may be regarded as ways in which individuals classify and categorise information. The functional model has always presented problems and, likewise, in mapping ego states (whether structural or functional) onto a behavioural stimulus-response paradigm Berne, probably unwittingly, created a possible category error implicit in transactional analysis proper. I offer an alternative approach: instead of functional ego states, the unit of observation for an analysis of the interaction between individuals is personalised roles underpinned by the notion of reciprocation.

Personalised roles occur at three levels (social, psychological and attitudinal) simultaneously (Barnes 1981) and may be identified behaviourally, socially, historically and phenomenologically. Behavioural recognition is based on words, tone of voice, postures, gestures and body movements and facial expressions that are characteristic .of the four categories of behaviour previously outlined – reactive, responsive, proactive, and inactive. Social diagnosis relies on the circular causality of role reciprocation. Historical diagnosis requires linking patterns of current and past role relations. Finally, at the heart of the observational matrix, is the phenomenological diagnosis: the use of the roles as the essence of a dialogical, interactive process.

Imagos

There are two reasons why I use imagos as an explanation for the influence of past events and relationships in preference to life script. The first is that the literature on scripts dwells largely on the extent to which children make self-limiting decisions in order to adapt to their perception of the world. Although Berne and other early writers refer to "winner's scripts" (Berne 1972) the bulk of his writing emphasises negative rather than positive connotations of scripts. Imagos on the other hand, are described in neutral terms:

> "Any mental picture, conscious, preconscious or unconscious, of what a group should be like". (Berne, 1963 p. 244)

The definition illustrates the second reason for using the concept; imagos are a specific aspect of a script that refers to an individual's perceptions of others in a *particular* situation. Massey links this process with the notion of expectations:

> "Humans develop expectations about self through ego states and script. These *expectations* are remembered and become the bases for relating from the time an infant develops the cognitive capacities of emotional object constancy and distinguishes familiar figures from strangers who evoke anxiety (Bower, 1977; Mahler, Pine and Bergman, 1975; Piaget, 1963). As the youngster bonds with significant others and as maturing individuals form attachments, a group-imago of one's intimate in-group evolves. The portrayal of *expectations* about others in a group imago provides a cognitive map or a set of anticipations that frequently become actualized in subsequent relationships. A group imago represents a higher level of abstraction than do ego states, for a group imago embodies a *blueprint* for interperception, interexperience, and the interaction with significant others". (Massey, 1995 p. 279: my italics)

Beyond transactional analysis, an imago is defined in very similar terms:

> "an unconscious, stereotypical set, based on a person's fantasies and distortions about a primary relationship experienced within the early familial environment; this set determines a person's reactions to others". (Agazarian and Peters, 1981 p. 277)

71

My use of the word "imago", although derived from Berne's use of the term, signifies the historical influences on internalised perceptions people have of each other in a group (Berne, 1963 p. 37). The "historical influences" are manifested in two ways – as "imago images" or particular beliefs associated with certain role behaviours, and attitudinally, as an individual's life position (Berne 1972, pp. 84-89). As such, my use of "imago" is consistent with the meaning ascribed to the term by Massey and Agazarian and Peters. In **Chapter 16** I elaborate on the links between roles, the beliefs attached to various "imago images" and underlying attitudes. Note that "images" is used figuratively rather than literally, denoting *every* historical factor having a bearing on an individual's imago.

Contact

It follows from the above comments on ego states, that ERICA is based on the analysis of communication between individuals that stem from interpersonal *contact,* rather than any specific interplay between ego states. In other words, the unit of analysis is derived from the reciprocity of roles and associated qualities of contact and imago images instead of transactional analysis proper. This is not to say that ERICA precludes the use of or need for an analysis of transactions. As will be shown, under certain circumstances, it is extremely useful to analyse the transactions involved; and for those practitioners who favour a particular approach or model of transactional analysis, conventional analysis of transactions and consideration of the associated communication rules remains an option. However, like many Bernean concepts transactional analysis proper, in my view, has its limitations.

In the first place, one has to consider the reasons why anyone would want or need to analyse transactions. There are at least two reasons that come to mind. The first relates to a fundamental understanding of transactional analysis as a theory and method of working with people. That is, having learnt that personality may be regarded as consisting of three systems (psychic organs that are manifested as ego states), one then proceeds to learn about the interaction of the ego states of two or more people and discovers that:

> "A transaction consisting of a single stimulus and a single response, verbal or nonverbal, is the unit of social interaction. It is called a transaction because each party gains something from it, and that is why he engages in it". (Berne 1972 p. 20)

Berne even goes as far as stating that:

> "Any system or approach which is not based on the rigorous analysis of single transactions into their component specific ego states is not transactional analysis". (Berne, 1972 p. 20)

This seems a somewhat unnecessary restriction and one that Berne himself did not follow explicitly – Formula G is based on an analysis of roles and does not use an analysis of ego states.

The second reason for using transactional analysis proper is for understanding the *minutiae* of interaction. This usually happens in supervision – but not always. Sometimes, a supervisor may judge that other concepts are more applicable. In other words, it is a question of what is the most useful unit of analysis for the purpose in mind.

Analogously, if you are a builder calculating the cost of a single dwelling, you are bound to have to consider how many bricks will be needed. If you are a property developer contemplating a ten acre housing estate, you are going to be thinking in terms of how many housing units will be needed. Of course, if necessary, you can translate this into how many billions of bricks will be needed. Likewise, if you're interested in going to the moon, you think of so many kilometres or miles. If you're reaching for the stars, light years are a more manageable unit of analysis.

It is not merely a question of scale; it also depends on what is being described. In my view, attempting to describe relationships by analysing transactions is not only clumsy, and likely to be confusing, it comes close to committing a category error. That is, you would be using a unit designed for analysis of one phenomenon (bricks for a single dwelling) to examine another phenomenon (houses for a ten acre estate).

There is also another reason why I include contact in the framework of a relationship. Personally, I believe this to be more important than any other reasons – but the idea has yet to be subjected to the fire of intersubjective discourse with other transactional analysts. This additional reason centres on how contact is defined and practiced. The traditional view of contact is as I have defined it – as "a dynamic pattern of experiencing and meeting a need" (Erskine. Moursund and Trautmann, 1999 p.8), is augmented by the concept of strokes - "a unit of recognition" (Berne, 1966 p. 230). In practice, the link between roles and strokes (contact) may be operationally defined and tracked by noting who asks for, offers, accepts, gives, receives, rejects or ignores positive and negative strokes. But there is an additional slant:

> "There is another aspect of contact, though, that is equally important: contact with oneself. Just as fully functioning humans are aware of and able to relate to the external world and the people in it, so they must also be aware of and relate to their internal world". (Erskine, Moursund and Trautmann, 1999 p.5)

Internal contact or "self stroking" is undeniably important. However, there is another aspect of contact that is often overlooked;

> "There is much more that could be said about the development of external and internal contact and how both change over the course of one's life. But this is a book is about psychotherapy and only generally about human development". (Erskine, Moursund and Trautmann, 1999 p.6)

The "more that could be said" is that there is another component of contact that operates at an energetic level that is largely out of awareness. Sometimes people recognise this as an unspoken "chemistry" between themselves and others, an almost irresistible pull to attachment (or otherwise). Undoubtedly, this is often erotic and/or transferential (and sometimes both). My experience is that there is more to it than this. Contact occurs at both an inter-personal and a transpersonal or "spiritual" level. I discuss this in more detail in **Part Six**.

This then, is the rationale for using different categories of *contact* associated with various role behaviours. As will be shown, like transactions, there are various distinctive categories (I call these "qualities") that obey different rules. Without pre-empting this discussion, it is not difficult to imagine that contact will be directly related to, and will vary with, different types of role behaviour – reactive, responsive, proactive and inactive – and associated imago images.

Key Points 7
7.1. ERICA distinguishes between formalised, personalised and situational roles for four
reasons:

- roles are a widely used concept and clarity about the ways in which I use the term will enable readers to make links with other approaches.
- the use of roles is an accepted aspect of transactional analysis theory and practice.
- Berne also wrote about roles both formalised and personalised without making clear the above distinctions; this oversight contributed to the difficulties TA theory encounters when attempting to relate persons to social structures.
- I have drawn on work by non-TA authors that throw new light on the traditional use of Drama Triangle roles and add a new dimension to both theory and practice.

7.2. As an alternative to functional ego states, personalised roles are presented as a higher order concept that offers a new level of analysis of social interaction.

7.3. Personalised roles occur at three levels (social, psychological and attitudinal) simultaneously.

7.4. I use imagos as an explanation for the influence of past events and relationships in preference to life script.

7.5. Imagos signify the historical influences on internalised perceptions people have of each other in a group.

7.6. Contact is a dynamic pattern of experiencing and meeting a need. This is a more appropriate **unit** for the analysis of **relationships** than transactional analysis proper.

7.7. Contact occurs at both an **inter-personal** and a **transpersonal** or "spiritual" level. I discuss this in more detail in **Part Six**.

Self Supervision Suggestions 7

7.1. Watch people in social situations and see if you can differentiate between formalised roles and personalised (Drama Triangle) roles.

7.2. Continue to practice spotting Drama Triangle roles.

7.3. Keep notes of the occasions when you adopted Drama Triangle roles. Use a format that gives a clear, *sequential* account of *observable* events. Include comments on how/when *you* can tell when you are in any of the roles *and* comments on how/when *an observer* could tell you are in any of the roles.

7.4. When in a new group of people meeting for the first time, have you ever noticed anyone who reminds you of someone you have met before in a totally different setting? If so, has this affected the way you relate to such a person?

7.5. On occasions when you are listening to someone telling you about something important to them, watch the pattern of their breathing very closely. Synchronise your breathing with theirs. Experiment with this idea/practice by changing your pattern(s) of breathing and keep a note of your reactions. Make sure you record which variable(s) you change.

7.6. Formulate a research proposal to investigate the relationship between strokes and Drama Triangle roles. Consider factors such as offering, accepting, giving, receiving, rejecting, and ignoring positive and negative strokes. Could you frame a hypothesis, and if so, what would it be? How would you 'control' situational variables? How would such an investigation be useful to anyone with responsibility for a) a group of junior school children, b) a residential home for elderly persons, c) a call centre in the telecommunications or IT industry?

Chapter 8

The Contact Cube

This Chapter presents the first of three models for describing relationships. The model enables us to formulate a method of observing relationships which can bridge the 'twin divides' of practice/research and health/pathology in transactional analysis.

The Contact Cube

The first model is called the Contact Cube (**Figure 8.1**) - a three dimensional role space representing psychological processes that describe the repertoire of role behaviours of a single individual. The assumption is that at any moment a person manifests a particular role profile – the enactment of personalised roles simultaneously at three levels. For the purpose of explanation roles are described in this Chapter as single entities.

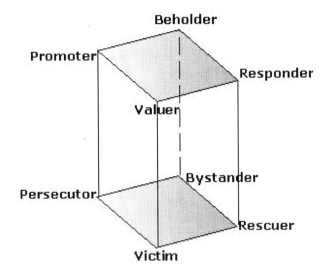

Figure 8.1

Conceptually, the Contact Cube stems from the hypothesis that relationships are characterised by behaviour that may be categorised as (1) reactive, (2) proactive or initiating, (3) inactive, and (4) responsive. These four features of behaviour constitute a particular way of describing human interaction. Reactivity is an aspect of our physiology and consciousness and therefore, but sometimes less obviously, behaviour that usually precedes the other three factors. Proactive/initiating and responsive are obviously opposites and in turn, are both the opposite of inactive. More formally, I am suggesting that at any moment, behaviour may be seen, literally, as the outcome of our capacity for reacting somatically and affectively, in the sense of being continuously open to the existence and impact of external and internal stimuli and disclosing our feelings thereon; OR our capacity to initiate action in situations devoid of any action OR our capacity to respond to action or stimuli external to ourselves, OR our capacity to do neither of the aforementioned. These basic interactional possibilities define the role categories of the Contact Cube.

The base and the top of the Contact Cube are referred to as the negative and positive Squares respectively. Each Square has four roles. Negative Square roles are based on discounting, not OK-ness, contaminations and exclusions. Adult may be experienced as Real Self, but Executive power is always in either Parent or Child. More usually, Real Self and Executive power are in Parent or Child. Positive Square roles do not entail discounting, contaminations or exclusions and there is always congruence between Real Self and Executive power.

Self Supervision Suggestion 8

8.1 If you don't find it easy to visualise two dimensional drawings in three dimensions, use any solid cube to represent the Contact Cube. Mark the roles on the sides at the top and base of the Cube.

8.2 Alternatively, make a model. Cut two 8.5 cm. squares of stiff card or balsa wood for the base and top, marking the positions as P-, R- etc.in the corners of each square. Use four 15 cm. rigid rods (drinking straws, thin dowels) for the vertical sides of the Cube. Glue the rods vertically to each corner of the base; allow to dry, postion and then glue the corners of the top square to the rods.

Drama Triangle roles (Karpman 1968, 1971; Choy 1990, Le Guernic 2004) are well documented and need little further elaboration beyond that given below. Apart from Jacobs (1987), English (1987) and Clarkson (1987, 1992) little has been written about Bystanders; my views build on their work. My understanding of the positive Square roles adds to Choy's and Le Guernic's perspectives (Choy 1990, Le Guernic, 2004).

Although the differences between Drama Triangle roles seems to be immediately obvious even to the uninitiated, it is surprising that no one apart from Kahler (1978), Clarkson (1987), Choy (1990) and Le Guernic (2004), seems to have described the Persecutor, Rescuer and Victim roles in anything more than general terms. Karpman himself seems to rely on a general understanding of the three words to convey the distinctions.

> "only three roles are necessary in drama analysis to depict the emotional reversals that are drama. These action roles ... are the Persecutor, Rescuer and Victim... Drama begins when these roles are established or are anticipated by the audience. There is no drama unless there is a switch in roles". (Karpman 1968 p 52)

In contrast, Kahler (1978, p. 60 – 64) gives a detailed exposition of the roles as "sequences", that is, as changes of "not-OK ego states" using the functional (behavioural) model. He identifies four 'non-reality beliefs', which he refers to as the four myths (Kahler 1977, pp. 275-280). Kahler maintains that:

> "The *myth* "I can make you feel good because I am responsible for your thinking" *is the belief that fosters rescuing.*
>
> The *myth* "You can make me feel good because you are responsible for my thinking" *is the belief that fosters being the victim of a rescuer.*
>
> The *myth* "You can make me feel bad" *is the belief that fosters being the victim of a persecutor.*
>
> The *myth* "You can make me feel bad but I can make you feel worse" *is the belief that fosters persecuting*". (Kahler1978, p. 275: my italics)

While there is an undoubted similarity between Kahler's use of "beliefs" and "myths" and my recourse to "expectations" in the definition of personalised roles, Kahler does not enlarge on the implicit links with Drama Triangle roles. Nevertheless, his description of the myths indirectly differentiates between the three roles and his use of the idea of myths seems to imply an element of expectation.

Apart from the standard application of Drama Triangle roles in Berne's Formula G analysis of games, the only other explicit example of their use is given in a few brief paragraphs in *The Cathexis Reader* (Schiff et. al., 1975 pp. 53-55), where they discuss the roles in relation to a person's frame of reference. Stewart and Joines (1987) give a succinct example that captures the essence of a frame of reference:

> "Suppose you and I stand outside a window and look at the room within. We report to each other what we see.
>
> I say: "It's a fairly small room. It is square in shape. There are people in it. The carpet is green and the curtain brown."
>
> You report: "It's a family scene. The whole atmosphere is warm. There's a Mother, Father and two kids, and they're talking and laughing. It's a big room so they have plenty of space."
>
> Judging by these reports a listener might think you and I were looking at two different rooms. But the room is the same. It is our perception of it that is different.
>
> Thus you and I differ in how we perceive the scene and how we respond to it".
> (Stewart and Joines 1987, p. 188)

They continue to point out that a person's script is that part of their frame of reference that entails discounting - or distorting some aspect of reality. In this respect a significant feature of the negative Drama Triangle is that all the roles involve a distortion of reality to fit the script. According to Mellor and Schiff (1975) this is particularly relevant to the ways in which people impose and/or adapt to frames of reference when playing games. Clarke (1996) has refined the Schiffs' description of the frame of reference by adding four additional components as in **Figure 8.2**:

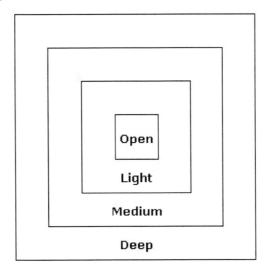

Figure 8.2

- "In the centre is an open area with the capacity to incorporate new information without trying to deflect it.

- Surrounding this is an area of light influence composed of values and assumptions that one holds but which one expects to examine and make decisions about routinely.
- The next area .. of medium influence holds assumptions about oneself and the world that grew out of experiences in early family settings. These ...are easily remembered and open to examination.
- The powerful outside section of the frame [of reference] is the area of deep influences. These firmly entrenched aspects are potent organizers of the individual's responses to life. They are automatic and often outside of awareness". (Clarke 1996, p.213)

In the context of our present discussion, personalised roles are located in the area of deep influences that are "automatic." [1]

The other writers who have made significant contributions to our view of the Drama Triangle are Choy (1990) and Le Guernic (2004) whose views are incorporated in the following descriptions. I have added my own views to their perspectives.

Rescuers

Rescuers over-identify with others and take responsibility for thinking for others or doing things for others without being asked to do so and without fully assessing the need for their acting on behalf of others. They feel obliged to do things for others in order to make others feel OK – often in the hope that their unsolicited or unnecessary efforts will make themselves OK. In more specific terms, they sometimes discount themselves by doing things that are asked of them even when they do not really want to do so. They do all this because they expect others not to be able to do things for themselves. Hence, for the same reason, they sometimes want to do things, whether gratuitously or not, but end up discounting others by doing things that others are capable of doing for themselves. Situationally, they often discount themselves, others and situations, by embarking upon unrealistic or impossible tasks that can only be undertaken by the person they are attempting to rescue. Rescuing is often based on the Biblical ethic of "doing unto others as you would have others do unto you," and, for many people, is seen as entirely legitimate. The underlying dynamic is that the Rescuer identifies with the Victim on the basis of beliefs such as "if that happened to me, I would want/welcome/need help". Others take the position "it would be selfish/ungenerous of me not to volunteer the information/help I think/know would provide a solution". Less magnanimous, is the view that "wont they think I'm nice/kind/helpful/clever if I tell them the answer," or, "they'll like me if I can give them the answer". In many instances, those who rescue others are unaware of the fact that they are doing anything that is inappropriate, or that may be a disservice to the other person.

Persecutors

Persecutors do not identify with others. They distance themselves from others by doing things to others in order to make others feel not OK about themselves, or to reinforce others' existing not OK-ness about themselves. They do things to others that are not needed, usually not asked for, or not wanted. They discount others and sometimes, situations, but do not

---

[1] The current description of the Contact Cube, essentially, is still a description of a *static* structure. The *dynamic* aspects of roles – changes from one role to anther – are described later in this Chapter.

discount themselves unless "out persecuted" by someone else. Their expectations may be categorised under three headings - self–centred, defensive and punitive. From the self-centred perspective, they appear to have little regard for how others see them and generally operate on the basis of competing for OK-ness by making others not-OK – with the expectation that, in any situation, someone has to be not-OK – a point of view that is often accompanied by the defensive stance of "and it's not going to be me". A mixed defensive/punitive belief is "if I've got to go down, I'll make sure I take them with me." A more blatant punitive, pro-active position is "I'll get them before they get me." A variation on this theme is the belief "they deserve what they going to get/ I gave them" or even "I'm going to enjoy getting them!"

Victims

Victims present themselves in ways that attract Persecutors and Rescuers. There is a built in reciprocity of the Rescuer - Victim roles and the Persecutor - Victim roles; both Rescuers and Persecutors need Victims in order to fulfil their expectations of the other. Energetically, Victims shift discomfort to others, thereby inviting symbiosis with anyone willing to take responsibility for thinking for them (usually Rescuers), or anyone willing to induce or further reinforce their helplessness and/or hopelessness (usually Persecutors). They discount themselves and others; the latter dynamic confirms their self-discounting and ensures that their Victim status is maintained in the short term. Victims genuinely believe that they are unable to, or are incapable of, solving their problems. They either expect others to be willing and able to solve the problem for them, and thus identify with Rescuers, or expect others to be unwilling and/or unable to solve the problem for them and thus identify with Persecutors. At best, Victims disclose their thoughts and feelings about themselves and invite but seldom directly ask others to respond to them in the *hope* that others will respond positively, but with the *expectation* that either they will not, or even if they do, it will be too risky to permit others to affect them positively. Thus the essence of the Victim role is to be affected by others negatively – to the extent that they do not permit others to affect them positively.

Bystanders

The inclusion of roles additional to Drama Triangle roles arose from my observation of the Bystander role, in conjunction with Clarkson's views (Clarkson 1987) and English's comments on Jacobs' analysis of autocratic power (English 1987, Jacobs 1987). Despite Clarkson's reference to the Bystander as the fourth role the Karpman Drama Triangle (Clarkson, 1987, 1992, p. 289), my experience is few trainers in the United Kingdom accord little more than passing reference to the significance of the role – a classic example of the theory/research divide.

Unlike English who regards Bystanders as falling into two *types* of people – Potential Protestors and Passive Acceptors – I regard the Bystander as a personalised role in its own right. The Bystander role is the position in the negative Square from which people either *move* to other roles (along the Promoter-Persecutor edge of the Cube or along the Responder-Rescuer dimension), or *compete* for Victim, Rescuer or Persecutor roles. In either case, a Bystander's move will usually be a response to an approach from another role. Bystanders seldom move of their own accord. Of these options a move to Victim is most usually in response to an approach from another Victim resulting in racketeering. Bystanders seldom compete for Rescuer or Persecutor roles. Thus the Bystander role is the role that fuels the creation of other roles – namely Protesters, Passive Acceptors, Resisters and Slaves.[1] I describe these roles below.

Clarkson, English and Jacobs (Clarkson 1987, English 1987, Jacobs 1987) draw on the work of Canetti (1962) and Latane and Darley (1970) to illustrate the role of the Bystander.

"A Bystander is considered to be a person who does not become actively involved in a situation where someone else requires help". (Clarkson, 1987 p. 82)

Clarkson's definition of a Bystander is clearly situational and behavioural and seems to be based on the moral imperative of helping others. Although I have no quibble with the values implicit in this statement and endorse all that Clarkson, English and Jacobs have to say about the social and political connotations of the Bystander role, the above description begs the question of who decides who needs help in any particular situation. Conceptually, Clarkson's argument seems to detract from the reality that for many people "bystanding games" are creative adaptations made at an early age and often under dire circumstances that enabled them to survive. Like all the roles in all games, the problem for Bystanders is that what was once a "solution", later becomes a problem. The following vignette illustrates this point.

Scenario 8.1

Harriet's University Tutor referred Harriet for therapy because of Harriet's failure to complete assignments. She was in her final year of training to become a teacher, specialising in physical education. She was a talented marathon runner who had represented the university at inter-varsity athletics meetings and was regarded by her coaches as a promising candidate for selection at national level. She was academically very able, although shy, and not particularly forthcoming in seminars and class discussions. Even in her first year, she was noted for her dedication to her sport and her ability to enthuse children about athletics. She had no particularly close friends, did not join in any of the social activities, and except for her reputation as a cross-country runner, and the general expectation that she had no time for anything other than the long hours she spent training, she passed largely unnoticed through her first two years. The crunch came early in the third year when the Dean of the Faculty, in reviewing performance ratings of various lecturers, identified Harriet as the common denominator that marred the Faculty's quality assurance ratings. It eventually transpired that the backlog of unfinished written assignments and incomplete practical work projects was so extensive that she was in danger of not being allowed to sit her final examinations. In attempting to retrieve the situation, Harriet's personal tutor discovered that Harriet had never actually asked for extensions beyond the deadline of the dates for submitting assignments, but somehow or other, over the years, various lecturers had come to expect that she would need extra time, and eventually, would even make allowances for her at the time they set dates for completion.

When faced with the situation Harriet was mortified and became significantly depressed. A later transcript (when she was in therapy) of her explanation was that "I knew they [the lecturers] were being kind to me. They didn't expect me to do all the training to be selected for the squad, as well as finish assignments on time, so when it came to the deadline, I would just sort of do nothing. Everyone expected me to do well in the cross country as well as go for the London marathon, so when they did nothing

---

[1] It is not clear whether or not Jacobs is describing the behaviour characteristic of particular types of *individuals* rather than behaviour associated with particular *roles* that may be enacted by anyone. I have retained his terms "Protester", "Passive Acceptor", "Resister" and "Slave" as terms for personalised roles.

or nothing much [about unfinished assignments], I still did nothing. Then I realised that they *couldn't* give me more time even if I'd asked for it. If they did there was a risk they'd get into trouble and the only way I could help them was not to ask for extensions. So I would end up not saying anything and hoping no one would notice."

Faced with the almost impossible task of completing her work in the available time, Harriet became increasingly withdrawn and her athletic performance dipped sharply. The Medical Officer prescribed anti-depressant medication to no avail, and rather than excluding her from further studies, the University referred her for therapy with the suggestion that she "may wish to consider the option of withdrawing from further studies until her health has improved"

In therapy it soon emerged that Harriet, her two brothers and her sister had been physically and sexually abused by their alcoholic father over many years. The family culture was characterised by the predictability of three outcomes. Depending on her father's level of consumption, he would "flake out, explode or 'be kind' to one of us [children]. So it was always the fear of waiting, waiting to see who would be 'it' for that night – to see who he would pick on. We all had jobs to do, so every night he'd ask what we'd done and then he'd inspect our work. If he was just a bit drunk, he would praise you and then take you upstairs to 'be kind' to you. That was the worst. If he was half drunk, he would explode and thrash you. If you were lucky and he was *really* drunk, he would just flake out before picking on one of us. So the best thing to do was to try not to be noticed and hope he wouldn't pick on you – or not do your job – or not do it very well. If he picked on one of the others, you'd feel guilty because you knew *they* were going to be 'it'. My one brother sometimes made it worse by playing up when I'd been 'it' for two or three nights in a row. Then he'd be 'it' and I'd feel it was all my fault. There was nothing any of us could do about it. My Dad made sure of that. Even when I was ever so little, he told me I should never ever tell anyone, not even my Mum, about what he did when he was being kind to me – because if I did, he would have to go to jail and *the whole family would suffer* - and I would get the blame."

A conventional TA approach would have designated Harriet's behaviour at university as a game of 'Kick Me', with Harriet having been rescued by her lecturers and thereby assigned the Victim role, and then later, about to be persecuted by the Dean. All this could be linked to the formation of her script where she became the victim of her father's abuse. Without going into further detail, closer analysis of her childhood script decisions - implicit in the above transcript - suggested that her way of coping with the intolerable family situation was firstly, to try not to be noticed and when this failed, to have already ensured a thrashing by not having done her chores properly, or not at all. The only other alternative was to wait for her father to pick on one of her siblings or for him to 'flake out'. Waiting became the watchword. Doing nothing became the strategy that sometimes enabled Harriet to avoid the other Drama Triangle roles. When the strategy failed she became a Victim.

At university Harriet avoided responsibility for keeping up with assignments by misperceiving her lecturer's expectations of her having to train hard as well as work hard. It seemed more than coincidence that five of her seven lecturers seemed to have behaved in ways that reciprocated her expectations. Arguably Harriet was not in a Bystander role – she was merely allowed and took a long time setting her self up to be a Victim. What she needed was genuine tutorial help in balancing academic demands against her sporting interests – rather than what probably originally started as flexibility of academic standards – but eventually became Rescuing.

When I reviewed the histories of thirty-nine clients with whom I had worked over an eight year period, I started to wonder whether or not there was more to the definition of bystanding than the view that Bystanders are those who do not become actively involved in a situation where someone else requires help. What intrigued me was the fact that seventeen of the twenty-one clients, who recounted situations involving bystander behaviour, described rescuing or persecuting behaviour of others that preceded the Bystander's move to a Victim role. In addition, there were reports (twelve out of seventeen) of an underlying theme of trying not to be noticed in order to avoid becoming a Victim. In two out of five cases, rescuing an actual or potential Persecutor consisted of over-adapting to perceived expectations or actual demands by doing nothing to resolve the situation. (For example, Harriet never considered telling her mother of the sexual abuse, partly because of her father's threat, but according to Harriet, mainly because she did not expect her mother to do anything – as was the case when any of the children received a thrashing.) In other instances, (three out of five cases), resisting potential or actual persecution was seen as a far less favoured option to doing nothing.

Based on these observations, my conceptualisation of the Bystander role seeks to preserve the expectation of *not being noticed*. At the same time I acknowledge that Bystanders evade any responsibility for helping others who seem to be in trouble (Clarkson 1992). This sometimes means that they remain in the Bystander role in the hope that someone else fills the Victim role, and, in this respect, their role may be seen as "negative" (rather than neutral) relative to the needs of the other person.

Thus my view of the Bystander role is that their generalised expectations consist of a proclivity for doing nothing in situations that require action to resolve a problem. Their expectations are that they will be able to avoid having to do anything, and that at best, others will not notice them, or if they do, will expect them not to do anything. At a more specific situational level, the Bystander role consists of a capacity to avoid engagement and remain behaviourally uninvolved in situations which affect, or are likely to affect, one's self and others with whom one has – or has not – significant relations.

I see the Bystander role dynamically as the position from which people move into or out of Victim, Rescuer or Persecutor roles. To do so requires them to be noticed or rejected, to become engaged, to disengage or remain unengaged. As is the case with all roles, this is a reciprocal process and it is often difficult to engage Bystanders without being seen (by them) to be persecuting or offering to rescue them. If they are noticed by anyone in any of the Drama Triangle roles, they will either over-adapt by moving from the "do nothing" form of passive behaviour (Schiff et. al. 1975) to versions of Persecuting or Rescuing or compete for the Victim position.[1] The latter possibility is least likely, arising only when racketeering strokes[2] offered by someone in the Victim role are no longer forthcoming.

Theoretically, Bystanders have one other option – not to move at all. Clinically, this is characteristic only of severely dysfunctional clients; even then, those who voluntarily seek individual therapy find it difficult to maintain the role for any length of time in the face of appropriate therapeutic interventions. In group therapy, Bystanders can sometimes maintain their role by pastiming or low key racketeering with other Bystanders or Victims. In organisations, Bystanders tend to have a much easier time. This applies even to well-

---

[1] I describe the changes from one role to another in more detail in **Chapter 9.**

[2] *Racketeering* is a concept used by English (1976a, 1976b) to describe a way of transacting that entails seeking strokes (recognition) for *racket feelings*. A *racket feeling* is "a familiar emotion, learned and encouraged in childhood, experienced in many different stress situations, and maladaptive as an adult means of problem solving". (Stewart and Joines, 1987 p.209)

managed companies where the skilful Bystander can get by in the short term. Indeed, bystanding is some times used as a tactic to evade deadlines, to buy time or generally "stall" pending the attainment of personal or sub-group agendas.

The characteristic way in which Bystanders are self-activating is for them to change to Victim. They seem to do this by initiating racketeering with other Victims or by moving directly into the Victim role and inviting others to persecute or Rescue them. Although it is theoretically possible for a Bystander to move directly from Bystander to Persecutor or Rescuer, I have not come across this in a clinical setting; it may be that such moves are more obvious in organisations. In either case, a Bystander will have had to collect sufficient stamps[1] to justify such a move.

Responders

Responsiveness to the perceived needs of others is the essence of the Responder role. Responders do not do anything they do not want to do and generally, do not do anything that others can reasonably do for themselves. Even then, Responders only do things that another person wants and clearly asks them to do.

How Responders do things is as important as what they do. The hallmark of the Responder role is that it is the basis of empathy. Responders are open and direct in ways that affirm their own and others OK-ness. They express their thoughts and feelings congruently and clearly in a manner that conveys their unconditional positive regard for others. Their style of communication is "contactful" in the sense that contact is a fundamental component of human interaction.

> "Contact occurs internally and externally: it involves the full awareness of sensations, feelings, needs, sensorimotor activity, thoughts and memories that occur within the individual and a shift to full awareness of external events as registered by each of the sensory organs." (Erskine and Trautmann 1996 p. 316)

The Responder role is invariably used as a stepping-stone to another role, often being interspersed between other roles in a role sequence. However, it is equally demonstrated by active listening, where non-verbal cues and responses play a crucial role. In essence, Responders:

- respond to a perceived need
- check the accuracy of their perception
- ask if assistance (from them) is needed
- acknowledge responses and/or respond to the perceived need
- check awareness of available resources
- if necessary, repeat one or more of the above steps
- do not confirm potential/actual discounting
- maintain their role throughout the interaction or change to another positive role
- invite a reciprocal role response that is open ended
- take account of any formalised role relationships and, where these exist, work within a contract or agreed understanding of a situation, or establish a specific contract
- only do things they genuinely want to do, or that they perceive are really necessary in the circumstances

---

[1] Stamps are unexpressed racket feelings that are "cashed in" (experienced *and* expressed) as a game payoff. (Stewart and Joines 1987 pp.217-129)

- take account of existing and/or future relationships
- take account of the context, the situational component, of the interaction
- operate from the existential, attitudinal stance of I'm OK-You're OK

All but the last five of the above points are directly observable; you would probably need to ask questions to evaluate the last five points accurately. The points do not need to be enacted in the above order providing all bases are covered.

The difference between the Responder and Rescuer roles is that Responders enact the belief that "people are responsible for themselves." Hence they expect themselves and others to take responsibility for their own thoughts, feelings and behaviour. The following scenarios illustrate these differences; to facilitate later discussion, I've added numbers in brackets at various points:

Scenario 8.2

John is standing outside a supermarket on a busy Saturday morning. The street is crowded with pedestrians and the traffic is heavy, stopping only when shoppers operate the push button lights at the pedestrian crossing. A little, old man comes out of the supermarket. He is leaning on a walking stick, while trundling a heavy looking shopping trolley and gripping a bulging plastic bag with the other hand. He approaches the kerb, is about to step off, falters in the face of the on coming traffic, steps back and nearly over-balances (1). Noticing this, John steps forward and asks; (2) "You look like you re trying to cross over?"
"Yeah. Traffic's too heavy." (3)
"Do you want me to help?" (4)
"Naah. I'll manage"
John nods, (5) but points to the lights and asks, "Can you manage the lights?" (6)
"Oh yeah. Didn't notice that button thing." (7)
The man tries to reach the push button with the hand in which he is holding his walking stick and says, "Can't reach." (8)
"Need a third hand?" asks John (9)
Before the man can reply a woman reaches over and presses the button. (10) "There we are, my dear! Traffic will soon stop. Sorry I can't be more of a help with your trolley, I'm in a bit of a rush; so much to do. (11) My, it looks very heavy (12)"
The man glares at her. (13) John says nothing. (14) The lights change. John says, "There you go. OK?" (15)
The man looks at John and says "I'll manage." (16)
John smiles. "'Bye. Have a nice day" (17)
"Yeah – you too" (18)

At point (1) it seems fairly clear that the man is struggling. He is elderly, walks with a stick and is heavily laden. Moreover, he appears to be about to embark upon a hazardous crossing without using the lights to stem the flow of traffic. In terms of the **Responder** role, John perceives a need for the man to be more careful. He therefore checks the accuracy of his perception (2). The man confirms this and also indicates that he is aware of the traffic (3). John asks if help is wanted (4) John acknowledges that help is not wanted (5), but again, checks to see if the man knows how to use available resources (6). It turns out that the man had not noticed the push button (7). This together with the seemingly true, but self-evident statement "Can't reach" (8) indicates discounting. The man a) has not noticed the push button b) is trying to push the button while gripping a walking stick in one hand and holding a shopping trolley/plastic bag in the other. Not surprisingly, he announces that he cannot reach the button. Written text omits the all important tone of voice/facial expressions and so on, but whatever these may have been, the man is clearly experiencing difficulty, but is not explicitly asking for help. He could be in, or is about to move to a **Victim** role, inviting John to rescue him. John maintains the **Responder** role (9).

At this point (10) the woman **Rescues** the man by pushing the button without waiting for him to respond to John's question (9). She is doing something not asked for, which, by definition, she doesn't know whether is wanted or not, is clearly unnecessary under the circumstances, and which the man could do for himself. That is, it seems reasonable to assume that a man who has apparently negotiated a crowded supermarket, emerged with his purchases, and is about to walk home or to a vehicle, is capable of pushing a button – even if he has to put down the trolley and bag. The woman seems not to have considered any of this; she **Rescues** (10) and thereby, defines the man as a **Victim**. She then immediately follows up with an apology for not being more helpful because she is so busy (11) – indicating that she too is, or could be, a **Victim**. Her final comment suggests that at another level she could be a **Persecutor**. (12)

At point (13) we do not have sufficient nonverbal data to interpret the man's glare – it could well be a switch in a potential game. The fact that the interaction does not continue, suggests that the man may have moved to a **Bystander** role. Meantime, John waits (14) (**Beholder**? see below) until again, as **Responder**, he checks with the "OK?" to see if the man wants anything else (15). Points (16), (17) and (18) illustrate another sequence of roles; I comment on this later in this Chapter.

Several points that indicate the basic differences between the Rescuer and Responder roles emerge from the above commentary. Firstly, from a mapping of the emboldened roles above with the italicised phrases and the listed bullet points from page 83, you will note that Responders:

- respond to a perceived need (1)
- check the accuracy of their perception (2) (3)
- ask if assistance (from them) is needed (4)
- acknowledge responses and/or respond to the perceived need (5)
- check awareness of available resources (6) (7)
- if necessary, repeat one or more a of the above steps (9) (15)
- do not confirm potential/actual discounting (8)
- maintain their role throughout the interaction or change to another positive role (14)
- invite a reciprocal role response that is open ended (16)
- take account of any formalised role relationships and, where these exist, work within a contract or agreed understanding of a situation, or establish a specific contract
- only do things they genuinely want to do
- take account of existing and/or future relationships (17, 18)
- take account of the context, the situational component, of the interaction
- operate from the existential, attitudinal stance of I'm OK-You're OK

As previously noted, most of the above points are directly observable. However, there are circumstances that require, if not demand, the omission of some factors. For example:

Scenario 8.3
A group of friends are chatting and laughing together in a hotel car park. They seem to be about to go their separate ways after a pleasant evening out. The atmosphere is friendly and relaxed. One couple are exchanging valedictory hugs, others are laughing

over something that happened earlier, three more are comparing diaries and one woman is standing a few feet apart talking into her mobile phone. No one notices a mini-van slowly reversing out of a parking space, directly towards the woman. She is right behind the van, which has only wing mirrors; the driver has not noticed her. Just as the van is about to knock her over a man who has just come into the car park, sees what is about to happen and shouts, "Watch out!" Everyone looks at him in surprise, except for the woman who continues talking into her mobile phone. The van continues to reverse. The man dashes forwards and drags the woman aside. The entire scenario is over in a matter of seconds; had the man not acted swiftly the woman would have been injured.

Here the man responded swiftly to a perceived need. He acted on the first and last of the above points, without waiting to check the intervening ones. His role was either Responder or Rescuer; the only way of telling the difference would be to obtain more information about the observable interaction that would have ensued immediately after the incident, as well as assessing the man's life position. A mismatch between these two sources of additional data would indicate a Rescuer role. Such additional checks constitute the essential information for differentiating the Responder role from what I have often heard being referred to as "legitimate rescuing"; in my view rescuing is always unnecessary and never "legitimate". This is not to say I never rescue anyone; my point is that one should acknowledge this as the enactment of the Rescuer role without any justification.

More general points arising from the above scenarios are firstly that the absence of nonverbal data underlines the importance of sensory based, observable data, as a foundation of any assumptions, descriptions, reports and interpretations of any role. Secondly, the commentary illustrates the distinction between thinking about roles rather than transactions. For newcomers to TA this is unlikely to be problematic. My experience is that those who are already attuned to tracking transactions need time to adjust their frame of reference.

Compared to Responders, Rescuers, at their most extreme, do none of the above summarised points except respond to a perceived need. Generally speaking their responses are often ill-timed and their definition of need is misperceived; they make little distinction between "want" and "need" and seldom explore the contextual aspects of their interventions. Starting from this position leaves little room for correction. Because they operate from life positions other than I'm OK-You're OK, discounting will always be present. In cases where the Rescuer appears to consider factors additional to perceived need, they do so from within a contamination or exclusion of Adult.

Given the above differences, it may seem difficult to imagine what Responders and Rescuers have in common. Indeed, you may have been misled by my use of terms that signify complete opposites; for example, I refer to positive and negative Squares and mirror image roles. Despite the appropriateness of these phrases, the two roles share a major feature of human interaction. I touched on this factor in **Chapter 6** in outlining a possible model for describing relationships. The characteristic that is common to both Responders and Rescuers is that they are *responsive* and the quality of contact is *co-operative*. I comment on the wider implications of this observation later in this Chapter and again in **Chapters 13** and **14**.

Promoters

Promoters promote the interests of self and others. The role has six components – *permission* and *protection*, (Crossman 1966), *potency* (Steiner 1971), *perception* and *practice* (Clarke 1996) - which I have widened to include role modelling applicable to any setting -

and a component that I call *prescription*. This is an elaboration of Steiner's description of the script antithesis or command as:

> "an emergency transaction from Parent to Child which is used to arrest or interfere with certain transactional sequences which the therapist feels are dangerous". (Steiner, 1974 pp. 305-306)

I use the term *potency* as meaning the ability to promote mutual OK-ness by intentionally influencing others to behave in a prescribed way. This is similar to Steiner's use of potency as "the therapist's capacity to bring about speedy improvement" (Steiner, 1974 p. 315),

The inter-relationship between the "6 Ps" is crucial to understanding the dynamics of the Promoter role. We can simplify this complexity by using a step-by-step approach to add each of the Ps to the basic template of the Promoter role

It is also worth noting that a person occupies a *personalised* role within the context of their role set (Merton 1957, 1968) and their role networks; the latter being sub-sets of the former. A role set consists of all the role relations a person has experienced and hence, all those with whom one has had significant *formalised* role relationships. For example, some of the role relations in my role set are as "father", "neighbour", "work colleague", "friend", "psychotherapist" and so on.

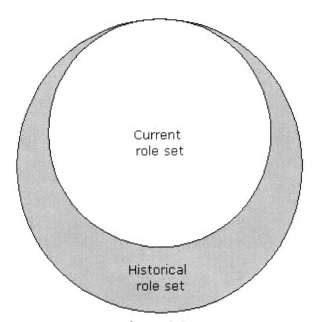

Figure 8.3

Role sets also embody a time dimension and thus, have historical and current dimensions. The boundary between the two is largely conceptual and in practice, is determined by frequency of contact and an individual's perception of the significance of the relationship. I discuss role sets extensively in **Chapter 15**, but touch on them at this stage because the idea is useful for illustrating the significance of the historical-current dimensions of role behaviour. The differentiation between the current and historical role sets is shown in **Figure 8.3**.

You may have noted from the above description of the 6 Ps that *perception* and *practice* are aspects of the Promoter role that, by definition, can only operate in the current role set.

This process is diagrammed in **Figure 8.4** where the hashed area denotes *perception* of the situation and role modelling as *practice* is shown by the circle with wavy lines. You will see that *practice* is shown within the *perception* boundary – indicating that people inevitably see and understand more than they act upon. To put this in another way, in any situation and for all roles, you will select and act upon a range of options from among the myriad variables you notice.

Clarke describes practice as:

"The opportunity to learn by direct experience. The educator:
- provides the opportunity to try out a new behavior or explore a new attitude in a safe setting.
- encourages participants to practice as much as they need to and strive for the degree of excellence that is appropriate for each of them". (Clarke 1996, p 217)

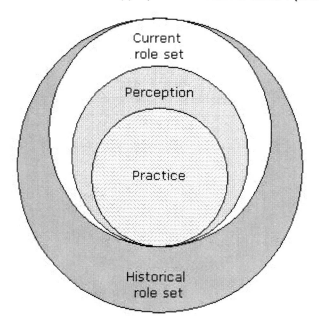

Figure 8.4

I have widened Clarke's definition of practice to include role modelling applicable to any setting. That is, anyone in a formalised group leadership role needs to practice what they preach. For example, it hardly encourages good practice for a Managing Director to send round a strongly worded memo about time keeping and then consistently turn up late for meetings. Likewise, a group therapist is unlikely to empower others if he or she does not model the Promoter role. The application of the practice component of the role is essential for demonstrating the other Ps.

I have also added another "P" - a component that I call *prescription*. This is an elaboration of Steiner's description of the script antithesis or command as:

"an emergency transaction from Parent to Child which is used to arrest or interfere with certain transactional sequences which the therapist feels are dangerous". (Steiner, 1974 pp. 305-306)

Steiner cites the examples of suicidal, violent or intoxicated clients who clearly need to be told to desist from certain behaviours. Kahler (1979) uses two similar therapeutic tactics he describes as interruptive and directive "channels of communication" (Kahler, 1979 pp. 5-6). Schiff et. al. regard the Parent ego state as that which "contains definitions of the world" and "gives prescriptions and advice" (Schiff et. al., 1975 p.23). All these writers share the view that under certain circumstances it is appropriate for a therapist to tell clients what to do. To date, clinical descriptions of this process are couched in terms of the ego states and the transactions involved. I have taken a somewhat wider view in two respects. The first is that I see prescription as a fundamental aspect of our expectation of others under certain circumstances, and hence, focus on prescription as an aspect of a role, rather than relating it to ego states and transactions. Secondly, societies could not exist without some or other prescriptive process being enacted at a macro level. Indeed we have elaborate institutional arrangements designed to ensure that individuals do what 'society' expects of its citizens. At the level of interaction between individuals, prescription is a taken for granted everyday occurrence. Teachers tell students what to do, parents are expected to 'control' as well as nurture their children and bosses are expected to be capable of giving instructions that workers will obey. When or where the prescriptive component of the Promoter role is necessary but not exercised or enacted with insufficient potency by those in formalised leadership roles, group or organisational norms, cohesion, morale and effectiveness are impaired. More simply relationships and eventually work effectiveness suffer.

Prescription as an aspect of the Promoter role is more evident in non-clinical settings than it is in the therapists' consulting rooms. Unlike teachers or bosses, therapists and even more so, counsellors, are loath to tell clients directly what to do – or not do. Nevertheless they do prescribe all manner of behaviours for themselves and their clients in relation to their formalised role relationship. In TA this is handled by way of the 'business contract' – an agreement that specifies times and frequency of session, fees and so on – and codes of ethics and professional practice. TA and some other models of therapy also use 'therapeutic contracts' – statements of what the clients would like to change, what they will do in order to effect such changes and what the therapist will do in order to facilitate the client's making changes. This too, is an aspect of the formalised role expected of TA therapists by their trainers and peers (but not necessarily by their clients). Not all models of therapy advocate such practice. In classical client-centred counselling or therapy, for example, the practitioner follows the client without first agreeing where they will be going. Psychodynamic therapists are traditionally 'non directive'. Nevertheless at a personalised level of role enactment all therapists prescribe the nature of the therapy they offer – even if it is done by way of believing and practising in a non-prescriptive manner. In short, in any interaction with others we contribute to what transpires and this may include defining or prescribing our expectations of others.

I enlarge on the prescriptive component of the Promoter role and the links between formalised and personalised roles in **Chapter 11;** for the time being it will suffice to note that prescription is the framework that enables potency, protection and permission to occur. In other words, I regard *prescription, permission, protection* and *potency* as interrelated components of the Promoter role, as shown in **Figure 8.5**.

Whereas *permission, protection* and *potency* sometimes accompany *prescription*, *potency* itself is always necessary for the other components to be effective. For example, the Chief Executive who firmly announces to senior managers "I want to thank you for your contributions to this discussion. You have all put forward your views and suggestions for what we should do next. Having listened to all your ideas, I have decided that we will ....
(continues to prescribe what will happen)." Here the CEO, having decided upon a particular

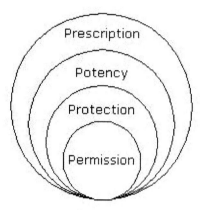

Figure 8.5

course of action, is enacting the Promoter role with *prescription* and *potency* as dominant features, *permission* and *protection* being technically submissive and practically irrelevant. Likewise, a therapist demonstrating *prescription* and *potency* may tell a distraught client to "stop working yourself up, and tell me what has been happening".

In these examples, *permission* and *protection* are implied rather than explicitly stated, but whether or not inferred by the recipients, the group leader's prescriptions would be largely ineffective without *potency*. If the CEO or the therapist delivers their message (the 'prescription') in an off-hand way (the 'potency' component) the recipients are unlikely take heed.

I use the term *potency* as meaning the ability to promote mutual OK-ness by intentionally influencing others to behave in a prescribed way. This is similar to Steiner's use of potency as "the therapist's capacity to bring about speedy improvement" (Steiner, 1974 p. 315), which he sees as a combination of the command, permission, protection, fun and work transactions. Whereas transactions are based on a stimulus response paradigm, roles arise from expectations. Without the mutual expectation that under some circumstances it is legitimate for one person to require another to behave in a particular fashion, we would probably not have evolved as a species much beyond the level of cave dwellers. At some time in our evolutionary history we discovered that some tasks could be more effectively accomplished by cooperative effort than by single or competitive endeavour. With this came the realisation that if we were to live, forage, hunt, and fight in groups it was inevitable that, at times, someone had to be in charge, someone had to give orders that had to be obeyed. Not much has changed since then but for some reason I have yet to fathom many clinicians seem to me to be remarkably reluctant to take on board the idea that relationships contain a power dimension. I discuss this more fully in **Chapter 11**; for the present, the point I'm making is that *potency* in any setting is no more than the appropriate use of the power dimension of relationships. Used appropriately it empowers both the user and others.

If we now enlarge and add the first two Ps – *perception* and *practice* – to the others, you will see that the six are arranged in order of inclusion as illustrated in **Figure 8.6**. This shows that the largest outer circle representing *perception* includes all the other circles. The hashed area denotes those aspects of a situation that are perceived but not acted upon. For

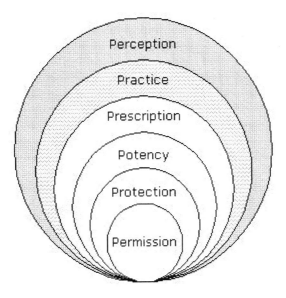

Figure 8.6

example, a teacher will notice which students form friendships in pairs or groups, those that are less sociably inclined and so on and not do anything about such patterns of classroom interaction unless they were to interfere with the educational task or general welfare of individuals. If it were necessary for the teacher to act upon his or her perception of these friendships – for example, to deal with bullying – this would fall within the second largest circle representing *practice* and shown in **Figure 8.6** as the area with wavy lines. Needless to say the teacher would have to role model ('practice') non bullying behaviour by prescribing (the third circle) appropriate constraints in a sufficiently potent (fourth circle) manner in order to provide the necessary protection. The teacher may even offer *permission*: "Anyone who is being bullied can come and talk to me in complete confidence about how to deal with the situation".

How a Promoter prescribes behaviours or offers *permission* and *protection* will depend on whether or not the permission and protection being offered is in relation to historical or current events. If we combine **Figures 8.4**, **8.5** and **8.6** we end up with **Figure 8.7**.

In **Figure 8.7** the dashed two-way arrows signify that the 6 Ps are enacted in the current role set, but impinge on material from the historical role set. In clinical work, I use the term "historical" as a prefix to *permission, protection, potency, prescription, practice* and *perception* to describe this process. To illustrate, I recall a client whose schizophrenic mother would never let my client play with other children without his having to suck a strongly flavoured cough lozenge, because she was convinced that the children would "pass on their germs" to my client. Such was the extent of her belief that she never left the house without a copious supply of mints, cough lozenges and as a last resort, garlic. The prospect of "catching germs" was held out to be a portentous, life threatening disaster waiting to happen. Of course, by the time my client started school he figured out that his mother had got it wrong and he adopted the sensible tactic of spitting out the lozenge as he turned the corner on his way to school. Thirty five years later when he sought therapy because he was overworked, stressed and increasingly prone to panic attacks, my client reported experiencing the taste of cough lozenges whenever he was about to have a panic attack.

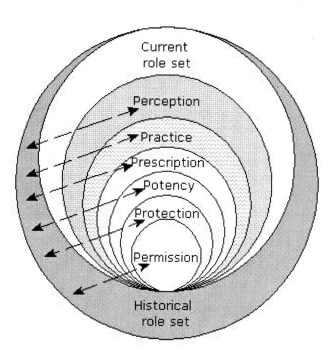

Figure 8.7

Here the historical *perception* was my client's mother's deluded view of the world; the historical practice was his mother's role modelling that accompanied the *prescription* of her insistence on his sucking lozenges. Historical *potency* was the genuine fear of a five year old about death from "catching germs"; historical *protection* (spitting out the lozenge) had been replaced by the taste of lozenges accompanying a panic attack. Historical *permission* was more obscure but turned out to be my client's five year old realisation that he himself could (indeed, had to) resolve situations that arose from his mother's irrational fears and bizarre beliefs.

All these historical factors were being played out in the client's current role set. Had I dealt with them by a purely here-and-now use of the Promoter role, I would have given him relevant information about the physiology of panic attacks, made little reference to the possible significance of childhood experiences and coached him on various techniques for breath control (thus role modelling the current situation), prescribed the use of this whenever he started having a panic attack, and given him appropriate information about the efficacy of this and other behavioural techniques along with re-assurance that he possessed the necessary resources to overcome his difficulties. I would probably not have been explicit about *permission*. All of this, delivered with sufficient *potency*, may well have sufficed. However being a clinician and acting upon what I perceived as my client's expectations, I did all the above, but in addition, praised his awareness/insight in linking his current panic attacks with his past history, discussed his childhood fears, stroked his five year old creativity in finding a solution to his mother's delusions and offered the suggestion that he need no longer use a solution that had now emerged as a problem. In both cases, throughout our interaction, the quality of contact and maintaining mutual OK-ness would have been/was a crucial factor.

Although deliberate use of knowledge of a client's past history is the distinguishing feature of clinical work, it clearly does not figure in a non-clinical setting. In other words, the

Promoter role may be enacted to equal effect, without invoking the historical dimension – as indicted below.

Promoters and Persecutors

The distinction between a Promoter and a Persecutor is usually easy to spot. This is clearly illustrated in the following *Scenario*:

Scenario 8.4

Manjeet works for a PR company as a clerk/word processor. She has been with the company for six months and is due for her first appraisal with her line manager and the Head of Administrative Services. This is a routine procedure in the Company; all new appointments have a six monthly probationary period and are subject to a satisfactory appraisal, before becoming eligible to join the Company's superannuation scheme. As a result of having completed in her own time an evening course on the use of the most up to date version of a word processing package, Manjeet is more knowledgeable than anyone else in the typing pool. Other older and more experienced staff, often turn to her for advice and information. Her line manager, Linda, regards this as "straying beyond her job description" but is otherwise satisfied. In adding her own views Manjeet has noted that "I did not think of helping other people as 'straying from my job description'

Siobhan, the Head of Administrative Services, starts the meeting by saying:

"OK, I've read your appraisal Linda – and the comments you've added Manjeet. The purpose of our meeting is to gives us all the opportunity of reaching an agreed view of your progress and future with the Company, Manjeet. (1) More personally I find these meetings also give me the chance to meet staff individually – rather than just exchanging 'hellos' when we happen to come across each other around the coffee machine. So, let's see what we've got here..." (2)

Siobhan glances through the papers; the other remain silent.

"You'll know Manjeet as this is your first appraisal one decision Linda and I have to make is about your eligibility to join the Company's superannuation scheme?"

"Yes".

"Of course this is an option – you do not have to join. You can decide to be what is known as 'contracted out'"

"I understand" says Manjeet

"Good. That would be best for you" says Linda condescendingly. (3)

"Oh" says Manjeet with a mixture of surprise and disappointment. (4)

"Do you want to say more?" asks Siobhan. (5) Manjeet shakes her head. (6) Siobhan turns to Linda and speaking slowly asks "Why?" (7)

"What I mean is that if she doesn't want to join the scheme, we don't have to make any decision about her eligibility." (8)

"True" agrees Siobhan (9) "And...?" (10)

"Well that way she can continue to pay into a contracted out scheme for another six months and wont lose out on long term contributions if we had decided she was not eligible for the Company scheme" says Linda with a smile. (11)

"Linda as far as I can see there's no question about her eligibility. In fact your appraisal makes no mention of this one way or the other. I took this to mean you had no objection. If I'm wrong and you are not recommending eligibility you should have included a statement to that effect in the appraisal, giving your reasons, so Manjeet could have responded." (12)

"They're in the appraisal report!" says Linda triumphantly. (13)

"What?" cries Manjeet. (14)

"I think you need to be more specific than that Linda. I am certainly not clear about whatever it is you are referring to in your appraisal. Please explain your position" says Siobhan firmly. (15)

"It's quite simple. She keeps on undermining my authority!" retorts Linda. (16)

"Linda I don't find that very explicit" says Siobhan "I hear you making a very general statement that has serious implications. Unless you can be very specific I am inclined to regard this as an over-reaction to whatever it is that has been happening over the past six months. Now, take your time (17) and tell me precisely in what way do you think Manjeet has been undermining your authority?" (18)

"If I've told her once, I've told her a dozen times it's not her job to be spending Company time telling other staff smarty pants ways to reformat documents or back up files or whatever else she's just learned at college!" (19)

"I can understand you may have been annoyed if Manjeet disregarded your instructions. (20) Is that what you mean by undermining your authority?" (21)

"It's my job to tell them what and when and how to do things! If anyone needs help with the new system they're supposed to ask me – not her! But what happens? She keeps coming out with 'see what I just learned on my course' ideas!" (22)

Siobhan (sharply) "There's no need for your sarcastic tone, Linda" ((23)

"Sorry" mutters Linda. (24)

"I agree you are responsible for telling your staff when and what to do" says Siobhan.(25) "I also think there's room for discussion about ways of co-operating to share new knowledge and skills." She pauses and then continues. "I think I now understand your position Linda (26) – and I have some ideas about how we can translate your views into an objective statement that will ensure that you, Manjeet, can have a fair appraisal.(27) Clearly, there is some miscommunication here; so much so Manjeet, that I am going to put your appraisal on hold so that we can all have a rethink before committing anything to paper.(28) I guess this has not been an easy situation for you and I reassure you both that for my part what has been said so far and the way it has been said, is not for discussion with anyone else. I expect the same from both of you (29).If it's OK with you Manjeet, what I suggest you do now is to take a break – freshen up, maybe get a coffee or whatever - but wait in the staff room. I want to talk to Linda for about ten minutes and then I'll come and fetch you. Are you OK with that?" (30)

Even without the nuances of tone, inflexion, speed of delivery and so on, the text alone reveals clear differences between the Promoter and Persecutor roles. To illustrate this you may want to do the following **Self Supervision Suggestions:**

Self Supervision Suggestion 8

8.3 Without re-reading *Scenario 8.4* which roles are enacted predominantly by each of the characters?

8.4 Give reasons for which of the points demonstrate the Persecutor role?

8.5 Give reasons for which of the points demonstrate the Promoter role ?

8.6 Which roles other than Promoter and Persecutor are indicated by which points?

8.7 Which points are linked with which of the 6 Ps of the Promoter role?

The answer to the first of the **Suggestions** is that Linda started as a Rescuer and later switched to Persecutor. Siobhan was the Promoter and Manjeet was probably in the Victim role. The question posed in this first **Suggestion** is by far the most important for three reasons. Firstly it requires you to make an overall appraisal of the whole Scenario thus capturing the reciprocity of roles. Secondly it will have encouraged you to answer quickly in an intuitive, 'first reaction' manner – which is always the best approach because thirdly, such an overall appraisal is the one that in practice is most useful. Everyday use of ERICA does not require the detailed level of analysis and discussion demanded by the answers to the remaining **Suggestions**; here they are included purely as a means of illustrating/teaching the various nuances of the Promoter role.

In reading the following commentary on the remaining **Suggestions**, you may need to exercise a little creativity in matching my interpretations of the various points with the written word.

At point 1 Siobhan uses the prescriptive component of the **Promoter** role to define the purpose of the meeting and seemingly role models the style of interpersonal contact she is seeking to establish. (2) Linda's first comment is probably enacted from a **Rescuer** role. Because she redefines the discussion from the possibility of Manjeet's being contracted out to what is 'best' for her, the statement is a discount; it is made without any reference to Manjeet's opinion or choice in the matter and clearly implies that Linda knows what is best for Manjeet. Manjeet is obviously surprised and disappointed. (3) The fact that she chooses not to ask for more information at this stage, (6) indicates she has accepted Linda's opening discount. She is probably in the **Victim** or **Bystander** role and if so, we would have beginnings of the classic formula for a game. Notice that Siobhan uses the **Responder** role (5) before moving on to deal with the ensuing game (7, 10). Linda maintains the **Rescuer** role (8, 11) by disregarding Siobhan's acknowledgement of the non-discounting element of her explanation, (9) until in the face of Siobhan's use of the perception component of the **Promoter** role (12) she switches to **Persecutor**. (13) From here on (16, 19, 22) Linda continues to Persecute and probably ends up as **Victim**. (24) Siobhan alternates between the **Promoter** role with prescription (15, 18) and with protection at (27, 29) while responding to the validity of some of Linda's statements. (20, 25, 26) She demonstrates her most prescriptive and potent use of the **Promoter** role at points (23) and (29).

You will note that I have not commented specifically on points (4), (6), (7), and (10) and not at all on (14), (21), and (30) which refer to roles we have not yet encountered; I discuss these in **Chapter 9**. In summary, Promoters:

- initiate action/discussion by stating their perception of a situation
- role model the nature/quality of contact they seek to establish
- prescribe behaviour that others are invited or required to follow
- offer and/or provide protection
- offer and/or provide permission
- demonstrate potency in enacting one or more of the above by
    i. acknowledging responses that do not contain discounts
    ii. inviting a reciprocal role response that is not open ended
    iii. confronting potential/actual discounting
    iv. if necessary, repeating one or more of the above steps
    v. use formalised role relationships in the expectation that others will comply with their requests, instructions or demands
- empower others by creating opportunities for them to practice roles in new ways
- maintain their role throughout the interaction or change to another positive role

- generally, only do things they genuinely want to do but sometimes act according to their formalised role even when they would personally prefer not to do so
- take account of existing and/or future relationships
- take account of the context, the situational component, of the interaction
- operate from the existential, attitudinal stance of I'm OK-You're OK

Beholders

The generalised expectations of the Beholder role consist of a proclivity for remaining neutral. At a more specific, situational level, the Beholder role consists of a capacity to postpone engagement yet remain alert in situations that affect or are likely to affect one and others with whom one has significant role relations. Beholders fuel the creation of other positive Square roles – namely Provocateurs, Active Acceptors, Announcers and Servants. I describe these roles below.

A significant difference between the Bystander and Beholder roles is that Beholders retain and eventually exercise their capacity for self-activation, whereas Bystanders rely upon others by virtue of their passive behaviours and symbiotic invitations of shifting discomfort and/or responsibility to others.

A feature of both the Beholder and Bystander roles is that there are remarkably few verbal transactions; both are verbally inactive for most of the time they occupy their respective roles. However the non-verbal behaviour accompanying both roles is significantly different. Beholders track whatever is going on around them. They do show non-verbal responses to the tone, affect and content of the dialogue that is either being directed at them or others in their presence, but only to the extent that such responses do not immediately provoke a role change in others.

Appropriate Beholder behaviour consists of whatever minimal comment it takes to stay in the role and keep the conversation going without the other person flipping in to another role in reaction to the Beholder's words. At times this may mean hanging back, postponing an intervention until one has sufficient information to be effective, being clear about the intent and likely outcome of the intervention and judging when to make the intervention. Whichever the display of verbal and nonverbal behaviour, the over-riding characteristic of the Beholder's role is a capacity for being present yet neutral, with an unspoken quality of alertness to and awareness of the environment.

The essence of the Beholder role is to be able to remain open and neutral. The skills of neutrality are highly sophisticated and the timing of a Beholder's move to another role is crucial. This is particularly important when the Beholder role is seen in relation to other roles. In such cases, the functions of the Beholder role often serve as a container not only for the interaction between two or more people, but also across boundaries within the self. I return to this point in later Chapters. Additionally, as will be seen in **Part Six**, the Beholder role is highly significant for contact at a transpersonal level.

Timing is also an important factor when enacting the Beholder role. This applies not only to knowing when to adopt the role, but also to being able to sustain it without seeming disinterested. Perhaps more so than with any other role, the Beholder role is what makes a person a "good listener". In this respect, the Beholder role plays a large part in the other person "feeling heard", being an essential vehicle for conveying respect and mutual OK-ness A practical example of enactment of the Beholder role is when a practitioner watches the development of a potential game but does not intervene until he or she has sufficient information to be able to confront the game effectively (Dusay, 1966). Additionally, the Beholder role is the gateway to transpersonal dimensions of experience and practice; this topic is covered in detail in **Part Six**.

Valuers

"Valuer" is a term that I have coined to describe a crucial feature of social relationships[1]. "Valuer" means being open to and valuing the emotional impact that people have upon each other. This is the human condition. We all affect or influence one another all the time. We react to others viscerally, affectively, cognitively and hence behaviourally. At times our behavioural reactions are more obvious than at others. Sometimes we are not aware of our reactions but they are always present. Perhaps more so than any other role, the expectations that accompany the behavioural enactment of the Valuer and the Victim roles are based on physiological processes. Our reactivity is 'hard-wired', so built in to our bodies that we have very little conscious control over our reactions; whatever 'control' we do exercise happens after we have reacted to a stimulus (LeDoux 1994, 1996). We adapt to our environment physiologically and psychologically. It is our adaptations that enable us to survive. Our reactions to particular events become automated and replayed as and when required to ensure survival. Normally we do not take much notice of such survival mechanisms – unless we have reason to.

Surprisingly, the Valuer role is a frequently overlooked aspect of social interaction. Many people find it difficult to "get their head around" the notion of a "positive" Victim and when faced with circumstances that engender "legitimate rescuing" it is easy to define others as Victims rather than regarding them as being circumstantially vulnerable.

Victims experience this normal openness to the environment as wounding, as betrayal by others. Hence they know that they are 'vulnerable', that they have been wounded but have been able to adapt by developing tactics and psychological strategies that enabled them to survive. It is (usually) when these strategies no longer work or become too onerous that they come into therapy. What Victims have lost (or never experienced) is the belief that healing is the mirror image of wounding. Whereas the Victim role has to do with the experience of being wounded by others in the past and defending against future wounding, the Valuer role denotes the opposite – the potential for or actual experience of healing oneself, healing others or being healed by others – or, simply, not having been wounded in the first place. In this context, "wounding" arises from the vulnerability of impairment to the healthy process of normal growth and development and "healing" denotes overcoming or correcting such impairments simply by virtue of being in contact with others and one's self.

The essence of the Valuer role lies in acknowledging our capacity to affect and be affected by others positively. Developmentally this is not possible without making contact with another person. Normally the infant's experience of such contact inculcates the expectation that they will or, at very least may, be affected positively by others. It is this very reactivity in us as biological organisms that underpins our intersubjectivity and the reciprocity of roles – that sparks reactivity in others. Babies cry, adults respond appropriately – and thus, we have the beginnings of intersubjectivity, the foundations upon which later expectations are based. It is from these beginnings that we formulate what later becomes the basis of self-esteem and realistic trust in others relative to the situation.

Behaviourally Valuers disclose their thoughts and feelings about themselves and invite or directly ask others to respond to them with the expectation that they themselves will or, at very least, may be affected positively by others. In contrast, Victims disclose their thoughts and feelings about themselves and invite but seldom directly ask others to respond to them, in the *hope* that others will respond positively, but with the *expectation* that either they will

---

[1] At one stage I considered using the term "Receptor" – implying the capacity of being receptive to others. For a while I used the term "Vulnerary"; feedback from clients indicated they were inclined to shy away from the connotations of being vulnerable.

not, or even if they do, it will be too risky to permit others to affect them positively. Likewise, the difference between Valuers and Responders is that the latter respond to the needs of others without necessarily disclosing their own thoughts or feelings about themselves.

In clinical practice, the frequency and extent of a therapist's enactment of the Valuer role is probably the major difference between Rowan and Jacobs's (2002) instrumental and relational styles of working with clients. When using the instrumental style, a therapist will probably seldom disclose their feelings or information about themselves, to the client. In a relational style, such information is a crucial aspect of the therapeutic work. I address these issues further in **Part Six.**

Contact and imago images

We have seen that the Contact Cube has positive and negative Squares; each Square has four roles. For both Squares there are two general guidelines about the nature of the *contact* associated with each of the eight roles

The concept of contact comes from Spitz's (1945) studies of infants' failure to thrive and was later invoked by Berne in developing the idea of strokes. Early Gestalt writers, (Perls, Hefferline and Goodman, 1951; Perls 1973) emphasise the way in which our awareness shuttles between internal and external stimuli. Bowlby (1969, 1973, and 1980) draws attention to the fundamental human need for contact and Fairbairn (1952) and Guntrip (1971) note how contact seems to be experienced as rewarding to infants.

From a transactional analysis perspective, Erskine (1994a, 1994b) describes interventions to heal the traumatisation that can arise from disrupted contact. Erskine, Moursund and Trautmann define contact as "a dynamic pattern of experiencing and meeting a need" (Erskine, Moursund and Trautmann, 1999 p.8) and view therapy as

"a relationship that can be used to heal the cumulative trauma of previous ruptures in relationships" .(Erskine, Moursund and Trautmann, 1999 p. 5)

They emphasise the role of internal and external contact and point out that contact is a dynamic, motivating process that can be used as the basis of a therapeutic relationship that can enable clients to expand their awareness and overcome the "fixed gestalten" of defences (Erskine, Moursund and Trautmann 1999 p. 2-16). Although they do not say so, their notion of "fixed gestalten" closely resembles the transactional analysis concept of a *script decision,* or the concept of *schemas* (Beck et. al., 1979).

Contact is a two way process; it is not something that happens to just one person. It is akin to the way in which Erskine, Moursund and Trautmann define contact as "a dynamic pattern of experiencing and meeting a need" (Erskine, Moursund and Trautmann, 1999 p. 8) and in turn, elaborate on "relational needs" (Erskine, Moursund and Trautmann, 1999 pp. 121-155). This two-person interaction between the personalised roles of two people is described by Law (2004); the present discussion focuses on what each person brings to the situation in which contact occurs. However, all contact has a biological basis and it is this that gives rise to the reciprocity of roles. Nevertheless, the environment has an equally important contribution to the formulation of roles and, for this reason I postulate the presence of four existential issues that feature in an individual's imago – the historical influences on a person's expectations.

Personalised roles arise from four classes or categories of role behaviour – reactive, inactive, responsive and proactive – located on the vertical edges of the Contact Cube. Each of these classes or types of behaviour is associated with the qualities of contact described as collaborative, co-existent, co-operative and compelling. The notion of the "qualities of contact" is similar to Berne's idea that strokes gleaned from games have "advantages" – they promote biological and psychological stability for individuals (Berne 1964, pp. 50-51). I have taken the view that homeostasis is not a one-sided affair. If we go along with the idea that the negative strokes yielded during games are "advantageous" in preserving or maintaining an individual's script, it is equally plausible to argue that positive strokes arising from other modes of time structuring also prevail and serve to maintain a person's frame of reference. Thus the qualities of contact and the associated existential issues I describe below have both positive and negative components.

There are four general guidelines about the nature of the contact associated with each of the eight Contact Cube roles. The first guideline comes from the Gestalt concept of the "cycle of interdependency of organism and environment" (Perls 1969) - more simply termed "the interactive cycle" (Zinker 1994) - and the second guideline is derived from the discounting matrix (Mellor and Schiff, 1975). The idea is that contact between individuals and their environment may be described dynamically as waves of contact and withdrawal.

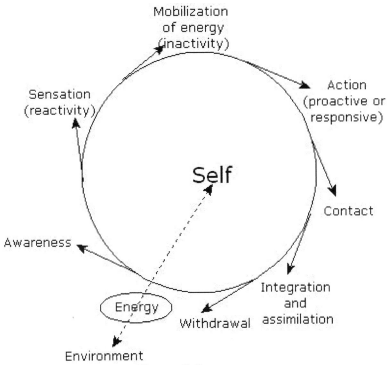

Figure 8.8

In **Figure 8.8**, I have slightly altered the interactive cycle to include my observation that sensation, as the first stage of the cycle, stems from an energy interchange that may originate internally or externally. Thereafter the cycle of events proceeds in a clockwise direction and the expectations associated with roles come into play at different phases of the cycle. The reactive Valuer and Victim roles are associated with the emergence of sensations. The largely behaviourally inactive roles of Beholder and Bystander are mapped onto the mobilisation of energy phase and the proactive (Promoter or Persecutor) or responsive (Responder or Rescuer) roles are linked with the action phase. Thus, the first the guideline governing the enactment of a role at the contact phase is that reactivity precedes inactivity which in turn, comes before pro-activity or responsivity

The second guideline is that which one of the reactive, inactive, pro-active or responsive pairs of roles eventually emerges as contact, will depend on the level of choice and/or discounting that is involved at the various phases of the cycle. Generally speaking, Victims tend to discount the existence of options, the significance of problems and the changeability of situations. Bystanders are prone to discounting themselves and others at a level of the significance of options, the solvability of problems and their own and others' ability to react differently. Rescuers characteristically discount others in terms of the other person's ability to resolve problems or exercise options. Persecutors will invariably behave as if they believe that the only way of relating to others is to make them feel bad. I am advancing these observations as a 'guideline' (rather than a 'rule') and it may not always be possible to identify precisely the discounting associated with any particular role – if only because discounting is an internal process. In practice it is more useful to identify the role behaviourally and then to use the 'guideline' to check observations.

The third guideline is that there is an association between roles and contact in terms of the stroke exchanges that are involved. Clearly, the enactment of negative roles is associated with *giving* negative strokes just as *giving* a positive stroke has to come from a positive role. Beyond this, it is all down to observation – as you may have discovered from **Self Supervision Suggestion 7.6**. People have highly individualised role reactions to stroke exchanges. You can test this by taking up **Self Supervision Suggestion 8.21.**

The final guideline is that contact is based primarily on awareness – an intuitive 'felt sense' of self (Gendlin 1981, Damasio 1999,) *in relation to* what is happening between you and another person. This is a non-cognitive "feel" or "quality" of your (plural) interaction and may be linked with English's motivators (English 2003). This appears to be a highly individualised experience – just as is the taste of apples, oranges, pears and peaches. We all know the *difference* between these tastes, but trying to describe them individually (beyond generalised descriptions such as "sweet", "sour"), is virtually impossible. Thus, although contact is a totally subjective experience, we can communicate about it because we can all recognise the differences. Hopefully, the following labels and descriptions convey the flavour of my palate.

'Collaborative' describes the nature of the contact along the Valuer-Victim or reactive dimension of the Contact Cube where the predominant behaviour consists of self-disclosure and sharing feelings. I use the term collaborative to describe the nature of the contact involved because the behaviour ranges from intimacy to racketeering. Affectively, both intimacy and racketeering stem from trust or mistrust and by definition, both behaviours require collaboration with another person.

The quality of contact that I refer to as *'co-existent'* implies minimal or no verbal contact. In terms of time structuring both the Beholder and Bystander roles may be regarded as examples of withdrawal (Berne 1964) or play (Cowles-Boyd and Boyd 1980). What contact does occur it is subtle and mostly non-verbal. Watching a group of two year olds playing in a sand pit brings home the fragility of the connotations of "playing alone together". Co-existent contact is similarly precariously maintained. Nevertheless, at the positive end of the continuum, the minimal external contact affords one time to become fully grounded and centred and reflect on future moves to other roles. The price tag of the Bystander role is the avoidance of contact. The existential issues seem to be related to recognition-anonymity.

Contact that that I describe as *'co-operative'* stems from the human need to bond, share with and care for others. Social level Rescuer-Victim reciprocity exists because of the desires to help and be helped - albeit inappropriately, because of the discounting involved. The empathy and altruism of the positive Responder role conveys to recipients the genuineness and "unconditional positive regard" described by Rogers (1951). Here the existential issue is attachment. Co-operative contact within the formalised role relationship between therapist and client is not only a major component of the value base of all counselling and psychotherapy, but also of most enduring interpersonal relationships. Society as a comparatively stable system of interpersonal relationships would not exist without co-operative contact between individuals.

'Compelling' contact is essential for self-expression. It is the basis of self-esteem, individuality, independence, creativity and ultimately, self-preservation. Compelling contact accompanies behaviour that ranges from survival of the fittest, winning a recreational game (such as tennis), or an argument, to merely stating a point of view or simply asking for what you want. I call all these compelling in the sense that only one person can initiate contact at any one moment in time, and that when one person initiates contact, the other person is more or less compelled to react either internally or externally. (For example, "don't think of a blue car"). Whatever form the contact takes, it is a manifestation of one's individuation – a statement of one's presence in the presence of another. Most compelling contact has to do with what one has to offer or what one wants – which may include information about self, others and the world. Ultimately, people are compelled to define reality for them selves – and in doing so, usually settle for affirmations of mutual OK-ness. The Promoter role promotes mutual OK-ness and the Persecutor role negates it.

I have described the essence of the four qualities of contact as though they are single entities. In reality contact is considerably more complex. We mingle the taste of our offerings. You bring an apple and I bring a pear. Perhaps, more subtly, you bring what, to you, is the taste of an apple... Most crucially, you can never be wrong about what, to you, is the taste of an apple. Moreover, some people have preferences and sometimes, you may yearn for a sweet tasting peach but somehow, end up with a sharp, tangy orange....

Less metaphorically, when two people make contact, each will bring a triadic combination of roles associated with the above qualities to bear upon the other. Likewise although I use Erskine et. al's. definition of contact as "a dynamic pattern of experiencing and meeting a need" (Erskine, Moursund and Trautmann, 1999 p. 8), the "dynamic pattern" is not confined to a single moment in time. In **Chapter 13** we will see that the interaction of roles and associated qualities of contact follow discernible patterns. For the moment it will suffice to say that the need that is experienced and met each time we make contact with another person, is none other than the need for homeostasis. Although I agree with the notion of relational needs (Erskine, Moursund and Trautmann, 1999 pp. 215-256), attempts to meet these needs are not only highly individualised – according to the ways in which individual imagos impinge on roles enacted in particular situations - but also, are not always successful. Underlying such attempts, and present in all situations is the process of how we influence others.

Persons				Relationships
Behaviours	Personalised roles enacted at the social level	Existential Imago images	Quality of contact based on attempts that are	Interaction based on an approach to another person that is
Reactive	Valuer	Trust	Collaborative	Positive (+1)
Inactive	Beholder	Recognition	Co-existent	Positive (+2)
Responsive	Responder	Attachment	Co-operative	Positive (+3)
Proactive	Promoter	Growth	Compelling	Positive (+4)
Reactive	Victim	Mistrust	Collaborative	Negative (-1)
Inactive	Bystander	Anonymity	Co-existent	Negative (-2)
Responsive	Rescuer	Detachment	Co-operative	Negative (-3)
Proactive	Persecutor	Survival	Compelling	Negative (-4)

Table 8.1

I develop the idea of influence in more detail in **Chapter 11**. In the meantime, we can see from **Table 8.1** that the Contact Cube offers eight ways of describing relationships in terms of the contact or interaction between two people. An individual has a choice of eight ways of relating to another person. Four of these are positive and four are negative. However the significance of **Table 8.1** lies not in the numbers, not in the arithmetic of how many ways there are of relating, but in the quality of the contact. I have attempted to convey this by assigning each of the four qualities of contact to both positive and negative Contact Cube roles.

In the Contact Cube, "contact" also describes the above qualities as a threshold between the positive roles and the negative roles. That is, because there is a threshold for changing from negative to positive roles, the four negative personalised roles located at the base of the Contact Cube are separated from the upper four positive roles by the 'Contact Plane'. The point at which contact with another person changes from positive to negative is located on the Contact Plane and is called the 'Critical' or 'Contact' point.

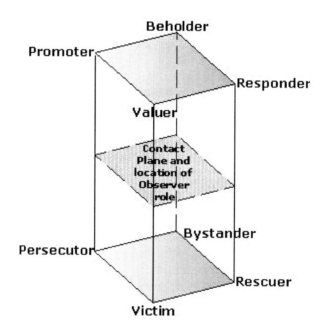

Figure 8.9

Dynamically, a Critical Point represents an existential moment of insight in the process of changing from negative to positive role expectations of self, others and immediate situations. The role associated with such moments is the Observer role, the capacity to be simultaneously in contact with self and others. It involves a self-reflective state of consciousness referred to as the Observer Self, or the Witness (Wilber 1985, 2000). The Witness is a state of awareness rather than a role that encompasses all that Berne wrote about on awareness as an aspect of autonomy (Berne 1964) yet, paradoxically, is often experienced as a fleeting still point, the crossing of a threshold en route to another role. It seems difficult to sustain the Observer role in its pure sense; epistemologically, as soon as one reaches the Critical Point, where subject and object are one, awareness of being at that point flips one into another role. Thus the Observer role ideally includes the capacity for self reflective awareness without identifying with or occupying any other role. Inasmuch as the Observer role differs in several respects from other Contact Cube roles, and is pivotal to changing from one Square to the other, **Part Six** is devoted entirely to describing this role.

Parameters of the Contact Cube

Having described each of the eight roles in some detail, I now point to some general, overall characteristics of the Contact Cube. I refer to these overall features as dimensions or parameters of the Contact Cube. Identifying these features gives an overall view of the Contact Cube that enables us to see that not only are the parameters themselves related to each other but, also that in understanding these connections, we can see more clearly the links between roles, contact and relationships

The *first parameter* of the Contact Cube is that the positive Square and the negative Square have four connecting bi-polar dimensions. In **Figure 8.1** (above) the vertical sides of the Cube define four bi-polar dimensions - Promoter – Persecutor, Responder – Rescuer, Valuer – Victim, and Beholder – Bystander. The implications of this parameter reveal a fascinating link between roles and relationships.

Firstly, what I have termed "bi-polar dimensions" would suggest that one is either a Promoter or a Persecutor on one dimension, either a Responder or a Rescuer on another dimension and so on for the remaining dimensions. In fact, my observations reveal a wider view of the four dimensions, namely that they are four continua that range from, for example, the Promoter role at one end to the Persecutor role at the other, *with additional roles in between*. Similar logic applies to the other three dimensions. In **Chapter 9**, I will explain how these intermediate roles located on each of these bi-polar dimensions emerge as an outcome of the dynamics of moves within the negative and positive Squares respectively.

The first parameter also highlights the fact that each continuum may be regarded as representing varying degrees of the four fundamental processes of human interaction outlined in **Chapter 6**. That is, interaction may be described behaviourally and psychologically as consisting of four mutually exhaustive and mutually exclusive processes - pro-active, responsive, reactive or non-active. In other words, the units of "behaviour" are the four sides of the Cube. At any moment in time, in any situation, individuals operate at a social level from one of these four mutually exclusive positions. One could even go as far as speculating

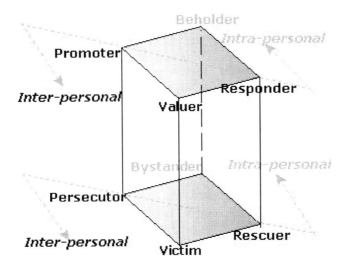

Figure 8.10

that there may be four fundamental ways or styles of relating characteristic of particular situations, occupations, formalised roles in management, models or types of therapy and so forth. I return to this point in later Chapters.

Figure 8.10 illustrates the *second parameter*, namely that there is a vertical intra/inter-personal dimension. The rear portion of the Contact Cube – the Beholder and Bystander roles are seen as *primarily* involving internal, intra-psychic processes; the remaining six roles are clearly enacted inter-personally. However the importance of non-verbal communication should not be overlooked. In addition, the outcome of such behaviour will be four different types of relationships – or, at least four basic ways of relating to others plus the associated qualities of contact.

The *third parameter* (**Figure 8.11**) refers to an attached-detached/active-passive horizontal dimension. The positive Square roles are regarded as active in that they are characterised by self -activation and intentionality that can be directed towards problem solving and satisfying relationships. The negative Square roles are 'passive' (Schiff et. al 1975) in a sense of inviting symbiosis, abdicating responsibility, shifting discomfort and generally creating rather than solving problems or correcting dysfunctional relationships. This parameter represents an elaboration of the idea that there are positive and negative Squares and roles

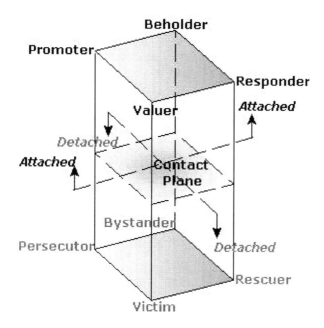

Figure 8.11

Figure 8.11 also shows that an additional horizontal dot-shaded plane has been inserted between the positive Square and the negative Square. All roles above this plane involve a drive to attachment and roles below the plane signify detachment. I refer to the intermediate plane as the Contact Plane and explain the connotations of this concept later in this Chapter.

These three parameters of the Conract Cube are structural in the sense that they define characteristics of the Cube as a whole and describe the overall "role space" in which the various parts (roles) are located.

The *fourth parameter* of the Contact Cube is as much dynamic as it is structural and, in this context, the psychological and behavioural processes involved are changes of role. You already know that this is what happens when people play games: a person will change roles from say, Persecutor to Victim. In the Drama Triangle the numbers of possible role changes are limited to six and it is comparatively easy to keep track of changes and even to be able to predict them; for each of the three roles there are two other change possibilities. Adding the fourth role (the Bystander) is also manageable; we have four roles each with three options for change – giving a total of twelve change possibilities. The same logic applies to positive Square roles. However, if we add the possibility that, when approached by someone in a role located in the same Square, there is no change then for each role there are four possible outcomes. This gives us sixteen change possibilities within each Square. Such changes are not random. I discuss the principle and rules that underlie the dynamics of changes within the positive and negative Squares in later Chapters.

Changes from the positive Square to the negative Square roles, are shown in **Figure 8.12**; this illustrates the *fifth parameter* of the Contact Cube. Conceptually this is the most significant parameter of the Contact Cube. In practice, it is the crux of the methodology of ERICA. Understanding the conceptual basis of this parameter is crucial to facilitating a client's capacity to change from negative to positive Square roles.

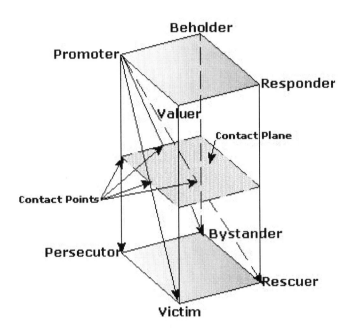

Figure 8.12

You will see that in **Figure 8.12** there are four arrows emanating from the Promoter role to each of the negative Square roles signifying that a person in the Promoter role has the choice of four negative Square roles. Obviously, this applies to the remaining positive Square roles and hence there are sixteen ways in which someone in the positive Square can change to negative Square roles. By the same token someone in the negative Square has a choice of four positive Square roles at any time and, similarly, there are sixteen possible changes from negative to positive Square roles.

Changing from one Square to another involves a role associated with a Contact (or Critical) Point. A Critical Point is a point or moment in time representing the capacity to differentiate between and be in contact with self and others and to change from one role to another. In **Figure 8.12** only four Critical Points are activated; these are located on the Contact Plane at the intersections (shown as the four Contact Points on the Contact Plane) of each arrow from the Promoter role to the four negative Square roles. Spatially, changing role from Promoter to Persecutor entails "crossing" the Contact Plane at the first (top) Contact Point. A move from Promoter to Bystander occurs at the second Contact Point and from Promoter to Victim at the third from top Contact Point. All these are on the perimeter of the Contact Plane. The fourth role change - indicated by the dashed-line arrow from Promoter to Rescuer – is "through" the centre of the Contact Plane at the fourth Contact Point. Activating all the Contact Points around the perimeter and in the centre of the Contact Plane would give the location of the sixteen Critical Points associated with all the change possibilities.

The *sixth parameter* is that all the Contact Cube roles include a dimension or component of *perception* and *practice* - as detailed in the above description of the Promoter role. Effectively, *perception* and *practice* determine the role a person chooses and acts upon. They are analogous to the Executive function of ego states. In practice it provides a useful index or operational definition of the autonomous choice of positive roles and the discounting involved in negative roles.

Summary

By way of summarising the material presented thus far, the following **Table** captures the essence of the Contact Cube roles.

Essential features of Contact Cube roles

Promoter	Responder	Valuer	Beholder
Provide self & offer to others: potent permission protection prescription, perception and practice. Potency always present. Two types of protection – historical and current	Empathic open & direct responses to others' needs; communication style is contactful; affirm own & others' OK-ness. Often used en-route to other roles	Openness to Physis and the potential for healing self others & being healed by others; based on trust. Believe (& will permit) others to affect them positively.	Stay neutral in situations that require action; have a capacity to be involved, yet postpone engagement. Assimilate information & can self – activate.
Don't identify with others; do things that are not needed, wanted, or asked for to make others feel not OK about them-selves. Compete for OK-ness on the basis of scar-city ("someone has to be not-OK & it won't be me").	Over-identify with others. Discount self others & situations. Feel obligated to take responsibility for others (usually by attempting to make others OK & thus, make them-selves OK.	Believe (& only allow) others to affect them negatively Discomfort is shifted to others. Often present do nothing type of passive behaviour. Invite others to racketeer with them or to persecute &/or rescue them.	Do nothing in situations that require action; have a capacity to remain un-involved & avoid engagement. Don't usually self –activate but are difficult to engage. Often move to Victim in order to racketeer with others
Persecutor	Rescuer	Victim	Bystander

Key Points 8

8.1 The **Contact Cube** is a three dimensional role space representing psychological processes that describe the repertoire of role behaviours of a single individual. A person manifests a particular role profile – the enactment of personalised roles - simultaneously at three levels. For the time being, we are considering only the social level.

8.2 The base and the top of the Contact cube are referred to as the negative and positive **Squares** respectively. In a person's frame of reference, personalised roles are located area of deep influences that are "automatic". Each Square has four roles:

- **Rescuers** over-identify with others and take responsibility for thinking for others or doing things for others without being asked to do so and without fully assessing the need for their acting on behalf of others.

- **Persecutors** do not identify with others. They distance themselves from others by doing things to others in order to make others feel not OK about themselves or to reinforce others' existing not OK-ness about themselves

- Energetically **Victims** shift discomfort to others thereby inviting symbiosis with anyone willing to take responsibility for thinking for them (usually Rescuers) or anyone willing to induce or further reinforce their helplessness and/or hopelessness (usually Persecutors).

- The **Bystander** role consists of a proclivity for doing nothing in situations that require action to resolve a problem. Their expectations are that they will be able to avoid having to do anything and that others will not notice them or, if they do, will expect them not to do anything. It is the position in the negative Square from which people either *move* to other roles (as will be detailed in **Chapter 9**) or *compete* for Victim, Rescuer or Persecutor roles.

- Responsiveness to the perceived needs of others is the essence of the **Responder** role. Responders do not do anything they do not want to do and generally do not do anything that others can reasonably do for themselves. The hallmark of the role is empathy.

- **Promoters** promote the interests of self and others. The role has six components – permission and protection, potency, perception and practice- and a component that I call prescription.

- The generalised expectations of the **Beholder** role consist of a proclivity for remaining neutral. At a more specific, situational level the Beholder role consists of a capacity to postpone engagement yet remain alert in situations that affect or are likely to affect one and others with whom one has significant relationships.

- **Valuers** disclose their thoughts and feelings about themselves and invite or directly ask others to respond to them, with the expectation that they themselves will, or may be affected positively by others role relations.

8.3 **Contact** is a dynamic pattern of experiencing and meeting a need. There are four useful guidelines for assessing contact:

- *reactivity precedes inactivity, which in turn, comes before pro-activity or responsivity,*

- which of the reactive, inactive, pro-active or responsive pairs of roles eventually emerges as contact, will depend on the *level of choice and/or discounting that is involved,*

- *stroke exchanges* are also relevant but highly individualised,

- an intuitive 'felt sense' of self *in relation to* what is happening between you and another person.

8.4   There are four **qualities of contact** – *collaborative* (for reactive roles), *co-existent* (for inactive roles), *compelling* (for pro-active roles), and *co-operative* (for responsive roles).

8.5   The point at which contact with another person changes from positive to negative is located on the Contact Plane and is called a '**Critical Point**'.

8.6   Dynamically, a **Critical Point** represents an existential moment of insight in the process of changing from negative to positive role expectations of self, others and situations.

8.7   Each Critical Point is associated with the **Observer** role, the capacity to be simultaneously in contact with self and others. It involves a self-reflective state of consciousness referred to as the **Observer Self**, or the **Witness**.

8.8   The Contact Cube has **six dimensions** or **parameters**:

- the first parameter is that the positive Square and the negative Square have four *connecting bi-polar* dimensions.
- the second parameter is that there is a vertical *intra/inter-personal* dimension.
- the third parameter is that there is an *attached-detached/active-passive* horizontal dimension above and below the Contact Plane respectively.
- the fourth parameter refers to changes of role *within* Squares.
- the fifth parameter illustrates that Contact Points are activated on the Contact Plane when a person changes roles *between* Squares.
- the sixth parameter refers to the components of *perception* and *practice* that determine the role a person chooses and acts upon. This is analogous to the Executive function of ego states. In practice this parameter provides a useful index or operational definition of the autonomous choice of positive roles and the discounting involved in negative roles.

Self Supervision Suggestions 8

8.7   Watch a film or TV soap and identify Contact Cube roles.

8.8   Repeat **8.7** and see if you can detect positive and negative role changes at the social level.

8.9   Repeat **8.1** and see if you can predict positive and negative role switches before they occur.

8.10   If you don't have time or access to TV, without intervening, observe people at work or in public places and apply **8.7** to **8.9**.

8.11   Watch a film or TV soap and identify different qualities of contact.

8.12   Repeat **8.11** and see if you can differentiate between positive and negative qualities of contact.

8.13   Repeat **8.11** and see if you can predict changes of positive and negative qualities of contact before they occur.

8.14   If you don't have time or access to TV, without intervening, observe people at work or in public places and apply **8.11** to **8.13**.

8.15   Repeat **8.7** to **8.14** together with someone else familiar with the Contact Cube and compare your observations.

8.16	On at least three occasions, systematically monitor your own behaviour in relation to social level roles, qualities of contact and any imago images of which you are aware. Make notes that will enable you to recount your observations to another person, giving a clear, *sequential* account of *observable* events. Include comments on how you were able to tell when you were in whichever of the roles, and how/when you experienced different qualities of contact. Pay particular attention to the Observer role.
8.17	Which of the Contact Cube roles do you most frequently enact in your **personal** relationships?
8.18	Which of the Contact Cube roles do you most frequently *have to* enact in your relationships at **work**?
8.19	Which of the Contact Cube roles do you find **easy/difficult** to enact in your **personal** relationships?
8.20	Which of the Contact Cube roles do you find **easy/difficult** to enact in your relationships at **work**?
8.21	Repeat **Self Supervision Suggestion 7.6** in relation to Contact Cube roles. Compare the two exercises and discuss the differences with someone who is familiar with the Contact Cube.
8.22	Repeat **Self Supervision Suggestion 7.5** in the light of your understanding of Contact Cube roles and qualities of contact. In particular, which role(s) are essential for you to enact during this exercise?
8.23	Repeat **Self Supervision Suggestion 7.5** deliberately using the Beholder role. Maintain this role and synchronise your breathing with the other person's breathing. Keep notes of your internal reactions to whatever happens as you adjust your pattern of breathing to match the other person's breathing.

Chapter 9

Second order analysis

This Chapter describes the changes from one role to another within Contact Cube and how the dynamics of such moves create additional roles located along the vertical sides of the Cube. Just as our options for using ego states are increased by Berne's sub-divisions of ego states as a "second order analysis" so, too, does an increase in the number of available roles enlarge our options for responding to the roles with which we are familiar.

Eight more roles

In **Chapter 8** I suggested that changes from Beholder and Bystander roles fuel the creation of additional Contact Cube roles. It transpires that the role enacted by the person who approaches the Beholder or Bystander is a crucial variable. In addition, the level of intensity with which that role is enacted makes a difference to the response enlisted from the Bystander and, to a lesser extent, from the Beholder. For example, if I am in the Bystander role and am approached by a Persecutor I have three options. I can remain in the Bystander role by doing nothing, I can resist or I can comply by moving to another role. This process is illustrated in **Figure 9.1** where the Protester and Resister roles are located along the Promoter-Persecutor side of the Cube while the Passive Acceptor and Slave are on the Responder-Rescuer dimension.

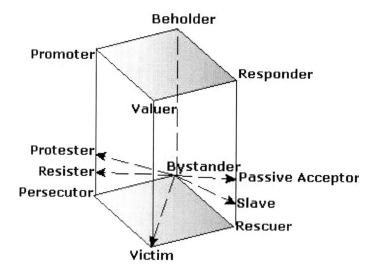

Figure 9.1

There are three factors that determine the nature of a Bystander's move to another role. The first is the level of intensity (as experienced by the Bystander) at which an approach by another person is made. Secondly, the role to which the Bystander moves will also depend on whether they resist or comply with whichever role is being enacted by the person who approaches them. The third factor is that the Bystander must have collected sufficient stamps (unexpressed racket feelings) in order to justify (to them selves) a move to another role. This is diagrammed in **Figure 9.2**.

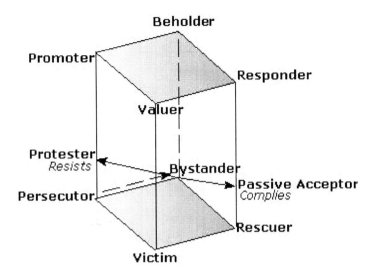

Figure 9.2

In **Figure 9.2** the dashed lines and arrows heads indicate an approach by a Persecutor. The diagram shows that if a Persecutor with a *low level of intensity* approaches (-----＞) a Bystander, the likely outcome is that the Bystander will move (——➤) to a Protester or Passive Acceptor position. Here the dotted horizontal lines represent varying degrees or levels of intensity of approach by a Persecutor – in this case, it is *low*. The general principle is that the outcome of a Bystander's move is determined by the extent to which the Bystander over-adapts. If the Bystander *resists*, the move will be to a position on the perimeter of the Cube that is nearest the position from which the approach was made. The most direct form of resistance (the highest level of intensity) to persecution is to meet it head on, to return it by competing for the Persecutor position. Bystanders seldom if ever do this. Instead, they make a token gesture of resistance by moving towards the Persecutor position. **Figure 9.2** shows a low level approach from Persecutor to Bystander; if the Bystander resists, they will move to the Protester role. If the Bystander complies, the move will be to Passive Acceptor.

English (1987) differentiates between individuals she terms Potential Protesters and Passive Acceptors from the Resisters and Slaves identified by Jacobs (1987). Jacobs uses life positions and symbiosis in his analysis of the use of autocratic power and although he appears to be writing about types of personality, his comments are equally valid as descriptors of role behaviour.

> "Resisters refuse to accept the symbiosis. Some are in a (+, +) life position but are forced through circumstances to take a (+, -) position... Other Resisters may be (+, -) in their position and seek revenge and power. Slaves are sought by the Master as a work force and as a symbol of strength ...When people are forced into servitude they manifest (-, -)". (Jacobs 1987 p. 69)

In ERICA the Resister and Slave roles may be seen as the outcome of more intense efforts to engage them. In **Figure 9.4**, if persecuted at medium level the Bystander resists, the move will be to the Resister role. If the Bystander complies, the move will be to Slave.

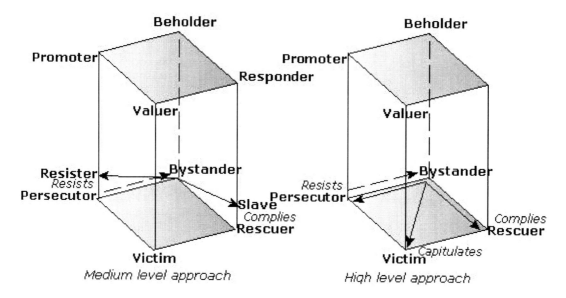

Figure 9.3   **Figure 9.4**

High intensity approaches by a Persecutor to a Bystander are shown in **Figure 9.4**. The strongest form of resistance is to compete for the Persecutor role. In my experience this is more usual in organisations than it is in a clinical setting. Compliance usually leads to the Victim role, but sometimes to Rescuer.

The same rules apply to approaches from a Rescuer but the outcome is "reversed". That is, in **Figures 9.2**, **9.3** and **9.4** when approached by a Rescuer the Bystander complies by moving nearer to the Rescuer and resists by moving away. On the other hand, it is not unusual for Bystanders to change to the Passive Acceptor role by over-adapting to their perception of what others expect of them before such expectations are expressed overtly. This illustrates the way in which expectations are based as much on fantasy as on situational demands of another's role.

Several colleagues have commented on the similarities of additional personalised roles in the negative Square to the roles and "types" described by English (1979, 1987) and Jacobs (1987, 1991b). Jacobs (1991b) uses life positions in parallel with Berne's dynamics diagram (Berne, 1963 p. 310). Conceptually, ERICA complements Jacobs' work, being based not only on concepts that include the existential level but, in addition, yield indices of role behaviours that permit ongoing measures of differentiation. However, in practice, the two methodologies are significantly different; Jacobs uses symbiosis (Schiff et. al. 1975) and Berne's schema for categorising life positions alongside post hoc historical analysis of events to generalise about large group, socio-political processes. ERICA was developed in a group/organisational setting, focuses on small group dynamics and uses in vivo coaching to teach clients how to analyse self-reported "Significant Incidents" that will enable them to learn new personalised role behaviours. Intuitively, I think that what is needed is a way of blending ERICA with aspects of Jacobs' work; I discuss this in **Chapter 12**. However there is a crucial distinction between the etymology of terms used by English (1979, 1987) and Jacobs (1987, 1991b) and similar terms used in ERICA. English describes two defensive existential life positions she uses to define "Type 1" and "Type 2" individuals (English 1979 p. 92). Later Jacobs refers to these as "Masters" and "Slaves" and then proceeds to write about such individuals or personality types without making clear that he is describing the behaviour characteristic of particular types of individuals rather than behaviour associated with particular personalised roles that may be enacted by anyone. My use of the term Bystander is as a personalised role entailing observable behaviour that may be enacted by anyone from time to time.

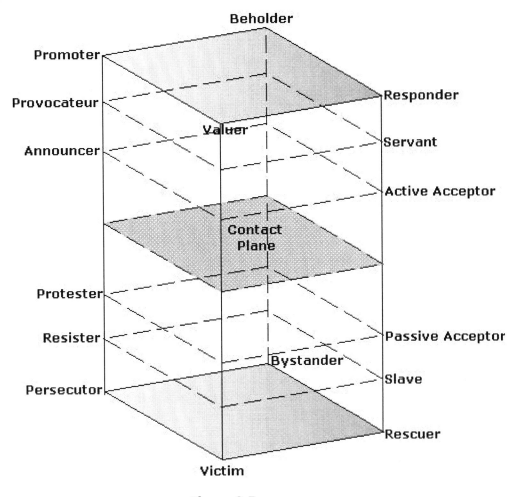

Figure 9.5

I have described the dynamics of the Bystander role in some detail because it illustrates the dynamics applicable to *all* personalised roles in both the negative Square and the positive Square. The approaches by and moves to roles in the positive Square follow the same principles as approaches by and moves to the bi-polar opposite roles in the negative Square. Just as the Bystander role fuels the creation of other roles in the negative Square, the Beholder does the same in the positive Square. I describe these other roles below. These roles lie along the vertical dimensions of the Cube as shown in **Figure 9.5**, where the positive Square roles are mirror images of the lower negative Square. The terms are chosen to reflect the main features of each role. The characteristics of each role are described below.

The dynamics of moves between personalised roles in both Squares

Provocateurs and Announcers are varieties of the Promoter role; Active Acceptors and Servants are seen as variations of the Responder role. Provocateurs and Servants lie on a horizontal plane shown by the dashed line diamond shape immediately below the positive Square. Similar horizontal planes link the Announcer and Active Acceptor, Protester and Passive Acceptor, and Resister and Slave roles. This arrangement preserves the dynamics of movements between the personalised roles within the resultant overall role space of the Contact Cube.

Announcers and Protesters

The bi-polar opposite of the Protester role is the Announcer. Announcers are factual and can be assertive. Unlike radio or TV announcers, who seldom if ever express their own opinions the Announcer role is the role through which the Self is most clearly defined. Joines' description epitomises the role.

> "Individuals in the I'm OK-You're OK quadrant [reference to Kaplan, Capace and Clyde, 1984, p. 116] have a clear sense of self, but there are spaces in their self-others boundaries that allow them to take in new information about themselves, which they can use for their growth. They also have clear boundaries between themselves and other people so they will not allow themselves to do things that are hurtful to others nor allow others to do things that are hurtful to them. At the same time, there are spaces in those boundaries that allow them to extend themselves out to others and to allow others in". (Joines, 1988, pp. 186-187)

They define themselves from an OK-OK position when put upon by others and at other times, ask for what they want in a clear, unequivocal and "straight" way. This role is similar to Choy's description of the Assertive role in the "Winners Triangle" (Choy 1987).

Protesters are low level Persecutors who tend to sulk ominously or whinge. They often are erstwhile Bystanders who change role by resisting Persecutors or complying with Rescuers.

Active Acceptors and Passive Acceptors

Active Acceptors accept others as they are; they engage with others by seeking information in a way that encourages and facilitates the other person to convey their point of view. The essential feature of the Active Acceptor role is inquiry by observation and questioning to confirm or dispel intuitive insights about how and why people are the way they are. It is important to understand that this process of inquiry should not be theory driven. That is, the questions asked need to be open-ended, and, as far as possible based only on the presupposition that the practitioner knows nothing about the client's experience. Hence questions need to be free from theoretically based assumptions. Close attention to the nature of the *contact* between therapist and client as well as exploration of the client's internal contact, is the fundamental requirement of the Active Acceptor role. Erskine, Moursund and Trautmann describe aspects of the Active Acceptor role (in conjunction with other positive roles), as the process of inquiry (Erskine, Moursund and Trautmann, 1999 pp. 19-45). I explain this process in more detail in **Chapter 10.**

Passive Acceptors are low level Rescuers. They sometimes are erstwhile Bystanders who change role by complying with Persecutors or resisting Rescuers; either way, they accept others' definitions rather than defining themselves.

Provocateurs and Resisters

The bi-polar opposite of the Resister (Jacobs 1987) is the Provocateur. Provocateurs challenge others in an OK-OK way. They do not immediately accept others as they are or seek to explore and understand their frame of reference (as do Active Acceptors). Instead they question apparent incongruities in others' frame of reference in ways that invite and often require others to respond ("don't think of a blue door"). Their repertoire ranges from low key observations, comments and remarks made as "asides", non sequitors and therapeutic ulterior transactions (Lankton, Lankton and Brown 1983), through to "soft" confrontations (Stewart 1996). They can spontaneously use genuine humour and have a capacity for eliciting Free Child in others. They love the world and, at the same time, can laugh at it and themselves in ways that confirm their own and others' OK-ness, yet questions the prevailing frame of reference. Along with an array of Ericksonian word plays, they may use surprise or shock, suspense, mystery, metaphors and indirect suggestions (Lankton and Lankton 1983 p. 86). They are creative and intuitive. Under appropriate circumstances, they may resort to explicit use of paradox and direct confrontation. Their overall effect on others is a disarming of Parent, destabilisation of Child and a challenge to Adult.

My impression is that the Provocateur role is under-developed or, at least, not much used in transactional analysis practice. Some forms of therapy, for example, psychodrama or the Aeskeleipion Game (Windes in Barnes, (ed.) 1977; Law 1978b) provide procedures, format and structures that make the use of the role more likely to emerge than in the average weekly therapy setting. Linehan has developed a range of "dialectical strategies" that use the Provocateur role to target the client-therapist relationship (Linehan, 1993 pp.205-219). Solution Focused Brief Therapy (O'Connell 1998, de Shazer 1996) makes extensive use of the Provocateur role. Like all the Contact Cube roles, judicious use of the Provocateur role, appropriately timed, under the right circumstances, remains an option.

Resisters are medium level Persecutors. They define themselves to a limited extent by making others not-OK. The role sometimes emerges when Bystanders change role by resisting Persecutors or complying with Rescuers.

Servants and Slaves

The Servant role is characterised by involvement with others and dedication to their needs over and above any more or less explicit agreement or, at the very least, common understanding between two parties within a given culture or society. The essence of the Servant role is that it extends beyond any agreed, implied, understood, hoped for or anticipated contractual conditions or formalised intersubjectivity. In its purest form, the Servant role involves altruism, kindness, compassion, caring or love for or towards another person, irrespective of any other role expectations that may exist. In many situations, the Servant role comes close to impinging on a formalised role relationship. For example, husband-wife employer-employee, doctor-patient, therapist-client are all examples of formalised roles that may be under-pinned by the personalised role of Servant. In these cases, enactment of the Servant role is not only for the benefit of the other party, but goes beyond the requirements of the formalised role requirements. However, genuine helpfulness or kindness towards a complete stranger without any expectation of recompense signifies acknowledgement of the stranger as a human being. The Buddhist notion of "random acts of kindness" epitomises the Servant role but most cases of the Servant role are usually based on longer-term relationships. When there is congruence between a formalised role and the Servant role, it is often difficult to discern whether or not any ulterior motive is present. For example, lavish lunches, unsolicited gifts or expensive holidays for business executives are sometimes offered under the guise of "customer care". Likewise, it is not unknown for a therapist to fall in love with a client and argue that consummation of the relationship was justified. Such concerns have lead to professional practice standards that explicitly forbid "dual relations". Sadly, this often makes therapists wary of overtly demonstrating compassion for their clients. Erskine, Moursund and Trautmann's description of the process of involvement embodies features of the Servant role (Erskine, Moursund and Trautmann, 1999 pp. 83-120).

The bi-polar opposite of the Servant is similar to Jacobs' description of Slaves (Jacobs, 1987). They are medium level Rescuers and sometimes erstwhile Bystanders who change role by complying with Persecutors or resisting Rescuers.

Table 8.2 Essential features of positive personalised roles

Promoter	Provocateur	Announcer	Beholder	Active Acceptor	Servant	Responder	Valuer
Provide and /or offer others Perception, Prescription, Practice, Potency Permission & Protection. Potency is always pre-sent. Two types of protection – historical & current	Challenge others in OK – OK ways; Use extensive repertoire for confronting incongruity in others' frame of reference, in ways that invite / require others to respond	Ask clearly for what they want in a straight way Can be assertive; but always define them selves & others from OK-OK position.	Stay neutral in situations that require action; have a capacity to be involved, yet postpone engagement. Assimilate information & can self – activate.	Others are accepted as they are; information sought by inquiry in ways that encourages & facilitates others to convey their views	Involvement & dedication over & above any prevailing contractual agreement for benefit of others. Kind-ness altruism compassion. May impinge on formalised role relation-ships	Empathetic; open & direct responses to others' needs; communicat-ion style is contactful; affirm own & others' OK-ness. Often used en-route to other roles	Openness to Physis and the potential for healing self others & being healed by others Believe (& will permit) others to affect them positively.

Table 8.3 – Essential features of the Contact Plane

CONTACT PLANE – location of the **CRITICAL POINTS** and the **OBSERVER** role. The Contact Plane has self-organised criticality that requires one either to be in the positive Square or the negative Square – but not both at the same time. The Critical Points represent a moment in time when a person changes from positive to negative roles, or vice versa. This requires use of the **Observer** role which is characterised by varying degrees of autonomy & balanced awareness of self, others. & the situation. Without this balance - & particularly, awareness of the situation, Contact becomes more historical than current. The Observer role is described in more detail in **Part Six**

Table 8.4 - Essential features of negative personalised roles

Don't identify with others; do things that are not needed, wanted, or asked for to make others feel not OK about them-selves. Compete for OK-ness on the basis of scarcity ("someone has to be not-OK & it won't be me").	Maintain a position of semi-independence & are able to define themselves to limited extent, but eventually accept Victim role Often rebellious; will Persecute when can "get away with it"	Vary from being passive –aggressive (sulking muttering glowering looks etc) in specific situations, to righteous protestation about generalised issues. May support legitimate or "alternative" fringe organisations	Do nothing in situations that require action; have a capacity to remain un-involved & avoid engagement. Don't usually self –activate but are difficult to engage. Often move to Victim in order to racketeer with others	Over adapt to poorly perceived external cues & approaches from others; operate largely from internal frame of reference & discount self & will comply with others even when this is clearly not in their own interests.	Go to extreme lengths to please others without questioning their motives or authority Dis count personal ability &/or existence of any options Seem unable to resist complying even when don't want to.	Over-identify with others. Discount self others & situations. Feel obligated to take responsibility for others (usually by thinking for them) attempting to make others OK & thus, make them-selves OK.	Believe (& only allow) others to affect them negatively Discomfort is shifted to others. Present do nothing type of passive behaviour. Invite others to racketeer o persecute &/or rescue them.
Persecutor	Resister	Protester	Bystander	Passive Acceptor	Slave	Rescuer	Victim

Key Points 9

9.1   Increasing the number of available personalised roles, widens our **options** for responding to any of the personalised roles with which we are already familiar.

9.2   The dynamics of interaction between roles in each Square illustrates the creation of **other personalised roles**. This process is illustrated by three factors that determine the nature of a Bystander's move to another role:

- the level of *intensity* (as experienced by the Bystander) at which an approach by another person is made.
- whether they *resist* or *comply* with whichever role is being enacted by the person who approaches them.
- the Bystander must have collected sufficient s*tamps* in order to justify (to themselves) a move to another role.

9.3   Just as the Bystander role fuels the creation of other personalised roles in the negative Square, the **Beholder** does the same in the positive Square.

9.4   **Eight additional roles** emerge along the vertical sides of the Contact Cube:

- **Provocateurs** and **Announcers** are varieties of the *Promoter* role; **Protesters** and **Resisters** are lesser versions of *Persecutors*
- **Active Acceptors** and **Servants** are seen as variations of the *Responder* role. **Passive Acceptors** and **Slaves** are varieties of the *Rescuer* role.
- *Provocateurs* and *Servants* lie on a horizontal plane immediately *below* the positive Square. Similar lower horizontal planes (just *above* the Contact Plane) link the *Announcer* and *Active Acceptor* roles.
- *Resisters* and *Slaves* lie on a horizontal plane immediately *above* the negative Square. Similar lower horizontal planes (just *below* the Contact Plane) link the *Protester* and *Passive Acceptor* roles.

9.5   **Announcers** are *low level* Promoters who are factual and can be assertive. This role emerges when a Beholder is approached by a Promoter or a Responder at a low level of intensity.

9.6   **Protesters** are *low level* Persecutors who tend to sulk ominously or whinge. They often are erstwhile Bystanders who change role by resisting Persecutors or complying with Rescuers

9.7   **Active Acceptors** are *low level* Responders who accept others as they are; they engage with others by seeking information in a way that encourages and facilitates the other person to convey their point of view. This role emerges when a Beholder is approached by a Promoter or a Responder at a low level of intensity.

9.8   **Passive Acceptors** are *low level* Rescuers. They sometimes are erstwhile Bystanders who change role by complying with Persecutors or resisting Rescuers; either way, they accept others' definitions, rather than defining themselves.

9.9   **Provocateurs** are *medium level* Promoters who challenge others in an OK-OK way. They do not immediately accept others as they are by questioning apparent incongruities in others' frame of reference in ways that invite and often require others to respond.

9.10 Resisters are *medium level* Persecutors. They define themselves to a limited extent by making others not-OK. The role sometimes emerges when Bystanders change role by resisting Persecutors or complying with Rescuers.

9.11 Servants are *medium level* Responders. The role is characterised by involvement with others and dedication to their needs over and above any more or less explicit agreement between two parties.

9.12 Slaves are *medium level* Rescuers. They are erstwhile Bystanders who change role by complying with Persecutors or resisting Rescuers.

9.13 Theoretically, a **further eight roles** exist on the *Beholder-Bystander* and the *Valuer-Victim* sides of the Contact Cube. These are not particularly helpful in clinical practice but could be crucial in an *organisational setting* where time scales are very different

---

Self Supervision Suggestions 9

9.1 In the light of your understanding of second order analysis of Contact Cube roles, repeat **Self Supervision Suggestions 8.7** to **8.15**.

9.2 On occasions when you are listening to someone enacting a **Victim role** to tell you about something important to them, adopt a **Beholder** role, and watch the pattern of their breathing very closely. Synchronise your breathing with theirs. Does this affect the way you feel about them? Experiment with this idea/practice by changing your pattern(s) of *non-verbal communication* and keep a note of your reactions. Make sure you record which variable(s) you change.

9.3 Repeat **Self Supervision Suggestion 9.2** in relation to **other negative** and **positive** Contact Cube roles and record your observations.

9.4 Using a full length mirror (or video camera) to **enact** and **practice** (by yourself) **all the Contact Cube roles** until you are able to adopt each one effortlessly. Which do you *most prefer* and *least prefer*?

9.5 Repeat **Self Supervision Suggestion 7.5** using the Beholder role. Maintain this role and synchronise your breathing with the *reverse* of the other person's breathing. That is, as they *exhale*, you *inhale*. Keep notes of your internal reactions to whatever happens as you adjust your pattern of breathing to match the reverse of the other person's.

9.6 Repeat **Self Supervision Suggestion 9.5** using the Beholder role. Maintain this role and synchronise your breathing with the *reverse* of the other person's breathing. That is, as they *exhale*, you *inhale*. Watch them closely and without saying anything, *internally* focus on the Responder role: you do this by *imagining* what you would say, feel and do if you were responding behaviourally. Keep notes of your internal reactions to whatever happens as you do this.

9.7 Repeat **Self Supervision Suggestion 9.6** using the Beholder role. Maintain this role and synchronise your breathing with the *reverse* of the other person's breathing. As they *exhale*, you *inhale*. Without saying anything, *internally* focus on the Responder role. Refine your awareness by imagining that as *they* *exhale* and as *you inhale*, you *absorb* their *energy*. Keep notes of your internal reactions to whatever happens as you do this.

9.8 Extend **Self Supervision Suggestion 9.7** by imagining that as you *inhale* and absorb their energy, you transmute this to care and compassion. As you *exhale* and they *inhale*, imagine your care and compassion is being conveyed to them. Keep notes of your internal reactions and any response they may show. **If necessary, discuss your reactions in supervision or your own therapy.**

Chapter 10
Working at three levels

This Chapter describes the way in which people change from roles in the negative Square to roles in the positive Square in response to an approach from another person. The components of the expected behaviours that constitute the basis of the processes of inquiry, attunement and involvement described by Erskine et. al. (Erskine, Moursund and Trautmann, 1999), are complemented by empowerment, assertion and challenge. Ways of identifying roles and adapting the use of the Contact Cube are discussed.

Roles, imagos and contact at different levels

Although I have indicated that personalised roles operate at overt, covert and existential levels, thus far the covert-existential aspect of the roles in both Squares has not been made explicit. Overt or social level and covert or psychological level roles are well understood in transactional analysis (Karpman 1968, Berne 1961, 1964, 1966, 1972). Barnes notes that:

> "As infants develop psychologically, they acquire the ability to understand and eventually use psychological level transactions. This birth takes place in the "period from about the fourth or fifth month to the thirtieth or thirty-sixth month, a period we refer to as the *separation–individuation phase* (Mahler, Pine and Bergman, 1975)". It is during this period that the injunctions seem to have a crucial effect upon the development of the infant. Before the fourth or fifth month, injunctions probably do not have a psychological impact upon the infant". (Barnes 1981 p. 23)

Barnes adds the somewhat radical observation that:

> "A role is given to an infant at birth and it is *fixed* by the strokes and other stimuli received by the growing child. This level of development is called the *social level* and begins with the biological birth of the infant. Babies are born to establish equilibrium in the family. They are born to be victims (to be cared for or persecuted), to make victims, or to help victims. The social level responds to stimulus and structure hunger". (Barnes 1981, p. 26)

While I accept the idea that babies could be said to be "born to establish equilibrium in the family", I think Barnes is overstating his case. There seems to be no *a priori* reason for claiming that babies "are born to be victims (to be cared for or persecuted), to make victims, or to help victims". It is equally plausible to claim that children are born with the potential of learning positive role responses. Furthermore, infants do not receive a 'diet' of exclusively *negative* strokes. I think it would be far more accurate to say that children respond to a mixture of positive and negative strokes and it is from this that they acquire a social level of later role enactment.

Barnes's position on this is point is a prime example of the practice/research divide. It also seems to be based on a frame of reference that does not appear to take account of the fact that children are born for biological reasons that require their being nurtured, *and* for their having to adapt, survive and perpetuate our species.

Nevertheless, Barnes continues to note that a second role level develops when infants learn to communicate at the psychological level[1]:

> "This role is decided upon by the child when he is responding to parental injunctions and developing rackets. It responds to stroke and recognition hunger". (Barnes 1981 p. 26)

Most significantly, it is during this period that children formulate script decisions in response to parental injunctions. In particular, it is at this stage that 'authentic' feelings are repressed, being replaced by racket feelings (Erskine and Zalcman, 1979). Along with this, core script beliefs and supporting script beliefs are established and, later, become the expectations of self, others and situations, that underlie role behaviours. Thus, by the age of four or five children have developed the capacity to operate or use roles at three levels. This age range is consistent with Piaget's stage of concrete operational thinking, where the child can begin to take the role of the other and begin to use rules (such as multiplication, division, class inclusion and so forth) in their cognitive functioning (Flavell, 1970; Piaget, 1977); it is also consistent with Wilber's writing on the development of levels of consciousness (Wilber 1979, 1983, 2000).

From a TA perspective, I agree with Barnes's view that the third level role coincidences with the adoption of the existential life position and "gives expression to one's attitude and beliefs. It responds to position hunger", (Barnes 1981 p. 26)

Several writers (White 1994, 1995a, 1995b, Erskine 1995, English 1995, Hine 1995, Jacobs 1997) have further developed Berne's concept of life positions; it is no longer regarded as an "either–or" concept. In other words, there are degrees of OK-ness. Nevertheless this does not detract from the gist of Berne's original ideas:

> "on the basis of these [positions] he makes his life decision.."(Berne 1972, p. 84).
> "Whatever the decision is, it can be justified by taking a position..." (Berne 1972, p. 85)
> "there can usually be detected one basic position, sincere or insincere, inflexible or insecure, on which his life is staked, and from which he plays out his games and script". (Berne 1972, p.87)

Despite these developments, I think that the existential level of role analysis has been underemphasised in the TA literature and it has been left to Hendrix (1992) to develop the idea in more depth. Hendrix expounds an approach he calls "imago relationship therapy"; essentially this is a method of couples counselling/therapy. Hendrix has worked extensively with couples and his approach hinges on the idea of the "Imago":

> "that unconscious by-product of your childhood experiences, the inner image formed by the confluence of childhood experience that powerfully influences your partner choice. With an Imago partner, someone whose character structure approximates your inner image of the significant other, you re-find the ambience of your childhood, and recreate the context in which you were wounded, in the hope that this time around, with this person who is the same-but-different, you can be healed". (Hendrix 1992, pp,55-56)

---

[1] As we saw in **Chapter 4**, the psychological level of a role comes into its own in the analysis of Drama Triangle roles (Karpman 1968, 1972) and was later included by Berne as a crucial part of his Formula G analysis of games.

Hendrix's thesis is that we need to be aware of our Imago, reclaim the split-off parts of our personality and arrive at the point where:

> "knowledge about your Imago is redemptive information. It has the power to heal you. The Imago is the key to your relationships and the basis for self-integration". (Hendrix 1992 p.221)

Hendrix's use of "the Imago" bears a close resemblance to Berne's description of the group imago – the internalised perceptions individuals in a group have of one another – and Berne's concept of life positions. Although Hendrix makes no reference to Berne's use of life positions, both are clearly covering the same ground. Terminology apart, their differences seem to be that Hendrix is more optimistic about the positive aspects of the Imago than Berne is about life positions. To put this in another way, I would suggest that the healing potential of the Imago parallels Berne's I'm OK-You're OK position. This provides the springboard for the idea that roles at the existential level embody the potential for recapitulating childhood wounding as well as present day healing.

Reciprocity

My use of the term "reciprocity" signifies a particular aspect of that which Hargaden and Fenton (2005) describe as intersubjectivity:

> "the crucial components of an intersubjectivity .... include the following:
> 1. It is an existential given.
> 2. It is a process of mutuality that is sometimes asymmetrical; in other words, mutuality does not imply equality.
> 3. It is an overlap of two minds, in a shared state of being, as in a meeting of minds in the in-between space that is sometimes described as a type of third intersubjectivity.
> 4. It involves both primary and secondary intersubjective relating, which are potentially self-constructive in nature, although they have qualities that impact on different domains of self.
> 5. It is a developmental achievement that involves the ability to recognise the existence of another subjectivity .... in the shared focus idea of secondary intersubjectivity.

> Most importantly, and continuing the relational tradition within transactional analysis, it immediately becomes apparent that the notion of pathology residing in the client alone is a reductionistic and clinically unhelpful notion. Instead, the theory of intersubjectivity emphasises the emotional environment – the intersubjective conditions – and requires us to analyse why and how experience is organised within the client, between client and therapist, and within the therapist". (Hargaden and Fenton, 2005, p. 179)

I use the term reciprocity because it constitutes an operational definition of intersubjectivity mediated by *roles*, rather than transactions. I explain the operational nuts and bolts of reciprocity in **Chapter 13.** For the present, it will suffice to note that in **Chapter 7**, I pointed out that social diagnosis of roles relies on the circular causality of role reciprocation, and that historical diagnosis requires linking patterns of current and past role relations. In other words, linking imagos with the existential level of personalised roles is a manifestation of role reciprocation. I extend this idea in **Chapter 13** by showing how during certain patterns of behaviour, the social level of a role is replaced by the role held at the psychological level, and finally, by the existential level role – thus confirming an individual's life position. For example, if a person is a social level Victim, a psychological level Rescuer and an existential level Persecutor, under certain circumstances they will end up occupying their erstwhile existential level Persecutor role at the social level. These dynamics are based on what I refer to as "reciprocity"[1] – more correctly, role reciprocation. In Cognitive Analytic Therapy (CAT) the therapist uses flowcharts and diagrams as:

> "a guide which can trace and make sense of the shifting parts played by the patient and the accompanying transference-countertransference variations. The developmental understanding points to the need to identify each role in relation to its reciprocal. ... a *role*, in this theoretical context, is understood to imply a pattern of action, expectation, affect and memory. Either pole of a core reciprocal role procedure may:
>
> 1. Be enacted towards others who will be induced to play the reciprocal.
> 2. Be enacted towards the reciprocal aspect of the self.
> 3. Be transformed into an alternative avoidant, symptomatic or defensive procedure.
>
> Core roles associated historically with unmanageable affects, or prohibited by their internalized reciprocating roles may either be elicited from others ('projective identification') or may be replaced by avoidant or symptomatic expressions, which involve modified behaviours and lessened affective arousal. Repression and other 'ego defenses' and 'compromise formations'; can be described in these terms.
>
> At its simplest, a Sequential Diagram describes a core reciprocal role procedure which generates two possible enactments. An individual could enact either role and in doing so would be seeking to elicit the corresponding reciprocal from another person or aspect of the self". (Ryle, 1997, p. 24)

I elaborate on the role reciprocity in **Chapter 13**, and for the present, my 'translation' of the CAT perspective is that a social level Rescuer will seek to "induce" others to "play the reciprocal" role of Victim, which is (probably) "the reciprocal aspect of the self" that is enacted or held at the psychological level. The existential level role (Persecutor of Bystander) is "transformed into an alternative avoidant, symptomatic or defensive procedure".

Likewise, the "accompanying transference-countertransference variations" are:

> "seen to be one particular example of the general meshing of reciprocal role procedures..... It is useful to distinguish two sources of countertransference. One, which may be called personal countertransference, will reflect the therapist's particular range of role procedures.... Such personal countertransference is not totally distinct from the specific reactions evoked by the particular patient, which can be called elicited

---

[1] It is perhaps as well to emphasize that my use of the term "reciprocity" differs from the *general* usage of the word in the transactional analysis literature, where reciprocity is described as:

> "a balanced interaction between two people in which there is mutuality and an equality of power, influence and openness to the other. Ideally a therapeutic relationship should involve reciprocity: however, the client often feels powerless when he of she enters therapy and has perceived the therapist as someone who has the power to help them. Transactional analysis stresses the importance of promoting AUTONOMY and empowering the client. The process of making a CONTRACT is important in this, as also is the sharing of theory with the client". (Tilney, 1998, p.102)

countertransference..... Within elicited countertransference reactions there is another useful distinction to bear in mind, that between identifying countertransference and reciprocating countertransference.... This distinction ... stems logically from the model of the dialogic self. A person enacting one pole of a RRP [reciprocal role procedure] may either (1) convey the feelings associated with the role to others, in whom corresponding emphatic feelings may be elicited, or (2) seek to elicit the reciprocating response of the other..... In the course of therapy, therapists can use their identifying countertransference to explore feelings which the patient is conveying non-verbally but does not acknowledge or experience consciously..... As regards reciprocating countertransference, the need is to recognise the pressure and to avoid reinforcing (collusive) responses". (Ryle and Kerr, 2003, pp. 103-105)

Levels of contact

In transactional analysis and most other humanistic psychotherapies, contact is usually regarded as a phenomenon that is discernible at the social level of interaction. This is in keeping with transactional analysis as an inter-personal model of interaction. In **Part Six** I extend this to include the notion that although contact occurs literally at a social level, it also exists at a transpersonal level. For the most part, this level of contact is out of conscious awareness.

Combining roles at the three levels

Although the roles of the Contact Cube are conceptualised and been described as separate entities, in practice they occur simultaneously at three levels – social, psychological and existential. This is in keeping with Karpman's observation that "once someone is in the [Drama] Triangle, they (and others) are all the roles at once" (Karpman 1973). In **Chapter 13** we will see how it transpires that the role that is being enacted occurs at the social level, the role a person moves towards occurs at the psychological level and the role a person defends against or seeks to confirm occurs at the existential level (Mellor and A Schiff 1975, Law 1979, Barnes, 1981 pp. 28-29). In other words, the observable role I enact behaviourally at the social level includes or is accompanied by two other roles that occur at the same time – one at the psychological level and the other at the existential level.

Certain combinations of roles - one role at each of the three levels - are referred to as a role profile. However, not all combinations are permissible. This is because the relationship between the Squares is governed by the psychological equivalent of what mathematicians and physicists refer to as a 'self-organised criticality'. In the present context, this means that one cannot occupy roles at two levels in one Square and a third role at another level in the other Square. Thus, role profiles with combinations such as social level Responder, psychological level Persecutor and existential level Victim are not psychologically possible. That is, phenomenologically and by definition, I cannot be genuinely emphatic towards another person and at the same time, harbour the ulterior motive of making them not-OK, as well as maintaining the existential position of I'm not-OK, You're not-OK. The transition from one Square to the other is therefore, "critical" in the sense that contact with another person can be based on *either* discounting *or* non-discounting, or as Erskine, Moursund and Trautmann describe the process, as "disruption to contact" (Erskine, Moursund and Trautmann, 1999 p.158). The "self-organising criticality" of transition from one Square to the other, means that "disruption" at one level of a role permeates the remaining levels.

On the other hand, changes of role between levels within the Squares are unfettered. Any combination of roles at each of the three levels is possible. However, a major difference between the Squares concerns changes from one role profile to another. In the positive Square a change from say, a Promoter, Responder, Valuer role profile to Beholder, Responder, Valuer profile requires an intermediate recourse to the integrated Adult capacity of the Observer role. In changing from a Persecutor, Rescuer, Victim role profile to Bystander, Rescuer, Victim profile in the negative Square, this intermediate step is either absent (and Adult is excluded) or is based on a contaminated Adult.

Uses of Contact Cube roles at three levels

Bearing in mind that the aim of the Contact Cube is to enable clients to use positive Square roles, one powerful way of doing this is for a therapist to model the process. Although they themselves do not use the term "discounting", Erskine, Moursund and Trautmann's (1999) book *Beyond Empathy* is a testimony to ways of respectfully enquiring about, resonating with and demonstrating willingness to involvement in understanding their clients' frame of reference. Rather than confronting discounting as described by Mellor and Schiff (1975), they make contact with their clients by acknowledging the validity of the client's ways of discounting within the client's frame of reference. Their work is couched in a "how to do psychotherapy" style with a prescriptive undertone on what they regard the formalised role of a competent psychotherapist should encompass behaviourally.

The Contact Cube adds a less prescriptive dimension by conceptualising the personalised roles involved. For example, the process of **inquiry** (Erskine, Moursund and Trautmann, 1999 pp. 19-45) may be described in terms of three of the positive Square roles as depicted in **Figure 10.1**. This represents the interaction between two people – a social level Bystander (person B) being approached by some one in the Active Acceptor (person A) role at the social level - as shown by the heavy black line and solid arrowhead. At the same time, the psychological level role of Beholder underlies the social level. This is depicted as a dashed line and solid arrowhead from Beholder to Active Acceptor. The role at the existential level is Valuer, signifying the protagonist's basic life position.

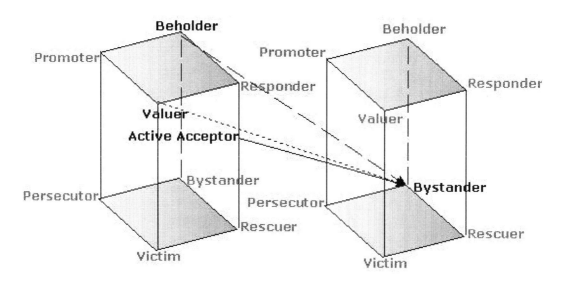

Figure 10.1

In a similar vein, the process of **involvement** (Erskine, Moursund and Trautmann, 1999 pp. 83-120) may be described as in **Figure 10.2** where the social level Active Acceptor role is replaced by the Servant role at the same level. The Beholder and Valuer roles at the psychological and existential levels, respectively, are retained and, as in the previous example, indicate ongoing monitoring of the other person (in this case, the Bystander) from the OK-OK life position embodied in the Valuer role. "Beholding" in this context, indicates ongoing awareness of self and the other person. The Valuer role implies open-ness, a willingness to be affected by the other person. Taken together the three levels constitute the therapist's autonomy and an invitation to here-and-now reparative contact that Erskine et. al. rightly emphasise.

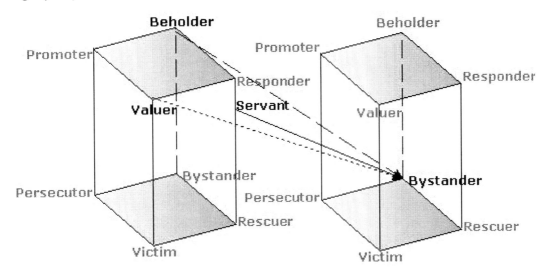

Figure 10.2

The personalised roles associated with **attunement** (Erskine, Moursund and Trautmann, 1999 pp. 46-82) may also be described in the same manner; this is illustrated by **Figure 10.3**. The hallmark of the Responder role is empathy, accompanied by responsiveness to the perceived needs of others. Responders are open and direct in ways that affirm their own and other's OK-ness. They express their thoughts and feelings congruently and clearly in a manner that conveys their unconditional positive regard for others. This matches Erskine, Moursund and Trautmann's description of attunement as

> "a two-part process. The therapist who is attuned to the client must first be aware of that client's sensations, needs, feelings, desires or meanings. Maintaining such awareness, the therapist must also communicate to the client that he or she is aware, does understand and is willing to shape his or her responses accordingly". (Erskine, Moursund and Trautmann, 1999 p.47)

My understanding of inquiry, involvement and attunement as described above is that they are *concepts* – terms for relating to others in particular ways. They are extremely useful, if not necessary therapeutic processes under certain circumstances. ERICA offers an additional perspective; it provides *operational definitions* that are situation and content free. Moreover, these processes are not the exclusive province of psychotherapy. The role profiles may be applied usefully in any setting.

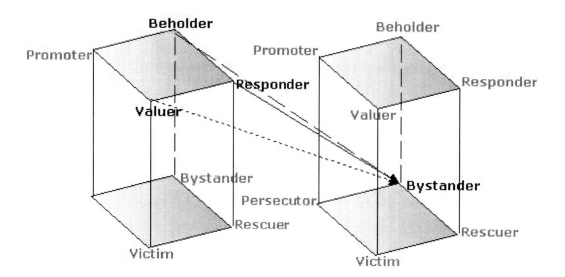

Figure 10.3

As indicated, inquiry, attunement and involvement all seem to involve roles at the social level located on the Responder-Rescuer dimension. This is not to say the above role profiles for inquiry, involvement and attunement are the *only* roles included in or constituting these processes. Attunement does not simply involve a series of Responder/Beholder/Valuer role profiles. There are undoubtedly many more role profiles that could legitimately be called "attunement". For example, there is a very subtle difference between the role profiles of a Responder/Beholder/Valuer and a Responder/Valuer/Beholder. Inquiry, involvement and attunement are *processes* – in the sense that they each consist of a characteristic cluster or group of role profiles described appropriately by Erskine et. al. in global terms, rather than as operational definitions of a single role profile. As we shall see in **Chapter 14**, these three processes require the choice of a particular cluster of role profiles that may be said to constitute a *role imago repertoire*.

The Contact Cube provides a conceptual framework for understanding the roles involved and indeed, generating a wide range of other role responses. For example, as indicated in **Chapter 8**, the Promoter role has six components - permission and protection, (Crossman 1966), potency (Steiner 1971), perception and practice (Clarke 1996) - which I have widened to include role modelling applicable to any setting - and a component that I call prescription. This is an elaboration of Steiner's description of the script antithesis. The Cathexis 'school' of transactional analysis (Schiff et. al., 1975, Barnes 1977) made extensive use of the prescriptive component of the Promoter role in defining the parameters of behaviour necessary in a therapeutic community. Indeed, one could speculate that some of the difficulties that arose within the Cathexis community (Barnes 1999a, 1999b, 1999c,) may well have involved the use of a prescriptive component of the Persecutor role.

Nonetheless, **empowerment** arises from appropriate use of the various components of the Promoter role. This yields a role profile that facilitates permission and protection, which, in turn, enable clients to claim their potency (Crossman, 1966; Steiner, 1979; Goulding and Goulding, 1979, Law, 2001). **Figure 10.4** shows the levels involved.

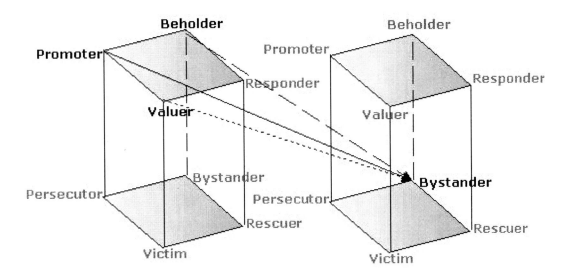

Figure 10.4

As shown in **Figure 10.5**, changing the Promoter for the Provocateur role at the social level would illustrate the role profile that would typically accompany **challenge** to a person's frame of reference. Almost by definition, any "cured" client has changed their frame of reference and my belief is that for some clients, challenging their frame of reference at some stage is entirely appropriate. For some clients, learning how to challenge others in OK-OK ways is often essential.

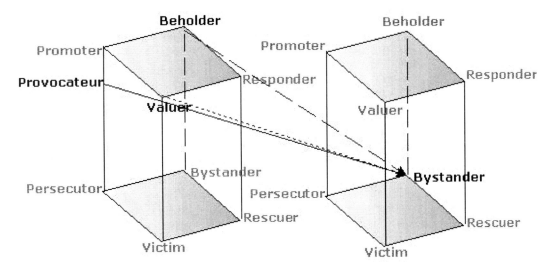

Figure 10.5

Under some circumstances, **assertion** is just as useful a role profile for people to have in their repertoire. Here the role at the social level is the Announcer, with Beholder and Valuer at the psychological and existential levels respectively. This process is shown in **Figure 10.6**

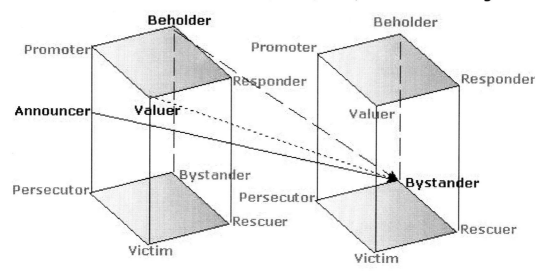

Figure 10.6

How the role profiles diagrammed in **Figures 6.1** to **6.6** are acquired, and when or why they may be best used is obviously a matter for more extensive discussion; the topic is taken up again in **Chapters 14, 18** and **19**. The Contact Cube suggests no more than the availability of the various roles that may emerge via the contact between people.

In my clinical experience, a therapist's use of roles at the social level located along the Responder-Rescuer continuum is helpful, if not essential, during most stages of therapy with clients who have schizoid and narcissistic personality adaptations. I suspect the same applies to clients with avoidant and dependent personality disorders or traits, but I have limited experience in working with such clients. Clients with borderline disorders constantly demand the Servant role and consistently invite Responder and Active Acceptor roles during the early stages of therapy. Later, they respond well to the Announcer and Provocateur roles and eventually learn to accept and use the Promoter role. Much the same may be said for clients with paranoid traits or disorders. In contrast, the overall therapeutic strategy for working with clients who have anti-social, passive-aggressive and obsessive-compulsive characteristics is to use positive Square roles located on the Promoter-Persecutor dimension.

These generalisations do not constitute a prescriptive treatment plan for working with any particular client group but serve merely to make the point that the Contact Cube provides a conceptual framework for therapeutic interventions. As such, the Contact Cube forms the theoretical basis of a way or method of mapping an individual's role expectations of self and whoever else comes within the individual's current role set. This process is applicable to individual and group therapy and may also be applied to work in organisations. I anticipate that the Contact Cube would be particularly useful for identifying factors such as management styles and patterns of role behaviour in an organisational setting.

One example of the practical application of Contact Cube roles is where the sequential nature of roles is the main focus of attention. For example, any reasonably competent transactional analysis practitioner will soon spot the games presented by clients with borderline issues. However, in working with such clients, my experience is that although it is necessary to be able to identify and deal with the game(s), this in itself is not always sufficient. What the Contact Cube offers is a methodology that provides not only an overall map of the sequence of games in which such clients become involved in an apparently haphazard fashion, but also the client's participation in charting the map, using the sequences of Contact Cube roles as the basic parameters for drawing these maps. In so doing, the Contact Cube becomes a methodology for teaching clients alternatives to hitherto dysfunctional roles. Inevitably, this requires a therapist to enter in a contactful relationship with a client. This process is described in more detail in **Chapter 17**.

Case Example

Part of the methodology of using Contact Cube roles is that therapists need to learn to think in terms of using roles to invite and maintain contact with clients. As previously indicated, Bystanders are not usually self-activating. By definition, their aim is to avoid engagement and remain uninvolved. A brief excerpt from a therapy group (run by a newly qualified TA practitioner) is shown below[1]. Although the focus is on tracking moves between roles, this obviously does not preclude noticing changes of ego states, transactions, redefinitions and all the other factors to which a therapist needs to pay attention. I would emphasise that this type of analysis is not a part of using ERICA, but is included here purely for the purpose of illustrating changes of role. In ERICA the unit of analysis is roles rather than transactions. However, at this stage of explaining Contact Cube roles, I show an analysis using each transaction at an overt level to illustrate the moves between Contact Cube roles enacted by the client and the therapist.

> **Therapist 1**: "I'm interested in what you said during check in. You said you've been working twelve hours a day and have been finding it difficult to concentrate?" (Offers social level Active Acceptor role; confirms psychological level Beholder role,)
> **Client 1**: "Mm". (Bystander)
> **Therapist 2**: "Maybe your body is trying to tell you that working these long hours means that you're doing too much.....Seems to make sense. (Provocateur ? Responder) I'm curious about what happens when you're so tired you can't concentrate". (Active Acceptor)
> **Client 2**: "Don't know really". (Bystander)
> **Therapist 3**: "Not knowing fits with being unable to concentrate". (Responder)
> **Client 3**: "My mind just goes blank". (over-adapts and moves to Passive Acceptor)
> **Therapist 4**: "Mm, that must make it difficult for you". (Responder)
> **Client 4**: "Yeah". (?Passive Acceptor?)

---

[1] The transcript highlights one of the difficulties encountered in using ERICA. As will be seen in **Chapter 17**, the methodology of ERICA enables clients to learn about their own role behaviour via discussion with the therapist about previous between-session situations. Eventually clients are able to recognise roles as they arise. However, when it comes to teaching, supervision and particularly, *writing* about roles, the limitations of text become all too obvious. Ideally, video recordings enable one to capture all the verbal and non-verbal cues needed for identifying roles. This is seldom a practical solution for most practitioners and in practice, audio recordings are the next best alternative; they are essential for detecting roles at the psychological level.

With transcripts I use the convention of "coding" them by showing the enacted role (at the social level only) in brackets after each statement – as shown above. Where more than one role is or may be involved the roles are both noted but interspersed with a "?" When there is no clear indication of what the role is or may become the assumption is that the person is in the same role as indicated by the previous statement. The same rule applies to statements that are ambiguous (e.g. grunts, sighs or single words without clear meaning within a given context). In both cases the role is indicated by a "?" before and after the observed/assumed role. Another convention is a short-tailed arrow to indicate "implies" or "likely to move to".

Therapist 5: "Maybe you're about tired enough to consider easing up a little". (Provocateur)

Client 5: "But I have to work longer because not concentrating means it takes longer to finish my assignments!" (Protester).

Therapist 6: "Okaay...I think I'm getting a feel for the way things work for you...(Responder). I'd be willing to work with you on this". (Servant)

Client 6: "Well, maybe ...OK..." (?Acceptor → Valuer?)

Therapist 7: "Great. I'm ready when you are (Responder). You take your time and let me know when you're ready". (Promoter)

Client 7: (Reportedly) looks relieved, says nothing, but nods. (? Valuer → Beholder?)

The transcript obviously fails to convey the all-important nuances of voice tone, speed of delivery, non-verbal gestures and so forth, but is sufficient to give the flavour of the therapist's changes of role that may not be captured by conventional analysis of the transactions. This is not to say that one or the other approach is better, but merely that they are different. That is, the vignette illustrates not only the difference in the unit of analysis, (roles rather than transactions), but also leads to consideration of several important aspects of the Contact Cube.

The first point is that the therapist's moves from one role to the next, provides data that may be used to confirm the theoretical basis of moves (by both parties) away from the Bystander role.

Secondly, someone in a positive Square role can begin to engage a Bystander by challenging the Bystander's symbiotic invitation in a way that confirms the Bystander's OK-ness without persecuting or rescuing him or her. In the above excerpt, for example, the therapist reframes the client's reported difficulty in terms of the possibility (Therapist 2: "Maybe ..) of a body-mind message that the client is "doing too much". This is a typical low-key Provocateur challenge that is immediately offset by the Responder comment implying that the client could be seen to be doing something sensible.

The therapist consistently refuses to accept the symbiosis, yet equally consistently acknowledges the validity of the symbiotic invitations within the client's frame of reference. The client's role responses may be seen as a potentially healthy attempt to return to an earlier stage of development in order to complete a normal developmental task, or in other words, to "heal" the original disruption of contact.

Although the above excerpt does not fully demonstrate a sustained positive Square role by the client the indications are that, in response to the therapist's use of the Servant role, the client seems to be about to move to the Valuer role. This, along with the client's previous responses gives invaluable data about the client's frame of reference. The therapist would have to explore such responses extensively before being in a position to begin formulating any characteristic response pattern for this particular client.

In the above example, the client is close to or has reached the Critical Point. This moment represents a single instance of the overall aim of the Contact Cube – to be able to reach and be aware of being at the Critical Point. The therapist chose not to point this out directly, but later in the session asks:

Therapist 8: " So how are you doing, Gerry?" (low-level Active Acceptor)

Client 8: "Well ...OK–ish".

Therapist 9: "Good for you....say more about the 'ish'". (Responder → Announcer)

Client 9: "Well .... I was waiting ... waiting for..."(Passive Acceptor?Valuer)

Therapist 10: (Pauses, speaks softly: "For some   ...thing.. some.. one?"(Active Acceptor? Rescuer?)

Client 10: (Exhaling)" For... for... for some space". (?Valuer Announcer?)
Therapist 11: "Great....You find your space .. Take your time... Is it OK for me to check with you now and then?" (Responder? Promoter → Active Acceptor)
Client 11: (sounds relieved) "That's OK". (?Announcer).

The example gives a flavour of "thinking in roles", a task which, interestingly, beginning trainees find easier than do many who are more advanced. Learning to identify changes in role profiles is a necessary precursor to using role profiles to map a client's characteristic patterns of role behaviour; detailed steps of this methodology will be given in a subsequent Self Supervision Suggestions.

Although the Contact Cube defines parameters and, as we will see in **Chapters 13 and 14**, may be used to provide a *theoretical* taxonomy of games and their positive counterparts (sets), the *practical* use of roles as a unit of analysis is best learned by *post hoc* matching of one's experience with whatever may be dictated by theoretical considerations. Supervision is almost always needed to monitor transferential issues.

Amending the Contact Cube
The flexibility of the Contact Cube at a conceptual and practical level is such that it may be adapted for a range of different uses. For example, the bi-polar opposite Responder- Rescuer dimension may be seen as underpinning varieties of attachment-detachment (Marrone 1998, Goldberg, Muir and Kerr 1995, Crittenden 1995, Main and Goldwyn 1994, Kaplan and Main, 1985). Likewise it is theoretically possible and sometimes useful in practice to regard the Bystander-Beholder dimension as degrees of activity-inactivity. Additional roles along the Valuer-Victim dimension of the Contact Cube could be postulated, but in practice I have not found them to be particularly helpful in a clinical setting. I imagine that practitioners working in an organisational setting may well wish to review this. For example, in a therapy group it is comparatively easy to make a distinction between the roles of Bystander and Beholder; a few well-directed questions will suffice. However in organisations differentiating between these roles is seldom a straightforward matter. This is partly because of the time scale involved but also because conceptually both roles are characterised by behavioural inactivity. Only by asking phenomenological questions that address expectations, is one able to discern which of the roles an individual is occupying. The paradox is that often the very act of enquiring results in a role shift; the caveat is not to ask such questions unless you are prepared to deal with the answers.

It is also sometimes useful to decide upon the level of analysis required in any situation. For example, do you need to use the first order model where you only have to deal with eight roles, or does the situation warrant the use of a second order analysis with sixteen roles? Likewise, some situations require analysis of behaviour at no more than the social level or at most, social and psychological levels. In practice I have found that these questions take care of themselves. Answers to these considerations emerge partly from the demands of the situation but also with experience of using Contact Cube roles. Clinically all three levels are frequently but not exclusively used. In my view, use of all three levels in settings other than clinical is contra-indicated

Identifying roles

You may recall from **Chapter 4** that roles may be identified at the social and psychological levels simply by observing the interaction between two people. For ease of reference, the relevant paragraphs read:

"The idea is simple, if not elegant – spot a Drama Triangle role and wait for one or other person to change to another of the three roles. If the change occurs, you are witnessing (or in) a game. If there is no change of role, then the interaction is either "pastiming" or "racketeering".

Merely by noticing non verbal cues such as tone of voice, body posture, gestures, facial expressions and so forth, it is also possible at the start of a game to predict the role to which a person will switch. There is a world of difference, for example, between someone using a soft, yet slightly patronising tone of voice, saying "Why don't you tell me what's been going on? I'm sure we can sort this out" and the person who uses exactly the same words but speaks firmly, if not sternly in a brusque, no nonsense manner. Even on paper and without taking account of the second person's response to this opening move, the prediction is that in the first case, the switch is likely to be from Rescuer to Victim; in the second it will be from Rescuer to Persecutor."

However, because we have included a fourth role in the both Squares, we now have first to identify a social level role and then identify one of three other roles. By definition, the Bystander role is characterised by behavioural inactivity and for most practical purposes may be disregarded at this stage. If (or when) a switch of roles occurs this will reveal the psychological level role. In other words, if there is a switch of roles you will be able to observe that the role that was at the psychological level, because it has now become the role at the social level. In short, roles may be identified at the social and psychological levels in much the same way as ego states – behaviourally, socially, historically and phenomenologically (see Stewart and Joines 1987, pp. 39-49). However there are some significant differences.

Identification of ego states – and hence transactions - happen in "real time". Irrespective of the method used, recognition of roles often requires a more extended time scale. This is partly because roles may be enacted from any ego state or indeed sequences of ego state changes, but also because one has to take account of the overall meaning of what is being said. Thus, the content of verbal statements may have to be assessed over a longer period and it is sometimes necessary to Beholder a series of transactions before being able to define the role. This has a number of advantages. In the first place, it means that you can take your time, you can listen to an audiotape, recall the particular incident, review your reaction and maybe even change your mind about what was going on.

Secondly, ERICA requires you to pay attention to both content and process. This is true of all therapy; ideally a good therapist will always pay attention to what people are saying as well as how they say it – along with whatever may be behind what is being said. Balancing attention to content and process comes with experience; most beginning therapists have to learn more about working with process than content. In ERICA you have to pay attention to both levels right from the start; you can't have one without the other. As you will see in **Chapter 17**, the methodology of ERICA requires the therapist and the client jointly to review a session and identify roles. Initially the 'reality' of the role sequences is co-created after the event; eventually clients are able to identify and make choices about their response in vivo. In a sense the above heading ("Identifying roles") is a misnomer. Any role that you or anyone else "identifies" is in fact "created" within the context of a relationship; this is certainly true of the methodology of ERICA.

These considerations apart, all the behavioural cues that are used for ego state diagnosis are relevant to roles – words, tone of voice, gestures, facial expressions and postures. However my experience is that the behavioural cues that accompany any particular role are highly individualised. Each person has their own characteristic range of behaviours that are associated with particular roles. Of course, the are obvious differences between positive and negative roles that apply generally, but in practice I have found the behavioural categories described in the Tables in **Chapters 8** and **9** to be the most useful guidelines for identifying the various roles.

Roles are also related to Kahler's mini-script. In particular, the transition from positive to negative Square roles is always accompanied by driver behaviour[1]. For therapists this links the skilled use of ERICA with all the armoury of the Process model (Kahler, 1978, 1979; Stewart, 1996, Joines and Stewart 2002) and locates ERICA firmly within the framework of TA clinical theory and practice. Identifying drivers in a TA model is essentially the same as spotting interruptions to contact in a Gestalt approach – a topic I address in more detail in **Chapter 13**. The absence of drivers or lack of any interruption to contact thus serves as the major indicator of positive Square roles. For non clinical practitioners, I would go as far as saying that the starting point for one of the major research challenges for TA is to link roles with personality adaptations and allowers - the opposite of driver behaviour.

Because of the reciprocal nature of roles, social diagnosis is usually straightforward and will often have a predictability of response, especially in the negative Square. For example, Victims "need" Rescuers but often "attract" Persecutors. Here the clue is to look for the role you most frequently encounter in your interactions with others when you are stressed. For example if you often seem to "find" or "attract" Victims, the chances are that you are often in the Rescuer role. Almost everyone is able to name someone who for the most part assumes a Victim role. If you know someone like this, watch closely to see how others respond.

Historical diagnosis is necessary for identification of roles at the existential level. As indicated in **Chapter 5,** the Observer role frequently leads to reflection on previous role performances or, in the present context, historical diagnosis. This has obvious implications for therapists who, by virtue of their contract with clients, are at liberty to explore issues originating in the historical role set. TA practitioners, who do not have therapeutic contracts with their clients and hence are not afforded such liberty, are obliged to exercise due caution and professional judgement. In other words, identifying roles at this level is one aspect of ERICA; working with existential level roles is another matter.

The nub of ERICA is a person's awareness of his or her own role profile - phenomenological diagnosis. This is a crucial aspect of identifying roles, especially when this involves transition from one Square to another.

Despite the similarity of using behavioural, social, historical and phenomenological ways of identifying ego states and roles at the social and psychological levels, it should be noted that roles are pitched at a higher level of abstraction than ego states and games. However for a full diagnosis of a persons' role profile, we need to take account of roles at the existential level - as illustrated in the above examples of roles at three levels that constitute the processes of inquiry, involvement, attunement, empowerment, challenge and assertion. In addition to these options, there are another a hundred and fourteen positive second order role profiles! The implications of this are discussed in **Chapter 14** where we shall be paying closer attention to role profiles and role imago repertoires.

---

[1] Drivers are a component of the not-OK mini-script (Kahler, 1978, 1979); they are short sequences of behaviour that occur within seconds that serve to counter the script proper. There are five drivers – "Be Perfect", "Please Others", "Try Hard", "Be Strong", and "Hurry Up". Each driver is characterised by distinctive verbal and non-verbal signals that may be correlated with script themes, rackets and games and overall personality adaptations or types (such as paranoid, hysteric etc.). Recognising drivers is a key skill in the use of the Process Communication model (Kahler 1979) for diagnosis and treatment planning. See Joines and Stewart (2002) for comprehensive coverage of the Process model.

Identifying roles – guidelines for researchers

The interface between formalised and personalised roles is especially relevant to researchers. Ideally research should be via video, thereby minimising (but not eliminating) the halo effect of in-situ observation. Nevertheless, both in-situ and retrospective observation of personalised roles goes beyond single individuals to consider what happens between two or more individuals - in this case, the observer and the observed. Moreover, personalised roles as behaviours based on expectations of self, others and situations, include both the variability and continuity of self, relative to other selves and situations. This is an intersubjective, phenomenological experience of self. The researcher's experience of self is held in the crucible of a latent relationship that becomes manifest in dialogue. Personalised roles are dialogically co-created but the researcher's formalised role precludes, or at least, constrains the extent of such co-creation. However, a researcher cannot escape being part of the process of co-creating whatever role they are observing (Etherington, 2004). For example, if I watch two people having an argument and discern one to be enacting a Persecutor role and the other in a Victim role, I have implicitly contributed to the 'creation' of these roles by virtue of the fact that I have observed a certain pattern of behaviour that I have defined as 'Persecutor' and you, the reader, have at least notionally accepted the validity of my perception and, maybe, even agree with my definition of persecutory behaviour.

This is the nature of research and the crux of the practice/research divide. The implicit contract between researcher and researched is witnessing-by-proxy. Inter-personally, the researcher needs to maintain the Beholder role at the social level.

The dilemma for researchers is that phenomenologically, the key to identifying roles in any relationship is the quality of contact This is the most immediate, intuitive and spontaneous way for a researcher to identify roles. It transpires that we can simplify relationships down to four categories or types of contact (positive-positive, positive-negative, negative-positive and negative-negative). Reactivity precedes inactivity - at which point the researcher needs to pause and shift rapidly to Beholder, rather than proceeding to either responsivity or pro-activity. Bearing in mind that, with the Contact Cube, the unit of analysis is the role profile of the researcher in relation to the role profiles of those under observation, the ideal role profile for a researcher is a continual, rapid shuttling between Valuer/Beholder/Announcer and Beholder/Announcer/Valuer.

Because of the reciprocal nature of roles, social diagnosis will often have a predictability of response, especially with negative roles. For example, Victims "need" Rescuers but often "attract" Persecutors. This is essential information for the observer as it provides both a check on the researcher's own initial phenomenological 'diagnosis,' but also constitutes the basis of predicting possible future role switches from one level to another. Social diagnosis is discussed further in **Part Four**.

Up to this point, a researcher can rely on his/her own reactivity, the above general behavioural descriptions of roles and confirmation thereof via social diagnosis; from here on, these guidelines become more transactional analysis model-specific.

Researchers need to be aware, as I have pointed out above, that despite the similarity of using behavioural, social, historical and phenomenological ways of identifying roles, roles are pitched at a higher level of abstraction than ego states and transactions. Identification of ego states – and hence transactions - happens within a stimulus-response paradigm in "real time". Irrespective of the method used, recognition of roles often requires a more extended time scale. This is partly because roles may be enacted from any ego state or indeed sequences of ego state changes but also because one has to take account of the overall meaning of what is being said. Thus, the content of verbal statements may have to be assessed over a longer period and it is sometimes necessary to monitor a series of transactions before being able to define the role.

All the behavioural cues that are used for ego state diagnosis are relevant to roles – words, tone of voice, gestures, facial expressions and postures. There are obvious differences between positive and negative roles – using a structural model; Parent or Child ego states signal negative roles and positive roles are always enacted from Adult. In practice, I have found that knowledge of Temple's Functional Fluency Index (Temple 1999) gives useful indicators for identifying the various roles. This association has yet to be verified empirically. Not all researchers will have (or need) this knowledge. Nevertheless, personalised roles may usefully be regarded as an alternative to functional ego states.

Negative roles are also related to Kahler's mini-scripts. In particular, the transition from positive to negative roles is always accompanied by driver behaviour. For therapists, this links the skilled use of the Contact Cube with all the armoury of the Process model (Kahler, 1978, 1979; Stewart, 1996, Joines and Stewart 2002) and locates Contact Cube roles firmly within the framework of transactional analysis clinical theory and practice.

Limitations and strengths of the Contact Cube

Even in a clinical setting the Contact Cube does not always provide clear evidence of historical factors that influence roles. Organisational, educational and to a lesser extent, counselling practitioners frequently do not elicit them and researchers often have to fall back on one or other of the two models to be discussed later for historical confirmation of roles.

This apart, the major limitation of the Contact Cube is that it does not by itself take account of formalised roles. This is a significant variable in organisational work and, to a lesser extent, in an educational setting. In private practice counselling and psychotherapy only two formalised roles are present. To some extent this shortcoming is offset by using Contact Cube roles in conjunction with Role Imago Templates – the third model in this series. A fuller account of integrating personalised and formalised roles and all the complexities of power and influence in organisations is given in **Chapter 11**.

If we go along with the idea that examining roles, contact and imago images is a useful way of describing relationships, it is not surprising to find we run the risk of reifying one or all of these. The only way out of is to bear in mind the dimensions of Wilber's AQAL model and view these processes as if we are both the parts and the whole.

Another constraint is that a focus on personalised roles can take precedence over contact and imago images. All three are of equal importance, and irrespective of setting, it seems that clients find the Contact Cube most useful when the emphasis is on relationships as a dynamic, phenomenological process rather than any hypothetical components.

Using role profiles instead of transactional analysis proper is a potential pitfall of method rather than the model itself. The two operations are based on different paradigms and have different purposes in both practice and research.

Despite these constraints the Contact Cube offers a framework for using roles, contact and imago images in ways that significantly redress the imbalance between a focus on functional and dysfunctional behaviours. The model offers concepts and operational definitions for observation, practice and formal research into the roles, contact and imago images that together constitute a way of viewing relationships.

Developing the Contact Cube as a research tool

The Contact Cube awaits further development as a research tool. Optimally the steps in such a venture would be to:

1. Use professional actors to make a video/DVD of scripted role plays to illustrate a) each role b) each role profile c) sequences of role interaction.
2. Use the video to train group(s) of experienced transactional analysis practitioners to identify roles, contact and imago images, establish inter-scorer reliabilities and confirm validity of a), b) and c).
3. Use this information to refine role plays and repeat 1) and 2) above.
4. Select role plays with best validity and use these to train researchers.
5. Devise and standardise indices of roles and correlate these with measures of contact and imago images.
6. Correlate 5 above with other transactional analysis-specific models/measures such as the Transactional Analysis Script Profile (Kahler, 1997), the Functional Fluency Index (Temple 1999) and the Joines Personality Adaptation Questionnaire (Joines, 2000).
7. Correlate 5 above with non-transactional analysis models such as Benjamin's Structural Analysis of Social Behavior instrument (Benjamin, 2003) and perhaps the Adult Assessment Interview (Kaplan and Main 1986, 1996).
8. In parallel with 1 to 7 above teach clients how to become researchers into their own behaviour. The rationale and methodology of doing this is discussed in **Part Five**.

Clearly steps 1 to 7 call for research beyond the resources of any single individual. They need to be widely and systematically applied, validated and reviewed. Step 8 requires little comment except to note that:

> "Eric Berne insisted that the client, as well as the practitioner, should have full information about what was going on in their work together. This follows from the basic assumptions that people are OK and that everyone can think". (Stewart and Joines 1987, p. 8)

In conjunction with appropriate technology (ideally, video linked with software for data analysis) the Contact Cube may be applied at two levels. At the interface with transactional analysis practice, it could provide for systematic meta-level reflection on interactive processes, as a tool for training and supervision and as a means of theory building within the framework of a transactional analysis or other theoretical models. At the interface with formal research, the model could provide a framework for the systematic collection of process data, providing for the development and testing of transactional analysis theory, and the systematic correlation of process variables with outcome data.

Key Points 10

10.1 Personalised roles operate at **overt, covert and existential** levels.

10.2 By the age of four or five children are able to use **roles at three levels**.

10.3 The existential level of role analysis has been underemphasised in the TA literature. The healing potential of the Hendrix's Imago parallels Berne's I'm OK-You're OK position. Roles at the existential level embody the potential for recapitulating childhood wounding as well as present day healing.

10.4 The *social* level role is accompanied by two other roles that occur at the same time – one at the *psychological* level and the other at the *existential* level. Certain *combinations of roles* - one role at each of the three levels - are referred to as a **role profile**. Not all combinations are permissible because the relationship between the Squares is governed by a 'self-organised criticality'.

10.5 The role profile associated with **inquiry** has the *Active Acceptor* role at the *social* level, the *Beholder* at the *psychological* and the *Valuer* at the *existential* level.

10.6 The role profile associated with **involvement** has the *Servant* role at the *social* level, the *Beholder* at the *psychological* level and the *Valuer* at *existential* level.

10.7 The role profile associated with **attunement** has the *Responder* role at the *social* level, the *Beholder* role at the *psychological* level and *Valuer* at *existential* level.

10.8 *Inquiry*, *involvement* and *attunement* all involve roles at the social level, located on the **Responder-Rescuer** dimension. The Contact Cube provides a conceptual framework for understanding the roles involved and generating a wide range of **other** role responses:

- **empowerment** arises from the role profile of social level *Promoter*, psychological level *Beholder* and existential level *Valuer.* This is the role that facilitates permission and protection, which, in turn, enable clients to claim their potency,
- **challenge** arises from the role profile of social level *Provocateur*, psychological level *Beholder* and existential level *Valuer.* For some clients, learning how to challenge others in OK-OK ways is often essential,
- with **assertion,** the role at the social level is the *Announcer*, with *Beholder* and *Valuer* at the psychological and existential levels respectively.

10.9 These generalisations do not constitute a prescriptive treatment plan for working with any particular client group. The Contact Cube provides **a conceptual framework** for facilitative interventions.

10.10 In practice**, clients participate** in *charting their own role profiles*. Thus, the Contact Cube becomes a *methodology* for teaching clients *alternatives to dysfunctional* roles.

10.11 All that has been said about roles applies equally to **contact,** which depends as much on the role of the observer as on the phenomena under observation. To use the Contact Cube effectively requires *appropriate contact*, in order to *be* the role - rather than *learn about* it.

10.12 The flexibility of the Contact Cube is such that it may be adapted for a range of **different uses** in different **settings**.

10.13 Roles may be *identified* at the social and psychological levels simply by *observing* the interaction between two people.

10.14 Roles **may be identified** at all three levels in much the same way as *ego states* – behaviourally, socially, historically and phenomenologically. However there are some *significant differences*:

- Identification of ego states and transactions happens in *"real time"*; recognition of roles often requires a *more extended time scale*.
- ERICA requires attention to *both content* and *process*.
- Roles are also related to Kahler's mini-script.

10.15 **Diagnosis of roles** at the *social* level is usually straightforward because of the reciprocal nature of roles:

- *historical* diagnosis is necessary for identification of roles at the *existential* level.
- *phenomenological* diagnosis is a person's awareness of his or her *own role profile*.

10.16 Roles are pitched at **a higher level of abstraction** than ego states and games.

10.17 The interface between *formalised* and *personalised* roles is especially relevant to **researchers** because:
- personalised roles involve an intersubjective, phenomenological experience of self,
- a research contract entails **witnessing-by-proxy**,
- the key to identifying roles in any relationship is the quality of contact,
- the **ideal role profile** for a **researcher** is a continual, rapid shuttling between *Valuer/Beholder/Announcer* and *Beholder/Announcer/Valuer*.

10.18 The **limitations** of the Contact Cube are that:
- it does not always provide clear evidence of *historical factors* that influence roles,
- it does not by itself take account of *formalised roles,*
- role profiles may be *reified*. Using Wilber's AQAL model enables us to view these processes as if we are both the parts and the whole,
- a focus on personalised roles can *take precedence* over contact and imago images,
- the use of role profiles instead of transactional analysis proper is a potential *pitfall of method* rather than the model itself.

10.19 The Contact Cube awaits further **development as a research tool**. Optimal steps are suggested, most of which are beyond the resources of any single individual.

Self Supervision Suggestions 10

10.1 Repeat **Self Supervision Suggestions 8.7** to **8.15** using role profiles at social, psychological and existential levels. Are you always able to identify the existential level solely by observation? If not, what would you need to know or do?

10.2 Using the suggested role profiles, **compose phrases** appropriate to the processes of inquiry, involvement, attunement, empowerment, challenge and assertion. Which other role profiles would be appropriate?

10.3 Start collecting role profiles for your most frequently used interventions.

10.4 Which role profiles do you consider most appropriate in working with various personality adaptations?

10.5 Observe a snippet of social conversation. As far as possible, analyse the role profiles and compare this with a similar account of Kahler's channels of communication.

10.6 Compose a two way dialogue that demonstrates intimacy and analyse this in terms of role profiles.

10.7 Write down all twenty four **first order role profiles** for negative *and* positive roles. (See **Chapter 14** if you get stuck!)

10.8 Using a full length mirror (or video camera), **enact** and **practise** (by yourself) as many of the twenty four **first order negative and positive role profiles** as you can manage until you are able to adopt each of these effortlessly. How many can you do? Which do you most prefer and least prefer?

Chapter 11
Adding formalised roles

This Chapter focuses on adding formalised roles to the Contact Cube. In the Contact Cube, the focus of attention was on what practitioners, clients or researchers would have to know and do in order to use roles, imago images and contact to influence relationships, thereby bridging the divides of practice/research and health/pathology in transactional analysis.

The Contact Cube emphasises personalised roles as behaviour derived from expectations of *self* and *others*, but says little about behaviour based upon expectations of *situations*. In order to illustrate how formalised roles, (as expected behaviours relative to situations) may be mapped onto personalised roles I use the notion of *Significant Incidents.* A Significant Incident is a participant observer's account of a particular situation. Thus this Chapter consists of various participant observer **Scenarios**, interspersed with a discursive account of:

- the nature of task and process variables in social interaction,
- ways in which power, influence and authority have a bearing on our expectations of situations and ultimately, our relationships.

Social interaction.

The addition of formalised roles to the personalised roles described so far highlights sociological processes common to all societies. Social interaction or relationships is one such process; a self-evident feature of all societies. The term denotes the reciprocal influencing of the acts of individuals and groups, usually mediated through communication.

Communication itself may be regarded as the activation of more or less enduring patterns of relationships. For example, every member of the International Transactional Analysis Association (ITAA) has a formalised role relationship with the President of the ITAA that is activated when some or other form of communication occurs. I describe these role relations as "formalised" because the two roles - "President" and "member" – exist within the ITAA as a set of codified expectations required of the role incumbents. That is, there is a written job description for the position of President and various articles of the ITAA's constitution spell out the requirements, rights, responsibilities and so forth of a member of the ITAA. Hence expectations at the formalised level always exist and do not depend on communication and by extension, contact. I refer to these as *generalised* expectations. Specific expectations and personalised roles on the other hand, come into play when the President communicates with a member. He or she does so in terms of two sets of expectations – his/her interpretation of those enshrined in the ITAA's statutes and those that emerge behaviourally as personalised roles in relation to the situation. In other words the President's behaviour may be described in relation to a role at two levels – expected or formalised and actual or personalised.

Have you ever met someone for the first time, chatted to them for a while and then discovered that their formalised role is important in some respect in one of the networks in your role imago repertoire? For example, say you are at a party having a lively conversation about a TV programme on legalising cannabis, and the person to whom you are talking turns out to be a doctor. If "doctors" feature significantly in your role imago repertoire, you are likely to be influenced by the new information. Even if members of the medical profession do not figure in your repertoire of roles, and for the purposes of illustration, assuming you are not medically qualified, the news that you are talking to someone who is likely to be more knowledgeable than you is bound to influence the subsequent conversation. Furthermore, the fact that the formalised role of a doctor has connotations of knowledge and the power to heal that have been institutionally legitimated in most, if not all, societies, may well influence your interaction with the person at the party – who also happens to be a doctor. In other words, knowing what a person's formalised role is in one setting will often have a bearing on your perception of them in another completely different setting. Knowledge of formalised roles as well as experience of personalised roles has a significant effect on behaviour

Berne addresses the ways in which we change our perceptions of people as we get to know more about them; he refers to this phenomenon as the group imago, which he defines as:

> "Any mental picture, conscious, preconscious or unconscious, of what a group is like or should be like". (Berne 1963 p 244)

His later definition:

> "a mental image of the dynamic relationship between the people in the group, including the therapist; idiosyncratic for each person present". (Berne 1966 p. 364)

This makes it clear that he is referring to "mental images" held by individuals within the context of a particular group. He continues to explain how the "images" held by individuals change as people get to know others in a group. First is the *provisional* imago – a view of a fantasised group based on previous experience of similar groups or situations - that is conjured up in anticipation of the group. At this point, an individual will have expectations of self, someone in a leadership role and a host of undifferentiated others who are likely to be in the group. Upon actually joining a group an individual forms an *adjusted* imago. Others become more differentiated according to whatever criteria are applied by the individual and specific expectations come into line with the 'reality' of the situation. The next stage of imago development is based on the extent to which the individual thinks he or she knows his or her place in the group leader's imago; Berne refers to this as the *operative* imago. The final stage of imago adjustment is the *secondarily adjusted* imago. This is characterised by the individual giving up aspects of his original imago and settling for the norms of the group.

Clarkson (1991) and Tudor (1999) draw attention to group leader roles at various stages of imago development. They show that the better an individual knows others, the more differentiated are their imagos, and hence, relationships. The process of getting to know others occurs within the context of one or more situations, and usually, over a period of time.

I have extended this idea by following Massey's comments; he gives a systems perspective on the way in which a group imago "serves as a bridge between the psychological and social-structural dimensions of therapy with individuals". (Massey 1995 p.271) He states that:

> "Humans develop *expectations* about self through ego states and script. These *expectations* are remembered and become the bases for relating from the time an infant develops the cognitive capacities of emotional object constancy and distinguishes familiar figures from strangers who evoke anxiety (Bower, 1977; Mahler, Pine and Bergman, 1975; Piaget, 1963). As the youngster bonds with significant others and as maturing individuals form attachments, a group-imago of one's intimate in-group evolves. The portrayal of *expectations* about others in a group imago provides a cognitive map or a set of anticipations that frequently become actualised in subsequent

relationships. A group imago represents a higher level of abstraction than do ego states, for a group imago embodies a *blueprint* for interperception, interexperience, and the interaction with significant others". (Massey, 1995 p. 279: my italics)

As indicated by my italics, Massey is implying that a group imago is a "blueprint" for expectations about social interaction. Thus, linking formalised roles and personalised roles offers a researcher a method of analysing ways in which roles are enacted reciprocally in relation to the *congruence* between expected and actual behaviour of individuals - not just in a therapy group, but in *all* situations. When formalised roles are activated by communication and personalised roles become operative, what I have termed "social interaction" ensues. Social interaction – and hence, relationships - may be seen as a dynamic pattern of relationships that constitutes the basis of societies, crowds, organisations, groups and dyads.

Social organisation

In social science usage, the term "organisation" or "social organisation" denotes the relatively enduring set of interrelations among component parts (relationships between individuals or groups) that results in *characteristics not present in the components and produces an entity in its own right.* The italicised words in the previous sentence may be equated with what in the psychoanalytic literature on groups is referred to as "the group-as-a-whole".

Although Berne (1963) gave a comprehensive scheme for categorising "social aggregations", the major blind spots in his analysis of groups and organisations are firstly, that he appears to regard "group authority" as stemming from only two sources – the leadership and the canon (Berne 1963 p.105). Secondly, Berne does not explore fully an important aspect of organisations – *the group-as-a-whole.* He writes about individuals in the context of the group-as-a-whole, (Berne 1963, p. 53-54) and initially, seems to spell out the connotations of the phrase.

"First there should be a model of the group-as-a-whole and then one of the individual personality. This makes it possible to consider the interplay between them: what such an ideal group does to the personality, and what such ideal personalities do in and to the group.... Such a theory helps to avoid errors in organization and in administrative procedures, to increase the effectiveness of group activities and to treat ailing groups and organizations. It makes it possible to predict to some extent what will happen to certain people in certain groups and what will happen to the group-as-a-whole. For instance, it offers a formula for predicting which patients will withdraw from psychotherapy groups". (Berne 1963, pp. 53-45)

In the psychoanalytic literature on groups, the phrase 'the group-as-a-whole' comes from the Gestalt idea that the sum of the parts is greater than the whole. Agazarian and Peters (1981) invoke Lewin to make the point that

"The whole is not 'more' than the sum of its parts, but it has different properties. This statement should be: The whole is different from the sum of its parts. In other words, there does not exist a superiority of value of the whole. Both whole and parts are equally real... the whole has definitive properties of its own". (Lewin, 1951 p. 146)

The common ground between the view that the sum of the parts is greater than the whole and the idea that the whole is different from the sum of its parts is that the whole has definitive properties of its own. We can see this in relation to roles by breaking down the definition of roles into expectations.

Expectations and imagos

The Contact Cube describes personalised roles largely in relation to the expectations of self and others- but not explicitly in relation to the expectations of situations. Adding formalised roles generally shifts the focus of our expectations in the direction of a group or an organisation. This is implicit in Berne's definitions of a group and various types of group structure:

> "A group may be defined as any social aggregation that has an external boundary and at least one internal boundary...the external boundary distinguishes between members and non members... the major internal boundary signifies that there are at least two classes of people in the group, the leadership and the membership. The organizational structure of a group is based on its constitution, the individual structure is made up of personnel who occupy the organizational structure at a given moment and the private structure is based on the personal feelings of each member". (Berne 1963, pp. 54–64)

He makes a further distinction by combining organisational and individual structures as the public structure and retains the group imago as an aspect of the private structure.

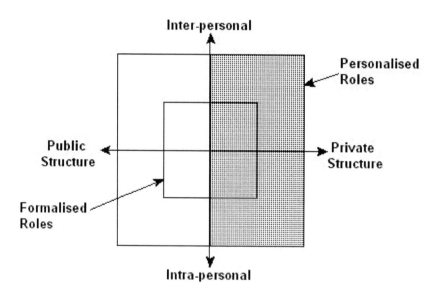

Figure 11.1

Figure 11.1 shows how formalised and personalised roles may be mapped onto Berne's description of structure. Formalised roles are represented by the small square, and personalised roles are shown as the larger outer square. The shaded portion of **Figure 11.1** is equivalent to Berne's group imago – which he designated as belonging to the private structure of a group. Each type of role operates in both the public and the private structure of a group. The intra-/inter-personal dimensions of behaviour are also associated with expectations. There are generalised expectations and specific expectations. The former are reminiscent of what Berne seems to have had in mind in describing the provisional group imago. As such, generalised expectations are usually intra-psychic phenomena often held out of conscious awareness. Specific or situational expectations are usually, but not always, inter-personal, and more amenable to direct observation, coming into play in later stages of group imago development

My choice of the term "role imago" attempts to capture both the formalised aspect of an individual's expected behaviour (Berne's public structure) and the personalised component derived from subjective expectations upon which role behaviours are based.

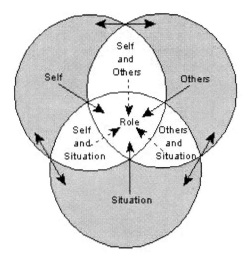

Figure 11.2

Examining the nature of expectations in more detail shows how they are linked with Berne's group imago and life positions. I diagram this process in **Figure 11.2** where the shaded areas represent generalised expectations. These are equivalent to Berne's provisional group imago. Such expectations are usually intra-psychic phenomena, often held out of conscious awareness. For example, if I am thinking of a family holiday my generalised expectations are likely to start with little more than something like "relaxation, fun with the kids, sometime this year". At this stage my personalised role at the social level will be Beholder, probably Responder at the psychological level and Valuer at the existential level. However all these expectations are relative – as indicated by the two-way arrows in **Figure 11.2**. That is, my expectations will combine roles, contact and relationships. In this case there is no actual contact with others, and although the situation is generalised the context includes my existing family relationships.

Considering the relativity of all these factors, you will recall that life positions embody values and beliefs about one's self and others that are used to justify decisions and behaviour. An existential life position:

"gives expression to one's attitude and beliefs.." (Barnes 1981 p. 26).

Thus imagos and life positions are included in generalised expectations and will have a bearing on my role behaviour. This is particularly important in clinical work and sometimes problematic in an organisational setting where the nature of a facilitator's contract with a group may not extend to dealing with intra-psychic phenomena; identifying Contact Cube roles offers a way around such issues.

When my wife and I discuss the topic (the single headed arrows in **Figure 11.2**) my expectations will probably extend to reminiscing about previous holidays, considering locations, costs and possible dates – all of which are still generalised. Behaviourally, my personalised role is likely to change to Responder or Announcer at the social level, Valuer at the psychological level and Beholder at the existential level.

Differentiating between generalised and specific expectations involves a move from past experience of a general class of events ("holidays") to consideration of a particular present, or proposed, event. Thus my generalised expectations become more refined as they veer towards specific expectations – as indicated by the dashed arrows emanating from each of the three outer non-shaded areas pointing to the central "Role" area in **Figure 11.2**. I am discussing my specific expectations of myself in relation to specific others and an increasingly specific situation. For example, my expectations of self, others and the situation may be influenced by considerations such "I'd (self) quite like a skiing holiday this year (situation) because one of the kids (others) has never been skiing before" (others and situation). Nevertheless the generalised expectations still remain as a backdrop to the current discussion.

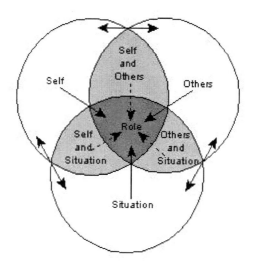

Figure 11.3

As the time of the holiday approaches my imago becomes more differentiated, and correspondingly, the more specific are my expectations – booking accommodation, making travel arrangements, ordering foreign currency and so forth. Although this is still within the bounds of Berne's provisional imago, my initial generalised expectations recede. In Gestalt terms they become the ground to the figure of my specific expectations as illustrated in the shaded areas of **Figure 11.3**

Changes in expectations and the idea of the group-as-a-whole are illustrated in **Scenario 11.1**. The story line in italics is interspersed with process comments (sometimes enclosed in square brackets) illustrating my changing expectations:

Scenario 11.1

I and my family decide on a skiing holiday in the Pyrenees. We have signed up for a two-week package with a company that has just opened a new resort in a hitherto unknown location. We check in at the airport and board the plane in the usual manner. The flight is largely uneventful, but by the time we arrive at an international airport in the south of France, my provisional imago has started to undergo adjustment. During the fight, I discern that not everyone is embarking on a skiing holiday. This is not unduly surprising and, although I had not given this much thought, I realise that I had previously assumed that everyone on the flight would be going skiing.

We are greeted at the airport by "Ski Guides" dressed in the ski company's livery, holding placards announcing "PyrenSki Tours - Check In Here". I had not anticipated this, but again, was not surprised.

The Ski Guides check off names and direct people to two waiting coaches. Note however that my expectations of the situation are now significantly differentiated. In terms of Berne's definitions, the **mass** of people at the airport changes to a **crowd.** [To Berne, a **mass** is "structureless congeries in which no member can predict with any degree of certainty to what class of people his neighbours at any given moment will belong" (Berne 1963, p. 246) and a **crowd** is "an aggregation with no external boundary but with a certain degree of predictability" (Berne 1963, p. 239). An **aggregation** in turn is "any collection of more than two people occupying a stated space" (Berne 1963, p. 238). A **group** is "a social aggregation that has an external boundary and at least one internal boundary" (Berne 1963, p.243), while a **boundary** is a "constitutional psychological or spatial distinction between different classes of membership – an **internal boundary** – or between members and non-members – the **external boundary**" (Berne 1963, p.238). In Berne's terms, the Ski Guides' directing people to the coaches is an example of the group's **external apparatus –** "the organ which deals with the external environment so as to minimise the threat of external pressure. Typically, it comprises procurement [as in this case] preventive and combat branches". (Berne 1963, p.238) In relation to my repertoire of roles, two formalised roles – the skiers and the Ski Guides - have been added to my active network.]

Significant Incidents and the group-as-a-whole

This Scenario clearly demonstrates that the adjusted imago emerges as soon as I am in situ. This may take a variety of forms but generally changes in expectations occur in all three areas – self, others and the situation. In ERICA, this material is elicited via the use of a *Significant Incident*.

A "Significant Incident" is an individual's perception of a situation. For the purpose of analysis the individual is called the "focal person". The term carries with it the pre-supposition that the "incident" is "significant" as defined by the focal person. The minimum requirements of a Significant Incident are a description by a focal person of an event or series of events that will enable a researcher/observer to identify formalised and personalised roles. Ideally, the description will provide sufficient information for a researcher to be able to relate the situation to a context, and discern or hypothesise about the goals of those involved and the likely outcome of the situation. Despite highly individualised descriptions of situations, it is possible to categorise Significant Incidents according to their outcomes. The rationale of this process may be illustrated briefly by reference to the following *Scenario*; numerals in brackets will facilitate subsequent discussion:

Scenario 11.2

Upon arrival at the ski location, it soon emerges that the facilities fall somewhat short of everyone's expectations (1). The shortfall mainly relates to two complaints – accommodation that is different to that which was advertised, paid for and, hence, expected and insufficient ski instructors (2) for those who had signed up for tuition, and had expected individual lessons everyday for a week. The first of these issues is apparent during the process of checking in and being allocated to rooms in the newly built hotel. The second problem emerges as people consult the roster of events scheduled for the next day. At first people attempt to deal with these complaints individually by berating (3) the hotel staff (4) and demanding (5) that the Chief Ski Instructor (4) reorganise (5) the roster to provide what is rightly expected. For a while, confusion seems to reign (6); some people (7) attempt to negotiate deals that are in line with what they have paid, (8) while others (9) seem to accept what is on offer (10). Some of us (11), my family included, have only signed up for the basic package – which specified no more than the cost of travel, accommodation, meals and hire of ski equipment, without the frills of en-suite rooms, excursions and instruction.

Eventually the Hotel Manager (8) calls everyone together (13) and apologises for the obvious dissatisfaction (14) of his guests (15). He explains that the hotel has only just been built and that we are the first group of holidaymakers (17) to use the facilities offered by the hotel and the Pyrenski tour operator (18). In the light of the many complaints he has taken the "liberty" of arranging for a Director of Pyrenski (19) to fly in from Barcelona and meet anyone (20) who is dissatisfied (21) at 10 a.m. the next day. Several people attempt to get the Hotel Manager (8.2) to commit to various demands in advance of the proposed meeting, but he deftly explains that he is not in a position to do so. He points out that the hotel has been asked to provide so many rooms at such and such a rate, and this they have done. He assures us that it is "obviously" in everyone's interest to find a solution "so you can all enjoy your holiday" (13). The meeting ends with most people adopting a "wait and see" attitude (14), some muttering about "passing the buck" (15) and one man spending considerable time during the rest of the evening on his mobile phone talking to his legal advisor (16).

Out of curiosity, I elect to attend the meeting while my family go off to hire equipment and explore the nursery slopes. The Director (19.2) arrives and gives a polished performance. He has an imposing appearance, speaks good English, and uses humour in a disarming way to defuse the anger behind the many complaints. He listens attentively to individuals, acknowledges the validity of the complaints, and expresses disappointment at his company's performance. He adds that he has not come with "hands that are empty". He offers full compensation for anyone who wants to return home immediately, a ten percent reduction for everyone and the assurance that by the next day, he will have arranged for two more ski instructors (2.2) to be flown in from another resort in the Alps. Most of the guests seem convinced (25), one or two are still disgruntled (26) but seem unable to find good reason for their dissatisfaction (27). The meeting is about to break up when a quietly spoken man (28) engages the Director (19.3) in a series of questions about compensation, Pyrenski's insurance cover, membership of the International Tour Operators Association and so on. The man speaks with authority and obviously knows the travel business. The Director (19.4) replies politely and answers all the questions briefly yet seemingly satisfactorily. The man (28.2) then turns to us (29) and explains that he is not personally affected by the disparity between what he's got and what he'd signed up for, but does not "fancy spending two weeks with a bunch of dissatisfied people." (30) He reckons he has something to contribute as he is in the travel business. He (28.3) is now satisfied that the Director's (19.5) offers are in fact, more than would be legally required under the circumstances, and although Pyrenski will lose money in the short term, the Director (19.6) is offering a win-win solution. One woman accuses him of being "in league with Pyrenski" and asks: "why should we believe you?" The man (28.4) shrugs and replies "Madam I guess maybe you'll find no reasons to believe me. Personally, I'm satisfied enough to accept ten percent and look forward to enjoying the company and the skiing." The Director (19.7) smiles, but remains silent. (32)

The next day two new Ski Instructors (2.3) arrive. No one accepts the full compensation offer, but over the next few days several people consult the travel agent (28.5) who spoke up at the meeting; he seems to give satisfactory assurances. After three more days everyone seems to have forgotten the potentially disastrous start of the holiday. The weather is ideal and the skiing is as good as anywhere else on the continent. The hotel is cosy, the staff are friendly and helpful and several sub-groups form among the guests. Two days before the end of the holiday the Director (19.8) returns unannounced to "make sure you all had good skiing." He circulates among the guests, offering a five percent reduction on the price of next season's tour. At least ten of the eighty or so guests accept the offer.

The Scenario accelerates us through all the remaining stages of imago development. Everyone had to make a major adjustment to his or her provisional imagos. The circumstances were such that the common plight for those most disconcerted took them rapidly into the operative phase of imago development (Berne 1963, p.164). In terms of personalised roles, they became proactive and the quality of contact was compelling, matching the behaviour of guests and hotel staff haggling over their contractual agreements. In Linton's terms they were enacting "the dynamic aspect of a status" which he defines as "a collection of rights and obligations" (Linton 1934, pp. 113-4). Those of us who were not affected by room allocation or instructor availability, were strongly compelled by the situation to adopt inactive Beholder personalised roles, with a corresponding co-existent quality of contact and hence, relationships with those who were more proactive. Our formalised roles as "satisfied guests" differentiated us from the "dissatisfied guests". The Hotel Manager (a formalised role) temporarily filled the leadership slot.

In **Scenario11.2**, I was the focal person and the situation described related to the context of a skiing holiday. We saw that there were formalised roles of satisfied and dissatisfied guests, the Hotel Manager, the Director, the man in the travel business and so on. Although we do not have details of the personalised roles enacted at various times by most of the individuals we can reasonably assume that the outcome of the incidents was positive for all concerned. That is, everyone seems to have attained or moved towards their presumed goals – an enjoyable holiday for the guests and good business for Pyrenski Tours and the hotel. **Scenario 11.2** provides a researcher with a good Significant Incident – a clear sequential account of events, identifiable formalised roles and indications of the personalised roles enacted.

Significant Incidents are merely a heuristic device – a means of procuring a clients' perception of a situation. But clarifying the notion of the group-as-a-whole requires more to than simply having a way of categorising the outcomes of Significant Incidents. Critical data about the group-as-a-whole is contained within or may be inferred from a well-written or narrated Significant Incident. Identifying such data requires consideration of three factors:

- the availability of roles in the situation and the function of the roles enacted at particular times in any situation or group,

- a theoretical model of group process, held or adopted by the researcher, and probably shared by some of the participants in the group or situation and,
- a schema for understanding power and influence.

Availability of roles and role functions

By "availability of roles" I mean the personalised roles that arise in or are "created by" a situation that invite, compel or require individuals to act in certain ways in order for the group to survive and attain its goals. To illustrate, in *Scenario 11.2* at point 13 the Hotel Manager assumed leadership of the situation. Later the Director took charge. Their status implied a "collection of right and duties" (Linton 1934), and was such that the guests expected them to enact "the dynamic aspects of a status", or what I refer to as formalised roles. Not unreasonably, the hotel guests assumed that the roles conferred by the positions of Director and Hotel Manager in the respective organisations carried with them access to or control of resources to which the guests regarded themselves as being contractually entitled. Resolution of the problem "required" the Director and Hotel Manager to fulfil the guests' expectations of their formalised roles; both did so by adopting positive proactive and responsive personalised roles.

Another example from point 11 of *Scenario 11.2* is that those who were not engaged in the melee of people attempting to get the rooms they were expecting, were "invited" or "compelled" to adopt Bystander or Beholder personalised roles, at least while waiting for the hotel staff to deal with the dissatisfied guests. Conceivably, the Beholders/Bystanders, at any time, could have became more assertive instead of waiting for their turn to be allocated to their rooms. Those who did wait and were allocated to rooms about which they had no particular expectations – or were not affected by the roster of skiing lessons – need not have attended the meeting with the Director but did so out of curiosity or because they had a wider agenda. For example, the man in the travel business who questioned the Director (point 28), was, in fact, a satisfied guest who we can assume had been happy to remain a social level Beholder until he had heard the Director's proposed solution. He then switched to a proactive role to check out the Director's offer, because he did not relish the prospect of spending two weeks with a "bunch of dis-satisfied people". The man further demonstrated the potency of his announcement by parrying the woman's accusation and role modelling his willingness to accept the Director's offer.

We can understand all this behaviour in terms of the Contact Cube roles adopted by various individuals. However from the perspective of the group process, the consequence or role function of the man's questioning the Director and responding to the woman was that most people – the group-as-a-whole - were satisfied. This is a somewhat literal view of the idea of the group-as-a-whole – implying "everyone in the group". A more integral perspective may be gleaned by considering task and process variables in a group.

Group process

Group process is a general term that refers to how people in a group are getting on together - how they do things together rather than what they do. These two aspects of group behaviour are often termed process and task variables. Groups and group leaders need to pay attention to the balance between these variables. Too much emphasis on the task carries the danger of "getting the job done", at the expense of "getting on with people". Reversing the emphasis often results in workers paying more attention to colleague relations than producing goods or providing a service. In TA the term "group process" is accorded a special meaning:

"The conflicts of forces resulting from attempts to disrupt, disorganize or modify the structure of a group. The **external group process** results from conflicts between external pressure and the group cohesion and takes place at the external boundary. The **major internal group process** results from conflicts between individual proclivities and the group cohesion as represented by the leadership and takes place at the major internal boundary. The **minor internal group process** results from conflicts between individual proclivities and takes place at the minor internal boundaries". (Berne 1963, p.244)

I have taken the view that allowing for differences in the nature of a group's task, process variables are relevant to *all* situations – and not just groups and organisations. That is, even in situations where the task is ill-defined and no group as such exists, may not form, or has yet to form, group process will still apply. What this means in practice is that groups or, more correctly, a collection of individuals, have to go through various stages of development before they become a group capable of attaining an optimal balance between task and process variables. The original idea stems from the work of Bion (1959) who postulated that a group could be regarded as either a "work group" when it was pursuing its primary task or a "basic assumption group" when it was not. By a "basic assumption group" Bion means that at times group members appear to share three types of emotional states that detract from the pursuit of group goals: these assumed emotions lead to behaviour that coalesce around pairing or forming sub-groups, dependency (on the group leader to make things happen) and the motif of fight or flight. Berne was aware of Bion's work (Berne 1963, pp. 212-215), but seems open minded about the usefulness of Bion's ideas:

"It remains to be seen whether the things Bion describes are always present in every group, or whether they only occur occasionally or in special kinds of groups: i.e. whether they are obligatory or incidental". (Berne 1963, p. 215)

Surprisingly, Berne does not refer to Bennis and Shepard (1956). They built on Bion's ideas and concluded that groups follow a sequence of development from their inception to their maturity. This process is in two parts – a phase featuring dependence and power relationships, and a second phase where interdependence and personal relationships predominate. Bennis and Shepard's model enables them to predict the behaviour of various types of individuals ("dependents", "counterdependents", "overpersonals" and "counterpersonals"), in relation to the phase of group development. If Berne had known about Bennis and Shepard's work he could have elaborated his description of a group imago to include the differentiation implicit in Bion's basic assumptions: namely that different types of people (dependents, counterdependents and so on), will pair or fight or take flight because they have made differentiations about each other at an unconscious level. I suspect that either Berne was not aware of Bennis and Shepard's findings, or simply chose to ignore them. Had he taken them on board, he would have been faced with the problem of accommodating unconscious process variables within the TA model.

Bennis and Shepard's sophisticated model was subsequently revived by Agazarian and Peters (1981), who incorporate systems theory concepts to complement their psychoanalytic framework. They make extensive use of the idea of the group-as-a-whole explaining that a group therapist needs to work at two levels. At one level, he or she must use inductive reasoning to argue from the particular to the general, and at the other level, the reasoning is deductive – from the general to the particular.

Psychoanalytic therapists place far more emphasis than do TA therapists on interventions intended to raise awareness of group process (Kapur and Miller 1987). Their end is therapy of the group; the means to this end is to progressively facilitate group members' working through defences associated with various phases of group development.

In most TA therapy groups the emphasis is on using the interaction between group members to achieve individual change. The means to this end is therapy through the group or, in some cases, therapy of individuals conducted in a group setting. Nevertheless, the TA model does take account of role functions as indicated by Clarkson's inclusion of "constructive" and "destructive" behaviours characteristic of each stage of imago development, and her emphasis on the leadership tasks at various stages of group development (Clarkson 1992 pp. 210-224) The distinction between roles as the observable behaviour of individuals and role functions as the consequences of such behaviour, is crucial not only to appreciating the significance of the formalised role of group leader (therapist/consultant/facilitator), but also to understanding the situational aspects of Contact Cube roles. That is, Contact Cube roles are behaviours based not only on our expectations of self and others, but also relative to our expectations of the situation in which the behaviours are enacted. In other words, Contact Cube roles describe roles *and* role functions. Thus, learning about Contact Cube roles in a group is a progressive process of mentoring that encourages clients to take responsibility for moving from negative to positive personalised roles. The relevance of the group imago to this process is that there are optimal stages of imago development for introducing and using Contact Cube roles explicitly as a means of teaching and heightening awareness of group process, as well as focusing on the attainment of individual goals.

All these accounts of group process constitute the theory of group development which I referred to above and that may be discerned by considering process variables. The group-as-a-whole is a particular example of process variables that Berne mentions, but does not fully develop. Although he makes it clear that imagos change in a predictable fashion, he does not explicitly emphasise the power struggles that arise during the various stages of group development.

While Berne's view of authority and likewise Clarkson's important description of leadership tasks are relevant to the structure and dynamics of groups and most organisations, they do not seem sufficient to account for the dynamics of all situations and particularly those where no leadership exists or is perceived to exist, and/or where there are no clearly stated or agreed goals. Understanding the availability of roles and group process enables us to use Significant Incidents to address the relevance of roles to relationships and in so doing, redress Berne's failure to examine critically the inter-relationship between power, influence and authority.

Power, influence and authority

Apart from the fact that Berne underplayed power as a variable in his analysis of groups and organisations, the topic has received a somewhat negative press in transactional analysis circles (Steiner 1974, 1981). Subsequent articles by Steiner (1987), Jacobs (1987) and English (1987) heralded a more extended account of power than Steiner's earlier work but, in my view, still tell only half the story.

Massey gives a glimpse of the other half of the story by contrasting Jacobs' historical analysis of autocratic power with a spectrum of power (May 1972) and in particular, the power to be which "encourages autonomy, intimacy and responsibility" (Massey 1987, p. 118). Massey's article lays the foundations for transforming TA as a "social psychiatry" (Berne 1964, p. 51) into a social psychology that "examines the interconnecting of persons and social structures" (Massey 1987, p. 108).

Inspired by Massey's comments what follows is derived from French and Raven (1959) and Handy (1976), I have amended their ideas to accommodate my own experience of small, large group, organisational and networking settings.

In the Contact Cube *power* is the ability to influence others. *Influence* is the process whereby one person modifies their behaviour in response to, or as a result of, the behaviour of another person, persons or the situation. There are various sources of power and different methods of influence. I discuss each of these definitions and categories in their own right but in doing so will cross-refer to the others. The inter-relationship between sources of power, methods of influence, modes of adaptation, likely outcomes and authority is outlined in **Table 11.1**.

Power source	Personal (personalised roles)		Resources domain/relevance/balance/ access/competence			Formalised roles Primary Secondary		
	Choice of role	Con-gruence	Physical	Material	Invisible	Social	Relational	Occupat ional
Methods of Influence	Persuasion based on use of positive roles Rhetoric based on use of negative roles		Age Gender Ethnicity Presentation Transactions Stroking Force	Exchange Environmental Negotiation Image Contractual		Cultural/social norms, culture, rules & procedures, information, networking access, social mobility, expertise		
Individual adaptation via process of	Leadership, role modelling, mentoring, counselling, therapy supervision, apprenticeship		Socialisation mortification	Reporting, monitoring, appraisal, mediation, arbitration, working to rule, official or wildcat strikes		Legal statutes, education training co-option promotion qualification, ethics complaints and grievance procedures, continuous professional development		
Likely outcomes	Identification		Adaptation/compliance			Internalisation		
Authority	A mode of securing assent among a group of people about behaviour in a particular situation relative to their goals; depends on congruence between power sources and use of appropriate method(s) of influence.							

Table 11.1

In the Contact Cube, influence is a multi-directional process. However, there is a subtle yet crucial difference between the *capacity* and the *ability* to influence others. Everyone has the capacity to influence others. In fact, no one has any choice about the matter. We all influence each other all the time. I believe that this is primarily an energetic process that mostly occurs beyond our conscious awareness; English gives an interesting account of how we are all influenced by three basic "drives" (English 1987, pp, 91-95).

In the Contact Cube, our capacity to influence and be influenced is significantly increased by learning how to use personalised roles; influence is latent, becoming manifest only when a personalised role is enacted. Personalised roles stem from personal power but are always underpinned by resources and formalised roles. It is this connection that takes the Contact Cube beyond a social psychiatry of intra- and inter-personal processes. Personalised roles alone do not fully bridge the gap between people and social structures in a way that would be useful to practitioners for whom consideration of group, inter-group and organisational dynamics are as important as individual proclivities.

The underlying logic of **Table 11.1** is that the three columns - *Personal* (personalised roles), *Resources* (domain / relevance / balance / access / competence) and *Formalised* roles - represent a way of thinking about power and influence – a matrix of inter-related factors. Although I explain the contents of each cell, my comments about any particular cell should not be seen in isolation. Change results from the activation of all three sources of power, in conjunction with one or more appropriate methods of influence. In other words, your ability to influence depends in the first place on your personalised role plus your resources plus your formalised role, together with whatever methods of influence you choose. Secondly, you have to take account of your situation – the context in which you are operating and the desired, or the likely, outcomes.

Before discussing each of the cells in **Table 11.1**, it should be noted that the framework gives no more than a conceptual overview of power, influence and authority – thereby linking the Contact Cube to organisational and social structures. The wider implication is that the application of these factors – the *tactics* involved in the use of power, influence and authority – that constitute the bread and butter of organisational development, are topics beyond the scope of this book.

Personalised roles

Taking the first of the power sources and methods of influence it should be noted that, although personalised roles invite a response from another person, an observer cannot definitively attribute causality to either. The roles are so defined that they reciprocally influence each other and "causality" becomes circular. It is in this sense that I say personalised roles imply a capacity to influence others. I would hasten to add that the definitions or descriptions of role behaviours are based on observations. This is not to say that individuals do not have a choice in the matter. Choice arises from the "self-transcending cognition" (Massey 1987 p. 111) of the Observer role. Indeed the entire point of the Contact Cube is that we do have choices about which personalised role we adopt. Choosing positive Square roles depends on our level or degree of autonomy and potentially transforms our capacity to influence into the ability to influence positively, which hopefully is congruent with the expectations of a formalised role. I say "hopefully", because for the use of power to be positive there needs to be sufficient and sometimes widespread public agreement about an appropriate role choice that ensures, or is based on congruence between a formalised role and the enactment of personalised roles. For example, you will recall from *Scenario 11.2* that the Director of the Pyrenski tour company dealt with the dissatisfied guests by enacting proactive personalised roles that were congruent with his formalised role, and the guests' expectation that he had the resources to back up his promises. His methods of influence were a combination of persuasion and negotiation. His use of power sources together with the methods of influence gave him considerable authority – a topic to which we will return later.

Persuasion

The method of influence that most often accompanies a personal power source is persuasion – information and (usually) argument based on facts supported by evidence. How information is presented will depend on which personalised roles are in play at all three levels. Autocratic leaders seldom use persuasion as defined above, tending to favour rhetoric based on propaganda along with negative Square personalised roles. However, even democratically elected leaders have problems with persuasion as a method influence, not least because the recipients are always cognisant of the leader's formalised role. Hence, decisions arising from genuine inter-personal exchanges based on rational discussion are often contaminated by a subordinate's awareness of the boss' position in an organisation, or even the need to use appropriate rules and procedures to implement the decision.

A double-edged feature of persuasion is that its use often leads to a recipient identifying with the source of influence. Indeed, the more potent the use of personalised roles, the greater the tendency for others to identify with the person – rather than the role. The role modelling that occurs as part of mentoring, counselling and psychotherapy will often lead to recipients identifying with the role model. The downside of this process is that influence leading to identification needs to be continuously maintained. Clinicians are familiar with this process as counter-script cure. The client makes changes in response to the therapist's interventions that counter unhelpful or self-limiting script messages, but until the new messages are internalised, reinforcement is usually necessary. In an organisational context, effective persuasion is often bolstered by apprenticeship leading to identification with an individual, task or group and sometimes, in turn, the need for project management. Effective as persuasion can be, identification is not self-maintaining. Contractual training in transactional analysis is an example of how an organisation seeks to ensure that values and skills are imparted; individuals are inducted into the norms of good practice but even after qualification regular supervision and 'continuous professional development' are considered necessary.

Resources
Attempts to influence others are seldom effective without resources. Examples spring readily to mind. The United Nations Organisation makes resolutions that are binding on member nations – but because UNO lack resources, resolutions cannot be enforced in cases where states choose to ignore them. Central governments pass legislation that requires implementation by local government, who plead lack of resources to do so. In commercial organisations, launching a new product requires appropriate investment in research and development, market research, advertising and so forth. The same principle applies at a more abstract level; if you are going to use roles to influence others, roles need to be accompanied by resources.

Broadly speaking, resources are anything required for implementing a role. However your resources have to be relevant to the issue in hand and valid in the domain in question. For example, if you want something when travelling in a foreign country, you would probably assume you could obtain it by exchanging money (the assumed relevant resource) for whatever it is you want. If this were the case, the money you tender would have to be a valid currency in the particular country (the domain). US dollars are valid currency in most parts of the world, but probably not worth much in a remote village in Madagascar. Alternatively, you may get a lot further in the village in Madagascar by offering a resource of different relevance - such as some other commodity or particular expertise that is in demand. Relevance and domain are obviously connected. If you go for a meal in a restaurant in provincial China, but don't speak Chinese, your ability to communicate with the waiter is likely to be restricted to non-verbal gestures – you would be lacking an essential relevant resource in that particular domain. Again, if you were applying for a job that specified "previous experience of such-and-such essential" and you had no experience of whatever such-and-such was, but had extensive experience in some related field, your power, your ability to influence, would be diminished and you would obviously have to couch your application in terms that you judge would sufficiently impress the prospective employer to grant you an interview. Here the balance of resources favours the employer; you want the job, but don't have the relevant resources that the domain requires. In the commercial field, another common strategy is to enlarge the domain by, for example, diversifying a product range, sources of outlet, or within a company, increasing a manager's span of control over products or personnel. In all cases, the balance of power is a cogent factor. A trade union, fearful of future redundancies, may object to a proposal to merge two departments accountable to one manager instead of two. The relevance of resources in any domain is always relative to a balance between who brings or wants what from the situation. As we shall see later, balance is a crucial variable when we consider issues of authority.

Over and above the variables of domain, relevance, and balance, you need the self-evident facility of access to whomsoever you are seeking to influence, and the competence to deliver whatever is on offer. Competence in this context means control of resources and whatever logistics or skills are required to deploy them. Examples of competence and access range from negotiating with terrorists who have hijacked a plane, to advertising products or services, circumventing bureaucratic channels to communicating directly with the right person and, ideally, face to face conversation with whomever you are seeking to influence.

Table 11.1 divides resources into three categories. As a way of thinking about power and influence rather than a matrix of watertight definitions, these categories have somewhat fuzzy boundaries. For example, there is an obvious overlap between resources that are physical and those that are material. The positioning of the three headings is of more significance than any precise definitions. That is, physical resources are listed nearest to personalised roles, implying that the impact of personal power relies more on the immediacy of physical resources than it does on material or invisible resources.

The methods of influence that fall under the heading of physical resources comprise factors such as age, gender, ethnicity and general presentation of self (Goffman 1959), whether in person, or via the media. While age and gender as methods of influence seem so self-evident and hence, scarcely worth mentioning, they are particularly significant in some situations. For example, when adults and children interact there are usually significant disparities of physical appearance, size, strength and level of energy. Pigmentation and dress are often the most immediate and obvious indicators of ethnic differences, coming even before language or accent. Note that these factors need not be evaluative to constitute a method of influence – as illustrated by the example of your going for a meal in an area where you are clearly a foreigner. Communication skills or, in TA terms, effective use of transactions, goes along with stroking. A person's stroke profile (McKenna 1974) – their characteristic ways of giving, asking for, accepting and refusing to give strokes – is a simple yet powerful way of influencing and being influenced. Note that this may include sexual interchanges and other forms of physical contact. The use of force is the crudest form of influence, often with the most immediate short-term payoff. Furthermore, a perceived or actual threat of force is sometimes a potent source of influence – stalking, harassment in the workplace, picket lines and mass demonstrations all contain incipient elements of force. However, the threat or actual use of force is not necessarily a negative factor. For example, parents sometimes forcibly prevent children from running into a road, lifeguards drag drowning swimmers from the water and forcibly resuscitate them, and police are permitted to use "reasonable force" to arrest suspected criminals. At the other extreme, big kids bully younger ones, muggers forcibly deprive you of your wallet, dictators deprive citizens of their liberty or lives, terrorists blow up themselves and innocent bystanders, and armies invade other nations. Note that the examples require progressively increasing levels of force and collective action – which in turn, invoke the use of resources and appropriate use of formalised roles. Although resorting to force is usually a last ditch method of influencing others, it is often invoked by those who feel impotent in situations where other methods of influence are ineffective because of gross imbalances of resources. The other side of the coin is that there is a circular causality about force, inasmuch as those who lack resources may see the use of force to have been provoked by those who control resources.

Access to material and invisible resources applies to both formalised and personalised roles. The most usual method of influence is financial exchange for goods or services. This often involves negotiation that may go beyond material resources to include *quid pro quo* behaviours that form the basis of the general class of events referred to as contractual methods of influence. These would include, for example, treaties between nations, business partnerships and less formal agreements or social liaisons between two or more parties. The contractual method of influence may also apply in conjunction with exchange. Environmental methods of influence include attention to health and safety issues, provision of appropriate working conditions, seating arrangements for meetings, and any other factors that contribute towards congenial physical conditions. All behaviour takes place in an environment, and it is often easier to adjust the environment in the hope of influencing behaviour, than to directly attempt to influence behaviour itself. For example, a physical layout that increases interaction will permit people to get to know each other, to form non-task related bonds that not only contribute to job satisfaction, but also make routine tasks less onerous. Likewise, the use of small group discussion is more likely to engage participants than large group meetings or committees. Nowadays, most if not all organisations pay considerable attention to creating a corporate image – not only for their products but also their personnel. Examples range from entire departments devoted to PR, along with the appointment of advisors and spin doctors employed to put the right gloss on a company's performance, or post hoc interpretations of public announcements by executives. Creating a desired image applies equally to the choice of headed notepaper used by a psychotherapist in private practice.

Adaptation and alienation

The outcome of the physical categories of resources and their associated methods of influence can be positive or negative; I term these extremes adaptation and alienation respectively. Socialisation is the process whereby individuals adapt to the norms of a group in order to gain approval. Throughout all societies, parenting is the prime example of a positive outcome of socialisation. However, socialisation applies equally to adaptation to less prolonged participation in all manner of social groupings. Most organisations have a variety of socialisation processes for inducting newly appointed personnel. At the other end of the scale I use Goffman's term "mortification" (Goffman, 1968) to describe processes that strip individuals of their dignity and liberty, leading at least, to compliance, or to alienation and even death. Sadly, from time to time unwarranted use of physical force in penal institutions, psychiatric hospitals, boarding schools, the armed forces and other total institutions, leads to public outcry in democratic societies, but goes largely unnoticed in dictatorships. Information about arms stock piling, arsenals of weapons of mass destruction and the atrocities that accompany ethnic cleansing and genocide are consistently suppressed by dictators, until revealed by foreign journalists or intelligence services.

Socialisation extends to accountability for material and less visible use of resources achieved by various forms of reporting, monitoring and appraisal, which, under some circumstances, may be countered by working to rule, or threatened or actual strike action. Mediation or arbitration represent attempts to restore adaptation and avoid alienation.

Formalised roles

Relationships exist within a matrix of formalised roles. For instance, if asked to group your role relations you may chose categories such as "friends," "neighbours", "work colleagues", "bosses" and so forth. I call some of these *primary* formalised roles and others *secondary* formalised roles. We have expectations about all manner of social gatherings that are not only generalised, sometimes emerge from the situation, but also include expectations that are no different from prevailing social norms. For example, what are the expected behaviours of people on a bus? What are your expectations of your neighbours – and how do these differ from your expectations of your friends? All these examples fall into the class of formalised roles that I refer to as primary formalised roles. Primary formalised roles are the expected behaviours of people with whom we interact without reference to their connection to any particular organisation.

In the Contact Cube primary formalised roles are differentiated from secondary formalised roles by virtue of the fact that the latter are correlated with designations or positions within a group or organisation, and are relevant to your interaction. If, for example, I have an active network that I have designated "work colleagues", I may further categorise those in that network according to some or other additional criteria. Where such criteria reflect some or other aspect of group or organisational structure relevant to our interaction, we may talk of secondary formalised roles. French and Raven (1959) and most other writers on organisations, call these secondary formalised roles *positions*. The term accurately reflects not only a formalised role, but also its location in the organisational structure. I use the term "position" synonymously with "secondary formalised roles" when referring to groups or organisations that have clearly defined goals, a written constitution and a more or less permanent organisational structure. As we shall see, the distinction between primary and secondary formalised roles is useful when it comes to considering methods of influence.

Unless or until you know a person's formalised role, your interaction will be based on personalised roles – actual behaviour enacted in a particular situation. To illustrate, recall the example cited earlier about a conversation with a fellow partygoer about legalising cannabis. Until it emerged that the person was a doctor you would probably have categorised his/her formalised role in a fairly general way, dictated by a mixture of expectations arising from self, others or situational cues – such as "what an interesting person", "reminds me of John/Mary", "knows a lot about cannabis", "just the sort of knowledgeable person I'd expect to meet at Jill and Peter's party" – and so on. When it was revealed that the person to whom you were talking was a doctor, your internalised perception of the person would immediately have undergone a change – something like "well, no wonder he/she is so knowledgeable about cannabis", "this is going to be interesting, I could learn something here" or you may even have recalled an incident when as an adolescent you argued with your own GP about the effects of smoking cannabis. Discerning formalised roles is no different from Berne's description of imago adjustment. You will recall from **Figure 11.1** that a group imago represents an individual's perception of the dynamic relationships between themselves and members of a group in terms of both personalised and formalised roles. Hence, in practice, behaviour in any situation is based on two separate sets of expectations – one in relation to a personalised role and the other in terms of a formalised role. Personalised roles are the actual behaviours enacted by individuals who occupy formalised roles, and it is the congruence, or otherwise, between personalised and formalised roles (along with imagos and the quality of contact), that form the basis of existing or subsequent relationships.

At the most general level the methods of influence associated with a power source based on formalised roles, stem from the cultural and social (including legal) norms of a particular country, region or society. In some cases sub-cultural norms may apply. The most obvious examples are financial transactions of any kind; your financial resources have to be deployed in accordance with various rules and regulations. More socially relevant examples are awareness of etiquette and social rituals or customs. In some countries, trying to make business appointments during siesta time is unlikely to be met with an enthusiastic response. As a rule of thumb, primary formalised roles that fall within the ambit of social and relational categories, are more closely linked with cultural and social norms than the other methods of influence in **Table 11.1**.

Secondary formalised roles are also part of an individual's expectations of the situation. Secondary formalised roles are expected behaviours of the incumbents of positions in groups, organisations and society that, in interaction, constitute the public structure of groups, organisations and society and carry with them obligations, rights and duties prescribed to a greater or lesser degree by sectors of society. In essence, positions exist, are created and sometimes, arise informally, in order to implement functions essential for the attainment of organisational goals. For example, if you want to set up a company to produce and sell widgets, you are likely to start with at least three functions - production, sales and finance – and probably, at least three positions. For each position you would have a person specification spelling out the knowledge skills, experience and so forth, of individuals who would be expected to carry out the responsibilities and duties at a specified level of performance. In effect, positions are expected behaviours associated with a function and a title – Director of Finance and so forth – or in other words, a secondary formalised role.

Positions, rules and procedures

Secondary formalised roles are the most distinctive source of power in organisations. That is, allowing for cultural and social factors, if you want to exert influence in organisations, you have to take account of positions. Together, positions and rules and procedures are probably the most powerful methods of influence in many organisational settings. All organisations have rules and procedures, if only as a convenient way of not having to repeat an increasing series of one-off decisions. Used sensibly they make for efficiency by virtue of everyone knowing what to expect or do under any given circumstances. Coupled with position as a power source, and backed with appropriate resources, rules and procedures yield legitimate decisions. Used effectively – that is, congruently with personalised roles appropriate to a given situation - they create little resistance and invite recipients to adapt to organisational norms via the process of internalisation. Indeed, they are rendered more effective and efficient if everyone contributes to their creation. Essentially rules and procedures prescribe what everyone in a certain position has to do under given circumstances. Thus procedures as a means of influence in organisations are inextricably linked with secondary formalised roles or positions. It follows that if you want to use rules and procedures to influence someone, you must occupy (or have the backing of someone else who occupies), a position that carries with it the right to institute a particular rule or procedure, as well as the resources and will to enforce the regulations. Influence associated with positions is pivotal to all the other methods of influence in organisations and many professional or occupational networks.

Networking

In most, and particularly in large organisations, one's position will often include access to networking opportunities that may be used legitimately as a method of influence to cut across formal channels of communication, without having to observe the protocol of following official procedures. Many boardroom decisions stem from interaction originating in corridors or on the golf course, yet again emphasising the importance of relationships as the fundamental component of influence. The mushrooming impact of the internet, intra-nets and the use of e-mail facilities in virtually all developed countries, makes access to or control of information an increasingly important aspect of organisational performance. The growth and flow of information exchange now possible via practices such as video-conferencing and home-working is already challenging traditional approaches to organisational structures and channels of communication. Harnessing new technologies as an aspect of networking is a method of influence that is as yet largely unexplored.

Social mobility

Table 11.1 includes social mobility as a method of influence. I am using the term somewhat liberally, if not metaphorically, to refer to the growing trend in patterns of employment characterised by short term and part-time contracts of employment, job sharing and the practice of individuals having more than one job at the same time. Dot com companies arise, fall or merge over short time scales, and globalisation seems to be bringing fluidity to social structures. The middle class aspiration of a 'job for life' has all but disappeared, and it is now not unusual in a single day to attend three separate meetings and a business lunch as part and parcel of working for four different employers. Along with these trends, there is the ever present need for inter-organisational collaboration both locally and on a multi-national scale, that will often spawn secondments to short lived, task-oriented projects as essential components of large scale contracts. All these developments point to decreasing reliance on positions within comparatively stable organisations and offer a secure base for networking as a method of influence. The aphorism that 'it is not what you know, but who you know' is taking on a new significance. Relationships may become as, if not more important than, formalised roles.

Expertise

Technical expertise in some particular sphere has always been a prized method of influence. Generally, people defer to those they regard as experts. However, expertise as a method of influencing others will remain credible only as long as it is demonstrably effective – which requires it to be recognised by others in the first place. Being acknowledged as an expert gives an individual a status that will sometimes exceed their actual position in the organisational structure. If such an individual continues to use skills and knowledge that are essential and cannot be provided by anyone else, they stand a good chance of being promoted, or even having jobs created for them in recognition of their expertise. However, using expertise as a method of influence does not always make for plain sailing. Even managerially approved experts meet resistance. It would seem that little but often is more effective than any approach that leaves others overly dependent on the expert.

Ways in which individuals adapt to the methods of influence associated with formalised roles, and the procedures that exist to facilitate such adaptation include a vast array of legal statutes and accompanying events. A marriage ceremony, for example, is a social ritual that is legally binding in most countries. Even something as innocuous as meeting a friend in a restaurant for coffee is surrounded by legalities prohibiting certain behaviours. The Courts, the police, and educational establishments, are all social structures that require, sanction or encourage individuals to internalise ways of adapting to defined standards of behaviour. Organisations provide in-house training to enable employees to improve their performance, and promotion to certain positions requires qualifications awarded by external bodies. Participation in decision-making via co-option onto or membership of working parties or committees further encourages and induces internalisation of organisational norms and values.

Likely outcomes

Internalisation is the psychological process whereby individuals adopt as their own the perceived attitudes, values and behaviours of others. In terms of a structural model of ego states, the content of Parent messages copied from others and the Child adaptations to these messages, having been evaluated by the Adult ego state, are integrated into and become an autonomous part of the Adult. When you internalise an expected behaviour, you adopt attitudes, values and behaviours because you *want* to – not because you are copying the behaviour of someone else whom you admire (which is identification), or because you want the approval of the other person (which is adaptation), or because it is in your immediate interest to do so despite your not wanting to do so (which is alienation). Professional bodies and organisations strive for, or, at least, tend to favour internalisation as a more stable state of affairs than any of the others, yet nevertheless provide fail-safe measures such as continuous professional development to ensure internalisation is reinforced. In counselling and psychotherapy ethics, complaints and grievance procedures further bolster expected behaviours.

Authority

Table 11.1 indicates that authority arises from a combination of power sources and methods of influence; authority is a function of power and how it is exercised. This interpretation of "authority" differs from the usual use of the word in the literature of organisations. The rationale of this view is outlined below.

In the literature authority is usually regarded as legitimated power. This view of authority is based on position power – the ability to influence that goes with a particular position in an organisation. The position gives the individual the right to make certain decisions. For example, a manager usually has the right to hire and fire, to allocate work, to appraise an employee's performance and so forth. This way of understanding authority requires agreement among participants about the relativity of positions in an organisation – bosses give orders that workers agree to obey. Thus, position in an organisation is regarded as a power source, and is usually accompanied by resorting to rules and procedures as the method of influence. The shortcoming of this way of defining authority is (logically) that "authority" exists only in organisations. However, my observations of social situations, informal groups and networks that do not have clearly demarcated positions with all the trappings of job descriptions, reporting arrangements and accountability, lead me to conclude that authority exists, can arise without discussion among participants, and is a valid (that is, effective) method of influence subject to the provisos I outline below.

In the Contact Cube congruence between a personalised role, a formalised role and resources, in conjunction with appropriate methods of influence, gives a person *authority*. That is, authority is regarded as a dynamic process that occurs when someone is allowed or permitted by others to behave in a certain way. Hence, authority is a mode of securing assent among a group of people about behaviour in a particular situation, relative to their goals. It is a special case of the dynamics implicit in the Joharri window (Luft 1969, 1970). Authority is a relative concept and its effectiveness is a matter of degree. It is a situational measure of the effectiveness of the methods of influence, relative to congruence between power sources, which include the balance of power held by others in the situation.

To illustrate how authority may be acquired let us return to ***Scenario 11.2***. You will recall that just as the meeting was about to break up, the man in the travel business intervened. Initially, he had assumed the personalised role of Beholder and, by virtue of his presence at the meeting, was probably regarded by the Director as a "dissatisfied guest". When he spoke up (personalised role as Announcer), it became apparent that he was using his knowledge of the travel business as a means of checking the Director's proposals. In terms of **Table 11.1**, he was using expertise and contractual methods of influence to check the congruence of the Director's proposition. He acquired the authority to do so by using methods of influence appropriate to the situation, as well as demonstrating congruence between his personalised role, his formalised role, and his invisible resources derived from the contract between Pyrenski and the guests. His closing riposte to the woman who challenged his acquired authority, demonstrated the role-modelling mode of influence. The effectiveness of his intervention may be judged from the fact that the other guests were apparently sufficiently impressed with the content of his comments and questions to the Director that they permitted him to continue, and, in this sense, legitimised his use of power. Having satisfactorily answered the questions, the Director wisely remained silent – allowing the man to retain his acquired authority. Later, several guests consulted the man. His acquired authority carried over until no longer relevant, but presumably would have been re-established had there been a hitch in the Director's proposals. By remaining silent the Director too was accorded authority by the guests, pending the addition of more ski instructors. True to his word, the Director provided what was wanted, and the question of authority fell into abeyance.

As a coda to the above comments on **Table 11.1**, note that in cases where there is gross incongruence between a personalised role and a formalised role, the more high profile the formalised role, the more likely will public opinion reflect the subsequent credibility or otherwise of the organisation or individuals involved. Affairs, extra-marital relationships and divorces between 'ordinary' members of society attract little attention compared to similar liaisons involving individuals holding high public office - the British monarchy and ex-President Clinton being cases in point. Lower down the social scale public service organisations and some professional bodies include blanket clauses making 'conduct likely to bring the organisation/profession into disrepute' a 'dismissible' act.

The consequences of incongruence between actual and expected behaviours will vary depending on the behaviour in question, as well as the publicity likely to be attracted by transgression of the expectations attached to a formalised role. However, there are differences between primary and secondary formalised roles. Primary formalised roles are defined loosely and sometimes by default rather than explicit statutes. As in the case of meeting a friend in a restaurant, there are no written statutes other than the constitutional rights of citizens which define how people *should* behave in restaurants. Indeed, most primary formalised roles rely on expectations that are socially construed as being to the advantage of all. Secondary formalised roles on the other hand, define specific task related behaviours, rather than general social behaviours. Here the assumption is that all secondary formalised roles define positive behaviours, provided that such behaviours contribute to organisational goals, and that there is agreement among members about goals. By and large, the assumption holds true for all organisations or groups that do not overtly transgress the law, but there are some special cases, such as penal institutions and psychiatric units, where the inmates are not committed to the organisations' goals. The assumption is also true of primary formalised roles where there are no goals other than social norms and customs which generally exist to promote or preserve social harmony.

Finally, it should be noted that all the power sources and methods of influence detailed above can be used positively or negatively depending on the outcome in mind. Therapists facilitate cure, managers motivate workers, spies infiltrate strategic intelligence or defence units, prisoners riot or go on hunger strikes; all these examples are instances of power as the ability to influence others.

Formalised and personalised roles and relationships

It behoves those who want to use roles to address the complexity of intra- and inter group and organisational dynamics, to have a conceptual schema for relating actual behaviour (personalised roles) to expected behaviours (formalised roles). Generally speaking, the expectations individuals have of another person depend as much on the relationship they have with the person as they do on their roles. The more or "better" you know someone the greater the likelihood that your expectations of them will be based on their use of personalised roles than on their formalised role. If you want to influence someone you cannot ignore your existing relationship. Relationships are the outcome of roles, imagos and contact; we can summarise the interconnection between persons and social structures as in **Table 11.2** where we can see that relationships are regarded as a variable connecting persons and social structures.

Persons				Relationships
Behaviours	Personalised roles enacted at the social level	Existential Imago images	Quality Of contact	Interaction based on relationship type
Reactive	Valuer	Trust	Collaborative	Positive +1
Inactive	Beholder	Recognition	Co-existent	Positive +2
Responsive	Responder	Attachment	Co-operative	Positive +3
Proactive	Promoter	Growth	Compelling	Positive +4
Reactive	Victim	Mistrust	Collaborative	Negative -1
Inactive	Bystander	Anonymity	Co-existent	Negative -2
Responsive	Rescuer	Detachment	Co-operative	Negative -3
Proactive	Persecutor	Survival	Compelling	Negative -4

Table 11.2

In **Table 11.2** the four vertical sides of the Contact Cube have been used to define the quality of contact and the imago images show the bi-polar factors associated with each of the eight roles. This forms the basis of mapping two person interactions. For example, if person A is a social level Valuer and person B is a social level Responder, we can describe their relationship simply as a "plus-one, plus-three" type of interaction. For dyads this gives 8x8 = 64 ways of categorising of relationships, but this can be simplified by grouping positive and negative relationships as in **Table11.3**

	Persons			Relationships	Social Structures	
Behaviours	Personalised roles enacted at the social level	Existential Imago images	Quality Of contact	Interaction based on relationships that are	Resources	Formalised roles
Reactive	Valuer	Trust	Collaborative	Positive	As defined in Table 2.1	As defined in Table 2. 1
Inactive	Beholder	Recognition	Co-existent			
Responsive	Responder	Attachment	Co-operative			
Proactive	Promoter	Growth	Compelling			
Reactive	Victim	Mistrust	Collaborative	Negative	As defined in Table 2. 1	As defined in Table 2. 1
Inactive	Bystander	Anonymity	Co-existent			
Responsive	Rescuer	Detachment	Co-operative			
Proactive	Persecutor	Survival	Compelling			

Table 11.3

Locating **Table 11.1** within **Table 11.2** (or vice versa) offers a framework for the analysis of relationships in groups, organisations and networks – as shown in **Tables 11.3** and **11.4**.

Power source	Persons as in Table 2. 2	Relation-ships as in Table 2. 2	Social structures					
			Resources domain/relevance/balance/access/ competence			Formalised roles Primary Secondary		
			Physical	Material	Invisible	Social	Relational	Occupational
Methods of Influence	Behaviours, personalised roles, imago images quality of contact	Positive	Age Gender Ethnicity Presentation Transactions Stroking Force	Exchange Environmental Image Negotiation Contractual		Cultural/social norms, rules and procedures, information, networking access, social mobility, expertise		
	Behaviours, personalised roles, imago images quality of contact	Negative						
Individual adaptation via process or function of	Leadership, role modelling, mentoring, counselling, therapy, supervision, apprenticeship		Socialisation mortification	Reporting, monitoring appraisal, mediation, arbitration, working to rule, official or wildcat strikes		Legal statutes, education training co-option promotion qualification, ethics complaints & grievance procedures, continuous professional development		
Likely outcomes	Identification		Adaptation/compliance			Internalisation		
Authority	A mode of securing assent among a group of people about behaviour in a particular situation relative to their goals; depends on congruence between power sources and use of appropriate method(s) of influence.							

Table 11.4

The addition of a conceptual schema for understanding the social psychology of power, influence and authority, will augment current thinking and practice and provide a basis for examining relationships as a major variable linking people and social structures. The schema will enable practitioners or researchers systematically to observe and compare differences between the use of personalised roles, imago images, quality of contact and hence, relationships, in clinics, schools, work units and so on, and relate these to differences in social structures.

To illustrate, I supervise a trainee who works in a correctional institution for juvenile offenders. In three of the four house units the "success rates" for inmates (as measured by a system of tokens awarded for good behaviour) was satisfactory, but appalling in the third house. The management redistributed the entire inmate population in an attempt to 'average out' the success rates across all four houses. Six months later success rates of inmates in the fourth house had fallen below those in the other three units. At that point, the managers redistributed the staff across all the house units. Over the next six months success rates in all four units were roughly the same, but still some twenty percent lower than the ratings that had prevailed in the beginning. My supervisee pointed out that the overall ethos of the entire establishment was geared to compliance. He suggested that more attention should be paid to leadership of the house units, and inter-personal relationships between staff and inmates. He proposed a series of training workshops for the staff based on the theme of I'm OK – You're OK. However, following a 'satisfactory' report by government inspectors, the managers settled for the status quo and decided that any further training would incur 'unwarranted expenditure'. My supervisee has now resorted to the more limited strategy of role modelling positive relationships and using supervision sessions to teach staff Contact Cube roles.

The example highlights the need to take account of both personalised and formalised roles and in turn, how these relate to situational variables – the expectations inherent in a behaviour modification regime that at best, would almost inevitably lead to adaptation and at worst, compliance or even alienation (in the fourth house). Initially, the managers of the institution focused on behaviour associated with one formalised role (inmates), and later another (staff), seemingly ignoring the interaction of the two variables (relationships). At the same time, in achieving a satisfactory report, the managers themselves may be seen as having successfully adapted to society's expectations of correctional institutions.

Although the application of personalised Contact Cube roles offers the practitioner a repertoire of interventions on a scale and of a type hitherto not systematically explored in practice or described by TA theory, personalised roles alone do not fully bridge the gap between people and social structures in a way that would be useful to practitioners for whom consideration of group, inter-group and organisational dynamics are as important as individual proclivities. Personalised roles stem from personal power, but are always underpinned by resources and formalised roles. It is this connection that takes the Contact Cube beyond a 'social psychiatry' model of intra- and inter-personal processes. In conjunction with Berne's group dynamics diagrams (Berne 1963), the schema outlined in **Table 11.4** offers an additional perspective for understanding the social psychology of power, influence and authority, and provides a basis for examining relationships as the major variable linking people and social structures

Implications for research

In addition to observation and categorisation of behaviours as described by the Contact Cube, a researcher may use a focused interview to elicit the expectations held by the client of relevant formalised roles. Ideally the client's description of the situation (a *Significant Incident*) together with documentary evidence (such as organisational charts, job descriptions and so on) will provide sufficient information for the researcher to be able to relate the situation to a context, and discern or hypothesise about the goals of those involved, as well as the likely outcome of the situation. In doing so it is helpful for the researcher to have a schema for understanding power and influence that will reveal the congruence (or otherwise) between personalised roles, relationships and formalised roles.

Key Points 11

11.1   **Significant Incidents** illustrate how formalised roles may be mapped onto personalised roles. A Significant Incident is a participant observer's account of a particular situation.

11.2   **Social interaction is** a dynamic pattern of **relationships** that constitutes the basis of societies, crowds, organisations, groups and dyads. It ensues when *formalised roles* are activated by *communication* and *personalised roles* become operative.

11.3   **Social organisation** denotes the relatively enduring pattern of relationships between individuals or groups that results in characteristics not present in the components, but which produces an entity in its own right – the *group-as-a-whole.*

11.4   Berne gave a comprehensive scheme for categorising "social aggregations" as an aspect of social organisation, but did *not pay much attention* to the **group-as-a-whole.**

11.5   Adding formalised roles generally shifts the focus of our expectations in the direction of the *group-as-a-whole*.

11.6   Formalised and personalised roles may be mapped onto Berne's description of structure. Examining the nature of **expectations** provides links with Berne's *group imago* and *life positions*

11.7   *Expectations* my be elicited via the use of a **Significant Incident**..

11.8   The minimum *requirements of a Significant Incident* are a description by a focal person of an event or series of events that will enable a researcher/observer to *identify formalised* and *personalised* roles.

11.9   Critical data about the **group-as-a-whole** is contained within or may be inferred from a well-written or narrated *Significant Incident*. Identifying such data requires consideration of three factors:-

- the availability of roles in the situation and the function of the roles enacted at particular times in any situation or group (detailed in **Chapter 12** as situational roles),
- the theoretical model of group process held or adopted by the researcher and probably shared by some of the participants in the group or situation and,
- a schema for understanding power and influence.

11.10 Understanding the availability of roles and group process enables us to *use Significant Incidents* to address the relevance of roles to relationships and in so doing, redress Berne's failure to examine critically the inter-relationship between power, influence and authority

11.11 **Power** is the ability to influence others. **Influence** is the process whereby one person modifies their behaviour in response to, or as a result of, the behaviour of another person, persons or the situation. Congruence between a personalised role, a formalised role and resources in conjunction with appropriate methods of influence gives a person **authority**.

11.12 The method of influence that most often accompanies a personal power source is **persuasion** – information and argument based on facts supported by evidence.

11.13 **Resources** are anything required for implementing a role. The use of physical categories of resources can lead to adaptation or alienation.

11.14 **Socialisation** is the process whereby individuals adapt to the norms of a group in order to gain approval. Most organisations have a variety of *socialisation processes* for inducting newly appointed personnel

11.15 Relationships exist within a matrix of **formalised roles**. *Primary* formalised roles are the expected behaviours of people with whom we interact without reference to their connection to any particular organisation. *Secondary* formalised roles are related to positions in an organisation

11.16 **Rules and procedures, expertise, social mobility, expertise** and **networking** are methods of influence related to primary and secondary formalised roles

11.17 **Relationships** are the variable that connects people and social structures.

11.18 Transactional analysis would benefit by taking more explicit of note of **cultural factors** via the application of models such as **Spiral Dynamics.**

Self Supervision Suggestions 11

11.1 Write a description of a work organisation with which you are familiar, in terms of three sources of power (personalised roles, resources and formalised roles) and the methods of influence outlined in **Table 11.1**

11.2 Write a description of a professional society or association to which you belong, in terms of three sources of power (personalised roles, resources and formalised roles) and the methods of influence outlined in **Table 11.1**

11.3 Formulate a research proposal to investigate the view that "*authority is a mode of securing assent among a group of people about behaviour in a particular situation relative to their goals; it depends on congruence between power sources and use of appropriate method(s) of influence*".

Chapter **12**

Adding situational roles

This Chapter rounds off the Contact Cube by adding situational roles or role functions – the consequences of the personalised role behaviours adopted by people in formalised roles at particular times in the life of a group that influence relationships.

ERICA, group dynamics and psychoanalytic group therapy

Agazarian and Peters (1981) relate aspects of group dynamics (Lewin 1951, Cartwright and Zander 1960) with the traditions of Bion (1959), Foulkes (1965, 1975) and Foulkes and Anthony (1973) and other psychoanalytically-oriented group psychotherapists. Their observations on roles are couched in terms of "visible" and "invisible" group processes.

By adopting a systems approach (von Bertalanffy, 1968, Ruben and King, 1975) in conjunction with Lewin's field theory (Lewin, 1951), Agazarian and Peters are able to demonstrate the knock-on effects of group processes. The following selective excerpts show how they arrive at the distinction between the visible and invisible group and how these concepts affect their understanding of roles.

> "Aristotle said that whatever you say a thing is, it is...Korzybski said that whatever you say a thing is, it is not....Although these two premises appear contradictory, in fact they are both true. Understanding this paradox requires understanding that different levels of abstraction provide different conceptual perspectives....By changing perspective it is possible to shift backwards and forwards between observing group level phenomenon that is 'not' individual, and individual level phenomenon that is 'not' group" .(Agazarian and Peters, 1981 p. 29)

They later proceed to invoke Lewin to make the point that "The whole is different from the sum of its parts ... the whole has definitive properties of its own" (Lewin, 1951 p. 146).

Their next step is to use systems theory notions of permeable/impermeable boundaries, input and output to demonstrate how one perspective (system) relates to another. They illustrate this with the analogy of a three-dimensional chessboard, where the boards are referred to in **Figure 12.1** as 'system 1', 'system 2' and 'system 3'.

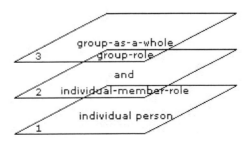

Figure 12.1

Fortunately, we don't have to understand three dimensional chess to follow their argument. They explain **Figure12.1** as:

"Three dynamic systems: 1, 2, 3, whose structure and function is isomorphically related and whose input and output-relationships are such that a change in any one system changes any other". (Agazarian and Peters, 1981 p. 41)

"When we talk about the relationship between system 2 and system 3, we talk about the 'group role' relationship to the 'group-as-a-whole'; and when we talk about the relationship between system 2 and system 1 we talk about an 'individual-member-role' relationship to the 'individual person'. A move (or change) in system 2 has a special meaning in system 2 and that same move has one kind of meaning in relationship to system 3, a different meaning in relationship to system 1 and still another overall meaning in terms of systems 1 and 2 and 3". (Agazarian and Peters, 1981 p. 41)

	Individual perspective		Group-as-a-whole perspective	
	Person	Member	Role	Group
Roles	Individual can be talked about independent of group in terms of any valid personality theory (like psycho – analysis) which yields definable personality styles (like hysteric, obsessive-compulsive, etc.)	Individual can be talked about independent of group in terms of (a) individual socio-psychological dynamics and overlapping membership roles; (b) roles developed as a functional transference in group; (c) membership responses to specific phases and group dynamic events	Role is a function of the dynamics of the specific group. Roles are clusters of definable behavior, independent of people that serve as driving or restraining forces in relationship to group goals; may be located in member, sub-group, or group-as-a-whole	Role dynamics can only be talked about in relationship to the inter- dependence of member roles specific to this particular group system and generalizable to group roles in general. Role behaviors serve as output of sub-systems and inputs to the group system. Group-as-a-whole in turn functions with a role in the system of which it is a component.
Commun-ication Behavior	Person communication behavior is a function of the person in interaction with their perceived environment, or: pcb=f(P,E)	Member communication behavior is a function of the member in interaction with the imagined group environment, or: Rcb=f(M,G_{im})	Role communication behavior is a function of the role in interaction with the group environment, or: rcb=f(P,E)	Group communication behavior is a function of the group in interact-ion with the environment, or: gcb=f(G,E)

Table 12.1

Their overall conclusions (Agazarian and Peters 1981 p. 122-123), are outlined in **Table 12.1** above. I would emphasise that these are selective quotes from Agazarian and Peters; their full Table additionally describes the column variables in relation to norms, goals, structure, cohesion and communication patterns. In essence, they put roles within the context of the major constructs of group dynamics, thereby emphasising what I refer to as the situational aspects of role expectations. Although theirs is a psychoanalytic orientation and thus includes aspects of unconscious behaviour that requires interpretation (usually by the therapist), it is a highly recommended work for anyone working with groups.

Berne, Agazarian and Peters and ERICA

Comparison between the first two of these approaches highlights the way in which I perceive and have attempted to incorporate differences The differences are more apparent than real[1]. That is, despite the disorganised way in which Berne presents his ideas, he covers all the ideas and concepts that Agazarian and Peters address in an academically considerably more polished manner, apart from the explicit attention which Agazarian and Peters pay to the group-as-a-whole. This is partly a matter of emphasis, but also of ideology, rather than an omission by Berne. Agazarian and Peters are psychoanalysts and, not surprisingly, espouse the unconscious and unconscious processes. In contrast, interpretations about the group-as-a-whole, or the invisible group, do not feature in Berne's writing in relation to imagos. (He does address aspects of group-as-a-whole but not specifically in relation to roles.) Nevertheless, this does not preclude a TA group therapist, for example, thinking about a group in terms of aspects of the group culture (technical, etiquette and character). Likewise, at a staff meeting in a multidisciplinary mental heath day centre, the same therapist may use Berne's dynamics diagram to understand and explain to colleagues, relationships between the TA group members and other clients at the centre.

Berne does not define or use personalised roles as a concept. However, as indicated above, personalised roles and expectations are subsumed in the concept of a group imago. In contrast, Agazarian and Peters use the concept in four ways as shown in **Table 12.1** above, but do not define roles per se. Rather they write about "dynamics", "functions" and "role dynamics" and, as evidenced by the following quotations, are clearly describing the way they think about and use roles.

> "From the perspective of the invisible group, a role is *a set of interrelated functions that contribute to group movement*. These functions can be located at the individual level, the sub-group level or group level. A role has flexibility of locus, that is, different members or combinations of members can perform it. It is this quality that makes it easy to understand a role as a function of the group rather than as idiosyncratic to an individual". (Agazarian and Peters, 1981 p.104: my italics)

Later they state:

---

[1] For example, an imago is defined as "an unconscious, stereotypical set, based on a person's fantasies and distortions about a primary relationship experienced within the early familial environment; this set determines a person's reactions to others" (Agazarian and Peters, 1981 p. 277) Earlier, Berne defined a group imago as "any mental picture, conscious, preconscious or unconscious of what a group is or should be like" (Berne 1963 p. 244). He uses the concept to describe four phases of group development – provisional, adapted, operative and secondarily adjusted. Tuckman and Jensen (1977) refer to stages of forming, storming, norming and performing.

"A role cannot exist in a group as a function of the *individual alone*. [original italics]. Every role in a group is not just a reciprocal relationship between two or more people, but is also a manifestation of the group dynamics". (Agazarian and Peters, 1981 p. 105)

Agazarian and Peters are writing about *role functions*, yet do not say explicitly what these functions are. Several authors on group dynamics have suggested functions necessary for group survival (Bales 1950; Hare 1962), outlining group task and group maintenance roles. More recently, Clarkson (1991) extends Berne's account of imago development by listing leadership tasks appropriate to each stage of Berne's imago development, and adding a fifth stage of mourning (Tuckman and Jensen, 1977). This highlights the main difference between Agazarian and Peters, and Berne.

The two approaches differ in relation to roles within a group, partly because Berne uses a four-stage model of differentiation of individual imagos, whereas Agazarian and Peters and Agazarian (1997) see roles as functions of a six-stage model of group development. This is derived from Bennis and Shepard (1956) and theoretically, if followed to its logical conclusion, dispenses with the therapist as group leader. This is not surprising as the groups studied by Bennis and Shepard (1956) were psychoanalytic therapy groups, where leadership style is deliberately non-directive, and the overall focus of attention is on the dynamics of the group-as-a-whole – rather than the progress or otherwise of individual members. Although Berne himself was sympathetic and largely adhered to this style of leadership (Berne 1970b), in many TA groups, the tradition is for the group leader to take major responsibility for role functions that ensure movement (back or forth) through stages of imago development (Clarkson 1991).

What emerges from these studies is that how roles in a group setting may be understood, depends on at least two related factors. The first is simply that we have to be clear about how we are using the term "role". Berne uses the term in two ways – as an aspect of group dynamics and as a manifestation of individual enactment of Drama Triangle roles - without making the differences explicit. Agazarian and Peters use the term to refer to *role functions* - the consequences of behaviour by individuals relative to their notion of their three tier configuration of individual, member roles, group-as-a-whole.

This leads to the second factor; we have to be clear about the *context* in which roles are enacted. ERICA deals with this first factor by noting that a role is defined generally as a disposition to act based on expectations of self, others and the immediate context. More specifically, roles are seen as operating in three domains.

Formalised roles exist as expectations held of individuals in positions in families, groups, organisations and social situations. *Personalised* roles constitute the actual behaviours of individuals; they emerge as part of normal growth and development. They occur at three levels (social, psychological and attitudinal) simultaneously and may be identified behaviourally, socially, historically and phenomenologically. Moreover because personalised roles are based on out of awareness hopes/expectations that other will reciprocate the roles we learned in childhood, relationships may be described in terms of attempts to confirm or deny mutual worth. In other words, the circular causality of role reciprocation leads to rules that enable one to predict the course of social interaction, in terms of the outcomes of various types of role sequences. *Situational* roles are a combination of the previous two domains - the dynamic outcome of formalised and personalised roles *in relation to* a particular group or situation at a particular time. Strictly speaking, situational roles are more correctly regarded as role functions – the consequences of personalised role behaviours.

The distinction between situational roles in relation to a "group" or "situation" is important because it means that situational roles are relevant to both group *and* two-person interactions. For the most part, the roles of therapist and an individual client scarcely warrant the additional dimension of situational roles. Nevertheless, conceptually, patterns of interaction change over time and what, for example, would be a typical role profile for a therapist during the early stages of therapy is bound to differ as time progresses. Indeed there are models that describe the changing pattern of client-therapist interaction (Hewitt 1995), albeit in broader terms than the outcome of role behaviours.

Situational roles

In order to describe situational roles, I have developed a model of group interaction consistent with both transactional analysis theory and practice as well as the major tenets of other group work approaches. This model addresses the **what, why, when, where, how** and **who** of being in a group. As such, it is a pragmatic classification of group process - rather than a comprehensive conceptualisation of group dynamics. A somewhat wider view may be found in Agazarian and Peters (1981) and Agazarian (1997); both these works combine up to date psychoanalytic and systems theory perspectives.

Perusal of the TA literature reveals that, apart from Berne's seminal works (Berne 1963, 1966), not much has been written by TA practitioners on group dynamics. Notable exceptions to this are Clarkson (1992) and Tudor (1999), who go beyond Berne's four stages of imago development to include further stages. Clarkson makes an important contribution by delineating 'constructive' and 'destructive' leadership tasks appropriate to each stage (Clarkson 1992 pp.) Tudor's work is considerably wider, drawing on the full gamut of social group work literature and research interspersed by reference to TA concepts. Hargaden and Sills (2002) give an all-too-brief Chapter on group psychotherapy and Sills (2003) draws attention to the phenomenon of "role lock".

Handling yourself in a group is not unlike playing with a Rubik Cube; change the pattern on one side and all the other sides are affected. A Rubik Cube has six sides; analogously these correspond to six fundamental group variables – *goals, norms, roles, cohesiveness, structure* and *communication*. The model outlined below touches on the major factors that need to be taken into account when working in a group setting (and to some extent, in individual counselling, psychotherapy or coaching). For example, *what* is likely to be going on in a group is always linked with the stage of a group's life cycle. *Who* you are in relation to the group immediately gives you a formalised *role*. For example, are you a group leader or a group member? In addition, at any time you have a choice of personalised roles (as described by the Contact Cube). How many formalised roles are there in the group/organisation? In addition, membership and participation in a group implies some or other commitment to group *goals* and contract – both are related to roles. (Prisons are the prime example of widely divergent types of commitment to group goals.) What happens in the group depends to some extent on how the group is *structured*. (Prisons are very highly structured.) Whenever you *communicate* by enacting a role, will be related not only to the group structure and your goals, but also to the *intention* behind whatever it is you do, which in turn, will influence *norms* and *cohesiveness*. (Prisoners can be compliant or disruptive.)

Figures 12.2 and **12.3** give a useful format for tracking and describing situational roles as an individual's interaction in a group - at any stage of group development. In other words, the diagrams are a visual aid that shows all the options everyone has at any time. Once you become familiar with the significance of each of the circles, you'll find you are able to use the categories to guide your interventions. Each of the circles represents a way of describing behaviour – according to the following descriptions:

1. The innermost circle has four sub-divisions representing the types of behaviour, associated qualities of contact and the bi-polar personalised roles. This is an easy way of tracking roles. At any moment you will be in one of the roles associated with the behaviours at the social level, another at the psychological level and in a third category at an existential level. However, for the purpose of describing situational roles, we will confine ourselves to behaviour at the social level - that is, proactive, inactive, responsive, or reactive. It is also important to bear in mind that roles are also associated with qualities of contact and imago images. In my experience, monitoring the contact between people in a group or organisation is often more important than simply focusing on social level roles. Under such circumstances the Beholder is the role of choice for the group leader. You need to know or hypothesise about what is going on before jumping in to avert even the most negative interaction between participants.

2. The second circle shows a variable related to the intentions of an intervention. The categories in **Figure 12.2** are those described by Heron (Heron 1990, pp.28-120, Heron 1989). Heron describes the categories in his Six Category Intervention Analysis model as:

> "The six-category system deals with six basic kinds of intention the practitioner can have in serving their client. Each category is one major class of intention that subsumes a whole range of sub-intentions and specific behaviours that manifest them". (Heron 1990, p. 4: my italics)

Heron divides the six categories into two groups – those that are "authoritative" and those that are "facilitative".

> "Authoritative
> 1. **Prescriptive**. A prescriptive intervention seeks to direct the behaviour of the client, usually behaviour that is outside the practitioner-client relationship.
> 2. **Informative**. An informative intervention seeks to impart knowledge, information, meaning to the client.
> 3. **Confronting**. A confronting intervention seeks to raise the client's consciousness about some limiting attitude or behaviour of which they are relatively unaware.
>
> Facilitative
> 4. **Cathartic**. A cathartic intervention seeks to enable the client to discharge, to abreact some painful emotion. primarily grief, fear and anger.
> 5. **Catalytic.** A catalytic intervention seeks to elicit self-discovery, self-directed living, learning and problem-solving in the client.
> 6. **Supportive.** A supportive intervention seeks to affirm the worth and value of the client's person, qualities, attitudes and actions".(Heron 1990pp. 5-6)

Heron's categories are designed to track the behaviour of a group facilitator, but there is no reason why they may not be applied to all group members. Heron gives a separate chapter on each of the six categories, with anything up to twenty sub-categories for each of the six basic types. Included in these descriptions are "degenerative and perverted interventions". These are "unsolicited; manipulative; compulsive; and unskilled". (Heron 1990, pp. 144-158)

Clearly, Heron is describing intentions that underpin positive Contact Cube roles – with the "degenerative and perverted interventions" matching negative Contact Cube roles. However, there is nothing sacrosanct about the Heron categories. In principle, any meta–level system of categorisation of intentions may be used. For example, one could just as easily substitute Berne's therapeutic operations (Berne 1966, pp.233-258) – as in **Figure 12.3 -** or Hargaden and Sills's reworking of these as "empathic transactions" (Hargaden and Sills, 2002, pp. 115-138). Indeed, either of the latter is eminently suitable for counselling, psychotherapy or coaching with individual clients. They may be used to equal effect in a group setting.

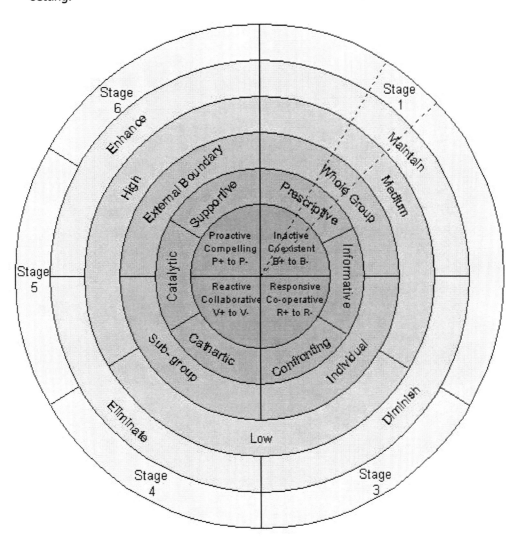

Figure 12.2

I have found the Heron categories useful for working with non-clinical practitioners, where consideration of group dynamics is important – and equally, with therapeutic groups where there is an emphasis on clients learning to work through group-as-a-whole issues, rather than solely focusing on their own individual goals. A useful guideline is always to bear in mind that situational roles are a reflection of the role functions of the group at a *particular* moment in time. As such, they will gives clues to *group* behaviour and motifs such as scapegoating, idealising (or denigrating) the leader, sub-group formation and so on, are only to be expected.

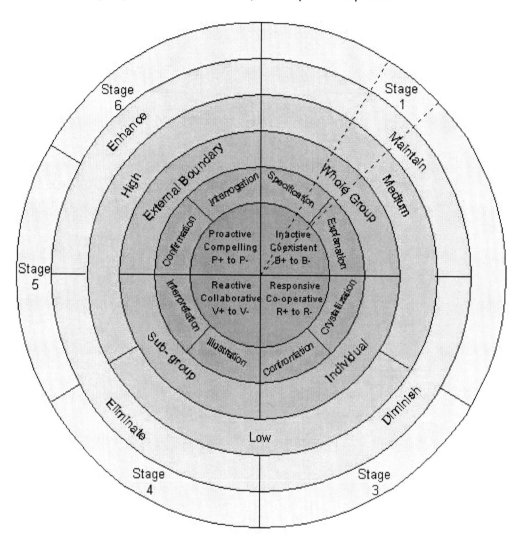

Figure 12.3

3. Interventions can be made at varying levels of intensity – shown above as high, medium, and low. What would be regarded as a medium level of intensity in a boardroom meeting would probably only qualify as 'low' in relation to a boisterous

group of adolescents. Likewise, the typical level of intensity in a classroom of A-level students is bound to differ over time in comparison to a Junior school class. Obviously, intensity is not the only factor that will contribute to group norms – but it is one that will always be present.

4. The next circle is a **where/who** factor. An intervention can be made in one of four directions. These are self-evident; you can address your intervention (enact your role in relation to) to an individual, a sub group, the whole group, or with reference to the external boundary of the group. The latter has significant implications for group **cohesiveness**. Notice however, that addressing an intervention to an individual does not occur in a vacuum; your intervention will impact on the whole group. In other words, these categories are exhaustive but not mutually exclusive.

5   The next circle is the one that is most open to 'observer bias'. This represents a **why** factor of crucial importance to the attainment of group **goals**. Metaphorically, the circle poses the question "using a particular role at a particular time in the life of the group, why make a particular type of intervention, at a given level of intensity, directed at whomever?" In other words, are you aiming to change or eliminate whatever is going on? Or do you merely want to tone it down; to diminish the effect of some or other behaviour? On the other hand you may want to maintain or even enhance the current proceedings. The difference between your intended and the actual outcome transforms this circle into a **what** variable.

6   The outer circle represents the fact that all the other variables are relative to the stage of the group's life cycle. I show this as a six stage model - giving the option of using Berne's four stages of imago development (Berne 1963), or Tuckman's six stage model and others referred to in Tudor's excellent treatment of the topic (Tudor 1999). Another option is to use the model described by Agazarian and Peters (1981, pp. 124-153) that draws on the work of Bennis and Shepard (1956) and Bion (1959). Despite the psychoanalytic orientation, I have found this a particularly useful model for long term psychodynamic psychotherapy groups and in working with organisations. Agazarian and Peters give six phases of group development that are far more sophisticated than Berne's account of imago development or Tuckman's model. In particular, they describe two stages each with three distinct phases. Stage One has phases of "dependence: flight", "counterdependence: fight", and "power-authority". Stage Two phases include "overpersonal enchantment", "counterpersonal disenchantment", and "interdependence work" Each of these stages is seen in relation to ten variables – Implicit group goal, Group organisation, Group role, Voice of group, Group theme, Group focus, Content themes, Group activity, Individual defences and Membership concerns. The latter proceed from Inclusion, Control, Power, Affection, Distrust to Trust. Even without descriptions or definitions of all these variables, the model is considerably more refined than the stages of development seen in typical transactional analysis groups – where the emphasis is on individual therapy in a group setting (Kapur and Miller, 1987).

7   There is also another circle that I've not shown; you have to visualise the final outer circle with five segments corresponding to the individual or self-centred system, the observing system, the member system, the subgroup system and the group-as a-

whole system.[1] This invisible circle represents the overall *structure* of the group. This is similar to the five stages of group imago development described by Clarkson, but is considerably more complex. The invisible outer circle, fittingly, is like Agazarian and Peters' invisible group; it exists as a set of ideas about how the energy within all the other circles comes together as a moving flux; being there, means that you cannot not influence what happens.

Situational Role Profile

Group: Malvern		Session No. 23		Date: 27 May 02		Recorded by: Gordon Law			

Stage/ Intervn. Time	Formalised Role and Name	Personalised Roles								Intentions						Direction				Intensity			Outcome			
		Positive				Negative																				
		P	B	R	V	P	B	R	V	P	I	C	C	C	S	I	S	W	E	H	M	L	M	D	N	E
2 / 17 1903	Client George	x								x						x					x				x	

Table 12.2

A situational role is thus described as a statement specifying the stage of group development/intervention, number/time, the formalised role and name of the individual, followed by a single variable for each circle in relation to each intervention. This information is recorded as a Situational Role Profile (SRP) score sheet as shown in **Table 12.2** above. This single line entry of a truncated version of the full SRP, shows that the particular group was at Stage 2, and the seventeenth intervention was made at 1903 hours by a client named George. He used the Promoter role, with prescriptive intent, in relation to another individual, at a medium level of intensity. The outcome was that the group process was enhanced.

Using situational roles

My experience is that clients soon learn to use Situational Role Profiles. It is also often a useful task to assign to a client on occasions when they have no particularly urgent issue to discuss. Likewise, in a well functioning, mature group, participants can take turns to act as the group apparatus (Berne 1963, p. 30) by using the SRP to track the group process; the last fifteen minutes of the group's time is given over to a review of this recording. Another option I often use is to invite trainees to participate in the group to observe, record, and provide feedback to group members.

Practicalities aside, situational roles are a convenient device for taking the pulse of a group. They provide a readily assimilated framework for understanding a complex process. Meticulously recorded over time, SRPs yield a wealth of data on a host of variables of interest to clients, practitioners, trainers, supervisors and researchers. For example, weekly SRPs may be easily copied into a database (or even a simple spreadsheet), and at the touch of a key, a breakdown of all the interventions made by any individual will appear on screen. Similarly, the database may be programmed to provide indices of whatever group phenomenon is of interest to a practitioner/researcher. As far as I know, no other comparable model exists that would readily provide indices such as differences between the interventions made by facilitators using different models of psychotherapy, correlations between any (or all) the

---

[1] Agazarian (1997) gives comprehensive tracts on all these factors; her *System-centered therapy for groups* is the best work I know on the dynamics of psychotherapy groups.

variables in a SRP, outcome measures of direct relevance to clients in educational or organisational setting and so on. The list is limited only by the discipline required to record the data. Moreover, SRPs are very flexible, "user friendly" and perhaps above all, cheap to use and analyse. All a researcher needs to have is an understanding of Contact Cube roles, the ability to recognise them and the other SRP variables *in situ,* and the time it takes to copy the data into a simple spreadsheet. The use of a lap top computer, instead of pen and paper for recording observations, makes the task even easier – as well as providing instant, ongoing feedback during the life of group.

In summary, situational roles may be employed:

1. As an appetiser – brief presentations to trainees/colleagues to provide a framework for understanding the range of options available to anyone in a group,
2. In depth – to teach trainees a) about group dynamics b) skills for making interventions in groups c) differences between schools of TA d) differences between various models of therapy e) differences between leaderships styles in various settings,
3. Over time – in group therapy, in supervision of group therapy and as a research tool.

The Contact Cube

The addition of situational roles to formalised and personalised roles completes the Contact Cube model. The advantages are many being both conceptual and practical. Although at first sight the Contact Cube may seem complicated, it is not rocket science; I seldom meet clients who are unable to grasp the idea within three or four sessions. Indeed, the Contact Cube is a model that adds little more to existing TA theory – but what is added has implications that are radical. To summarise:

*   The Drama Triangle with *personalised roles at three levels* is *expanded to include the Bystander role* and thus, forms the base of the Cube.
*   Four mirror image *positive roles* form the top of the Cube. The way in which these are conceptualised and function at three levels is entirely new, fully redressing the hitherto one-sided emphasis on negative aspects of social interaction.
*   Equally novel is the notion of the Contact Plane and the emphasis on the four *qualities of contact* associated with the four positive-negative dimensions of behaviour.
*   *Formalised roles* may be added to address the relevance of *power, influence* and *authority* in groups, organisations and social situations.
*   *Situational roles* and *Situational Role Profiles* enable one to locate formalised and personalised roles in relation to stages of group development and other group variables
*   The lynch-pin of the Contact Cube is *a learned Observer role* and the capacity of the *Observer self* for self-reflective awareness, without identifying with the content of one's awareness. Detailed consideration of this is postponed until we reach **Part Six**. However, the Contact Cube as described up to now, may be applied as a "stand alone" model to identify and choose between roles and the associated qualities of contact, imago images and hence, relationships.

The limitations of the Contact Cube are that it does not take account of the background, the historical factors that impinge on observable role behaviours. This is covered by the models presented in **Part Four** and **Part Five**.

Key Points 12

12.1 Berne's writing on groups and group dynamics parallels that of **Agazarian** and **Peters.** They define a *role* is a set of *interrelated functions that contribute to group movement* and add that "A role cannot exist in a group as a function of the individual alone. *Every role* in a group is not just a reciprocal relationship between people, but *is also a manifestation of the group dynamics*".

12.2 ERICA caters for this by adding **situational roles** to the Contact Cube - the *dynamic outcome* of formalised and personalised roles *in relation to* a particular group or situation at a particular time.

12.3. Situational roles are related to six fundamental group variables – *goals, norms, roles, cohesiveness, structure and communication.*

12.4. We can **track situational roles** by observing types of *behaviour*, associated qualities of *contact* and the bi-polar *personalised roles*, the *intention* behind an intervention, the *direction, intensity* and *outcome* of an intervention - relative to a six stage model of the stage of group life.

12.5. Situational Role Profile (SRP) score sheets may be used by group members or a researcher to record this information.

Self Supervision Suggestions 12

12.1. It may be helpful to make an actual model of the circles. Copy each circle (and sub-divisions) onto a different coloured card and cut away the outer edges so you end up with six different sized and coloured circular sheets. Pierce the centre of each circle and stack them one on top of the other – with the largest circle on the bottom Make a seventh circle out of clear plastic - such as an OHP transparency. Make this the same size as the largest circle but with no radial sub-divisions except a dotted line "V" shape from the edge to the centre – like the dotted lines in diagram **12.2**. Position the seventh (plastic) circle on top of all the others. Push a drawing pin through the centres of all the circles and pin them on a suitable surface (a square of corrugated cardboard will do nicely - or a cork floor tile if you want a luxury model). This will enable you to rotate each circle independently.

12.2. Sit in any group, twirl the circles around and see if you can come up with an intervention matching whatever appears in the "V". Would it be relevant to the group you're in? If so, try it and see what transpires. If not, why not? What *would* be relevant?

12.3. Watch what is going on in the group and categorise interventions by rotating each circle so that the relevant variable in the circle is aligned with the "V".

12.4. Using the Situational Role Profile (SRP) score sheet, formulate a research proposal for participant-observation of role interventions in a group. Would you be able to relate any results to Berne's diagrams about group processes? What time scale would be needed? Would you be able to hypothesise differences between (which) variables in a psychodynamic group and a TA group? List the potential benefits of this type of research to a) a commercial organisation, b) an educational establishment c) a psychotherapy group.

Chapter 13

Role Sequences

This Chapter presents the second of the models that contribute to bridging the divides. Because the Contact Cube focuses on the role imago repertoire of a single individual, a second model - Role Sequences - is needed to describe more precisely the interaction between two or more people. Role sequences place equal emphasis on positive and negative aspects of social interaction, thereby widening our understanding of relationships.

As much of the theory behind the model is new, the Chapter details somewhat more than the essential information a researcher (or client) would need; I clarify this distinction towards the end of the Chapter.

Reciprocals and role sequences

Personalised roles at three levels form a person's role profile. The combination of person A's role profile with person B's role profile is referred to as a reciprocal (**Table 13.1**) signifying the effect one role profile has on the other and vice-versa. A reciprocal is a unit of interaction between the personalised role profiles of two people, relative to the situation.

Person	Reciprocal	
	A	B
Social	V-	R-
Psychological	P-	V-
Existential	R-	P-

Table 13.1

At any given moment an individual has a choice or repertoire of twenty four positive and twenty four negative role profiles. Thus there are 24x24=576 reciprocals or ways in which two people may interact when using negative roles. However, if the order of who starts the interaction (person A or person B) is ignored, this figure may be reduced to 300. Likewise, there are 300 reciprocals for positive roles – plus a further 300 reciprocals where one person uses positive and the other uses negative roles. These 900 reciprocals constitute a complete theoretical taxonomy of social interaction. (**Chapter14** explains how I arrive at these figures).

Options for research

Given the somewhat daunting figure of 900 reciprocals the tradition in transactional analysis for the 'typical practitioner' is to use these pragmatically. A more 'research-oriented' practitioner would at the very least examine each of these three categories to see what they have in common, whether they may be further simplified and what 'evidence' is to hand that will demonstrate how they 'work' in practice. For example, the literature on roles reveals that Berne (1963, 1964) Kahler (1978), Mellor and Sigmund (1975), Law (1978a) English (1987), Jacobs (1987), Clarkson (1987), Choy (1987) and Le Guernic (2004), all focus on roles as a property of individual behaviour. Law (1979, 2001, 2004), Barnes (1981), Schwock (1981), and Hine (1990), give a more interactional view of roles. Most significantly Gilbert notes that:

"Our internalised network of relationship dynamics will include the 'games' we learnt to play in childhood in imitation of, and in response to our parents. We have in our internal world a record of all the roles in a particular game and when we move into Victim we will project onto the other protagonist the role of Persecutor or Rescuer, or the reverse may apply. This relates directly to Ryle's concept of internalised reciprocal roles. The reciprocal roles that form part of our internalised experience of relationship networks, subconsciously influence the manner in which we engage with new relationships (Ryle 1992)". (Gilbert, 2003, p. 243)

Observations reveal that reciprocals across all three categories may indeed be reduced to distinctive patterns that follow specific rules based on principles consistent with existing transactional analysis theory and practice. What follows are the salient points of a more detailed account of this 'practice-research' (rather than 'pure' research) given by Law (2004).

Role sequences - general considerations

Combinations of reciprocals are called role sequences. A role sequence is a series of reciprocals that confirms or denies the mutual OK-ness of both parties and thereby affects their future relationship. This is a temporary "working definition". There are "indeterminate" role sequences that neither confirm nor deny mutual OK-ness. I describe these later and will add an additional phrase to the above definition to account for indeterminate role sequences.

Role sequences are defined by outcome, the roles contained in the reciprocals at the end of the role sequence. Thus there are negative outcome role sequences (NORS), mixed outcome role sequences (MORS) and positive outcome role sequences (PORS). With NORS, both people end up using negative roles. In **Scenario 1** and **Table 13.2** both parties are using negative roles that preclude mutual OK-ness.

Scenario 13.1
Person A says "I just don't know what to do! I've installed the new software exactly as instructed and the damned thing doesn't work!!"
Person B replies "It works OK on my machine. I'll show you how to do it." B moves towards A's machine, but A retorts "Look, I don't need you to show me! If it was any good it would have come with decent instructions that don't need a nerd to make them work! I'll work it out myself."
B shrugs and walks away.

Person	Reciprocal 1		Reciprocal 2	
	A	B	A	B
Social	V-	R-	P-	B-
Psychological	P-	B-	B-	P-
Existential	B-	P-	V-	R-

Table 13.2

With a little theatrical licence you can see how the above **Scenario** may be played out to fit the reciprocals in **Table 13.2**.

With MORS, one person ends up using negative roles and the other occupies positive roles. To illustrate, consider the following:

Scenario13. 2
Person A says "I just don't know what to do! I've installed the new software exactly as instructed and the damned thing doesn't work!!"

Person B replies "It works OK on my machine. I'll show you how to do it?" B waits for A's response, but A retorts "Look, I don't need you to show me! If it was any good it would have come with decent instructions that don't need a nerd to make them work! I'll work it out myself." B shrugs and walks away.

Person	Reciprocal 1		Reciprocal 2	
	A	B	A	B
Social	V-	R+	P-	B+
Psychological	P-	B+	B-	P+
Existential	B-	P+	V-	R+

Table 13.3

While the content of the verbal interaction between A and B remains the same in **Scenario 13.2** and **Table 13.3**, person B's non verbal behaviour indicates that B's roles are positive. The subtlety of difference between B's social level Rescuer with the emphasis on "I'll" in **Scenario 13.1** and the Responder role in **Scenario 13.2** lies mainly in B's tone of voice where the phrase "I'll show you how to do it" implies "Do you want me to show you how to do it?" followed by the non verbal "B waits for A's response." There is no confirmation of mutual OK-ness because person A starts and ends with negative roles.

With PORS, both people end up in positive Square roles. We would have to alter A's verbal utterances completely for them to reflect positive roles.

Scenario 13. 3
Person A says "I just don't know what to do! I've thought I'd installed the new software exactly as instructed but I still can't get it to work!!"

Person B replies "It works OK on my machine. I'll show you how to do it?" B waits for A's response, but A replies "No thanks. The instructions seem to be quite clear so I must be missing something. I'd like to have one more go."

B says "OK" and walks away.

Person	Reciprocal 1		Reciprocal 2	
	A	B	A	B
Social	V+	R+	P+	B+
Psychological	P+	B+	B+	P+
Existential	B+	P+	V+	R+

Table 13.4

Here mutual OK-ness is confirmed - both parties are using positive roles.

Indeterminate outcome role sequences (IORS) appear to fulfil the important function of linking positive, negative and mixed outcomes. They are associated with reciprocals that have either the Bystander role or the Beholder role at the existential levels. Because of the behavioural inactivity associated with these roles OK-ness is neither confirmed nor denied. Thus the full the formal definition of role sequences is:

*A **role sequence** is a series of reciprocals that confirms or denies the mutual OK-ness of both parties. Indeterminate role sequences do not confirm or deny mutual OK-ness, but in all cases, the future relationship is affected.*

Role sequences that start and finish with the same type (positive or negative) of reciprocals, (as in all the above **Scenarios**) - are *invariable* role sequences. Role sequences where one or both parties change reciprocals from positive to negative or vice versa somewhere between the start and finish fall into a variable class. This distinction has important practical consequences when it comes to developing indices of role sequences to describe individual and group behaviour.

Variable reciprocals are likely to be of particular interest to practitioners aiming to facilitate change. Conceptually they may be regarded either as a class in their own right that would be expected to predominate where one or both parties have changes of the type of reciprocal from positive to negative or vice versa, somewhere between the start and finish of a role sequence, OR as two separate reciprocals enacted in succession. I touch on this below in describing mixed outcome role sequences. That apart and, pending further research, this Chapter is focused entirely on invariable role sequences.

Duration, degree, density and diversity of role sequences

It seems that the factors that would enable a researcher to compare the above four types of role sequences are the duration, degree, density and diversity of a role sequence The "4D's" of role sequences are offered as suggestions for researchers to investigate, replicate, validate and review the use of role sequences.

Duration refers to how long a role sequence persists, as 'measured' by the number of reciprocals in a role sequence. The above **Scenarios** all have a 'duration' of 2. A two hour business meeting may have a total role sequence duration of 1000, consisting of varying numbers of role sequences of each type. Comparatively speaking, Quaker meetings probably have lower duration role sequences. Duration enables researchers to concoct all manner of indices to account for the variability of situations.

The degree of a role sequence refers to extent of mutual OK-ness involved. Mutual OK-ness means that both parties have to end up in positive roles and that OK-ness occurs at or is reflected by the existential level of the reciprocals at the start of a role sequence. "OK-ness" in this context refers to a refinement of Jacobs' notion of "calibrated positions" (Jacobs 1997, p. 204). Jacobs suggested that by "calibrating" the vertical and horizontal axes of the OK diagram, an individual's view of OK-ness could be seen in relative terms. For example, I would probably regard my spouse as "more OK" than my brother and he in turn, as "more OK" than my neighbour. Although OK-ness is subjectively defined, life positions are concepts that reflect both the "quantity" and the "quality" of an individual's valuing of self and others. Hence, the concept of first, second or third degrees of a role sequence is a way of describing the interaction between two people in terms of their respective definitions of OK-ness at the existential level. In other words, the degree of mutual OK-ness is a relational concept. However, OK-ness also depends on who defines OK-ness. This is the crux of the practice/research divide; researchers need to be aware that they have to view other people's perceptions of OK-ness, but can only do so only via their own view of OK-ness (see Etherington, 2004.) To be of practical use the idea of first, second and third degree role sequences needs an observable index. Possible candidates may be measures derived from the Stroking Profile (McKenna 1974), the Functional Fluency Index (Temple 1999) or even an inverse index of discounting implicit in the "Keyhole" diagram (O'Reilly-Knapp and Erskine, 2003). It remains for researchers to devise indices that take account of the fact that, irrespective of the subjectivity of who defines OK-ness in any situation, there is a one in four chance that any particular role sequence will be characterised by both people having positions in the same OK-ness quadrant and a one in sixteen chance that such a position will confirm mutual OK-ness.

The density of a role sequence is a simple ratio of the above two factors. For example, the reciprocal "You're so beautiful!"/"I do love you!" does not have the same 'density' as a Shakespearean love sonnet. It may be possible for researchers to relate the notion of the density of a role sequence to ways of time structuring.

The diversity of a role sequence is determined by the number of protagonists. The more people involved the wider the diversity and measures of duration, degree and density will be 'diluted' or 'inflated' accordingly.

Role sequences and time structuring

The link between role sequences and Berne's modes of time structuring, including two others identified subsequently - play (Cowles-Boyd and Boyd, 1980) and racketeering (English 1976) - is shown in **Table 13.5**.

Type of outcome	Roles	Time Structure
Negative (NORS)	Negative	Games Racketeering
Positive (PORS)	Positive	Activity Sets Play Intimacy
Mixed (MORS)	Positive &/or Negative	Activity Games Sets (Play) Racketeering Pastimes
Indeterminate (IORS)	Positive &/or Negative	Withdrawal (Play) Rituals Pastimes Racketeering

Table 13.5

This locates role sequences within the overall framework of transactional analysis. A new category of time structuring termed "sets" is also included. Sets are the positive counterpart of games. All games are played with negative roles; sets are comprised of positive roles. This is a totally new concept that will have far reaching if not radical implications for transactional analysis. Sets are discussed below

Principles

There are two principles and associated rules that underpin the dynamics of all role sequences. The first principle is a general "world view" that asserts that, although we are unique individuals who create our own "reality", we affect others and are affected by others. In terms of the Contact Cube, whenever I enact a particular role I invite others to reciprocate. Although based on observations, the roles are so defined that causality is circular – an observer cannot definitively discern which of any two people 'caused' the other to respond in a particular way.

The second principle is that people interact on the basis of attempts to affirm their own and others' OK-ness. When such attempts fail, we refer to them as games. Sets are the opposite – successful attempts to affirm the OK-ness of both parties. This is the crux of the health/pathology divide in transactional analysis. Although founded on a value base of OK-ness the balance between concepts derived from functional and dysfunctional behaviours has tended to favour the latter.

Patterns and rules

Because of the reciprocity of roles, predictable patterns of relationships exist. In transactional analysis these are known as "contaminations", "discounting", "racketeering" and "games". Cognitive Analytic Therapy describes similar processes as "snags", "traps", "dilemmas" and "target problem procedures". (Ryle 1995, Ryle and Kerr 2002) In addition:

> "The developmental understanding points to the need to identify each role in relation to its reciprocal. ... a *role*, in this theoretical context, is understood to imply a pattern of action, expectation, affect and memory. Either pole of a core reciprocal role procedure may:
>
> 1. Be enacted towards others who will be induced to play the reciprocal.
> 2. Be enacted towards the reciprocal aspect of the self.
> 3. Be transformed into an alternative avoidant, symptomatic or defensive procedure.
>
> Core roles associated historically with unmanageable affects, or prohibited by their internalised reciprocating roles may either be elicited from others ('projective identification') or may be replaced by avoidant or symptomatic expressions, which involve modified behaviours and lessened affective arousal. Repression and other 'ego defenses' and 'compromise formations' can be described in these terms.
>
> At its simplest, a Sequential Diagram describes a core reciprocal role procedure which generates two possible enactments. An individual could enact either role and in doing so would be seeking to elicit the corresponding reciprocal from another person or aspect of the self". (Ryle, 1997, p. 24)

Extending this type of categorisation to include role sequences and sets derived from positive roles yields a classification of non-pathological interaction, which potentially, describes the full spectrum of relationships. I say "potentially" as a reminder that role sequences are associated with characteristic qualities of contact and imago images. Relationships are by no means as cut and dried as a taxonomic series of Aristotelean categories, but include an individual's "phenomenological experiences and inter-subjective relationships [that] determine his or her sense of self-in-the-relationship at the current moment" (Erskine 1995 p. 237). Nevertheless, discernible patterns exist, perhaps most noticeably in games analysis.

The idea that roles operate at two levels is a well-established method of game analysis (Berne, 1970). Here the rule is that the role occupied, that is, being enacted, occurs at the social level, whereas the role to which a person will switch occurs at the psychological level.

A third level of analysis may be added (Law 1979, Barnes 1981). With positive roles, the role a person *expects/hopes* others will reciprocate occurs at the existential level. With negative roles, the role a person *defends against* in others or seeks to confirm for him or her self occurs at the existential level. Similar logic may be applied to the psychological and attitudinal levels.

The dynamics of the process (**Table 13.6**) is illustrated by Barnes's description of a client who:

> "occupies the role of Rescuer on the Social level and moved externally toward a Social Victim. Internally she defended against Social Persecutors. Psychologically she assumes [occupies] the role of Victim, the role she moved toward socially, and she defended against or moved away from Rescuers. Existentially, she occupies the Persecutor role,

moved toward Rescuers (for reinforcement of her life position) and defended against Victims (to avoid a challenge to her life position). The role she moved toward existentially (Rescuer) is the role she occupies socially." (Barnes, 1981 p. 29)

Barnes' description may be translated into the moves shown in **Table 13.6**. Note that **Table 13.6** only shows the roles for one person. Likewise, the roles occupied at the Con are not shown as they are the same as those for those during the Response. Similarly, roles for the Gimmick are subject to slightly different rules – which I explain later – that involve the roles exhibited by the second person in the interaction. Note too, that the shaded areas represent aspects of the interaction that are not immediately or directly discernible to an observer. This signifies that the social level is what everyone can *see* and *hear*. The psychological level may be intuited from non verbal postures, gesticulations, facial expressions and tone of voice.

Rule	Level	Response Role occupied at each level	Switch Previously occupied role moves to (level)	Cross-up Internally seeks to confirm in self & defends against (moves away from) in others	Pay-off Role finally occupied at each level
S→ E → P	Social	R	V	P	P
P → S → E	Psycho-logical	V	P	R	R
E → P → S	Existential	P	R	V	V
NU	Not used	B	B	B	B

Table 13.6

1. The solid arrows show that the role occupied at the *social* level (Rescuer in the above quotation) is the role a person will move towards at the *existential* level. It is also the role (in others) that is defended against, but the role the person seeks to confirm for him or herself and finally occupies at the *psychological* level. I refer to this as the **sep** dynamic rule

2. The dashed arrows show that the role occupied at the *psychological* level (Victim in Barnes' example) is the role a person will move towards at the *social* level. It is also the role (in others) that is defended against, but the role the person seeks to confirm for him or herself and finally occupies at the *existential* level. This is the **pse** dynamic rule.

3. The dotted arrows show that the role occupied at the *existential* level (Persecutor in the above example) is the role a person will move towards at the *psychological* level.

It is also the role (in others) that is defended against, but the role the person seeks to confirm for him or herself and finally occupies at the *social* level. This is the **eps** dynamic rule.

4. The role **not** used (but existing as an additional option at a *fourth* level) is the role that is avoided in self and may be projected onto others. This is the **nu** dynamic rule.

I refer to these rules are the **sep-pse-eps-nu** rules for NORS; they hold true for most of the negative reciprocals and provide extremely useful predictors. Once we know a person's role profile, we can predict the "payoff" or Closure. A simple way of remembering this is to visualise that "existential goes up and the other two go down".

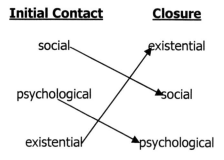

Initial Contact   **Closure**

social   existential

psychological   social

existential   psychological

Table 13.7

Identifying levels

A researcher has four options for detecting the existential level of a person's role profile during a negative or a positive outcome role sequence. The first is by observing the social level role and inferring the role at the psychological level and then hypothesising which of the two remaining roles is likely to be at the existential level. For example, if someone is a social level Rescuer and a psychological level Victim, they will be either an existential level Persecutor or an existential level Bystander. Secondly, if there is a switch of roles a researcher will observe that the role that was at the psychological level becomes the role at the social level. At that point the researcher will then be able to discern the new psychological level role – which previously, had been held at the existential level.

These two ways of identifying the role held at the existential level rely on a switch of roles – a person will switch or "move up" the psychological level role to the social level. We can see this by comparing the first two columns of **Table 13.6.** The erstwhile social level Rescuer "moves down" to become the role at the existential level – which is the sep dynamic rule. In accordance with the pse dynamic rule, the Victim role occupied at the psychological level becomes the person's social level role; diagrammatically it has "moved up". So too, according to the eps dynamic rule, the existential level Persecutor "moves up" to become the role at the psychological level.

In situations where there is no role switch we have to fall back on hypothesising what the existential level role might be. Obviously, it is one of two remaining roles – but which one? Barnes gives us a clue:

> "The third role is decided upon by the child when the basic life, or existential, position is adopted. The role on the existential level gives expression to one's attitudes and beliefs and determines the nature of the transactions at this level. It responds to position hunger.

Key issues are How to maintain a sense of worth and dignity and How to choose people to say hello to who will complement one's position, reinforce it, or oppose it. The Existential Persecutor's attitude is "I'm OK, you're not-OK", the Existential Rescuer's attitude is "I'm not-OK, you're OK", and the Existential Victim's attitude is "I'm not-OK, you're not-OK"" (Barnes 1981, p. 26).

This leaves the Bystander role. The Existential Bystander's attitude is "I'm not-OK, you're Irrelevant" (White 1994, 1995). Barnes also cites the following questions and answers to illustrate a person's role profile:

"(1) Why did your parents have you? (Social Role) – "They had me to keep them together. I always knew it was my responsibility to take care of my mother. Now I give my life for others" (Social Rescuer)

(2) What was the worst thing your parents ever said or did to you? "When I was fourteen my mother told me that I was born to keep her and my father together. They were married two months before my birth."

(3) What did you feel? (Psychological Role) – "I felt betrayed and hurt. (Psychological Victim) Before therapy I felt I must disappear. I was using drugs to kill myself"

(4) What did you think in your head? – "I know I will always come out alright." (Existential Persecutor)" (Barnes, 1981 p. 31).

Note that Barnes' suggestions require the formalised role of a participant/observer and, as such, fall outside simple observation of role sequences. Nevertheless, knowledge of the above patterns and rules is crucial information for an observer as it provides both a check on the researcher's own initial phenomenological 'diagnosis,' and also constitutes the basis of predicting possible future role switches from one level to another.

The fourth option is for the researcher to make a judgement about the transferential nature of the role enactment under consideration. This is far less "objective" than the other three options, since it demands differentiation between three categories – personal countertransference of the researcher, the identifying countertransference evoked by the act of observation, and the apparently desired or reciprocating countertransference manifested by those under observation. Again, I cite the Cognitive Analytic Therapy perspective:

"transference and countertransference are seen to be one particular example of the general meshing of reciprocal role procedures….. It is useful to distinguish two sources of countertransference. One, which may be called personal countertransference, will reflect the therapist's particular range of role procedures [reciprocals and role sequences]…. Such personal countertransference is not totally distinct from the specific reactions evoked by the particular patient, which can be called elicited countertransference….. Within elicited countertransference reactions there is another useful distinction to bear in mind, that between identifying countertransference and reciprocating countertransference…. This distinction … stems logically from the model of the dialogic self. A person enacting one pole [role profile] of a RRP [reciprocal] may either (1) convey the feelings associated with the role to others, in whom corresponding emphatic feelings may be elicited, or (2) seek to elicit the reciprocating response of the other….. In the course of therapy, therapists can use their identifying countertransference to explore feelings which the patient is conveying non-verbally but does not acknowledge or experience consciously….. As regards reciprocating countertransference, the need is to recognise the pressure and to avoid reinforcing (collusive) responses. (Ryle and Kerr, 2003, pp. 103-105).

In practice, and as we shall see in **Chapter 17**, with ERICA, the majority of role profiles are identified *after* the action has occurred. Thus there is always the opportunity for the practitioner to check his or her perceptions during supervision before recording them. Furthermore, the rules form the basis of detecting meta-level patterns of bilateral interaction.

Bilateral analysis of negative outcome role sequences

Zalcman's review and critique of racket and game analyses highlights the fact that Berne's various accounts of games (Berne 1964, 1966, 1972), give an incomplete picture of the inter-action between two players. Hine's account of the bilateral nature of games (Hine 1990), significantly corrects the theoretical shortcomings of Berne's Formula G formulation of games (Berne, 1970) as a process from the perspective of only one player:

> "The fact that Formula G is neither completely one-handed nor a true bilateral picture with mutual responsibility should, in a sense, imply two Formula Gs superimposed. The bilateral nature of games is better shown in Karpman's Drama Triangle (1968) (Hine 1990, p.29),"

Superimposing roles at three levels on Berne's Formula G (Berne 1972), as shown in **Table 13.8**, gives a bilateral account of a game that follows the sep-pse-eps-nu rules exactly. In **Table 13.8** the roles are negative and the shaded areas signify stages of the sequence that are not observable. It echoes the Bernean format of a game, but does not show the complexity of analysis inherent in Hine's formulation, with links to other transactional analysis concepts (Hine 1990). Nevertheless, it is entirely compatible with Hine's bilateral analysis of games, and, as such, complements her observations. Likewise, it fits with Schwock's observations that role changes from social to psychological level, and from psychological to an existential level, are accompanied by rackets and drivers (Schwock 1979, 1980, cited in Barnes, 1981 p. 28).

Con		Gimmick		Response		Switch		Cross-up		Payoff	
A	B	A	B	A	B	A	B	A	B	A	B
V	P	P	V	V	P	P	V	R	R	R	R
P	V	V	P	P	V	R	R	V	P	V	P
R	R	R	R	R	R	V	P	P	V	P	V

Table 13.8

Note that **Table 13.8** also illustrates a role sequence with a negative outcome. Negative outcomes of a role sequence (NORS) are similar to games. However, they differ from games as defined by Berne at various times, in as much as they are bilateral; they are units of analysis that fully describe the interaction between two or more people. Examining the processes underlying role sequences with negative outcomes (NORS), serve also to elucidate the analysis of bilateral games.

Contact, Communication and Confirmation

Role sequences all share the same underlying process. This is in three stages – Contact, Communication and Confirmation. Each stage has two further sub-divisions, and these

(**Table 13.9**) may be added to the Formula G format given in **Table 13.8**. The additional headings show how the three stages relate to the revised Formula G.

Contact		Communication		Confirmation	
Con	Gimmick	Response	Switch	Cross-up	Payoff
A	B	A	B	A	B	A	B	A	B	A	B
V	P	P	V	V	P	P	V	R	R	R	R
P	V	V	P	P	V	R	R	V	P	V	P
R	R	R	R	R	R	V	P	P	V	P	V

Table 13.9

Table 13.10 gives the full format applicable to an analysis of positive, negative and mixed role sequences. Bearing in mind that each phase has two sub-phases, the entire process may be conveniently referred to as the 3Cs ("the three Cs").

Contact		Communication		Confirmation	
Con	Gimmick	Response	Switch	Cross-up	Payoff
External	Internal	Emergent	Revealed	Options	Closure
A	B	A	B	A	B	A	B	A	B	A	B
V	P	P	V	V	P	P	V	R	R	R	R
P	V	V	P	P	V	R	R	V	P	V	P
R	R	R	R	R	R	V	P	P	V	P	V

Table 13.10

The division and transition from one phase to another are not rigidly demarcated. Formal definitions of each of the three stages of a role sequence serve as a useful starting point for examining further the practical and conceptual distinctions between the phases.

- Contact is the mutual acknowledgement between two people of each other's presence. Figuratively speaking, contact raises the question *"How do you say hello?"*
- Communication entails the mutual inter-change of a message. Here the question is *"What do you say after you say hello?"*
- Confirmation involves the mutual acknowledgement of the impact of the Contact and the Communication. At this point the question becomes *"How's our relationship now?"* Or perhaps more definitively, a statement emerges, *"Okay I got the message. This is how our relationship is/will be next time"*

Contact

Contact consists of the mutual acknowledgement between two people of each other's presence. Contact involves an exchange of strokes, which conceptually, are regarded as separate from whatever communication may follow. The degree of attachment and bonding (Benjamin 1993, 2003) involved is a significant factor in determining the quality of the Contact that is established. In turn, the quality of contact influences any subsequent Communication. Berne (1972) addresses the very issue of contact. His comments on "how do you say hello?" (Berne 1972, pp. 3-5), "the handshake" and "friends" (Berne 1972, pp.8-10), and his tongue in cheek account of the six different ways of answering the question (Berne 1972, pp.440-441), capture the profundity that belies the apparent simplicity of Contact.

External Contact is what an observer may see and each of the players experience in the role sequence. It is similar to, but significantly different from Berne's notion of the "con" (Berne 1971 p.23), with the most important distinction being that, following Hine's suggestion, both parties have, and present to one another, their individual role profiles.

The salient feature of the External aspect of Contact in a negative role sequence is the presence of discounting. This may – and often does - include ulterior transactions, but they are not a defining characteristic. Transactionally (or externally), discounting may be detected by redefining or blocking transactions (Mellor and Schiff, 1975). All the negative roles contain a discount. Enacting a social level Rescuer role discounts the other person by defining him or her as a Victim – and so on.

Internal Contact is non-observable and hence, strictly speaking, remains a hypothetical state of affairs. One hypothesis is that one or both players identify with each other. Another hypothesis is that projective identification based on negative roles, applies to a negative role sequence, whereas empathy predominates in role sequences with positive roles.

Establishing the nature of Internal Contact requires a research design beyond mere observation. The indications are that identification is a complex process and that "identification" may be projective, retroflective, introjective or confluent, with each of these disruptions of contact matching various negative role profiles.

Communication

There are three factors that contribute to the continuation of a role sequence beyond the Contact phase into the process of Communication. The first is the nature of the Internal component of Contact. This probably involves identification with the role profile of the other person. If I identify with someone else, I take on their role and am likely to want to continue beyond our initial contact. If I do not identify with the other person, our interaction is likely to peter out. This is consistent with English's concept of racketeering, where person A seeks strokes from person B by presenting racket feelings. English points out that the process will continue until person A withdraws or person B stops stroking (English 1976). There may be ulterior transactions, but no switch of roles, and therefore, no game ensues. Role sequences add an additional perspective; the interaction does not continue because person B probably does not identify with person A.

Secondly, the intention of psychological games is implicit and all such encounters convey a common message – one or both players are, or become, not-OK in the eyes of the other. Players do not necessarily start (make Contact) with the conscious or explicit intention of making him or herself or the other person not-OK. However, if there is discounting by one or both players during the Contact phase, together with the internal process of identifying with the role of the other, the stage is well set for the interaction to continue on into the Communication phase. Having negotiated the way in which they have said hello, and thus, reached the beginning of the Communication phase, the players then have to deal with the question of what they say after they have said hello. In **Table 13.10** this is represented as the "Emergent" sub-phase of a role sequence leading to a negative outcome.

If, at the start of the Communication phase, there is no explicit purpose or intention behind whatever message the players are in the process of conveying, *or* if the purpose of their interchange is based on discounting, the players' intentions will be ambiguous. More especially, discounting if not already present during the Contact phase, will emerge as redefining, blocking and/or ulterior transactions, along with an ostensible purpose. The players' roles will be the same as those occupied during the External Contact sub-phase with the hypothesised process of mutual identification having taken place during the Internal

Contact. Thereafter the players will maintain their starting roles while exchanging a series of transactions, each of which is aptly described by Hine as a "provocative stimulus" (Hine 1990 p. 30). Eventually, one player switches and the other follows suit – as indicated by the role profiles during the Revealed sub-phase of Communication. At this point it becomes apparent that the ostensible message is not the "real" message.

Along with these possibilities, my account of the switch is that one or both players are following the sep-pse-eps-nu rules diagrammed in **Table 13.5**. The players move to the roles they occupied at the psychological level at the start of their interaction. The role switches are usually accompanied by crossed transactions. Which person switches first, seems to make little difference. It is also at this point that the existential roles become more explicit; they "move up" or change to the psychological level and what previously had to be gleaned from knowledge of the players' scripts may now be inferred from their rackets (Schwok, 1980 in Barnes, 1981 p. 28)

Confirmation

In **Table 13.10 t**he internal or intra-psychic Options component of Confirmation is based on speculation consistent with the dictum that the roles at the social level are the roles hitherto occupied at the psychological level. This is Rescuer for player A and Persecutor for player B. In both cases, these are the roles against which each player originally defended in another person or sought to confirm for themselves. This poses the double bind of having to adopt their own existential level role, or the alternative of switching to the existential level roles occupied at the end of the Revealed sub-phase of Communication (Victim and Rescuer for players A and B respectively). The latter option, presumably, is discounted on the basis of having had these negatively reinforced during the Emergent sub-phase. The observable resolution or Closure is to revert to the role profiles prevailing at the Revealed sub-phase, thereby externalising blame and confirming the "real" message that in the eyes of the other, each player is not-OK.

Bilateral analysis of role sequences with positive outcomes

All that has been said about role sequences with negative outcomes applies to role sequences with a positive outcome – with four crucial differences. The *first* and most obvious difference is that the roles involved are positive and hence contact is not based on discounting or transferential factors.

The *second* difference is that the Internal Contact sub-phase probably arises out of identification with another person based on empathy rather than projective identification. Obviously there are degrees of empathy, albeit difficult to categorise, but all require positive roles. Thus pastiming, for example, may be characterised by varying degrees of "lesser" empathy, with intimacy representing the acme.

The *third* difference between NORS and PORS is that the role switches are experienced in very different ways. In both cases, there are switches or changes of roles at the Revealed stage of the interaction (the Switch in Berne's Formula G). With NORS the switch is disconcerting, to say the least. It is at this stage that what was previously 'out of awareness' comes into conscious focus; individuals who are familiar with the theory of games, realise they are in a game (Berne's "cross-up"). Those who have no TA background feel confused, deceived, cheated. "I thought you were supposed to be helping – but now you're having a go at me" is a typical internal response. Mutual not-OK-ness is confirmed.

None of this happens with PORS. More correctly, there *are* role changes, but they are not experienced as disconcerting. In fact, they are either not even noticed, or are experienced as positive; mutual OK-ness is confirmed. And just as in games, NORS and PORS occur at varying levels or degrees of intensity. First degree NORS (games) are neither here nor there; people feel annoyed, irritated, miffed or "put out". This doesn't last for long. They 'unload' by relating the incident to someone else, mutter under their breath, avoid each other for a while, and generally, subsequent contact is tinged with wariness. Second degree games are more serious – the sort of row people would not wish the neighbours to overhear. Third degree NORS end up in fisticuffs, court, hospital, police stations, or the mortuary. First degree PORS often have monosyllabic endings – "OK", "Good", "Thanks", and "Great!" They represent the bread and butter of general, "normal" social interaction. Second degree PORS are characterised by comments such as "Thanks, that's very helpful", "I feel good about that", "I knew I was right", "Good for you", "Well done!" They result in people looking forward to their next meeting. Third degree PORS touch the soul, or end with the time structuring of intimacy.[1] During each of the three degrees of PORS, there is nothing duplicitous about PORS.

Along with these differences a *fourth* crucial factor is that with PORS, the sep-pse-eps-nu rules that apply to NORS do not operate in the same way, being based on entirely different expectations. That is, the dynamics of Options and Closure columns of **Table 13.6** operate in a totally different way - as in **Table 13.11.**

Rule	Level	Emergent Role occupied at (level)	Revealed Previously occupied role moves to (level)	Options Role hopes others will reciprocate	Closure Role finally occupied at
S→E→P→S	Social	R	V	P	R
P→S→E→P	Psychological	V	P	R	V
E→P→S→E	Existential	P	R	V	P
NU	"Not used"	B	B	B	B

Table 13.11

---

[1] In citing these somewhat anodyne examples it is important to remember that role sequences are based on reciprocals – the combined role profiles of (at least) two people. Reciprocals are not the same as single transactions between ego states which depend on a stimulus-response paradigm; reciprocals have circular, rather than linear, causality. Hence many of the examples I give are potentially misleading. All the personalised roles are relative; any one role exists at any level only in relation to the other roles. They are manifestly co-created, yet have to be presented sequentially in the text. Conceptually, they have the status of the union of two symbols in a (mathematical) set. Thus one cannot be defined without another. An analogy may be helpful. In certain ball games (such as cricket and baseball) a player may be dismissed in several ways. For the purpose of the analogy, let us confine this to four ways of being dismissed. Readers unfamiliar with the laws of cricket or baseball will still be able to grasp the point, namely, a player can only be dismissed as the result of the action of another player. It takes two players to create each one of four modes of dismissal – just as it takes two people to create a role (even if the second person is not physically present, or exists only in fantasy). In addition, the multi–level nature of reciprocals makes it extremely difficult to give meaningful examples simultaneously at all the levels of a reciprocal. For these reasons I have chosen mostly to present only the symbols, leaving it to readers to create their own examples.

This requires that the sep-pse-eps-nu rules for NORS have to be re-phrased for positive roles:

1.   The role occupied at the *social* level is the role a person will move towards at an *existential* level and the role which the person expects/hopes others will reciprocate at the *psychological* level, but finally returns to and occupies at the *social* level.

2.   The role occupied at a *psychological* level is the role that a person will move towards at the *social* level and the role a person expects/hopes others will reciprocate at the *existential* level, but finally returns to and occupies at the *psychological* level.

3.   The role occupied at the *existential* level is the role a person will move towards at the *psychological* level and the role which a person expects/hopes others will reciprocate at the *social* level, but finally returns to and occupies at the *existential* level.

4.   The role *not used* (but existing as an additional option at a *fourth* level) is the role that is avoided in self.

These are the SEPS-PSEP-EPSE-NU dynamic rules for this type of PORS which I refer to as **Type One** sets. The nature of the Contact and subsequent Communication is qualitatively different. The intentionality of the message emerges and is manifestly co-created during the Revealed sub-phase. In Bernean games and bilateral analysis of NORS, the disconcerting feature, indeed the drama, comes from the unexpected switch of roles and the revelation of the "real" message.

As in games, in Type One sets, there is a change of role from social to psychological level, but this emerges from the preceding interaction and comes without drama as a joint exchange – rather than as something unexpected. The rationale of this is implicit in the SEPS-PSEP-EPSE-NU rules; when enacting positive roles, people are operating on the assumption that others will reciprocate their OK-ness and thus, whatever messages are exchanged, are presented as an affirmation of the parties' mutual OK-ness. This dynamic occurs despite the role switches at the Revealed sub-phase and hypothetically, during the Options. Apart from the fact that positive roles are being used, the sequence looks very much like a game where the players do not accept the payoff (Stewart and Joines, 1987 p. 255). Observation of positive outcome role sequences confirms that the Revealed sub-phase usually consists of a joke, an aside, a light hearted comment, or the main topic of conversation being interspersed by reference to some other topic. The players do not go along with the new topic but retain their OK-OK positions and perhaps more importantly, their relationship is fostered. The Contact, Communication, Confirmation format of the interaction is preserved. Despite the fact that the Revealed sub-phase of Communication is often disregarded, or sometimes redefined (in a non-pathological sense of the word), and thus becomes redundant, the link between the Contact phase (role expectations) and the Confirmation phase of the relationship, is not threatened.

Type One sets represent "normality" – in a statistical sense. They occur most frequently and are the equivalent of first degree games. Most people do not even notice Type One sets. Generally speaking, what we seem to notice is *differences* – but not differences or changes of *role*. Roles are derived from expectations; we only classify them as such when we *think* about them. Expectations are that which one does not have until something *other* than the expected occurs. What we notice is differences or changes of *contact.* Given that the normality of social interaction is preserved when positive roles are enacted, by the time the Revealed stage of the 3Cs format is reached few people are sufficiently emotionally attuned to notice changes in the *quality* of positive contact – particularly when at the Closure, both people revert to the roles they adopted at the start of the role sequence.

Type Two sets mirror the dynamic rules for NORS, but with positive roles and no discounting. The difference between Type One and Type Two sets is that during the latter the participants *do* notice the difference of contact and usually role, at the Revealed stage. This sub-phase typically consists of new information, new insights and opportunities for growth and the relationship between the parties is heightened.[1] The Closure consists of confirmation of the role initially held at the existential level.

Accordingly, we have to amend the SEPS-PSEP-EPSE-NU rules to read:

1. The role occupied at the *social* level is the role a person will move towards at the *existential* level. It is also the role the person seeks to confirm for him or herself and finally occupies at the *psychological* level.

2. The role occupied at the *psychological* level is the role a person will move towards at the *social* level. It is also the role the person seeks to confirm for him or herself and finally occupies at the *existential* level.

3. The role occupied at the *existential* level is the role a person will move towards at the *psychological* level. It is also the role the person seeks to confirm for him or herself and finally occupies at the *social* level.

4. The role *not used* (but existing as an additional option at a fourth level) is the role that is avoided in self.

I write these as the SEP-PSE-EPS-NU2 rules, or more simply, remember them and refer to them verbally as **Type Two** set rules. They are the positive counterpart of second degree games, indicating an increased level of affective contact. My impression is that Type Two sets are culturally bound. That is, they involve a degree of openness that in Western society is restricted to particular situations such as therapeutic exchanges that depend, at least to some extent, on the formalised roles of the protagonists.

There is possibly a further version or type of PORS that warrants brief mention at this point. I say "possibly" for reasons that will become apparent as I explain the nature of this type of role sequence. In a *Type Three* set the extent or degree of openness is supplemented or accompanied by spontaneity. Up to the Revealed stage, the process pans out in the same way as a Type Two set. What follows is more like a climax than the usual Closure. Instead of the role that was at the psychological level during the Revealed stage appearing as the social level Closure, the role that was previously at the *fourth "not used"*

---

[1] Resolution of a Type II impasse (Goulding and Goulding, 1979), where the *therapist* gives new information to the client's A$_1$, is a good example - provided that the client is not enacting negative roles (which would be an example of a mixed outcome role sequence). Most excerpts from audio-tapes prepared for and presented to Exam. Boards during the Certified Transactional Analysis oral examination process, have the format of a Type Two set. Most trainers exhort trainees to select tapes that demonstrate a definite, if only momentary, change in the client's (audible) behaviour.

level, emerges as the social level Closure – together with the original, initial social level role at the psychological level. **Table 13.12** shows this process:

Rule	Level	Emergent Role occupied at	Revealed Previously occupied role moves towards	Options Internally seeks to confirm in self	Closure Role finally occupied at
S→ N→ E → P	Social	R	V	P	B
P → S → N → E	Psycho-logical	V	P	B	R
E → P → S → N	Existential	P	B	R	V
N → E → P → S	Not used	B	R	V	P

Table 13.12

Provisionally, the dynamic rules for Type Three PORS are:

1 The role occupied at the *social* level is the role a person will move towards at the hitherto *not used* level. It is also the role a person seeks to confirm for him or herself at the *existential* level, but finally occupies at the *psychological* level.

2 The role occupied at the *psychological* level is the role a person will move towards at the *social* level. It is also the role that a person will seek to confirm for him or herself at the *not used* level, but finally occupies at the *existential* level.

3 The role occupied at the *existential* level is the role a person will move towards at the *not used* level. It is also the role a person will seek to confirm for him or herself at the *social* level and finally relinquishes to occupy at the *psychological* level.

4 The role *not used* during the Emergent stage (but existing at a *fourth* level) is the role that is progressively claimed and the role that the person will seek to confirm for him or herself at the *psychological* level and finally occupy at the *social* level.

This is a tentative interpretation of observations of interaction where there is this level of affective impact. My observations suggest that this type of role sequence is characteristic of intimacy as a mode of time structuring. However, it is particularly important to note that the roles at the various levels during the shaded Options area in **Table 13.12** are "theoretical" and can be confirmed only by introspection. The reasoning behind my interpretation of this type of set is that instead of the initial existential level Promoter being confirmed at the Closure, the individual exercises the option of activating the "not used" level of the role profile. I discuss Type Three set further in **Chapter 14**, and, in **Chapter 22**, reflect upon possible unconscious processes that may be involved.

Clearly, the above "rules" constitute no more than the basis of a series of hypotheses. In reality, relationships do not come in neatly packaged parcels labelled "PORS", "NORS" "MORS" or "IORS". More so than with negative outcome role sequences PORS exist within a tangle of indeterminate outcome role sequences. Nevertheless, because the Type One and Type Two rules apply to all PORS, we can apply the rule to any role profile. This is bridging the practice/research divide in action. Once we know a person's role profile we can use the rules to predict not only the roles to which they are likely to move during the ensuing interaction, but also to hypothesise about contact, and the imago images and life position held at the existential level.

The significance of sets as a major component of role sequences with a positive outcome warrants serious consideration. Sets are the operational antidote to the divide of health/pathology in transactional analysis. In terms of the practice/research divide they present a challenge to practitioners and researchers alike of identifying, categorising and naming them. Again, I would emphasise that the Type One and Type Two rules are more difficult to detect than NORS (Bernean games), because of the drama associated with the role switches in the latter, and the fact that PORS always exist within a tangle of IORS.

Nevertheless, one of Zalcman's recommendations arising from her critique of games and rackets (Zalcman, 1990) was that "we need to include behaviors that are "healthy" or "non problematic" and which are useful in understanding desirable functioning" (Zalcman, 1990 p. 11). She concludes:

> "concepts and techniques which focus on normal or mentally healthy behavior and change (not just those focusing on problems or pathological development) are needed" (Zalcman, 1990 p. 17).

Sets clearly fill this gap and I would anticipate that they would be particularly useful in organisational work. For example, it would be far more useful for a CEO to know the distribution of work time in a company in terms of PORS, NORS, MORS and IORS than an account of time devoted to rackets and games. Practicalities aside, sets have other implications, namely, the extent to which they are consistent with and are related to other concepts in transactional analysis.

Hitherto, transactional analysis has been adept at describing how needs are not being met. A spin-off of sets is that they demonstrate how in everyday life, people have their "relational needs" met (Erskine, Moursund and Trautmann. 1999 p. 122-151). That is, when expectations are met (via contact) relational needs are satisfied. In other words, we now have a theoretical concept (sets) and an operational definition (the dynamic rules) for testing the hypothesis that mutual OK-ness is the cornerstone of non-clinical social interaction.

Historically I do not think it was that Berne overlooked the existence of sets – but that he discounted their significance. That is, although purely speculative, I imagine that having identified withdrawal, rituals, pastimes, games and rackets and intimacy as the major ways of structuring time, Berne lumped together anything left over into the category of activity. It is only when we take account of the distinction between formalised and personalised roles (Law 2004) that we can apply the dynamic rules to dyadic interaction in relation to the 3Cs, and conclude that sets represent a refinement of Berne's notion of activity as being a goal-directed mode of time structuring. Indeed, one may argue that unlike Berne's other categories, activity is not an exclusive category – it is an amorphous catch-all account of how people get strokes while engaged in anything that may be said to be goal directed. In contrast, sets have exclusive parameters derived from specific, observable behaviours amenable to empirical research. Moreover like all role sequences, they are based not on the predictability or otherwise of stroke exchanges, but on confirmation of mutual OK-ness.

Mixed outcomes

Role sequences with mixed outcomes (MORS) occur when one player ends with a negative role profile and the other with a positive role profile.

Contact				Communication				Confirmation			
External		Internal		Emergent		Revealed		Options		Closure	
A	B	A	B	A	B	A	B	A	B	A	B
V-	P+	P+	V-	V-	P+	P-	V+	R-	R+	R-	P+
P-	V+	V+	P-	P-	V+	R-	R+	P-	P+	V-	V+
R-	R+	R+	R-	R-	R+	V-	P+	V-	V+	P-	R+
B-	B+	B+	B-	B-	B+	B-	B+	B-	P+	B-	B+

Table 13.13

In **Table 13.13** there is no mutual agreement between the players about their OK-ness. Throughout the sequence player A occupies negative roles, while player B consistently maintains positive roles.

Theoretically, role sequences with mixed outcomes are just as likely to occur as are sequences with negative outcomes (racketeering or games) and those with positive outcomes (pastiming or sets). Thus, with mixed outcomes it is possible for one person to be playing a game while the other does not – as shown above. However, in practice such sequences are often resolved enroute, ending up either with both players in negative roles or both with positive roles. This raises the possibility referred to earlier of "variable" role sequences; an issue I have shelved pending further research.

In these cases, situational variables such as setting and time scale also play a part. For example, I imagine that the incidence of mixed outcome role sequences over comparable time scales is higher in an organisational setting than in a therapy group. The competent therapist would succeed in inviting player A into positive roles and thus the potential mixed outcome would become a sequence with a positive outcome. Middle of the road competence will spawn MORS. An incompetent therapist would end up in a game within a sequence with a negative outcome.

My experience of organisational settings is that there is a greater likelihood of a mixed outcome scenario occurring more frequently or continuing for longer than in clinical settings. Factors such as the time a manager is able to devote to single instances of dysfunctional behaviour, the diversity of organisational tasks, the variability of modes of time structuring and so forth, make some aspects of the average manager's task comparatively more complex than the therapist's who is operating in a once a week group.

Indeterminate outcome role sequences

These outcomes occur most frequently. They do not confirm the participants' mutual OK-ness or not OK-ness and the quality of the contact involved depends largely on the setting. Unlike positive, negative and mixed outcomes of role sequences, indeterminate outcomes do not have role switches from one level to another. Likewise complementary, crossed and ulterior transactions may be included and the associated communication rules (Berne 1961) apply –

but without role switches in relation to ulterior transactions. For negative roles, blocking, redefining transactions and racketeering abound, while with positive roles, rituals and pastiming most frequently yield manifestations of indeterminate role sequences.

Role sequences with indeterminate outcomes do not conform to the three C's of Contact, Communication and Confirmation. These role sequences are usually restricted to the first of these phases of interaction. For negative roles, Contact is characterised by racketeering and, sometimes, rituals of the social type. Pastiming and rituals are linked with positive roles and the Contact phase of interaction. Where the interaction continues beyond the Contact phase, activity and play are the modes of time structuring most usually associated with the indeterminate outcome of a role sequence. The following example illustrates a typical Contact-Communication snippet of interaction.

> Person A: "Hi. How are you doing?"
> Person B: "Fine. You?"
> Person A: "Okay."
> Person B: "I e-mailed the London supplier. Waiting for them to get back to me".
> Person A: "Good. Keep me posted"
> Person B: "Will do"

The first three lines of the conversation are Contact and the last three are Communication. They match with ritual and activity as ways of time structuring. Although the roles are positive, the type of role sequence is indeterminate. Because there is no shift of role, no change from psychological to social level, OK-ness is implied rather than *confirmed* or *denied* at the end of the sequence. Whether or not this may be regarded as a role sequence with a positive outcome is a matter of definition. To date, the comparatively high incidence of IORS suggests that they are of sufficient importance to warrant differentiation from other types of role sequences.

Other common features of role sequences

The above '3Cs' not only parallels Hine's treatment of dyadic interaction (Hine 1990) but also corrects Berne's one sided description that Zalcman highlighted:

> "the dynamic, interactional quality of games is missing", (Zalcman, 1990 p. 10)

All 900 reciprocals are amenable to the application of the positive and negative sets of dynamic rules. The 3Cs method of analysis means that PORS, MORS and NORS can all be treated in the same way using non-pejorative terms to describe each phase. In other words, we have the basis of a complete taxonomy of bilateral dyadic relationships for role sequences with negative, positive and mixed outcomes. Note too that role sequences are vastly different from Berne's concept of games. The latter concept is largely deterministic – people play games to 'get' a negative payoff that will advance the 'negative' aspects of their script. Role sequences describe patterns of social interaction based on co-created (reciprocal) role behaviours, which, in turn, appear to be linked with positive or negative life positions.

In addition to the above principles and rules that govern the dynamics of role sequences, other common features exist. These are largely of a statistical nature concerning the theoretical distribution of the each of the three groups of 300 reciprocals. For NORS these may be further reduced to six types of Bernean games and two types of racketeering. Three of the types of games have social level Bystander roles for one or both parties and thus the Bernean payoffs are not directly observable. Indeed, it transpires that only a third of all reciprocals are fully fledged bilateral games and/or racketeering that lead to fully observable payoffs. This does not mean that the remaining two thirds are not amenable to research, but rather, that a researcher would have to intervene in the interactive process to be able to identify partially observable configurations. A more extended discussion of the characteristics and distribution of the eight types of reciprocals is given in **Chapter 14**.

Implications for practice and research

As previously stated, relationships do not consist simply of a series of role sequences neatly packaged as PORS, MORS, and NORS interspersed with IORS These are the components of an observational model – Role Sequences – that need to be systematically researched to establish the frequency of occurrence, validity and reliability of all these patterns of interaction. The suggested 4Ds parameters of duration, degree, density and diversity are a useful starting point.

One of the predictable issues will be whether IORS are sufficient for determining when one role sequence starts and finishes and when the next one commences. This is an area of enquiry that has been extensively researched in Cognitive Analytic Therapy (CAT) where the use of "Self States Sequential Diagrams" or SSSDs is a central feature of the method:

> "Once the different self states [roles] have been identified, transitions between them can be monitored and a Self States Sequential Diagram (SSSD) can be constructed. The SSSD plots the patient's self state, the transitions between them and the procedures generated by each, and allows the events or procedures triggering state shifts to be monitored" (Ryle, 1997 p. 27).

The methodology of CAT requires clients to identify "target procedures" (dysfunctional roles) and "reformulate" these by devising "exits" from them. The parallels between SSSDs and role sequences are obvious. Procedures are similar to games and the CAT account of role reciprocation is enriched by the dynamics of Contact Cube roles. Most strikingly, however, the CAT process of identifying "procedures" and reformulating these as "target procedures" with "exits", confirms that even severely dysfunctional borderline clients become engaged and benefit from the process. This holds considerable promise for clinical transactional analysts. The prospect of teaching clients about personalised roles and role sequences in other settings is equally tenable.

Essential information for researchers and clients

In addition to the observational skills for identifying Contact Cube roles, the essential information about role sequences a researcher or client needs to know is that the unit of analysis is a reciprocal and these come in four varieties. Potentially, the dynamic rules kick in at certain stages of some role sequences. Knowledge of the rules is crucial information for an observer as it provides both a check on the researcher's own initial phenomenological 'diagnosis,' but also constitutes the basis of predicting possible future role switches from one level to another

Recapitulation

Because of the newness of the ideas advanced in this Chapter a brief recapitulation seems warranted:

197

- The Chapter builds on the Contact Cube model by adding four new concepts – reciprocals, role sequences, the three Cs and sets, all of which are linked by the associated dynamic rules. All these concepts rest on the assumption that relationships are based on confirmation or otherwise of mutual OK-ness.
- I have also touched on a theoretical classification and distribution of racketeering and games. The same logic may be applied to categorisation of pastiming and sets as well as a mixture of positive and negative role sequences.
- Although the ideas in this Chapter have been presented as theoretical concepts consistent with existing transactional analysis theory, they are all based on observations gleaned from practice. Clearly, further research is needed. However we don't need to re-invent the wheel; many of the research challenges posed by role sequences have already been tackled by Cognitive Analytic Therapy.

The Chapter has emphasised the importance of observation in balancing practice with a research-orientated mind set. The concepts described above call for research beyond the resources of any single individual. They need to be widely and systematically applied, validated, and reviewed. As will be described in **Part Five**, the application of the concepts to practise is based on a methodology that teaches clients to become researchers into their own characteristic use of Contact Cube roles and patterns of reciprocal interaction with others.

Key Points
13.1 Because the Contact Cube focuses on the role imago repertoire of a single individual, a second model - **Role Sequences** - is needed to describe more precisely the interaction between two or more people.
13.2 Personalised roles at three levels form a person's role profile. The combination of person A's role profile with person B's role profile is referred to as a **reciprocal**
13.3 Combinations of reciprocals are called role sequences. A role sequence is a series of reciprocals that confirms or denies the mutual OK-ness of both parties and thereby affects their future relationship.
13.4 There are negative outcome role sequences (**NORS**), mixed outcome role sequences (**MORS**) and positive outcome role sequences (**PORS**). Indeterminate role sequences (**IORS**) do not confirm or deny mutual OK-ness, but in all cases, the future relationship is affected. In all, there are 900 reciprocals that constitute a complete theoretical taxonomy of social interaction.
13.5 Consideration of the duration, degree, density and diversity of a role sequence permits comparison of the four types of role sequence.
13.6 There is a link between **role sequences** and Berne's modes of **time structuring,** including two others identified subsequently – play and racketeering.
13.7 Whenever people enact a particular role they invite others to reciprocate, in attempts to affirm their own and others' OK-ness. With NORS this process follows a **set of rules**: • The role occupied at the *social* level is the role a person will move towards at the *existential* level. It is also the role (in others) that is defended against, but the role the person seeks to confirm for him or herself and finally occupies at the *psychological* level. I refer to this as the **sep**

dynamic rule.
- The role occupied at the *psychological* level is the role a person will move towards at the *social* level. It is also the role (in others) that is defended against, but the role the person seeks to confirm for him or herself and finally occupies at the *existential* level. This is the **pse** dynamic rule
- The role occupied at the existential level is the role a person will move towards at the psychological level. It is also the role (in others) that is defended against, but the role the person seeks to confirm for him or herself and finally occupies at the social level. This is the **eps** dynamic rule.
- The role **not** used (but existing as an additional option at a fourth level) is the role that is avoided in self and projected onto others.

13.8 Superimposing roles at three levels on Berne's Formula G gives a bilateral account of a game that follows the above **sep-pse-eps-nu** rules exactly.

13.9 Role sequences all share the same underlying process. This is in three stages – **Contact, Communication** and **Confirmation.** Each stage has two further sub-divisions and these may be added to Formula G:
- Contact is the mutual acknowledgement between two people of each other's presence.
- Communication entails the mutual interchange of a message.
- Confirmation involves the mutual acknowledgement of the impact of the Contact and the Communication.

13.10 The **3cs** formula applies to negative and positive outcome role sequences. This is an alternative to Berne's one-sided description of games.

13.11 There are also rules for PORS. **Type One** set rules state:
- The role occupied at the social level is the role a person will move towards at an existential level and the role which the person expects/hopes others will reciprocate at the psychological level, but finally returns to and occupies at the social level.
- The role occupied at a *psychological* level is the role that a person will move towards at the *social* level and the role a person expects/hopes others will reciprocate at the *existential* level, but finally returns to and occupies at the *psychological* level.
- The role occupied at the *existential* level is the role a person will move towards at the *psychological* level and the role which a person expects/hopes others will reciprocate at the *social* level, but finally returns to and occupies at the *existential* level.
- The role *not used* (but existing as an additional option at a *fourth* level) is the role that is avoided in self.

13.12 Type Two set rules are:
- The role occupied at the social level is the role a person will move towards at the existential level. It is also the role the person seeks to confirm for him or herself and finally occupies at the psychological level.
- The role occupied at the *psychological* level is the role a person will move towards at the *social* level. It is also the role the person seeks to confirm for him or herself and finally occupies at the *existential* level.
- The role occupied at the *existential* is the role a person will move

towards at the *psychological* level. It is also the role the person seeks to confirm for him or herself and finally occupies at the *social* level.

- The role *not used* (but existing as an additional option at a fourth level) is the role that is avoided in self.

13.13   Provisional **Type Three** PORS have the following rules:

- The role occupied at the *social* level is the role a person will move towards at the hitherto *not used* level. It is also the role a person seeks to confirm for him or herself at the *existential* level, but finally occupies at the *psychological* level.

- The role occupied at the *psychological* level is the role a person will move towards at the *social* level. It is also the role that a person will seek to confirm for him or herself at the *not used* level, but finally occupies at the *existential* level.

- The role occupied at the *existential* level is the role a person will move towards at the *not used* level. It is also the role a person will seek to confirm for him or herself at the *social* level and finally relinquishes to occupy at the *psychological* level.

- The role *not used* during the Emergent stage (but existing at a *fourth* level) is the role that is progressively claimed and the role that the person will seek to confirm for him or herself at the *psychological* level and finally occupy at the *social* level.

13.14   **Sets** are the operational acme of the twin divides.

13.15   Relationships do not consist simply of a series of role sequences neatly packaged as PORS, MORS, and NORS interspersed with IORS. These need to be systematically researched. For **researchers**, knowledge of the four types of reciprocals and the relevant dynamic rules is essential.

13.16   The **methodology of CAT** holds considerable promise for clinical transactional analysts.

Self Supervision Suggestions 13

13.1   Identify a game and analyse it using **Berne's Formula G**

13.2   Superimpose the **3Cs formula** on the **13.1** result.

13.3   Observe snippets of social interaction and use **reciprocals** to analyse these.

13.4   Start documenting examples of the **four types** of role sequences. Note the frequency of occurrence of each type.

13.5   See if you can find links between the data from **Self Supervision Suggestion 13.4** and the **3Cs formula**.

13.6   Watch a ten minute excerpt from a film or a soap and do a **complete role sequence analysis**. If possible, get someone else to watch the same film/soap and compare your results.

13.7   Formulate a research proposal to investigate the **duration, degree, density** and **diversity** of role sequences in at least two different settings.

Chapter 14

Role Imago Repertoires

An important practical consideration is that individuals display a repertoire of role profiles and reciprocals, giving a characteristic "thumbprint" of their relationships. This Chapter examines the rationale behind this idea and describes ways of identifying and using these patterns to improve relationships. In particular, I describe eight distinctive types of negative outcome role sequences and demonstrate how they parallel role analysis used in Cognitive Analytic Therapy (CAT) with clients with borderline issues.

This Chapter is essential for trainers and researchers, but less so for anyone wanting to use ERICA to facilitate clients researching their role relationships. Information about the types of role sequences I will be explaining are not a necessary component of or requirement for clients being able to apply ERICA to their own circumstances.

Role profiles

In **Part Three** we saw that at any moment individuals have a choice of four positive and four negative roles at each of the social, psychological and existential levels. Each of these combinations of roles is called a role profile. They are germane to four types of role sequences, but to simplify matters in this Chapter we will confine ourselves largely to discussion of the four negative roles.

The total number of any four things taken three at a time (a "combination") is twenty-four. If you tackled **Self Supervision Suggestion 10.3**, you will already have written them out as twenty-four role profiles, but probably not in the same order as shown in **Table 14.1**.

Rescuer Cluster						Persecutor Cluster						Victim Cluster						Bystander Cluster					
1	2	3	4	5	6	7	8	9	10	11	12	13	14	15	16	17	18	19	20	21	22	23	24
r	r	r	r	r	r	p	p	p	p	p	p	v	v	v	v	v	v	b	b	b	b	b	b
v	b	v	p	b	p	v	b	r	b	v	r	b	r	p	r	b	p	v	p	r	p	r	v
p	p	b	b	v	v	r	r	v	v	b	b	p	p	b	b	r	r	r	r	v	v	p	p
b	v	p	v	p	b	b	v	b	r	r	v	r	b	r	p	p	b	p	v	p	r	v	r

Table 14.1

Table 14.1 shows all the role profiles in four "clusters" or groups. The second row of **Table 14.1** assigns a number to each role profile - from 1 to 24. The third row of **Table 14.1** represents the social level. The fourth row shows the psychological level and the fifth row gives the existential level. The last row represents the role that is not used.

Note that the order in which the profiles are arranged is not arbitrary; they are grouped (clustered) with the first six profiles having the Rescuer role at the social level; the next six profiles (numbers 7 to 12) have the Persecutor role at the social level – and so on.

How, one may ask, is **Table 14.1** going to help us understand relationships?

- In **Chapter 13** we saw that the 3Cs formula gives a useful way of looking at social interaction – a dynamic process that proceeds in stages. Simply by considering the social level of any of the twenty four role profiles we can predict the apparently desired reciprocal role; Rescuers and Persecutors "need", "look for", "invite" Victims

– and so on. Knowledge of role profiles implies that there is more to relationships than the initial, observable social level role.

- The psychological level indicates the role to which an individual will 'switch' if the interaction continues beyond the Emergent stage of a role sequence.
- The existential level signifies the Closure – the role a person seeks to confirm their life position.
- The role that is not used is the role that is likely to be projected onto others.

In other words, even before a second person responds, we will be able to apply the sep-pse-eps-nu rule to the role profile. As soon as the second person responds, we will be able to discern the nature of the forthcoming role sequence.

- If there is a discount, a negative outcome role sequence (NORS) is likely to ensue.
- If there is no discount, a mixed outcome role sequence (MORS) or an indeterminate outcome role sequence (IORS) is on the cards.
- We may have wait for the Emergent phase of the interaction to be able to judge whether an indeterminate outcome role sequence (IORS) will prevail.

Of course, in all the above instances, we will also be able to track the qualities of contact that are on display. Sometimes the content of the interaction will give us a glimpse of the imago images that may be around.

Reciprocals

This is where we have to go beyond immediate observation to consider what happens when two people interact, each having a choice of twenty-four role profiles. The seemingly daunting prospect of 24 x 24 = 576 reciprocal looms, but need not deter us. A simple example will show how this figure may be significantly reduced.

Take two people A and B. Give each person a choice of six items – designated 1 to 6. We can quite easily write out all the possible choices in a table with six rows and six columns; rows represent the choices made by A and columns show choices made by B.

	Choice 1	Choice 2	Choice 3	Choice 4	Choice 5	Choice 6
Choice 1	1:1	1:2	1:3	1:4	1:5	1:6
Choice 2	2:1	2:2	2:3	2:4	2:5	2:6
Choice 3	3:1	3:2	3:3	3:4	3:5	3:6
Choice 4	4:1	4:2	4:3	4:4	4:5	4:6
Choice 5	5:1	5:2	5:3	5:4	5:5	5:6
Choice 6	6:1	6:2	6:3	6:4	6:5	6:6

Table 14.2

Thus, for example, in **Table 14.2** "4:2" signifies that person A made Choice 4 and person B made Choice 2. In all, there are 6 x 6 = 36 combined choices. However, notice that "4:2" is the same as "2:4"; the only difference is that person A's choice (Choice 4) is shown first, followed by person B's choice (Choice 2). If we reverse this, we have person B's choice (2) and then A's choice (4). This means that if we are not interested in who was first to make their choice, we can ignore all the shaded cells or almost half the total number of cells in **Table 14.2**. In other words, we only have to examine the non shaded cells (36 - 15 = 21). We arrive at this simply by counting these - or by adding the number of choices (6) minus the number of shaded cells (5 for row 1, 4 for row 2 and so on).

There is a simple way of applying the same logic to any combination of rows and columns. Just as in **Table 14.1** where we counted (added) 6 + 5 + 4+ 3+ 2+ 1 = 21, with *twenty-four* choices, we have to add 24 + 23 + 22 + 21, continuing all the way down to 1, giving a total of 300, which is already considerably less than 576.

In addition, if we consider the *nature* of all the 576 reciprocals, there are some reciprocals where the role profiles of both parties have the Bystander role at the social level. You can see this by referring back to the Bystander cluster in **Table 14.1.** To illustrate, let us assume person A has role profile 21 (Bystander, Rescuer, Victim and Persecutor at the social, psychological, existential and the "not used" levels respectively), and person B has a Bystander, Victim, Rescuer and Persecutor role profile (number 19). Berne's term for this is "solitaire" or "skull games" – games that are played internally (Berne 1970, p.189). An observer would see only non-verbal behaviour - there would be no words and the all important tone of voices by which to judge the roles. This reduces the observable number of reciprocals by thirty-six reciprocals – or twenty-one if we disregard who "started" the interaction.

It turns out that if we examine the full matrix of 576 reciprocals we can eliminate 396 or two-thirds of these that involve reciprocals with the Bystander role at either the social or psychological levels.[1] This works out as 201 of the 300 reciprocals - disregarding the order of who starts the interaction. Within the two-thirds (201), there are further divisions (which I describe below), but a crucial point to note at this stage, is that this is as far as one can go merely by *observing* social interaction. To establish the reciprocals characterised by Bystander roles at the social and psychological levels, a researcher has to ask questions. The very act of so doing is likely to colour the response. In other words, if you want to change this aspect of a relationship, you have to *be in* the relationship.

It is also sobering to note that two-thirds of our role relationships stem from interaction that is largely non-verbal.

There is a further way of understanding the number of reciprocals that are amenable to observation only. We can see this by grouping reciprocals that have the same combinations of roles at the *social* and *psychological* levels. I call these groupings *configurations.* Each configuration has variations at the existential level.

Role profile #	Variation 1		Variation 2		Variation 3		Variation 4	
	1	9	1	12	3	9	3	12
Persons	A	B	A	B	A	B	A	B
Social level	r	p	r	p	r	p	r	p
Psychological level	v	r	v	r	v	r	v	r
Existential level	p	v	p	b	b	v	b	b

Table 14.3.

To illustrate, the reciprocals in **Table 14.3** have Rescuer and Victim roles at the social and psychological levels for person A and similarly, Persecutor and Rescuer roles for person B. If we keep these constant and only vary the roles at the shaded existential level, we end up with one configuration and its four variations. This is not a purely theoretical consideration –

---

[1] You would have to examine the matrix of 576 reciprocals if you wanted to verify this. Research-minded readers can obtain a colour–coded Excel spreadsheet by emailing me at gordon.law1@btopenworld.com

the social and psychological levels are what we *see* at the start of a snippet of interaction (unlike the existential level which has to be inferred).Taking account of the configurations permits our mapping all the possible combinations of these reciprocals and grouping them according to various criteria. Eight distinctive patterns emerge. I detail these below, bearing in mind that we are dealing with reciprocals that comprise the entire distribution of varieties of negative outcome role sequences (NORS).

Rationale

Readers may query the point of categorising and naming various role sequences. Even Berne did not get around to anything more than distinguishing between practical and theoretical game analysis:

> "Practical game analysis deals with special cases as they appear in specific situations. Theoretical game analysis attempts to abstract and generalize the characteristics of various games, so that they can be recognized independently of their momentary verbal content and their cultural matrix". (Berne 1964, p. 52)

Zalcman notes that:

> "Using this [above] distinction, I think that Berne's contributions were largely practical (or clinical), *not* theoretical (or conceptual)". (Zalcman 1990, p. 6)

Yet the question remains: what is the point of categorising and naming various role sequences – and in particular, the theoretical distribution of role sequences? The answer is that we do this in order to "test" a "theory". That is, based on observations of behaviour (proactive, reactive, etc.) ERICA proposes a *theory* of role interaction that enables us to make certain predictions about relationships. More specifically, the theory predicts the *existence* of 576 role sequences, some of which may not be readily discerned by observation. If the theory is going to be useful in our understanding of relationships, we need to determine *by observation* how frequently each of the role sequences occur under certain circumstances, for which groups of people, or indeed, for which individuals. This follows logically from Zalcman's critique of games as a concept and practical tool in transactional analysis (Zalcman 1990)[1]. ERICA seems to be following many if not all Zalcman's suggestions for a "make-over" of games analysis – particularly those suggestions that will widen the application of analysis to settings that require "the inclusion of transactional sequences that are not necessarily problematic or pathological" (Zalcman 1990, p. 11).

Names and definitions

There are many ways of categorising role sequences. For example, one could categorise the entire distribution according to the social level roles occupied by the protagonists at the start (or the end) of a role sequence. This type of categorisation is not particularly useful because the groupings exceed reasonable limits for parsimony. Moreover, as we have seen, two-

---

[1] Another reason is that ERICA has many similarities with Cognitive Analytic Therapy (CAT). CAT has demonstrated that it is possible to work with clients with a DSMIV diagnosis of Borderline Personality Disorder on a comparatively short term basis. The CAT claims appeal to me because their outcome studies cover a wide range of conditions and are solidly backed by research findings (see Ryle and Kerr 2002, pp.131-174).

thirds of the role sequences are not directly observable – to identify them requires active intervention that, by itself, is likely to change the variables under consideration.

Accordingly, I show below the eight divisions of NORS as the modern equivalent of Berne's concepts of rackets and games, using the yardstick of "observable". That is, they are categorised according to what an observer will actually *see and hear* – rather than what is theoretically possible, but needs questioning to confirm. Thus, in relation to all the stages of the 3Cs format described in **Chapter 13**, the three categories, range from "***fully observable***", to "***partially observable***" and on to "***not directly observable***". **Appendix C** gives detailed descriptions, examples and statistics of the distributions of each category.

Sub-categories of NORS

The first sub-category of NORS contains three varieties or types of ***bi-lateral*** interaction. The characteristics of bi-lateral NORS are that initially, there are no Bystander roles at the social and psychological levels; the interaction between *both* parties is *fully observable* throughout all the stages of the 3Cs format

- **Competitive NORS** have one person who either starts as a Victim, or one person who ends up as either a Victim or a Bystander.
- **Confluent NORS** have the same role for both players at social and psychological levels. Even at the Revealed stage and Closure (the Switch and Payoff in Berne's Formula G), the players share the same roles at two and sometimes three levels.
- **Reversed NORS** have only two of the four possible roles at social and psychological levels, but with the social level of one player matching the psychological level role of the other. The players swap roles at the Revealed stage of the role sequence. Reversed NORS are actually subtle varieties of Competitive NORS – one person ends up as a Victim or a Bystander.

The next sub-category involves ***racketeering*** - Fanita English's term for a series of transactions where both people withdraw instead of switching to Persecutor, Rescuer or Victim roles (English 1976, 1977a, 1977b, 1977c, 1988). Thus what is observable lasts only up to the Revealed stage of the 3Cs formula.

- **Confluent Racketeering** NORS arise when the players occupy the *same* role at the social level. Being Bystanders at the psychological level, they withdraw instead of switching to Persecutor, Rescuer or Victim roles.
- **Mutual Racketeering** NORS arise when both players have *different* roles at the social and/or existential levels and Bystander roles at the psychological level. Instead of switching to Persecutor, Rescuer or Victim roles, both players withdraw.

The final sub-category is what I call ***unilateral*** NORS. They have the common feature of one or both people being a social or psychological level Bystander; the interaction does not start at all, or, if it does, it does not go beyond the Revealed stage of the 3Cs formula.

- **Single Exit** NORS occur when one player is a psychological level Bystander who attempts to racketeer but withdraws at the Revealed stage.
- **Bystander** NORS. One player is a social level Bystander and/or the other is a psychological level Bystander - who racketeers and withdraws at the Revealed stage of the role sequence.

- **Reciprocal Skull** NORS. This is "Solitaire" or "skull games" - Berne's term for games (NORS) that are played internally (Berne 1970, p. 189). Here both players are Bystanders at the social level and so there is no observable interaction.

These categories cover all 576 reciprocals and all are amenable to the application of the sep-pse-eps-nu rules. In other words we have a complete **taxonomy of bilateral dyadic relationships** for role sequences with negative outcomes. The same logic may be applied to the other types of role sequences.

Statistics

The distribution of the eight categories of NORS is shown in **Table 14.20** and depicted graphically in **Chart 14.1**. The areas of the Chart follow the same order as the columns in **Table 14.4**, starting at twelve o'clock and continuing in a clockwise direction.

	Bilateral			Racketeering		Unilateral			
	Competitive	Revers-ed	Confluent	Confluent	Mutual	Single Exit	Bystander	Reciprocal Skull	Totals
Configurations	12	3	6	3	3	18	27	9	81
Totals	21			6		54			81
Variations	48	12	18	9	12	72	108	21	300
Totals	78			21		201			300
	16%	4%	6%	3%	4%	24%	36%	7%	100
	26%			7%		67%			100

Table 14.4

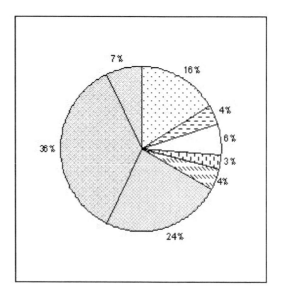

Chart 14.1

Only 26% of the reciprocals result in fully fledged observable bilateral NORS with a Closure comparable to the traditional Bernean games payoff. Numerically, there are only three types of basic bilateral NORS with 21 configurations having the same roles at the social and psychological level and 78 variations at the existential level.

In a Bernean analysis of games, the Bystander, Reciprocal Skull and Single Exit categories of interaction that contribute 67% to the total distribution, are not readily observable. This does not mean that they are not amenable to research, but rather, that a researcher would have to intervene in the interactive process to be able to identify partially observable configurations.

These figures represent the entire distribution of NORS. Needless to say, systematic research is needed to establish the frequency of occurrence, validity and reliability of all these patterns of interaction. Before outlining the beginnings of this process, the following general comments are worth noting:

- Although role sequences stem from a revision of Berne's Formula G, conceptually and in practice, games and role sequences represent very different levels or orders of analysis. Berne's analysis of games, and the focus on highly specific aspects of dysfunctional social behaviour, is principally practical; ERICA offers both a theoretical and practical schema for describing *relationships* as the major variable connecting people and social structures.
- The negative payoff of games is seen as the motivation for advancing one's script. ERICA posits four types of role sequences whose outcome is confirmation or otherwise of mutual OK-ness.
- The process of observing behaviour and formulating concepts to explain the observations is not without precedent in transactional analysis; it is precisely what Berne did with ego states and Kahler has done with drivers – to cite but two obvious examples. Both Berne and Kahler demonstrated the usefulness of their original concepts. With ERICA I am following the same path – with some way yet to go. The rest of this book demonstrates how ERICA works in practice. What is still needed is systematic observation to establish the frequency of occurrence of the various types of role sequences as a means of establishing their validity and reliability and eventually, usefulness in practice. An initial contribution to this process is given in **Appendix C.**
- All that has been said about role sequences with negative outcomes applies to role sequences with a positive outcome. I have yet to complete a comparable scheme for naming and describing the eight patterns of positive outcome role sequences, but at present see no reason why this is not conceptually possible.

Role imago repertoires

The eight categories of NORS provide a springboard for the concept of role imago repertoires. The rationale of this is that individuals have a characteristic range of reciprocals they "occupy" or employ in most situations. In some respects, they are not unlike egograms (Dusay 1966) and the Stroke Profile (McKenna 1974) – diagrams created by clients or practitioners to depict particular aspects of behaviour that (usually) are a target for change. Everyone has a role imago repertoire in the sense that it is no more than a pattern of reciprocals that comprise role sequences. These, in turn, are repeated in various combinations that, together, constitute the individual's role imago repertoire.

Individuals who characteristically enact a narrow range of preferred role profiles have fewer options for satisfactory relationships than those who demonstrate wider and more flexible role behaviours. Identifying role imago repertoires enables them to understand the repetitive patterns of dysfunctional role sequences. Instead of attempting to teach the full gamut of positive, negative and mixed role sequences, the aim is to home in on those that occur most frequently and create most difficulty. Engaging clients in researching their own role imago repertoires is easy, efficient and essential – as described in **Chapters 15** to **17.**

Evidence supporting the notion of role imago repertoires comes from Hine (1990) and Cognitive Analytic Therapy (Ryle 1997, Ryle and Kerr 2002). I discuss each briefly and then explain how these independent views of social interaction mesh with ERICA.

Significant aspects of Hine's TAJ article are that she presents a *bilateral* analysis of games that "shows the interlocking of each players' cons and gimmicks, and the build up to the familiar climax of the switch, the crossup and payoffs" (Hine, 1990, p. 29). She proceeds to discuss each of these variables and demonstrates the ongoing nature of games:

> "After the switch, cross up and payoffs, the players may (and usually do) continue to play with each other, as in a tennis match where the set and match are comprised of many games. The process is described as an ongoing game. ... the players may move onto new partners, as in a tennis tournament. They may do this immediately or after a lapse of time, which can be a matter of minutes, hours, days or months. Games can also be taken up again after an interval at the place where they were left off. Some people give up in a huff after each payoff and move onto new partners for each episode. This is however, still a continuation of what they were doing with their last partner". (Hine 1990, p. 35)

Hine presents practical examples and diagrams to illustrate all the stages of Formula G for both players, which convincingly makes a solid case for the view that the ongoing and cumulative nature of the game phenomenon is "unstoppable". This is precisely what is meant by the notion of role imago repertoires – with an important twist, as explained below.

Cognitive Analytic Therapy seems to have reached exactly the same conclusion as Hine – albeit by using very different terminology and methodology. As previously indicated, CAT theory is based on the way people define themselves. They refer to this as a "state" or as "self states" which are linked with roles.

> "Roles are defined as combining memory, affect and action organized in relation to a search for, or the experience of, reciprocation. A *self state* will therefore be described in terms of its reciprocal role pattern, either pole of which may be subjectively identified with and experienced as a state". (Ryle 1997, p. 27)

CAT therapists use sophisticated psychometric measures to plot the states/roles in various diagrams and flow charts termed a *Self States Sequential Diagram* (or SSSD). In essence, these are equivalent to role imago repertoires; they are a diagrammatic way of representing ongoing games described by Hine. She diagrams "stacks" of games – that is, game 3 stacked upon (following on from) game 2, which follows game 1. In a similar fashion, because ERICA has reciprocals as the components of role sequences, it is possible to map *sequences* of role sequences. I call these *rounds.* There are predictable patterns. Indeed, simply by noting the first round, one is sometimes able to predict as many as the next two rounds. In other words, role imago repertoires embody a recursive pattern. The Closure of the first role sequence becomes the External Contact or start of the second role sequence. The Closure of the second role sequence becomes the start of the third role sequence. The Closure of the third role sequence becomes the start of the fourth role sequence – *which is the same as the first role sequence*

We can see the whole process by combining three role sequences. In **Table 14.5** the Emergent, Revealed and Closure stages of each negative outcome role sequence are abbreviated "E", "R" and "C" respectively. For each person – A and B - the three role sequences constitute a round in their role imago repertoires.

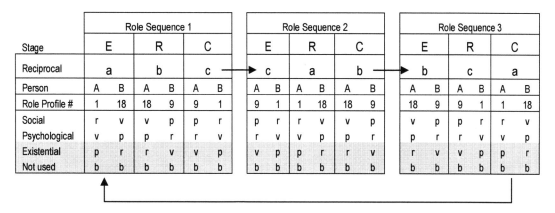

Stage	Role Sequence 1						Role Sequence 2						Role Sequence 3					
	E		R		C		E		R		C		E		R		C	
Reciprocal	a		b		c		c		a		b		b		c		a	
Person	A	B	A	B	A	B	A	B	A	B	A	B	A	B	A	B	A	B
Role Profile #	1	18	18	9	9	1	9	1	1	18	18	9	18	9	9	1	1	18
Social	r	v	v	p	p	r	p	r	r	v	v	p	v	p	p	r	r	v
Psychological	v	p	p	r	r	v	r	v	v	p	p	r	p	r	r	v	v	p
Existential	p	r	r	v	v	p	v	p	p	r	r	v	r	v	v	p	p	r
Not used	b	b	b	b	b	b	b	b	b	b	b	b	b	b	b	b	b	b

Table 14.5

Needless to say, social interaction is not as deterministic as the above pattern may suggest – for several reasons. The first reason concerns the intrapsychic dynamics involved. Hine explains these under four headings – contact and distancing, the racket system, the cognitive aspects of an individual's frame of reference, and time structuring as behavioural and social ways of defending a frame of reference.[1] The first of these illustrate a salient feature of role imago repertoires:

> "games visibly lead to distancing, and I suggest that the pain of successive payoffs (the cumulative negative charge) escalates in time into something like a climax for each partner. This may not be simultaneous, nor be lived out in the same way for each person. To continue the tennis metaphor, at this climax the player finishes the match with one person, causing a break in attempts to relate with that individual similar to the communication break which follows a crossed transaction. .. This break may be accompanied by despair or triumph, but will, in any case, be a script milestone where injunctions and their accompanying beliefs and early decisions will be confirmed. This homeostasis helps maintain the individual's own frame of reference". (Hine, 1990, p. 36)

Secondly, from my experience, it would seem that imago images are an important variable that explains the shift from one round to another. Pursuing Hine's tennis metaphor, it is as if an individual is playing in more than one tournament before finishing the first. One situation or round of role sequences may touch upon imago images relating to recognition. For example, a person may have "collected stamps" (unexpressed racket feelings) about his or her treatment by colleagues at work. In parallel with this, the same individual may be experiencing relationship difficulties at home with their partner.

---

[1] Hine stops short of describing the recursive nature of games and, in this respect, the details of her exposition need not detain us. Nonetheless, they are among the best insights I have come across in the TA literature, and are a "must read" item for anyone wishing to explain or teach role imago repertoires.

The third reason why social interaction is not as straightforward as may be inferred from ERICA's account of the theoretical distribution of NORS, is the fact that rounds are interrupted by the presence or operation of the Bystander role. This means that with Single Exit, Bystander and Reciprocal Skull role sequences the 3Cs format is truncated, in the sense that the Revealed stage merges with and becomes the Closure. The detail of this is given in **Appendix C**.

The upshot of this is that with NORS, an individual's role imago repertoire is peppered with truncated role sequences. Rounds prevail only when the parties are involved in Competitive, Confluent or Reversed NORS. As yet, I have not formulated a firm rule to cover the bridge between a truncated role sequence and the start of the next role sequence. Racketeering NORS add further variety. The obvious way forward is to accumulate more data. **Chapters 15** to **17** give examples of how this may be done in practice.

Another reason for not over-simplifying social interaction and more particularly, the rounds of a person's role imago repertoire is that most people have a balance between positive, negative and mixed outcome role sequences. This adds the final twist.

The recursive property of role sequences operates differently with positive outcome role sequences (PORS). This is not surprising since they are based on a different dynamic - the Type One, Type Two and the tentative Type Three set rules. You may recall from **Chapter 13** that at the Closure in a Type One set, the players return to the roles that prevailed at the start of the interaction. Hence a Type One set consists of a single role sequence. A Type Two PORS follows the same dynamic rules as a NORS, but with positive roles and no discounting. Thus a Type Two set has three role sequences.

Table 14.6 shows four Type Three positive outcome role sequences.

Role Sequence 1						Role Sequence 2						Role Sequence 3						Role Sequence 4					
E		R		C		E		R		C		E		R		C		E		R		C	
a		b		c →		→ c		a		d →		→ d		c		b →		→ b		d		a	
A	B	A	B	A	B	A	B	A	B	A	B	A	B	A	B	A	B	A	B	A	B	A	B
3	17	13	12	9	24	9	24	3	17	20	5	20	5	9	24	13	12	13	12	20	5	3	17
R	V	V	P	P	B	P	B	R	V	B	R	B	R	P	B	V	P	V	P	B	R	R	V
V	P	B	R	R	V	R	V	V	P	P	B	P	B	R	V	B	R	B	R	P	B	V	P
B	R	P	B	V	P	V	P	B	R	R	V	R	V	V	P	P	B	P	B	R	V	B	R
P	B	R	V	B	R	B	R	P	B	V	P	V	P	B	R	R	V	R	V	V	P	P	B

Table 14.6

As indicated in **Table 14.6** it takes longer for the protagonists to return to their starting points than it does for Type One and Type Two set. Note that with Reciprocal "b" at the "R" (Revealed) stage of the third role sequence, person B enacts the Beholder role. What an observer would see is person B waiting - alert, receptive and fully attentive to person A. Because both people are using positive roles, the interaction continues to the Closure. In contrast, were negative roles prevailing, person B would withdraw – intra-psychically and inter-personally – and the round would become truncated. The Beholder role does not seem to have the effect of truncating a round. I comment on the significance of the differences between Beholders and Bystanders in **Appendix C.**

To complete the picture of role imago repertoires, we need to consider what happens with mixed outcome role sequences (MORS). Again, I comment on this in **Appendix C**, but for the present, suffice to say that in a combination of NORS and both Type One and Type Two PORS, each MORS have three role sequences in a round. Type Three sets have six.

Application to practice

In practice and irrespective of setting, ERICA provides a test-bed for confirming (or rejecting) the above hypothesised patterns of social interaction. As previously stated, the aim is to enable clients to identify those aspects of roles, contact and imago influences that interfere with their relationships. They identify these patterns by teaching a practitioner how they (clients) describe their own experiences across various situations. They do this by recounting Significant Incidents that occur between sessions. Invariably these narratives are comprised of less than satisfactory relationships. Over four to eight sessions a pattern emerges that enables client and practitioner to identify recurring themes, imago images, role sequences and associated qualities of contact. In short, they map their role imago repertoire.

Throughout this process, the practitioner has to give his or her primary attention to three crucial variables:

- The quality of contact.
- The language used by clients in describing their experiences.
- The nature of the interaction between client and practitioner. The task is for the client to teach the practitioner how they see the world. The practitioner has to assimilate information without reciprocating negative roles.

This process is described in detail in **Chapter 17** with case examples.

Key Points 14

14.1 Individuals display a **repertoire** of role profiles and reciprocals, giving a characteristic "thumbprint" of their relationships.

14.2 If we examine the full matrix of 24 x 24 = 576 reciprocals we can eliminate 396 or two-thirds of these that involve reciprocals with the Bystander role at either the social or psychological levels. Disregarding the order of who starts the interaction we reduce this to 300 reciprocals, of which 99 are observable.

14.3 A further way of understanding the number of reciprocals that are amenable to observation only is by grouping reciprocals that have the same combinations of roles at the *social* and *psychological* levels. I call these groupings *configurations.*

14.4 Configurations enable us to map all the possible combinations of these reciprocals and group them according to various criteria. **Eight distinctive patterns emerge** in relation to all the stages of the 3Cs. The three sub-categories range from "**fully observable**", to "**partially observable**" and on to "**not directly observable**".

14.5 The first sub-category of NORS contains three varieties or types of *bi-lateral* interaction. Initially, there are no Bystander roles at the social and psychological levels; the interaction between *both* parties is *fully observable* throughout all the stages of the 3Cs format.
- **Competitive NORS** have one person who either starts as a Victim, or one person who ends up as either a Victim or a Bystander.
- **Confluent NORS** have the same role for both players at social and

psychological levels. Even at the Revealed stage and Closure (the Switch and Payoff in Berne's Formula G), the players share the same roles at two and sometimes three levels.

- **Reversed NORS** have only two of the four possible roles at social and psychological levels, but with the social level of one player matching the psychological level role of the other. The players swap roles at the Revealed stage of the role sequence. Reversed NORS are actually subtle varieties of Competitive NORS – one person ends up as a Victim or a Bystander.

14.6   The next sub-category involves *racketeering* NORS, where both people withdraw instead of switching to Persecutor, Rescuer or Victim roles; that which is observable, lasts only up to the Revealed stage of the 3Cs formula.

- **Confluent Racketeering** NORS arise when the players occupy the *same* role at the social level. Being Bystanders at the psychological level, they withdraw instead of switching to Persecutor, Rescuer or Victim roles.
- **Mutual Racketeering** NORS arise when both players have *different* roles at the social and/or existential levels and Bystander roles at the psychological level. Instead of switching to Persecutor, Rescuer or Victim roles, both players withdraw.

14.7   The final sub-category is what I call *unilateral* NORS. They have the common feature of one or both people being a social or psychological level Bystander; the interaction does not start at all, or, if it does, it does not go beyond the Revealed stage of the 3Cs formula.

- **Single Exit** NORS occur when one player is a psychological level Bystander who attempts to racketeer but withdraws at the Revealed stage.
- **Bystander** NORS. One player is a social level Bystander and/or the other is a psychological level Bystander - who racketeers and withdraws at the Revealed stage of the role sequence.
- **Reciprocal Skull** NORS. This is "Solitaire" or "skull games" - Berne's term for games (NORS) (Berne 1970, p. 189) that are played internally. Here both players are Bystanders at the social level and so there is no observable interaction.

14.8   **Appendix C** gives detailed descriptions, examples and statistics of the distributions of each category. In brief, only 26% of the reciprocals result in fully-fledged, observable bilateral NORS with a Closure comparable to the traditional Bernean games payoff. Numerically, there are only **three types of basic bilateral NORS** with 21 configurations having the same roles at the social and psychological level and 78 variations at the existential level.

14.9   The eight categories of NORS provide a springboard for the concept of **role imago repertoires**, giving a characteristic "thumbprint" of their relationships

14.10 It is possible to map *sequences* of role sequences. I call these *rounds*. There are predictable patterns. Role imago repertoires embody a **recursive pattern**.

14.11 The *recursive property* of role sequences operate differently with **positive outcome role sequences** (PORS); they are based on a different dynamic - the *Type One, Type Two* and the tentative *Type Three* set rules.

14.12 At the Closure of a role sequence in a **Type One** set, the players return to the roles that prevailed at the start of the interaction. Hence a **Type One** set consists of **a single role sequence**.

14.13 A **Type Two PORS** follows the same dynamic rules as a **NORS**, but with positive roles and no discounting. Thus a **Type Two** set has a round of **three role sequences.**

14.14 A **Type Three** set has a round of **four role sequences**.

14.15 With **mixed outcome role sequences** (MORS), a **combination** of **NORS** and both *Type One* and *Type Two* **PORS**, each **MORS** has **three role sequences** in a round. **Type Three** sets in **combination** with **NORS** have six **role sequences** in a round.

Self Supervision Suggestions 14

14.1   Read the examples of the eight types of NORS in **Appendix C**. Watch films, videos, TV soaps or documentaries and collect one or more examples of each of the eight types of NORS.

14.2   Observe "real life" social interaction and collect one or more examples of each of the eight types of NORS.

14.3   Keep an ongoing record of the types of NORS you observe (as per **Self Supervision Suggestion 14.2**), noting the frequency of occurrence of each type.

14.4   Note your own interaction with others and identify the reciprocals. Keep an ongoing record of the types of NORS you identify. For each reciprocal, note the quality of contact and the imago images that may be involved. Note your role imago repertoire for NORS.

14.5   Using the material from **Self Supervision Suggestion 14.4** keep an ongoing record of the types of PORS you identify. Devise alternative names for these. For each reciprocal, note the quality of contact and the imago images that may be involved. Note your role imago repertoire for PORS.

14.6   Repeat **Self Supervision Suggestions 14.1** to **14.4** and identify one or more of the eight types of PORS. In particular, note the frequency of occurrence of Type One, Type Two and Type Three PORS.

14.7   There are eight types of NORS and eight types of PORS. Theoretically this means there are sixty four types of MORS. Work out as many *theoretical* examples of these as you can manage. Keep a separate note of these and add to it from time to time.

14.8   Keep an ongoing record of the types of MORS you identify *by observation*. Devise a system for naming them. For each reciprocal, note the quality of contact and the imago images that may be involved.

14.9   Start to categorise the MORS you identify by observation. Do this by noting the frequency of occurrence of Type One, Type Two and Type Three PORS in combination with NORS

14.10 Start keeping notes on your role imago repertoire for MORS.

14.11 Watch films, videos, TV soaps or documentaries and collect examples of IORS.

14.12 Observe "real life" social interaction and collect examples of IORS.

14.13 Note the occurrence of IORS in relation to various types of NORS, PORS and MORS.

14.14 Observe "real life" social interaction and identify the opening reciprocals of potential role sequences. Practice predicting the ensuing reciprocals and compare your predictions with observations of the complete role sequences. Do this for each of the eight types of NORS, PORS and MORS.

Chapter **15**

Role Imago Templates

This Chapter gives an account of the third of the models used for mapping relationships.

Preamble

Although the Contact Cube focuses on the role profile of a single individual, and Role Sequences describe the interaction between two or more people, neither model takes account of the context in which relationships occur. A researcher or an observer needs knowledge of first and second order Contact Cube roles and how these are linked with reciprocals and various types of Role Sequences. However, even in a clinical setting, the Contact Cube and Role Sequences do not always provide clear evidence of historical diagnosis of personalised roles. Organisational, educational and to a lesser extent, counselling practitioners, frequently do not elicit them and researchers have to fall back on a third model, Role Imago Templates (RITs), not only for historical confirmation of roles, but also for identifying the parameters of role behaviour that make possible comparisons within and beyond transactional analysis practice. The following overview explains these links and the ways in which RITs maybe used in practice and research.

Role Imago Templates

A basic role imago template - a BRIT (**Figure 15.1**) - is a diagnostic tool for observing and mapping formalised role relations. It is a heuristic device that describes the context in which an individual's (or an observer's) account of a "Significant Incident" occurred. It is similar to a script matrix (Steiner, 1966) and may be used as the basis of a case formulation (Benjamin 2003, Law 2004).

The BRIT is the basic tool used for understanding and mapping role relations. In a clinical setting, the client and therapist compile BRITs jointly over a period of time; initially the therapist coaches the client to give a clear, sequential account of one or more Significant Incidents. The next stage is for the therapist to help the client identify the personalised roles of the protagonists involved in a Significant Incident. Thereafter the client comes to be able to recognise roles him/herself and eventually, evolves strategies for formulating more satisfactory personalised role responses.

A person occupies a focal role within the context of their *role set* (Merton 1957, 1968) and their *role networks,* the latter being sub-sets of the former. A role set consists of all the role relations a person has experienced and hence, all those with whom one has had 'significant' role relationships. For example, some of the role relationships in my role set are as "father", "neighbour", "work colleague", "friend", "psychotherapist" and so on.

Role sets also embody a time dimension and thus, have historical and current dimensions. In **Figure 15.1** the historical role set is represented by the large shaded circle; within this the current role set is shown as the non-shaded circle. The boundary between the two is largely conceptual and in practice is determined by frequency of contact and the focal person's perception of the significance of the relationship.

For example, I left High school nearly fifty years ago and have since had virtually no contact with my former schoolmates. Hence, I regard my school friends as falling within my historical role set. My wife on the other hand, still has periodic contact with five people with whom she went to school. One lives nearby and they meet every two or three weeks. All these school friends are part of my wife's current role set; the remaining members of the class who graduated with her are part of her historical role set.

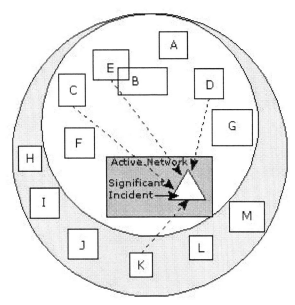

Figure 15.1

Role sets may be further sub-divided into role networks. These may be regarded as being either active (the shaded rectangle in **Figure 15.1)**, or influencing (A to G in **Figure 15.1**). Some influencing networks are operative and transferential (C, D and E) and may be located in the focal person's current network or their historical network (as in K). Other networks merely exist as potential sources of transferential, influencing networks (A, B, F, and G in the current role set and all but K in the historical role set).

An active network is the network or situation experienced by the focal person at any particular time. By definition it is constantly changing and may be regarded as the (changing) network a person "carries around" with them. Thus time and place and the immediate context largely determine the nature of one's active role network. All the roles in a BRIT are formalised roles; they become personalised roles when enacted as a Significant Incident in the active role set.

The distinction between an active role network and a current role set is that "active" refers to whatever particular here and now network or situation a person is in. Once the situation - say a meeting at work - changes, the erstwhile active role network becomes part of the current role set and the next situation - say, having tea at home - becomes the active role network.

A similar dynamic applies to influencing networks. For example, I may be chatting to a group of friends, but am pre-occupied by what may take place the next day at work. Here the actual active role network is "friends" but to some extent, my behaviour will be coloured by the operative "work" role network. Both networks are in the current role set.

Additionally, role networks sometimes overlap. If I work with someone who is also a personal friend, my "work" and "friends" networks overlap (as in B above). Which of the two networks is active at any time will depend on our topic of conversation.

Compiling a basic role imago template profile

Early on in therapy I use the following questions to elicit a basic role imago template. In some cases I give clients a homework assignment consisting of an A4 page with the following instructions and diagram (**Figure 15.2**)

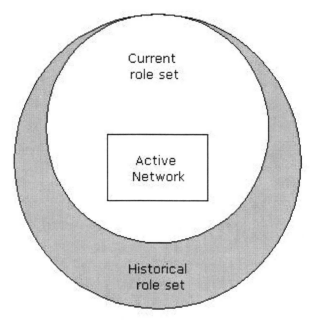

Figure 15.2

1   Make a list of the people (and/or events) in your life – past and present - which you would regard as significant to you. (You may find it easier to do **2** first or combine **1** and **2** by doing them together.)

2   Examine your list and, using small adhesive stickers that can later be stuck onto a large sheet of paper, transfer (re-write) names under headings or categories such as "family", "friends", "neighbours", "work" and so on. Use one sticker for each category. Use whatever categories seem most appropriate, but create categories for everyone on your list. In some cases you may only have one person in a category.

3   Examine the categories. If necessary, add additional names to each category; you may remember people who were not on your original list, or you may want to add other categories. You may also want to refine a particular category – for example, you may want to break down the category "work colleagues" into more than one category, such as "current work colleagues", "work colleagues in London" or "work colleagues 1980-90". If you cannot remember someone's name, use a brief phrase to describe them.

4   By now you should have categories and names of those who were or still are significant to you. If need be, amend your adhesive stickers to take account of any period in your life that is not covered. There may be one or more periods during which you had no significant relationships or no new significant relationships; use dates to note these (e.g. '1969 – 71 no new relationships').

5   Review the names within each category and select no more than ten names from each category, of those people whom you regard as most significant. For categories

with more than ten names, cross out the names of those who you regard as least significant.

6   Divide the categories into two groups – those which represent current relationships and those which you would regard as representing past relationships.

7   Review each group (current relationships and past relationships) and select no more than fifteen categories from each group that you regard as most significant. If either group has more than fifteen categories, discard the stickers with the categories that you regard as least significant. Thus for either or both groups with up to fifteen categories, you should now have two set of stickers – those that are most significant current relationships and those that are most significant past relationships.

8   For each category in your current relationships give an estimate of a) the time (in hours) you have spent in contact with the each person in each category over the past year and b) the time (in hours) you are likely to spend in contact with the each person in each category over the coming year

9   Using an A2 size sheet of paper draw a large circle to represent your historical role set. Draw a smaller inner circle for your current role set (see example below). In the inner circle paste the stickers for each of the categories with most significant current relationships. Include a blank sticker for details of an "Active network" rectangle to be added later. Paste the stickers for each of the categories with most significant past relationships in the large circle.

10   Using a soft pencil, draw dotted line arrows from any names in the historical networks to the blank Active Network sticker that may have had a bearing on the way you have compiled your BRIT. Do the same for your current network. Keep your BRIT in a safe place and bring it to your next therapy session.

For trainees I add additional items/questions such as:

11   How might a BRIT be used in conjunction with injunctions/counter injunctions typically shown in a script matrix?

12   How might a BRIT be used in conjunction with McKenna's stroke diagram and what additional information would you need to elicit to the information required to link the two diagrams??

13   Discuss the possible links between a BRIT and the Racket System.

14   Answer ONE of the following;
   • How would you amend **1** to **10** to be able to use a BRIT with junior schoolchildren, adolescents, and an elderly person and/or in an organisational setting?
   • What indices could be derived from a BRIT and for what purposes would you use them?
   • How might the information yielded by **1** to **10** be used to devise indices or measures to compare individuals, families or other groups?

Figure 15.3 gives an example of the categories I would use in my own BRIT profile; space does not permit the normal procedure of showing names in each rectangle. Likewise, names would normally be shown in the two overlapping networks. This is a basic RIT (a BRIT) and the Significant Incident is the task of compiling the diagram.

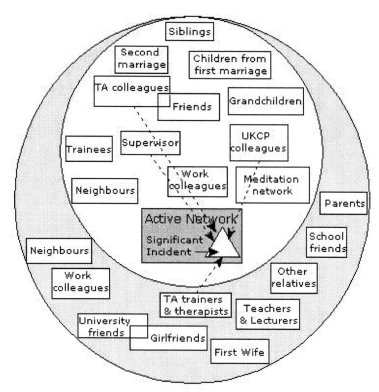

Figure 15.3

The categories in a BRIT always refer to formalised roles.[1] As a reminder, formalised roles are *expected* rather than *actual* behaviours that are linked to occupations or relationships.

To summarise, these essential components of the BRIT are illustrated in the following scenario, where the story line is interspersed with elements of the BRIT in italic parenthesis.

Scenario 15.1

My wife (*the focal person*) tells me about her meeting (*the Significant Incident*) with her old school friend (*active network = my wife and school friend*). Among other topics, they chat about their children and also about their mutual friends from their school days with whom they are in contact (*two influencing networks in the current role set = children and other school friends*). This leads to their reminiscing about their schooldays and trying to recall who else graduated with them (*influencing network in historical role set = graduate class of 1963*)

A BRIT is a diagnostic tool that may be used in several ways. For example, even without names in the various categories, one of the indices that may be derived from **Figure 15.3** is the ratio

---

[1] See page 62 above, where I state that formalised roles *"are legitimated within groups, organisations, a culture or society and carry with them consensually agreed and often legally prescribed, obligations, rights and duties. In organisations these roles usually emerge from the existence or creation of specific positions and are characterised by a range of expected attitudes and behaviours, together with socially legitimated sanctions and rewards. Formalised roles are similar to Linton's sociological view of a "unit in society" (Linton 1936) and Berne's notion of roles as an aspect of the public structure of a group (Berne 1963). These roles usually vary from one situation to another and are certainly influenced by cultural factors. Broadly speaking there are two main categories of formalised roles – relational (such as husband, wife, friend, neighbour) that describe interpersonal relationships and occupational (manager, teacher, engineer). Arguably there is a third category – recreational or social – that is neither relational nor occupational."*

between categories in the current and historical role sets. Carefully designed and clearly specified, such indices may be used for many purposes. It may, for example, turn out that depressed clients have more categories in their historical than current role sets. Likewise, the number of names in various categories in the current role set will give an indication of a person's role and stroke repertoire. To establish reliable indices of this nature will require agreement among practitioners about the definition and purpose of such indices, systematic data collection, correlation with other relevant measures routinely used in (and beyond) transactional analysis, and so forth.

Like most practical tools, the BRIT was devised for particular purposes and rests on certain assumptions. The BRIT was developed to track role relationships - to provide a baseline for exploring relationships and changes in relationships. The assumption is that roles plus imagos and contact is a valid way of describing relationships. It further assumes that the request to "Make a list of the people (and/or events) in your life – past and present - which you would regard as significant to you" is a meaningful question. Obviously the significance of 'significant' will vary from one person to another.

To illustrate, I once had a client whose BRIT showed three networks in both his current role set and in the historical role set. The current role set networks were labelled "work", "friends" and "them". The work network had one name – that of his supervisor with whom he had very little contact; the client worked as a night watchman at a military installation. "Friends" consisted of seven email addresses – people with whom the client communicated or "chatted" with via websites devoted to UFO watching. "Them" consisted of a local psychiatrist, a general practitioner and a community psychiatric nurse – each of whom the client saw monthly. The historical role set showed "the wife" (who had died thirty three years ago), "comrades" with whom the client had been interned in a concentration camp in Burma during the Second World War, and "the visitation" – that referred to an event where the client had been taken on board a UFO and "befriended" by "beings" shortly after his wife had died.

Clearly, this client had an idiosyncratic definition of "significant", but his categorisation did actually match for him the reality of his circumstances. And undoubtedly, for almost everyone, 'significant' will vary *between* categories. For example "neighbours" are significant to me in as much as I "see them every day", whereas "friends" are significant because they are "reliable", "loving" or "stimulating", and so on. Personal Construct theory (Kelly 1955, Winter 1992) gives a host of techniques for investigating such perceptions, most of which go beyond roles to include other personality variables.

In its simplest form, a BRIT is a flexible tool that gives a snapshot view of a person's formalised role relationships, a frozen picture of an ongoing dynamic process.

Contextual Role Imago Templates

A further refinement of the BRIT is a cRIT or Contextual Role Imago Template that focuses on the particular context in which relationships occur. cRITs highlight two points. The first is that all interaction exists and takes place in a particular context and secondly, aspects of context frequently overspill into the transactional analysis process itself and/or are presented and (usually) dealt with in supervision as examples of 'parallel process'. Not only does a cRIT provide a baseline of an individual's repertoire of role behaviours relative to a particular context, it enables the practitioner, researcher or supervisor to identify the influencing networks extraneous to the interaction of the Significant Incident per se. For example, if a researcher is interested in the role profile of a particular individual in a work setting, he or she can elaborate the person's work network to include tasks, designations or positions of various colleagues.

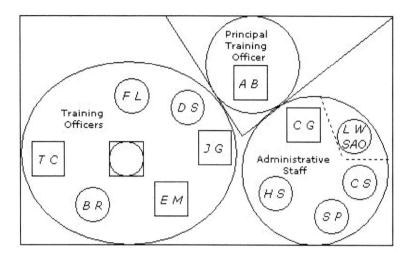

Figure 15.4

To illustrate, **Figure 15.4** shows three formalised roles in a work network – Principal Training Officer, Training Officers and Administrative Staff. This effectively equates the BRIT with Berne's diagram for the organisational structure of a group (Berne 1963, Fox 1975 p. 349). I have also further differentiated between individuals, by using circles to depict females and squares for males and showing the initials of each person, thereby adding the equivalent of Berne's individual structure (Berne 1963, Fox 1975 p. 349). External group boundaries are obviously depicted by the perimeter lines of a network and the major internal boundaries are shown by the solid lines separating the person in the leadership slot (the Principal Training Officer) from the two categories of membership – Training Officers and Administrative staff. Note that the leadership slot has a solid boundary, as does the sub leadership slot for LW the Senior Administrative Officer (SAO). The unfilled slot in the Training Officers' team is shown as a circle within a square – indicating a vacant Training Officer post. Minor internal boundaries are drawn with dashed lines. A cRIT may be enlarged to show other influencing network roles by including arrows between interacting networks

A more elegant (and cheaper) research design would be for an employer to train individuals to recognise Contact Cube roles and compile their *own* BRITS and/or cRITs. Such a change in focus from an observer to a participant-observer format rests on the cusp of the practice/research divide. Practitioners trained in this manner would enhance their capacity for reflective awareness of the interactive process applicable to their own model of practice.

Dynamic Role Imago Templates

Both a BRIT and a cRIT map formalised roles, yielding a static picture of role influences against which the Significant Incident may be seen. cRITs can easily be extended to include personalised roles and hence, actual behaviours; this transforms the cRIT into a Dynamic Role Imago Template (a dRIT). The following example of a Significant Incident illustrates this process.

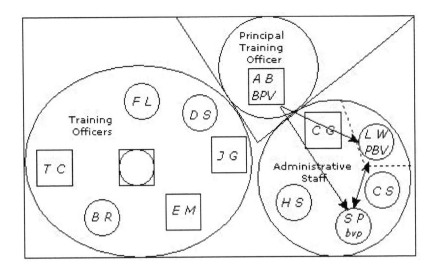

Figure 15.5

Figure 15.5 is a dRIT that shows the interaction between three people - AB as the Principal Training Officer, LW the Senior Admin Officer and SP, a member of the Admin Team. These are all formalised roles. The two-way arrows signify the enactment of personalised roles at social, psychological and existential levels by each person according to the focal person (AB) who defined the role profiles. These are shown below each person's initials. To complete the picture AB would write a brief 'narration' of the Significant Incident (SI 1). AB's narration reads ***SI 1:*** *Sat in on a meeting where LW gave SP a verbal warning for repeated instances of poor timekeeping. SP probably Bystander and LW did not check her response. I did not intervene but will discuss with LW in the next supervision session*

The role profiles for AB, LW and SP are a shorthand way of recording a single Significant Incident. In this case it shows a role sequence with a mixed outcome and the detail of the interaction could be further analysed using the phases of Contact, Communication and Confirmation or as the moves in a bilateral game (Hine 1990). A wider perspective emerges if we continue to map further Significant Incidents over a specified time scale.

Group Role Imago Templates

A transcript of an excerpt from a newly formed group is shown below:

> *Tr1:.14.36* **Dave:** I still feel shaky, but I'm going to stick with my decision. **VPR/Therapist1:** Good for you. **RVB**
> *Tr1:.15.03* **Barbara:** I know what it's like. I used to get terrified when my grandmother started up, just like your mother. **vpr/ Therapist1:** Your grandmother's the one you described as a nasty old witch? **RVP**
> *Tr1:.15.11* **Jeff: (Barbara)** I don't know why you always chip in so inappropriately with your own stuff. **pvr/ Barbara:** I could never get anything right. She was such an old witch I always felt terrified. **vbp**
> *Tr1:.15.19* **Prue.** Yeah, whatever. But is Jeff...**rpv/ Barbara**....(sighs) **bpv**

Tr1:.15.27 **Jeff:** Anyway, there's something else I want to check with you. **pvr/ Barbara:** What .. what is it? **rvb**

Tr1:.15.35 **Jeff:** Three or four times now that I've been able to smell that you've been drinking. I don't know if anyone else noticed, but last week it was so bad that I even changed my chair part way through. It's not like you've said you have a drink problem – like Simon. He's out front with it – He's told us that he goes to AA. But you must be drinking just before you come to group. Either that, or you've been really tipping it back a lot, earlier, to smell that much. But it's not like you're totally pissed. I don't know if anyone else could smell it and I know I'm extra sensitive, what with my old man and that. It's quite disgusting! I don't think, like maybe, you should be excluded for the session – but maybe there should be a rule about drinking before group. Else what's the point of coming to group? **pvr/ Barbara:** But I *need* to be in group and anyway, I only have two or three sherries – just to get my confidence up. Sometimes I don't have anything before group. **vbr**

Tr1:.17.16 **Jeff:** Well maybe I'm over-reacting. I feel like guilty about bullying you **vrp/ Barbara: bvr**

Tr1:.17 19 **Prue (**to **Jeff)** So where do you think this is getting you? Look what.. **pvr/ Therapist1:** Will you hold fire a bit, please Prue? **RPV**

Tr1:.17.22 **Therapist1** Given that you feel strongly about this, how else could you have made your point – without ending up feeling guilty about "bullying" Barbara. **PRV/ Jeff** I suppose ... maybe I could have said I felt angry. **rvp**

Tr1:.17.31 **Therapist1:** Yeah, that would have been one way. **RPB +.** Do you remember the first transaction – the opening line? **PBR Jeff:** Mmm – think so. **rvp +** I said she was always chipping in at the wrong time and I wanted to check something with her. **RVP**

Tr1:.17.39 **Therapist1:** Good, that's it. **RPB +** So, could you diagram that? **PRB + (Whole Group).**This is how we can all learn from this kind of experience. **PVB + (Jeff).** The pen's down there. **PBR /Jeff:** I'll use the blue one. **RPV....(Whole Group).**O.K. this is me and this is Barbara. **PVB**

Tr1:.18.21: **Therapist1:** O.K., say the first line – just the way you said it. Use the present tense, then draw the diagram. **PBV /Jeff:** I've got something I want to check with you. **PVR**

Tr1:.18 28 **Therapist1:** My recollection is there was another line before that. **PRB/ Jeff:** Oh! Yes - I don't know why you always chip in like that. **RVB**

Tr1:.18.34 **Dave:** Not like that! You were a *lot* more *angry*. **PVR /Therapist1. (Whole Group** We could re-run the mini-disc, but that'll take a lot of fiddling about. **PVB + (Jeff)** Think back to how you were feeling when you started. **PVB**

T*r1:.18 49* **Jeff:** I don't know why you always chip in like that. **pvr/ Therapist2:** That's it! **RVP**

Tr1:.19.00 **Prue:** So which ego states are involved? **PVB/Jeff:** Adult, but with a hidden P and maybe C, I guess. **RVB**

Tr1:.19.05 **Therapist1:** I reckon your guess is right. **RVP/Jeff:** I can see it now. **PVR +** It's like when my Dad used to come home pissed out of his head and there were *terrible* rows. **VRP**

Tr1:.19.11 **Therapist1:** Sounds like the beginnings of a useful insight. **RVB/Jeff:** Yeah, I need to think about it – perhaps I'll tackle it next week. **RVP + (Barbara)** Sorry about that. It's my stuff, really. **VPR**

Tr1:.19.18 **Therapist2:** Good work. **RVP/ Jeff: BVR**

Tr1:.19.22 **Simon:** Yeah, well done. **RVP/Jeff: BVR**

Tr1:.19.24 **Dave:** You're cool, man. **RVP/ Jeff: BVR**

Tr1:.19.25 **Prue:** I'm glad you got there – in the end. **rpv** + **(Barbara)** So how are you now? **rvp/ Barbara:** I'm alright. **rbv**

Tr1:.19.31 **Therapist2:** Well, you don't *look* alright. You've gone all hunched up. **RPB/ Barbara:** I'm O.K. – really. **rbv**

Tr1:.19 42 **Dave:** Come on Barbie! There aint no witches around here! Sit up straight! **PVR/ Barbara:** I know that. I've accepted Jeff's apology and I'm O.K. now. **RVP**

Tr1:.19.50 **Therapist2:** Good. You're looking better now. **RPV/ Barbara:** It's just that I get scared if I'm told I've done something wrong. Then I go quiet 'til I think it through. **VPR**

Tr1:.19.56 **Therapist1:** Good. It's helpful for us to know the strategies that work for you. **RPV** + **(Whole Group)** O.K. – we've tidied up the process. Let's move on and discuss whether or not there should be 'rules' prescribing what you can or can't do outside group. **PVR**

Figure 15.6 is a therapist's coding of the reciprocal roles enacted in a group setting, showing the formalised roles of everyone's BRITs together with the personalised roles of the Contact Cube; the diagram is called a Group Role Imago Template or gRIT. The following conventions are used for gRITs:

Each person's BRIT is shown according to their position in the room (cf. Berne's seating diagram – Berne 1963 p. 8). Individuals are depicted by first names followed by their attendance relative to the total number of sessions to date. The circular shape of the BRIT has been amended to show gender differences; males are shown as squares and females as circles. Absent members (Siobhan) are shown with a dashed border; group therapists have a heavy border. The upper half of each BRIT is the current role set and the shaded lower half represents the historical role set. The categories in each person's BRIT are referenced alphabetically, followed by the number of people in each role network. Rudimentary measures may be added, according to the researcher's interests; for example, the ratio of current to historical categories. The space in the middle of the page is used for recording by a participant-observer, or for transferring the role profiles recorded by an observer using a video or mini-disc transcript. In this central space italicised text refers to the track as per the mini-disc recorder. First letter abbreviations are used for names and role profiles are shown in bold. Once these have been noted, frequencies of occurrence of each role at each level may be added. Using an Excel spreadsheet for recording a gRIT and transferring the data to a group Role Imago Matrix (a gRIM) makes handling of numerical data possible.

The coding of the transcript and the gRIT shown in **Figure 15.6** were compiled by Therapist1 to whom the clients were known and who was, therefore, easily able to discern the existential level roles. A researcher lacking this clinical knowledge of the clients may need to code this level as "?" until later role switches confirm the above mentioned sep-pse-eps-nu rules. This does, in fact occur in the example at *15.35* (J, pvr /B. vbr), and *17.16* (J. vrp /B. brv). That is, at *15.35* Jeff is clearly enacting a social level Persecutor role – with Barbara in Victim. This profile changes at *17.16*; Jeff's social role moves to the existential level, his psychological role moves up to become overt as the social level Victim and the hitherto attitudinal level Rescuer becomes the new psychological level role. Barbara responds similarly by withdrawing (social level Bystander).

The transcript is probably fairly typical of a transactional analysis therapy session in the early stages of a group's life. This is indicated by the notation within each individual BRIT; the group has been in existence for twelve sessions with an average attendance rate of 10.9. You can see from the key to the notation in **Figure 15.6**, that the therapists have recorded a "C/H" measure that expresses the ratio of networks in the current and historical role sets. The closer this figure is to unity, the more numerically "balanced" is a person's current-past role influences.

One may, for example, postulate that someone with very few networks and people in their current role set is likely to be less outgoing than someone whose current role set contains several networks and a large number of people. Obviously, one would have to collect data from

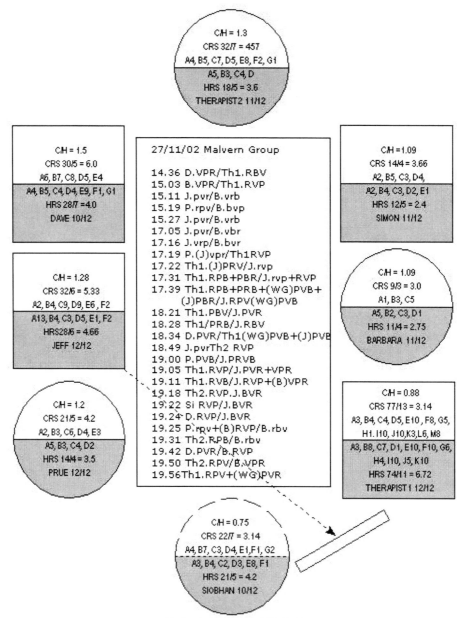

Key to Notation within each BRIT
CRS=Current Role Set, HRS=Historical Role Set.
C/H=Ratio of number of Networks in Current to Historical Role Sets.
HRS14/4 = 3.5 signifies that there are a total of 14 people and 4 networks
in the Historical Role Set. A5 = Network A with 5 people, B3 = Network B with 3 people and so on

Figure 15.6

a large sample of clients before any conclusions could be drawn. The point is that the therapists are on the way to making data collection a normal part of their practice.

Figure 15.6 is an alternative to the use of Situational Role Profiles (described in **Chapter 12**), and a practitioner's choice between the two will depend on the use to which the instruments are to be put – and for, or by, whom. My experience is that clients are most interested in the gRIT, particularly where this can be linked to modern technology capable of showing behaviour in a group in relation to individual dRITs. Situational Role Profiles on the other hand, are of more use in supervision or research. The extent to which either or both will be used by colleagues remains to be seen.

Key Points 15
15.1 A **basic role imago template** (a BRIT) is a diagram for mapping current and past role relations. The components of a BRIT include:
- The client as **the focal person,** who is required to report on a series of **Significant Incidents**.
- A **role set** consisting of all the roles a person has occupied throughout their life; role sets have *historical* and *current* dimensions and may be further sub-divided into **role networks**.
- An **active network** as the network or situation experienced by the focal person at any particular time.
- An **influencing network** as the network or situation that influences the focal person's behaviour in their active network.
- **Overlapping networks** which exist where two or more people are members of more than one network.

15.2 The categories in a BRIT always refer to formalised roles.
15.3 A further refinement of the BRIT is a cRIT or **Contextual Role Imago Template** that focuses on the particular context in which relationships occur.
15.4 A **cRIT** provides a *baseline* of an individual's repertoire of role behaviours relative to a particular context. It enables the practitioner, researcher or supervisor to identify the influencing networks extraneous to the interaction of the Significant Incident per se.
15.5 cRITs can easily be extended to include personalised roles and hence, actual behaviours. This transforms the cRIT into a **Dynamic Role Imago Template** (a dRIT).
15.6 A Group Role Imago Template (a gRIT) may be used to depict role interaction by showing:
- individual BRITs as per Berne's seating diagram with circles for females and squares for males
- various measures indicating attendance, the number of networks (and the number of people in each network) in the current and historical role sets
- a notated transcript of role profiles and reciprocal role interactions.

15.7 Rudimentary numerical data may be added by using a spreadsheet to compile a **Group Role Imago Matrix** (a gRIM).

Self Supervision Suggestions 15
15.1 Compile your own BRIT using instructions **1 to 10** and the diagram in **Figure 15.3** above.

15.2	Using instructions **1 to 10** and the diagram in **Figure 15.3** above compile BRITs for two or three other people and discuss these with them.
15.3	How would you:

1. Identify, develop and standardise measures for BRITs?
2. Link these with measures of statistical indices for Contact Cube roles, reciprocals and role sequences?
3. Use 2 above to identify, develop and standardise measures for cRITs, dRITs and gRITs?
4. Develop and standardise software packages for in-putting data from RITs to Role Imago Matrices (RIMs) and Group Role Imago Matrices (gRIMs) thus enabling easy transfer of ideas, data and results between researchers? [Note that Cognitive Analytic Therapy (Ryle and Kerr 2002) has a raft of instruments routinely used for recording and analysis of the type of data that could be yielded by RITs. (Tschudi, 1990)]

Chapter **16**

Identifying imago images and qualities of contact

This Chapter examines individual imagos and qualities of contact and the idea that they may be linked with roles as major components of relationships. This is especially relevant in clinical work and in counselling, particularly when there are recurrent patterns of reciprocals in an individual's role imago repertoire. Given the licence of an appropriate contract, organisational and educational specialists may also pursue contact and imagos to the benefit of individuals and work groups.

The nature of imagos

Imagos are the historical influences on the internalised perceptions that individuals have of others in social situations (Berne, 1963 p. 37). The "historical influences" are manifested in two ways – as "imago images" or particular beliefs associated with certain role behaviours, and attitudinally as an individual's life position (Berne 1972, pp. 84-89). As such, my use of "imago" is consistent with the meaning ascribed to the term by Massey (1995 p. 279) and Agazarian and Peters (1981 p. 277).

Expressing all this in another way, imagos give a measure of people's *changing* perceptions of others in a group. Although these perceptions stem from an individual's early family experiences and resultant life position, the perceptions change as relationships in the group become more differentiated. Thus imagos are more refined aspects of script decisions or injunctions; the latter two imply 'pathology' and a need for change. Imagos reflect more flexibility and a capacity to establish, maintain and adjust current relationships.

Including imago images as a component of relationships, implies a need for an operational definition of imagos. This is a complex variable whose validity has yet to be established to my satisfaction. What follows is an account of my thinking to date – rather than a definitive statement of how to "measure" or establish any sort of reliable index.

The fundamental problem is not only have roles, role profiles and reciprocals been defined as operating at three levels, but also that imago images are both multi-directional and multi-faceted. That is, they should reflect changing perceptions *and* whatever "historical influences" prevail at any time. By defining imago images as a blend of Berne's attempt to capture role differentiation over time with Massey's emphasis on the historical influence of early relationships, I have saddled myself with a composite variable that is difficult and, maybe, even impossible to define in operational terms.

For example, if I am in a group with six others I am bound to have *different* perceptions of others in relation to *particular* topics at *different* times. Thus, I may agree with three others' views on say, euthanasia, while vehemently disagreeing with three others who have different or even opposite views. Clearly, some of this may be transferential and some not. Hopefully, the more blatant transferential factors will be reflected in an individual's dRIT or gRIT. But this still leaves the problem of demonstrating ongoing changes in relationships. Again, gRITs hold the promise of providing an answer. By comparing the reciprocals between each and every member of a group for each session, over time, one would be able to track changes in the frequency/type of role interactions that would reflect changing nature of relationships. Of course, this would demand sophisticated statistical analysis of such data, and would undoubtedly be the province of researchers rather than everyday practitioners. That said, I know from my own experience of group work as well as from supervising trainees, that "everyday practitioners" *do* detect this level of changing relationships. It is not unusual for a trainee to bring "an issue about group dynamics" to supervision. My recollection of the most recent example was along the lines of *"I'm not too bothered by what's happening in the group, but I can't put my finger on it. It may be that Jon is no longer projecting his sister onto Angie – well, not so much - after he did that major redecision work about three weeks ago. But they're getting on fine together now. And this probably means that Steve's no longer got an excuse for zapping Jon like he used to. So I'm curious about the process".*

It is on such occasions that longitudinal data would enrich discussion and indirectly, relationships among the clients. However, all is not lost and even allowing for the way in which I have framed imago images as an important part of relationships, ERICA includes meta-level and more qualitative indicators of the significance of imago images. That is, in previous Chapters I suggested that roles are underpinned by four generalised, bi-polar imago images – recognition-anonymity, trust-mistrust, attachment-detachment, and growth-survival. This is a *developmental* line of reasoning, with clear implications for the nature of the contact and roles required to engender the positive ends of the polarities. In other words, I am claiming that it is likely, if not necessary, for people to have *experienced* the above positive imago images, in order to establish and maintain positive relationships with others.

In addition to the information that may be impressionistically gleaned from inspecting dRITs or gRITs, I have explored other avenues for assessing an individual's perceptions of self in relation to others. While Berne's life positions seemed an obvious candidate for this, my observations lead me to conclude that they are too general for discriminating between the four imago images hypothetically associated with behavioural roles. That is, someone who shows a preponderance of positive role behaviours, has an overall OK-OK position in relation to *all four* dimensions of behaviour. While questions such as "when I am in a Valuer (etc.) role I am ..." held short-lived promise, the obvious drawback is that these questions presuppose a common understanding or definition of each role. Moreover, the responses I got to this type of question varied tremendously from items such as "happy", "a bit scared", "caring for others" and so on. Nevertheless, these answers appeared to be tapping underlying ways in which people value themselves. This, in turn, reminded me of Jacqui Schiff's notion of ego state networks – the ways in which the content of ego states is hierarchically structured. Theoretically, these could be indexed using techniques such as Kelly's Repertory Grid (Kelly 1955) – which is a sophisticated package of personality variables that does not lend itself to self-administration by clients.

Fortunately, and to my delight, a possible solution came from a client who, in describing a Significant Incident, was talking about being assertive versus "being a doormat". The phrase he used was "what that [being assertive] does for me is that I feel important". For some reason I asked "what does that do for you?" and the reply was "I feel like other people are taking notice of me". Again, I asked "what does that do for you?" I don't remember the reply, but certainly recall that what emerged, what was co-created, was a loop – a series of statements that came back to being important and being noticed. I have followed this up, both theoretically and in practice. Theoretically, the answers to this sort of repetitive question are akin to the notion of "core states" of self (Andreas and Andreas, 1994), Polster's concept of "animating" self (Polster 2003) and Kelly's "core role" which:

> "consists of those fundamental constructions of the construing of other people which determine the person's characteristic ways of interacting with others". (Kelly 1955, p. 503)

In practice I have pursued this by asking clients to write up to ten phrases or statements that represent their values and beliefs about themselves, which elicit experiences or feelings of self worth. I then use the repetitive question to explore the loop of related states. There are two patterns of response. The first is a series of linked statements that return to the first statement (as above). The second type of response is where one phrase leads to another phrase on the client's list. In both cases, the end product seems to reflect a "core state" of self or the "core role" as described by Kelly. In short, my client and I had found a way of eliciting the experience of a positive self-image.

More often than not, clients relate negative experiences as their chosen "Significant Incident". When a client has acquired the knack of relating such an incident in clear, sequential steps of what happened, who said what and so on, and is able to identify accurately the reciprocals involved, I ask them to identify a positive role they *could have* enacted at a particular point, and then, in the therapy session, ask them to access the most appropriate positive self state they *would have liked* to have experienced during the incident, that would match the positive role. Alternatively, I ask these questions in the reverse order – first to access the positive self state and then match it with a role.

A variation on this procedure that I learned from Ken and Elizabeth Mellor is to use positive *and* negative self-descriptions: *"Write five statements or qualities that describe yourself positively, and five statements or qualities that describe yourself negatively. Talk to a partner about each one in relation to the question 'how did this statement or these qualities serve you in the past and how do they serve you now?' Your partner must simply keep repeating the same question'."*

On balance, the Mellors' format is more open-ended than the first procedure, and comes closer to the "historical influences" included in the above definition of imagos. The answers to the discussion on each of the five positive and negative statements can be linked with roles by posing questions such as, *"So which of these statements were you following when you were in a Victim (etc.) role?"* I detail this process in **Chapter 17**.

My experience is that the first procedure is well suited for work in organisations and an educational setting; it emphasises positive self states and avoids the need to delve into historical factors. The second procedure is recommended for clinicians and counsellors; it yields historical information that sometimes throws light on further or unexplored issues.

At this stage, I do not have sufficient evidence to support the view that the imago images of recognition-anonymity, trust-mistrust, attachment-detachment, and growth-survival are *consistently* related to the four vertical dimensions of the Contact Cube for *all* people. The most that can be said is that clients *do* show characteristic patterns of role behaviours and core self states. For example, one of my clients consistently experiences herself as "confident" when in the Promoter role, "close to others" with the Responder role, "feeling alive" as a Beholder, and "reassured" in a Valuer role. Significantly, these are relative to the role profile of whoever the client is relating – as illustrated by the comment *"I felt reassured when she said she could see my point of view. She was warm and kind and I sensed we'd sort of clicked".* Interpreting this as an example of the imago images of trust and attachment may seem plausible, but scarcely warrants the claim that those imago images, as elicited by the above procedures, are always representative of the positive ends of the four polarities.

Nevertheless, the procedures do elicit data that has the potential for linking historical influences with roles. This is still "work in progress" and it remains to be seen whether there is any clinical advantage in having some or other empirical measure of imago images. Currently, my position is that the above procedures are definitely helpful in providing clients with a springboard for changing from negative to positive roles. In practice, knowledge of a person's negative imago images enables them to identify with, own and where necessary, resolve these before moving to positive roles. For these reasons I have incorporated the above procedures in ERICA, along with life positions as indicated by the roles held at the existential level

Qualities of contact

In earlier Chapters I suggested that roles located on the four vertical dimensions of the Contact Cube are associated with different qualities of contact. I described these as *co-existent, co-operative, collaborative* and *compelling.* Clearly these are my descriptions of a meta-level process, rather than words used by clients to describe the nature of affective relationships. To date, the most I have done by way of verifying clients' experience of contact as a component of relationships is to ask questions such as *"Would you describe your contact with x as positive or negative?" "How would you describe your relationships with colleagues?"* Although answers to these sorts of questions are useful in an organisational setting as a guide to what might be expected (or can be checked by observation), the responses are predictably bland and not particularly inspiring in terms of linking contact with roles. Like imago images, I have yet to be convinced of the practical usefulness of any *empirical* measure of contact.

When I was in my thirties and all fired up with enthusiasm for the "meaning" behind statistics, one of my tutors (a Yorkshire man) was looking at work I had submitted. He seemed favourably impressed – but then pointed to a column of figures and shook his head. "You'll have to take them out, lad. There's nowt you can do with them here, not in this paper. You know the saying 'where there's muck, there's brass'? Them's like brass, lad, so you have to treat them like brass, outside all this muck". I looked at him, puzzled by the metaphor. "Quality, lad, quality, not quantity. Speaking proper-like, them's better dealt with qualitatively".

Key Points 16

16.1   **Imagos** are the *historical influences* on the internalised perceptions that individuals have of others in social situations.

16.2   **Historical influences** are manifested in two ways – as *imago images* or particular beliefs associated with certain role behaviours, and *attitudinally* as an *individual's life position*.

16.3   Imagos give a measure of people's changing perceptions of others in a group.

16.4   *Imago images* are multi-directional and multi-faceted

16.5   *Roles* are underpinned by four generalised, bi-polar *imago images* – **recognition-anonymity, trust-mistrust, attachment-detachment, and growth-survival**.

16.6   **Repetitive questions** may be used to identify *imago images*. These questions are akin to the notion of "core states" of self (Andreas and Andreas, 1994), Polster's concept of "animating" self (Polster 2003) and Kelly's "core role."

16.7   To assess **life positions**, I ask clients to write up to ten phrases or statements that represent their values and beliefs about themselves, which elicit experiences or feelings of self worth.

16.8   A variation on this procedure that I learned from Ken and Elizabeth Mellor, is to use **positive and negative self descriptions**.

16.9   The first procedure (**16.7**) is well suited for work in organisations and an educational setting; it emphasises positive self states and avoids the need to

---

delve into historical factors. The second procedure (**16.8**) is recommended for clinicians and counsellors; it yields historical information that sometimes throws light on further or unexplored issues

16.10 **Qualities of contact** are described as *co-existent, co-operative, collaborative* and *compelling.* These are meta-level descriptions of a process and not amenable to quantitative analysis.

Self Supervision Suggestions 16

16.1   How would you describe your imago images?

16.2   Write up to ten phrases or statements that represent experiences or feelings of self worth.

16.3   For each of these phrases, ask your self "What does this do for me?" Take the answer to this question and keep repeating "What does this do for me?" until you can go no further. Write down your answers on a large sheet of paper and see if you can detect a pattern.

16.4   Write five statements or qualities that describe yourself positively, and five statements or qualities that describe yourself negatively. Talk to a partner about each one in relation to the question 'how did this statement or these qualities serve you in the past and how do they serve you now?' Your partner must simply keep repeating the same question.

Chapter **17**

ERICA with individual clients

This Chapter details ways of teaching clients to use the three models. As previously indicated and in Rowan's terms, the Contact Cube, Role Sequences and Role Imago Templates, may be used instrumentally, relationally and (as we will seen in **Part Six**), transpersonally. In this Chapter the models are presented as if the practitioner were operating instrumentally and relationally.

Overview

In a clinical setting, the client completes a BRIT as part of the intake process. This would be the first post-contracting task in an educational or organisational setting. I use the questions following on from **Figure 15.2** to elicit a basic role imago template. In some cases I give clients a homework assignment consisting of an A4 page with instructions and diagram similar to **Figure 15.2**.

BRITs should not be seen in isolation. They are part of the assessment or diagnostic phase of a facilitative relationship. In a clinical setting I frequently use BRITs in conjunction with other diagnostic tools – such as a script matrix, or racket system analysis.

Having compiled a BRIT with the client, the practitioner coaches the client to give a clear, sequential account of one or more Significant Incidents. They are defined according to whatever the client has experienced during the week as "significant". This is usually a version of the reinforcing memories in their racket system (Erskine and Zalcman, 1983). In this way, data is systematically accumulated to demonstrate the client's characteristic role sequences over an extended period. It is the sequential nature and revision of roles that is of interest. I discuss Significant Incidents in considerable detail below.

Thereafter client and practitioner compile dRITs jointly over a period of time based on the client's reports of "Significant Incidents". Significant Incidents (the white triangle in **Figure 15.1**) are the basic parameters for drawing a dRIT, yielding a diagrammatic representation of the focal person's role profiles, mode of time structuring and stroke exchanges.

The next stage is for the practitioner to help the client identify the roles of the protagonists involved in a Significant Incident. Thereafter, the client comes to be able to recognise roles him/herself and eventually, evolves strategies for formulating more satisfactory role responses.

The point of mapping role sequences is to give a base line of the characteristic pattern of role sequences for any individual or group. Involving clients in this process means that they gradually acquire a meta-perspective of their own behaviour and in so doing, move to the Beholder and, optionally, the Observer roles. This is usually a necessary precursor to using positive roles to reformulate previously dysfunctional behaviours. Client-participation is a crucial factor in compiling dRITs.

The general purpose of teaching RITs is to enhance relationships by understanding and appropriately using the links between roles, contact and imago images. More specifically, the practice of compiling a weekly dRIT based on Significant Incidents, results in an accumulated record of reciprocal role relations, which clients use as data for identifying their characteristic responses – their role imago repertoire. Effectively clients are undertaking research into their own behaviour – and the twin divides of practice/research and health/pathology cease to be issues.

Significant Incidents

Introducing clients to the practice of reporting Significant Incidents is a staged process – contracting, learning, reviewing and charting, revising, identifying and considering the consequences of options and finally, agreeing an "authorised version". The stages have "fuzzy" boundaries; they merge imperceptibly according to the interaction between client and practitioner. It is important to follow the above sequence yet avoid the theory getting ahead of the process. Significant Incidents are a means of data collection about the client's frame of reference – their view of the world. They should include coverage of the "3Rs" - Rackets, Resources and Resilience. I expand on these factors below.

Data collection is based on the following overall contract:

- The client and the practitioner agree that throughout the following processes, they will discuss any miscommunication and/or differences of their respective points of view; the motto is "openly agreeing to agree, and openly agreeing to disagree".
- The client "teaches" the practitioner about their way of seeing the world, by relating to the practitioner an incident that occurred between sessions, which the client regards as significant.
- The practitioner listens and feeds back to the client what has been learned.
- The client corrects any inaccuracies and an agreed account of the incident is logged; client and practitioner keep copies of the log.
- After sufficient data has been collected, the log is reviewed and a simple flow chart diagram is jointly compiled.
- The practitioner gives the client feedback on how the client seems to have learned what he or she has been teaching. The flowchart is revised in the light of agreement about the practitioner's feedback.
- The process continues with the addition of the client's perceptions of options and their possible consequences.

Complex as this may seem, the process soon becomes routine - often taking no more than ten minutes. Invariably, clients report versions of their racket system - the first of the 3Rs. It is vital to encourage reports of "the good news" and include a balance of positive and negative items in the practitioner's feedback; this addresses the second of the 3Rs. Resilience too, needs to be highlighted and stroked. Evidence of Resilience is the client's reporting an Incident that includes or replaces behaviours that were previously unhelpful. This usually emerges during the review and options stages.

The downside of Significant Incidents is that they make labour intensive demands on the practitioner. It usually takes me fifteen minutes between sessions to re-play the audio disc and reflect on what I have learned during the previous session. The advantages are that clients report "feeling valued", "being taken seriously", "like taking charge of my own therapy", and, above all, "like being involved."

The following excerpts from sessions with a client, Freda, illustrate how information about Significant Incidents may be introduced and accumulated. The vignettes are edited transcripts (with editing being the removal of most of the "ums", "ers" and other monosyllabic utterances), prepared for training sessions with advanced level trainees. Some include *post hoc* speculations, hypotheses and comments on the process, shown in italics within square brackets; the symbol -> means "leading to":

Transcript 1

GL: So ... How are you doing? ... *[Promoter]*

Freda: OK *[doesn't look or sound OK; Victim? I should have commented on this.]*

GL: Good. I've been pretty busy. Tell me about how you've been getting on during this past week.

Freda: OK – I suppose. *[Victim inviting Rescuer?]*

GL: Say some more. *[Open ended Announcer]*

Freda: There's not a lot to say, really. *[still Victim looking for a Rescuer?]*

GL: Well that's OK for the time being. Part of being in therapy involves learning – for both of us. Learning about how we're going to proceed, about what you want to talk about – about what you want or expect from me. *[I am starting to feel a little anxious.]*

Freda: (says nothing) *[passive behaviour; Bystander?]*

GL: Everyone I see is different. Each person has their own story, their particular concerns. I have to learn – learn about how the world works for you. You already know; you have to teach me.

Freda: (remains silent) *[I am not sure what she is experiencing at this point – back to Bystander? about to switch? I continue feeling uneasy.]*

GL: You've already told me a great deal. Your depression... your ex-husband running off with your best friend .... the divorce .... how much you wanted a child .... and your family .... your hopes when you left school .... and a lot more. *[I still feel slightly uncomfortable; probably should have said "I'm feeling anxious. What's going on for you?"]*

Freda: I *know* all that – *and* I've told you! Now you want to know what I've been doing all week! What's the point? *[Persecutor -> Bystander as suggested by "what's the point?"?]*

GL: It sounds as though you're angry with me? *[soft tone Responder attunement; important not to reinforce negative role]*

Freda: (says nothing) *[still Persecutor -> Bystander? – but maybe, Valuer??]*

GL: Are you angry? *[inviting Valuer – or Promoter]*

Freda: (shrugs) *[From her body language, I sense she wants to respond positively]*

GL: Coming to therapy and then not talking is rather like going to your doctor and expecting him or her to cure you without knowing what's wrong with you – without answering when he or she asks questions. *[Announcer using illustration (c.f. Berne's therapeutic operations)]* .... Are you angry with me?

Freda: I was – a bit. But not just with you ... *[Her tone suggests Responder/Valuer]*

GL: Now we're making progress. Even though we're only five or so minutes into the session and it may have been a little uncomfortable, I think you've already taught me something important.

Freda: What – that I don't stay angry for long? *[sharp tone – still Persecutor?]*

GL: Well that's another thing I've learned! But not just that. *[I redefine possible invitation to reciprocate a negative role by reframing]*

Freda: What d'you mean?

GL: I think I missed my cue early on. You came in looking rather miserable – your body language seemed to suggest you were in need of what you referred to last week as "a little tlc – and needing a shoulder to lean on or cry on". Remember that? Last week?

Freda: (nods)

GL: I missed those signals today – or rather, I noticed the body language, but didn't acknowledge the message. Am I on the right track?

Freda:	Yeah – maybe
GL:	Instead, I jumped ahead – said something like "what have you been doing this last week?" and you were non-committal.
Freda:	Well – so what? *[still slightly sharp tone – wary, but curious?]*
GL:	I think... *maybe* this is a similar pattern of behaviour. I mean, you've already told me about desperately wanting to get pregnant. You were feeling "down", "neglected". Jim [her ex-husband] didn't seem to recognise you were wanting to be "coddled" – I think that was the word you used. He said you were getting too anxious about starting a family – that it would happen when it was supposed to happen. Just forget about it until it did happen; *"let it be"* he would say. So you did – or tried to – but began to get depressed. And then you discovered that Sandra [her "best" friend] was expecting - and Jim was the father-to-be. So you threw him out.
Freda:	I don't see the connection... *[now engaged; positive role Announcer?]*
GL	Maybe there *isn't* a connection – but there is a similar pattern – a sequence. Wanting to be acknowledged, cared for... When it doesn't happen - when your feelings are not recognised - you go quiet. Later, you get angry. But I think you are right to suggest there isn't necessarily any *connection*.
Freda:	And so? *[Promoter]*
GL:	The point is that I mustn't jump too far ahead without acknowledging what you've already taught me. It's not just what you say – or don't say. It's also about body language and feelings. I didn't respond to your non-verbal messages. That's a whole *new* language, *another* language I need to learn. That was my mistake. Sorry about that ... *[Promoter -> Valuer->Responder]*
Freda:	That's OK.
GL:	Thanks ....I need – we need to learn from each other. We have to collect the data, marshal the facts. Do you remember that last week we spoke about "mapping the territory" - and how we could use everyday events to do that? *[Promoter]*
Freda:	You said every time I come, I should pick out one incident and tell you what happened. *[Responder]*
GL:	You got it!
Freda:	But the letter... (referring to a "no send" letter she was to have written to her ex-husband as homework). *[Anxious, please me? - low key Victim?]*
GL:	Sure – that's what we agreed last week – to discuss the letter today. *[Responder]* We'll do that in a moment. *[Promoter]*
Freda:	I have done it – and I brought it with me, like you said. *[AC tone/posture – wants/needs strokes]*
GL:	Good for you! Well done! *[Responder]* What I suggest is that we finish off talking about using everyday incidents to 'map the territory', and then we spend the rest of the time on the letter. Are you OK with that? *[Promoter inviting Responder/Promoter/Valuer]*
Freda:	Fine. *[Responder]*
GL:	Good! This won't take long.... The idea is to use your descriptions of current events to teach me three things. First, who you *are,* and how it is for you to *be* the way you are. I want and need to know how things work for you, what it's like to be in your skin. I need to know your reactions – your behaviour – your feelings, your thinking, your hopes, your resources. It's not good enough for me to guess all this – for me to make interpretations. You need to *teach* me. You're the expert on this – no-one knows more

235

about *you,* than you do. Does that make sense? *[Promoter – needing to get bilateral contract]*

Freda: Yeah... I got that.

GL: Good. Second thing is: what's the best way for me to relate to you – so that I don't reinforce the ways of communicating and relating that are not helpful to you? Again, you have to teach me, and maybe you have to learn what it is that I have to learn – rather as we've done today, but a lot more openly.

Freda: How do you mean?

GL: We have to agree to talk about what's going on between us if either of us think or feel we're not communicating clearly. For example, if I say something you don't understand, you need to say so - there and then – or at least, as soon as you realise we're not on the same wavelength.

Freda: Right.

GL: Or it might be that I ask you to think or talk about something painful. You may not want to do that at the time – when I ask. Maybe it's something you're not ready to talk about – something you've always known, but don't like to even *think* about – let alone talk about to someone else. Now that's OK – people only talk about difficult issues when they're ready to. And if that's the case, you need to say so. You have to say "No" – or "Not now" Do you see what I mean?

Freda: Yes.

GL: And what do you think about what I'm suggesting?

Freda: Erm ... It's all right – seems a good idea - in principle. Perhaps I'll think otherwise once I've tried it! (laughs)

GL: And that would be fine – provided you say so at the time.

Freda: Right

GL: Good. And ...Oh yes ...There's another aspect of this same idea.. It ties in with the first point – about your teaching me about your way of seeing the world. Say I ask about something to do with your childhood in Upton that you'd find difficult or painful to discuss – and you say "No". I may then follow that up and say "OK that's fine with me for now. But tell me - what happened inside you when I asked about Upton? What was your immediate reaction? What came to mind? What did you feel?" Do you see what I mean - and would you be OK with that?

Freda: Yeah that's OK

GL: Finally...third point. This one's a lot more like two-way traffic. As you teach me and I learn, I'll also teach you – so you'll be learning too.

Freda: Mmm .. yeah?

GL: It's actually a lot easier than it may sound – believe me. The way I'll be teaching you is by giving you feedback – as we go along. I'll be telling you what I've learned about your way of experiencing things – and you'll be able to say "Yes, that's right" or "No, that's not how I was feeling"

Freda: I'm starting to get the picture...

GL: In fact, we did a bit of this today. I said I could see a *connection* between my missing my cue earlier on today, and some of the experiences you'd told me about in our earlier sessions. Right?

Freda: I'm with you so far.

GL: And you said maybe there *isn't* a connection!

Freda: Your point being?

GL:	That we had two-way communication – we'd made a feedback loop. *I'd thought there was a connection – you* weren't sure. That's the way forward. You tell me about your experiences, I learn and feed back what I've learned, you agree or correct. And then we log it. We make diagrams – flowcharts – this bit of information connected to that bit – and so on.
Freda:	Then what?
GL:	We build up information over four, five perhaps even ten sessions – however long it takes. Then we review it all and we'll be able see the patterns. One guy who did this described it as like being able to control the weather….
Freda:	*What?!*
GL:	Yeah … I thought it sounded a bit strange at first! He explained that looking at all the charts we'd made, was like looking at a satellite view of the clouds over the Atlantic. He said: "You can see a storm brewing out there – and you know it's coming this way. And then you start to think what can you do to keep the sun shining."
Freda:	Go on holiday?!
GL:	Exactly! Great option! Barbados! Morocco! But seriously – once you recognise the patterns, you'll start to think about options. You'll start thinking "what if…"
Freda:	I do a lot of that already – all the time…
GL:	Great! You're already part way there! But ….I'll bet your 'what ifs' are mostly about the past?
Freda:	True…
GL:	So *what if* you had options about what to do - how to be - in the future?
Freda:	That'd be alright – it'd be great!
GL:	That's how it works! Each week you come along and tell me about one event – one thing – could even be a thought, a mood - anything you like. I have a one page leaflet with guidelines for how to do this. *[I offer the leaflet to Freda].*
Freda:	Thanks.
GL:	Have a quick skim through that …… Anything there that's not clear to you?
Freda:	(Reads)…. No – it's all OK … Well, except for the heading…
GL:	"Significant Incidents?"
Freda:	Yes
GL:	What's the problem with that?
Freda:	What if I tell you something that you don't think is significant?
GL:	Forget about me. Whatever is "significant" is what *you* regard as being significant.
Freda:	Mmm …You might think I being really silly – or stupid – or …something….
GL:	That's not what it's about. You're not supposed to be impressing me – you're *teaching* me how things work for *you.*
Freda:	Well … I can see that …mmm… Yeah …OK then
GL:	Good – how about … You take the leaflet, read through it again and then do one incident for next week as a trial run?
Freda:	OK …yeah …that's fine
GL:	Good ..that's the deal then. Now …. are you ready to go onto the letter?

[My overall impression is that her role profile was probably Victim/Bystander/Persecutor with Rescuer being the role she projected onto me during

first part of the transcript. This could be regarded as an example of a Single Exit mixed outcome role sequence. The latter part of the transcript demonstrates the use of positive roles/reciprocals during the explanation/contracting about the homework of composing a Significant Incident, She is bright, quick on the uptake, well motivated; her job (accountancy) suggests she will have no difficulty doing dRITs]

The leaflet I gave to Freda reads:

Significant Incidents

The aim of this "homework" is to collect information in a systematic way that will enable you to identify your distinctive style of perceiving and reacting to ongoing events or experiences. All you have to do during the coming week is to select one incident that you will be asked to describe briefly at the beginning of your next session.

Whatever you choose as "significant" and as an "incident" is entirely up to you. Indeed, the whole point of the exercise is to accumulate a record of *your* views. However, to make your account of incidents comprehensible to others, it is suggested that you present your experience of events or aspects of an Incident in a temporal sequence – experience A, then experience B, and so on. Note that an Incident does not have to be a series of external *events*, such as "I went to the shops, and bought some food and when I got home, I phoned my friend". An Incident could be thoughts, feelings, fantasies or memories – or any combination of 'external' and 'internal' experiences. The emphasis is on your *experience.*

It is also suggested you select the *most* Significant Incident that occurred during the week. This may mean discarding an initially selected experience that, for example, happened on a Monday, in the light of a subsequent experience on, say, the Friday.

Keep a brief written and dated note of the Significant Incident in a booklet, for future use in compiling diagrams of your characteristic patterns.

I comment later in this Chapter on alternative ways of compiling data for Significant Incidents.

The transcript of Freda's first Significant Incident reveals her level of engagement with the task that is typical of clients on their 'trial run':

Transcript 2

Freda:	I did both lots of homework *[referring to the Significant Incident and another assignment]*
GL:	Good for you. You sound pleased.
Freda:	I was ... I am – and a bit worried.
GL:	Uhu?
Freda:	Worried about what you'll think.
GL:	Not unusual with a trial run. You have to think of it as an exercise in teaching me about your experiences
Freda:	I know ... but still....
GL	Come to think of it, *I'm* the one who should be worried! You're setting the work for *me* to *learn* and *I* could be getting worried about not getting it right!
Freda:	You're having me on?
GL:	Well – only a bit...

Freda:	Whatever.....
GL:	So .... what did you come up with as a Significant Incident?
Freda:	It's not a lot really – only four and a bit lines – I wrote it out. Was that alright?
GL:	Fine. Let's have it
Freda:	I'll read it ...."I was taking Tammy for his evening walk and he cocked his leg against my neighbour's gate. I waited for him to finish his business and my neighbour opened the window and started shouting at me. I ignored her and waited until Tammy had finished. Then I walked on. She was still yelling about not being able to keep my dog under control. I was fuming but didn't say anything."... That's all.
GL:	Good – very clear. One thing, then the next. I can just visualise the scene.
Freda:	Is that like I was supposed to do it?
GL:	It's absolutely fine. The way this process works, you can't go askew – whatever you do will be valid.
Freda:	What about ... erm ...feedback?
GL:	Ha! early days yet. What would you say I could learn about you from this Incident?
Freda:	Don't know really ...Well, I suppose you could say I don't always say so when I'm angry
GL:	Is that what *you'd* say or is it what *I "could say" about you?*
Freda:	No ..I mean ... that's what I'd say about me.
GL:	Great! so that's my first lesson!
Freda:	Is that it?!
GL:	Yep – As they say, "no big deal"
Freda:	What about the ..um ..the flowchart?
GL:	Right – well done for remembering that. Not yet, is the short answer. We need more information, more data. You have actually already done one kind of chart. Remember? - about three or four sessions ago – your BRIT. Remember that?
Freda:	Oh – yes
GJL	That gave us a great deal of background information – it split current circumstances from what I call historical data. That's all incredibly useful, but it's all top down stuff. It's all based on *general* categories. What we've done is fit your experiences into the circles provided by the 'theory'. What we're doing now is bottom up stuff. Absolutely vital. We need to build a 'theory' of *your* world; for you to teach me about *your* experiences, your own *personalised* picture. Later on, we'll cross check with the top down information... So, are you up for doing the same again next week?
Freda:	Another Significant Incident?
GL:	That's it
Freda:	I'll have a go.
GL:	Good. Now, let's move on to...

[A good 'trial run']

The next transcript illustrates Freda's growing familiarity with the process:

Transcript 3

GL:	What have you got today?

Freda:	A puzzle – I think. I mean …I've been thinking …Before – up to now - and even when I was a kid, when I was feeling …like I was upset – like what we've logged as "feeling hollow" and no-one took any notice, I would "shrivel up" and feel angry, but not show it. Right?
GL:	I'm with you.
Freda:	So is that what you call a pattern?
GL:	Yes.
Freda:	Well that's the puzzle! It's got mixed up…
GL:	*"It's"?*
Freda:	OK – I ..me …I've got mixed up.
GL:	Fascinating. Say more…
Freda:	It's in my SI.
GL:	Which is?
Freda:	I've been getting angry – all over the place. Well, more like tetchy …at work, in the supermarket. But it's a different kind of angry that…
GL:	Mmmm …it does sound like a 'mixed up' SI.
Freda:	OK, OK. Don't get sarcy! I'll do it properly….. On Wednesday at work my boss was in a flap because he had to give a report to the Finances Committee at short notice. He asked me for some figures, so I asked the filing clerk to get me the files, while I logged onto the network. Then I heard her laughing and giggling next door and I started to feel *really* irritated. By the time I'd fired up my PC she hadn't brought the files, so I went next door to get them myself. She was just standing there - still telling the other girls what her idiot boyfriend had done the night before! They were giggling like schoolgirls. I told her off really sharply and grabbed the files myself. Everyone went quiet. Even my boss looked surprised. I went back to my room. I was feeling scared …a kind of sinking in my stomach. I wished my boss would come in and tell me it was OK. I started to work on the files. It only took ten minutes, but it seemed ages. I was dreading going next door again and having to face everyone. I did nothing for *another* ten minutes and then the phone rang. After that I was OK.
GL:	So what do you make of all that now?
Freda:	I thought – I was hoping …hoping you'd tell me …Yeah, yeah, yeah - I know …I'm the expert about myself!
GL:	(chuckles)
Freda:	It's all the other way round!
GL:	Like?
Freda:	Sharp – angry that is. Then scared and needy and couldn't face them…
GL:	Is *needy* my word or yours?
Freda:	Yours – but you don't have copyright!
GL:	Good …Good…And the phone?
Freda:	Couldn't face them until I'd made contact with John – he was the guy on the phone.
GL:	*I'd* made contact?
Freda:	Until he'd made contact with me.
GL:	Congratulations!! Great lesson!
Freda:	But I was puzzled ..I couldn't….
GL:	Don't knock it! – Let's log it! What shall we put?
Freda:	Sharp-angry, scared-needy, do nothing until contacted.
GL:	Is *do nothing* the same as *couldn't face them*?

Freda:	No, not quite – but it was there ….I'll put both.
GL:	Good. What's next?

[Probably more than ready for Review; will explain/suggest this next session]

Transcript 4

Freda:	I had a wobbly this week.
GL:	What was that?
Freda:	You won't believe it. I promise!
GL:	I can't wait!
Freda:	This is the biggie – my most Significant Incident ever! Today I'm going to teach you something about me that's not been there for ages …..
GL:	I did wonder when you said "wobbly". That's not a word I've heard you use before.
Freda:	Spot on! In fact, it's been *years* since I was like that. I remember that my brother and I used to talk about being pimply and wobbly because…
GL:	Is this part of….
Freda:	No, it isn't part of my Significant Incident – but it *is* relevant. Probably what you'd call a "historical factor" – or whatever.
GL:	Oooh - great stuff!
Freda:	Anyway … where was I? …Yes, we used talk about wobbly – as against pimply. Pimply means shivering and being scared – Wobbly's the same – or *starts* the same – but then it goes SPLASH! You know, like "wibble-wobble jelly on a plate" – and then the jelly slips off and splashes – smashes - *all over* the floor!
GL:	Wow! I'm feeling the energy – the excitement …
Freda:	That's *your* feelings – not mine!! Listen to teacher! It's ANGER!!
GL:	I seeeee… You're shaking now?
Freda:	Yes… I have to clench my hands – my fingers - together without my palms touching - like this..
GL:	Maybe you don't … stay with whatever this means for you…Take your time.
Freda	(low voice ----)
GL	(waits)
Freda:	I said *'I know you're going to ask if I want to work on this now'* – but I don't. Maybe later … I want to tell you the Significant Incident.
GL:	Sure?
Freda:	Of course I'm sure – so no need to ask if I'm avoiding something! OK?
GL:	Fine
Freda:	It's a rather longer than usual ….So here goes …On Friday I had a call from my solicitor to say that the final divorce papers had come through and she was sending them on for me to sign. She was a bit brusque, but explained about a *decree nisi*. That means it's final – kaput, over, no going back. I was upset… On the Saturday I was watching out the window - waiting for the postman because I knew he'd ring the bell - the papers would be Recorded Delivery and I'd have to sign for them. I knew what to expect and I was quite calm. I knew exactly what I was going to do – wait for the doorbell, shut Tammy in the front room – he always barks his head off at the postman – and open the door. Then I'd sign, say "Thank you" and he'd give me the envelope. So, like I said, I was watching out the window…. You can see the postman coming because he does the opposite side of the street first – and then down a side road – then crosses over to my side and

241

does three houses up the street before he gets to me. So I knew I'd have to watch for a good five minutes before he'd ring the bell. Then I saw him down the street and I could feel myself going tense in my hands and arms. It was the *walking* postman – not the *running* postman!! – We have two postmen. I call the young bloke the *running* postman because he runs from door to door; we joke about it. He has another part-time job, so he has to finish his rounds by twelve o'clock. The other fellow's the *walking* postman – ever so friendly, but *incredibly slow;* takes ten minutes before he gets to me. - I watched him and was getting more tense. Then he stopped to chat to someone down the side road and I was thinking *"Why can't you just shut up, you silly old cow, so as he can get on with it!"* By the time he rang the bell and Tammy was barking no end, I was so uptight that I flung open the door and yelled *"Give me the f..ing pen!"* He was so startled that he just stared at me with his mouth open. I grabbed the pen and pad and scrawled my name. He shoved the envelope into my hand and scuttled down the path before I'd even thought of apologising. I was shaking all over and went all goosey. I closed the door and felt *absolutely furious* for about half a minute - I could hear my brother laughing and taunting *"wibble-wobble wibble-wobble, jelly on a plate!"* when I was having a temper tantrum because my mother refused to let me have a second helping. Then I sort of heard her joining in with the laughter, and I felt of totally lost.....

GL:	(waits)
Freda:	That's it.
GL:	Thank you... I am humbled ...is there anything you want from me now?
Freda:	No ... just be you ... just be here
GL:	I am ...Let me know what next...

[Later, did chair work resolving Don't be close injunction. This SI confirms previous hypothesis A re VBP with Rescuer at 4ᵗʰ level? Last comments interesting - "just be there". Indications are she is able to access Valuer in presence of Beholder?? Significant Learning for me is "That's your feelings – not mine!! Listen to teacher!"]

The notion of "Significant Learning" in the last line of my comments refers to a catchphrase used by client or practitioner to indicate the most relevant aspect of what had been learned during a Significant Incident. In this case, it demonstrates that Freda is operating at a sophisticated level of correcting my jumping to the conclusion that the 'jelly on the plate' episode was exciting for *her.* The excitement was *my* feeling; hers was anger. Her riposte, enacted from the Provocateur role implicit in the phrase "Listen to teacher", suggested she was well able to start making links between the items we had logged thus far. This was confirmed two sessions later when she responded to my opening line by saying:

Transcript 5

Freda:	I've been thinking about my patterns. So I've started a flow chart.
GL:	Wowee! Let's see!
Freda:	Three patterns – and some loose ends that I haven't allocated yet. The first pattern is *feeling hollow, shrivel up* and *angry but don't show it.* The second pattern is *angry sharp, scared-needy,* and *couldn't face them and do nothing until contacted.*
GL:	That's brilliant!
Freda:	And I've not forgotten the good news ... See ... here in the middle....
GL:	Wow! This is *very* good.

Freda: I didn't quite know what to do with these others…on the right … and down at the bottom … they're not really Significant Incidents. These on the right … they are like "unallocated items"… I mean … At work, when we have income -   or more often, like when the Council vote through expenditure - there's always some monies we know we're going to have to spend, but

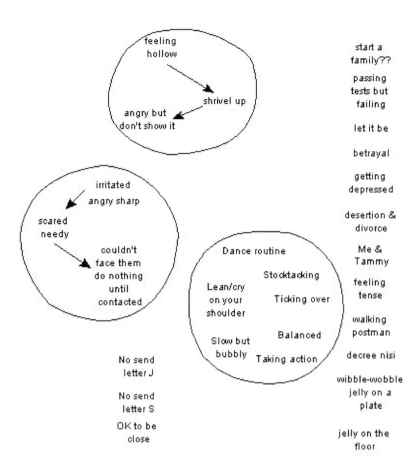

Figure 17.1

they've not yet been allocated to a budget heading. So I haven't got patterns for these yet. I thought we could talk about them today. You know, decide where they should go ….

GL: Freda, this is astounding! You've done what most people take twice as long to do! And you've done it off your own bat! What a star!!

Freda: Thanks … It's alright then is it?

GL: Well? !!

Freda: Yeah, I know - *what do I think?* I think it's alright except for the unallocateds. I don't know enough about how the system works, to be able to allocate …to know what to do with them. Overall – now that I've done this – as I sit here now, looking at the piece of paper… I … I …

GL: Am feeling?

Freda: Pleased ... and a bit scared... and strange ... sort of distant. Yeah distant... Is that a feeling?

GL: Not ...really...

Freda: It's like ... June 2001, eleven fifteen - I'm 29. Here I am, sitting in a room with a man I've known for less than three months - and a piece of paper. And there it all is – on the paper – everything that's happened, that I've said was *significant* because you asked me to, and I thought it would be a helpful exercise.... Yeah distant ... and a tat scary .....and pleased!.... What now?

GL: We discuss.

*[Her flow chart is shown above as **Figure 17.1**]*

During the ensuing discussion the flowchart went through several changes. The outcome is shown in **Figure 17.2,** warranting brief explanation.

 The left hand rectangles identified by Freda remain unchanged, being the two patterns

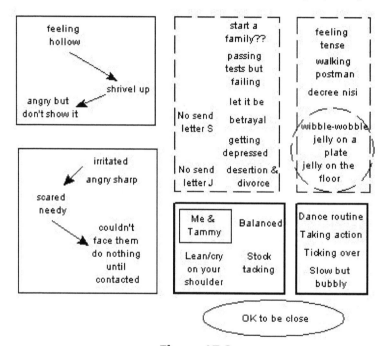

Figure 17.2

detailed in the ***Transcripts 4***.and ***5***. The rectangles in the lower right of the diagram are two motifs derived from the "*good news*" circular shape in Freda's original flow chart, together with the "*Me and Tammy*" item from her "unallocated" list. Her criteria for differentiating these heavily bordered items was that the left hand one was labelled "*as of now*", with "*future dreams*" on the right. These two positive aspects of Freda's experience are spanned by the ellipse representing her redecision work.

 The upper two rectangles with dashed line borders, are both "pending" (Freda's term), indicating that they would be discussed further. The difference between these two rectangles is that the right hand one was derived from the "*walking postman*" Incident (the circle represents an "historical factor"), whereas the other emerged from other, (non Significant Incident) work. The "*passing tests but failing*" item signified that Freda and her ex-husband had both undergone medical examinations that revealed no reason for her not falling pregnant. The *"let it be"* phrase represented her ex-husband's stance on her failure to conceive. *"Betrayal"* and the *"No send letter S"* to her (then) best friend Sandra, led to Freda's depression and the subsequent *"desertion and divorce"*, which was what she referred to in the first transcript as "the letter".

The revised flow chart highlights the co-created nature of this stage of the work. Freda continued relating Significant Incidents for a further four sessions, each time revising her flowchart, before we did a final "authorised version" of her experiences, as depicted in **Figure 17.3**. Comparison between this and her previous chart reveals important changes.

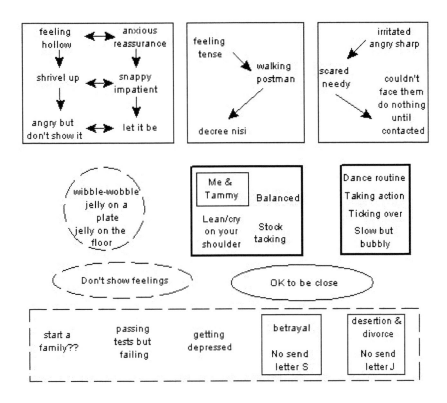

Figure 17.3

The previously unallocated items *"start a family??"*, *"passing tests but failing"* and *"getting depressed"* are still categorised as "pending", along with *"betrayal"* and *"desertion and divorce"*. Although the latter two experiences had been dealt with by way of their respective "no send" letters, Freda sensed that "there's something else there", and accordingly, allocated them to the dashed line rectangle at the foot of the diagram.

Another unexplored issue was a possible "don't show feelings" injunction which Freda thought was connected with the "jelly" scenario, and the top middle rectangle with the *"walking postman"* experience.

Transcript 6 describes how the changes to the previously identified pattern *"feeling hollow"*, *"shrivel up"* and *"angry but don't show it"*, were created:

Transcript 6

GL: Right, we're nearly done

Freda: I thought we had? This was supposed to be the final version, and we've made all the changes I can see. What else?

GL: This one here – *feeling hollow*

Freda: But we did that, *ages* ago! And anyway, it's not something I want to change

GL: No, this is different...

Freda: What?

GL: Remind me, when you were *feeling hollow* – that was before the divorce, with Jim?

Freda: Yes

GL: And you'd been trying for a family and it wasn't working?

Freda: I'd had all those tests and gynae examinations and they said everything was OK. They saw Jim too.. He doesn't fire blanks – so we just had to keep trying.. I felt – still feel - such a failure....

GL; Sure .... I can't pretend to know how that *felt* – but I *know* that your reactions were completely natural... understandable ...

Freda: Yeah .... (sighs deeply)

GL: OK?

Freda: Yeah ... That's all down here – bottom of the chart, in "pending" - *passing tests but failing*. That's not what you were asking about? – The *feeling hollow* was afterwards when I just used to get that sort of hollowness – like there was nothing inside me – which there wasn't, of course! And I'd get all weepy and sorry for myself.

GL: So this is what I mean when I say there something different: there's a whole new angle on all the experiences that we've not touched on yet.

Freda: Oh ...like what?

GL: Up to now we've been tracking *your* experiences. You've been teaching me, I've been learning – and so on. What you've been teaching me is *your* angle, *your* experiences. That's fine – entirely appropriate. What you've not yet taught me *explicitly* is how the *other* person *reacted* to your experiences. Like the walking postmen ..Let me see..(I consult my notebook). Hang about. ... Right *"He was so startled that he just stared at me with his mouth open."* That's what I'm getting at.

Freda: Okaay...

GL: We've got most of this in the notes – but we haven't shown it on the chart

Freda: I see.

GL: I'll say more about why we need to do this in a moment. My question is – when you were *feeling hollow*, how did *Jim* react?

Freda: Right, got you..

GL: What did he do – or say – or what do *you reckon* he was feeling?

Freda: He would try to reassure me that it'd all work out. But it - he was..... Well ... not phoney... but like he didn't quite believe what he was saying... No, that's not quite right ... He was anxious

GL: So what phrase should we log – add to the chart?

Freda: *Anxious re-assurance.*

GL: Good ... OK, and...

Freda: Then I'd go quiet because I *wasn't* feeling re-assured. There was no way he or anybody else could re-assure me. He'd get impatient and rather disapproving – not nasty, but just snappy. By then, I'd had enough, so I

	would give long, hard, warning glares - but not say anything. And he'd just shrug and mutter about biding our time and letting things be – and then walk out in case I was going to explode.
GL:	Great description. You've got the idea.
Freda:	So let's log *snappy impatient* and … I'm thinking … Right – it's *let it be.* See, here in the unallocateds.
GL:	Write those two into the chart - that's it.
Freda:	There. We've done!
GL:	Yep – we've done….Now; we still have a little under twenty minutes … I want to summarise for a bit and then look ahead to the next stage. Are you OK with that?
Freda:	Yes.
GL:	What you've achieved so far is really important. You have your two good news patterns down here, and at the top the three negative experiences. Then there's the pending items, the possible injunction and the jelly scenario – all waiting to be dealt with - really, really excellent progress. In particular, this one, with you experiencing *feeling hollow*, and Jim as *anxious re-assurance* – this illustrates the way forward. We don't have experiences in a vacuum. Significant Incidents occur in a context – in relation to something, to other people. Are you with me so far?
Freda:	I'm following
GL:	Good. So from now on, we need to include other people's reactions in the Significant Incidents. You'll see why in a moment. You've now reached a stage where you can make a choice. We'll go on with the Significant Incidents – just as we've done up to now – but include other people's reactions. And we'll tackle the injunction, plus anything else outstanding and whatever else you want to throw in. But this means the charts are going to get cluttered. And in any case, we don't want to get bogged down by over-detailing the map - the territory. The choice is for you to decide if you want a shortcut. If you do, I'll suggest one next week. If you want to go on the way we've been doing so far, that's fine. You don't have to decide now. What'll probably be helpful is for me to tell you a bit more about the shortcut.
Freda:	Yeah… What is it?
GL:	The shortcut is that I'd teach you a different way of looking at your experiences and other people's reactions. It's like you've got a good command of English and can now start learning French – if you want. That's perhaps not a good example – the shortcut is miles easier than learning French. You only have to understand the meaning of eight words that you'd be able to use to describe ways of thinking, feelings and behaviour - just like I explained the idea of permissions and injunctions. *Don't show feelings* – just three words that signify an *incredibly* complex process. In accountancy, you have the same sort of idea. You know, like *income* and *expenditure.* You have these two categories and all sorts of *items* in each category. To make sense of items, it helps if you know how to deal with them - as *income from* or *expenditure on* … whatever. Everyone has *items* of income and expenditure, just like everyone has their own *descriptions of experience.* The shortcut I have in mind gives four *categories* for positive descriptions of experience and four *categories* for negative descriptions of experience.
Freda:	Sounds like a good idea. I like categories – makes sense to use them.

GL:	As long as we remember they're just a shorthand way of describing *experiences*. We still need your descriptions. You can learn how to package them and label them – but without the descriptions, the labels are meaningless. I can tell you about the labels - that is, if you want to?
Freda:	I'm game.
GL:	So next week, are you willing for us to spend the whole session on learning the shortcut?
Freda:	You got a deal.
GL:	Not yet. There's one more thing. Have you heard the saying *"If it works, don't fix it"*?
Freda:	Yeah.
GL:	When I tell people about these shortcuts I always point out the there's a follow up saying *"If it doesn't work, throw it away"*. I'm sure you won't forget to remember that, or even if you don't remember to forget that – or what ever makes sense to you - the important thing is to use whatever's useful for you.

We spent most of the next session on an explanation of the Contact Cube. Towards the end, Freda commented:

Transcript 7

Freda:	It's really dead easy.
GL:	So let's apply the signposts – the labels – to the chart.
Freda:	OK.
GL:	Take this one – *feeling hollow.*
Freda:	Right … Let me see … I'm the Victim, Jim's Rescuer.
GL:	Good – if that's how you read it.
Freda:	Then I go to … to Bystander and Jim moves over to Persecutor?
GL:	You're teaching me how you learn. And finally?
Freda:	Persecutor and … and… and he goes .. Well .. he buggers off – so it's Bystander!
GL:	And so your role profile is..?
Freda :	Victim, Bystander, Persecutor – and Jim is Rescuer, psychological … Persecutor, and the Bystander.
GL:	Great lesson! Now, for homework…
Freda:	I can guess! … Do the other role profiles!
GL:	You guessed right. Do the usual Significant Incident, and then we'll add the role profiles, together, next session.

Freda duly completed the role profiles for the remaining Significant Incidents on her chart. Understandably, she was able to identify only her own profile for the office scenario and the two good news scenarios. The role profiles of others in the office scenario and with the walking postman would have required more information than that provided by Freda when she related these Incidents. Nevertheless the role profiles identified from the feeling hollow scenario enabled me to *hypothesise* one round of her role imago repertoire for negative outcome role sequences. This is shown in **Table 17.1**, where the shaded areas signify aspects of the interaction that were insufficiently described in the original relating of the Significant Incidents to merit assigning roles to them.

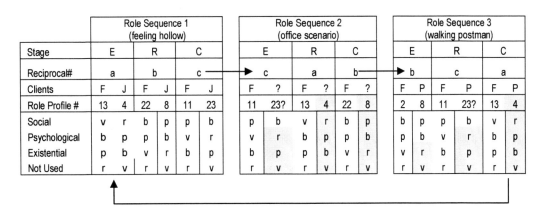

	Role Sequence 1 (feeling hollow)						Role Sequence 2 (office scenario)						Role Sequence 3 (walking postman)					
Stage	E		R		C		E		R		C		E		R		C	
Reciprocal#	a		b		c		c		a		b		b		c		a	
Clients	F	J	F	J	F	J	F	?	F	?	F	?	F	P	F	P	F	P
Role Profile #	13	4	22	8	11	23	11	23?	13	4	22	8	2	8	11	23?	13	4
Social	v	r	b	p	p	b	p	b	v	r	b	p	b	p	p	b	v	r
Psychological	b	p	p	b	v	r	v	r	b	p	p	b	p	b	v	r	b	p
Existential	p	b	v	r	b	p	b	p	p	b	v	r	v	r	b	p	p	b
Not Used	r	v	r	v	r	v	r	v	r	v	r	v	r	v	r	v	r	v

Table 17.1

I cannot emphasise too strongly that assigning roles and role profiles to data derived from Significant Incidents, needs the utmost methodological rigour and restraint. I would have waited for least another three examples of each of the above role sequences, before asking Freda whether she could discern any links – without saying what I thought the links appeared to be. Freda and I never got that far. When she progressed to the next stage of assigning roles to Significant Incidents in relation to her BRIT, she focused increasingly on the "good news" patterns (lower right of the chart in **Figure 17.3**) and made redecisions based on her perception of the links between her historical and current role sets. Just when I was speculating about strategies for identifying further rounds of her role imago repertoire, she announced that she was going to take time out from "dredging dRITs" and instead, had signed up for ceroc dance classes, and in therapy, wanted to focus on improving social skills. When I asked what she thought she had learned by compiling dRITs she said something along the lines of: "Personally, incredibly helpful, especially at first; gave me a way of making sense of my feelings. But now it's getting a drag – writing out those narrations. At work, the Cube is a revelation – to see the roles all happening outside therapy - where ordinary people are doing their jobs". Reluctantly but thankfully, I heeded her final salutary lesson.

Principles

While the above transcripts reflect my style of working with a *particular* client, I would emphasise that there is no "formula" for how to elicit descriptions of Significant Incidents. This is because the aim, the object of the exercise, is to get 'bottom-up' information about the *individual* client's frame of reference – to *co-create* a model of the client's world; the practitioner has to work in a way unique to each client. "Reality" is "agreed intersubjectivity" – or even, "contextualised agreed intersubjectivity". However, there are several principles that I have found useful:

- The primary aim of the first stage of practice is to **elicit collaboration**. To do this, the practitioner needs to make clear to the client that the "deal" is *"you teach me about your model of the world; I tell you what I have learned; where necessary, you correct my learning. I give you feedback on the way I see your learning, and you may choose to amend your model in the light of my feedback. To do all this, we have to agree to agree, or agree to disagree".* Generally, I prefer a low key approach – what Ericksonian practitioners refer to as a one-down position – implying low key use of the prescriptive component of the Promoter role. *"This is what I suggest, Do you want to do this (have a 'trial run'/ do an experiment etc.)?"*

- Once embarked upon the next stage, there are all manner of options for **clarifying what is being learned by the practitioner**. Most have the logical form of "If this, then that", or "when A and B, then C and D". For example, *"when you get upset, you 'go all quiet'?"* At this stage it is important to use phrases such as *"I wonder if..., It seems that... ,Am I right?...Perhaps you..., Maybe..., I may be wrong,".* Even more powerful is *"What do you think?..., What's your take on this?"* In terms of the facts – the *content* of what has been learned, the aim of this stage is to establish the accuracy, or otherwise, of the practitioner's perceptions. In terms of the *process,* the aim of this stage is to establish/consolidate two-way communication. The most helpful role profile for the practitioner to adopt during this stage is Active Acceptor/Beholder/Valuer, with judicious switches to low key Provocateur/Beholder/Valuer.

- The next stages are focused on **reaching agreement and/or disagreement**. Again, it is important for the practitioner to model the process in a non-competitive way. *"So are we agreed that?...,I accept your point that..., I think that's right..."* Even when disagreeing with the client, the practitioner needs to give precedence to the client's point of view. *"We have different views on this one, but I'm willing to go with yours..., What should we put here? (referring to the flow chart)".* During this stage, the practitioner may also start introducing options. *"Do you think an option here would be for you to do what you did when..., What options to you think you had at this point?".* The practitioner's predominant role profile during this stage should vary between Announcer/Beholder/Valuer and Responder/Beholder/Valuer.

- The aim of the next stage is to identify and anticipate the **likely consequences of options:** *"What do you think would happen if you were to...? What would he think/do/feel ...? What would he think/do/feel, if you were to ...? What would that do for you...? (followed by the repetitive question, "And what would <u>that</u> do for you"? until the 'loop' is completed by returning to the first answer). So what do you think about doing...?"* Again, the practitioner's predominant role profile needs to be flexible, varying between Active Acceptor/Beholder/Valuer, or Announcer/Beholder/ Valuer, and Responder/Beholder/Valuer.

- The final stages are aimed at **reviewing** the previous stages and **consolidating the learning** achieved to date. This may involve a re-cycling of the third and fourth stages. It is at this point (and not before) that it is appropriate to introduce the client to Contact Cube roles and use the material elicited to date from Significant Incidents to illustrate roles. In most, if not the majority of cases, by the time the work has reached the review stage, clients will be using characteristic phrases of their own that fit the definitions of Contact Cube roles. For example *"Being a wimp, doing a grovel, whinging, wailing and whining"* are all phrase used by clients that correlate with what *for them* constitutes the equivalent of the more general term "Victim" .*"Going mega"* or *"going into mega mode, putting my foot down, going ape, over the top, I used both barrels"* all seem to suggest a Persecutor role. *"Biding my time, taking time out, staying cool, hanging loose"* imply enactment of the Beholder role. Needless to say, cultural, class and ethnic variables are always at play in the client's use of language. For example, practitioners need to be aware that phrases such as *"bringing dishonour to my family"* has very different connotations for clients coming from different backgrounds. As far as possible, the review stage should include evidence of the client's *consistent* use of their own positive and negative phrases, which suggests patterns that may be summarised as one or more of the Contact Cube roles. It is not enough for the practitioner gleefully to seize on one or two such phrases and present them as "evidence" of, or substitutes for, Contact Cube roles. Each of the phrases needs to be checked out in relation to the behaviours, feelings, thinking (and combinations thereof) that prevailed at the time. *"So when you were what you describe as 'being a wet dishcloth' what were you doing? What would I have seen if I was a fly on the wall? What's it like to be a wet dishcloth? You often use the phrase 'being a wet dishcloth'; does that always mean the same/that you are feeling/thinking/ behaving in the same way? What way is that?"* It is imperative that this course of action is *offered* to the client as *a new contract* – rather than simply tacked on in the guise of feedback implicit in the previous contract.

Unpalatable as it may seem to "objective" researchers, and admirers of "grand" theories, at present the Contact Cube is a fragile structure, born out of consensus between practitioner and client. What is needed is a thesaurus of phrases used by clients that may be correlated with Contact Cube roles. If, and only when such empirical measures may be rolled out, will the Contact Cube attain stability by communication and consensus between practitioners. This is the practice/research divide in action.

Over and above and throughout the above stages, there is a meta-level of communication relating to the interaction between the client and the practitioner. Practitioners ignore this at their peril. Roles are based on the notion of reciprocity. Not examining and addressing the occurrence of negative roles and the possible extent to which a practitioner is reinforcing their own, or the client's, negative roles, results only in replaying the client's and/or the practitioner's racket systems. Herein lies the dilemma: Significant Incidents (usually) elicit rackets as *content*, presented via the enactment of a role as *process.* If the content is rackety, the role will be negative. The practitioner's task is to learn about the content, *without reciprocating a negative role.* Learning to learn is primarily experiencing a process, and coincidentally, acquiring information about content. Likewise, learning about a client's view of the world should not obscure the need for the practitioner to expand his or her own view of the world.

Failure to address this dynamic is probably the single most frequently endorsed way of perpetuating the health/pathology divide. In my experience there are three ways of averting this. The first is not to discount self. The second is not to discount others. The third is not to discount situations. These three solutions stand in ascending order of difficulty. Practitioners may guard against these possibilities by exercising obvious basic routines – personal work, supervision and continuous professional development.

Even then, there is a continuous need to be alert to levels of discounting, bearing in mind that the overall aim is to learn about the client's frame of reference. In other words, if the practitioner consistently attempts to confront or "correct" every discount presented by the client, there will be no learning. All that will have happened is a role reversal - the client is "learning about" (adapting to) the practitioner's frame of reference. Not only do practitioners have no control over the client's predilection for discounting, they also are faced with the reality of the situation. By this I mean that clients and practitioners bring to their conversation their respective expectations that include life long histories of discounting. Inevitably, discounting and transferential/countertransferential issues will exist.

Under these circumstances, the facilitative reframe is to *accept* this, to *monitor* levels of discounting, *rather than* embarking on any corrective manoeuvers. The Contact Cube permits this. Victims look for a quality of contact that is co-operative - the role reciprocation of Rescuers *or* Responders. The bottom line is for the practitioner to maintain positive roles, while accumulating sufficient data to identify the client's role imago repertoire. Thus, the basic tactic for dealing with rackets, discounting and transferential issues in relation to the *process* of data collection about Significant Incidents, is to draw attention to the nature of the reciprocal roles involved. For example, *"I notice that when I ask a question and you don't answer, I feel (anxious, compassionate etc.) and am inclined to offer a solution. This is invaluable learning for both of us. It tells us how we expect others to relate to us".* However, not all clients respond to rational explanations. Sometimes the practitioner has either to ignore such questions (not a preferred tactic in my book) or simply reaffirm the contract. *"Our contract is for you to teach me, not to ask for my opinions".*

The other side of the coin is for the practitioner to deal with their own discounting (or mistakes) by apologising. This has the dual advantage of modelling good communication, as well as implicitly drawing attention to the reciprocals involved (as in the example of *"missing my cue"* during the first transcript of the work with Freda). Over and above all this, there is the need for the practitioner to highlight the client's resources, by including reference to the client's positive modes of communication. Without these, client and practitioner co-create the negative aspects of the health/pathology divide.

Working on Significant Incidents at this meta-level is an option that nudges the application of ERICA towards the relational end of Rowan's classification. This is probably not as necessary in organisational or educational settings. And even in therapeutic work, it is a matter of degree; most experienced therapists employ both instrumental and relational styles of relating to clients. The guiding principle is to use the approach best suited to the client's needs at different times.

Alternative approaches

An alternative way of using Significant Incidents is for the practitioner to carefully note all a client's experiences and offer feedback as and when appropriate. For example, ask any client questions such as *"How are you? How are doing? What have you been doing since our last session?"*, and you will find that most clients reply in terms of the reinforcing memories of their racket system. If the practitioner tracks such responses, over time an overall pattern emerges. This is a perfectly legitimate way of proceeding, but lacks the advantage of a clear contract, and, perhaps above all, is less likely to engage the client in owning their behaviour. It also carries the danger of perpetuating the health/pathology divide. In practical terms, it requires the practitioner to review audio recordings and keep at least outlined notes of the reported Incident.

Another option is to use the range of diagnostic tools favoured by Cognitive Analytic Therapists (Ryle 1997, Barkham et. al. 1998, Pollock et. al. 2001) and the "psychotherapy file" (see Appendix 2 in Ryle and Kerr, 2002 pp. 232-240). Such an approach makes for a more formalised style of working and would require some training in interpreting the results of these measures.

Teaching

Teaching clients to understand and apply dRITs to their own circumstances proceeds in tandem with understanding and using BRITs, cRITs and whatever "non-ERICA" work has been done to date. Irrespective of setting, it is important to emphasise that the purpose of the exercise is a mapping of the client's characteristic patterns of *relationships* – and that roles, qualities of contact and imago images are no more than convenient stepping stones from past to future improved relationships.

Once clients are familiar with Significant Incidents and have been introduced to Contact Cube roles (as described above), a new contract is agreed to cover the following procedures:

A dRIT is done jointly during the first twenty minutes (or less) of each session. Clients keep a copy of the dRIT and complete the "Narration" as part of their homework. As the client becomes proficient at recognising roles, they bring their Narration and a provisional dRIT to their session for discussion, agreement, amendment or 'agreed disagreement'. Client and practitioner keep copies of the agreed dRITs and Narrations.

In parallel with these, ideally, *Significant Learning Logs* (SLLs) are kept by both client and practitioner. Use of SLLs is an option commanding considerable discretion by the practitioner and is contra-indicated for, and hence not offered to, some clients. The aim is to record information relevant to the client's progress. Anything relating to the client's work that is regarded as "significant learning" by client or practitioner may be recorded. They are compiled independently, are not open to negotiation, but have to be shared each week. The 3Rs applicable to Significant Incidents, which constitute general guidelines for the practitioner and are not explicitly shared with clients, is replaced by the 3Rs of Significant Learning Logs; the motto is Respect, Record, and Reveal. I elaborate on this below.

I have adopted some simple conventions for drawing dRITs with individuals (**Figures 17.4** and **17.5**). The large circle represents the historical role set; the inner circle is the current role set. Role networks are named within rectangular boxes; networks within a network (sub-networks) are named within dashed line rectangles inside the larger network. The active role network is shown with a heavy border. People are represented as squares (male) and circles (female). Where necessary, an individual's formalised role is in bold type. The focal person is shown with a heavy border. Interaction between the focal person and others within each network follows the solid arrowheads, representing Significant Incidents. The first Significant Incident is labelled "SI-1". By following these, one can map the client's interaction with others during the period covered by the dRIT. Dashed arrows link influencing networks and Significant Incidents to distinguish them from interactions within a network; historical influences are shown using dotted line arrowheads. The role profiles associated with each Significant Incident are shown within the relevant square or circle. Positive roles are in uppercase font and the focal person's role profile is underlined.

Examples of dRITs and the 3Rs for Significant Learning Logs

Mark has schizoid traits and prefers to work alone. He came into therapy because his level of anxiety and periodic outbursts of frustration with people who did not understand him were affecting his work performance. He has been in therapy for fifteen sessions and this is his seventh dRIT. He finds it easy to talk to his therapist, but is still wary of discussing feelings. He is about to join a group run by his therapist and is learning to do dRITs. He is now able to compile his own dRIT in session with his therapist and has just started compiling them between sessions as homework. Mark's Narration for the session reads:

*"The first SI was a game with my boss. He wanted to be sure I had all the details of the new project ready for the meeting. I hadn't quite finished what I should have done and the boss got shirty. Told me I've got to pull my weight. **SI2** was OK but Cliff had to go out on a call so we didn't have much time. I felt a bit down when he left, so I phoned my wife **(SI3)** – that was OK, I guess. In the meeting (SI4), set up with the guy from (Company B) everything seemed to be OK until he was making out he didn't understand*

253

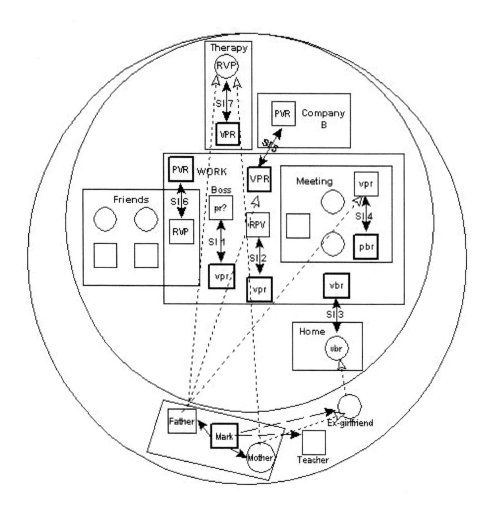

Name: Mark Brown			Date(s) 27/11/99 8h30m				Practitioner Sharon Howard		Ref: 7/15/65	
Sig/Inc.	1	2	3	4	5	6	7	8	9	10	11	12
R/Profile	1 8 ?	1 8 6	1 7 7	1 1 8 8	1 8 7	7 1	1 8 1					
Social	v p	v R	v v	p v	V P	P R	V R					
Psych.	p r	p P	b b	b p	P V	V V	P V					
Exist.	r ?	r V	r r	r r	R R	R P	R P					
N/used	b ?	b B	p p	v b	B B	B B	B B					
R/Seq.*	N	M	N	N	P	P	P					
S/type**	**Comp**	S/Ex	Rcon	S/Ex								
Current	Work	Work	Home	Work	Work	Frnd	Thrpy					
Hist'cal		Tchr.	Exgfd	Fthr	Fthr		M/F					
Notes: N=3, M=1, P=3												
Roles: lower case = negative; UPPER case = positive *Use bold font to code R/Sequence NORS; PORS; MORS; IORS ** Use bold to code **Comp**etitive; **R**eversed; **C**onfluent; **Rcon**fluent; **Rm**utual; **S/Ex**it; **By**stander; **R/Sk**ull												

Figure 17.4

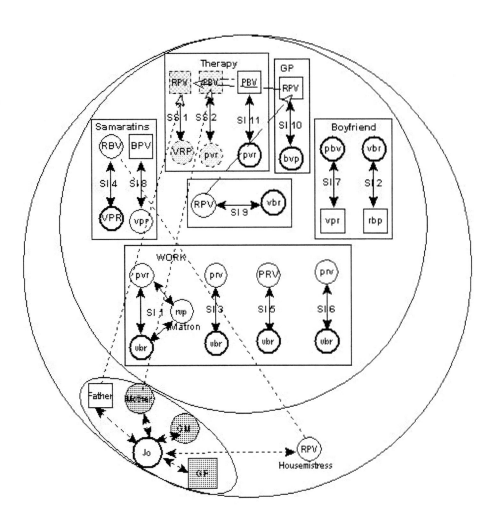

Name: Jo Green		Date(s): 17/01/00 – 21/01/00 - 5 days				Practitioner: Simon Pollock				Ref: 4/11/55	
Sig/Inc.	1	2	3	4	5	6	7	8	9	10	11	
R/Profile	1 7	7	1 7 1	1 7 9	1 8 5	1 7 9	1 7 9	1 0 1 8	1 8 2 2	1 7 2 2	1 9 6	7 1 0	
Social	v p	v r	v p	V R	v P	v p	p v	v B	v R	b R	p P	
Psych.	b v	b b	b r	P B	b R	b r	b p	p P	b P	v P	v B	
Exist.	r r	r p	r v	R V	r V	r v	v r	r V	r V	p V	r V	
N/used	p b	p v	p b	B P	p B	p b	r b	b R	p B	r B	b R	
R/Seq.*	N	N	N	P	M	N	N	M	M	M	M	
S/type**	S/EX	Rmut	S/Ex		S/Ex	S/Ex	S/Ex	Comp	S/Ex	Bystd	Comp	
Current	Work	B'Fr'd	Work	Samar	Work	Work	B/Fr'd	Samar	RMate	GP	Thrpy	
Hist'cal				Hmistr								
Notes: N=5/5, M=5/5, P=1/5 17/9 occurs X 3												
Roles: Lower case = negative; UPPER case = positive *Use bold font to code R/Sequence **NORS; PORS; MORS; IORS**												
** Use bold to code **Comp**etitive; **R**eversed; **Conf**luent; **Rconf**luent; **Rmut**ual; **S/Ex**it; **Byst**ander; **R/Sk**ull												

Figure 17.5

my proposal, so I had a go at him. Then I got scared and backed off when he started to have a go at me. After the meeting (SI5), I got a call from another guy in (Company B). He was really great! Made my day! I'll log this as my Significant Learning L. They're very impressed with the Delphi programme I've been doing. He said his boss wants to meet me and my boss, to talk about a joint project. Afterwards I went for a late lunch with my friend (SI6). I worked on my own all afternoon and was last to leave. Came direct to therapy session. (SI7) We looked at my RITs for past week and did my RIT for today and I reckon I'm getting the hang of this now."

Mark is clearly entering the second of a five stage process: recognising the components of his RIT, joint discussion thereof with his therapist (mentoring/coaching in an organisational setting), identification of in-session roles enacted by practitioner and client, anticipation of role sequences with negative outcomes and finally, devising strategies for "converting" these to role sequences with positive outcomes.

I comment on Mark's dRIT later – in comparison to **Figure 17.5**; this shows how a dRIT may be used in conjunction with other therapeutic interventions.

Jo is a twenty-two year old Nursery Nurse working for a small private Nursery. Despite her father's desertion when she was fifteen months old she has an idealised view of him as a father "who always looked after me financially". When Jo was almost two, her mother was killed in a car crash, amidst speculation that the event may not have been an accident. Her maternal grandparents raised Jo; she describes her grandmother as "strict and distant". Her grandfather was "a kind man", who nevertheless appears to have abused Jo systematically until he had a heart attack when she was nine. He died three months later and Jo was sent to an expensive boarding school. Her father paid for her education but always resisted any attempt to make contact with her. Her grandmother died when Jo was thirteen and a kindly Housemistress became her only source of adult support during adolescence.

In the latter stages of training as a Nursery Nurse, Jo became depressed; she started having flashbacks and began contemplating suicide when she heard that her ex-Housemistress had retired and moved away. She became extremely anxious about her final exams and began to mutilate herself as a means of tension reduction. Her General Practitioner referred her for psychiatric assessment but she did not attend appointments. Passing her exams and meeting a new boyfriend seemed to bring some stability into her life, but she continued to "fall out" with colleagues at work. Her boyfriend eventually persuaded her to seek therapy.

Jo's dRIT in **Figure 17.5** differs from the situational focus of Mark's dRIT in that the focus is on relationships over a five day period. Jo's dRIT uses the conventions described above but additionally, show "Shadow Scenarios" (SS) in relation to particular relationships. These represent either transferential phenomena or indirect contact. For example, Jo idealises her relationship with her therapist (SS 1) in roles she describes as "caring - cared for", but later (SS 2) sees him as "controlling". Jo's Narration reads:

*"Not a good week. **SI1** was a row with Amanda, (Work SI1) but Matron took my side. **SI2** was when I whinged a bit to Tony (Boyfriend SI 2) afterwards and he was sweet. Tuesday was no better - **SI3**. Silly cow Betty thinks she might be pregnant and had to go to the clinic for tests. She was away all morning! Matron out so I was left with TWO groups. When Betty came back she started moaning at me because I hadn't had time to tidy up her group room (Work SI 3). Tony out all evening so **SI4** I spoke to Jane (Jo's "regular" Samaritan SI 4) for a bit. Wednesday no better. **SI5** was Matron (Work SI 5) telling me off about forgetting to collect the dinner money. **SI6** on Thurs.*

was when had to work late because Mary P's. mum was "delayed" (again!!). Then I couldn't remember how to set the alarm & had to phone the security company. Took them 2 hours to send an engineer to fix my mistake. Matron's going to slay me tomorrow! SI7 Was late meeting Tony. We had a row & I walked out (Boyfriend SI 7) so SI8 phoned Jane (Samaritan) but had to speak to that stupid man Peter (Samaritans, SI 8) – he's not at all sympathetic, just listens and hardly says anything. When he does he asks things I've already told Jane and I hate having to explain everything all over again. In the end I hung up. Tried to phone Tony but got the answerphone. Felt a migraine coming on and was scared Tony's going to dump me. Then SI9 Sue [Jo's room-mate] started fussing around – said she was worried about me. She wouldn't let up so I locked myself in the loo. Felt like my head was going to burst. Wanted to slash myself but know I mustn't – would screw things up with me and Simon [Jo's therapist]. Anyway, didn't have anything. Started sobbing, banging on the door. Must have passed out. SI 10 next thing I knew Dr. G was talking to me through the door. Apparently Sue panicked & phoned Simon. He sent Dr. G around. I was mad at Simon (SS2). He's very controlling at times. Dr. G. was very calm. Examined me, made me go to bed, & gave me 2 tabs. Told me to take day off. Was going to go to work but didn't wake up until 9.20. Wanted to call Tony [an engineer] but know he's out on site all day, so stayed in bed. Pottered around in afternoon. Nearly didn't go for session with Simon SI 11 I thought he was going to terminate with me, so I said straight out that I was finishing therapy. He just gave me a soppy look and said he doesn't give up that easily so we'd better get down to work! (Therapist SI 11) Made me do this week's template thingy [the dRIT]. He does listen but can be very insistent in a quiet sort of way. We argued a bit about some of the roles. He said I must start to spot when I am cognitively distorting. I could see what he was getting at but wasn't going to say so. I still don't think he should have called out Dr. G. but it shows he can get serious when he thinks he has to & I know where I stand with him."

Compiling dRITs does not operate in isolation. Progress through the above stages will still need "standard" operations such as decontamination, de-confusing the Child, re-aligning cognitive distortions, redecision work and so on.

In **Part Three**, we saw that with the Contact Cube, the focus of attention – the operational unit of analysis – is personalised and formalised roles and role functions along with the qualities of contact and associated imago images. In **Part Four**, the emphasis was on reciprocals and role imago repertoires as the unit of analysis. Now, in **Part Five**, the general, structural concepts are role imago templates, derived from the particular Significant Incidents recounted by individuals. The unit of analysis is an amalgamation of dRITs that emerge from conversations. The notation I have used above is self-evident, representing the minimum information required to track changes, but may be varied according to the nature and purpose of the dynamic RIT. Indices may be devised to suit clients' circumstances and/or the practitioner's research interests. dRITs are usually reviewed every four sessions; this gives sufficient time to arrange data in simple frequency tables and detect overall patterns.

The most immediate difference between Mark and Jo's dRITs is that Mark's covers one day and Jo's is spread over five days. However, at this point, my aim is not to compare the two 'results' item by item, but to illustrate two very different applications of ERICA.

The "Ref:" for Mark (7/15/65) signifies that this is his seventh dRIT, that he has had fifteen sessions of therapy and that he has a rating of 65 on the Global Assessment of Functioning (GAF) Scale (Luborsky et. al., 1962). This indicates "Some mild symptoms OR some difficulty in social, occupational, or school functioning, but generally functioning pretty well, has some meaningful interpersonal relationships."

In contrast, Jo has completed four dRITs during her eleven weeks of therapy. Unlike Mark, who is still at the stage of compiling a dRIT covering a single day, Jo has been pushed to compiling a dRIT each day. The usual time scale is for the therapist to spend four sessions collecting descriptions of the client's experiences (as I did with Freda) before introducing the Contact Cube. After another four sessions of writing Narrations and compiling dRITs jointly during the first twenty minutes of a session, most clients progress to coming to sessions with fully completed Narrations and dRITs. In Jo's case, her GAF Scale rating of 55 ("Moderate symptoms OR moderate difficulty in social, occupational, or school functioning"), together with her "acting out" seemed to indicate a need for a more structured approach[1]. Note too, that Jo is already showing a tendency to gravitate towards a "17/9" reciprocal. That is, her Victim/Bystander/Rescuer/Persecutor role profile links with the other person's Persecutor/Rescuer/Victim/Bystander profile on three occasions; she starts as social level Victim finding (or being found by) a Persecutor, and then withdraws. This is consistent with the potential for a Rescuer payoff at the Closure and her "not used" role of Persecutor being projected onto others.

Another factor that is not apparent from Jo's dRIT is that her therapist has not (yet) suggested that he and she should use the convention of a **Significant Learning Log** – as is the case with Mark. Introducing the idea of Significant Learning Log is a matter of clinical judgement, should always be discussed in supervision, and be subject to a specific bilateral contract. It is a powerful therapeutic tool that needs to be used sensitively and with discretion, not least because it requires the practitioner to be scrupulously honest in revealing to the client what he or she (the practitioner) has learned that would be therapeutically advantageous for the client. My stance is that entries should always be discussed beforehand in supervision, thereby minimising the possibility of inappropriate disclosure, which, at worst, could lead to a formal complaint. For example, it would have been unwise for Jo's therapist to state *"when Jo's room mate called, I realised Jo could be at risk of harming herself and that I needed to exercise my duty of care by asking Dr. G to make an emergency visit"*. Entries in a Significant Learning Log should always be based on what the client and the practitioner need to share that will improve their relationship.

Not all clients benefit from compiling dRITs. Of the thirty nine clients with whom I have worked systematically using the ERICA models[2], seventeen received no instruction or information about dRITS[3]. Of the remaining twenty two, seven progressed no further than did Freda. Fifteen compiled dRITS and for eleven of these, ERICA and dRITS was the major focus of their therapy. Regrettably, I did not obtain informed consent in all cases and am unable to report their progress as the outcome of a formal research project. And even if I had, the models kept changing, as I learned about how the clients were learning. This is the standard dilemma for research-oriented practitioners; clinical priorities and ethical principles take precedence over research. Suffice it to say that thirty-four were "satisfied" or more than satisfied" with what they learned; four were "less than satisfied" and one thought dRITS were "a waste of time and too much work". Arising from this, the following Guidelines give indications and contra-indications for teaching the ERICA models as an adjunct to other transactional analysis concepts and techniques.

---

[1] This is supported by the standard procedure in Cognitive Analytic Therapy with borderline clients; using a raft of diagnostic tools, therapists complete the client's "reciprocal role procedures" (roughly equivalent to ERICA's role imago repertoire) in as few as four sessions.
[2] Additionally, in developing ERICA, I have used various aspects of the models with 105 clients.
[3] A description of ERICA as a method of "brief therapy" is given in **Chapter 22.**

Guidelines

A comprehensive checklist for teaching clients to research their own behaviour, requires a client to:
- understand the components of a BRIT;
- compile their own BRIT;
- be willing and competent to enter into a *"openly agreeing to agree, and openly agreeing to disagree"* contract as described earlier in this Chapter;
- understand and be able to describe sequences of events that represent a Significant Incident;
- understand and identify Contact Cube roles, qualities of contact and imago images at the social level;
- recognise use of their own roles at the social level and apply this knowledge to Significant Incidents;
- identify role switches and understand psychological level roles;
- recognise use of their own roles at the psychological level and apply this knowledge to Significant Incidents;
- understand the significance of role reciprocation between therapist and themselves;
- understand and identify roles and imago images at the existential level;
- recognise use of their own roles at the existential level and apply this knowledge to Significant Incidents;
- understand and identify types of role sequences;
- recognise use of their own role sequences and apply this knowledge to Significant Incidents;
- formulate and enact alternatives to negative and mixed outcome role sequences;
- understand the three stages of relationships– Contact, Communication, Confirmation and where relevant, apply this to Significant Incidents;
- use existing strategies/capacity to access the Observer role;
- use specific techniques of grounding, centring, goal setting and witnessing (Wilber 1985, 2000, Mellor 2002, Law 2003) to access the Observer role.

The last two of the above points are covered in **Part Six.**

For most clients in a clinical setting, I teach the above sequence as a 'Seventeen Step Programme' which requires clients to contract to complete all seventeen steps, but not necessarily in the above order. The criterion of suitability for undertaking such a programme is the capability of completing the first four steps and the motivation to complete homework. Thereafter, the basic requirement is for clients to demonstrate competence at each step before being 'promoted' to the next level. Crises, failure to complete homework and/or other deviations from contract delay promotion. Clients are encouraged to set their own time scales for progression from one level to another and cite specific evidence of readiness to move up to the next level".

In educational or organisational settings, individuals can demonstrate competence by participating in experiential exercises related to each step. A typical programme would consist of three one day events spread over six weeks interspersed with self-selected daily, weekly or fortnightly homework assignments. This may be supplemented where necessary, or if requested, by individual coaching and/or mentoring. However, I would emphasise that I have limited experience of using ERICA in a non-clinical setting.

How the steps are taught will vary according to the client and setting, bearing in mind the following guidelines:

- Establish clear, attainable and behaviourally verifiable contracts.
- Seek routinely informed consent to use the results of RITs for research
- Emphasise positive outcomes – such as 'growth', 'enhancing relationships' – rather than pathology. This is particularly important in organisational work.
- Especially during initial sessions, emphasis on relationships and contact are the crucial factors in engaging clients' interest and willingness to embark upon the learning process involved in compiling dRITs.
- Learn to compile a dRIT as an educational task. Although the client is responsible for completing each of the seventeen steps, even in a clinical setting the transactional analysis practitioner has to assume the formalised role of teacher, instructor or coach – as well as therapist. In practice it is often necessary to do decontamination work as part of the teaching process.
- Lead the client's narration of Significant Incidents and the identification of reciprocals towards specific, sensory based stimuli and a subsequent response. For example, if a client reports that *"I was really upset because he was being so vile"*, it is entirely inappropriate to jump to *"So you were Victim and he was Persecutor?"* Preferable by far would be questions such as *"What was it that he said?"* followed by *"And how did you feel?" "What did you experience in your body when you were feeling X?"* and so on, eventually leading to *"What roles were involved in this incident?"*
- Tailor teaching to the needs of individual clients. Some clients prefer their own definitions or names for roles. I go along with this and gradually get the client to compare the roles with the labels used in the Contact Cube. I have found this approach particularly useful in working with clients who have a dissociative identity disorder.
- Exercise flexibility and be creative. Teaching and learning is based on *joint* participation in compiling dRITs. Having clients come up with their own suggestions is preferable to imposing rules.
- Model the process and positive roles you are aiming to teach. The other side of the coin is to reinforce clients' use of positive roles whenever these occur and, at the same time, use the client's BRIT (and/or dRITs) to relate current behaviour to historical role relations. Non-clinical practitioners need to exercise due caution in this regard.
- Use indices to give feedback. Ideally, get clients to devise the indices that will indicate progress. Group therapy provides fertile ground for using all the models and the learning/teaching progress is accelerated. If possible, in an organisational setting, use relevant routine measures of performance or productivity and correlate these with dRIT indices. In one instance a work group correctly predicted that absenteeism and the incidence of positive outcome role sequences (Law 2004) within the group over six months would be inversely related. Unfortunately the programme was aborted after thirteen weeks because of redundancies – despite the fact that the predictions were panning out.
- Constantly ask questions such as *"How did you experience your contact with X?" "What did you feel when Y occurred?" "What would you have preferred as the outcome?" "What options do you think you had at that point?" "What could you have done differently?"* In other words, dRITs have tremendous potential as indicators for therapeutic direction and treatment planning. For example, if a client consistently reports Significant Incidents with a Persecutor, Rescuer, Victim,

Bystander role profile, a therapist will be able to demonstrate how the application of the sep-pse-eps-nu rules lead to the racket feelings that accompany the Victim role at the Closure phase (the payoff in classical Bernean terms) of the role sequence with a negative outcome. Asking such questions will often lead to contracting for specific therapeutic operations, such as two chair work, redecision work and so forth. The caveat is not to permit the compilation of dRITs take precedence over therapeutic opportunity.

In summary, for clients, using dRITs is a five stage process: recognising the components of a dRIT, joint discussion thereof with the therapist (mentoring /coaching in an organisational setting), in-situ identification of role sequences, anticipation of role sequences with negative outcomes and finally, devising strategies for "converting" these to role sequences with positive outcomes. Compiling dRITs does not operate in isolation. Progress through the above stages will still need "standard" operations such as decontamination, de-confusing the Child, re-aligning cognitive distortions, redecision work and so on.

The downside of using dRITs with individuals or in a group setting is the potential for what I call "therapeutic bureaucracy" – a variation of the Psychiatry game. Client and therapist give undue time and attention to the diagram and "homework" at the expense of more important issues.

Key Points 17

17.1   ERICA enables offers **three ways of working** with clients - instrumental, relational and transpersonal. The latter way is discussed in **Part Six**.

17.2   In a clinical setting, the client completes a BRIT as part of the **intake process**. The purpose of the exercise is a mapping of characteristic patterns of *relationships*

17.3   **Initially** the therapist coaches the client to give a clear, sequential account of one or more Significant Incidents. The **next stage** is for the therapist to help the client identify the roles of the protagonists involved in a Significant Incident. **Thereafter** the client comes to be able to recognise roles him/herself and eventually, evolves strategies for formulating more satisfactory role responses.

17.4   Data collection is based on the following overall contract:

- The client and the practitioner agree that throughout the following processes, they will discuss any miscommunication and/or differences of their respective points of view. The motto is "**openly agreeing to agree, and openly agreeing to disagree**".

- The **client teaches the practitioner** about their way of seeing the world, by relating to the practitioner an incident that occurred between sessions, which the client regards as significant.

- The **practitioner listens and feeds back** to the client what has been learned.

- The client corrects any inaccuracies and an **agreed account** of the incident is logged; client and practitioner keep copies of the **log**.

- After sufficient data has been collected, the log is **reviewed** and a simple flow chart diagram is **jointly compiled**.

- The practitioner gives the client **feedback** on how the client seems to have learned what he or she has been teaching. The flowchart is **revised** in the light of **agreement** about the practitioner's feedback.

- The process continues with the addition of the client's perceptions of **options** and their possible **consequences**

17.5 In compiling dRITs there is a **meta-level of communication** relating to the interaction between the client and the practitioner.

17.6 An **alternative way of using Significant Incidents** is for the practitioner to note carefully all a client's experiences and offer feedback as and when appropriate. Another option is to use the range of diagnostic tools favoured by Cognitive Analytic Therapists.

17.7 Teaching clients to understand and apply dRITs to their own circumstances **proceeds in tandem** with understanding and using BRITs, cRITs and whatever "non-ERICA" work has been done to date.

17.8 Once clients are familiar with Significant Incidents and have been introduced to Contact Cube roles, a **new contract** is agreed.
- A dRIT is done jointly during the *first twenty minutes* (or less) of each session. Clients keep a copy of the dRIT and complete the *"Narration"* as part of their homework.
- As the client becomes *proficient* at recognising roles, they bring their *Narration* and a *provisional* dRIT to their session for discussion, agreement, amendment or 'agreed disagreement'.
- Client and practitioner keep *copies* of the agreed dRITs and Narrations

17.9 In parallel with these, ideally, **Significant Learning Logs** (SLLs) are kept by both client and practitioner. SLLs are **not used with all clients**. The "**3Rs**" of Significant Learning Logs are *Respect, Record, and Reveal*. Introducing the idea of SLLs is a matter of *clinical judgement*, should always be discussed in *supervision*, and be subject to a *specific bilateral contract*.

17.10 I have adopted some **simple conventions** for drawing dRITs with individuals

17.11 Compiling RITs does not operate in isolation. Progress through the above stages will still need "standard" operations.

17.12 I teach the above sequence as a **'Seventeen Step Programme'** which requires clients to contract to complete all seventeen steps, but not necessarily in the prescribed order.

17.13 **Guidelines** for a Seventeen Step Programme are outlined.

Self Supervision Suggestions 17

17.1 Write your own Significant Incidents, identify the reciprocals, and draw flow charts. Compare your charts with the role imago repertoire and imago images you identified for yourself in **Self Supervision Suggestions 14.4 to 14.6**.

17.2 Contract with a work colleague to teach them how to compile their BRIT.

17.3 Observe people with whom you have frequent contact and note the phrases they use that would enable you to identify their role imago repertoire.

17.4 Establish a contract with an experienced supervisor for supervision of your doing **Self Supervision Suggestions 17.5 to 17.8.** Note that the aim of **Self Supervision Suggestions 17.5** to **17.7** is for you to learn the steps of compiling Significant Incidents and dRITS. This should be reflected in your contracting with anyone else.

17.5 Contract with a client, a friend or a work colleague to collect information for Significant Incidents over sufficient time to draw, discuss and agree flow charts.

17.6	Contract with the same client, friend or work colleague to teach them Contact Cube roles and how these may be used with Significant Incidents.
17.7	Contract with the same client, friend or work colleague to teach them how to compile their dRITS.
17.8	Correlate elements of the dRITS of the same client, friend or work colleague with other TA theoretical concepts and measures.

Chapter 18

Reflections

In this brief Chapter, I reflect on what has been presented so far. The Chapter also provides a bridge between the personal and transpersonal aspects of experience.

The models and their application

With the Contact Cube, the focus of attention is personalised and formalised roles, and role functions, along with the qualities of contact and associated imago images. In the second model – Role Sequences - the emphasis is on reciprocals and role imago repertoires as the unit of analysis. The third model – Role Imago Templates – provides structural concepts derived from the Significant Incidents recounted by individuals. The unit of analysis is an amalgamation of dynamic Role Imago Templates (dRITs) that emerge from conversations.

The models address relationships by linking roles, contact and imago images. They may be applied irrespective of setting to teach clients to research their own behaviour. They may also be used as formal research tools, bridging theory specific models of the interactive process, as well as observational tools for the purposes of training and supervision.

Inasmuch as the models include both positive and negative aspects of individual behaviour and social interaction, they avoid the divide of health/pathology. Likewise, application of the models generates a wealth of data amenable to empirical research. Finally, the models encourage diversity – they may be applied according to the practitioner's preferred style of working.

Teaching and learning the models

The process of teaching/learning all three ERICA models depends on the practitioner's values, philosophical orientation and preferred style of relating to others.

Allowing for these factors, one way of teaching clients to research their own behaviour, is to follow Benjamin's stages of *collaboration, learning about old patterns, enabling the will to change versus clinging to old wishes, blocking manipulative patterns,* and finally, *learning new patterns* (Benjamin, 2003). I have adopted the stages identified by Benjamin at this general, conceptual level, as a useful meta-level framework for the stages of learning implicit in the application of the ERICA models. This is a largely cognitive-behavioural approach, ameliorated by Benjamin's emphasis on the importance of empathic attunement, especially during the collaborative and 'blocking' stages[1]. Teaching all the ERICA models may be facilitated in this way.

A constructivist approach to the teaching and learning of ERICA is based on the view that models are subjective constructions, rather than objective reflections of "reality". This takes account of the process of reaching consensus about shared concepts (Berger and Luckman, 1966). Likewise, Pask's "Conversation Theory" provides a sophisticated formal

---

[1] Benjamin's emphasis on the three copy processes – (1) "Be like him or her", (2) "Act as if he or she is still there and in control", (3) "Treat yourself as he or she treated you" – warrant further research. The hypothesis would be that the copy processes are directly related to Contact Cube roles. Benjamin also gives step-by-step guidelines for each of the various stages of therapy (collaboration, learning about old patterns of behaviour, and so on), and insightful examples of applying her model to work with the full gamut of personality disorders as per DSMIV criteria. The downside of Benjamin's Structural Analysis of Social Behavior (SASB) and Interpersonal Reconstructive Therapy (IRT) models is that both involve a complex system of coding social interaction, which is likely to tax all but experienced researchers.

model of such "conversational" interaction that ends in an agreement over shared meanings (Pask 1975, 1976). The fundamental idea of the theory is that learning occurs through conversations about a subject matter which serves to make knowledge explicit. The critical method of learning according to Conversation Theory is "teachback", in which one person teaches another what they have learned.

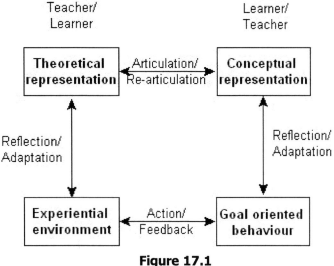

Figure 17.1

The application of Conversation Theory in an educational setting is illustrated by Atherton (2005), who draws attention to the work of Laurillard (2002) and Thomas and Harri-Augstein (1985):

> "Gordon Pask's work stands rather outside the mainstream of the psychology of education, but is immediately recognised by many learners and teachers in adult education as being very significant. He was a cyberneticist rather than an educationalist, and developed a systems approach to learning which is highly abstract and difficult, although rewarding: it is reflected in the "conversational" models of learning of Laurillard and Thomas and Harri-Augstein" (Atherton, 2005)

According to Atherton, Laurillard's view is that the pattern of the conversation needs to be:

> "At the "lower" level (on the diagram) the student is engaged in the goal-oriented behaviour of trying to master the topic of learning, while the teacher is providing the experiential environment within which this can happen, including managing the class or tutorial, setting tests, delivering resources, etc. As this is going on, the teacher and learner are engaged in a conversation about it, exchanging their representations of the subject matter, and their experience of the lower level, and adapting each to the other. This process of talking about what you are doing is one of <u>reflection</u>, and modification of what you are doing in the light of the talk is <u>adaptation</u>." (Atherton 2005)

This is reminiscent of Bateson's notion of "learning to learn" (Bateson, 1972) and germane to conversations about Significant Incidents. Thus in ERICA, the client teaches the practitioner what he or she has learned about relationships, and the practitioner teaches the client how he or she (the practitioner), has learned how the client has learned to learn. This process continues in a circular fashion that, over time, becomes a spiral, affording both parties further learning about the process of their conversation. Inevitably, learning about learning, leads to change. Whether consciously or not, each person reflects on their learning and adapts their conversational interaction to that of the other, revising or re-articulating the subject matter in the light of their respective experience of their own, and the other's, actions. Consensus is attained by agreeing to agree and agreeing to disagree. All this takes place within a context, defined partly by agreement between the parties about whatever it is they are doing (therapy, counselling, mentoring, education), but also in relation to societal consensus about what it is the individuals are doing.

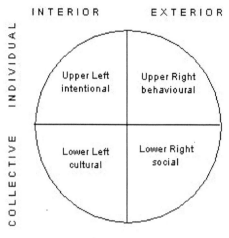

Figure 18.2

We can depict this particular aspect of ERICA diagrammatically as a *process,* by adapting Wilber's AQAL ("all quadrants, all levels") epistemological model, which we touched on as far back as **Chapter 3**. Recall that **Figure 3.2** depicted three versions of his basic model (Visser 2003). The first most general version is shown in **Figure 18.2**. If we regard **Figure 18.2** as representing person A, we can, likewise, imagine a second person, B. Exercising considerable

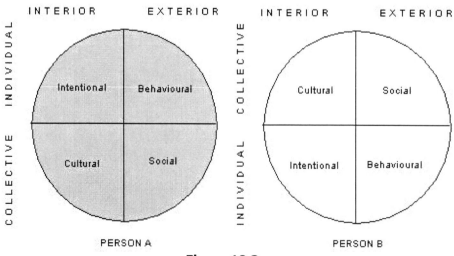

Figure 18.3

epistemological licence we can depict them, metaphorically so to speak, standing side by side Permitting ourselves even further leeway, let us invert the horizontal dimension for person B – as in **Figure 18.3.** If we then merge the two halves of **Figure 18.3** by overlapping the cultural/social dimension of each person, we have a diagrammatic schema of the *process* of the relationship between the two people.

In **Figure 18.4**, the shaded, upper circle represents person A; the lower circle signifies person B. **Figure 18.4** is symbolic, rather than mathematically correct. Nevertheless, it illustrates the way in which areas of disagreement and adaptation together constitute a conversation that forms the basis of the relationship. Depending on the topic and the social context, this may be called therapy, or counselling, or education and so on. The two-way arrows show the "circuitry" of the feedback. Note that I also show the influence A has on B and vice-versa. This idea flies in the face of Barnes' exhortation to expunge "theory-centered psychotherapy" from transactional analysis and replace it with "conversations" that do not

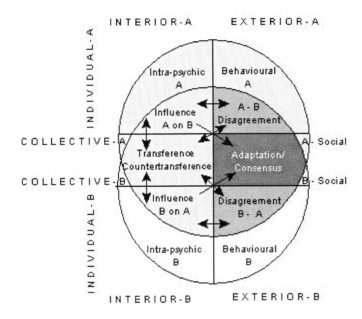

Figure 18.4

impose their theories on the client in ways that makes them not-OK (Barnes, 2004).[1]

---

[1] While fully endorsing Barnes's position that all people are OK, I think he comes close to advocating throwing the baby out with the bathwater. That is, he uses a specific aspect of second-order cybernetics to demonstrate the flaws in Berne's "grand personality theory" (Barnes, 2000, 2004). However, reifying a concept does not necessarily invalidate the concept. My point is that second-order cybernetics, itself, is a theory, and in this respect, Barnes is merely replacing one theory by another. Even then, I am not entirely convinced by the cybernetic logic of Barnes' argument. Eleanor Rosch (1994) draws on Buddhist metaphysics to "deconstruct" the notion of causality by identifying general forms of explanation in terms of "cause and effect" (or, equivalently, "process and product") and demonstrating that they are all essentially circular tautologies. She notes in particular the poverty of explanation in cognitive and behavioural sciences, which employ cause-effect models, pointing out that all attempts to give coherent accounts of phenomena in causal terms lead to circularities or tautologies, in the explanation chains.

My stance on this is that transactional analysis practitioners and their clients need *something* to talk about while relating to one another. It could be the weather, or stock exchange prices, or a theory of how people relate to other people under certain circumstances. Usually, conversations have a purpose. I would even go as far as saying that conversations always have a purpose, in the sense that they represent attempts to confirm mutual OK-ness. For me, the purpose of therapy is for clients to talk about which model of the world works best for them. Given that we all influence each other all the time, how people converse is as important as what they talk about. Mutual OK-ness seems to be a pre-requisite for productive conversations – or at least, for one conversation to lead to another. My task as a therapist is to keep the conversation going until a client has decided upon a model of the world that works best for him or her. In doing so I may seek clarification, pose questions about consequences, or refer to alternative ways of seeing the world. And all the time I am doing this I am being influenced by, and am influencing my client. Reality is defined by consensus, by the intersubjectivity of our communication. I expand on this point below.

Figure 18.4 depicts this approach symbolically. Three aspects of the processes involved are worthy of note. The first is that there is considerable fluidity of role functions. It is not that one person is "teaching" and the other is "learning". Inasmuch as one person is teaching *while* the other is learning, both functions co-exist at the same time.

Secondly, client and practitioner are active-observers and anyone else is a non-active-observer. This includes anyone "accessing" the conversation either directly as a participant, or indirectly as an influence. The class of active-observers is those who participate in the conversation. The class of non-active observers is those who do not participate, but influence, or attempt to influence, or are perceived by the conversationalists to influence, or be attempting to influence, the conversation. It follows that *everyone* is an observer, including anyone who reads or thinks about the conversation.

However, there are constraints. The first is epistemological, being well-illustrated by the following comment:

> "one of the dimensions of a metamodel might be the degree to which an observation affects the phenomenon being observed, with classical, observer-independent observations at one extreme, and quantum observation closer to the other extreme. Since a metamodel is a still a model, built by an observer, it must represent itself. This is a basic form of self-reference. Generalizing from fundamental epistemological restrictions such as the theorem of Gödel and the Heisenberg indeterminacy principle, Lars Löfgren has formulated a *principle of linguistic complementarity*, which implies that all such self-reference must be partial: languages or models cannot include a complete representation of the process by which their representations are connected to the phenomena they are supposed to describe. Although this means that no model or metamodel can ever be complete, a metamodel still proposes a much richer and more flexible method to arrive at predictions or to solve problems than any specific object model." (Heylighen and Joslyn, 2001).

The second constraint is more practical:

> "some people feel that the second-order [cybernetics] fascination with self-reference and observers observing observers observing themselves has fostered a potentially dangerous detachment from concrete phenomena. The only influence this outside world has on the system's model is in pointing out which models make inaccurate predictions" (Heylighen and Joslyn, 2001).

Acknowledging the abstract yet important principle of "linguistic complementarity", the constraint implicit in the second quotation is the predictive utility of the ERICA models. In other words, do the models, and how they are presented, contribute anything useful to a client's model of the world?

The third feature of **Figure 18.7** that merits elaboration refers to the significance of the arrows. These indicate not only the flow of information between person A and person B, but also highlight each of the areas. And by "information" I mean *everything* that transpires when two people interact. The areas shown In **Figure 18.7** represent experiences. These areas exist – that is, may be experienced – in a number of different ways. The most obvious and most "out front" experience is the area labelled Adaptation/Consensus, which in ERICA is the agreed outcome that is recorded as the reciprocals of a dRIT. However, it is useful to differentiate between "adaptation" and "consensus". What emerges as consensus is the result of agreement without negotiation or discussion of different viewpoints. Adaptation in this context is agreement resulting from discussion; A or B, and sometimes both, change their views to accommodate the other. Much the same applies to the areas labelled "Disagreement", although there is less incentive to be open about these – if only because there is less pressure to negotiate.

Influence is the process whereby one person modifies their behaviour in response to, or as a result of, the behaviour of another person, persons or the situation. Influence is a double-edged factor; one side of the coin. I can never fully know what influence I have on others. I have only a 'more or less' idea of how others are influencing me. The other side of the coin is presence. Presence simply is. I cannot influence someone without presence.

I regard influence as a process that is separate to and different from transference and/or countertransference. To argue otherwise is to take the position that adults influence their offspring and thereafter, everything else is transferential and/or countertransferential. The logic of this line of thought is that mothers relate to their babies in these ways, and that only babies have presence. I suspect those who take this view minimise the significance of their own presence. Traditional psychoanalysis seems to have adopted this view, and it is only now that the movement is grappling with alternative perspectives.

Adaptation/Consensus and Disagreement represent experiences that are manifested externally as behaviours discernible to non-active observers. The "interior" processes take us into altogether different areas. They are subjective and intersubjective, the latter being the coalescence of the subjectivities of both people. My experience of meditation leads me to believe that these experiences are different from what I have experienced as transference and/or countertransference.

When I think about these matters – or when you read about them – another factor comes into play. I think of this as the relativity of focus and position. *Focus*, as clarity of perception, and *position*, as active-observers or non-active-observers, are always related. The more precise the focus, the less is known about position – and vice versa. To explain this idea, and bearing in mind that **Figure 18.4** is a diagram about knowledge – about what you know, and how you know what you know - I proffer the following scenarios:

Scenario 18.1
Imagine you are looking at **Figure 18.4** from a great height, using binoculars. You are in a bird's-eye position. From this position, you understand that you are looking at a representation of the interaction between person A and person B. This requires you to think dispassionately in abstract terms.

Scenario 18.2

Now, as you continue looking at **Figure 18.4** through the binoculars, imagine you are person A and person B is a client. This may require you to dissociate mildly, and for some people, it becomes more difficult to maintain the dispassionate bird's eye position. They feel pulled closer to their actual experience; they are "nearer" the memory of being in the conversation as active-observers. Additionally, they may also find it more difficult to maintain an *overall* view of the diagram. Metaphorically speaking, they have to adjust the focus of the binoculars.

Scenario 18.3

Now imagine that you (still as person A) are even closer to the diagram, so much so that you can no longer see the whole diagram. Your field of vision has narrowed and you can only focus on parts of the diagram at any one time.

Scenario 18.4

You are now so close to the diagram that you are virtually in it. No matter how you adjust the focus of your binoculars, you find that there are certain areas of the diagram that are extremely fuzzy. Fortunately, you know - in theory - how the diagram should look. You also are able to call upon someone else who is more experienced, further away and likely to see more of the diagram than you can. However, this means you have to rely on their reports of what they can see, and their interpretation of what you could see if you were to adjust the focus of your binoculars in certain ways.

Finally, add another fantasy factor. Imagine that you always have to look at the world through binoculars. The binoculars represent consciousness. They are fitted with a lens called awareness. They gather the light of knowledge. Crucial questions are: What is the nature of this instrument? What does it reveal, and what does it not reveal? And how does anyone arrive at answers to these questions?

Key Points

18.1   **Role Imago Templates** provide structural concepts derived from the **Significant Incidents** recounted by individuals. The unit of analysis is an amalgamation of dRITs that emerge from conversations.

18.2   One way of teaching clients to research their own behaviour, is to follow **Benjamin's stages** of collaboration, learning about old patterns, enabling the will to change versus clinging to old wishes, blocking manipulative patterns, and finally, learning new patterns. This is a **largely cognitive-behavioural approach**. Teaching all the ERICA models may be facilitated in this way.

18.3   A **constructivist approach** to the teaching and learning of ERICA is based on the view that models are subjective constructions, rather than objective reflections of "reality".

18.4   **Learning to learn** is germane to conversations about *Significant Incidents*.

18.5   In ERICA, the **client teaches the practitioner** what he or she has learned about relationships. The **practitioner teaches the client** how he or she (the practitioner) has learned how the client has learned to learn.

18.6   **Consensus** is attained by agreeing to agree and agreeing to disagree.

18.7   Transactional analysis practitioners and their clients need something to talk

---

about while **relating** to one another.

18.8   ERICA accommodates considerable **fluidity of role functions**. Teaching and learning co-exist at the same time

18.9   *Client* and *practitioner* are **active-observers** and *anyone else* is a **non-active observer**. Experiences occur in a number of different ways.

18.10 **Influence** is a double-edged factor; one side of the coin. The other side of the coin is **presence.**

18.11 I regard *influence* as a process that is **separate to and different from** *transference and/or countertransference.*

18.12 I suspect those who take the view that everything is transference and/or countertransference, **minimise** the significance of their own **presence.**

18.13 **Focus,** as clarity of perception, and **position**, as active-observers or non-active-observers, are always related. The more precise the focus, the less is known about position – and vice versa.

Chapter 19
The transpersonal dimension

This Chapter takes us beyond the divides in transactional analysis to an emphasis on consciousness per se – rather than the content thereof. The starting point of this process is a wider view of contact, consideration of consciousness per se, an appreciation of the distinction between autonomy and interdependence, the nature of self, and our capacity for self-reflective awareness.

Contact

The three models presented in **Parts Three** to **Five**, encompass a range of theoretical concepts that offer an orientation that in practice is primarily relational. This is because reciprocals (and hence, role sequences) as the basic unit of social interaction, arise from the circular causality of role reciprocation. This is vastly different from Berne's model of transactions between ego states that are grounded in a stimulus-response paradigm. In particular, personalised roles are associated with qualities of contact and imago images that together form the bedrock of relationships.

Role reciprocation is a process that is not only built-in to our physiology, but also our psyche. An interactive process commences from the moment of conception. Long before infants acquire language and later, are able to take the role of the other:

> "'protoconversations' between mother and infant … and the reciprocal role relationships they embody, … are the major determinants of the development of personality, involve pre-linguistic mediating tools and are, as a result, largely unavailable to conscious reflection" .(Ryle and Kerr, 2002, p.41)

These authors give an extended account of the development of the self (Ryle and Kerr, 2002, pp. 33-60) that emphasises a dialogic model of role reciprocation, underpinned by an even more fundamental variable:

> "Just as the body is formed initially in the mother's womb (body), a person's consciousness awakens wrapped in another's consciousness". (Bakhtin 1986, p. 138)

Numerous others have attested to the fact that there is a level of contact that exists beyond the "normal" contact recognised in transactional analysis under the headings of transactional analysis proper and strokes.

> "The idea often is that certain boundaries are quite different at this level, and may even disappear altogether. We suggest that much of the therapeutic process is done at the level of ordinary thinking, with the therapist using skills and knowledge of ordinary thinking and a certain degree of self-perception …. and that a smaller amount of therapy – but still a substantial amount - takes place at the level of authentic consciousness, ….. A smaller amount again of therapy is done at the level of more subtle form of consciousness ……
>
> One of the essential features of this form of subtle consciousness is that one's whole sense of boundaries is radically revised. At all the earlier stages we take it for granted that we end at our skins. What is inside my skin is me, what is outside my skin is not me. This is not only common sense; it is existentialist philosophy. But at the

subtle stage, this does not hold. At a surface level, we are certainly separate; but at a deeper level, we are one. One analogy that has been used is that we are like islands that were originally hills overlooking a plain: the sea rose, the plain sank, and the newly formed islands started to become more and more different and distinct. But they are still part of the same land". (Rowan and Jacobs, 2002 pp. 71-72)

Evidence of this type of contact comes from Bion's concept of 'O' (Bion 1970, Symington and Symington, 1996); Field – who explains projective identification as a potentially healing process that requires the therapist to *merge* with the client at an unconscious level (Field 1996); Thorne who describes his own experiences of a "spiritual" connection between himself and his clients (Thorne, 1991); Mearns, who cites clients' accounts of the process (Mearns, 1994); Mahrer who details "experiential listening" as an example of this type of involvement with others (Mahrer, 1996); van Deurzen-Smith, who extends Buber's existential ideas to encompass "the perfect merging of two beings who totally identify with each other and who operate in absolute self-forgetfulness, aiming at something that transcends their separateness and thus binds them together" (van Deurzen-Smith 1988, pp. 208-209); and Jungian accounts of states of consciousness where visions and imagery take precedence over words (Corbin 1969, Hillman 1975, Samuels 1989, Schwartz-Salant 1991). Rowan and Jacobs note that:

> "we can subsume all these phenomena under the heading of 'linking' Linking is that way of relating that refuses to take separation seriously, and assumes instead that the space between therapist and client can be fully occupied and used by both, to the advantage of the therapeutic work. This can only be done in a state of consciousness where the fear of relating at such a depth can be overcome or set aside, or just not experienced. ... It is not a new therapy or a new technique, but simply recognition of a relatively unfamiliar human relationship, which has been formally researched and described in a number of sources.
>
> Budgell describes 'linking' as:
>
>> "The experience is described as near fusion, a communion of souls or spirits and a blurring of personal boundaries. To achieve this, both parties have to give up something of themselves while remaining separate. It is not symbiosis, but the other end of the spectrum, as described by Wilber (1980a). It is the transpersonal sense of relinquishing self. Symbiosis is about being cosy, but this is about working through pain and fear. It is a sacred experience and yet natural and there all the time. It comes from the spiritual or transpersonal realm, being a step beyond empathy and the natural plain". (Budgell 1995:33)
>
> Budgell found over and over again that therapists who had had these experiences did not want to reduce them to something which could be controlled". (Rowan and Jacobs 2002, pp. 82-83)

Personally, I have to acknowledge that had I not been practising meditation for many years, I would probably not have paid much attention to my early experience of this type of contact with clients. At first I put this down to intuition – and felt chuffed when I seemed able to part-anticipate what clients were about to discuss – or avoid. After a while this type of event seemed to lose its element of surprise and I often withheld this potential linking from clients. One day, a client was regaling me with the latest chapter in the saga of her divorce proceedings – much of which I'd heard several times before. My attention was starting to wander and I realised that my vision was becoming blurred. I tried to focus on her face and head outlined against the window and garden beyond, but the figure seemed to start shimmering until it was transformed into an image of a deep blue/indigo pansy with a yellow centre. In the background there was a sonorous choral harmony, which I recognised as Fauré's Requiem. At this point the client said something like "Sorry, I've told you all this before. You must be getting really bored with me going on like this". I told her I was fascinated rather than bored, because I'd had an image of a deep blue flower with a brilliant yellow centre. She startled, and said "That's really spooky! When I was ever so little and was really, really upset I used to hide in the garden. I remember once I did this and consoled myself by lying with my face close to the flowers so that I couldn't see anything else. Like you say, I can see that deep blue and the yellow, smiley face. .. I feel so sad now.." Months later, the same client gave me an audio-tape of her favourite music for me to record a voice-over of a relaxation meditation we had done previously in the therapy group. "It's a Requiem – my favourite – by Fauré" she said. Regrettably, I did not say anything about my earlier experience.

While this type of experience may seem unusual, my guess is that is that no one knows for certain how widespread the phenomenon of "linking" is between therapists and their clients. What I do know is that it seems to be a manifestation of consciousness at a transpersonal level – the psychic and subtle stages in Wilber's terms (Wilber 1986, p. 178; and 2000, pp.220-221, 244-245) involving the therapeutic exploitation of intuition, imagery, and symbolism. In my experience, these capacities emerge naturally, yet may be both evoked and honed by ongoing meditational practice. In terms of Contact Cube roles, the starting point of linking experiences is the Beholder role and, beyond that the Observer role – as we shall see in subsequent Chapters. For the present, suffice to say that initially, the linking relationship can be scary, and the pitfalls therapists need to be aware of are discounting the significance of these stimuli, and/or the narcissism of assuming that they (the therapists) have special skills or power.

Similar experiences of linking, in combination with training in Ericksonian trance work, led me to start exploring the literature on altered states of consciousness.

Consciousness

Berne appears not to have considered consciousness or any of its connotations (such as trance) in his thinking about ego states. The nearest he comes to this is his brief description of awareness which is subsumed as an aspect of autonomy. Subsequent transactional analysis practitioners have referenced trance states and other hypnotic phenomena (Lankton, Lankton and Brown 1981, Allen and Allen 1984, Conway and Clarkson 1987, Price 1987, Avary and Milhollon 1997, van Beekum and Lammers 1997, Porter-Steele 1997), but generally speaking, trance and other altered states of consciousness are not widely used by transactional analysis practitioners – probably because of an emphasis on the importance of the here-and-now awareness of the Adult.

I think the price tag of potentially over-rigid attempts to fit clients' experience into an ego state (or any other) model, is that transactional analysis has missed out on significant aspects of what clients will often present. In this respect, paying attention to consciousness itself as well as its contents is a powerful therapeutic ally largely unengaged by our current repertoire of transactional analysis knowledge and skills.

"Transpersonal experiences may be defined as experiences in which the sense of identity or self extends beyond (trans-) the individual or personal to encompass wider aspects of humankind, life, psyche and cosmos.... Transpersonal therapy is therapy informed by a transpersonal perspective, which recognizes the value and validity of transpersonal experiences and development. The transpersonal model clearly holds consciousness as a central dimension. Traditional Western schools of psychology have held differing positions with regard to consciousness. These range from behaviorism, which ignores it, to psychodynamic and humanistic approaches, which pay more attention to its contents than to consciousness itself.

A transpersonal model views "normal" consciousness as a defensively contracted state of reduced awareness. This normal state is filled to a remarkable and unrecognized extent with a continuous, mainly uncontrollable flow of fantasies which exert a powerful though largely unrecognized influence on perception, cognition and behavior. Prolonged self-observation inevitably reveals that normal experience is perceptually distorted by the continuous, automatic and unconscious blending of inputs from reality and fantasy.

Optimum consciousness is viewed as being considerably greater than normal consciousness and potentially available at any time, if the defensive contraction is relaxed. Growth, therefore, involves letting go of this defensive contraction and removing obstacles to the recognition of the ever-present expanded potential. This is achieved by quieting the mind and removing the perceptual distortion and constriction imposed by the fantasies ...". (Walsh and Vaughan 1996, p. 17-18)

Understanding this point of view calls for an appreciation of our capacity for self-reflective awareness. I refer to this as the Observer self – a state of awareness rather than a role. Both the Observer self and the Observer role require autonomy and lead to interdependence.

Autonomy

Autonomy has a special significance in transactional analysis, largely because it is the acme of the psychotherapeutic process of "cure" as defined by Berne (1972). He gave a four stage model of the process of cure and describes the final stage as script cure:

"At a certain point, with the help of the therapist and his own Adult, [the patient] is capable of breaking out of his script entirely, and putting his own show on the road, with new characters, new roles, and a new plot and payoff. Such a script cure, which changes his character and his destiny, is also a clinical cure, since most of his symptoms will be relieved by his redecision". (Berne, 1972, p. 362)

He suggested that script cure can sometimes be achieved quite suddenly and describes this as "flipping in." More usually, script cure takes longer and needs reinforcement (Pulleyblank and McCormick, 1985). However as noted by Stewart:

"the achievement of autonomy must be closely related to script cure, or perhaps is even identical with it, though Berne never drew out the connection explicitly". (Stewart 1992, p. 83)

Unfortunately, Berne did not define autonomy but indicated that it:

"is manifested by the release or recovery of three capacities: awareness, spontaneity, and intimacy....Awareness means the capacity to see a coffeepot and hear the birds sing in one's own way, and not the way one was taught...Awareness requires living in the here and now, and not in the elsewhere, the past or the future......Spontaneity means option, the freedom to chose and express one's feelings from the assortment available (Parent feelings, Adult feelings and Child feelings). It means liberation, liberation from the compulsion to play games and have only the feelings one was taught to have......Intimacy means the spontaneous, game-free candidness of an aware person, the liberation of an eidetically perceptive, uncorrupted Child in all its naiveté living in the here and now". (Berne 1964 pp 158-160; my italics)

The first and last of these three capacities – awareness and intimacy – are topics of enormous magnitude; systematic training and instruction in the development of awareness and the practice of mindfulness are the basis of all forms of meditation and obviously beyond the scope of our present discussion. In addition, Berne's view of autonomy is essentially individualistic – in contrast to the notion of intersubjectivity and role reciprocity between people. Comparatively speaking, Berne has more to say about spontaneity, albeit indirectly, in his description of the self.

The self in transactional analysis

Inasmuch as the definition of roles is based on expectations of self, it would seem that some awareness of self is a pre-requisite of such expectations. In TA, self is seen in relation to ego states.

> "The Self, in some existential sense, is recognized and highly regarded by transactional analysts. The Self is experienced as that ego state in which free energy resides at a given time". (Berne 1966 p. 306)

In other words, the Self moves from one ego state to another:

> "At the moment the person is expressing Parental anger, he feels "This is really me" even though the Self resides in a borrowed ego state. At another moment, when he is objectively adding his client's accounts, he again feels "It is 'really me' adding these figures". If he sulks just like the little boy he once actually was, he feels at that moment "It is 'really me' who is sulking". In these examples, the free energy, which gives rise to the experience of "really me", was residing in the Parent, Adult and Child, respectively". (Berne, 199 pp. 306-307)

Berne later describes this as the "moving self" – the process of the Self moving from one ego state to another in order to maintain the script (Berne, 1972 pp. 248-254). I refer to this as Berne's *dynamic model* of ego states to distinguish it from the more usually referenced structural model (Stewart and Joines 1987, pp. 14-20, 30-37). The significance of this in the present context is that Berne's dynamic model gives a definition of self as a *process*. His reference to "free energy" harks back to his earlier formulation of the existence, distribution and dynamics of different types of "psychic energy" (Berne 1961 pp. 37 – 43). He uses this model to explain particular clinical syndromes, but also to relate the dynamics of ego states to their structure. Although he devotes only one Chapter to the topic, he outlines a complex, if not profound model that is logically and theoretically entirely consistent with the notion of ego states as three systems or ways of classifying and storing information - the structural model (see Stewart and Joines 1987).

The shortcoming of the dynamic model is that it does not explain how energy gets translated into information (Barnes 1999). While this is true, I think Berne's recourse to three types of "psychic energy" is a model that has been overlooked for far too long. I resurrect it *en passant* in **Chapter 20**, and for the present, note that the brevity of his comments on varieties of energy (Berne 1961 pp. 37 – 43) and autonomy (Berne 1964 pp 158-160), has as much to do with conceptual difficulties of accommodating unconscious processes in an ego state model, as it has to do with the question of self.

Nevertheless, Berne links spontaneity with options and contrasts this with the use of self to maintain the script. Thus, Stewart notes:

> "the essence of autonomy, as of script cure, lies in the person's freedom to choose in the here-and-now. In Berne's words; 'What the Adult acquires is not exclusive dominance, but increasing option' (Berne, 1961: 153, emphasis in original)". (Stewart, 1992 p. 85)

Although Berne appears to make the link between spontaneity and the moving self, he quite clearly evaded defining it and regarded self as being beyond the province of psychiatry and presumably, therapy:

> "The inherent paradox that "the patient" can control "his Self" is by no means more resolvable in transactional terms than in philosophical or existential ones. What transactional analysis offers is a method for exploiting this paradox to increase autonomy and authenticity. The "Self" and "free energy" are left open as an experience and a construct, respectively, whose ultimate definition and reduction belong outside the province of psychiatry. This is an invitation to philosophers, theologians and creative and interpretative artists of all kinds to participate with psychotherapists in giving meaning to ultimate values". (Berne, 1966 p. 307)

Several other TA authors address the concept of self (James and Savary, 1977; James, 1981; Porter-Steele, 1990, Hargaden and Sills, 2002). Clarkson and Lapworth (1992) give an excellent and succinct coverage of the self from a transactional analysis perspective that includes other mainstream therapeutic disciplines. They introduce their presentation of six "different but interrelated concepts of the self in TA" with the observation that whatever happens to the self during the process of therapy may be regarded as:

> "epiphenomena of other structural changes in the personality; for example, the direct psychotherapeutic work with ego states. However, one of the reasons for the fact that the self is so hard to define may be because it is not referred to as a structural entity but as a quality or experience. . The idea is therefore offered for consideration that reparative work on the self is usually done indirectly and as a concomitant effect of psychotherapy". (Clarkson and Lapworth 1992 pp 176-177)

They agree with Berne's view that "we will need the participation of others outside psychotherapy to help us in this endeavour [of understanding self]" (Clarkson and Lapworth, 1992 p. 203). The indications are that some such "help" may come from a synthesis of Western and Eastern views of self.

Transcultural views of Self

In Western psychology and psychotherapy, self is a general term that refers to the manifestation of any of the "characteristics of the self-system" (Wilber 1986). These include a locus of identity (Freud S., 1923, Wilber 1986), an organising principle which "gives unity to the mind" (Brandt, 1980), the locus of will or free choice of ego state cathexis (Berne 1961), normal use of defence mechanisms (Freud A. 1946), metabolisation of "self-objects" to form structure (Guntrip 1971) and navigation from one stage of development to the next (Wilber, 1986). Wilber's explanation of the process of identification and navigation (Wilber 1986) are crucial aspects of the self in relation to the Observer role.

However, Porter-Steele, while acknowledging the formation of identity and the attainment of object constancy[1] as necessary stages of psychological development, challenges the concept of self, and takes the (Buddhist) view that the self is illusory:

> "There is a huge flaw in the assumptions upon which almost all psychotherapy is based. What is it? The notion that there is or has ever been such a thing as self".
> (Porter-Steele, 1990 p. 56)

In advancing this (particular) Buddhist view of "no-self", Porter-Steele is presenting a *transpersonal* view of self to challenge the use of self as an *interpersonal* concept. Engler counter-balances this apparent choice between self and no-self:

> "you have to be somebody before you can be no-body. The issue in personal development as I have come to understand it, is not self or no-self, but self and no-self. Both a sense of self and insight into the ultimate illusoriness of its apparent continuity and substantiality are necessary achievements. Sanity and complete psychological well-being include both, but in a phase-appropriate developmental sequence..". (Engler, 1986 p49)

Engler's comments seem to raise two points. The first is that Porter-Steele's "huge flaw" has the logical form of "self *or* no-self". Developmentally, it is not that self changes into no-self, but that when self reaches a certain stage, no-self "emerges" and exists alongside self.[2]

The second point is that while Eastern traditions have little to say about child development, Western theories of development tend to run out prematurely; they do not describe levels of consciousness beyond the inter-personal realm. Almaas gives an eloquent description of the "dimensions of self realization" which includes an account of the seemingly paradoxical experience of "non-conceptual reality" where:

> "there is no sense of individual or self, but no sense of their absence, for either would be a concept. Everything appears to be part of this immense clarity, which is totally itself, without it needing to be conceptualized. All objects and persons appear as part of this transparent clarity, pervaded with, constituted of it, but only as transparent patterns in this nameless reality. Thus, duality is transcended before it is even conceptualized". (Almaas 1996 p 412)

Later in describing another level of consciousness (the Absolute), Almaas states:

> "Perhaps the best description of this state is its absolute and total intimacy, for we are directly in touch with the inmost of everything we experience. We may recognize it as the self, but there is no feeling of "I", identity, or self. This recognition has no

---

1 *Object constancy* is a psychoanalytic concept that refers to a child's capacity to accept the ambivalence of others – "the mother who frustrates is also the mother who nurtures". (Tilney, 1998 p. 80)
2 Wilber points out that the 'self – no self' argument is a view held by one particular Buddhist school; other schools espouse a more relativistic doctrine.

conceptual quality. There is only the direct and clear perception that it is none other than one is" (Almaas 1996 p 425).

Almaas writes from a Sufi orientation in which this level of reality is referred to as "dhat"; he notes that:

"the closest English equivalent is the word 'ipseity'. In the experience of ipseity, duality ends as we perceive that the identity and nature of everything, including ourselves, is inseparable from everything". (Almaas 1996 p 425)

He makes two additional crucial points:

"we feel utter spontaneity, where each thought, word and activity arises before there is any recognition. [This] is due to the fact that, in this condition of self-realization, there is absolutely no self-consciousness. This clarifies the observation that one of the main sources of narcissism is the self-reflective capacity of the normal self. More precisely, one of the main characteristics of narcissism is self-consciousness, an outcome of the normal self's capacity for self-reflection. It is only at the level of the Absolute that this characteristic disappears". (Almaas 1996 p 425)

The first point is Almaas' reference to the normal self's capacity for self-reflection. I develop this aspect of the self later as the process of witnessing.

The second point arising from consideration of Eastern traditions, is that the Observer role does not require an "altered state of consciousness" – which is what Almaas is writing about – that is, states of consciousness that differ from our normal waking state. Moreover, there is a distinction between the Observer role and altered states of consciousness. The latter are *not based on expectations* and thus, move beyond the concept of roles. Such states of consciousness range from substance–induced states of mind through to unfocused "natural" reveries, normal sleep, dreams, near death experiences (Atwater and Morgan, 2000) and various forms of explicitly taught/learned methods of concentration, contemplation or witnessing that form the basis of most meditative practice. Although the latter are all based on "awareness" in all the meditative traditions particular emphasis is placed on the absence of expectations.

In contrast to a transpersonal view of consciousness, transactional analysis is a Westernised view of the world that emphasises the pre or *intra-personal* (ego states, scripts) and *interpersonal* (transactions and games) aspects of human interaction. Despite recent suggestions by Hargaden and Sills (Hargaden and Sills 2002) with which I disagree, on the grounds that I do not regard self as a structural entity, mainstream transactional analysis thinking, by admission of some authors (Berne 1966 p.307, Clarkson and Lapworth. 1992 p. 176), lacks a comprehensive view of self.

Key Points 19

19.1 Transpersonal experiences may be defined as experiences in which the sense of identity or **self extends beyond** (trans-) **the individual** or personal to encompass wider aspects of humankind, life, psyche and cosmos.

19.2 A transpersonal model views **"normal" consciousness** as a defensively contracted state of **reduced awareness.**

19.3 Working with clients in a transpersonal way involves contact (**linking**) that goes beyond normal, everyday inter-personal interaction.

19.4   Berne appears not to have considered **consciousness** in his thinking about ego states.

19.5   The hallmark of the **Observer role** is **autonomy.**

19.6   Autonomy has a special significance in transactional analysis, largely because it is the acme of the psychotherapeutic process of "cure".

19.7   **Roles** are based on **expectations of self**. In TA, **self** is seen in relation to **ego states.**

19.8   Self is a general term that refers to the manifestation of any of the "characteristics of **the self-system**" (Wilber 1986). These include:
   - a locus of **identity**,
   - an **organising principle** which gives unity to the mind,
   - the locus of **will** or free choice of ego state cathexis,
   - normal use of **defence mechanisms**,
   - metabolisation of "self-objects" to form **structure**,
   - **navigation** from one stage of development to the next.

19.9   Wilber's explanation of the process of **identification** and **navigation** (Wilber 1986) are crucial aspects of the self in relation to the **Observer role.**

19.10 Porter-Steele presents a *transpersonal* view of self to challenge the use of self as an *interpersonal* concept.

19.11 When self reaches a certain stage, no-self "emerges" and exists alongside self.

19.12 Transactional analysis lacks a comprehensive view of self.

Chapter **20**

The spectrum of consciousness

This Chapter relates stages and states of consciousness to various characteristics of self. In particular, we will examine the nature of trance, identity and dissociation – a defence mechanism where facets of self are split off while consciousness is still identified with them.

Consciousness and self

Ken Wilber has addressed the issue of self in terms of a *spectrum of consciousness* that covers the life span (Wilber 1977). Wilber gives a panoramic view of consciousness that is based on various developmental stages of self (Wilber 1986 pp 267- 291). He has the knack of stating crucial aspects of a highly complex process simply, yet without oversimplification. His writings about the self should be seen in relation to the *development* of consciousness, or as he puts it, *the spectrum of consciousness.*

In essence, the spectrum of consciousness is a model of human development that integrates "standard" Western theories of development with contemplative (mostly Eastern) traditions. I outline these in order to provide a context for Wilber's discussion of self. My summary gives no more than a glimpse of Wilber's work and barely does justice to the quality of his extensive coverage (Wilber 1977, 1981, 1983, 1986, 1991, 1995, 1998, 2000).

- There is a pre/perinatal level of consciousness of profound significance to transpersonal dimensions of experience. (See Wilber 1980, Chapter 16 and 1997, pp. 180-185.)
- The first and most primitive level of waking consciousness – the *sensoriphysical* - corresponds with Piaget's (1963) sensorimotor stage of the development of intelligence and includes little more than the body as matter, plus sensation and perception.
- At about seven months there then develops the second level – the *phantasmic-emotional* – or the level of impulses and emotions.
- The third level or stage is what Piaget calls pre-operational thinking. Wilber's term is *rep-mind,* signifying the emergence of symbols (at two to four years) and concepts (which emerge between the ages of four and seven).
- Level four prevails between seven and eleven; this is Piaget's concrete operational thinking or, in Wilber's scheme, the *rule/role mind.* He chooses this term because this is the first stage at which a child can "take the role of other, or actually assume a perspective different from its own" (Wilber 1998 p. 71) – in addition to being able to think concretely about sensory experience.
- Next is the *formal-reflexive* level, where children are capable of hypothetical reasoning, testing propositions against evidence and, in short, thinking about thinking. This is Piaget's formal operational thinking; it emerges during adolescence.
- Level six is existential or what Wilber terms *vision-logic* – "a very integrative structure, capable of integrating the mind and body into a higher order union – which I call the 'centaur'" (Wilber 1998 p. 71).
- From level seven onwards, we encounter transpersonal stages of development – the *psychic* or beginning stages of spiritual contemplation.

- Thereafter is the *subtle* – or intermediate stage of spiritual development wherein one encounters archetypes and a personal God.
- Level nine is the *causal* or "the pure unmanifest source of all the other and lower levels" (Wilber 1998 p.72).
- The final level "represents ultimate reality, or absolute Spirit, which is not a level among other levels, but the Ground and Reality of all levels". (Wilber 1998 p.71)

Wilber not only describes each level in great detail; he outlines the type of pathology that can arise, and his assessment of the types of therapy best suited for each stage (Wilber 1983, 1986). Interestingly, he regards transactional analysis as the therapy of choice for issues up to and related to level five of the spectrum (Wilber1981, p. 103). The implication is that training in transactional analysis does not equip a therapist to deal with problems at or beyond level six. For these levels Wilber cites Gestalt, bioenergetics, psychosynthesis, a Jungian approach, Almaas' Diamond approach and varieties of yoga and meditation as appropriate treatment modalities. Disregarding this as a theoretical point by a non transactional analysis academic constitutes a potential ethical dilemma for the transactional analysis community.

Against this background, Wilber commences his view of self by noting that:

"as various structures, processes, and functions emerge in the course of development, some of them remain in existence some of them pass". (Wilber, 1983 p. 267)

He cites the contrast between Piaget's (1977) four stages of cognitive development (which all remain) and Kohlberg's (1981) levels of moral development, where lower levels are replaced by higher levels. Wilber calls the latter "transition stages" and the former "basic structures ". To these he adds functions and gives the following analogy to illustrate the links between the three factors.

"take the growth of the United States by the annexation of new territories. Hawaii used to be a sovereign and autonomous nation itself [with] its own sense of 'selfhood' - or nationality - and its own basic geographical structures. When annexed the basic geography remained the same [but] the nationality - its existence as an exclusive nation - was simply and completely dissolved. It was replaced". (Wilber, 1983 p. 269)

Wilber suggests that once acquired, basic structures, like geographical features, tend to remain in existence as relatively autonomous units or sub-units in the course of subsequent development. On the other hand, transition stages involve "phase-specific" and "phase-temporary" structures that tend to be more or less entirely replaced by subsequent phases of development - (like the replacement of one nationality by an entirely different one). To basic structures and transition stages, Wilber adds the self (which he sometimes refers to as the *self-system*), which he regards as having six characteristics or functions. (I will return to discuss these functions – particularly *identification* and *navigation*.)[1]

---

[1] It is interesting to note that Levin's account of child development and the various stages that she claims are recycled throughout life (Levin 1982, 1988), is not all that far removed from the first five stages of Wilber's account of the development of consciousness. The obvious difference is that like most other Western accounts of personality development, Levin's model does not include either specific consideration of the development of consciousness or cover stages of development beyond early adulthood. Instead, she recycles earlier stages. The extent to which her second and subsequent recycled stages map onto Wilber's model warrants closer examination.

Wilber's notion of "basic structures" is the above levels of consciousness or stages of normal development which support the phase-specific transitional stages. In his earlier writing (prior to 1995) Wilber uses a metaphor where the basic structures are like a ladder, each rung of which is a level of consciousness; the self is the climber of the ladder. Progression from one rung to the next brings a new perspective or view of reality, with a different sense of self-identity (cf. Loevinger, 1976), a different set of self needs (cf. Maslow, 1954), and a different type of morality (cf. Kohlberg, 1981). Ascending the ladder requires the self to replace one perspective with the next. Nevertheless, on any rung of the ladder, it is possible to have fleeting glimpses of the world from the perspective of a 'higher' rung, or, indeed temporarily descend (regress) and occupy lower rungs.

More recently, Wilber has elaborated the metaphor of the self climbing a ladder (of consciousness) and relates consciousness to his "all-quadrants-all–levels model (AQAL) or "world view", encompassing dimensions that are *intentional, behavioural, cultural* and *social* (Wilber 1998, 2000; see too, **Chapter 3** above). More significantly for our purposes, he expands upon his conceptualisation of the self – the climber of the ladder:

> "If you get a sense of your self right now – simply notice what it is that you call "you" – you might notice at least two parts to this "self": one, there is some sort of observing self (an inner subject or watcher); and two, there is some sort of observed self (some objective things that you can see or know about yourself – I am a father, mother, doctor, clerk: I weigh so many pounds, have blond hair, etc.). The first is experienced as an "I", the second as a "me" (or even "mine"). I call the first the *proximate self (since it is closer to "you"),* and the second the *distal self* (since it is objective and "farther away"). The both of them together – along with any other source of self-ness – I call the *overall self.*
>
> These distinctions are important because ...during psychological development, *the "I" of one stage becomes a "me" at the next* (original italics). That is, what you are identified with (or embedded in) at one stage of development (and what you therefore experience very intimately as an "I") tends to become transcended, or disidentified with, or dis-embedded at the next, so you can see it more objectively, with some distance and detachment". (Wilber, 2000 p. 33)[1]

Thus, under normal circumstances a child will progress from one developmental stage (rung of the ladder) to the next. His/her proximate self identifies with the rung of the ladder, the content of his/her current experience. From there, the child is able to "look down" to the previous rung – the distal self without having to identify with it.

> "For example, a young infant is identified almost solely with its body – the body is the infant's self or subject (the proximate I), and thus the infant cannot really stand back and objectively observe its body, and as a body it looks at the world. But when the infant's verbal and conceptual mind begins to emerge, the infant will start to identify with the mind – the mind becomes the self or subject (the proximate I), and the infant can then, for the first time, start to see its body objectively (as a distal object or "me") – the body is now an object of the new subject, the mental self. Thus the subject of one stage becomes an object of the next. The overall self, then, is an amalgam of all these "selves" insofar as they are present in you right now: the proximate self (or "I"), the distal self (or "me"), and, at the very back of your awareness, that ultimate

---

[1] Wilber's distinction between proximate and distal self is similar to object-relations writers who differentiate between *self-representations* and *object representations.*

Witness (the Transcendental Self, antecedent Self, or "I-I"). All of these go into your sensation of being a self in this moment". (Wilber, 2000 p. 34)

Wilber's reference to identification leads us to the next step in understanding the dynamics of the Observer self and what I later describe as the Observer role.

Identification

It is our identification with our experience, personal history and memories that provides a sense of self-recognition, a sense of self. Berne explains this - albeit indirectly - in his structural model of ego states where Parent and Child are relics of the past in contrast to Adult. In this respect, Berne's account of archaic ego states parallels Wolinsky (1991), who refers to those aspects of our identity that are not based on here and now information as trance identities:

> "In psychology it is common to talk about how one's sense of self is formed – one's identity. What is uncommon is the realization that many of the identities that people casually own as being representative of who they are, are actually trance identities... a trance identity is created by the child as a means of self-preservation and to handle various problems and traumas. The identity is comprised of the child's assumptions and beliefs about his interactions with his parents. Psychologically speaking, the child fuses with the parents and creates an identity that reacts, thinks, sees, and hears either like the fused parents or in resistance to the fused parent. As adults, these identities remain on "automatic pop-up" and continue to function, seemingly autonomously[1], in relation to the early family context". (Wolinsky, 1991 p. 217)

Wolinsky's description of "an identity that reacts, thinks, sees and hears either like the fused parents or in resistance to the fused parents", bears close resemblance to the following accounts of Parent and Child ego states:

> "the Parent ego state means the entire set of thoughts, feelings and behaviors which you have copied from parents and parent-figures. Thus in the structural model, the content of the Parent is defined as the set of memory traces of these parental thoughts, feelings and behaviors." (Stewart and Joines 1987 pp. 31-32: original italics)

> "We define any stored experience from the person's own childhood as being part of the content of the Child ego state". (Stewart and Joines 1987 p. 34: my italics)

In short, Wolinsky is saying some of that with which we identify is a "trance identity". Stewart and Joines (and Berne) categorise this as the content of Parent and Child. The only difference between the two points of view is that, in transactional analysis, the classification is of *ego states*, whereas Wolinsky identifies four categories or ways of classifying *trance identities*.[2]

---

[1] Note that Wolinsky's phrase is "seemingly autonomously". His use of the word "autonomously" should not be confused with Berne's use of "autonomy"; the latter refers to the three capacities of awareness, spontaneity and intimacy. Hence, for "seemingly autonomous", read "not autonomously" – or "automatically" - as meaning outside, or beyond the conscious (volitional) control, of one's will.

[2] It is interesting to note that at about the same time that Berne was formulating the basic concepts of TA, two other therapists independently developed an entire system of theory and therapeutic method based on hypnotic work with ego states. This seems to have been largely unrecognised by the TA community – probably because a full account of their work has only recently become available in a single volume (Watkins and Watkins 1997), but perhaps also because Watkins and Watkins regard ego states as aspects of unconscious processes.

"*Role identities* include all our social and familial functions: mother, father, wife, husband, stepmother, stepfather, community leader, environmental activist. It is easiest to see the identification with role identities in families – usually with the parents – when they have little or no sense of themselves as separate from the activities, accomplishments, problems, and dreams of their children.

Professional identities span the gamut from plumber to professor, from dancer to electrician, from editor to gardener. We all have work/career identities of one sort or another.

"*Self image identities* reflect our core beliefs about our performance and worth as a person. These self-image identities are almost always formed early in childhood, primarily as a result of parental influences. Whenever the identity is "negative" or uncomfortable, the child also forms a compensatory oppositional identity". (Wolinsky, 1991 pp. 218-220)

Taking account of Stern's four domains of self – the emergent sense of self, the core self, the intersubjective self and the verbal self - Wolinsky's use of the terms self image and oppositional identities, as a parallel formulation of the process involved in cathecting Parent or Child, merits consideration of the nature of trance.

The nature of trance

There are two general types or states of consciousness – natural and altered or "non-ordinary". Natural states are waking, dreaming and deep sleep; altered states include trance, drug-induced states, peak experiences (Maslow 1954), near death experiences (Atwater and Morgan 2000), and meditative states. A trance is a non-ordinary but brief state of consciousness in which attention is not only inwardly directed, but also narrowed.

"Trance is a condition wherein there is a reduction of the patient's foci of attention to a few inner realities; consciousness has been fixated and focused to a relatively narrow frame of attention rather than being diffused over a broad area". (Erickson and Rossi, 1980 p. 448)

There are numerous examples of similar "naturally occurring" trance phenomena. That is, trance states occupy the boundary between the natural and altered states of consciousness. For example, have you ever watched the flickering flames of an open fire? Recall the changing colours, the moving shapes, the warmth and maybe even the smell of wood smoke... Pretty soon you become fascinated (consciousness is becoming fixated). You watch, wondering.... Then you seem to drift off.... still watching the flames, but 'find' yourself thinking about some totally unrelated topic. Other examples abound. Have you ever driven from A to C on a journey you've made hundreds of times before and, arriving at C, have absolutely no recollection of say, crossing the bridge at point B, en route?

Another characteristic is that the *experience* of being in or going into a trance, is that it *happens* to you.

"Hypnotic response [i.e. a trance] is an expression of behavioral potentials that are experienced as taking place autonomously". (Erickson and Rossi, 1979 p. 4)[1]

---

[1] Erickson and Rossi's use of the word "autonomously" should not be confused with Berne's use of *autonomy"*; the latter refers to the three capacities of awareness, spontaneity and intimacy. Hence, for "autonomously" read "automatically" - as meaning outside or beyond the conscious (volitional) control of one's will.

This is particularly significant when it applies to our trance identities. Ask yourself if you have ever been in the Victim role (or Rescuer, or Persecutor). Then answer the question: how did you get there? Chances are that you may have been aware of being in one or other of these roles – either at the time or afterwards, but would be hard pressed to say how or when you got there.

The point of all this is that trance occurs "naturally"; it does not have to be deliberately induced. It is characterised by a narrowing, shrinking or fixated focus of attention. There are also degrees of being in a trance state - a light trance, a deep trance. Likewise, duration varies – from seconds to minutes or less usually, longer. Recall of having been in a trance is not difficult – providing you already know what constitutes a trance state.

Similarly, if I consider a formalised role such as "I am a psychotherapist" (Wolinsky's *professional identity*) then by definition, I have narrowed my focus of attention (the first characteristic of trance phenomena) and if, in addition, I allow my selfhood and worth to depend *solely* on my status/ability as a therapist, it is highly likely that I will have slipped into the identity "seemingly autonomously" (to use Wolinsky's term). Likewise, with a self-image identity such as "I'm no good" it is easy to imagine the "automatic" quality of the immediate *oppositional identity* response of "I'll show you".

An important factor in all the above examples is the extent or degree of identification we feel. The more we are wedded to a particular trance identity, the more "seemingly autonomous" and restrictive the experience is likely to be.

A third consideration is that trance is characterised by the spontaneous emergence of other hypnotic phenomena such as losing track of time, or awareness of your body, psychologically (and usually, behaviourally) reverting to an earlier stage of development and so on. Milton Erickson was especially adept at using one of the most frequently occurring hypnotic phenomena - dissociation. Understanding the differences between identification, disidentification and dissociation is essential for understanding and teaching others to recognise the Observer self and use the Observer role.

En passant, it is as well to note that all the above comments about trance are relative to the stage of development and hence, a level of consciousness attained by most adults. More specifically, my assumption is that anyone capable of Certified Transactional Analyst status is operating at Rowan's "instrumental" level of self-awareness. Qualifications apart, there will undoubtedly be many who have the capacity for the "authentic" or "relational" use of self, and first hand experience of self at a transpersonal level. Take note, however, that these categories are no more than convenient shorthand for describing the process of normal growth and development. My point is that many people take their level of consciousness as a given, as a self-evident feature of experience, beyond which no further growth is possible; my experience is that it is inevitable.

Dissociation and the self

It is the function and origins of dissociation that are relevant to our use of the Observer self. This is most dramatically illustrated by the accounts of adults who were abused or traumatised in childhood. They use phrases such as "moving out of my body", "floating on the ceiling", "switching off my feelings", and "going numb all over". The capacity to dissociate from painful experiences enables children to survive. Moreover, the experiences need not be life threatening; it is the child's perception of the level of threat – real or imagined – that will trigger the "discovery" of dissociation. Once elicited for self-preservation, the process may be repeated; the greater the perceived threat, the better the mechanism works. Eventually it becomes "automated" and operates as a defence mechanism accompanying or leading to a trance identity.

Dissociation means not associating with some internal feeling, emotion or belief, or some part of the body, or some or all external stimuli. It is a special, if not extreme, case of discounting selective aspects of self at a level of existence. Exclusion or "shutting out" one or more ego states is a similar process (see Stewart and Joines 1987 pp. 53-55). Likewise, when I am in one ego state and aware of the content of other ego states I may be said to be dissociating. This is supported by Berne's view that the peak of personal development is characterised by an integrated Adult ego state that incorporates useful components of Parent and Child – implying some connection in the here and now with other time frames (Berne, 1971). To this we may add the possibility that when a person identifies with the content of their Parent or Child ego state they are using or are in a trance identity that may have been triggered by dissociation.

Several transactional analysis authors address aspects of dissociation (Allen 1981, Price 1988, Erskine 1988, 1993, Hyams 1998, Karol 1998, and Hudson 2000). Of these Price (1988) and subsequently, Avary and Milhollon (1997), and Porte-Steele (1997), give a more focused account of the mechanism of dissociation in relation to Self. Price notes that with:

> "normal transition between alternate ego states…. boundaries … are permeable, such that a flow of active cathexis is possible between them. Thus under different sets of circumstances, different personalities emerge (alters). However, the boundaries between such encapsulated alternating selves are also impermeable in the sense that information exchange between them is minimal. This leads to a discontinuity in the perception of a unified self due to amnesia about events occurring during the emergence of secondary selves. The person … is thus left with no experience of a temporal continuance of events between alternating aspects of self…". (Price 1988, p. 232)

Caloff notes that dissociative disorders:

> "fall along a continuum of dissociation. That continuum ranges from everyday experiences to the dissociative disorders. Dissociation is a very valuable skill that we all have to a greater or lesser extent. We couldn't navigate in the world without it because if we didn't have it, we would have to take in all the data that impinges on us all at once…. Next along the continuum are dissociative episodes or experiences. Here, a typical example might be someone who develops a retrograde amnesia following a severe trauma… [for example, accident and sexual assault victims].. Next are atypical dissociative disorder and then dissociative disorder…. A much more significant step is from dissociative disorder to multiple personality disorder. This is a very important distinction. Multiples split off parts of the self that contain information that is ego alien and very difficult for the self to accept… This information is contained in split-off parts of the personality. The difference between dissociative disorder and MPD is that the dissociative more or less knows about the parts, and the parts are, for the most part, incapable of taking executive control of the body. Most of us know about our parts and can more or less associate to them. In a multiple, however, certain alter personalities can take executive control. They can run the body resulting in an amnestic period for the personality who was displaced… There's another important distinction… I have seen .. individuals who were fully multiple as children during their years of abuse..[but] when they were leaving home and starting their own families, some kind of manager

personality developed [and] stayed out almost exclusively from that point forward". (Caloff 1993 pp. 5-9)

Thus there are degrees of dissociation, and the use of dissociation as a defence mechanism can vary over time. As we shall see in **Chapter 23**, this is relevant to teaching the Observer role to those who use dissociation defensively.

Although dissociation is a self-protective mechanism, it may be exploited therapeutically. An essential ingredient of Erickson's work was the way he used dissociation to split off the conscious from the unconscious mind. To illustrate, as part of a trance induction he would make suggestions such as "You may wish to pay close attention and even consciously remember what I am saying, while your unconscious mind is doing something else..." He went as far as maintaining:

> "Deep hypnosis is that level of hypnosis that permits the subject to function adequately and directly at an unconscious level without interference from the conscious mind". Erickson and Rossi, 1980 p. 146)

Wilber's explanation of what happens when people dissociate is that:

> "A dissociated subpersonality results when facets of the "I" are split off while consciousness is still identified with them. They thus become, not unconscious objects, but unconscious subjects...This is the key, in my opinion, to distinguishing between repression and transcendence. That is, dissociation (or repression) occurs when a proximate I is turned into a distal I; whereas transcendence occurs when a proximate I is turned into a distal me. In the former, the subjective identification/attachment (or I-ness) remains, but is submerged (as an unconscious subject); in the latter, the subjective identification is dissolved, turning the unconscious subject into a conscious object, which can then be integrated......Therapy involves converting hidden subjects to conscious objects". (Wilber 2000 p. 247 – original italics)

Wilber's account of dissociation seems to be based on Rowan's work on subpersonalities (Rowan 1997) and the conceptualisation of ego states advanced by Watkins and Watkins (Watkins and Watkins 1997). Allowing for the fact that Wilber mistakenly regards all *three* Bernean ego states as *subpersonalities,* and seems to have overlooked the fact (or doesn't know) that ego states, or, more particularly, the structural model of the Adult ego state, as conceived by Berne, has observable, here-and-now behavioural correlates, and does not involve unconscious processes, I think Wilber's sub-division of self into the proximate, distal and overall self has much to offer transactional analysts.

If we accept his view that one of the functions of the self is to *navigate* from one level of development to the next, and that *identification* is part of this process, then we may postulate that identification with the content of Parent and Child is evidence of, or represents the operation of, the distal self. The implication of this is that we would have to regard Parent and Child as mildly dissociated states of consciousness. In addition, we would also have to postulate that the operation of the proximate self comes into play via or alongside identification with the content of Adult. To complete the picture we would add the presence of the overall self.

This point of view is not all that far removed from Berne's "moving self" or *dynamic* model of ego states; instead of types of psychic energy, we will have substituted varieties or aspects of self. The logical extension of this point of view is that transactional analysis could embrace a transpersonal view of consciousness that is entirely consistent with existing transactional analysis theory. It is at this point that we are able to go beyond – or, more correctly, refine - aspects of Wilber's model. However, to do so requires a refinement of one of the most hallowed gospels of transactional analysis – ego states.

To me, transactional analysis theory does not adequately account for the *development* of ego states. That is, it offers a very plausible description of second-order analysis of ego states[1], and although there are accounts of the growth and development of the ego states of children through infancy, latency, adolescence to adulthood (Schiff et. al. 1975, Levin 1982), these stages are presented as "givens". True, they may be mapped with stages of growth and development described by other writers (Anna Freud 1963, Piaget 1952), but unlike Wilber, these writers do not correlate psychological development with stages of the development of consciousness. In other words, as suggested by Wilber, it is *because* self *identifies* with a particular stage of development, integrates, differentiates and eventually, dis-identifies that it is able to proceed or "navigate" to the next level. Pursuing the metaphor of self climbing the rungs of a ladder (stages of the development of consciousness) Wilber describes the *navigation* of self from one stage of consciousness to another as follows:

> "At any rung on the developmental ladder (except the two end points), the self is faced with several different "directional pulls". On the one hand, it can (within limits) choose to remain on its present level of development, or it can choose to release its present level of development in favor of another. If it releases its present level, it can move up a hierarchy of basic structures or it can move down. *On* a given level, then, the self is faced with preservation vs. negation, holding on vs. letting go, living that level vs. dying at that level, identifying with it vs. dis-identifying with it. *Between* levels the self is faced with ascent vs. descent, progression vs. regression, moving up the hierarchy to levels of increasing structuralization, increasing differentiation-and-integration, or moving down to less differentiated and less integrated structures. .
>
> As the basic structures or rungs begin chronologically to emerge and develop, the self can *identify* with them (becoming, in turn, a physical self, an emotional self, a mental self, and so on). Once centrally identified with a particular basic structure, the self, or the self's preservation drive, will seek to consolidate, integrate, and organize the resultant overall complex. This initial identification with a particular basic structure is normal, necessary, and phase-appropriate, and it gives rise to the particular self-stage (impulsive, conformist. individualistic, etc.) associated with or supported by that basic structure. ...
>
> If, however, the central self is to ascend the hierarchy of basic structural development – to grow – then eventually it must release or negate its *exclusive* identification with its present basic rung in order to identify with the next higher rung in the developmental ladder. It must accept the "death," negation, or release of the lower level – it must dis-identify with or detach from an exclusive involvement with that level – in order to ascend to the greater unity, differentiation, and integration of the next higher basic level.
>
> Once identified with the new and higher basic structure, a new and phase-specific self-state swings into existence: a new self-sense, with new self-needs, new moral sensibilities, new forms of life, new forms of death, new forms of "food" to be metabolized, and so on. The lower self-stage is (barring fixation) released and negated, but the lower basic structure remains in existence as a necessary rung in the ladder of consciousness, and must therefore be *integrated* in the overall newly configured individual. Once on the new and higher level, the self then seeks to

---

[1] See Stewart and Joines, 1987 Chapter 2, and all the references cited on p. 306 and p. 308. In particular, I find Woollams and Brown, 1978, Chapter 2, most coherent.

consolidate, fortify, and preserve *that* level, until strong enough to die to that level, *transcend* that level, (release or negate it), and so ascend to the next developmental rung. Thus, both preservation and negation (or life and death) apparently have important phase-specific tasks to accomplish". (Wilber 1986, pp.80-81)

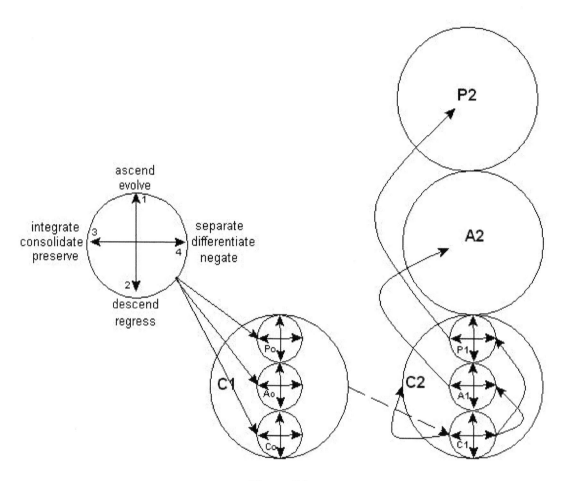

Figure 20 .1

So there we have it; for "self" read "self in relation to ego states". In **Figure 20.1**, self is represented by the "crossed" vertical-horizontal arrows shown within the circle on the left, together with the explanatory text and numbered "directional pulls". These are present at each stage of physical growth and development, and the concomitant development of ego states from C_0, A_0, P_0 to C_1, A_1, P_1 and so forth. (Note that the diagram does not show second order structure for Adult and Parent.) However, because, in my view, self is a *process*, it cannot be permanently located in one or more ego states; the experience of self "moves" between ego states – as described by Berne's account of Mrs. Tettar (Berne 1961, pp. 41-43 and Berne 1972, pp. 248-254). Nonetheless, add to this Wilber's more recent notion of *proximate* (subject), *distal* (object), and *overall self* (witnessing), and we have a potential enrichment of transactional analysis theory.

Moreover, this works both ways; we also have a potential enrichment of Wilber's spectrum model. That is, ego states have "phenomenological reality" (Berne 1961), which is Wilber's AQAL model, upper-left quadrant. They may also be diagnosed behaviourally – AQAL upper-right. And so on, for social and historical diagnosis. In other words, transactional analysis offers an *operational definition* that may be useful in thinking about the proximate and distal self.

However, a word of caution is not amiss. In my view, ego states are not the same as self. And before we go any further, there is another necessary stage - *a communal strand* (Wilber 1983 p.33). I may be the first to express, in writing, the possibility of these links, but it remains for the idea to be tested by a community of like-minded (trained) individuals within the TA community.

There is also another important strand of the link between self and ego states that is related to the process of identifying and dis-identifying with any particular level of consciousness – the capacity of self-reflective awareness.

Key Points 20

20.1 Self may be seen in relation the development of consciousness - a **spectrum of consciousness** - that covers the life span.

- There is a **pre/perinatal** level of consciousness of profound significance to transpersonal dimensions of experience.
- The **first stage** of waking consciousness – the **sensoriphysical** - corresponds with Piaget's (1963) sensorimotor stage of the development of intelligence and includes little more than the body as matter, plus sensation and perception.
- At about seven months there then develops the **second stage** – the **phantasmic-emotional** – or the level of impulses and emotions.
- The **third stage** is what Piaget calls pre-operational thinking. Wilber's term is **rep-mind**, signifying the emergence of symbols (at two to four years) and concepts (which emerge between the ages of four and seven).
- **Stage four** prevails between seven and eleven; this is Piaget's concrete operational thinking or, in Wilber's scheme, the **rule/role** mind. This is the first stage at which a child can take the role of other, or actually assume a perspective different from its own– in addition to being able to think concretely about sensory experience.
- **Stage five** is the **formal-reflexive** level, where children are capable of hypothetical reasoning, testing propositions against evidence and, in short, thinking about thinking. This is Piaget's formal operational thinking; it emerges during adolescence.
- **Stage six** is existential or what Wilber terms **vision-logic** –an integrative structure, capable of integrating the mind and body into a higher order union.
- **Stage seven** is the **psychic** or beginning stages of spiritual contemplation.
- **Stage eight** is the **subtle** – or intermediate stage of spiritual development wherein one encounters archetypes and a personal God.
- **Stage nine** is the **causal** or pure unmanifest source of all the other and previous stage or lower levels
- **Stage ten** is absolute Spirit - which is "not a level among other levels, but the Ground and Reality of all levels". (Wilber 1998 p.71)

20.2   Wilber differentiates between **basic structures** that *tend to remain* in existence as relatively autonomous units, and **transition stages** that *tend to be* more or less entirely *replaced* by subsequent phases of development.

20.3   The **basic structures** are like a ladder, each *rung* of which is a *level of consciousness*; the **self** is *the climber* of the ladder.

20.4	Progression from one rung to the next (a basic structure) brings a new perspective or view of reality - with a different (transition stage) sense of self-identity, a different set of self needs, and a different type of morality.
20.5	Ascending the ladder requires the self to replace one basic structure with the next. Nevertheless, on any rung of the ladder, it is possible to have fleeting glimpses of the world from the perspective of a 'higher' rung, or temporarily descend (regress) and occupy lower rungs. Thus a child will progress from one developmental stage (rung of the ladder) to the next.
20.6	His/her **proximate self** *identifies* with the rung of the ladder, the content of his/her current experience. From there, the child is able to "look down" to the previous rung – **the distal self** *without having to identify* with it.
20.7	**Identification** with our experience, personal history and memories that provides a sense of self-recognition, a **sense of self.**
20.8	Wolinsky identifies four categories or ways of classifying **trance identities** - some of that with which we identify is a "trance identity". In TA we categorise these as the content of Parent and Child. The only difference between the two points of view is that, in transactional analysis, the classification is of *ego states*, whereas Wolinsky classifies *trance-identities.*
20.9	There are two basic **states of consciousness** – natural and altered. *Natural* states are waking, dreaming and deep sleep. *Altered* states include trance, drug-induced states, peak experiences, near death experiences, and meditative states. *Trance states* occupy the boundary between the natural and altered states of consciousness.
20.10	The **characteristics of trance** are that: <ul><li>it **occurs "naturally"**; it does not have to be deliberately induced</li><li>it is associated with a narrowing, shrinking or fixated **focus of attention**,</li><li>the more we are wedded to a particular trance identity, the more **restrictive** the experience is likely to be,</li><li>trance is also **linked with** the spontaneous emergence of **other hypnotic phenomena** such as losing track of time, or awareness of your body, psychologically (and usually, behaviourally) reverting to an earlier stage of development and so on.</li></ul>
20.11	**Dissociation** means not associating with some internal feeling, emotion or belief, or some part of the body, or some or all external stimuli.
20.12	The function and **origins** of dissociation are relevant to our use of the **Observer self.**
20.13	A dissociated subpersonality results when facets of the "I" are split off while consciousness is still identified with them. They thus become not unconscious objects, but unconscious subjects. Therapy involves converting hidden subjects to conscious objects.
20.14	Transactional analysis theory does not adequately account for the **development of ego states**. Wilber's account of the development of self in relation to the spectrum of consciousness offers a possible explanation.

Chapter **21**

Witnessing, the self, and the Observer self

This Chapter introduces the notion of witnessing as an aspect of our capacity for self-reflective awareness. This leads to a re-evaluation of self as currently understood in transactional analysis.

Witnessing

My refinement of Wilber's model may be regarded as a process of 'secondary identification'. That is, we all have the capacity to witness our own experience – *without* having to use dissociation as a defence mechanism or having to identify with the object of our attention.

By 'secondary identification' I mean that there is a process within each stage of development that ultimately emerges as the Witness, but is ordinarily experienced as a mere act of perceiving – awareness of awareness. That is, when identification is extended to include awareness that I am the author of my own perception and categorisation of events, I need no longer identify with the content of my experience – I merely observe or 'witness' it. This is the hallmark of the Observer self.

In everyday terms, not identifying, or 'disidentifying' with an object of attention, but observing or witnessing it, is that aspect of the self that represents our capacity for self-reflective awareness. For example, I have no difficulty in looking at my desk in the knowledge that it is I (subject) who is looking at the desk (object).

> "If you said "I have a pen", you would never then proceed to identify yourself with the pen. The pen is something you have; you are larger than the pen....Grasping the notion of the "you behind the trance" is the corridor to the no-trance state of expanded awareness, where who you are remains a fluid and ongoing experience. Entrance to the corridor is gained by becoming familiar with the process of picking up and putting down identities and roles, by beginning to experience a new psychological limberness and flexibility.
>
> Volumes of literature exist in the area of object-relations theory concerning the creation of "false selves" that operate autonomously.[1] The "true self," from my point of view, is that which created these false selves". (Wolinsky, 1991 pp. 222-223)

The process of witnessing is not a concept that is included in Berne's theoretical framework. Indeed, Drego (1979, 2000), Hine (1997), Steinfeld (!998) and Tudor (2003) seem to be the only transactional analysis authors to have documented this capacity of the Adult ego state. Drego's comments invoke a spiritual dimension:

> "As an Indian and a student of Eastern spiritual traditions, I have found the dispassionate *observer* aspect of the Adult to be an ideal of harmony and self-actualization that is consonant with mysticism and God-experience". (Drego, 2000, p. 204: my italics)

---

[1] For Wolinsky's use of "autonomously" read "automatically", as meaning outside or beyond the conscious (volitional) control of one's will.

Drego also refers to the "Photographic Adult" that:

> "provides an additional spiritual dimension as the *witnessing self* or the *see*-er in Indian spirituality and has the same sense of non-interpretive, even-toned response to both intrapsychic reality and external reality". (Drego 2000, p. 204 – original italics)

Hine comes closer to a secular view of the concept of self-reflective awareness:

> "One perceives a more autonomous state [than Parent or Child] when one observes oneself and others in the Adult state of the ego. A person is more focused and more concentrated when the Adult ego state network is activated, and they experience less emotional reaction and more sense of separateness. In this ego state the person can be like an observer, a self who can think about its own ego states and observe other people's ego states". (Hine 1997 p. 285)

Steinfeld (1998) touches on "witness consciousness" and a "non judgemental observer" without further elaboration. Likewise Tudor, in describing the "integrating Adult", makes passing reference to "reflective consciousness" as the ability to "reflect on different aspects of ourselves". (Tudor 2003 p. 218)

My use of the term should not be equated with Almaas' descriptions of witnessing that require altered states of consciousness that are explicitly taught in meditative practices, nor, indeed, of Wilber's account of the "Ultimate Witness". In other words, my conceptualisation of witnessing exploits the natural capacity for self-reflective awareness, but does not involve teaching or learning witnessing as described by Engler, Almaas and many others that require altered states of consciousness. Wolinsky captures the essence of this distinction:

> "The moment you step outside of your problem to observe it, you create a larger context for it. Observing or witnessing thus becomes a key activity of therapy.
>
> Witnessing ... does not involve a sense of splitting or depotentiating different regions of the mind. It is a unified perception that allows and embraces without limiting and shrinking one's focus of attention. Emphasis is placed on awareness of the Self or being behind the ongoing activity, rather than on portioning out and labelling different aspects of mental functioning". (Wolinsky 1991, p.61-62)

Witnessing and other therapeutic approaches

Several other therapies (psychosynthesis, hypnotherapy, NLP and perhaps to a lesser extent, psychodrama) include and use witnessing and/or dissociation either explicitly or indirectly. I mention these briefly, partly to place ERICA's use of witnessing in context, but also to draw attention to potential shortcomings of particular approaches. This overview is by no means exhaustive.

Role play and various other techniques used in psychodrama have obvious links with all the Contact Cube roles. A therapist will often assign "observer" roles, alter-ego functions and so on, to protagonists. This does, of course, require a group work setting and provides the opportunity for valuable feedback; the techniques are easily adapted for individual clients.

Cognitive behavioural therapy bristles with procedures for enabling clients to identify and interrupt patterns of thinking, feeling, beliefs and thus, behaviour. To my knowledge, apart from the "mindfulness" of Segal, Williams and Teesdale (2002), they do not use specific techniques for dealing with dissociation. It is perhaps for this reason that Linehan (1993) has developed what she terms Dialectical Behaviour Therapy (DBT). Within this framework, Linehan teaches clients to use their "wise mind" to synthesise "reasonable mind" and "emotional mind". Using this process is not the same as witnessing, but can sometimes be taught as a precursor to witnessing.

Most forms of bodywork stress the somatic aspects of witnessing. For example, bioenergetics, emphasise the need to be "grounded" - that is, for me to be aware of the contact with whatever is supporting me (a chair or the ground). Remaining grounded is an essential component of using the Observer role; it provides a powerful here-and-now anchor, encourages the use of the Adult ego state and obviates the use of dissociation as a defence mechanism.

Psychosynthesis therapists will routinely facilitate their client's awareness of their "higher self" – thereby eliciting a conceptual and usually, visual experience of witnessing. They also emphasise 'dis-identification' or visualisation without resource to a higher self as one of the ways of eliciting witnessing within the Observer self.

My impression is that Gestalt therapists emphasises contact more than witnessing. This is perhaps because they have an intersubjective, phenomenological concept of self:

> "The self is not aware of itself abstractly but only as contacting something or someone. 'I' exists in contrast to 'you' or 'it'". (Mackewn, 1997 p.74)

Perhaps more so than any other approach, Gestalt therapy is conceptually well placed in relation to the Beholder role. That is, their orientation to self is, by definition, couched in terms of a relationship with someone or something. Nevertheless, because of this orientation, they do not appear to make explicit therapeutic use of dissociative phenomena; their tendency is to *counter* dissociation by emphasising contact. However, they do acknowledge the importance of awareness as attention to the flow of experience in the here-and-now. Hycner (1988), for example, explicitly advocates teaching clients to "slowly observe all his actions without being attached to them".

I have already discussed the use of witnessing in hypnotherapy. This undoubtedly represents the most explicit and sophisticated use of dissociation for therapeutic purposes. However the distinguishing feature of hypnotherapy is the use of altered states of consciousness and in this respect, the utilisation of trance states to elicit witnessing differs from exploiting the more everyday experience of self-reflection.

Neuro-linguistic programming (NLP) has a range of techniques and procedures that draw upon witnessing. Many of these are presented in a "user friendly, DIY" style with a minimum of theory, few references and little indication of any indications or contra-indications for use. Some appear to make glib statements about profoundly complex processes. For example, Andreas and Andreas (1994) describe five "core states" as "the deepest level of what our parts [of ourselves] want for us" (Andreas and Andreas, 1994 p. 20). They maintain that the five core states are being, inner peace, love, OKness and oneness and present a ten stage, step-by-step procedure for attaining these states. While I have considerable reservations about the "anyone can do it" nature of this approach, the technique clearly makes explicit use of witnessing and altered states of consciousness.

Self as process

Allowing for the fact that "self" is a topic of enormous complexity, I use the following as a "working definition" of self *as a process*.

Self is the process of identifying with one's experience as ongoing awareness of one's own presence or existence, and one's capacity to define one's self in relation to a context – a unit of consciousness with the capacity for self-activation. And in this respect, consciousness is simply the ultimate relationship – the relationship between dual and nondual awareness[1].

Here 'awareness of one's own presence' refers not only to awareness itself, but also to one's ontological existence and evaluation thereof in terms of one's life position. Note too, that I have included 'experience' as well as 'awareness'; for many people the two are not synonymous. Awareness of my own presence or existence is both a phenomenological and an ontological view of self. That is, sentient beings cannot (rationally) deny that they exist. No one can even imagine a state where basic awareness is not - because they would still be aware of the imagining. That said, 'experience' might be favourable or otherwise. Both experience and awareness are relative to one's level or stage of development and state of consciousness.

The connotations of 'define' or defining one's self include the concepts of expectations, roles, contact and relationships. 'Context' refers not only to one's self and others, but also any situation, relative to a given culture.

Arguably, the most important words in the above definition are "in relation to a context". This is because I have taken a wider view of self than that hitherto accepted by most TA practitioners. That is, the traditional as well as the most recent TA view of self (Hargaden and Sills 2002), is related to how self may be accommodated within a model of ego states. I disagree with the idea that self is a structural entity. My view is that ego states are a "container" for self, which is a higher order concept – rather than the other way around. Almaas (1996) captures this particular flavour of the self.

> "[Self] refers to an actual ontological presence, not a construct... the self is a living organism that constitutes a field of perception and action... Fundamentally, it is an organism of consciousness, a field of awareness capable of what we call experience – experience of the world and of self-reflective awareness of itself.   In addition to the realms of mental, emotional and physical experience, the self has access to the realm of Being, that is, it can experience directly rather than indirectly, its own presence as existence". (Almaas 1996 pp 13-14)

These comments on the Observer self, and the techniques used to develop witnessing that I describe below, would seem to require a re-evaluation of self as currently understood in TA theory.

Like most conundrums, it is easier to say what is not, than what is, "self". In my view, self is not a structural entity on a par with ego states. You cannot fit self into one or other ego states. Metaphorically, if ego states are like the drawers in a filing cabinet (Stewart and Joines 1987), self is not simply in one particular drawer of the filing cabinet. It is not even one particular folder that is somehow present in whatever drawer is opened at any time (Berne's "moving self"). A question that is nearer the mark, is, *who* is opening the drawers? Better still, *who* defines the whole shebang as a filing cabinet with drawers? Self is both an ontological experience and a relationship; it is the experience of one's ongoing existence in relation to whom or whatever one is relating. As such, self is intra-personal, inter-personal and transpersonal.

Observer self and witnessing

It follows from the above discussion of self that we can think of the Observer self in terms of the *experience* of the "I" in the phrase "I am singing" (or walking, talking, drinking, coffee,

---

[1] See page 382 for an elaboration of my understanding of consciousness as the ultimate relationship.

hot, tall, a psychotherapist etc.)". In other words, what I refer to as the Observer self is the *experience* of "I" in *relation to* whatever it is I "am" (being/doing). It is a state of awareness equivalent to Wilber's proximate self; the "I" that is the "navigator" (Wilber 2000, p.35), and similar to the psychosynthesis notion of 'I'". (Hardy and Whitmore 1988, p.207)

To put all this in another way, the Observer self is what you *don't* have when you are asleep. It is, for example, what you are sometimes *aware* of as you drift off to sleep; you lie drifting in and out of waking consciousness and think "I'm going to sleep". On such occasions, when you *do* go to sleep, you relinquish volitional control over the navigator. Of course, you can over ride this by force of will – but with difficulty, as anyone who has tried to stay awake beyond normal limits can attest.

The Observer self is also what you partially have during lucid dreaming (LaBerge 2004, Wangyal, 1999)[1]. Lucid dreaming is dreaming *with* awareness; dreaming while knowing that you are dreaming and being able to 'control' the events in a dream. Not everyone has lucid dreams "naturally", but the "technique" has a long history and is easily learnt. Note that I am not advocating that readers learn lucid dreaming in order to understand the Observer self.

Several forms of psychotherapy explicitly harness the Observer self and exploit the potential of the "awake" version of lucid dreaming. For example, in Gestalt "dream-work", dreams are re-experienced in the here-and-now. Clients are exhorted to use personal pronouns, the present tense, and to identify with particular elements of the dream (for example, "be the most powerful thing in the dream" or, more directly, "be the sky") and "make the dream come out the way in which you would like it to end".

Another instance of the Observer self is that it is what you have to use when you are awake and take a meta-perspective. However, it is not the meta-perspective itself; it is the *taking* of the meta-perspective that is invoked by the Observer self.

Maintaining a meta-perspective without identifying with the focus or content of your awareness, is what I refer to as "witnessing". In other words, it is awareness not only of one's self, the other person and the situation*, but also the experience of knowing that it is "I" who is aware of me, the other person and the situation*, that signifies the function of what I am referring to as *witnessing*.

In evolutionary, biological terms, we survive by noticing what is relevant and doing something about it. In other words, we adapt. However, it is not always as straightforward as this may sound. For instance, sometimes we *do* something, and *then* notice it. For example, I scratch my nose - and *then* notice it was itchy. All this is part of the "normal" experience of consciousness, with identifiable neuro-physiological correlates. Sometimes the process goes awry. In the face of genetic and environmental factors, and/or neurological damage, individuals learn for example, obsessive behaviours, overuse of the capacity to dissociate, and so on. Nevertheless, they survive, at a price of self-limiting adaptations, or, in TA terms, "script decisions". Fortunately we are able to counteract such adaptations through psychotherapy and/or other forms of realisation and healing.

The extent of our conscious experience of witnessing seems to depend on our awareness of difference and the degree of importance, significance or investment in any particular issue. To illustrate, I look around the room and notice a plethora of familiar objects. I don't consciously attempt to label or categorise them in my mind – because there are so many objects, all are familiar to me (it is my room) and right now, I do not have any burning investment in any particular objects, other than the keys on the keyboard and what

---

[1] See too, www.dreamviews.com for an informed discussion of the phenomena. There is a veritable 'cottage industry' on the internet devoted to information and products purporting to facilitate lucid dreaming; some sites are more responsible than others. There is also a natural progression from lucid dreaming to the Tibetan Bön tradition of dream yoga (Wangyal, 1999).

appears on the screen. If, in addition to all this, I am able to hold in my awareness the ongoing experience of "I" as the author of my perceptions, I may be said to be witnessing. In short, witnessing is an ordinary, everyday and largely subliminal experience, yet is also something we can do at will.

Although witnessing does not *require* an altered state of consciousness, learning to witness via altered states (as described in **Chapter 23**) is probably the easiest way of being able to do so "automatically", that is, simultaneously while engaged on some other task. This is facilitated and accelerated by being grounded and centred.

Witnessing and the paradox of change

Choice and indirectly, change, is primarily a cognitive process. More correctly, we tend to think of choice as a cognitive process, or even more explicitly, we experience ourselves as "making a choice" when we use our cognitive capacities to complement or supplement somatic and/or affective processes.

Consider for example, the following internal monologue. "Shall I go to London via the motorway or across country? The motorway is fast – but boring. The route through the Cotwolds is slower, but so much more interesting; all the spring blossoms will be out in the Vale of Evesham and it looks as though it's going to be a sunny day."

We are constantly making such choices with varying degrees of conscious awareness. Transactional analysis practice is about making choices, about changing old ways of being and relating. TA tends to favour, if not inculcates, conscious choice. As Barnes points out, historically much of what has been written about how to do TA therapy implicitly followed Berne's 'grand personality theory' rather than a 'theory of therapy' which involves:

> "making psychotherapy dialogical so that we think in terms of communication and patterns – patterns of emotions, behavior and beliefs or attitudes – and patterns of messages". (Barnes 2000, p.244)

I like to think that ERICA goes a step further. Whether or not it does, depends on the client's readiness for change, and to a lesser extent, on the practitioner's ability to recognise and support such change. People change when they are sufficiently uncomfortable, or when they give up striving to become something or someone they are not. The first type of change is often costly and usually temporary. Berne referred to this as "counter-script cure". Given the right conditions, the second type of change is inevitable:

> "Change occurs when one becomes what he is, not when he tries to become what he is not." (Beisser 1970, p.77).

Implicitly, ERICA embodies the 'change strategy' outlined by Benjamin (2003), but enlarges the final stage ("learning new patterns") by introducing the additional options of grounding, centring, witnessing and intentionality as outlined below. As will be seen in **Chapter 23**, these techniques are specifically designed for acceptance of what is.

Key Points 21

21.1   Our capacity for **self-reflective awareness** means we are able to witness our own experience – *without* having to use dissociation as a defence mechanism or having to identify with the object of our attention.

21.2	Several other therapies (psychosynthesis, hypnotherapy, NLP and perhaps to a lesser extent, psychodrama) include and use witnessing and/or dissociation either explicitly or indirectly.
21.3	In ERICA, **Self** is the process of identifying with one's experience as ongoing awareness of one's own presence or existence, and one's capacity to define one's self in relation to a context – a unit of consciousness with the capacity for self-activation. Consciousness is the relationship between dual and nondual awareness.
21.4	The **Observer self** is the experience of "I" in relation to whatever it is I "am" (being/doing). It is a state of awareness equivalent to Wilber's proximate self; the "I" that is the "navigator".
21.5	The Observer self is also what you partially have during **lucid dreaming** and the Bön training in dream yoga.
21.6	TA tends to favour, if not inculcate, conscious **choice.**
21.7	People **change** when they are sufficiently uncomfortable, or when they give up striving to become something or someone they are not.
21.8	Change occurs when one becomes what one is, not when one tries to become what one is not. ERICA facilitates this **paradox.**

Chapter 22
People have bodies – and shadows

This Chapter covers the above two topics in no more detail than is necessary for understanding the Observer role. Volumes of literature exist on the therapeutic use of both somatic processes and the shadow, and there seems little point in replicating this here. Most of the techniques for harnessing somatic processes are relevant to any level of development of consciousness.

Unconscious process

Apart from highlighting the need for transactional analysis to review the way in which self is formulated, the link with transpersonal levels of consciousness raises a wider issue – the status of unconscious processes.

Berne did not debunk the Freudian notion of *the* unconscious; he regarded such consideration as the province of psychoanalysis, and focused instead on phenomenological, here and now awareness of ego states. Ever since then, transactional analysts have used the term "out of awareness" rather than "unconscious". Despite such caution, psychoanalytic concepts and terminology have crept into both the literature and indeed, practice. For example, the use of concepts such as transference and countertransference, have undoubtedly brought richness and diversity to transactional analysis. However there is a price to pay – or at least, there are two potential pitfalls. The first is Zalcman's caution that:

> "the reframing of TA into psychoanalytic and neopsychodynamic terms, often to make it "more respectable," ... has resulted ... in the outcome ... [that] concepts and techniques borrowed from other methods have been taken out of context and introduced into TA, often without adequately examining their implications for or consistency with TA values, theory or practice". (Zalcman, 1990, p.5)

Nevertheless, in an editorial article of the Transactional Analysis Journal, guest editor Helena Hargaden, wrote:

> ".. we highlight a variety of ways in which authors seek to incorporate the unconscious into their work. .... [The current] articles ...reflect a thirst within the transactional analysis community to find a voice in the world of depth psychotherapy". (Hargaden, 2005, p. 106)

In this respect, raising the issue of unconscious processes in transactional analysis could be seen as a trans-generational echo of parallel process. For example, Berne appears not to have considered the shadow or any of its connotations in his thinking about ego states. The nearest he comes to this is his brief reference to the persona as an aspect of roles (Berne 1963, p. 38). This is perhaps not surprising as the major thrust of Berne's thinking about ego states represented a move away from classical psychoanalytic concepts. Nevertheless, vestiges of Berne's training as an analyst under Erikson and Federn and the influence of Fairbairn have filtered down, inasmuch as Fairbairn (1952) amalgamated the functions of Freud's psychic organs or structures (id, ego, and super-ego) into three *functions* of ego. Thus, properly speaking, transactional analysis is derived from an ego psychology that describes the human personality in terms of ego *functioning*. As such, it does not encompass "the unconscious" as a distinct, well formulated concept.

> "In *Principles of Group Treatment* .... His description of the "private structure"
> "smells" a good deal like an unconscious structure, as does much of Berne's later
> terminology about script. But there was no explicit theory of the unconscious
> articulated in his writings". (Cornell, 2005, p.121)

Referring to processes or phenomena that are "out of awareness" is thus tantamount to
semantic sleight of hand. As noted by Cornell: ""out of awareness" is not quite the same as
"unconscious" " (Cornell, 2005, p. 120). At the very least, the phrase poses the question of
whether or not ego states "contain" or are capable of processing "memories and strategies"
that are 'out of awareness'.

> "The functional model classifies observable behaviors, while the structural model
> classifies stored memories and strategies". (Stewart and Joines 1987, p. 36: see also
> Joines 1976)

This leads us back to Berne's view of how ego states are energised or "cathected" (Berne
1961, pp. 40-41). I believe that his writing about bound, unbound and free energy, Real
Self and the ego state which has "executive power" at any moment, is an aspect of theory
that warrants further consideration. That is, the notion of free energy as the equivalent to
conscious awareness, unbound energy being sub-conscious, and bound or latent energy as
the unconscious (or, maybe, even transpersonal), seems to offer a possible way of further
illuminating unconscious processes within an ego state model. However, apart from the
comments accompanying **Figure 20.1** and as ego states are somewhat peripheral to
ERICA, I have side-stepped dealing with the issue in these terms, at least for the time
being.

Instead, and in line with the notion of the development of consciousness, it is
essential to view unconscious processes developmentally[1]. This is consistent with the
development of self and therefore pertinent to ERICA - if only inasmuch as roles are based
on expectations of self, others and the situation.

In particular, several colleagues have enthusiastically suggested that the role that is
not occupied at the social, psychological and existential levels during negative outcome role
sequences (NORS and, more traditionally, Bernean games), *must exist at an unconscious
level as the shadow*.

I regard the suggestion with some caution, for two reasons. In the first place, the
shadow is a concept derived from the Jungian view of the psyche in terms of balance or
imbalance. Thus, psychopathological imbalance arises when there is:

> "rejection of instinctuality; hence a depotentiating of the personality or a projection of
> unacceptable facets of the personality onto others. ... It is also possible to identify
> with the shadow – a form of negative inflation such as self-deprecation, lack of self-
> confidence, a fear of success (and a peculiar 'analytic' state in which everything is put
> down to dark and nasty unconscious motivations)". (Samuels 1985, p.93)

Hence, regarding the shadow as any sort of variable in a "traditional" TA model is
theoretically dubious – unless, of course, one is able to locate the shadow structurally.
Additionally, in developmental terms, the shadow is a "personal aspect of the repressed
submergent-unconscious" (Wilber1983, p. 110), where the submergent-unconscious is "that

---

[1] For a succinct and striking account of six types of unconscious processes and development of self, see Chapter
11 in Wilber (1980) and Chapters 3 and 4 in Wilber (1983). In Wilber's frame of reference, "the unconscious" is
consciousness without awareness. This is entirely compatible with both Freudian and Jungian views.

which was once unconscious, in the lifetime of the individual, but is now screened out of awareness" (Wilber 1983, p.108). This, of course, requires us to "adjust" Berne's original model – which poses all sorts of epistemological problems.

Roles are manifested - begin to be enacted - during Piaget's concrete operational thinking stage (Wilber's rule/role mind stage), and it is conceivable that aspects of role behaviour become "screened out of awareness", that is, repressed, and become the shadow. Just as likely in my view, is the operation of projection as a defence mechanism. In other words, the role not used (but existing as an additional option at a fourth level), is the role that is avoided in self and projected onto others. Projection is a defence mechanism that develops later than repression.

However, the second reason for my caution in regarding the role that is not used as a *shadow level* role, is the need to address a second potential pitfall, namely, the possibility of the "pre-trans fallacy" (Wilber 1983, pp. 201-246, 1992, pp. 187-189).

The "pre-trans fallacy" is a term used by Wilber to highlight the difficulty inherent in interpretations of unconscious processes. All too often psychotherapists unfamiliar with the idea of a spectrum of consciousness are prone to attributing anything and everything that appears not to be at an inter-personal level, to a pre-personal realm of consciousness[1]. Clearly, roles apply to inter-personal interaction. By the same token, roles hitherto not used, must be at an inter-personal level. This is a developmental line of reasoning, and as previously indicated, it is essential to view unconscious processes developmentally. To put this another way, what do we know about the development of consciousness in relation roles? Again, I (selectively) cite Wilber's view that the self progresses through various stages or milestones:

> ""it first identifies with a new level, then disidentifies with and transcends that level, then includes and integrates that level from the next higher level". (Wilber, 2000, p. 92)

Wilber refers to this process[2], these milestones, as "fulcrums"; he abbreviates them F-0, F-1, and so on up to F-10. He continues to explain what he terms the archaeology of Spirit (which is F-10, the ultimate level or stage of consciousness):

> ""the more superficial layers of the Self are peeled off to expose increasingly deeper and more profound waves of consciousness. .... At the beginning of F-1 ... the worldview of this stage is *archaic,* and this archaic consciousness, if not differentiated (transcended) and integrated (resolved), can lead to primitive pathologies....
>
> With F-3, the early mental self (the early ego or persona) first begins to emerge and differentiate from the body and its impulses, feelings and emotions, and attempts to integrate these feelings in its newly conceptual self .....
>
> This early mental self is at first a simple name self, then a rudimentary self-concept, but it soon expands into a fully-fledged *role self* (or persona) with the

---

[1] I would strongly urge anyone working with unconscious processes to familiarise them selves with transpersonal approaches to psychotherapy. Rowan (1993 and the 2005 second edition of the same book) gives a good introduction; Boorstein (1996) is a "must read". Working with unconscious processes without having read Freud and Jung would be unthinkable. To my way of thinking, the previous sentence should read "...without having read Freud, Jung and Wilber *is* unthinkable". Of Wilber's early work, *"No boundary: Eastern and Western approaches to growth"* is eminently readable. A more up to date account of his work is the equally readable *"A theory of everything: an integral vision for business, politics, science, and spirituality".* Of more interest to clinicians is *"Integral psychology: Consciousness, spirit, psychology, therapy".* For a historical survey and chapter-by-chapter guide to his major works, see Reynolds, 2004. Visser, 2003, provides similar, yet more critical, coverage.
[2] Recall that I have suggested that this process is linked with the development of self in relation to ego states, as in **Figure 20.1**.

emergence of the rule/role mind and the increasing capacity take the role of the other (F-4). The worldview of both late F-3 and early F-4 is *mythic,* which means that those early roles are often those found displayed in the mythological gods and goddesses, which represent the *archetypal roles* available to individuals. That is, these are simply some of the collective, concrete roles available to men and woman .... which are often embedded in the world's mythologies. .... Jungian research suggests the archetypal mythic roles are *collectively* inherited; but let us note, for the most part they are *not* transpersonal (a confusion common in Jungian and New Age circles)....

These preformal, archetypal roles are bolstered by the specific cultural roles that the child begins to learn at this stage – the specific interactions with family, peers, and social others. As these cultural scripts are learned, various problems and distortions can arise, and these contribute to what we have generically been calling script pathology. Since the worldview of this level is *mythic* (mythic membership), therapy at this level, by whatever name, often *involves uprooting these myths and replacing them with more accurate, less self-damaging scripts and roles* [my italics]. Even the Jungian approach, which sometimes overvalues mythic displays, proceeds in a similar fashion, by differentiating-and-integrating mythic motifs and thus both honoring them and transcending them". (Wilber2000, p. 102-105)

This gives credence to perhaps my most radical speculation: Drama Triangle and the Bystander roles are archetypal displays of a mythic worldview. ERICA *"involves uprooting these myths and replacing them with more accurate, less self-damaging scripts and roles"*, or, in other words, with positive roles. Perhaps it is not entirely coincidental that Karpman's original TAJ article was entitled *"Fairy tales and script drama analysis"* (Karpman, 1968), suggesting a mythological origin. Conceivably, the archetypal role that is "not used", is simply one that was either not learned, or, for whatever 'Jungian' reason, is not displayed under varying circumstances. However, I would be the first to acknowledge that I am insufficiently familiar with the Jungian literature to gauge the validity of such conjecture.

It is also possible that roles are related to the three "motivators" or drives postulated by English (1971, 1972, 1976, 1979, 1987, 2003). Her account of the motivators is that they are unconscious processes that influence all conscious behaviour – and hence could be applied to any transactional analysis concept. They are described as instrumental, expressive and quiescent. Instrumental *may be* correlated with compelling contact along the Promoter-Persecutor dimension of the Contact Cube. Less obviously, the same may be said of the expressive drive. The quiescent drive appears to underlie Beholder-Bystander behaviours. Although they constitute a useful backdrop to understanding ego states (English 2003), interpretations of their clinical or practical significance is likely to be particularly prone to the pre-trans fallacy. My difficulty with the motivators is that their origin is unclear and it is difficult to judge their relevance to a developmental view of unconscious processes.

It is at this point that I return to my basic hypothesis. That is, Contact Cube roles are based on *observable behaviours* - proactive, reactive, responsive and inactive. In particular, babies are just as prone to these phenomena as are adults. In other words, we can regard the strokes received by babies as a reinforcement schedule for establishing their social level transactional and role responses. As noted by Barnes, this process commences at birth (Barnes 1981, p. 26). To this we can add Bakhtin's (1986) observations on proto-conversations between pregnant mothers and their unborn child, Vygotsky's (1937) notions of the zone of proximate development and internalisation, and the Cognitive Analytic Therapy (CAT) model of role reciprocity, and we have a reasonable case for arguing that although roles do not emerge *behaviourally* until at least three and a half years of age, certain components or aspects of roles are *formulated* considerably earlier. For example, if we consider the origins of expectations as a specific aspect of the development of roles, I think there could be a case for examining possible links between roles and shadow phenomena. However, we can only use this idea if we are willing to acknowledge that shadow phenomena arises from the operation of repression and the return to the unconscious of material that was once conscious.

The universality of Persecutor, Rescuer, Victim and Bystander roles, and the way in which they are enacted without here and now awareness of the consequences, strongly suggests that there is something untoward going on during a negative role sequence that does not happen with positive role sequences. As we saw in **Chapter 13**, the major differences are that four levels of role are available during a positive outcome role sequence (PORS), whereas in negative outcome role sequences (NORS) only three levels of role are used. In addition, the specific aspects of roles that need to be taken into account are the *expectations the protagonists have of themselves* rather than those they have of each other. Most significantly, it is during the period that children formulate script decisions that 'authentic' feelings are repressed, being replaced by racket feelings (Erskine and Zalcman, 1979). Along with this, core script beliefs and supporting script beliefs are established.

The racket system is an accepted canon of transactional analysis, and it seems plausible to argue that script beliefs include expectations of self, others and situations, that later, underlie role behaviours. In other words, it is conceivable that these early self-expectations will include a *predisposition* to behave or not behave in certain ways.

To illustrate, the following example is taken from a researcher's coding of personalised roles observed during clinical work with a couple. (Positive roles are in upper case; negative roles are in lower case)[1].

> **Therapist:** What are the issues you two want to resolve? **PVR**
> **Bryn:** Boyo, it's getting me down! No matter what I say Megan thinks I'm gay! **vp?**
> **Megan:** That's because you go red! You blush whenever we see anyone who's even the slightest bit camp. It just proves.. **pv?**
> **Bryn:** But I've explained that <u>hundreds</u> of times and you <u>still</u> don't believe me! **vp?r**
> **Therapist:** For my benefit, what's the explanation you offer to Megan? **PVR**
> **Bryn:** When we first started going out, I was so low in self esteem I would do anything to prove she didn't really want to go out with me. So I'd tell her all sorts of lies – about all the woman I'd had who still wanted me and even that there were some blokes who fancied me. **vpr**
> **Megan:** So if it's not true, if you've got yourself sorted out since you've been seeing that counsellor woman, why are you still blushing? **pvr**
> **Bryn:** When that happens it's because I'm scared you're going to up and off. I don't blush unless I know you're watching me. As soon as we see anyone like that, then I think... I think that you're going to be watching me to see if I blush and if you do, and maybe if I do blush because you're watching, then you'll think that I fancy him and if I tell you I don't fancy blokes, you're not going to believe me. Then I find myself blushing and I get <u>more</u> scared. **vpr**
> **Megan:** So why can't you just be honest and admit you <u>could </u>be gay? **pvr**
> **Therapist:** How would you feel if he were gay? **PMR Megan:** Scared he'd leave me and the girls. **vpr**
> **Therapist:** And if he was gay and didn't leave you and the girls? **PBR**
> **Megan:** It's really scary, but I guess I'd have to take the girls and leave him. **vpr**

---

[1] The shortcomings of text alone are immediately apparent; audio recording is needed to detect the nuances of voice tone, emphasis, rhythm and speed of delivery of the words. A video of the session would add the necessary non verbal clues that would be used to arrive at the notated coding. For example, the therapist's first question could be delivered in a number of ways, simply by varying the inflexion and/or tone of voice.

Therapist: So what you have in common is that you each believe the other person is going to leave you? **PBR**

Bryn: When I tell the truth, she doesn't believe me! If I lie and say I'm gay, she's going to leave! **pvr**

Megan: And I can't live with a closet poof! What are we going to do? **vpr**

Therapist: What we've not yet explored is what each of you expects of me. **PVR**

Bryn: We're *paying* you to .. Well, to sort it – us- out. **prv**

Megan: Tell us what to do that would get us out of this mess! **vrp**

Therapist: What I can tell you at this stage is how I see the situation. That's not going to 'sort you out' or 'tell you what to do', but it will give you some ideas about how to find those kinds of answers for yourselves. **RPV +** Do you want to go in this direction, or do you each have ideas about what would be a satisfactory solution as far as *you're* concerned? **PVR**

The transcript shows that at a social level, Megan is enacting the Persecutor role and Bryn is the in the Victim role. They later change their role profiles and both expect the therapist to be the Rescuer. Predictably, the competent transactional analyst would establish a clear contract and then proceed to point out the moves of the game.

Assuming the therapist establishes an appropriate contract, there seem to be at least five ways for Bryn and Megan to resolve their impasse. The first is for the therapist to resort to a traditional TA approach – such as exploring the origins of the couples' unhelpful symbiosis, their early script decisions, injunctions, drivers etc., and then proceed with decontamination, de-confusion, redecision work and the like.

A second type of intervention is for the therapist to follow the standard ERICA method of accumulating sufficient information to establish their preferred role profiles. In other words, is there at least a reasonable probability that they *characteristically* attempt to confirm their respective life positions via the use of the Rescuer role? If so, the strategy would be to teach them how to access the Beholder and then consider their options in terms of other positive Contact Cube roles. This is a largely cognitive-behavioural approach. The downside of the approach is that it takes time to gather sufficient data required to establish the links between role profiles, quality of contact, imago images and so on. However, there is a "short cut" component of ERICA that may be invoked on occasion. I describe this below as a "brief therapy" approach.

The third option is to skip the data collection stage and simply teach the meditational techniques I describe in detail in the next Chapter. The rationale of this would be that use of these techniques would enable the couple (and therapist) at least, to buy time while pursuing either of the first two strategies, and at most, even resolve the problem. Clearly this is a "nothing to lose" strategy.

The fourth course of action is to focus initially on the first two stages of Berne's view of "cure" as a progressive process that entails four stages – social control, symptomatic relief, transference cure and script cure (Berne 1961, pp. 160-175. Berne 1971, pp. 362-364). ERICA incorporates a particular approach to social control and symptomatic relief based on addressing somatic processes. I outline these below.

The fifth option is for the therapist to use a "scatter gun, catch–all" tactic by combining some or all of the previous options. This requires flexibly steering a pragmatic course, and does demand an experienced therapeutic hand on the tiller.

ERICA as a brief therapy

In **Chapters 13** and **14** we saw that we can very quickly predict the likely course of events. Simply by considering the social level of any of the twenty-four role profiles we can foretell the apparently desired reciprocal roles at each level. That is, the psychological level indicates the role to which an individual will 'switch' if the interaction continues beyond the Emergent stage of a role sequence. The existential level signifies the Closure – the role a person seeks to confirm as their life position. And more significantly in the present context, the role that is not used is the role that is likely to be projected onto others.

With ERICA, the aim of the 'brief therapy' approach is simply to exploit a natural capacity for dispassionate awareness of external events. Everyone has this capacity, and it is particularly well suited to circumstances where one or both individuals have a Bystander role at the fourth level of a reciprocal.

The opening lines of the above transcript show that Bryn is enacting a social level Victim and a psychological level Persecutor role. Megan is a social level Persecutor and a psychological level Victim. This suggests a Reversed negative outcome role sequence, probably at a second degree of intensity. Later, when the therapist asks what they expect of her, Megan ("Tell us what to do that would *get us out* of this mess!") is a social level Victim and a psychological level Persecutor) and Bryn ("We're *paying* you to .. Well, to sort it – us- out") is a social level Persecutor and a psychological level Victim: both invite the Rescuer role at the psychological level. This seems to confirm the view of a Reversed NORS with Rescuer as the *existential* level roles for both individuals. The existential level of a role profile is the role that people seek to occupy for themselves, yet defend against or move away from in others. In other words, Megan and Bryn each identifies with Persecutor, Rescuer and Victim roles - but not with the Bystander role. Arguably, this is the role they have repressed, with which they identify at an unconscious level, and *may* be projecting onto the other. At this point the therapist has enough information to formulate the working hypothesis that the first reciprocal is as in **Table 21.1.**

Stage	E	
Reciprocal #	a	
Clients	B	M
Role Profile #	18	7
Social	v	p
Psychological	p	v
Existential	r	r
Shadow	b	b

Table 21.1

Subsequent supervision with Bryn and Megan's therapist confirmed that their inter-locking role imago repertoire was a series on ongoing role sequences:

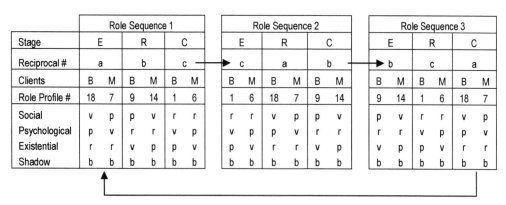

Stage	Role Sequence 1						Role Sequence 2						Role Sequence 3					
	E		R		C		E		R		C		E		R		C	
Reciprocal #	a		b		c		c		a		b		b		c		a	
Clients	B	M	B	M	B	M	B	M	B	M	B	M	B	M	B	M	B	M
Role Profile #	18	7	9	14	1	6	1	6	18	7	9	14	9	14	1	6	18	7
Social	v	p	p	v	r	r	r	r	v	p	p	v	p	v	r	r	v	p
Psychological	p	v	r	r	v	p	v	p	p	v	r	r	r	r	v	p	p	v
Existential	r	r	v	p	p	v	p	v	r	r	v	p	v	p	p	v	r	r
Shadow	b	b	b	b	b	b	b	b	b	b	b	b	b	b	b	b	b	b

Table 21.2

Although the therapist did not immediately home in on the Bystander roles at the fourth level of the initial reciprocal (she used a "tapping" technique, which I describe later in this Chapter), it would not have been entirely inappropriate for her to have done so. In other words, under such circumstances, there is nothing to be lost by targeting *the positive counterpart* of the role at the "not used" level *at a general level* – rather than in relation to the particular problem presented by the couple.

The Beholder role is the easiest of the Contact Cube roles to engage, being a resource that everyone uses in innumerable ways on a daily basis. With this 'brief' approach, there is no need to explain or teach anything about roles or imago images. My preferred way is to blend a mild trance induction into the normal discussion during the second or third therapy session. This may be done either as an uninterrupted three or four minute intervention - as outlined below with a client, Jack, who sought therapy for "a relationship problem"– or with snippets of the whole statement being interspersed between discussion of other matters:

> "One of the resources or *skills you already have* is an idea I call "what you notice is what you get". What this means is that we all *notice* all sorts of things about *what's going on* around us *without getting upset*. Like you notice a bus going down the road – you don't even *think* "Oh, there's a bus going down the road" – you simply *notice* it and continue with whatever else you're doing. Just look out the window – what do you see, what do you notice? Trees, the grass - maybe a bird. … and you're not getting upset. … But you could see a bus going down the road and think, "Oh, there's a bus going down the road. Just like those poor people in London and the suicide bomber". If you did that, you'd probably start feeling sad – or angry – or scared. But there's nothing in the garden that is *actually* scary – or sad. So just as an experiment, keep on looking out the window to see what you can notice while I'm talking. Most of the people who come to see me get confused about what's outside and what's not – it's natural to get upset when you think of upsetting things … of times when things are not going the way you want.. Keep on looking out the window – *that's good* practice for seeing what you notice - So *you already know* how it's useful to be able *to notice* things without getting upset. You also know how to *notice* that you're noticing *things* that are or *are not upsetting*. You don't have to do this consciously – you *just notice* what it is that you're doing or thinking or feeling – just like you notice the bus going down the road without thinking about it. And later on – maybe next week – I'll teach you a very easy and specific way of taking notice of what's happening. In the meantime you may want to consider just how much you *do notice* – *ordinary* things – like what's happening in the garden? - and how much you *notice* that you're noticing what's going on outside and on the inside. In fact, you can even get curious enough to be able to *fantasise* that you're noticing *yourself* – like watching a video of yourself. And of course, you'll *know* that it's not a *real* video – just a fantasy visualisation you've made up for yourself. Even as a kid, I used to have all sorts of fantasies – like I could watch myself playing football and scoring goals – and you'll know that I knew that it was really only what I was making up. Of course, you can watch a *real* video of yourself – like your holiday – if you've got one. Or you can make one up – just like you want it to be. That's what I mean by what you notice is what you get. What you get – what you want to get – comes later. Learning how to get what you want to get is what brings you here in the first place. Learning to notice when you're noticing is the start. Like I said, *next week* I'll teach you a very simple way for all this when *you'll tell me* what you've noticed during the week. Right now, I'm curious about what you have noticed in the garden."

This type of intervention takes less than five minutes and "seeds" the beginnings of more explicit use of the Beholder role. It also serves as an introduction to the grounding technique that is explained in a later Chapter. Obviously, it does require the therapist to have the appropriate training and skills to be able to blend this type of Ericksonian "conversational induction" (see, for example, Lankton and Lankton 1984 pp. 178-246) into the therapeutic hour.

The fact that Jack responded to the embedded suggestions and was able to start using the Beholder role, does not necessarily confirm the idea that the fourth level of a role profile is held at an unconscious level or has been repressed as shadow material; it merely attests that people are able to access resources "naturally" in response to appropriate stimuli. I illustrate the process of this type of enquiry in the following paragraphs by drawing on comments spread over three sessions with Jack.

In the subsequent post-trance sessions, I offered Jack the opportunity to "*run a video of the good times you've had together.... And as you're watching the video, tell me what's happening - just as it happens*".

The next phase was to move on to "*Now run a video of how your relationship is at the moment ....And as you watch, tell me what's happening*". The third "video" was "*how you want your relationship to be*". Throughout all this, I was shuttling between social level Promoter and Responder, giving plenty of strokes, firmly correcting, reframing and even refusing to accept redefinitions or deviations from the task. Along with all this, I used a variety of techniques to heighten affective responses, and noted potential imago images, contaminations, injunctions and so on, for possible future exploration. For example, "*now freeze-frame the video and zoom in. That's right ... so you're there in the living room and you've just said ...... Strikes me there's something else here you've maybe not noticed..... So choose something you think could just be right for you and tell me about it...*"

Likewise, I periodically interrupted: "*Well, maybe I'm not getting the right message... Perhaps it's something about the way you're trying to tell me what's going on. Like it's the **impression** you want me to have – rather than the way it is for **you**. Or maybe it's **me** – just the way **I'm** hearing you. We'll discuss this later...Remember this is **your** video, **your** fantasy. It's all about learning that what you notice is important for you. So you can make it be anyway you want it to be*".

The penultimate phase was to "review" the three videos. "*We'll do it like this for each video - I'll tell you what's happening – and as I'm doing this, you're in charge of the 'pause button'. So you can stop me anytime you like – especially if I'm not telling it like it is. Of course, I'll have to refer to the notes I've made from the mini-discs. And when we've gone through all three videos, we can discuss any changes you may like to make – like you're editing the videos. And next week we'll move up a level. We'll start to put together what we've learned about how you notice yourself*"

The last two sentences set the scene for the final phase where the focus was an exchange of what Jack has learned about observing him self, *and* what I learned about Jack's capacity to enact the Beholder role. In addition I used the session to start the process of "*moving up another level*" – *of learning about patterns of behaviour you seem to use*". Using examples of Jack's descriptions of his and his wife's behaviours (taken from the mini-disc recordings of Jack's reported "videos" he had "watched" during previous sessions), I started adding to my initial hypotheses about Jack's role imago repertoire. The following transcript of the fourth session with Jack shows the hypothesised components of the couple's role profiles in bold text:

GL: "So when you say [on the mini-disc] '*She's being a right nag bag again. The moment I come in, she starts banging on about me coming in at all hours and what I expect her to have ready for my dinner*', [**Wife ->**

Persecutor]	you go on to say *"I'm starting to feel murderous, and I'm trying to tell her about the traffic along the Chelmsley Road, but she's not listening. So I start doing my nut. I'm slamming the door* **[Jack -> Persecutor]** *and going down the pub for a quiet meal".* **[Jack -> Bystander]** Now, I'm curious about this, because I'm beginning to see a pattern: you come in late, she nags, doesn't listen to your explanation and you "feel murderous" and "start doing your nut". Is that right?
Jack:	Yeah, that's right.
GL:	There're two things that interest me here. First, what's "doing your nut" mean for you?
Jack:	Just that – I do my nut, go bananas.
GL:	Say some more…
Jack:	Like the other day – at work. There was…
GL:	We'll come back to that – if it's important. What I'd like is for you to describe in more detail what the words on the disc "doing your nut" means. Are you OK with this?
Jack:	Sure …. She's shrieking and I do my nut?
GL:	Yes.
Jack:	I get angry and I shout and swear.
GL:	And when you do that, what's happening in your body?
Jack:	Well it's a sudden rush - in my head. I feel like I'm going to explode…Want to throttle her. But I don't – because I start to feel like I've got to get out - get away from the shrieking. So I'm scared, but I shout and swear and bang the door.
GL:	OK - thanks. I'll write that down. **[I write down "Doing my nut" and note the number on the mini-disc recorder, add "J->P", signifying Jack -> Persecutor]**. Second thing - you say *"As soon as I'm away from her shrieking, I just want to shrivel up and hide, not even talk to anyone".* **[Jack -> Bystander]** What I'm curious about here, is what do you guess she'd be doing and thinking or feeling at this point?
Jack:	Well, she's back at the house – but I know she'd be all sorry for herself. and shit scared I'm not going to come back. I did that once before – booked into a B-and-B. So I guess she'd be thinking *"I got to be nice to him when he comes back".* And she is. **[Wife -> Rescuer]**
GL:	What happens?
Jack:	She's over the top apologetic and then starts coming on – just a bit sexy **[Wife -> Rescuer]**. I play stumm for a bit. **[Jack -> Bystander; start of next role sequence?].**

Note that at this point we had moved away from directly induced hypnotic phenomena and were engaged in here-and-now discourse similar to the discussion of Significant Incidents described in **Chapter 17**. The salient points about this process are:

- This is a *joint* exercise; Jack is teaching me about his role behaviours. I am learning about his model of the world.
- The data are from Jack's narrative of "*how your relationship is at the moment*" – told in his own words. We are using the data to track his capacity to "notice" and report on his own behaviour. Additionally, we have started the process of *"moving up another level"* – *of learning about patterns of behaviour you seem to use".*
- Jack's account of the "videos" required him to dissociate in order to comply with *"as you're watching the video, tell me what's happening - just as it happens".* Jack was

able to do so and, during the current session, demonstrates sufficient stability of cathexis to engage in a here-and-now (Adult ego state) discussion of his behaviour, thoughts and feelings.

- At times I query Jack's account of the "video" – *"maybe I'm not getting the right message... Perhaps it's something about the way you're trying to tell me what's going on. Like it's the* impression *you want me to have – rather than the way it is for* you. *Or maybe it's me –just the way* I'm *hearing you".* As indicated in **Chapter 17**, it is essential not to collude with a client's attempts to elicit a desired reciprocal role.

The remainder of the session was devoted to graphical mapping of the role sequence – couched entirely in Jack's words on the mini-discs. Our homework was to listen to the other recordings and compare similar diagrams during the fifth session. We agreed a joint version, and in the sixth session, I was about to suggest we start to look for a "meta-pattern", namely, the reciprocals we had tentatively identified thus far. Jack interrupted me and said:

> "I think we have a breakthrough. I must tell you.... Over the week-end we started rowing again. She was working up her shrieking and I was thinking *'Oh no! Here we go again'.* Then I sort of heard you saying *"Tell me what you notice about the good times".* I looked at Peg and she was all angry and tearful and I thought *"what you notice is what you get"* and I said to myself *"Just notice ... just notice the bus going down the road. I don't have to think ... just notice the good times".* I felt all shaky, but I grabbed her and looked at her – close up. I think she was surprised - and scared – but she stopped shrieking. So I started playing the good times video while I was looking at her. It was .... it was like ... like I was noticing myself noticing the good times while I was looking into her eyes. It was weird. Then she sort of melted and went all floppy, so I hugged her. I was coming out of re-playing the good times video and I heard the neighbour's dog barking. After a while we started talking and I showed her our charts. She was fascinated and we spent another two hours and a bit - just talking about the good times and discussing the last one [chart] we – you and me – did. She wants us to do another one together – for us both".

I did not proceed to explain anything about roles, reciprocals or imagos. Jack had another six sessions, during which I taught him the grounding and centring techniques and supported his improving marital relationship. He explored and cleared up a 'Don't be close' injunction over two sessions, and spent the final two sessions consolidating and reviewing progress.

Although I describe this type of work as "brief therapy", the between-sessions homework for both therapist and client can often take as long as the therapeutic session itself. As with all audio-recorded work, the therapist needs either to review the recording and make copious notes, or to call upon secretarial services for a typed transcript.

Clearly, not all clients are as well suited to the ERICA version of brief therapy as was Jack. Since my work with him, I have worked "briefly" with seventeen clients solely by facilitating their use of the Beholder role, and without going as far as naming or interpreting their role imago repertoires in terms of Contact Cube roles. With ten of these clients I have also used the grounding and centring techniques in conjunction with the use of "videos". With four of the remaining seven clients, I taught these techniques *after* reviewing the "videos".

Contraindications for using this brief approach apply to clients:

- With a rating lower than 40 on the GAF scale (Luborsky et.al. 1962; see also American Psychiatric Association, 1995, pp. 30-32).
- Difficulty in maintaining Adult ego state cathexis.
- A level of discounting in more than five out of ten transactions as evidenced by redefining.
- Clients who demonstrate frequent recourse to third degree games as a coping strategy, in conjunction with:
- Frequent and spontaneous regression and/or dissociative states they find difficult to manage –as well as:
- Complex role imago repertoires with more than three rounds (ongoing series of role sequences) evident after two assessment sessions.
- Last, but not least, the therapist's inexperience of trance work in conjunction with unavailability of readily accessible supervision by an experienced supervisor.

Clearly, this brief approach does not fit with "conventional" or "traditional" transactional analysis practice. It is a blend of Rowan and Jacobs's instrumental and relational approaches, with equal emphasis on technique and relational constructs of non-collusive role reciprocation. What it illustrates also is the significance and explicit use of unconscious processes, framed within the client's definitions of their situation, and only marginally in relation to theoretical constructs provided by the therapist[1]. This demonstrates not only the flexibility within the ERICA model, but also confirms the view in Cognitive Analytic Therapy that:

> "transference and countertransference are seen to be one particular example of the general meshing of reciprocal role procedures….. It is useful to distinguish two sources of countertransference. One, which may be called personal

---

[1] Parenthetically, I used ERICA as a framework in conjunction with 'hypnotic' techniques, over a three year period for working with a client who had a dissociative identity disorder. She was a tremendously courageous woman who held her life together until her two children had left home. She routinely dissociated as a means of coping with her job, and within two sessions of starting individual therapy, would regress at the drop of a hat, as other sub-personalities "popped out". She had five major role imago repertoires with several sub-personalities and throughout the therapy we referred to each by her names for them. There was "the Actress", "the Nurse" and "Mother Earth" (Rescuers); "Sulky Susie", "SillyShillySally" and "the Lady-by-the-Pool" (Victims): "the Void", "the Abyss" and "HideyHoleHenry" (Bystanders); "the Demon", "the Dark Cloud" and "the Thing" (Persecutors). Some of these (the Nurse, Mother Earth, the Lady-by-the-Pool) doubled by enacting positive roles most of the time, and there were additional positive role sub-personalities – "the Guide" and "the Wise One" (Promoters).

There were also two, fourth level, sub-personalities that occasionally emerged when she was particularly stressed – "the Mountaineer" and "the Angel". These two would never "talk" to me except to announce they were taking her "beyond" for "respite care" during the remainder of a session. I suspect the "respite care" involved aspects of transpersonal dimensions of consciousness; she maintained a self-induced, silent trance for the rest of the therapy session. Much of the communication between me and several of her other sub-personalities was done by her ("their") presenting symbolic doodles or sketches; often she, the Guide, or the Wise One, were unable to add meaningful verbal interpretations.

As we neared the planned end of therapy, I was concerned to provide an additional cognitive structure, and offered to explain Contact Cube roles and reciprocation as an alternative to her "keeping the conversation going" with her "characters". She listened politely, but after less than five minutes said "So that's your story - but I'm going to stick to mine".

She finished therapy, took early retirement and now spends much of her time sketching, rock climbing and working as a volunteer for a wildlife preservation society. For eight years I got Christmas cards from "all of us"; in the ninth year there was a post script that read "HideyHoleHenry has grown up and left home". Two years after this, the annual card was signed "just ME". After another three years the cards stopped coming; the last was signed only with her name and the words "Thanks for everything".

At one stage during therapy, she resolved to write about her "characters" for the benefit of "other people's characters", but later, changed her mind. Instead, I report this with her permission ("in no more than 500 words"). I am tremendously indebted to her for all I learned about myself, personally and professionally.

countertransference, will reflect the therapist's particular range of role procedures [role imago repertoire].... Such personal countertransference is not totally distinct from the specific reactions evoked by the particular patient, which can be called elicited countertransference..... Within elicited countertransference reactions there is another useful distinction to bear in mind, that between identifying countertransference and reciprocating countertransference.... This distinction ... stems logically from the model of the dialogic self. A person enacting one pole [role profile] of a RRP [reciprocal] may either (1) convey the feelings associated with the role to others, in whom corresponding emphatic feelings may be elicited, or (2) seek to elicit the reciprocating response of the other..... In the course of therapy, therapists can use their identifying countertransference to explore feelings which the patient is conveying non-verbally but does not acknowledge or experience consciously..... As regards reciprocating countertransference, the need is to recognise the pressure and to avoid reinforcing (collusive) responses". (Ryle and Kerr, 2003, pp. 103-105)

Somatic processes – 'people have bodies'

Although Berne touches on the significance of somatic processes in script formation, not many transactional analysis practitioners consistently and explicitly use "bodywork" as a therapeutic tool. Early examples of this integration are Cornell (1975), and Cassius (1980) who explicitly link Reichian character analysis with aspects of (Bernean) scripts under the umbrella of the *bodyscript* (Cassius 1980, pp. 223-244). More recent interest is described by Childs-Gowell and Kinnaman (1992) and Erskine, Moursund and Trautmann (1999) with their inclusion of physiology as one of seven "major facets of intervention". (Erskine, Moursund and Trautmann 1999, p.337)

With ERICA I follow a slightly different path – it is not "bodywork" in a Reichian sense of the term, but it is based on somatic processes. My interest in this stems from the well established idea that scripting is not just something that happens in our heads; script decisions are holistic processes that impinge on body and mind. In psychoanalytic terms, resolution of unconscious intra-psychic conflict – a Type 3 impasse in transactional analysis - requires a healing of the splits between persona and shadow, ego and body. All this takes time. In the meantime, 'people have bodies'. They present themselves for therapy, travailing tales of trouble in mind, body, and soul – usually in that order

In addition, I have drawn upon my personal experience of "energy classes" as taught by a Mongolian Qigong master, Ambaa Ragchaa. I was singularly impressed by his ability to detect and accurately interpret subtle energy fields, based upon his understanding of the flow of energy along (through) the meridians used in Chinese medicine. [1]

"Although the methods of energy psychotherapy are very new, the ideas and knowledge are also ancient and are found in many parts of the world (Gallo, 1999). Subtle energy, known as *chi* in the Chinese system, and *prana* in the Indian yoga

---

[1] Ambaa Ragchaa speaks very little English – a fact that doubly impressed me. I have seen him teaching a group of nearly fifty people various exercises that are not unlike Tai Chi movements/postures. During the course of his instruction, he periodically pointed to different members of the class and (via an interpreter) identified various "energy problems" ("Lady in blue dress has problem with throat", "Man over there has energy problem in back") In all, he picked out nine people with various maladies, and in each case, his "diagnosis" was confirmed by the individuals concerned. In individual "treatments", Ambaa Ragchaa demonstrates a similar uncanny accuracy of assessment. Without any words, he gazes intently at his patient from a distance of about two metres and then, without touching, he will simply run his hands over the person's body, pausing every here and there. He then tells the interpreter to ask a series of leading questions (such as "When you little, you break bone in leg?") that without fail, receive affirmative replies. "Treatment" consists of a (usually vigorous) whole body massage similar to shiatsu.

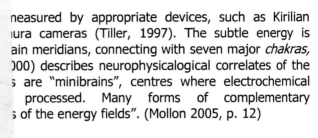

neasured by appropriate devices, such as Kirilian
iura cameras (Tiller, 1997). The subtle energy is
ain meridians, connecting with seven major *chakras,*
)00) describes neurophysicalogical correlates of the
; are "minibrains", centres where electrochemical
processed. Many forms of complementary
; of the energy fields". (Mollon 2005, p. 12)

developments in two such fields - eye movement
mply, EMDR, (Shapiro 1995, Shapiro and Forrest,
ques, - EFT, (see Lammers and Kirchner 2002,
's website www.emofree.com) – that are largely
i my Mongolian mentor. I duly undertook training in
que in conjunction with the other ERICA models to

:fers to a genre of therapies that link psychological
turbances and blockages in the subtle energy fields
...Usually the approach is for the client to stimulate
n mind a particular aspect of distress or emotional
ns but the two most well known now are "thought
)01], and a modified and simplified version of this
Je" (EFT) [Carrington and Craig, 2000].
:ations of Callahan's and Craig's clinical findings is
urbance may not lie essentially in the person's
neurobiology, their traumatic memories, cognitions, internal models of relationships,
persisting phantasies, and so on, but most fundamentally in their energy fields. The
patterns of information in the energy fields then determine the recurrent
reverberations throughout the psychosomatic system. It is hard to escape this
conclusion if the reports of extremely rapid and lasting changes, brought about by
stimulating the energy meridians, are to be taken seriously. Thus, Callahan argued
that the root cause of emotional distress is a *perturbation* in the thought field....
Similarly, Craig in his teaching material presents the formula: 'The cause of ALL
negative emotions is a disruption in the body's energy system'". (Mollon 2005, pp. 11-
12)

Mollon gives an extensive and excellent account of EMDR and EFT; his work is a radical yet
seamless integration of energy therapy and Freudian psychoanalysis. For anyone interested
in these developments, Mollon's work is a "must read" account of a burgeoning new field of
research and practice. He gives succinct summaries of the EFT treatment protocol (Mollon
2005, pp. 67-70) and a "schematic summary of the therapeutic process" (Mollon 2005, pp.
250-251). The latter demonstrates the integration of the energy therapies and a
psychoanalytic orientation.

Shapiro, the originator of EMDR, presents a likewise well-researched account of her
method. Independent research has demonstrated that EMDR is the most effective form of
treatment for post traumatic stress disorder (Mollon 2005, pp. 253-255). Training in EMDR
is not yet widely available internationally, but is of excellent quality.

EFT and other variants of the "energy therapies" present a somewhat mixed picture of
enthusiastic reports of seemingly amazing results and, in some cases, increasingly
expensive training opportunities open to anyone. Unfortunately, not all training
opportunities come with the standards of rigour one would expect of a methodology that

purports to be as potent as its practitioners claim it to be. The dilemma for trainers is that the technique is simple, easily learned, and according to most trainers, may be applied to *any* constellation of symptoms. As far as I know, such claims have yet to be validated by the findings of independent research.

A notable exception to the trend towards expensive training is Gary Craig's website, where extensive training material is available for a reasonable price, along with free initial tutorial advice and a regular (free) newsletter. Most importantly, the website includes appropriate caution regarding the innovative status of the method, and listings of qualified EFT practitioners.

My own experience is that EFT is undoubtedly effective, and used responsibly in conjunction with another therapeutic approach, constitutes a tremendously empowering technique. The relevance of EFT to ERICA is that for some clients, it is an optional component of the overall process of teaching them to research their own behaviours. In particular, the technique is easily adapted to ameliorate the influence of negative roles. The standard treatment protocol is based on identifying the feelings associated with a distressing experience and getting the client to rate this on a 0 to 10 scale of intensity. The therapist then formulates a "set up" phrase based on the logical form of "*Even if I feel (sad, angry, jealous etc.) I totally and completely accept myself*" and coaches the client to memorise the words. The client then repeats this phrase internally while tapping a sequence of acupressure points associated with each of the meridians. The client is then asked to give a new rating of the experience. The procedure is repeated until the intensity is reduced to zero. Clients are not only able to use this technique during therapy sessions, but more importantly, on their own between sessions.

This is no more than a bare bones outline of the procedure. There are numerous refinements.[1] My point is that:

> "Although the reasons these energy methods seem to work so well is still unclear, they do several things that may prove to be significant for the healing process:
>
> 1. They separate the person's identification with his or her problem from who he or she is...
> 2. They help the person to move into the area of emotional distress rather than developing his or her unique style of avoidance. This embracing of the problem is crucial for the healing process to occur....
> 3. They help the person stay in the here and now .... (Steinfeld 2004, p. 5)

These comments bring to mind the phrase that "therapy involves converting hidden subjects to conscious objects" (Wilber 2000, p. 247). Whether or not the "hidden subjects" represent shadow phenomena, depends on one's acceptance (or not) of unconscious process and the dynamics of repression as a defence mechanism. An alternative point of view is to adopt a more pragmatic position. That is, is it *useful* to regard the role that is not used as representative of shadow phenomena? For me, an affirmative answer to this is a perfectly tenable position – pending further research. By this I mean that one would have to demonstrate empirically that people characteristically avoid a particular role, and secondly, that at certain stages in their development, acquire the ability to avoid this role

---

[1] Rather than re-inventing the wheel, I would urge readers interested in exploring EFT techniques to obtain the free Manual on CD-ROM from Gary Craig's website (see www.emofree.com). For readers with an interest in the physics and neuro-scientific aspects of the "energy therapies" see http://www.emofree.com/articles/physicist.htm

more often than not. An equally tenable hypothesis is that imago images, rather than roles, are the dominant variables.

Be this as it may, let us return to the example of the impasse between Bryn and Megan. The therapist's last comment is replicated below followed by an edited transcript showing how the therapist proceeded:

Therapist: What I can tell you at this stage is how I see the situation. That's not going to 'sort you out' or 'tell you what to do', but it will give you some ideas about how to find those kinds of answers for yourselves. **RPV +** Do you want to go in this direction, or do you each have ideas about what would be a satisfactory solution as far as <u>you're</u> concerned? **PVR**

Megan: I just want us to be like we used to.

Therapist: If that were so, how would *you* want to be?

Megan: Loving and accepting ... even if ...

Therapist: Even if?

Megan: Even if ... even if he does blush.

Therapist: Good ! And Bryn?

Bryn: Well, I am interested in how you see us, but what I really want is just to be the way I am at any time and still be accepted.

Therapist: No matter what? ...whatever you're doing .. or saying?

Bryn: Well, sure, if there's a problem .. then we can talk. I just want her to love me, to accept me no matter what....

Therapist: Okay Maybe I'll want to clarify that a bit more later. At the moment you – both of you - seem to be in a log jam – and no way out. So I think it may be useful for you to do an experiment.

Bryn: I'm up for anything that'll help.

Therapist: Well, no guarantees. That's why I call it an experiment.

Megan: So what is it?

Therapist: I'll talk you through a simple exercise. All you have to do is to follow my instructions. And then we see where you get to, how you are at the end of the experiment.

Bryn: Sounds okay to me.

Megan: I don't see how ...But what do we have to do?

Therapist: Let me explain a bit more. And then you decide whether you want to do it or not. By "experiment" I mean ... It's something you do to see if it works. No big deal, no matter if it doesn't. This experiment is dead easy. Its safe and .. my guess is that maybe it'll help you get out of the log jam - so there's nothing to lose. When people get upset, when they go round and round and can't sort things out, they get out of balance. So this experiment is designed to get you both in balance again. When you argue, you generate a lot of energy – negative energy - energy that pushes the other person away. So this is a hands-on experiment that clears the negative energy. All you have to do is to stimulate parts of your face and hands – I'll show you how. But first you have to take a reading – give a rating on a nought to ten scale of how you feel when you've been arguing. Then when you done the experiment, you give yourself another rating. Are you willing to go ahead?

Bryn: I'm ready

Megan: Well... yeah, okay.

Therapist: Good! One other thing: you have to be honest with yourself. And it pays to be curious! Ask yourself 'is there *really* a difference?' You'll see what I mean as we go along. So Megan, tell me – when you feel *scared*, and you think you'll have to take the girls and leave, where do you feel that *scare* in your body?

Megan: Well, all over really ... but in my stomach .. and in my shoulders... a bit.

Therapist: So focus on that scare ... in your stomach .. and shoulders. And the thought 'I'll have to take the girls and leave'. Just stay with the scare ... Good .. That's it ..You can close your eyes and still listen to me ... So while you're feeling that scare rub along your upper chest - from left to right, just below the collar-bones. That's right, .. use your middle finger .. Now somewhere there, you'll find a spot .. a spot that's more tender than anywhere else .. That's good .. Just hold it there just keep stimulating that spot and let yourself feel that *scare* while I talk to Bryn for few seconds ... Now Bryn, when you blush and feel scared Megan is going to up and off, what happens in your body?

Bryn: It's my arms .. and there's a sort of 'dong' sound in my head .. and my chest goes sort of tight.

Therapist: So feel that *scare* in your arms ... and the tightness in your chest ... and hear the dong in your head ... the thought Megan is going to up and off. Now find that spot on your chest .. just like I told Megan .. That's it .. good ..focus on the scare .. Now Megan, are you still in touch with that scare?

Megan: Uh-hu.

Therapist: And Bryn?

Bryn: Yes.

Therapist: Okay – Both of you, on a scale of nought to ten how scared are you?

Megan: Eight... no, nine.

Bryn: About seven ... seven-ish.

Therapist: Now Megan, rub that spot .. round and round and repeat out loud after me *Even if I feel scared and have to take the girls and leave,*

Megan: *Even if I feel scared and ....*

Therapist: *have to take the girls and leave,*

Megan: *and have to take the girls and leave*

Therapist: *I fully and completely accept myself,*

Megan: *I fully and completely accept myself,*

Therapist: Okay again ... Together with me.

Therapist/Megan: *Even if I feel scared and have to take the girls and leave, I fully and completely accept myself.*

Therapist: And again .. so you remember it ,, keep rubbing.

Therapist/Megan: *Even if I feel scared and have to take the girls and leave, I fully and completely accept myself*

Therapist: Good .. keep rubbing gently ... and keep repeating that phrase silently to yourself ... Now, Bryn [The therapist gives Bryn similar instructions using the phrase *Even if I feel scared she is going to up and off. I fully and completely accept myself* Bryn repeats the phrase].

Therapist: Now both stop rubbing and watch me. You use two fingers - middle and your forefinger – like this. Now your tap ... You are going to tap on each of the points I'm going to show you ... And as you tap, you repeat the phrase silently to yourself. Watch me, and I'll tap along with you. The first point is here .... close your eyes and tap while you say your phrase *Even if I feel ...* Open your eyes when you've said the phrase to yourself ... Now the next point ... over here .... Close eyes ... tap and *Even if I feel* .... Open eyes ... now the next point .... [The therapist continues to work through all the points and then asks], Okay Megan, on the same nought to ten scale, how do you rate your scare now?

Megan: Wowwww ! That's amazing! I .... it's almost not there .... only about one

Therapist: And Bryn?

Bryn: Ermmm nothing ... not a thing!

Therapist: Right – let's go again Megan. Bryn, you tap along with Megan but this time you use another phrase *Even if I feel scared and I blush, I fully and completely accept myself* ... Here we go .. first point, end of eyebrow - at the junction of eyebrow and the bridge of your nose ... *Even if I feel scared ....*

The therapist takes them through another round of tapping; both give a zero rating. The therapist congratulates them and gives instructions for using the procedure. The trigger for the procedure is whenever Bryn blushes - according to Megan. "And Bryn, the more you blush the more you can both practice getting the scare down to zero." The couple contract to use the procedure in this way. The therapist adds a "fail safe" clause *(Even if I still feel scared, I fully and completely accept myself)* that they are to use if either has not reduced their scare to zero after four rounds of tapping. The therapist also stresses the "experimental" nature of the technique and hints that at the next session, they will "review the situation" and "maybe start on learning other useful techniques – as well as learning to recognise the bigger picture – learning about other roles you can use". The therapist's closing comment is, "I think you've both done pretty damn well. Remember, it was an experiment – but, on the basis of what you've done to today, I reckon you're more than capable of cracking this one for good".

I would add that this is rather more than the usual use of EFT. Normally, the technique is used with individuals, and usually, with a lot more exploration of the central issue. It is frequently the case that there is more than one source of energetic disturbance. A succinct account of the efficacy of EFT in conjunction with redecision therapy is given by Porter-Steele (2005). This, and the above transcript, is typical of the effectiveness and rapidity of EFT, aptly illustrating how the approach may be used as an adjunct to ERICA. As noted by Steinfeld (2004), it is empowering, encourages the use of here-and-now awareness, and focuses on a positive outcome. I leave it to readers to judge the relevance of the technique to the shadow and unconscious processes.

Other bodywork techniques

I encourage clients to use two other techniques. The first is a sequence of six exercises described by Ken Mellor that offer a "unique contribution to physical health, personal well-being and rejuvenation" (Mellor 1996). They involve little more than adopting various simple postures typically used in Hatha yoga; they are graduated in a way that permits one to do as many of each of the six exercises as suits one's level of fitness, and then increase this over time. Without exception, I have found that the simple act of taking charge of their own bodies in this way, builds increasing confidence and the ability to deal with other aspects of their lives.

The second technique is more therapeutically oriented, having to do with dissolving muscular tensions that mask particular emotions. The essential steps are to lie down and simply *notice* your body – without trying to change anything. The next step is to breathe deeply - all the way down into your abdomen. This is variously known as "belly breathing" or "ballooning"; it takes a little practice to inhale and simultaneously extend the abdomen without straining. Once you have acquired a rhythm that enables you to breathe in this way without straining or holding your breath, you simply focus on your breathing, noticing the "naturalness" of the entire cycle of inhaling – and exhaling. Maintain this awareness for three or four in-breaths / out-breaths so that your awareness is as much physical as it is cognitive. That is, be aware of *the bodily sensations* that accompany inhalation and exhalation. Focus on these and affirm their "naturalness", the "comfort" of breathing in –

and breathing out. And as you continue to breathe like this – naturally and comfortably - allow the comfort to spread throughout your whole body. As you breathe out, feel the comfort spreading. As you breathe in, feel your breath as a life force connecting you to the entire cosmos. With each exhalation the comfort, the pleasure, spreads through your entire body – and out into the world. Let yourself experience the simple physical pleasure of breathing.

Gradually begin to notice differences in various areas of your body. Notice the areas - without trying to change anything. Pinpoint the parts – and as soon as you do, you'll automatically have begun labelling them – stiff neck, tightness in my shoulders, numbness in my legs – and so on. These sensations, these blocks in the flow of comfort and pleasure, are no more than the visceral location of disowned aspects of one's self. They are muscular tensions created by suppressing muscular discharge of the energies associated with thoughts and feelings. For example, when I feel slightly angry, I hold my breath briefly, clench my fists and curse under my breath. If I am more than slightly angry, I am likely to swear out loud, thus partially discharging the accumulated energy. To clench my fists I have to tighten the muscles in my hands, lower and upper arms, shoulders, neck, throat jaw and face; less obviously, the muscles in my chest, abdomen, leg and feet contract. Energy builds up, ready to be discharged in defence of my physical body, my territory, my kith and kin and everything I hold dear to myself. This is a natural, biological function, designed to ensure survival. A similar process applies to all feelings, although the physiology – the 'route' of the energy and muscular tensions from contraction to discharge – varies. For example, when sad, there is a different configuration of muscular tension-discharge. If, however, I deny my anger (scare, sadness, jealousy etc.) there has to be an interruption, a blocking of energy. But it does not simply evaporate. It has to go somewhere. It does. It gets held in the body. It is held by muscular tension. Again, this a natural process, but if consistently repeated, reinforced in relation to a particular issue that is too uncomfortable, too threatening or too traumatising for me even to *think* about it, the thought gets split off, suppressed, or even more drastically, repressed. It becomes part of my shadow. I am not consciously aware of this part of my subjectivity; it has become split of as an unconscious subject. One way of accessing this is via the location of bodily tensions.

Locating the sources of tension is one thing; dealing with them is another. The way to do this is to focus on the tension and consciously attempt *to increase it*. Do this by slowly and deliberately tightening the muscles in question. As you do this, bear in mind that you are also using the very same muscles to hold back that which has been split off. Acknowledge this as you tighten your muscles – and then slowly, start releasing them. Be open to whatever next arises.

Depending upon their history, I almost always urge clients not to undertake this journey on their own.[1] This is because whatever it is that was disowned, split off or suppressed, occurred at an earlier stage of development, at whatever level of development had been attained at the time. Recovering repressed relics results in regression – which needs to be supported. Usually the type of support most helpful is non-verbal, physical holding – as one would hold a young infant.[2] That said, more often than not, this type of

---

[1] Needless to say, similar caution applies to readers

[2] There are several techniques or postures for holding adults. I learnt most of these from working with Jacqui and Shea Schiff who pioneered "regressive work" with very dysfunctional clients in a therapeutic community setting. I routinely use these with most clients in a weekly therapy group. This is quite literally, hands on work. However, I would caution anyone who has not previously used such procedures, firstly, to seek instruction (and regular supervision) on their use from someone experienced in such matters, and, secondly, to give clients full information about the techniques and obtain informed consent. Even then, holding following particular periods of therapeutic work, should always be within a specific contract negotiated *before* the therapeutic work as an option for the client to invoke after the talking has been done.

bodywork is 'no big deal', often being no more than a sense of relief as energy now flows 'through' the previously constricted points of tension. It also often takes time; unblocking tensions that have existed for years may take weeks or even months. Along with the recovery the re-emergence of potential shadow material, there is usually a process of cognitive reconstruction that eventually leads to take a third person perspective – which becomes encapsulated in the Observer role.

Contact and the fourth level of role enactment

Reflecting on all the above considerations, and drawing on my experience of this potential shadow level of role enactment, leaves me with the following far from conclusive thoughts:

- There is a level of contact between people that exists at a transpersonal level.
- Generally, awareness of this level arises unbidden. For me, it seems to have developed gradually over a ten year period, usually accompanied by intuitive insights about what may have been occurring.
- I have simply allowed this process to occur, to "grow", and it has gradually taken the form of imagery (and sometimes sounds or fragrances) that often seems unrelated to anything that may be happening in the here-and-now.
- I *think* the most frequently occurring role profile associated with this is Beholder/Valuer/Responder – but I have not systematically checked this. Sometimes the reciprocal has been Valuer/Beholder/Responder for the client and Valuer/Responder/Beholder from me.
- Likewise, I have not always confirmed what may have been happening with my clients on these occasions. (Audio recording is essential; video is even more helpful.)
- As I became more confident about this process, I started using the material by disclosing to my clients what I had just experienced.
- With positive reciprocals (PORS), I now simply disclose the content of my imagery and feelings and leave it to the client to respond.
- When negative roles are involved there is almost always shadow material lurking at this fourth level – either for me, my client or both of us.
- Not all interaction carries this quality of "linking".
- I suspect that whereas mixed outcome role sequences (MORS) and negative outcome role sequences (NORS) indicate the need for work to occur at a pre-personal level, positive outcome role sequences (PORS) and, interestingly, indeterminate outcome role sequences (IORS), indicate linking at a transpersonal level. This could be a useful marker for avoiding Wilber's pre/trans fallacy.
- The ERICA 'brief therapy' approach facilitates the use of the Beholder role. This, in itself, is not sufficient evidence for arguing that the role held at the fourth level represents shadow phenomena. This *may* apply to negative roles, and if so, the hypothesis would be that positive roles represent the emergence of roles previously held at a transpersonal level of consciousness.
- Clearly, further systematic research is needed. Psychotherapy is not necessarily the best arena for this endeavour.

Key Points 22

22.1 Consideration of the *shadow* and *somatic processes* raises the status of **the unconscious.** Transactional analysis does not encompass "the unconscious" as a distinct, well formulated concept. TA practitioners tend to talk about issues that are "out of awareness". It is essential to view unconscious processes developmentally.

22.2   It has been suggested that **the role** that is *not occupied* at the social, psychological and existential levels during negative outcome role sequences, *must exist at an unconscious level as the shadow.* I regard the suggestion with some caution:

- because of the "pre-trans fallacy" or difficulty inherent in interpretations of unconscious processes.

- because we can only use this idea if we are willing to acknowledge that shadow phenomena arises from the operation of repression and the return to the unconscious of material that was once conscious.

22.3   A developmental view of consciousness suggests that Drama Triangle roles and the Bystander role may be regarded as **archetypal roles**. Speculatively, ERICA *involves uprooting these myths and replacing them with more accurate, less self-damaging scripts and roles*, or, in other words, with positive roles.

22.4   ERICA may be used as a **brief therapy** involving visualisation, the therapeutic use of trance and other hypnotic techniques. This usually requires the practitioner to be able to work at the transpersonal level.

22.5   Not many transactional analysis practitioners consistently and explicitly use **"bodywork"** as a therapeutic tool.

22.6   **EFT** facilitates symptom relief for clients. This constitutes a tremendously *empowering* technique.

22.7   Simple **yoga postures** and other techniques having to do with *dissolving muscular tension* that mask particular emotions are also helpful; the latter should be used with caution.

22.8   **Contact** at the fourth level of role enactment needs to be systematically researched.

Chapter 23

The Observer Role

This Chapter describes the Observer role – the capacity to take a meta-perspective on other roles either in relation to the Contact Cube, reciprocals, role sequences and dRITs.

Preamble

Understanding Contact Cube roles requires individuals to adopt a first person perspective. Using Contact Cube roles to understand reciprocals leads to a second-person perspective – the ability to take the role of the other. Moving on to an understanding of role sequences provides the springboard for the transition to a third-person perspective. In this respect, ERICA involves a "re-engineering" of normal developmental processes. That is, children "learn about" or acquire the capacity to use roles as part of the process of normal growth and development. Most adolescents are able to take a third–person perspective and for the most part, enact Contact Cube roles "naturally" without conscious awareness. ERICA provides a framework for re-learning a normal developmental task by correcting dysfunctional role behaviours. This learning is not solely cognitive and behavioural; roles have associated qualities of contact and imago images. And as we have seen in the previous Chapter, re-aligning energetic and somatic processes brings us closer to a holistic view of humankind.

Like all roles, the Observer role is based on expectations. Expectations are complex phenomena, ranging from the expectations others have of us that we have taken on board, through to promises, good intensions, social norms or simply strategies for dealing with unpredictable circumstances. For the most part, we do not ordinarily think about our expectations; they exist as part and parcel of whatever level or stage of consciousness has been attained. The expectations associated with the Observer role arise from a combination of familiarity with Contact cube roles and what Wilber refers to as vision logic:

> "whereas the formal mind establishes relationships, vision-logic establishes *networks* of those relationships. This, obviously, is a highly *integrative* structure; indeed, in my opinion, it is the highest integrative structure in the *personal* realm... (Wilber 1986, p. 72)

Teaching clients to access various roles via the Observer role is the crux of the methodology of ERICA; it involves being simultaneously grounded and centred and knowing how to witness - techniques I describe below. These techniques provide a trigger for the Observer role as *a meta-perspective of their relationships.*

These three techniques are presented in the sequence in which they are taught to clients. For the reasons stated below it is important to start with grounding before proceeding to centring and witnessing.

Grounding

Being grounded entails being simultaneously aware of internal sensations and external events. It is a sensory-based experience. Some people are able to ground themselves without explicit instructions, merely by noticing what they can see, hear, feel (are touching), smell, or taste as well as noticing what they are thinking/feeling internally. Try it and you will realise how simple it is. At the same time you will soon discover how subtle the process is and just how easy it is to become ungrounded – for your attention to be *either* externally focused *or* internally focused.

Grounding requires the use of the integrated Adult ego state. For people who cannot readily cathect their Adult, learning to become grounded is essential before tackling the other two techniques. In my experience, only severely dysfunctional clients are unable to ground themselves when given appropriate coaching, and even for those who are able to learn the technique (with or without coaching), the most frequently occurring difficulty is not cathecting Adult, but maintaining the cathexis. Routinely teaching all clients how to ground themselves, by itself, is a useful therapeutic practice.

Grounding involves shuttling from paying attention to *internal* thoughts, images and bodily-sensations, to sensory based awareness of *external* events. This process is repeated and refined and eventually, the focus of attention is directed simultaneously to both internal and external experience. The basic steps are:

- Sit in a comfortable position and close your eyes.
- Be aware of the contact of your body and whatever is supporting you.
- Focus on your body, noticing different sensations (hot, cold, tense, relaxed, tight and so on) in various parts. Simply note these sensations; *don't try to change them.*
- Open your eyes and select an object within arm's reach. Focus on the object and describe it to yourself *in visual terms.* For example, what colour is it? Is it the same colour all over – or is it differently coloured in various areas? Is it shiny – or dull? What shape is? Regular? Circular? Angular? How many planes does it have/can you see? Is it large? How large – in inches/centimetres?
- Now close your eyes again. Focus on your body, noticing different sensations. Are these sensations different from your memory of the sensations you had when you first closed your eyes? What are the sensations you experience – and in which parts of your body do you experience them?
- Open your eyes and focus on the same object – but this time, reach out and touch it. Explore it tactilely by describing it to yourself in tactile words. For example, is it hard? Is it soft? Is it rough? Is it smooth? Does it feel the same all over its surface(s) – and so on?
- Now close your eyes again. Focus on your body, noticing different sensations. Are these sensations different to your memory of the sensations you had the last time you closed your eyes? What are the sensations you experience – and in which parts of your body do you experience them?
- Open your eyes again, and select an object two or three yards from you. Focus on the object and describe it to yourself *in visual terms.* For example, what colour is it? Is it the same colour all over – or is it differently coloured in various areas? Is it shiny – or dull? What shape is? Regular-shaped? Circular-shaped? Angular-shaped? How many planes does it have/can you see? Is it large? How large – in inches?
- Now close your eyes again. Focus on your body, noticing different sensations. Are these sensations different to your memory of the sensations you had the last time you closed your eyes? What are the sensations you experience – and in which parts of your body do you experience them?
- Open your eyes and focus on the same object – but this time, get up and move over to it, reach out and touch it, Explore it tactilely by describing it to yourself in tactile words. For example, is it hard? Is it soft? Is it rough? Is it smooth? Does it feel the same all over its surface(s) – and so on?
- Now, standing where you are, close your eyes again. Focus on your body, noticing different sensations. Are these sensations different from your memory of the sensations you had the last time you closed your eyes? What are the sensations you experience – and in which parts of your body do you experience them?

- Open your eyes again, and select another object two or three yards from you. Move over to it and start to explore it in visual *and then* tactile terms. And as you do this, let your self be simultaneously aware of *internal* sensations

Once you get the hang of shuttling between awareness of *internal* and *external* sensations and using *sensory based* words for describing your experience, you'll find you can dispense with the above detailed instructions and simply close your eyes for five to ten seconds, open them, focus on an object, describe it visually/tactilely and while doing so, be simultaneously aware of *internal* sensations. At an advanced level, you can ground yourself almost instantly, without words. When learning the technique it is often helpful to set your watch to beep every hour, and then spend three minutes grounding yourself. Another useful aid is to obtain a recording of the process; Ken Mellor has recorded an audiotape/CD (Mellor, undated) that gives step-by-step instructions and guidelines for their use.

I have also found that some people benefit from using grounding in conjunction with the EFT tapping technique – particularly when they are unable to get their self rating down to zero. The usual EFT strategy on these occasions is to resort to the ploy of *"Even if I still have some (anger, sadness etc) left …"* If this is immediately supplemented by grounding and then another round of EFT tapping, the subjective stress rating usually reaches zero.

Parenthetically, there are no contra-indications for learning to ground one's self. You don't have to be "in therapy" to benefit from the procedure. Rowan gives a good chapter on using meditation and grounding in conjunction with therapy (Rowan 1993, pp. 80-92). Likewise, Kornfield (1994, 2000) gives a useful introduction to meditational practices.

Centring

Once a person can become grounded at will, they are ready to move on to centring. Centring entails being grounded, being aware of a sense of self (or becoming aware of a sense of self) and then locating this sense of self in (or in relation to) your body. For many people the sense of self is located in their head, for others it is in their stomach or chest. Some people have a sense of self located outside their body and some locate self in more than one part of the body. In addition the location of a sense of self varies over time.

Once a person has located a sense of self in (or in relation to) their body they are ready to move into using the capacity for self reflective awareness – the "I" that is aware of whatever it is of which *I* am aware; this is referred to as the Observer self. The final step is to align the Observer self with your bodily sense of self. Note that *awareness* simply is; it is automatic and instantaneous and most people are centred or partially centred most of the time. However many people become partially de-centred as they grow up. Energetically, this de-centring arises as a result of our in-built capacity to preserve homeostasis in the face of intensity. This is the energetic accompaniment to the standard transactional analysis explanation of this process - that is, that children adapt in order to survive and that such adaptations, or script decisions, are self-limiting. Centring is the energetic equivalent of restoring the original connection with self by aligning the Observer self and one's body.

Metaphorically, centring involves connecting (accessing the Observer self) a plug (awareness) to a power source (self). If you are so inclined, you can expand the metaphor to read, "connecting (accessing the Observer self) a plug (awareness) to a wall socket (self) wired to a power source (Physis)". Again, Ken Mellor has recorded a CD with detailed instructions and guidelines that provide the opportunity for listeners to understand and refine their own particular style of centring (Mellor 2002).

Witnessing

The third technique essential to learning the Observer role is an extension of the first two. In meditation, witnessing involves a state of consciousness where you do not identify with whatever it is you are noticing. Optimally, it goes beyond centring, or the witnessing described below, inasmuch as it involves awareness without labelling or categorising the object of your awareness. It requires sustained concentration on a single object (a mantra, a mandala, a candle flame, your breath, or an affirmation), without making judgements, until observation is experienced purely as a mental process or function, instead of the activity of self; the observer becomes the "thing" observed and experiences "self" as part of the observation as well as that which is being observed. I mention this for four reasons. The first is that for most people the ability to blend observer and the observed usually takes months (or even years) of practice under the guidance of an experienced teacher.

Secondly, because "witnessing" as described below is an aspect of "the ultimate Witness" mentioned by Wilber, many clients opt to pursue meditation classes with an experienced teacher in addition to therapy.

Thirdly, for some people, witnessing can sometimes lead to dissociation – which is why being grounded should be presented as a precursor to being able to centre or witness. That said, there's no rule that prohibits dissociation; as previously suggested, Parent and Child are mildly dissociated ego states – but knowing how to witness gives people more conscious choice between ego states, roles and pre-, inter- and transpersonal levels of awareness.

Finally, experiencing transpersonal realms of awareness is a natural, if not inevitable, outcome of normal development. Virtually everyone has had dreams or peak experiences (Maslow 1954) where one's sense of self seems to encompass everything else. Witnessing as described below is simply a shortcut to such experiences. However, taking the shortcut is pointless unless you are ready to do so – just as trying to teach a five year old calculus before they have grasped the rudiments of arithmetic, is probably futile and boring for the five year old, and frustrating for the teacher.

The witnessing technique I describe below is a derivative of Wilber's reference to the "ultimate Witness" (Wilber, 1985 pp.128- 132, Wilber, 1998 pp.36 – 40, Wilber 2004, pp. 1-31), The techniques involve being grounded, *not* being centred and then using the capacity for self-reflective awareness, to simply notice whatever is in awareness. A brief outline of the essential steps is as follows:

- Sit in a comfortable position and become fully grounded – simultaneously aware of internal and external events. Note that 'internal events' will include body sensations, thoughts, feelings, images and maybe even smells or tastes. External events usually amount to what you can hear, see or touch. The contact of your body with whatever you are sitting on is an obvious bridge between the external and internal; more refined examples of contact are the sensation of clothes on your body, the air on exposed areas such as your face and hands.
- Close your eyes and notice your internal experiences. These will include bodily sensations as well as thoughts, memories, images and self-talk, in all manner of combinations.
- A useful guideline at this stage is "***Now*** *I am aware of (whatever you are experiencing)",* or *"**Now** I see (am feeling, thinking etc)".* Use this, or a similar, phrase to capture your *present awareness.*
- Gradually direct your awareness on the location of your self– which is usually in your body. This requires you to de-centre, to separate "I" from whatever is in your

awareness. A useful idea at this point is to become aware of the "I" behind whatever is in your awareness.

- It may also be helpful to focus on the idea that "*I am **not** the (whatever thoughts, feelings, sensations, smells, tastes, images, sounds you are experiencing). I am **having** the (thoughts, feelings, sensations, smells, tastes, images, sounds) but I am **not** the (thoughts, feelings, sensations, smells, tastes, images, sounds)*".

- As you become more efficient at *noticing* thoughts, feelings or images, gradually decrease the verbal labelling of the thoughts and feelings, and increase the emphasis on "I am", and within that , emphasise the "I".

- Maintain and amplify "I" until you are able to observe the comings and goings of sensations, feelings, images, ideas and internal dialogues

- Affirm that "*I am more than*" the comings and goings of sensations, feelings, images, ideas and internal dialogues.

The above are the essential steps of the witnessing process. It is a powerful technique that not everyone is able to follow precisely at a first sitting. The usual pitfalls are either that you may get lost in the content of your thoughts and/or feelings, or that you struggle to maintain contact with your body and/or your surroundings. A combination of these two factors leads to dissociation. Some people find it is helpful to sit with closed eyes, focusing solely on internal events, but periodically, opening their eyes, becoming fully grounded and then closing their eyes and returning to experiencing internal events, along with the above *I am* statements. Note that the emphasis is on the "I" rather than the "am." An alternative to opening and closing your eyes is intermittently to re-affirm your awareness of your bodily contact with whatever is supporting you, and incorporate this awareness in your internal dialogue - "*I am feeling my back against the chair and I am not that feeling."*

An alternative to the above format is to break the entire process into smaller chunks, practising each one until you can do it with ease, before progressing to the next stage. For example, in this approach, you close your eyes, become fully grounded and then focus on your breathing. Watch and/or feel your breath rise as you inhale. Watch and/or feel your breath fall as you exhale. Notice that there is a momentary pause, a space between the rising and falling of your breath. The next step is to notice that there is a space between the cessation of one thought and beginning of the next thought you have.

> "As you observe your thoughts passing, watch very sensitively for the moment, when one thought fades and another arises. This transition is very quick and subtle, but involves the momentary availability of a space which you can contact and expand. This space has a quality of openness, free from the usual discursive and discriminative thinking" (Tarthang, 1977 p. 58)

Once you are able to verify this by your own experience, you ask yourself "To where does that thought go?" This exercise and the question therein, require you to create a division between subject and object in order to answer the question. That is, you have to separate from a thought in order to watch it, to notice where it ends and the next thought begins. This separation, this deliberate division of subject and object, reduces or lessens your identification with the thought. It is the beginning of the process of learning to observe without identifying with the content of your observation. In short, you are acquiring the capacity to enact the Observer role[1].

---

[1] For those who find the above brief exercises helpful, I would strongly recommend Wilber (2004, pp. 1-31) and Wolinsky's book *"Quantum Consciousness"* (Wolinsky 1993). Wolinsky gives guidelines for a series of short, "do-it-yourself" exercises that cover the process of witnessing in an eminently user-friendly style (Wolinsky 1993 p. 25-50). If you have access to the internet take a look at Frank Visser's website www.integralworld.com for a series of

Learning about witnessing is not only an opportunity for personal growth, it enables a practitioner to be better equipped to recognise and explore spiritual issues with those clients who present them. I teach clients grounding, centring and witnessing in conjunction with Contact Cube roles, but the techniques may be taught appropriately in conjunction with routine therapeutic interventions, such as decontamination, de-confusion, redecision work and so on, or as 'stand alone' methods for self-affirmations and relaxation. Teaching clients grounding, centring and witnessing is a task within the skills repertoire of any competent practitioner and, for many clients, will lead naturally to increasing use of self-reflective awareness, being no less than that of which everyone is already capable, but do not necessarily use deliberately or mindfully. However, I would caution practitioners not to embark on this type of instruction before they have mastered the techniques themselves. For those who take to the techniques and wish to pursue this interest seriously, I recommend an experienced meditation teacher.

There are no clients to whom I would not teach grounding. There are some clients with whom I will take time before teaching centring. And there are some clients with whom I proceed very cautiously in teaching witnessing. The criteria for these exceptions are that in all cases, grounding has to precede centring, and centring has to be mastered before tackling witnessing. Additionally, I advocate not teaching centring or witnessing to clients who use dissociation as a defence mechanism (or who are prone to discounting at a high level), until they have mastered grounding. These clients need to be able to ground themselves at will, and ideally, need to be able to dissociate at will. Then and only then, are they ready to combine the two procedures – which effectively, means they are able to become centred. For psychotic clients who experience difficulty in differentiating between external and internal reality, the watchwords are grounding, grounding, grounding – along with meticulous attention to redefining transactions and levels of discounting.

All three techniques – grounding, centring and witnessing - overlap the fuzzy boundary between psychotherapy and meditation.

> "meditation is not a structure-building technique, nor an uncovering technique, nor a script-analysis technique, nor a Socratic-dialoguing technique. It cannot substitute for those techniques, nor should it be used to "spiritually bypass" (Welwood, 1984) any major work needed on those levels. In *conjunction* with analysis or therapy, however, it apparently can be very useful in most forms of ....pathology, both because of its own intrinsic merits and because it tends to "loosen" the psyche and facilitate derepression on the lower levels [of consciousness], thus contributing in an auxiliary fashion to the therapeutic procedures on those levels" (Wilber, 1983 p.156).

That noted, learning the above techniques, at minimum, enables one to choose whether or not to identify with the object or content of awareness; optimally it leads beyond "a defensively contracted state of reduced awareness" (Walsh and Vaughan 1996, p. 17). This is the use of the Observer role *par excellence* – consciously and deliberately to access transpersonal realms of awareness

---

meditations based on Ken Wilber's work. Likewise, if you are interested in a more extensive account of grounding, centring and the wider aspects of meditation, Ken and Elizabeth Mellor publish weekly "e-meditations". The entire series will take you over two years (and counting!) to work through. You can signup for free weekly editions at www.biamenetwork.net. If you prefer a more personal touch, *before* committing yourself to anything – or anyone, read *"Halfway up the mountain"* (Caplan, 1999) and *"Do you need a guru?"* (Caplan, 2002). Many teachers of meditation operate within a structure that invites, or, indeed, inculcates symbiosis and there is a fine line between learning meditational techniques and inadvertently ending up doing therapy without a clear agreement to do so. In my view, anyone embarking upon learning meditation is likely to need recourse to psychotherapy at some stage of their journey. The optimum strategy is to find someone sufficiently experienced/qualified in both areas. For a good integration of spirituality and everyday life, see Kornfield (2000) and Richo (2002).

Intentionality

There is another technique that I teach most clients to round off enactment of the Observer role. This technique has as much to do with intentionality as it is related to expectations. Similar techniques are routinely taught in various yoga traditions and often used by psychologists for creating a positive mind-set. I present the exercise to clients as a routine for goal setting.

Start by getting fully grounded – simply noticing thoughts, feelings, sensations, internal images, sounds, smells, tastes and so on, without trying to change anything. Even if you are agitated and worrying about a forthcoming event, simply notice your *internal* processes – and the contact of your body with the external world. Then switch your awareness to building a *fantasy* - a fantasy that will lead to the ideal outcome you would like to have. This is *your* fantasy; you are completely in charge and can fantasise *anything* you want. Fantasise the situation/events as though they are happening *now*. Then return to awareness of your body, and notice any *differences* between the present and your previous sensations. Continue in this way, switching between grounding and your fantasy until your body is completely relaxed and your fantasy is completely fleshed out to your full satisfaction. Finally, make a decision about one small step you can take as soon as possible, that will contribute to the manifestation of your fantasy; decide what this is, and when you will take it. Again, Ken Mellor has a "Creative Release" CD that gives similar instructions (Mellor, 2002.) Dyer offers an entire book and a six CD set (Dyer, 2004).

The technique is a useful adjunct to grounding, centring and witnessing and may also be used as a stand-alone exercise for any clients. As such, it is "very instrumental – a typical example of trying to use Subtle or even Causal insights in the service of the ego" (Rowan; personal communication). Beyond this, the optimal step is harnessing the Observer role and intentionality: this is the acme of ERICA as a method of influencing relationships.

The Observer role

People acquire the capacity to take a meta-perspective of issues or situations as part of the transformation from one stage of consciousness to another. When harnessed with awareness of roles, either in relation to the Contact Cube, a reciprocal or a role sequence, the enactment of this capacity is what I refer to as the Observers role. It is a personalised role like any of the other Contact Cube roles, but with an important difference.

The characteristic that enables me to differentiate between any other role and the Observer role is that in the latter case, I do not immediately identify with the content of my experience and thereby, lose sight of the fact that I have created whatever expectations I have of the other person, the situation and myself. In other words, the essence of accessing the Observer role lies in inculcating an *expectation that I am more than my expectations*. Moreover, it is *I* who created the expectations and *I* who can change them. In other words, individuals create their own reality, and thus, the Observer role is the gateway to choice between the other roles. Hence, it is always juxtaposed in between other roles.

Although this process leads one into the Beholder role, reflection on past role relations from the perspective of the Observer role, is a crucial aspect of the Contact Cube. The aim is to move from identifying patterns of past role relations, to reformulating one's own part of the reciprocal role(s), in order to be able to identify them in real time and enact other roles differently. This is the crux of the methodology of using Contact Cube roles. The Observer role and the capacity to take a meta-perspective, is the starting point of the reformulation process. Essentially, the Observer role is a set of expectations that fleetingly triggers instantaneous grounding, centring and witnessing and all the associated features of dis-identification. However, the ebb and flow of normal relationships seldom affords time for prolonged reflection and for most people, the Observer role is sustained consciously only for relatively brief periods. As soon as I relate my experience to a context – another person or a situation – the tendency is for me to identify with the other role. Nevertheless, it is precisely because, with practice, one can become grounded, centred and attain witnessing in a matter of seconds, that by definition, the Observer role triggers a dis-identification process. Metaphorically, it is not unlike learning to swim or to ride a bike. Once you have acquired the knack of keeping your balance, practice leads only to greater proficiency.

Because of the nature and brevity of the Observer role, it is not directly amenable to observation. Indirect indicators are *post hoc* accounts of the expectations people have of themselves in decision-making situations. It would seem that many people probably use the Observer role without having been taught grounding, centring and witnessing. My experience from asking questions such as "what were your expectations of yourself?", "how did you reach your decision?" is that those who make decisions congruently with the executive power of an integrated Adult ego state, do so when they are grounded and centred and *in situ,* and are able to thinking about their thinking. (Clearly, it is well-nigh impossible to discern witnessing in others; it is essentially an internal process.) It is when people are *not* grounded and centred that they use negative roles and upon enquiry, were operating from a contaminated Adult, or from Parent or Child. Although I have not systematically compared the frequency of positive vs. negative roles used by those who have been taught the meditative techniques, my impression is that "meditators" are more likely than non-meditators to give coherent accounts of self-expectations, use more positive than negative roles and generally, pay attention to grounding and centring.

Even a fleeting or "minimal" experience of the Observer role seems to have a profound effect. Many clients who learn the techniques described above, continue to meditate after completing their therapy. The reasons for this may be because accessing the Observer role is an affirmation of one's very existence. My guess is that most transactional analysis practitioners would probably describe this as an affirmation of being (Levin 1988, Clarke 1998) or a permission to counter a "don't exist" injunction (Goulding and Goulding, 1979), but I think there is more involved. Using or exercising one's self reflective awareness without identifying with the content of one's experience, is a serious therapeutic tool. Learning to witness one's experience implies not just insight into or dispassionate awareness of one's own process, but the beginnings of using insights to make new choices. For those who use dissociation as a means of dealing with their experience, learning to "witness", to dis-identify with or from their experience, while remaining grounded or in contact with another person, is often the nub of their subsequent growth.

The Observer role, self and contact

As described in **Chapters 8** and **9**, the Contact Plane represents a threshold between positive and negative roles. It is also the location of the Observer self and the Observer role, the locus of which will depend on different ways of conceptualising and using self. Extending Rowan and Jacobs's three way categorisation of the use of self to include practitioners in educational and organisational settings, **Figure 23.1** shows how the Observer role may be incorporated in (or on) the Contact Plane.

In **Figure 23.1** the Contact Plane has three areas of contact corresponding to different ways of understanding and using self. Rowan and Jacobs "call these 'possibilities' or 'positions': they may often be referred to as 'levels', but we do not wish to suggest that any one is superior to another" (Rowan and Jacobs 2002, p. 4). In **Figure 23.1**:

- The outer area represents the transpersonal use of self and in particular, contact that is probably associated with the fourth level of role enactment. This is full-blown use of ERICA including attention to somatic processes and the meditational techniques described above. The distinguishing characteristic is an embracing of the transpersonal dimension where the normal boundaries of time and space no longer apply. Self is defined in intersubjective terms as a process.

- The middle area refers to the relational use of self [1] – epitomised by the recent interest in the "relational tradition in transactional analysis" (see the April, 2005 issue of the Transactional Analysis Journal). Contact is associated with roles at the social, psychological and existential levels. Self may be defined in structural terms – either in the traditional Bernean sense of the moving self, or as a discrete entity advocated by Hargaden and Sills (2002).

- The inner area represents the instrumental use of self. In educational and organisational settings, contact is linked with roles at the social and psychological levels, and may be extended by therapists and counsellors to accommodate the existential level. Self may be defined in the traditional Bernean sense of the moving self.

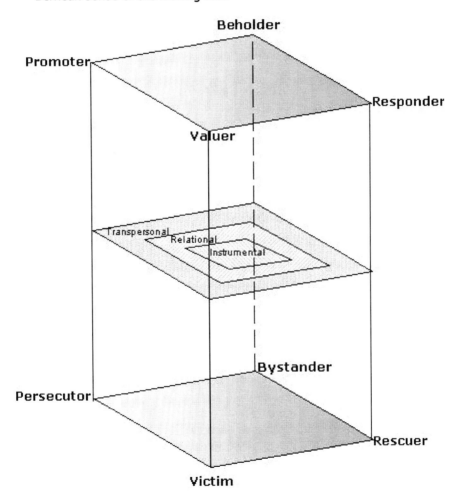

Figure 23.1

---

[1] I prefer "relational"; "authentic" seems to imply that the transpersonal and instrumental levels are somehow "inauthentic" in the everyday sense of that word.

329

The inner area is contained within the middle area, which, in turn falls within the outer area. This implies that a practitioner holding a transpersonal position may comfortably operate in the other two areas. Someone operating from a relational position is unlikely to want, or be able, to use the transpersonal dimension. Similarly, exponents of the instrumental position are unlikely to be able to extend themselves into the relational and transpersonal areas.[1]

However, I would caution against taking these positions too literally or simplistically; Rowan and Jacobs devote an entire volume to these complex features of relationships, and their views have all manner of implications for training counsellors and psychotherapists (for example, see Rowan 2005). The most extreme position is that anyone practicing a relational approach would need to undertake personal psychoanalysis. Personally, I don't believe this to be the case; sustained meditational practice is an equally tenable option that leads naturally to transpersonal dimensions. Personally, I think a combination of personal therapy and meditation is probably necessary. However, this debate is beyond the scope of this book. My point is that ERICA accommodates all three uses of self and the Observer role is the variable, conceptually and in practice, that permits the practitioner to move freely about the Contact Plane – according to the nature of the relationships in which they are involved.

Review of Part Six

In contrast to a *transpersonal* view of consciousness, transactional analysis is a Westernised view of the world that emphasises the pre or *intra-personal* (ego states, scripts) and *interpersonal* (transactions and games) aspects of human interaction. Viewing human development as a spectrum of consciousness leads to an understanding of identity, trance, dissociation and the self, that includes the Observer self and the capacity for self-reflective awareness.

The concept of the shadow and its resolution via body/mind unity is not addressed in any depth by transactional analysis theory. Some of the recently developed energy therapies offer one way of tackling this issue. The indications that contact at a transpersonal level are relevant to shadow phenomena, warrants further exploration.

Grounding, centring and goal setting are techniques that can be taught routinely to facilitate witnessing – an extension of one's natural self-reflective awareness. Witnessing represents the beginnings of deliberately exploring aspects of consciousness at a transpersonal level where "normal" consciousness no longer has to remain "as a defensively contracted state of reduced awareness" (Walsh and Vaughan 1996, p. 17).

All this is encapsulated in the Observer role. The Observer role is not an esoteric abstract concept and involves more than self-reflective awareness. It is a set of expectations that operate catalytically at the transpersonal level of consciousness to trigger access to positive Contact Cube roles. Self is experienced ontologically and epistemologically as a *relational* process. Such a view of self is consistent with existing transactional analysis theory and, additionally, legitimates the use of transactional analysis at a transpersonal level to explore aspects of spirituality that at present lie beyond the 'orthodox' model of transactional analysis. The implications of such a view of self is that transactional analysis can 'take on board' the notion of unconscious processes that go beyond roles, yet enrich relationships at the inter-personal level.

---

[1] Another useful way of thinking about the Contact Plane is to consider the notion of memes (Beck and Cowan, 1996) outlined in **Appendix B.** Essentially, Beck and Cowan describe levels of consciousness as a spiral of values and behaviours characteristic of individuals within a given culture. They refer to these as "memes" and use colours as a way of differentiating between levels. Without pre-empting familiarity with this material, Rowan's instrumental and relational positions are green and the transpersonal is yellow. See **Appendix B** for details of each colour.

Key Points 23

23.1   **ERICA** involves a "re-engineering" of normal developmental processes – a framework for **re-learning** a *normal developmental task* by correcting dysfunctional role behaviours.

23.2   The **Observer role** is based on **expectations**. Grounding, centring and witnessing provide a trigger for the Observer role as *a meta-perspective of their relationships*.

23.3   Being **grounded** entails being simultaneously aware of internal sensations and external events.

23.4   **Centring** entails being grounded, being aware of a sense of self in relation to your body.

23.5   **Witnessing** involves a state of consciousness where you do not identify with whatever it is you are noticing.

23.6   For most people the ability to **blend observer** and the **observed** usually takes months (or even years) of practice under the guidance of an experienced teacher.

23.7   Many clients opt to pursue **meditation classes** with an experienced teacher in addition to therapy.

23.8   For some people, *witnessing* can sometimes lead to **dissociation** – which is why *being grounded* should be presented as *a precursor* to being able *to centre or witness*.

23.9   Experiencing **transpersonal** realms of awareness is a natural, if not inevitable, outcome of normal development.

23.10 Grounding centring and witnessing may be taught **in conjunction** with Contact Cube *roles* and other *routine therapeutic interventions,* or as 'stand alone' methods for *self-affirmations* and *relaxation*.

23.11 Learning about **witnessing** is not only an opportunity **for personal growth**, it enables a practitioner to be better equipped to *recognise* and explore *spiritual issues* with those clients who present them.

23.12 **Teaching** clients *grounding, centring* and *witnessing* is a task within the skills **repertoire** of any competent practitioner, and for many clients, will lead naturally to increasing use of *self-reflective awareness.*

23.13 I would **caution** practitioners not to embark on this type of instruction before they have **mastered** the *techniques themselves.*

23.14 For those who take to the techniques and wish to pursue this interest seriously, I recommend an experienced **meditation teacher**.

23.15 Another technique for **goal setting** rounds off the enactment of the Observer role. Harnessing the Observer role and **intentionality** is the acme of ERICA as a method of influencing relationships.

23.16 The essence of *accessing* the **Observer role** lies in inculcating an *expectation that I am more than my expectations*. Moreover, it is *I* who created the expectations and *I* who can change them.

23.17 The Observer role is the variable that permits practitioners to move freely within the Contact Plane according to the contact implicit in **different uses of self.** Hence the Observer role is a set of expectations that operate **catalytically** at a transpersonal level of consciousness to **trigger** access to positive Contact Cube roles.

23.18 The Observer role legitimates the exploration of spirituality that at present lie beyond the 'orthodox' model of transactional analysis.

Chapter **24**

Coda

This closing Chapter gives a brief review of the main features of the models described in earlier Chapters and ends with a comment by a client on what he had learned about relationships.

Bridging the divides

Parts One to **Five** of this book offer a method of observing relationships which bridges the divide of health/pathology and practice/research in transactional analysis. In doing so, I have sought to diversify transactional analysis theory, practice and research, while avoiding the pitfalls of competitive labelling. The three models – the Contact Cube, Role Sequences and Role Imago Templates – facilitate the observation of any sequence of interaction, irrespective of setting or specialism. They are derived from existing transactional analysis concepts and similar ideas used in Cognitive Analytic Therapy. The scale and coverage of the models is extensive, but may be summarised as follows:

1. The models are presented in a series of logical steps that progressively bridge the triple divides by describing:
    - expected behaviours as formalised roles and actual behaviours as personalised roles and,
    - the Contact Cube as a three dimensional role space with,
    - positive and negative personalised roles linked by,
    - the Observer role, which implies,
    - a reformulation of self and the capacity for self-reflective awareness of,
    - four fundamental dimensions of relationships that give rise to,
    - the dialogical co-creation of reciprocal roles along these dimensions, characterised by,
    - distinctive qualities of contact associated with,
    - various bi-polar imago images.
2. The addition of formalised and situational roles to the personalised Contact Cube roles leads to:
    - a conceptual schema for examining power and influence and,
    - ways of categorising relationships as a variable linking persons and social structures,
    - a pragmatic way of tracking role functions in a group, relative to the stages of group development.
3. Behaviourally, personalised roles are enacted at three levels, referred to as a role profile giving a repertoire of:
    - twenty four role profiles for a single individual and hence,
    - the unit of interaction between the role profiles of two people is a reciprocal and,
    - a role sequence is a series of reciprocals that confirms or denies the mutual OK-ness of both parties.
4. Role profiles provide an immediate and powerful way of role modelling:
    - the process of inquiry, involvement and attunement,
    - at least three other role profiles that extend a person's behavioural repertoire of roles to include empowerment, challenge and assertion.
5. Reciprocals and role sequences are related to modes of time structuring revealing:

- an additional way of structuring time referred to as 'sets' – the positive counterpart of games,
- the duration, degree, density and diversity of role sequences are offered as suggestions for researchers to investigate, replicate, validate and review the use of role sequences.

6. Two principles and associated rules underpin the dynamics of all role sequences enabling us to:
   - superimpose role sequences on Berne's Formula G to formulate,
   - a three stage pattern of relationships of Contact, Communication and Confirmation yielding,
   - a bilateral account of games that follows the rules exactly.

7. If we map all the possible combinations of reciprocals and group these according to various criteria, eight distinctive categories of role sequences emerge covering:
   - all 24x24=576 reciprocals giving,
   - a complete taxonomy of bilateral dyadic relationships for role sequences with negative outcomes. The same logic may be applied to role sequences with mixed and positive outcomes, enabling us to identify and describe sets – the positive counter-part of games.
   - Effectively, the taxonomy of role sequences offers a means of bridging the divide of health/pathology.

8. Full blown application of all three Models integrates TA and aspects of Cognitive Analytic Therapy (CAT).
   - A basic role imago template (a BRIT) is used for understanding and mapping role relations. Heuristically it is similar to a script matrix (Steiner, 1974).
   - A Contextual Role Imago Template (cRIT) focuses on a particular context in which relationships occur giving a static picture of expected behaviours.
   - A Dynamic RIT (dRIT) combines the use of role sequences with the BRIT. dRITs are similar to the Self States Sequential Diagram (SSSD) used in Cognitive Analytic Therapy.
   - dRITS may be upgraded to a Group RIT (gRIT) for use in a group setting.

9. Client and practitioner contract for the client to teach the practitioner their model of the world by giving brief accounts of "Significant Incidents" that occurred between weekly sessions; "significant" is defined by the client.

10. Descriptions of the Significant Incidents are logged and later reviewed; patterns are identified – using the client's words/phrases.

11. Using dRITs is a five stage process: recognising the components of a RIT, joint discussion thereof with the practitioner and in-situ identification of role sequences, anticipation of role sequences with negative outcomes and finally, devising strategies for "converting" these to role sequences with positive outcomes.

12. Guidelines are described for teaching clients seventeen steps for compiling dRITs.

13. Teaching clients to compile their own RIT entails the use of a research-oriented methodology that bridges the divide of practice/research.

14. All the concepts are described in ways that are consistent with the fundamental TA values of mutual OK-ness. Relationships are seen as ongoing attempts to affirm mutual worth.

15. The methodology of regular reporting on Significant Incidents provides a steady stream of empirical data; this holds considerable promise for research into a wide range of phenomena.

The models enable a researcher to observe any number or type of Significant Incidents either *in vivo* or via audio-visual recording – irrespective of the interactive setting (individual, dyadic or group), transactional analysis specialism, or theory-specific model of interaction. All manner of research projects spring readily to mind. For example, one could compare the role profiles of a psychodynamic therapist and a Gestalt therapist; predictably the former would be less proactive than the latter. Such measures could be correlated with indices of outcome. Likewise, comparisons within a given model of psychotherapy or counselling may be used to compare the characteristic styles of different therapists and counsellors. Treatment regimes for different groups in a clinic or therapeutic community could be evaluated and compared. In an educational setting, one would expect a high correlation between positive Contact Cube roles and measures of Functional Fluency (Temple 1999). Similarly, indices of productivity, time keeping, and absenteeism and so on for individuals or work teams within and between companies, could be compared.

For all such ventures, the minimum requirements of a researcher would be an understanding of the Contact Cube model, the ability to identify the various levels of role enactment, understanding and being able to differentiate between types of Role Sequences and the operation of the dynamic rules, understanding a BRIT and the ability to conduct a focused interview or administer and interpret a BRIT questionnaire. The somewhat lesser demands for clients learning to research their own behaviour require the ability to identify the various levels of role enactment, and apply this knowledge via Significant Incidents as a dRIT. Once researchers and clients have achieved the above requirements, clients may concentrate on producing dRITS and researchers may focus on collating and analysing data.

Throughout **Parts One** to **Five** I have emphasised the need for a research-oriented mind set in advancing and developing new concepts. The scale of the research suggestions I have made will far exceed the resources of a single individual. If only for this reason, I urge colleagues and particularly new entrants to the field, to respond to the challenge of testing the models I have advanced. They are anything but complete and perhaps best regarded as a potential new direction in transactional analysis that, while correcting some of Berne's oversights and introducing alternative ideas, nevertheless, preserves the value base of TA.

Beyond the divides

Part Six extends the theoretical base of transactional analysis beyond inter-personal interaction into the realms of transpersonal experience. Again this is a logical sequence of ideas that unfold in the following order:

1. Transactional analysis does not pay much attention to transpersonal levels of awareness.
2. During transpersonal experiences one's sense of identity or self extends beyond (trans-) the individual.
3. Roles are based on expectations of self. The hallmark of the Observer role is autonomy, interdependence and an intersubjective sense of self. In TA, self is seen in relation to ego states. However, transactional analysis lacks a comprehensive view of self.
4. Self may be seen in relation the development of consciousness - a spectrum of consciousness – with ten stages that cover the life span.
5. Within the spectrum there are basic structures that tend to remain in existence and transition stages that tend to be replaced by subsequent phases of development.
6. The basic structures are like a ladder, each rung of which is a level of consciousness; the self is the climber of the ladder.
7. Progression from one rung to the next (a basic structure) brings a new perspective or view of reality - with a different (transition stage) sense of self-identity, a different set of self needs, and a different type of morality.

8. Everyone progresses from one developmental stage (rung of the ladder) to the next. One's proximate self identifies with the rung of the ladder, the content of current experience. From there, one is able to "look down" to the previous rung – the distal self without having to identify with it.

9. Identification with our experience, personal history and memories provides a sense of self-recognition, a sense of self. Wolinsky defines aspects of our self image identities as "trance identities". In TA we categorise these as the content of Parent and Child. The only difference between the two points of view is that, in transactional analysis, the classification is of ego states, whereas Wolinsky classifies trance-identities.

10. There are two basic states of consciousness – natural and altered. Natural states are waking, dreaming and deep sleep. Altered states include trance, drug-induced states, peak experiences, near death experiences, and meditative states. Trance states occupy the boundary between the natural and altered states of consciousness and are linked with the spontaneous emergence of other hypnotic phenomena, such as dissociation.

11. The function and origins of dissociation are relevant to our use of the Observer self. A dissociated subpersonality results when facets of the "I" are split off while consciousness is still identified with them. Therapy involves converting hidden subjects to conscious objects.

12. Our capacity for self-reflective awareness means we are able to witness our own experience – without having to use dissociation as a defence mechanism or having to identify with the object of our attention.

13. Several other therapies (psychosynthesis, hypnotherapy, NLP and perhaps to a lesser extent, psychodrama) include and use witnessing and/or dissociation either explicitly or indirectly.

14. In ERICA self is a *process* - the experience or ongoing awareness of one's own presence or existence and one's capacity to define one's self in relation to a context – a unit of consciousness with the capacity for self-activation. This is very different to the traditional TA view of self. The development of ego states parallels the development of self.

15. People change when they are sufficiently uncomfortable, or when they give up striving to become something or someone they are not. Change occurs when one becomes what one is, not when one tries to become what one is not. ERICA facilitates this paradox.

16. Consideration of the shadow and somatic processes raises the issue of the unconscious. It is essential to view unconscious processes developmentally. Historically, transactional analysis does not encompass "the unconscious" as a distinct, well formulated concept.

17. It has been suggested that the role that is not occupied at the social, psychological and existential levels during negative outcome role sequences, must exist at an unconscious level as the shadow. I regard the suggestion with some caution because:
    - of the "pre-trans fallacy" or difficulty inherent in interpretations of unconscious processes,
    - we can only accept this idea if we are willing to acknowledge that shadow phenomena arise from the operation of repression and the return to the unconscious of material that was once conscious.

18 It is helpful to regard "the unconscious" as consciousness without awareness, and to think about unconscious processes in developmental terms. In this respect, negative roles may be regarded as displays of an archetypal mythic worldview.

19 For some clients, ERICA may be used as a brief therapy in conjunction with hypnotic techniques that exploit unconscious processes.

19. Not many transactional analysis practitioners explicitly use "bodywork" as a therapeutic tool.

20. ERICA uses EFT to facilitate symptom relief for clients. This is a tremendously empowering technique.

21. Simple yoga postures and other techniques having to do with dissolving muscular tension that mask particular emotions are also helpful; the latter should be used with caution.

22. Systematic research is needed to explore the contact associated with the fourth level of role enactment.

23. ERICA involves a "re-engineering" of normal developmental processes – a framework for re-learning a normal developmental task by correcting dysfunctional role behaviours. Experiencing transpersonal realms of awareness is a natural outcome of normal development.

24. The Observer role is based on expectations. Grounding, centring and witnessing provide the basis of the Observer role as a meta-perspective of relationships.

25. Being grounded means being simultaneously aware of internal sensations and external events. Centring entails being grounded, being aware of a sense of self and then locating this sense of self in relation to your body. Witnessing involves a state of consciousness where you do not identify with whatever it is you are noticing.

26. For some people, witnessing can lead to dissociation. Grounding should be taught as a precursor to centring or witnessing.

27. Grounding, centring and witnessing may be taught in conjunction with Contact Cube roles and other routine therapeutic interventions, or as 'stand alone' methods for self-affirmations and relaxation. Practitioners are advised not to embark on this type of instruction before they have mastered the techniques themselves.

28. Goal setting is a useful adjunct to the three meditative techniques described above.

29. The Observer role inculcates an expectation that I am more than my expectations. It is I who created the expectations and only I who can change them. The Observer role is a set of expectations that operate catalytically at the transpersonal level of consciousness to trigger access to positive Contact Cube roles.

30. The Observer role, and the associated view of self, legitimates the use of a transpersonal level of awareness to explore aspects of spirituality that, at present, lie beyond the 'orthodox' model of transactional analysis. The implications of such a view of self is that transactional analysis can 'take on board' the notion of unconscious processes that go beyond roles at an inter-personal level.

ERICA - limitations and future developments

The limitations of this volume's account of ERICA are mainly that I have not explored the many nuances of contact that accompany roles as a major component of relationships. The notion of qualities of contact barely scratches the surface that the depth a more extensive description will add. The foundations are laid and future developments will need to focus on more explicit descriptions of defence mechanisms associated with types of role sequences and, within these, various clusters of reciprocals. Likewise, in relation to positive roles, there will need to be parallel accounts of openness and intimacy and similar non-defensive varieties of contact. Educational and organisational practitioners of transactional analysis are particularly well placed to contribute to such developments. In more precise terms, I anticipate a link between learning about roles and the neuroplasticity of affective states (Goleman, 2003 – a crucial reference for specialist researchers).

Secondly, imago images need to be fleshed out to encompass a thesaurus of items correlated with role sequences and reciprocals, which take account of developmental factors, cross cultural variables and differences, and possibly, gender differences. The demands of any such endeavours will challenge practitioners and researchers of all persuasions and specialisms.

Both these areas of interest as well as the detailed suggestions for further development scattered throughout previous pages, are beyond the resources of individuals isolated from a community of practitioners professionally committed to exchanging research-oriented accounts of practice. My hope is that this book will have contributed to this process.

Apart from the quotations at the very end of this book, I have not explicitly addressed soul and Spirit per se. Personally, I am most interested in this area of development – developing skills for honing the capacity to communicate and relate to others at a transpersonal level in addition to "normal" interpersonal contact. This is something we all do all the time. My aim is to do so more consciously and in a way that would integrate many of the widely available meditational exercises with therapeutic practice. Effectively, most teachers of meditation teach protégés how to manage trance states for the purposes of growth, rather than therapy. Harnessing such skills for therapeutic ends seems relatively unexplored. However, relating to others at a 'spiritual' level, demands reflexive research (Etherington, 2004) and probably renders distinctions between models and therapeutic modalities redundant.

The final frontier of development for furthering the efficacy of ERICA concerns mind-body holism. My fantasy is that there has to be distinctive patterns of bodily energy and sensations associated with various roles, imago images and qualities of contact that are sufficiently general across populations to be identified and systematically mapped. There is already a wealth of such information that forms the basis of various body therapies such as Radix, Rolfing, bioenergetics and the like. But I think the net may be cast even wider than this. My limited experience of Qigong and the emerging fields of energy therapies suggest a richness of resources awaiting exploration and ethical exploitation for healing.

An integral approach to relationships

Integral means "of or pertaining to a whole". Approach means "move towards, come or draw near". The object of the phrase is "relationships". I have shown that relationships may be described in terms of roles, imagos and contact. My hope is that readers will agree – or at least agree in part. I have also detailed ways of teaching clients to research their own behaviour and explored ways of how this maybe done in parallel with/by using TA concepts at a transpersonal level.

One of my clients, on leaving the therapy group, commented:

"I've been in the group now for nearly two years and I've seen people come and go – leave the group. So I know what you're going to ask me – what have I learned? Well, I've learned lots about different words that mean that things we do, have names – like strokes and roles and things like that. But the most I learned, what I know now about me and other people, is about relationships. Relationships is what matter most; not just me and other people, but also everything else – like what goes on in the whole world. I don't know how to say it properly, but there's nothing else – like me or you - that's important like relationships. What I mean is that there is no real me or you, without relationships."

Appendix A

Structure of the Contact Cube

The aim of this Appendix is to consider the psychological assumptions upon which the Contact Cube is based and consider how these may be most meaningfully depicted.

Analogies and metaphors

Analogies and metaphors need to be alike in some respects that are clearly understood: and unlike in other respects that are clear also. The boundaries between ego states, for example, are like the boundaries between circles. TA has a long tradition of representing psychological processes in diagrammatical form. However, the choice of any particular two-dimensional shape to represent a theoretical concept, thereby aiding our understanding of the written text, is somewhat arbitrary. It is only by agreement within the TA community that particular symbols have become standardised and immediately recognisable, the use of circles to represent ego states being the most obvious examples. Here circles are used as symbols and have no mathematical relevance in respect of size, relative location or, indeed shape; Berne could just as well have used triangles rather then circles and there is no particular reason why the circles are stacked one above the other. Nevertheless, in depicting Parent, Adult and Child as three separate circles, Berne was making the point that there is a fundamental psychological principle involved; the circles represent boundaries. They symbolise different and separate psychological processes.

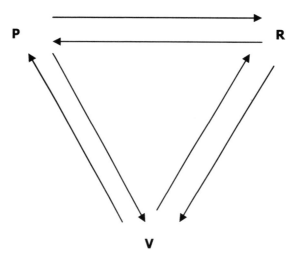

Figure AA.1

Since Berne's first use of symbols in this fashion, TA writers have continued to represent psychological processes without paying too much attention to the format of their diagrams and particularly, the mathematical implications of any chosen shape. For example, the Karpman Drama Triangle in **Figure AA.1** shows, or at least, implies that the relative positions of the roles, form an isosceles triangle - as shown in **Figure AA.2**.

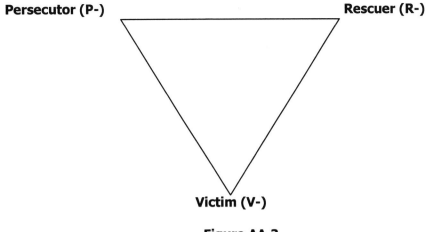

Figure AA.2

Mathematically, the distinguishing feature of an isosceles or equilateral triangle is that all the angles are equal to 60° and all the sides are the same length. In choosing this shape to depict the relationship between the roles, was Karpman implying anything more than the fact that people switch from one role to another in a fairly predictable fashion during a game? Probably not, but the layout does incline one to some interesting speculations. For example, are the three roles psychologically 'equidistant', or, to put it another way, is the change from say, Rescuer to Victim the same as a change from Rescuer to Persecutor? There is no a priori reason for assuming such changes are not in themselves the same phenomenon – a change from one role to another. In all probability, the diagram was never intended to illustrate anything more than the fact that role switches may occur in various ways; empirical data indicating additional features of the role relationships either warrant a different diagram or written commentary explaining how the new features may be accommodated in the existing diagram. Clearly, if one is starting to use diagrams to postulate more precise relationships than those normally used in the TA literature, then the need for the relationship to be accurately reflected by its pictorial representation, becomes more demanding.

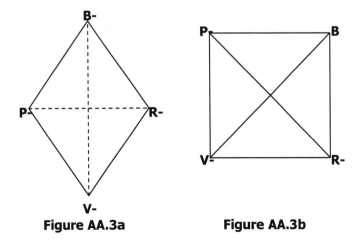

Figure AA.3a   **Figure AA.3b**

Throughout this book, in explaining the relationship between Contact Cubes roles, I have referred to *positive* and *negative* roles and secondly, described their relative positions as the corners of two squares that form the base and top of the Cube. While this is a sufficient and accurate enough description for adding a visual dimension to the written account of the roles, it does not explicitly address the psychological assumptions upon which a graphical depiction of the processes involved are (or are not) founded. For example, if one extends the Drama Triangle by simply adding the Bystander role, the result is either a diamond or a square – as shown in **Figures AA.3a** and **AA3b**

The diamond shape preserves the original Drama Triangle and adds a second triangle (P-, B-, R-), but locates the Bystander role further away from Victim than from Persecutor or Rescuer. A square has all four roles equal distances apart around the perimeter, but because the diagonals of a square are greater than the sides, the roles at opposite corners (P- and R-, B- and V-) appear to show, or at least imply, that a change from Persecutor to Rescuer (for example) is somehow different to a change from Persecutor to Bystander.

But does it matter if the diagram is not a 'true' representation of the processes involved? As long as we are clear that the diagram is no more than an illustration, a metaphor for the psychological processes involved, then we need not bother with the mathematics, providing we specify what the 'psychological processes' are. Given that in many respects we do not know precisely what the psychological process are the most we can do is make assumptions and attempt to illustrate these in ways that are not wildly incongruous. For example, it would have been incongruous for Berne to have depicted Parent and Child as circles and Adult as a triangle; quite reasonably, readers would have wondered what was special about Adult that did not apply to the other ego states.

Models

In contrast to analogies and metaphors, models go beyond like and unlike features of the psychological processes they represent. In addition to like and unlike aspects of whatever they represent, good models have an additional feature: they should not merely seek to summarise what is known, but should give scope for further exploration. The model itself can be studied for its properties and this may suggest new possibilities (or otherwise) and raise new questions. With appropriate yet cautious mathematical consideration, the Contact Cube may be treated as such a model. In so doing, I need hardly point out that it is a fundamental mistake ever to identify a model for "reality". Even in the pure sciences, the mathematical constructs of physics, for example, are so beautiful and effective that it is an occupational hazard to suppose that they are the reality.

In much the same way as Berne consistently portrayed ego states as separate but related concepts, I have used shapes to represent the ways in which Contact Cube roles are related: I have referred to the roles forming positive and negative squares. However, it is mathematically more accurate to regard the roles as forming two prisms. The rationale of this view is outlined below.

If we assume that changes from one role to another all entail psychologically identical processes, it makes sense to think of them as psychologically separate yet related and therefore locate them equidistantly. The only way in which we can do so is to use three dimensions. This is difficult to illustrate in two dimensions, but you can make a simple model by drawing a four triangles each with 60 ° angles as shown in **Figure AA.4.** Cut out the large triangular shape (BBB) and fold upwards along the dashed lines. Tape the sides together so that point B+ becomes the apex of the PRV based prism. Make another prism, using lower case notation for the negative roles

Mathematically, each prism with four planes (surfaces or sides), four vertices (formed at the points where three planes meet), and six edges (formed where two planes meet), and is known as a tetrahedron.

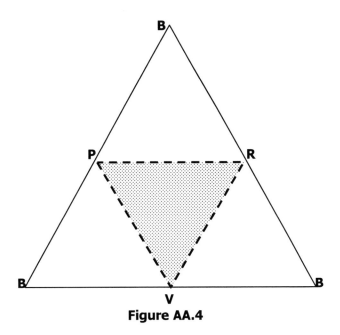

Figure AA.4

The way in which the two prisms are related is considerably more complex. Locating four points equidistantly from each other on three planes requires the two prisms to become enmeshed, resulting in a twenty-four sided star shape with eight vertices. Hence attempting to represent psychological "distance" between the roles, makes the "Cube" a complex polyhedron – mathematically referred to as a stella octangula[1]. The price tag of this solution is that the roles can only be regarded as equidistant if one accepts the restriction that "movement" between roles is confined to the surface of the polyhedron, or through the common origin of all the vertices.

While the planes of the polyhedron permit the co-planar roles to be equidistantly located, they also preserve the other psychological assumptions made about the location of roles in the Contact Cube, most notably, that there are four bi-polar dimensions all of which require "crossing" the Contact Plane. However the Star seems to impose a restriction; the roles can only be equidistantly located from one another if one assumes that "movement" from one role to another is confined to or bounded by the surface of the Star. This restriction provided the inspiration for the idea that the Observer role may be located meaningfully on the Contact Plane at two Contact Points for each role – or at the origin of all the points; a single point right in the middle of the Contact Plane. This raises fascinating challenges for further research into the psychological processes involved.

Although the mathematical relations between the dimensions of the Star aided my thinking about the psychological processes involved, there came a point where the model, like scaffolding used in building a house, needed to be discarded. Given the level of analysis involved, I settled for replacing the complexity of the polyhedron, with the metaphor of a cube. Research-minded readers with a mathematical bent may wish to consider the trigonometry of a stella octangula and use catastrophe theory (Poston and Stewart 1996) to explore changes of roles at three levels.

---

[1] A wireframe version of the stella octangula is sometimes known as the merkaba and imbued with mystic properties; see http://mathworld.wolfram.com/StellaOctangula.html or http://www.korthalsalters.com for a origami model.

Spiral Dynamics

Spiral Dynamics is the term coined by Beck and Cowan (1996) for their elaboration and documentation of the work of Clare Graves. They describe him as "an obscure professor of psychology in the years following World War II". He died in 1986 and only now are his ideas becoming widely known and recognised as an overarching system that explains how we can integrate the complexities of a biological, psychological and sociological view of humankind. The basis of his theory is that:

> "..the psychology of the mature human being is an unfolding, emergent, oscillating spiraling process marked by progressive subordination of older, lower-order behavior system to newer, higher order systems as an individual's existential problems change. Each successive stage, wave, or level of existence is a state through which people pass on their way to other states of being. When the human is centralized in one state of existence, he or she has a psychology particular to that state. His or her feelings, motivations, ethics and values, biochemistry, degree of neurological activation, learning systems, belief systems, conception of mental health, ideas as to what mental illness is and how it should be treated, conceptions of and preferences for management, education, economics, and political theory and practice are all appropriate to that state". (Graves, 1981)

Extensive research by Beck and Cowan (1996) has added to Graves' original ideas:

> "The theory of human emergence, change and transformation he proposed has been richly fleshed out and validated rather than replaced by contemporary research. Once you start thinking `like a Gravesian,' you will find this point of view has the power and precision to deal with people and social forces of all kinds, from hostile warlords and virulent `-isms' to the relief agencies caring for their victims and peace-keepers befuddled by the mess.
>
> The same principles of Spiral Dynamics apply to a single person, an organization, or an entire society. Since it describes human nature in a universal sense rather than through personality types or racial, gender, and ethnic traits, the model provides a common language for grappling with both local and global problems. It offers a unifying framework that makes genuinely holistic thinking and actions possible". (Beck and Cowan, 1996 pp. 29-30)

In practice Spiral Dynamics is used primarily as a means of facilitating organisational transformation. A central concept of Graves' work is the notion of "vMEMEs"

> "In *The Evolving Self* (Harper Collins, 1993), Mihaly Csikszentmihalyi uses the expression `memes' to contrast with `genes' in identifying the origins of human behavior as opposed to physical characteristics.
>
> The term itself was first introduced a number of years ago by Richard Dawkins who abbreviated the Greek root, `mimeme.' He and others have used it to describe a unit of cultural information such as a political ideology, a fashion trend, language, usage, musical forms, or even architectural styles. In the March 1994 issue of *Wired* magazine, John Perry Barlow states that: Dawkins' idea involves

'... self-replicating patterns of information that propagate themselves across the ecologies of mind, a pattern of reproduction much like that of life forms ... They self-reproduce, they interact with their surroundings and adapt to them, they mutate, they persist. They evolve to fill the empty niches of their local environments, which are, in this case, the surrounding belief system and cultures of their hosts, namely, us.'

Thus, what biochemical genes are to the DNA, memes are to our psycho-cultural 'DNA.' Genes are the information units of our physical nature derived from genetic contributions of mom and dad and properties inherited from our species. Memes are born, Csikszentimihalyi notes, 'when the nervous system reacts to an experience.' (*Evolving Self*, p. 120) They are the information units in our collective consciousness and transport their views across our minds.

A meme contains behavioral instructions that are passed from one generation to the next, social artefacts, and value-laden symbols that glue together social systems. Like an intellectual virus, a meme reproduces through concepts like dress styles, language trends, popular cultural norms, architectural designs, art forms, religious expressions, social movements, economic models, and moral statements of how living should be done.

Memes act much like particles. Spiral Dynamics proposes the existence of another kind of wave-like meta-meme, a systems or 'value meme' (ᵛMEME). These ᵛMEMEs are organizing principles that act like attractors for the content-rich memes Dawkins and Csikszentimihalyi describe. Big ᵛMEMEs are the amino acids of our psycho-social 'DNA' and act as the magnetic force which binds memes and other kinds of ideas in cohesive packages of thought. While they are initially shaped in each human mind, ᵛMEMEs are so vital they reach across whole groups of people and begin to structure mindsets on their own. ᵛMEMEs establish the pace and process for gathering beliefs. They structure the thinking, value systems, political forms, and world views of entire civilizations. ᵛMEMEs are linchpins of corporate cultures that determine how and why decisions are made. Our individual ᵛMEME stacks are central to our personalities and set the tone for relationships and whether we are happy campers or restless souls.

While genes evolve slowly, the decision systems formed by ᵛMEMEs are always on the move. ᵛMEMEs can be so dominant they seem like archetypes and are easily misinterpreted as 'types' of people. When several are in harmony, ᵛMEMEs resonate like the notes in a musical chord. However, ᵛMEMEs in conflict lead to troubled individuals, dysfunctional families, corporate malaise, fractured churches, and civilizations in decline and fall. Since they are 'alive,' vMEMEs can ebb and flow, intensify and soften like a string of Christmas tree lights on a dimmer. Several different ones may line up in support of a specific issue, idea, or project because: they share the values contents. At other times, people with essentially the same ᵛMEME decision-making frameworks may disagree violently over details of beliefs and what is 'the good', degenerating into holy and un-civil war.

We can have toxic, dangerous genes that predict physical troubles ahead. (How to deal with this knowledge may be the single biggest issue confronting medical ethicists today.) We can have nasty, unpleasant memes nestled among our attitudes, beliefs, and behaviors. Likewise, you may find misfit ᵛMEMEs in control of individuals, organizations, or cultures. The forces that enable us to respond to new problems in the environment can also block successful adaptation if the vMEMEs are unhealthy. Any strength, taken to the extreme, becomes a weakness. No wonder so many great cultures fade into historical footnotes. Their ᵛMEMEs wore down long before their monuments.

The ᵛMEMEs encode instructions for our world views, assumptions about how everything works, and the rationale for decisions we make. To clarify with an illustration, think about a fast-track, highly competitive, self-directed and status-sensitive Yuppie you have known. He or she strongly expresses what we will color-code as the **ORANGE** ᵛMEME. It often attracts things like dressing for success, driving the prestigious motor car, being seen in the right places, displaying the upscale spouse or partner, making the right career moves, and seeking autonomy along with the pot of gold.

As long as that ᵛMEME flashes and repeats its messages, the pattern will continue. It may be passed right on to the children who translate it into their own special music, fashion statements, and attitudes at the mall. The ᵛMEME's processes may be dominant throughout a neighborhood and central to the politics of a community. It may often, remain steady, or become even more intense. **ORANGE** is only one of eight principle ᵛMEMEs attached to the Spiral.

ᵛMEMEs are like a parallel life form. We are barely aware of their power because we can only infer their existence from behavioral displays and the artifacts swirling around them. But like the intestinal *compadres* that digest food for us, ᵛMEMEs assist the wetware of our minds to sort out what world is `really' like. *Spiral Dynamics* describes how they act at three different but clearly interrelated levels:

- **Individuals** possess dominant ᵛMEMEs which shape their life priorities and values, from most basic survival to global villager and beyond. Child development involves the awakening, guidance of, and learning to express ᵛMEMEs in healthy forms at appropriate times. The appearance of ᵛMEMEs often provokes a personal crisis in family and work relationships. Executive careers are highly vulnerable to these conflicts and overloads.
- **Organizations** have the ᵛMEMEs that will determine their success or failure in the competitive marketplace or the court of social responsibility at their basic cultural `DNA' level. While the task of O.D. (organization development) has long been to refine or realign the nuts-and-bolts of what companies do, it is quickly coming to include the awakening of new ᵛMEMEs. Memetic change is a greater challenge by far than just `working harder and smarter.'
- **Societies**, whether local or national, toss to and fro unless firmly grounded in the critical ᵛMEMEs which are congruent with the kind of worlds they occupy. Both upheaval and stability are products of ᵛMEMEs on the move, though few analysts manage to look through the fog of confusing ideas to see them.

These are only a few manifestations of the core ᵛMEMEs in action. The dynamic Spiral is the framework on which ᵛMEME awakenings expressions hang. It is the organizing principle that pulls the "Why?" from apparent chaos and translates our values languages. Instead of categorizing behavior or classifying people -- there are plenty of other models that do that - Spiral Dynamics will guide your search for the invisible, living ᵛMEMEs that circulate far deeper within human systems and pulsate at the choice-making center in the core intelligences of every person, organization, or society". (Beck and Cowan, 1996 pp.30-33)

Another extended quotation – this time, from Wilber (2000) - succinctly describes the first six of the eight `colours' of the memes.

"*1: Beige: Archaic-Instinctual*. The level of basic survival; food, water, warmth, sex and safety have priority. Uses habits and instincts just to survive. Distinct self is barely awakened or sustained. Forms into *survival bands* to perpetuate life.

Where seen: First human societies, newborn infants, senile elderly, late-stage Alzheimer's victims, mentally ill street people, starving masses, shell shock. Approximately 0.1 percent of the adult population, 0 percent power.

2: Purple: Magical-Animistic. Thinking is animistic; magical spirits, good and bad, swarm the earth leaving blessings, curses and spells which determine events. Forms into *ethnic tribes*. The spirits exist in ancestors and bond the tribe. Kinship and lineage establish political links. Sounds 'holistic' but is actually atomistic: "There is a name for each bend in the river but no name for the river."

Where seen: Belief in voodoo-like curses, blood oaths, ancient grudges, good-luck charms, family rituals, magical ethnic beliefs and superstitions; strong in third world settings, gangs, athletic teams, and corporate "tribes." 10 percent of the population, 1 percent of the power.

3. Red: Power Gods. First emergence of a self distinct from the tribe; powerful, impulsive, egocentric, heroic. Magical-mythic spirits, dragons, beasts, and powerful people. Archetypal gods and goddesses, powerful beings, forces to be reckoned with, both good and bad. Feudal lords protect underlings in exchange for obedience and labor. The basis of *feudal empires* – power and glory. The world is a jungle full of threats and predators. Conquers, outfoxes and dominates; enjoys self to the fullest without regret or remorse; be here now.

Where seen: the "terrible twos", rebellious youth, frontier mentalities, feudal kingdoms, epic heroes, James Bond villains, gang leaders, soldiers of fortune, New-Age narcissism, wild rock stars, Attila the Hun, *Lord of the Flies*. 20 percent of the population, 5 percent of the power.

4. Blue: Mythic Order. Life has a meaning, direction and purpose, with outcomes determined by an all-powerful Other or Order. This righteous Order enforces a code of conduct based on absolutist and unvarying principles of "right" and "wrong." Violating the code or rules has severe, perhaps everlasting repercussions. Following the code yields rewards for the faithful. Basis of *ancient nations*. Rigid social hierarchies; paternalistic; one right order; impulsivity controlled through guilt; concrete-literal and fundamentalist belief; obedience to the rule of Order; strongly conventional and conformist. Often "religious" or "mythic" [in the mythic-membership sense; Graves and Beck refer to it as the "saintly/absolutistic" level], but can be secular or atheistic Order or Mission.

Where seen: Puritan America, Confucian China, Dickensian England, Singapore discipline, totalitarianism, codes of chivalry and honor, charitable good deeds, religious fundamentalism (e.g., Christian and Islamic), Boy and Girl Scouts, "moral majority", patriotism. 40 percent of the population, 30 percent of the power.

5. Orange: Scientific Achievement. At this wave the self "escapes" from the "herd mentality" of blue, and seeks truth and meaning in individualistic terms – hypothetico-deductive, experimental, objective, mechanistic, operational – "scientific" in the typical sense. The world is a rational and well-oiled machine with natural laws that can be learned, mastered and manipulated for one's own purposes. Highly achievement orientated, especially (in America) toward materialistic gains. The laws of science rule

345

politics, the economy, and human events. The world is a chessboard on which games are played as winners gain pre-eminence over losers. Marketplace alliances; manipulate earth's resources for one's strategic gains. Basis of *corporate states*.

Where seen: The Enlightenment, Ayn Rand's *Atlas Shrugged*, Wall Street, emerging middles classes around the world, cosmetics industry, trophy hunting, colonialism, the Cold War, fashion industry, materialism, secular humanism, liberal self-interest. 30 percent of the population, 50 percent of the power.

6. Green: The Sensitive Self. Communitarian, human bonding, ecological sensitivity, networking. the human spirit must be freed from greed, dogma and divisiveness; feelings and caring supersede cold rationality; cherishing of the earth, Gaia, life. Against hierarchy; establishes lateral bonding and linking. Permeable self, relational self, group intermeshing. Emphasis on dialogue, relationships. Basis of *value communities* (i.e., freely chosen affiliations based on shared sentiments. Reaches decisions through reconciliation and consensus (downside: interminable "processing" and incapacity to reach decisions). Refresh spirituality, bring harmony, enrich human potential. Strongly egalitarian, antihierarchy, pluralistic values, social construction of reality, diversity, multiculturalism, relativistic value systems; this worldview is often called *pluralistic relativism*. Subjective, nonlinear thinking; shows a greater degree of affective warmth, sensitivity, and caring, for earth and all its inhabitants.

Where seen: Deep ecology, postmodernism, Netherlands idealism, Rogerian counseling, Canadian health care, humanistic psychology, liberation theology, cooperative inquiry, World Council of Churches, Greenpeace, animal rights, ecofeminism, post-colonialism, Foucault/Derrida, politically correct, diversity movements, human rights issues, ecopsychology. 10 percent of the population, 15 percent of the power. (Wilber 2001 pp. 9-11)

The waves are hierarchical in the sense that individuals, organisations and societies proceed or develop the above characteristics sequentially. Moreover, each of the above "waves" includes all the characteristics of its predecessors. In addition, waves go "down" as well as "up"; lower or earlier level waves are activated according to circumstances. Once established, all the memes are available to everyone at anytime. However, unless appropriately managed, the above six memes do not mix well – as evidenced historically on a global scale. The Middle East, for example, is a complex morass of ethnic red, patriarchal blue, orange techno-rationality and green pluralism – none of which take kindly to the points of view of the others. However, the fact that much of Beck and Cowan's work was undertaken in post-apartheid South Africa bears testimony to the validity of the approach.

The first six waves or colours are regarded as "first-tier" thinking, which fails to appreciate the significance and validity of other memes. In contrast, "second-tier" thinking appreciates the necessary role played by other memes. Second-tier thinking is described as the yellow and turquoise memes:

"7. *Yellow: Integrative.* Life is a kaleidoscope of natural hierarchies [holarchies], systems and forms. Flexibility, spontaneity, and functionality have the highest priority. Differences and pluralities can be integrated into interdependent, natural flows. Egalitarianism is complemented with natural degrees of ranking and excellence. Knowledge and competency should supersede power, status, or group sensitivity. The prevailing world order is the result of the existence of different levels of reality (memes) and the inevitable movement up and down the dynamic spiral. Good governance facilitates the emergence of entities through the levels of increasing complexity (nested hierarchy). 1 percent of the population, 5 percent of the power.

8. *Turquoise: Holistic.* Universal holistic system, holons/waves of integrative energies; unites feeling with knowledge; multiple levels interwoven into one conscious system.[13] Universal order, but in a living, conscious fashion, not based on external rules (blue) or group bonds (green). A "grand unification" ...... is possible, in theory and in actuality. Sometimes involves the emergence of a new spirituality as a meshwork of all existence. Turquoise thinking uses the entire Spiral; sees multiple levels of interaction; detects harmonics, the mystical forces, and the pervasive flow-states that permeate any organization. 0.1 percent of the population, 1 percent of the power". (Wilber, 2000 pp. 12-13)

I have deliberately cited Beck and Cowan (1996) and Wilber (2000) at length. To me, it is surprising that seasoned TA practitioners - and especially those involved in working with organisations - have not gleefully seized upon Graves's, Beck and Cowan's work, pointing out the obvious parallels between memes and ego states. In other words, I am suggesting (if not claiming) that the above accounts of the bio-social memes are not all that far removed from Berne's accounts of a psychological concept – namely, ego states – the corner stone of transactional analysis. Memes are nothing less than a bio-sociological description of what Berne was writing about at the same time as Graves was propounding a strikingly, if not exactly, similar idea. Nevertheless, differences prevail. Ego states are conceived of phenomenologically in Wilber's upper-left "I" language; memes tend to be pitched in third-person "it" terminology, and "as such, are a classic examples of subtle reductionism" and "the vast majority of scientists reject the concept of memes because of its lack of operational specificity" (Wilber 2000, p. 147).

However, help is at hand. Careful reading of Wilber's comments (Wilber 2000, pp. 146-149) and Drego's inclusion of the cultural influences on ego states (Drego, 1983) in conjunction with direct experience of using TA concepts in an organisational setting, holds the promise of harnessing Beck and Cowen's strategies for organisational change with all the potency of transactional analysis. I anticipate that this will herald an era of unparalleled expansion of the organisational application of TA. An "off the top" example is that the worldwide TA community is primarily green but struggling to contain pockets of regressive blue memes. Orange memes are in short supply. One of the characteristics of green meme organisations is an in-built resistance to progress to second-tier yellow memes.

Anyone grappling with a mapping of memes and other TA concepts has to resort to second-tier, yellow thinking to appreciate the validity, or otherwise, of the contention that ego states and memes are different sides of the same coin. At the very least, this could pose a challenging hypothesis for TA organisational practitioners to refute – or otherwise.

Appendix C

Role Sequences - Examples

The purpose of this Appendix is to describe the types of negative outcome role sequences identified in **Chapter 14**, the way in which some of these are truncated and how this accounts for differences between negative and positive outcome role sequences.

Examples of the eight types of NORS

The three hundred reciprocals that comprise the entire distribution of NORS may be categorised in relation to all the stages of the **3Cs** format described in **Chapter 13**, according to the yardstick of "*fully observable*", "*partially observable*" and "*not directly observable*".'

Competitive NORS have no Bystander roles at the social and psychological levels. There will always be one person who either starts as a Victim or one person who ends up as either a Victim or a Bystander – which is why I refer to these NORS as "competitive".

	Contact				Communication				Confirmation			
	External		Internal		Emergent		Revealed		Options		Closure	
Person	A	B	A	B	A	B	A	B	A	B	A	B
Profile #	1	9	9	1	1	9	18	1	9	18	9	18
Social	r	p	p	r	r	p	v	r	p	v	p	v
Psychological	v	r	r	v	v	r	p	v	r	p	r	p
Existential	p	v	v	p	p	v	r	p	v	r	v	r
Not used	b	b	b	b	b	b	b	b	b	b	b	b

Table AC.1

Table AC.1 shows the full 3Cs format for this type of role sequence. Note that the shaded areas signify non-observable processes. Bearing in mind that the reciprocals of the External phase are replicated at the Emergent stage, we can dispense with non-essential information and retain only that which is directly observable; we end up with **Table AC.5**

	Contact		Communication		Confirmation	
	External		Revealed		Closure	
Person	A	B	A	B	A	B
Role Profile #	1	9	18	1	9	18
Social	r	p	v	r	p	v
Psychological	v	r	p	v	r	p
Existential	p	v	r	p	v	r

Table AC.2

Remembering that role analysis usually requires more than the analysis of simple transactions, imagine a conversation along the following lines that match the reciprocals in **Table AC.2**:

Scenario AC.1

A: *"Poor dear! You can't reach! (sighs) I guess I'll have to get it for you"* **B:** *"Push off you interfering busybody!"*

A: *"Well I know when I'm not appreciated!"* **B:** *"Sorry, OK, you can get it. I can't reach".*

A: *Get it yourself – or wait till I'm ready!"* **B:** *"I'll just have to do without – that is, until you're ready".*

There are twelve Competitive NORS *configurations* – role sequences with reciprocals that have the same combinations of roles at the *social* and *psychological* levels. Each of these has four *variations* at the existential level. For example, in **Table AC.2**, person A is a social level Rescuer and a psychological level Victim; person B is a social level Persecutor and psychological level Rescuer. **Table 14.3** gave the four existential level variations for this configuration – replicated here for ease of reference:

	Variation 1		Variation 2		Variation 3		Variation 4	
Role profile #	1	9	1	12	3	9	3	12
Persons	A	B	A	B	A	B	A	B
Social level	r	p	r	p	r	p	r	p
Psychological level	v	r	v	r	v	r	v	r
Existential level	p	v	p	b	b	v	b	b

Table 14.3

With twelve configurations of Competitive NORS, each with four variations at the existential level, there are a total of forty-eight variations – an impossible number to visualise. For the record, and the benefit of research-minded readers, I list the configurations without their variations in **Table AC.3** – using the (by now) usual convention for rows – role profiles, social, psychological, existential and "not used" levels (both shaded).

Config. 1		Config. 2		Config. 3		Config. 4		Config 5		Config. 6		Config. 7		Config 8		Config. 9		Config. 10		Config. 11		Config. 12	
1	4	1	7	1	15	3	9	4	7	4	14	6	15	9	7	9	14	14	7	18	9	18	14
r	r	r	p	r	v	r	p	r	p	r	v	r	v	p	p	p	v	v	p	v	p	v	v
v	p	v	v	v	p	v	r	p	v	p	r	p	p	r	v	r	r	r	v	p	r	p	r
p	b	p	r	p	b	b	v	b	r	b	p	v	b	v	r	v	p	p	r	r	v	r	p
b	v	v	b	b	r	p	b	v	b	v	b	b	r	b	b	b	b	b	b	b	b	b	b

Table AC.3

Fortunately, you don't have to try to remember all these – for two reasons. In the first instance, forty of these variations involve the Bystander role – which means that what an observer will see is one, and sometimes two people withdrawing at the Closure stage of a role sequence. Of the remaining eight variations, four have Victim-Persecutor roles and four have Victim-Rescuer roles at the existential level.

	Variation 1		Variation 2		Variation 3		Variation 4		Variation 5		Variation 6		Variation 7		Variation 8	
Social	r	r	r	p	v	r	v	p	r	v	p	p	r	p	p	v
Psychological	v	p	v	r	r	p	r	r	p	p	r	v	p	v	r	p
Existential	p	v	p	v	p	v	p	v	v	r	v	r	v	r	v	r

Table AC4

Table AC.4 shows these eight variations. This underlines the point that Victims need (find) people who will either persecute or rescue them, but there are only eight ways of achieving this in a fully-fledged manner without resorting to the Bystander role. Note, however, that as soon as you can identify all three levels of a role sequence, you can predict the Closure. For example, in **Scenario AC.1**, the line *"Well I know when I'm not appreciated!"*, that occurs at the Revealed stage, implies a social level Victim and a psychological level Persecutor – which had hitherto been held at the existential level.

In more general terms, we know from the sep-pse-eps-nu rules described in **Chapter 13**,[1] that the existential level roles eventually become the social level roles at the Closure. Applying the rules to the starting reciprocals for each of the role sequences shown in **Table AC.4**, we see from the variations in **Table AC5**, that the Closures) all involve Victim roles.

Social level role at	1		2		3		4		5		6		7		8	
Emergent phase	r	r	r	p	v	r	v	p	r	v	p	p	r	p	p	v
Revealed phase	v	p	v	r	r	p	r	r	p	p	r	v	p	v	r	p
Closure phase	p	v	p	v	p	v	p	v	v	r	v	r	v	r	v	r

Table AC.5

The second reason for not having to keep track of all forty-eight variations is that with practice, the existential level may be intuited before the Revealed phase. In fact, detection of Competitive NORS is easier in practice than it may seem from the theory. The yardstick is the sense of competitiveness between the individuals – someone has to have their not-OK-ness confirmed. Judicious enquiry at the start or Emergent phase of the role sequence will often avert the payoff. To illustrate, if, upon hearing the opening line of **Scenario AC.1**, the

---

[1] The role occupied at the *social* level is the role a person will move towards at the *existential* level. It is also the role (in others) that is defended against, but the role the person seeks to confirm for him or herself and finally occupies at the *psychological* level. I refer to this as the **sep** dynamic rule.

The role occupied at the *psychological* level is the role a person will move towards at the *social* level. It is also the role (in others) that is defended against, but the role the person seeks to confirm for him or herself and finally occupies at the *existential* level. This is the **pse** dynamic rule.

The role occupied at the *existential* level is the role a person will move towards at the *psychological* level. It is also the role (in others) that is defended against, but the role the person seeks to confirm for him or herself and finally occupies at the *social* level. This is the **eps** dynamic rule.

The role **not** used (but existing as an additional option at a *fourth* level) is the role that is avoided in self and projected onto others.

therapist were to say, *"It seems you are in a social level role of Rescuer and a psychological level of Persecutor. What's your prediction about how this will end?"* The answer will often be sufficient to avert the otherwise inevitable persecutory Closure.

The upshot of all this is that in the ERICA revision of Berne's analysis of games, there are no more than two Closures for Competitive NORS – Persecutor-Victim and Rescuer-Victim. I have not attempted to assign colloquial names, but imagine them to variants of NIGYSOB-Kicked, and I'm only trying to help-Why don't you, Yes but …

Reversed NORS have only two of the four possible roles at social and psychological levels, but with the social level of one player matching the psychological level role of the other. The players swap roles at the at the Revealed stage of the role sequence. Like Confluent NORS, they have no Bystander role at the social or psychological levels. They represent a special case of Competitive NORS, with the switch of roles at the Revealed stage taking a surprising turn. For example, consider the following:

Scenario AC.2
A: *"Poor dear! You can't reach! I guess I'll have to get it for you"* **B:** *"I don't manage too well these days. I'm nowhere near as mobile as I used to be".*
A: *"I always seem to end up doing everything!!"* **B:** *"You take a break! I'll wait - until you're ready".*
A: *Remains silent; continues own activity.* **B:** *"I'm waiting!"*

	Contact		Communication		Confirmation	
	External		Revealed		Closure	
Person	A	B	A	B	A	B
Role Profile #	3	14	18	1	9	18
Social	r	v	v	r	b	p
Psychological	v	r	b	p	r	v
Existential	b	p	r	v	v	r

Table AC.6

The **Scenario** illustrates a distinctive feature of Reversed NORS – the presence of tangential transactions:

> "Tangential transactions are transactions in which the stimulus and response address different issues or address the same issue from different perspectives.… The participants appear to "talk past" each other and not "to" each other". (Schiff et. al. 1975, p. 58)

In practice, identifying roles requires more than consideration of a stimulus-response transaction. The brevity of **Scenario AC.2** gives a somewhat exaggerated example of tangential transactions involving the opening social level Rescuer-Victim roles. This is perpetuated by the redefinition accompanying the Revealed stage role switch. Usually, the psychological level role that accompanies a social level Rescuer-Victim pairing will have at least one person in the Persecutor role. This is not to say that redefining (tangential and blocking transactions) do not occur in other types of role sequences; they do. However, with Reversed NORS, tangential transactions provide useful confirmation of the defining characteristic – role reversal at the psychological level.

There are twelve Reversed NORS variations that are derived from only three configurations:

	Configuration 1		Configuration 2		Configuration 3	
Reciprocal #	3	14	4	9	11	15
Social	r	v	r	p	p	v
Psychological	v	r	p	r	v	p
Existential	b	p	b	v	b	r
Not used	p	b	v	b	r	b

Table AC.7

For each configuration, the Closure for three of the four variations involves Bystander roles. The fourth variation is a pairing at the Closure – Persecutor-Persecutor, Victim-Victim and Rescuer-Rescuer. Therapeutic options for responding to Reversed NORS at an early stage are in line with routine ways of dealing with tangential transactions.

Confluent NORS have the same role for both players at social and psychological levels. Even at the Revealed stage and Closure (the Switch and Payoff in Berne's Formula G), the players share the same roles at two and sometimes, three levels.

	Contact		Communication		Confirmation	
	External		Revealed		Closure	
Person	A	B	A	B	A	B
Role Profile #	1	9	18	1	9	18
Social	r	r	v	v	p	b
Psychological	v	v	p	b	r	r
Existential	p	b	r	r	v	v

Table AC.8

Again, allowing for the over-simplification of single transactions, imagine a conversation along the following lines that match the first reciprocal in **Table AC.2**:

Scenario AC.3
A: *"Poor dear! You can't reach! (sighs) I guess I'll have to get it for you".* **B:** *"Sorry, I'll wait till you're finished – or just get used to doing without".*
A: *"Why do I always end up having to do everything? – especially when I'm not appreciated!"* **B:** *I just have to get used to managing without".*
A: *"Stop whinging - and wait till I'm ready!"* **B:** *Says nothing.*

There are six Confluent NORS *configurations* – role sequences with reciprocals that have the same combinations of roles at the *social* and *psychological* levels – as shown in **Table AC.9**. Each of these has three *variations* at the existential level.

Unlike Competitive NORS, the Confluent variety does not have Drama Triangle payoffs for both parties. As we shall see, they end up with roles that are similar to those at the start of Bystander NORS.

	Config. 1		Config. 2		Config. 3		Config. 4		Config. 5		Config. 6	
Reciprocal #	1	3	4	6	7	11	9	12	14	16	15	18
Social	r	r	r	r	p	p	p	p	v	v	v	v
Psychological	v	v	p	p	v	v	r	r	r	r	p	p
Existential	p	b	b	v	r	b	v	b	p	b	b	r
Not used	b	p	v	b	b	r	b	v	b	p	r	b

Table AC.9

For example, in **Scenario AC.3** and the first configuration in **Table AC.9**, what an observer (researcher) would note at the Closure is person A clearly persecuting Person B. With person B in a Bystander role, the observer would have to decide whether to simply note the non-verbal behaviour (sighs, shrugs, walking away and so on), or proceed to ask relevant questions (such as *"What were you thinking/feeling at that time?"*). As previously suggested, this could well be an unwarranted change of the observer's formalised role.

And there is an additional twist. Although not apparent from **Table AC.6**, twelve of the eighteen variations have the same role profiles for both people at all three levels.

	Variation 1		Variation 2		Variation 3	
Reciprocal #	1	3	1	6	1	11
Social	r	r	r	r	r	r
Psychological	v	v	v	v	v	v
Existential	p	b	p	p	b	b

Table AC.10

To illustrate, **Table AC.10** gives the three variations for Config.1 of **Table AC.9**. Variation 2 shows a social level Persecutor-Persecutor payoff. In Bernean terms of colloquial names, this is Uproar. Similar pairings (Rescuer-Rescuer and Victim-Victim) at the social level arise from the other configurations. Matters start to get a little tricky at this point; you would need to write out all the variations to see how with Confluent NORS there are six ways of reaching the same social level payoffs of Bystander-Bystander.

In practice, people who get into Confluent NORS live up to the name I have assigned - roles become enmeshed. Because of this, these NORS are easily recognised. The therapeutic strategy for undercutting the payoffs consists of early interventions along the lines of *"It seems you are both social level Rescuers and psychological level Victims. What I want to know from each of you separately is how is this a problem for you?"*

My experience is that many people use the Bystander-Bystander payoffs of Confluent NORS as a way of withdrawing and sulking. Some Rescuer-Rescuer payoffs lead to the protagonists resolving to 'try harder next time'. Clients with borderline issues revel in the acting out potential of persecutory Closure or slide towards racketeering.

Racketeering NORS share the feature of having Bystander roles at the psychological level for both parties. By definition the observable interaction runs out at the Revealed phase of a role sequence.

Up until now I have used the term "racketeering" in the sense originally expounded by English (1971, 1972, 1976, 1979, 1987) – as a way of eliciting strokes for racket feelings. As such, racketeering is a process defined in terms of switches between ego states. Although these may be present in racketeering NORS, the emphasis is on a switch of roles rather than ego states. More specifically, racketeering NORS are a sub-category of negative outcome role sequences that are terminated at the Revealed stage, where the reciprocals have social level Bystander roles. From here on, I use the phrase "Racketeering NORS" ("Confluent Racketeering" and "Mutual Racketeering") in terms of this definition, and will continue to refer to "racketeering" a la English's concept where appropriate.

Confluent Racketeering NORS arise when the players occupy the *same* role at the social level. Being Bystanders at the psychological level, they withdraw instead of switching to Persecutor, Rescuer or Victim roles.

	Contact		Communication		Confirmation	
	External		Revealed		Closure	
Person	A	B	A	B	A	B
Role Profile #	2	2	(20)	(20)	(11)	(11)
Social	r	r	b	b	p	p
Psychological	b	b	p	p	r	r
Existential	p	p	r	r	b	b

Table AC.11

Scenario AC.4 is a minimalist account of Confluent Racketeering NORS that fits the reciprocals in **Table AC.11**. The shaded areas represent roles that are not immediately apparent.

Scenario AC.4
A: *"Poor dear! You can't reach! I'll get it for you". **B:** "Sorry, I'll wait till you're finished".*
A: *Continues own activity in silence, (but thinks "Damn nuisance!") **B:** Waits in silence (but thinks "Come on, hurry up and get finished.")*

Normally Confluent Racketeering has a more extended Emergent phase, which is roughly equivalent to the Response in a Bernean game. In a clinical setting, one therapeutic strategy is to interrupt the exchange of racketeering strokes. Another is to draw attention to the roles and explore predictions of the Closure and the associated imago images.

	Configuration 1		Configuration 2		Configuration 3	
Reciprocal #	2	2	8	8	13	13
Social	r	r	p	p	v	v
Psychological	b	b	b	b	b	b
Existential	p	p	r	r	p	p
Not used	v	v	v	v	r	r

Table AC.12

There are three configurations. Each has three existential level variations and all may occur in conjunction with English's concept of racketeering. I think English's sub-types (Helpless, Helpful, Bratty and Bossy) are similar to Confluent Racketeering, - but with two crucial differences. English's examples of the sub-types are couched in terms of ego state switches (rather than roles), and secondly, her concepts apply to a racketeer and a *non-racketeer*. In ERICA, *both* parties switch roles.

Mutual Racketeering NORS differ from Confluent Racketeering inasmuch as both players have different roles at the social and/or existential levels and Bystander roles at the psychological level. Instead of switching to Persecutor, Rescuer or Victim roles, both players withdraw, as in **Table AC.12**.

	Contact		Communication		Confirmation	
	External		Revealed		Closure	
Person	A	B	A	B	A	B
Role Profile #	2	8	(20)	(23)	(12)	(4)
Social	r	p	b	b	p	r
Psychological	b	b	p	r	r	p
Existential	p	r	r	p	b	b

Table AC.12

The detailed parameters of Mutual Racketeering differ from **Table AC.13** only inasmuch as there are different (rather than paired) roles at the social and existential levels. Additionally, there are four variations at the existential level for each of the three configurations.

	Configuration 1		Configuration 2		Configuration 3	
Reciprocal #	2	8	5	13	10	13
Social	r	p	r	v	p	v
Psychological	b	b	b	b	b	b
Existential	p	r	v	p	r	p
Not used	v	v	p	r	v	r

Table AC.13

These configurations are partially correlated with English's concept of racketeering in that the ego state switches occur at the same time as the role switches. The difference is that, as with Confluent Racketeering, *both* people switch to the Bystander role. With racketeering, there is only one person who switches ego states.

These fine grained distinctions have practical implications for trainers and practitioners. Students already familiar with racketeering are used to identifying ego state switches; with ERICA they need to "think meta" in terms of reciprocals. I have found it helpful to urge students to watch out for the mutuality of Mutual Racketeering – to see the process as the interaction between two people – a Bossy *and a* Bratty, for example. And this is not merely an academic or an educational point. Identifying Racketeering NORS has far reaching practical implications and applications. Together with indeterminate outcome role sequences (IORS), Racketeering NORS are by far the most frequent type of role sequence identified by the thirty nine clients I have taught to use ERICA. Moreover, clients with a history of symbiotic relationships seem to depend largely on racketeering and pastiming as modes of time structuring. Changing such patterns of relationships is a central feature of personal growth.

Unilateral NORS have the common feature of one or both people being a social or psychological level Bystander; the interaction does not start at all, or, if it does, it does not go beyond the Revealed stage of the 3Cs formula.

Single Exit NORS occur when a psychological level Bystander withdraws at the Revealed stage.

	Contact		Communication		Confirmation	
	External		Revealed		Closure	
Person	A	B	A	B	A	B
Role Profile #	1	8	(18)	(23)	(9)	(4)
Social	r	p	v	b	p	r
Psychological	v	b	p	r	r	p
Existential	p	r	r	p	v	b

Table AC.14

Scenario AC.6

A: *"Poor dear! You can't reach! (sighs) I guess I'll have to get it for you". **B:** Push off you interfering busybody!"*
A: *"Well I know when I'm not appreciated! **B:** Says nothing (but thinks" I hope I've not upset her too much.")*

I list the eighteen configurations: each has four variations at the existential level:

Config. 1		Config. 2		Config. 3		Config. 4		Config 5		Config. 6		Config. 7		Config 8		Config. 9	
4	2	3	5	4	8	1	8	4	9	2	11	4	17	1	13	5	14
r	r	r	r	r	p	r	p	r	p	r	p	r	v	r	v	r	v
p	b	v	b	p	b	v	b	b	r	b	v	p	b	v	b	b	r
b	p	b	v	b	r	p	r	p	v	p	b	b	p	p	p	v	p
v	v	p	p	v	v	b	v	v	b	v	r	v	r	b	r	p	b

Table AC.15a

Config. 10		Config. 11		Config. 12		Config. 13		Config AC		Config. 15		Config. 16		Config 17		Config. 18	
2	15	9	8	11	8	9	13	7	13	8	14	8	18	16	13	15	13
r	v	p	p	p	p	p	v	p	v	p	v	p	v	v	v	v	v
b	p	r	b	v	b	r	b	v	b	b	r	b	p	r	b	p	b
p	b	v	r	b	r	v	p	r	p	r	p	r	r	b	p	b	p
v	r	b	v	r	v	b	r	b	r	v	b	v	b	p	r	r	r

Table AC.15b

At this point, the way in which I have conceptualised and named role sequences – along with the truncated, if not over-simplified, single line 'transactional' examples – becomes an issue. That is, I have consistently emphasised that the unit of observation and analysis is the reciprocal, and, secondly, that we need not concern ourselves with who (person A or person B) starts the interaction. As far as we are concerned, reciprocals are isomorphic – AB is the same as BA. Provided we stick to this principle, there is no problem – conceptually. In practice, often, when person B withdraws at the Revealed stage, person A persists with their interaction. **Table AC.14** illustrates the case in point. Person B withdraws at the Revealed phase switch. If person A continues with their role profile 9 (observably, social level Persecutor, psychological level Rescuer), whether or not B responds (with whichever role), this should be treated as the start of another role sequence. This means that with Single Exit role sequences the 3Cs format is truncated, in the sense that the Revealed stage merges with and becomes the Closure.

Bystander NORS come in two varieties. The first are role sequences where one person is a social level Bystander who simply does not get started. The second is where one person is a Bystander at the psychological level. **Tables AC.18** and **AC.19** and the accompanying **Scenarios** illustrate these differences.

	Contact		Communication		Confirmation	
	External/Emergent		Revealed		Closure	
Person	A	B	A	B	A	B
Role Profile #	1	20	(18)	(9)	(9)	(2)
Social	r	b	v	p	p	r
Psychological	v	P	p	r	r	b
Existential	p	r	r	b	v	p

Table AC.16

Scenario AC.6
A: "Poor dear! You can't reach! (sighs) I guess I'll have to get it for you" B: Says nothing (but thinks "Interfering busybody!")

The non-shaded areas in **Table AC.16** are all that an observer would actually see. At most, the observer would have the tonality and body language of person A's opening statement with which to hypothesise about their psychological level role. With person B, the observer is on shakier ground in interpreting non-verbal behaviour as persecutory – as indicated by the medium shaded area. All the other shaded areas are hypothetical. Hence, even though one has prior indication of person A's social and existential level roles at the Revealed phase (as per the heavily shaded areas), there is at present insufficient hard data to justify anything other than regarding the role sequence as 'truncated'. If it transpires that sufficient evidence is accumulated by person A's clearly continuing with a verbal statement to which person B responds verbally, we would have to re-assess the status of this type of role sequence.

	Contact		Communication		Confirmation	
	External		Revealed		Closure	
Person	A	B	A	B	A	B
Role Profile #	2	12	(20)	(2)	(12	(20)
Social	r	b	b	p	p	b
Psychological	b	p	p	v	r	p
Existential	p	v	r	b	b	r

Table AC.17

Scenario AC.7
A: "Poor dear! You can't reach! I'll get it for you". *B:* "Says nothing (but thinks! "Interfering busybody!")
A: Says nothing (but thinks "Not likely - you do it yourself!")

The above argument holds even more so for the second type of the Bystander role. Person B's silence following A's initial verbal non-response makes the interpretation even more difficult. Clearly, we need empirical data before formulating more specific ground rules.

In all, there are 108 Bystander NORS, 72 of the first type and 36 of the second. They all have four variations at the existential level. I comment on the significance of these figures below.

Reciprocal Skull NORS are non-events as far as an observer is concerned. Both people are social level Bystanders. Fortunately there are not too many and for our purposes, we can simply note that there are nine configurations, some with three, two and one variations, giving a total of twenty one.

Table AC.18 gives rudimentary comparisons of observed and theoretical distributions of the various types of NORS based on data collection over an eleven year period.

Negative Outcome Role Sequences	Bilateral NORS			Lateral NORS			Racketeering NORS		Totals
	Competitive	Confluent	Reversed	Single Exit	Bystander	Reciprocal Skull	Confluent	Mutual	Predicted # NORS = 300
Variations # Observed # Theoretical	31 48	9 12	10 18	61 72	66 108	9 21	7 9	8 12	198 300
Total #s Observed Theoretical	47 78			136 201			15 21		198 300
Observed as % Theoretical Variations	64.5	75.0	55.6	84.7	61.6	47.2	78.9	66.6	66.0
Total Observed as % Theoretical Variations	60.3			67.7			71.40		66.0

Table AC.18

These figures represent little more than the fact that I have observed two-thirds of the theoretical distribution of NORS. In other words, **Table AC.18** gives a count, but says nothing about the frequency of occurrence of particular reciprocals. What is needed is clearly defined criteria for establishing inter-scorer reliabilities for categorising observed frequencies of occurrence of the types of reciprocals. Previous Chapters have laid the foundations for such a venture; my hope is that researchers will build upon these. In particular, I anticipate rich pickings for researchers interested in exploring, naming and describing the circumstances giving rise to the distribution of mixed and positive reciprocals.

References

Adler, A. (1963). Individual psychology. In Levitas, G. (Ed.) *The world of psychology.* New York: Braziller.

Agazarian, Y. (1997). *Systems-centered therapy for groups.* New York: Guildford.

Agazarian, Y. and Peters, R. (1981).*The visible and invisible group,* London: Karnac Books.

Agel, J. (1971). *The radical therapist.* New York: Ballantine.

Allen, J. R. (2000). Biology and transactional analysis 11: A status report on neurodevelopment. *Transactional Analysis Journal 30, pp. 260-26.8*

Allen, J. R. (2003). Concepts, competencies and interpretive communities. *Transactional Analysis Journal 30, 260-268.*

Allen, J. R. and Allen, B. A. (1991). Concepts of transference: A critique, a typology, an alternative hypothesis and some proposals *Transactional Analysis Journal 21, 77-91*

Allen, J. R. and Allen, B. A. (1997). A new type of transactional analysis and one vision of script work with a constructivist sensibility, *Transactional Analysis Journal 27, 89-98*

Almaas, A. H. (1996). *The point of existence – Transformations of narcissism in self-realization,* Berkley: Diamond Books.

American Psychiatric Association, (1995). *Diagnostic and statistical manual of mental disorders; DSM-IV.* Washington, DC: American Psychiatric Association.

Andreas, C. and Andreas, T. (1994). *Core transformations: Reading the wellspring within.* Real People Press: Moab, Utah.

Atherton, J. S. (2005). *Learning and Teaching:* Conversational learning theory; Pask and Laurillard [On-line] UK: Available at http://www.learningandteaching.info/learning/pask.htm

Atwater, P. M. H. and Morgan, D. H. (2000). *The complete idiot's guide to near death experiences,* Indianapolis: Alpha Books.

Avary, B. and Milhollon, B. (1997). The altered state: A missing link in ego state theory? *Transactional Analysis Journal, 27, 295-298.*

Bakhtin, M. M. (1986). *Speech genres and other late essays.* Austin: University of Texas Press.

Bales, R. F. (1950). *Interaction process analysis: A method for the study of small groups.* Cambridge, Massachusetts: Addison-Wesley.

Bannister, D. and Fransella, F. (1986). *Inquiring man.* London: Croom Helm.

Barkham, M., Evans, C., Margison, F., McGrath, G., Mellor-Clark, J., Milnes, D. and Connel, J. (1998). The rationale for developing and implementing core outcome batteries for routine use in service settings and psychotherapy outcome research. *Journal of Mental Health. 6, 35-37.*

Barnes, G. (1981). On saying hello: The script drama diamond and character role analysis. *Transactional Analysis Journal, 17, 22-33.*

Barnes, G. (1999a). About energy metaphors 1: A study of their selection, defense and use in Berne's theory. *Transactional Analysis Journal, 29:3, 96-108.*

Barnes, G. (1999b). About energy metaphors 11: A study of Schiff's applications *Transactional Analysis Journal, 29:3,186-187.*

Barnes, G. (1999c). About energy metaphors 111: Basic conceptual issues. *Transactional Analysis Journal, 29:4, 283-291.*

Barnes, G. (2000). Retrieving a flourishing psychotherapy: A transactional-cybernetic meditation on Transactional Analysis. *Transactional Analysis Journal, 30:3, 233-247.*

Barnes, G. (2002). *Psychopathology of psychotherapy: A cybernetic study of theory.* Unpublished doctorial dissertation, Royal Melbourne Institute of Technology, Melbourne, Victoria, Australia.

Barnes, G. (2004). Homosexuality in the first three decades of transactional analysis: A study of theory in the practice of transactional analysis psychotherapy. *Transactional Analysis Journal, 34: 126-155.*

Barnes, G. (1977). (Ed.) *Transactional analysis after Eric Berne : Teachings and practice of three TA schools.* New York: Harper's College Press.

Basch, M. F. (1988). *Understanding psychotherapy: The science behind the art* New York: Basic Books.

Bateson, G. (1972). *Steps to ecology of mind.* New York: Ballantine Books.

Beck, D. E. and Cowan, C. (1996). *Spiral dynamics: Mastering values, leadership and change.* Oxford: Blackwell Publishing.

Beisser, A. (1972). The paradoxical theory of change – in Fagan, J. and Shepherd, I. L. (Eds.) *Gestalt therapy now.* New York: Harper and Row.

Bennett, D. and Parry, G. (1998). The accuracy of reformulation in cognitive analytic therapy: A validation study. *Psychotherapy Research, 8, 64-103.*

Benjamin, L. S. (1993). Every psychotherapy is a gift of love. *Psychotherapy Research 3, 1-24.*

Benjamin, L. S. (1994). SASB: A bridge between personality theory and clinical psychology. *Psychological Inquiry 5, 273-316.*

Benjamin, L. S. (1996a). An interpersonal theory of personality disorders. In Clarkin, J. F. (Ed.) *Major theories of personality disorder.* New York: Guildford Press.

Benjamin, L. S. (1996b). *Interpersonal diagnosis and treatment of personality disorders.* New York: Guildford Press.

Benjamin, L. S. (2003). *Interpersonal reconstructive therapy: Promoting change in nonresponders.* New York: Guildford Press.

Bennis, W. G. & Shepard, H. A. (1956). A theory of group development. *Human Relations 9.4, 415-437.*

Berger, P. and Luckman, T. (1966). *The Social Construction of Reality: A Treatise in the Sociology of Knowledge.* Garden City, NY: Doubleday.

Berne, E. (1958). Transactional Analysis: A new and effective method of group therapy. *American Journal of Psychotherapy 12, 735-743.*

Berne, E. (1961). *Transactional Analysis in psychotherapy: A systematic individual and social psychiatry.* New York: Grove Press.

Berne, E. (1963). *The structure and dynamics of organizations and groups,* New York: Ballantine Books.

Berne, E. (1964). *Games people play. The psychology of human relationships.* Harmondsworth: Penguin Books.

Berne, E. (1966). *Principles of group treatment,* New York: Grove Press.

Berne, E. (1970, 1973). *Sex in human loving,* New York: Simon and Schuster.

Berne, E. (1971). *A layman's guide to psychiatry and psychoanalysis,* Harmondsworth: Penguin.

Berne, E. (1972). *What do you say after you say hello? The psychology of human destiny,* New York: Grove Press.

Bion, W.R. (1959). *Experiences in groups,* London: Tavistock.

Bion, W.R. (1970). *Attention and interpretation.* London: Tavistock.

Boholst, F.A. (2003). Effects of transactional analysis group therapy on ego states and ego state perception *Transactional Analysis journal. 33, 254-261.*

Bower, T. G. R. (1977). *A primer of infant development.* San Francisco: Freeman.

Bowlby, J. (1969). *Attachment. Volume I of Attachment and loss.* New York: Basic Books.

Bowlby, J. (1973). *Separation: Anxiety and anger. Volume II of Attachment and loss.* New York: Basic Books.

Bowlby, J. (1977). The making and breaking of affectional bonds *British Journal of Psychiatry 130. pp. 201-210.*

Bowlby, J. (1980). *Loss: Sadness and depression. Volume III of Attachment and loss*. New York: Basic Books.

Brandt, A. (1980) Self-confrontations *Psychology Today, Oct. 1980.*

Buber, M. (1923, English translation 1958). *I and thou*. New York: Charles Scribner and Sons.

Budgell, R. (1995). Being touched through space. Unpublished dissertation, Regents College, London.

Callahan, R. J. (with Trubo, R.) (2001). *Tapping the healer within*. Chicago: Contemporary Books.

Caloff, D. L. (1993). *Multiple personality and dissociation: Understanding incest, abuse and MPD.* Hazelden: Minnesota.

Campbell, J. (1949). *The hero with a thousand faces*. New York: Pantheon.

Campos, L. (2003). Care and maintenance of the tree of transactional analysis. *Transactional Analysis Journal, 33, 115-125.*

Canetti, E. (1973). *Crowds and power.* Harmondsworth: Penguin.

Caplan, M. (1999). *Halfway up the mountain: The error of premature claims to enlightenment.* London: Hohm Press.

Caplan, M. (2002). *Do you need a guru? Understanding the student teacher relationship in an era of false prophets.* London: Thorsons.

Carrington, P. and Craig, G. (2000). A meridian-based intervention for the treatment of trauma. *Journal of the International Society for the Study of Subtle Energies and Energy Medicine, 148-151.*

Cartwright, D. and Zander, A. (Eds.) (1960). *Group dynamics: Research and theory*, New York, Macmillan.

Cassius, J. (1980). *Horizons in bioenergetics: New dimensions in mind/body psychotherapy.* Memphis: Promethean Publications.

Childs-Gowell, E. and Kinnaman, P. (1992). *Bodyscript blockbusting: A transactional approach to body awareness.* Seattle: Good Grief Rituals.

Choy, A. (1990). The Winner's Triangle. *Transactional Analysis Journal, 20, 40-45.*

Clarke, J. I. (1996). The synergistic use of five transactional analysis concepts by educators, *Transactional Analysis Journal, 26, 214-219.*

Clarke, J. I. (1998). *Self esteem: A family affair*. Hazelden: Minnesota.

Clarkson, P. (1987). The bystander role. *Transactional Analysis Journal, 17, 82-88.*

Clarkson, P. (1991). Group imago and the stages of group development. *Transactional Analysis Journal, 21, 36-50.*

Clarkson, P. (1992). *Transactional analysis psychotherapy: An integrated approach*. London: Tavistock/Routledge.

Clarkson, P. and Gilbert, M. (1988). Berne's original model of ego states. *Transactional Analysis Journal, 18, 20-29.*

Clarkson, P. and Lapworth, P. (1992). The psychology of the self in transactional analysis. In: Conway, A. and Clarkson, P. (1987). Everyday hypnotic inductions. *Transactional Analysis Journal, 17, 17-23.*

Corbin, H. (1995). Creative imagination in the Sufism of Ibn 'Arabi. Princeton, NJ: Princeton University Press.

Cornell, W. F. (1975). Wake up "sleepy": Reichian Techniques and script intervention. *Transactional Analysis Journal, 5 144-147.*

Cornell, W. F. (2005). In the terrain of the unconscious: The evolution of a transactional analysis therapist. *Transactional Analysis Journal, 35, 119-131.*

Cornell, W. F. and Hargaden, H. (2005). *From transactions to relations: The emergence of a relational tradition in transactional analysis*. Chadlington: Haddon Press.

Cowan, C. and Todorovic, N. (2005). (Eds.) *The never ending quest: Dr. Clare W Graves explores human nature*. Available at http://www.clarewgraves.com

Cowles Boyd, L. and Boyd, H. S. (1980). Play as a time structure. *Transactional Analysis Journal, 10.1, 5-7.*

Craig, G. (undated).*The EFT Manual*. Available at http://www.emofree.com

Crittenden, P. M. (1995). *Attachment and Psychopathology* – in Goldberg, S., Muir, R. and Kerr, J. (1995) *Attachment theory: social, developmental and clinical perspectives*. Hilldale, N. J: The Analytic Press.

Crossman. P. (1966). Permission and protection. *Transactional Analysis Bulletin, 5, 152-154.*

Damasio, A. (1999). *The feeling of what happens: Body and emotion in the making of consciousness*. London: William Heineman.

Davis, J. (2004). (Ed.) *Diversity and shared identity*. Unpublished monograph.

de Shazer, S. (1996). *Words were originally magic*. Norton: New York.

Drego, P. (1978). The basis of structural analysis in transactional analysis in India today. *Souvenir ITAC 1, 70-71.* New Delhi: TASI.

Drego, P. (1979). *Towards the illumined child: An Indian study of ego states*. Bombay: The Grail.

Drego, P. (1983). The cultural parent. *Transactional Analysis Journal 13, 224-227.*

Drego, P. (1999). *Building family unity through permission rituals; Permissions and ego state models*. Mumbai: Alfreruby Publishers.

Drego, P. (2000) Towards an ethic of ego states *Transactional Analysis Journal 30.3, 192-206.*

Dusay, J. M. (1966). Response. *Transactional Analysis Bulletin 5, 136-137.*

Dyer, W. W. (2004). *The power of intention: Learning to co-create your world your way*. Carlsbad, CA.: Hay House Inc..

Engler, J. (1986). Therapeutic aims in psychotherapy and meditation: Developmental stages in the representation of self - in Wilber, K., Engler, J. and Brown, D. (1986). *Transformations of consciousness; Conventional and contemplative perspectives on development*. Boston: New Science Library.

English, F. (1971). Rackets and real feelings, Part I. *Transactional Analysis Journal, 2, 27-33.*

English, F. (1972). The substitution factor: Rackets and real feelings, Part II. *Transactional Analysis Journal, 4, 27-33.*

English, F. (1976). Racketeering. *Transactional Analysis Journal, 6, 78-81.*

English, F. (1979). Talk by Fanita English on receiving the Eric Berne Memorial Scientific Award for the concept of rackets as substitute feelings. *Transactional Analysis Journal, 9, 90-94.*

English, F. (1987). Power, mental energy and inertia. *Transactional Analysis Journal, 17, 91-98.*

English, F. (1995). Commentary on Tony White's article "I'm OK, You're OK: Further Considerations". *Transactional Analysis Journal, 25, 239-240.*

English, F. (2003). How are you? And how am I? Ego states and their inner motivators. In: Hargaden, H. and Sills, C. (2003). (Eds.) *Key concepts in transactional analysis. Contemporary views; Ego states.* London: Worth Publishing Ltd.

Erickson, M. H. and Rossi, E. L. (1979). *Hypnotherapy: An exploratory casebook.* New York: Irvington.

Erickson, M. H. and Rossi, E. L. (1980). Two level communication and the micro-dynamics of trance – in Rossi, E. L. (Ed.) *The collected papers of Milton H. Erickson on hypnosis 1: The nature of hypnosis and suggestion.* New York: Irvington.

Erskine, R. G. (1988). Ego structure, intrapsychic function and defense mechanisms: A commentary on Eric Berne's original concepts. *Transactional Analysis Journal 18, p. 15-19.*

Erskine, R. G. (1993). Inquiry, attunement and involvement in the psychotherapy of dissociation. *Transactional Analysis Journal, 23, 184-190.*

Erskine, R. G. (1994a). Therapeutic intervention: Disconnecting rubber bands. *Transactional Analysis Journal, 24, 172-173.*

Erskine, R. G. (1994b). Shame and self-righteousness: transactional analysis perspectives and clinical interventions. *Transactional Analysis Journal, 24, 86-103.*

Erskine, R. G. (1995). Commentary on Tony White's article "I'm OK, You're OK: Further Considerations". *Transactional Analysis Journal, 25.2, 236-238.*

Erskine, R. G. (1997). *Theories and methods of an integrative transactional analysis: a volume of selected articles.* San Francisco: TA Press.

Erskine, R. G. and Moursund, J. P. (1988). *Integrated psychotherapy in action.* Newbury Park, CA: Sage Publications.

Erskine, R. G. and Trautmann, R. L. (1996). Theories and methods of an integrated transactional analysis. *Transactional Analysis Journal,* 26, 316-328.

Erskine, R. G. and Zalcman, M. J. (1979). The racket system: A model for racket analysis. *Transactional Analysis Journal 9, 51-59.*

Erskine, R. G., Moursund, J. P. & Trautmann, R. L. (1999). *Beyond empathy: A therapy of contact-in relationship,* Philadelphia: Brunner/Mazel.

Etherington, K. (2004). *Becoming a reflexive researcher: Using our selves in research.* London: Jessica Kingsley Publishers.

Fairbairn, W. R. D. (1952). *An object-relations theory of the personality.* New York: Basic Books.

Federn, P. (1952). *Ego psychology and the psychoses.* New York: Basic Books.

Field, N. (1996). *Breakdown and breakthrough.* London: Routledge.

Flavell, J. (1970). *Concept development* - in Musson, P. (Ed.) *Carmichael's manual of child psychology, Volume 1.* New York: Wiley.

Foulkes, S.H. (1965). *Therapeutic group analysis.* New York: International Universities Press.

Foulkes, S.H. (1975). *Group analytic psychotherapy: Method and principles,* London, Gordon and Breech.

Foulkes, S.H. and Anthony, E.J. (1973). *Group psychotherapy: The psychoanalytic approach,* Harmondsworth, Penguin.

Fox, E. M. (1975). Eric Berne's theory of organizations. *Transactional Analysis Journal 5, 345-353.*

Fransella, F. and Dalton, P. (1990). *Personal construct counselling in action.* London: Sage.

French, J. R. P. and Raven, B. (1959). *The basis of social power.* In: Cartwright, D. and Zander, A. *Group dynamics: Research and theory.* London: Tavistock Publications.

Freud, A. (1946). *The ego and mechanisms of defense.* New York: International Universities Press.

Freud, S. (1900). *The interpretation of dreams.* In: *The standard edition of the complete works of S. Freud, Volume 4,* London: Hogarth Press.

Freud, S. (1923). The ego and the id. *The standard edition of the complete works of S. Freud, Volume 19,* London: Hogarth Press.

Gallo, F. P. (2000). *Energy: Diagnostic and treatment methods.* New York: Norton.

Gendlin, E. (1981). *Focusing.* New York: Bantam.

Gilbert, M. (2003). Ego states and ego state networks: some considerations for the practitioner. In: Hargaden, H. and Sills, C. (2003) (Eds.) *Key concepts in transactional analysis: Contemporary views; Ego states.* London: Worth Publishing Ltd..

Gildebrand, K (2003). An introduction to the brain and the early development of the Child ego state. In: Hargaden, H. and Sills, C. (2003) (Eds.) *Key concepts in transactional analysis: Contemporary views; Ego states.* London: Worth Publishing Ltd.

Goffman, E. (1959). *The presentation of self in everyday life.* New York: Doubleday.

Goffman, E. (1968). *Asylums.* Harmondsworth: Penguin Books.

Goldberg, S., Muir, R. and Kerr, J. (1995). *Attachment theory: social, developmental and clinical perspectives.* Hilldale, N. J: The Analytic Press

Goulding, M. M. and Goulding, R. L. (1979). *Changing lives through redecision therapy,* New York: Brunner/Mazel.

Graves, C. W. (1981). Summary statement: The emergent, cyclical, double-helix model of the adult human biopsychosocial systems," handout for presentation to World Future Society, Boston, Mass. Available at http://www.clarewgraves.com

Goleman, D. (2003). (Narrator) *Destructive emotions and how we can overcome them: A dialogue with the Dalai Lama.* London: Bloomsbury

Grégoire, J. (2000). About the link between ego state models. *EATA Newsletter 77.* EATA: Geneva.

Grégoire, J. (1990). Therapy with the person who meditates: Diagnosis and treatment strategies. *Transactional Analysis Journal, 20, 60 -76*

Grégoire, J. (2004). Ego states as living links between current and past experiences. *Transactional Analysis Journal, 34, 10-29.*

Groder, M. (1978). Asklepeion: An integration of psychotherapies. In: Barnes, G (Ed.) *Transactional analysis after Eric Berne : Teachings and practice of three TA schools.* New York: Harper's College Press.

Grudermeyer, D. (2002). Getting on the same page: How all the energy psychology approaches fit together. In: Lammers, W. and Kirchner, B. *The energy odyssey: New directions in energy psychology. 123-126.* Eastbourne: Dragon Rising.

Guntrip, H. (1971). *Psychoanalytic theory, therapy and the self.* New York: Basic Books.

Handy, C. B. (1976). *Understanding organisations,*: Harmondsworth: Penguin.

Hare, P. A. (1962). *Handbook of group research.* New York: Macmillan.

Hardy, J. and Whitmore, D. (1988). Psychosynthesis. In: Rowan, J. and Dryden, W, (Eds.) *Innovative therapy in Britain. 202-204.* Milton Keynes: Open University Press.

Hargaden, H. and Fenton, B (2005). An analysis of nonverbal transactions drawing on theories of intersubjectivity. *Transactional Analysis Journal, 35,* 173-186.

Hargaden, H. (2005). Letter from the guest editor: All that jazz. *Transactional Analysis Journal, 35, 105-109.*

Hargaden, H. and Sills, C. (2002). *Transactional analysis: A relational perspective.* Hove: Brunner-Routledge.

Hargaden, H. and Sills, C. (2003). (Eds.) Key concepts in transactional analysis. Contemporary views; Ego states. London: Worth Publishing Ltd.

Harris. T. A. (1973). I'm OK- You're OK. London: Pan Books.

Hendrix, H. (1992). *Keeping the love you find: A personal guide.* New York: Pocket Books.

Heron, J. (1990). *Helping the client: A creative practical guide.* London: Sage.

Hewitt, G. (1995). Cycles of psychotherapy. *Transactional Analysis Journal, 25, 280-207.*

Heylighen F. and Joslyn C. (2001). Cybernetics and Second Order Cybernetics. In: R.A.

Hillman, J. (1975). *Re-visioning psychology.* New York: Harper Colophon.

Hine, J (1990). The bilateral and ongoing nature of games. *Transactional Analysis Journal, 20, 28-39*

Hine, J. (1995). Commentary on Tony White's article "I'm OK, You're OK: Further Considerations". *Transactional Analysis Journal, 25, 240-241.*

Hine, J. (1997). Mind structure and ego states. *Transactional Analysis Journal, 27, 278-289.*

Horowitz, M. J. (1979). *States of mind.* New York: Plenum Press.

Hudson, S. (2000). Working with dissociative identity disorder using transactional analysis *Transactional Analysis Journal 30, 91-93.*

Hyams, H. (1998). Dissociation: definition, diagnosis, manifestations and therapy, with special reference to cults/sects *Transactional Analysis Journal 28, 234-243.*

Hycner, R. H. (1988). *Between person and person.* New York: Gestalt Journal Publications.

Jacobs, A. (1987). Autocratic Power *Transactional Analysis Journal, 17, 59-71.*

Jacobs, A. (1990). Nationalism *Transactional Analysis Journal, 20, 221-228.*

Jacobs, A. (1991). Aspects of survival: Triumph over death and onliness. *Transactional Analysis Journal, 21, 4-11.*

Jacobs, A. (1992). Autocracy: Groups, organizations, nations and players. *Transactional Analysis Journal, 21, 199-206.*

Jacobs, A. (1994). Theory as ideology: Reparenting and thought reform *Transactional Analysis Journal, 24, 39-54.*

Jacobs, A. (1997). Berne's Life Positions: Science and morality *Transactional Analysis Journal, 27-3, 197-206.*

James, M. (1981). *Breaking free: Self-reparenting for a new life*: Reading, Massachusetts: Addison-Wesley.

James, M. and Savary, L. (1977). *A new Self: Self therapy with transactional analysis.* Reading, Massachusetts: Addison-Wesley.

Jayyusi, L. (1984). *Categorisation and the moral order.* London: Routledge and Kegan Paul

Jefferson, G. (1988). On the sequential organisation of troubles talk in ordinary conversation. *Social Problems 35(4) 418-422.*

Joines, V. (1986). Using redecision therapy with different personality adaptations. *Transactional Analysis Journal 18:3 185-190.*

Joines, V. (1988). Diagnosis and treatment planning using a transactional analysis framework. *Transactional Analysis Journal, 18. 178-190.*

Joines, V. and Stewart, I. (2002). *Personality adaptations: A new guide to human understanding in psychotherapy and counselling,* Nottingham: Lifespace.

Jung, C. G. (1946). *Psychological types.* New York: Harcourt Brace.

Kahler, T, (1982*). Personality Pattern Inventory Validation Studies.* Kahler Communication, Inc.

Kahler, T. (1972). *Predicting academic underachievement in ninth and twelfth grade males with the Kahler transactional analysis script checklist.* Dissertation, Purdue University.

Kahler, T. (1978). *Transactional analysis revisited.* Little Rock: Human Development Publications.

Kahler, T. (1979). *Process therapy in brief,* Little Rock: Human Development Publications.

Kahler, T. (1997). *The transactional analysis script profile (TASP^{TM)}*.Little Rock: Tabi Kahler Associates , Inc.

Kahler, T. and Capers, H. (1974). The miniscript. *Transactional Analysis Journal, 4, 26-42.*

Kaplan, G. C. and Main, M. (1985). *An adult attachment interview.* Unpublished M.S. University of California, Berkley.

Kaplan, K. J. Capace N. K. and Clyde, J. D. (1984). A bidimensional distancing approach to transactional analysis: A suggested revision of the OK corral. *Transactional Analysis Journal, 15, 114-119.*

Kapur, R. and Miller, K. (1987). A comparison between therapeutic factors in TA and psychodynamic therapy groups. *Transactional Analysis Journal, 17, 294-300.*

Karol, J. A. (1998). Confluence, isolation and contact in psychotherapy with clients who dissociate. *Transactional Analysis Journal, 28, 111-120.*

Karpman, S. B. (1968). Fairy tales and script drama analysis. *Transactional Analysis Bulletin, 7, 39-43.*

Karpman, S. B. (1973). Eric Berne memorial scientific award lecture. *Transactional Analysis Journal, 3, 73-78.*

Kelly, G. A. (1955). *The psychology of personal constructs.* New York: Norton.

Klein, M. (1949). *The Psycho-analysis of children.* London: Hogarth Press.

Klein, M. (1961). *Narrative of a child analysis.* London: Hogarth Press.

Kohlberg, L. (1981). *Essays on moral development: Volume 1.*Harper & Row: San Francisco.

Kornfield, J. (1994) *A path with heart: The classical guide through the perils and promises f spiritual life.* New York: Bantam Books.

Kornfield, J. (2000) *After the ecstasy, the laundry: How the heart grows wise on the spiritual path* .New York: Bantam Books.

Kovel, J. (1975). *A complete guide to psychotherapy.* Harmondsworth: Pelican.

LaBerge, S. (1985). Lucid dreaming. New York: Ballantine.

Lammers, W. and Kirchner, B. (2002). *The energy odyssey: New directions in energy psychology.* Eastbourne: Dragon Rising.

Lankton, S. R. and Lankton, C. H. (1983). *The answer within: A clinical framework of Ericksonian hypnotherapy,* New York: Brunner/Mazel.

Lankton, S. R. Lankton, C. H. and Brown, M, (1981). Psychological level communication in transactional analysis, *Transactional Analysis Journal, 11,* 287-299.

Latane, B. and Darley, M. (1970). *The unresponsive bystander: Why doesn't he help?* New York: Appeleton-Century Crofts.

Laurillard, D. (2002). *Rethinking University Teaching: a framework for the effective use of educational technology (2nd edition)* London; Routledge-Falmer.

Law, G. C. (1978a). Cathexis. *Transactions – Journal of the Institute of Transactional Analysis, 4, 13-18.*

Law, G. C. (1978b). The game. In: Moiso, C. (Ed.) *T.A. in Europe: Contributions to E.A.T.A. summer conferences, 1977-1978.* Rome: EATA.

Law, G. C. (1979). Models for analysis, extension and use of drama triangle roles. *Paper presented at Fifth European Transactional Analysis Conference, Aix-en-Provence, 1979.*

Law, G. C. (2001). Role Imago Analysis - In *ITA Conference Papers, Volume 5 – Keele University,* United Kingdom: Institute of Transactional Analysis.

Law, G. C. (2003). Self, the Observer role and transpersonal awareness in transactional analysis. In: *ITA Conference Papers, Volume 7.* United Kingdom: Institute of Transactional Analysis.

Law, G. C. (2004). *Bridging the divides: Observational methods for a relational model of transactional analysis.* Fremantle, Australia: Fremantle Publishing.

Le Guernic, A. Fairy tales and psychological life plans. *Transactional Analysis Journal, 34, 216-222.*

LeDoux, J. (1996). *The Emotional Brain: The mysterious underpinnings of emotional life.* New York: Simon and Schuster.

Leiman, M. (1994). The development of cognitive analytic therapy. *International Journal of Short-Term Psychotherapy, 9.67-82.*

Lepper G. (2000). *Categories in text and talk.* London: Sage Publications.

Levin, P. (1982). The cycle of development. *Transactional Analysis Journal, 12, 129-139.*

Levin, P. (1988). *Becoming the way we are.* Pampano Beach: Health Communications.

Lewin, K. (1951). *Field theory in social science,* New York: Harper & Row.

Linehan, M. M. (1993). *Cognitive-behavioral treatment of borderline personality disorder.* New York: The Guildford Press.

Linton, R. (1936). *The study of man*, New York: Appleton-Century.

Lister-Ford, C. (2002). *Skills in transactional analysis counselling and psychotherapy.* London: Sage Publications.

Loevinger, J. (1976). *Ego development.* San Francisco: Josey-Bass.

Loewenthal, D. and Winter, D. (2006). (Eds.) *What is psychotherapy research?* London: Karnac.

Loria, B. (2003). Wither transactional analysis: obsolescence or paradigm shift. *Transactional Analysis Journal, 33, 192-200.*

Luborsky, L. (1962). Clinician's Judgements of Mental Health. *Archives of General Psychiatry. 7, 407–417.*

Luft, Joseph (1969). *Of Human Interaction.* Palo Alto, CA.: National Press Books.

Luft, J. (1970, 2nd Ed.) *Group processes; an introduction to group dynamics.*: National Press Books: Palo Alto, CA.

Mackewn, J. (1997). *Developing gestalt counselling.* London: Sage.

Mahler, M. S. (1975) *The psychological birth of the human infant.* New York: Basic Books.

Mahler, M. S., Pine, F. and Bergman, A. (1975). *The psychological birth of the human infant: Symbiosis and individuation.* New York: Basic Books.

Mahrer, A. (1996). *The complete guide to experiential psychotherapy.* New York: Wiley.

Main, M. and Goldwyn R. (1994). *Adult attachment interview scoring and classification system* (version 8.0). Unpublished manual, University College, London.

Marrone, M. (1998). *Attachment and interaction.* London: Jessica Kingsley.

Maslow, A. (1954). *Motivation and personality.* Harper & Row: New York.

Massey, R. F. (1987). Transactional Analysis and the social psychology of power: Reflections evoked by Jacobs' "Autocratic Power". *Transactional Analysis Journal, 17, 107-121.*

Massey, R. F. (1995). Theory for treating individuals from a transactional analysis/systems perspective. *Transactional Analysis Journal, 25, 271-284.*

Masterson, J. F. (1981). The narcissistic and borderline disorders: An integrated developmental approach. New York: Brunner/Mazel.

May, R. (1972). *Power and innocence: A search for the sources of violence.* New York: W.W. Norton & Co. Inc.

McFarlane, T. J. (2004). The integral sphere: A mathematical mandala of reality. Available at http://www.integralscience.org/sphere.html

McKenna, J. (1974). Stroking profile: Application to script analysis. *Transactional Analysis Journal 4, 20-24.*

McLeod, J. (2000). *Qualitative research in counselling and psychotherapy.* London: Sage Publications Ltd.

McLeod, J. (2003). *Doing counselling research.* London: Sage Publications Ltd.

Mead, G. H. (1934). In: Morris, C. W. (Ed.) *Mind, self and society.* Chicago: The University of Chicago Press.

Mearns, D. (1994). *Developing client-centred counselling.* London: Sage.

Mellor, K. (1996). *Another day younger.* Available at http://www.biamenetwork.net

Mellor, K. (2002) *Centering meditation.* Biame Network Inc. Available at http://www.biamenetwork.net

Mellor, K. (2002) *Creative Release meditation.* Biame Network Inc. Available at http://www.biamenetwork.net

Mellor, K. (undated). *Grounding meditation.* Biame Network Inc. Available at http://www.biamenetwork.net

Mellor, K. and Schiff, E. (1975). Discounting. *Transactional Analysis Journal 5, 295-302.*

Mellor, K. and Sigmund, E. (1975). Redefining. *Transactional Analysis Journal 5, 303-311.*

Merton, R. K. (1957). *Social theory and social structure,*: Glencoe, Ill.: The Free Press.

Merton, R. K. (1968). Role sets: *Social theory and social structure.* New York: Free Press

Moiso, C. (1985). Ego states and transference. *Transactional Analysis Journal, 25, 194-201.*

Mollon, P. (2005). *EMDR and the energy therapies: Psychoanalytic perspectives.* London: Karnac.

Mothersole, G. (2001). TA as a short-term cognitive therapy. In: Tudor, K. (Ed.) *Transactional analysis approaches to brief therapy. 54-82.*London: Sage.

Nadel, S. F. (1957). *The theory of social structure.* Glencoe, Ill: The Free Press.

Novellino, M. and Moiso, C. (1985). The psychodynamic approach to transactional analysis. *Transactional Analysis Journal, 15, 194-201.*

Novey, T. B. (2002). Measuring the effectiveness of transactional analysis: an international study. *Transactional Analysis Journal. 32, 8-24,*

O'Connell, B. (1998). *Solution focused therapy.* London: Sage.

O'Reilly-Knapp, M. and Erskine, R. G. (2003). Core concepts of an integrative transactional analysis. *Transactional Analysis Journal 33, 168-177.*

Ohlsson, T. (2002). Effects of transactional analysis psychotherapy in therapeutic community treatment of drug addicts. *Transactional Analysis Journal. 32, 153-177,*

Oller-Vallego, J. (2000). In favour of preserving the functional model. *EATA Newsletter 77. EATA: Geneva.*

Oller-Vallego, J. (2002). In support of the second-order functional model. *Transactional Analysis Journal, 32, 178-183.*

Oller-Vallego, J. (2003). Three basic ego states: the primary model *Transactional Analysis Journal, 33, 162-167.*

Pask, G (1975). *The Cybernetics of Human Learning and Performance* London: Hutchinson.

Perls, F. S. (1969). *Ego hunger and aggression* New York: Vintage Books.

Perls, F. S. (1973). *The Gestalt approach and eyewitness to therapy.* Palo Alto: Science and Behavior Books.

Perls, F. S. Hefferline, R. F. & Goodman, P. (1951). *Gestalt therapy: Excitement and growth in the human personality.* New York: Julian Press.

Pert, C. (1997). *The Molecules of Emotion: Why You Feel the Way You Feel.* New York: Scribner's.

Piaget, J. (1963). *The origins of intelligence in children,* New York Basic Books.

Piaget, J. (1977). *The essential Piaget.* In: Gruber and Voneche (Eds.) New York: Basic Books.

Pollock, P. H., Broadbent, M., Clarke, S., Dorrian, A. J. and Ryle, A. (2001). The Personality Structure Questionnaire (PSQ): A measure of the multiple self states model of identity disturbance in cognitive analytic therapy. *Clinical Psychology and Psychotherapy. 8, 59-82.*

Polster, E. (1995). *A population of selves; A therapeutic exploration of personal diversity* San Francisco: Jossey-Bass.

Porter-Steele, N. (1990). Response to over the border: The nonreification of "Self" *Transactional Analysis Journal, 20, 56-59.*

Porter-Steele, N. (1997). Comments in response to "The altered state: A missing link in ego state theory?" *Transactional Analysis Journal, 27, 297-299.*

Porter-Steele, N. (2005). *Blending Redecision Therapy with EFT- a creative way to uncover core issues.* Available at http://www.emofree.com

Poston, T. and Stewart, I. (1996) *Catastrophe theory and its applications.* New York: Dover.

Price, R. (1987). The legacy of Milton H. Erickson: Implications for transactional analysis. *Transactional Analysis Journal, 17, 11-16.*

Price, R. (1988). Of multiple personalities and dissociated selves: The fragmentation of the child. *Transactional Analysis Journal 18, p. 231-237.*

Pulleyblank E. and McCormick, P. (1985). The stages of redecision therapy. In: Kadis, L. (Ed.) *Redecision therapy: Expanded perspectives.* Watsonville: Western Institute for Group and Family Therapy.

Rank, O. (1910). *The myth of the birth of the hero.* New York: Nervous and Mental Disease Monographs.

Richo, D. (2002) *How Be To An Adult in Relationships.* New York: Shambhala.

Rizzolatti, G., Luppino, G., & Matelli, M. (1998). The organization of the cortical motor system: New concepts. *Electroencephalography and Clinical Neurophysiology, 106*(4), 283-296.

Reynolds, B. (2004). *Embracing reality: the integral vision of Ken Wilber: a historical survey and chapter-by-chapter guide to Wilber's major works.* New York: Jeremy P. Tarcher/Penguin

Rogers, C. (1951). *Client centred therapy.* London: Constable.

Rosch, E. (1994). Is causality circular? Event structure in folk psychology, cognitive science and Buddhist logic. *Journal of Consciousness Studies, 1 (1),* pp. 50–65.

Rowan, J. (1993). *The transpersonal: Psychotherapy and counselling.* London: Brunner-Routledge.

Rowan, J. (1997). *Subpersonalities.* London: Routledge.

Rowan, J. (2005). *The future of training in psychotherapy and counselling: Instrumental, relational and transpersonal perspectives* London: Routledge.

Rowan, J. and Jacobs, M. (2002). *The therapist's use of self.* Buckingham: Open University Press.

Ruben, B. and King, J. Y. (1975). (Eds.) *General systems theory in human communication.* Rochelle Park, NJ: Harden Book Co.

Ryle, A. (1979). The focus in brief interpretive psychotherapy: dilemma, traps and snags as target problems. *British Journal of Psychiatry 153, 443-458.*

Ryle, A. (1982). Psychotherapy: *A cognitive integration of theory and practice.* London: Academic Press.

Ryle, A. (1990). *Cognitive analytic therapy: Active participation in change,* Chichester: Wiley.

Ryle, A. (1995). *Cognitive analytic therapy: developments in theory and practice.* Chichester: Wiley.

Ryle, A. (1997). *Cognitive analytic therapy and borderline personality disorder: The model and the method,* Chichester: Wiley.

Ryle, A. and Kerr, I. B. (2002). *Introducing cognitive analytic therapy: Principles and practice.* Chichester: John Wiley and Sons.

Sacks, H. (1992a). *Lectures on conversation. Vol. 1* Ed. G. Jefferson. Oxford: Blackwell.

Sacks, H. (1992b). *Lectures on conversation. Vol. 2* Ed. G. Jefferson. Oxford: Blackwell.

Salters, (2004). Personal communication.

Samuels, A. (1985). *Jung and the post-Jungians* Routledge and Kegan Paul: London.

Schiff, J. L. with Schiff, A., Mellor, K., Schiff, E., Schiff, S., Richman, D., Fishman, J., Wolz, L., Fishman, C., and Momb, D. (1975). *The Cathexis reader: transactional analysis treatment of psychosis,* New York: Harper & Row.

Schwartz-Salant, N. (1991). in Schwartz-Salant, N. and Stein, N. (Eds.) *Liminality and transitional phenomena.* Wilmettee: Chiron.

Schwock, B. (1979). Les roles victimie, persecuteur, sauveur et la dynamique de la "matrice scenarique dramatique". *Paper presented at 5th Conference of the European Association of Transactional Analysis: Aix-en-Provence.*

Schwock, B. (1980). Script drama diamond. *Paper presented at 5th Conference of the European Association of Transactional Analysis: Aix-en-Provence.*

Segal, Z. V., Williams, J. M. G. and Teesdale, J. D. (2002). *Mindfulness-based cognitive therapy for depression.* New York: Guildford.

Shapiro, F. (2001). *Eye movement desensitization and reprocessing.* New York: Guildford.

Shapiro, F. and Forrest, M. (1997). *EMDR* New York: Basic Books.

Sills, C. (2003). Role lock: When the whole group plays a game. *Transactional Analysis Journal, 33, 282-287.*

Sills, C. (2004). Celebrating differences. *Keynote speech at the ITAA/CHILD Conference, Bangalore, India.*

Silverman, D. (1997). *Discourses of counselling.* London: Sage.

Silverman, D. (1998). *Harry Sacks and conversation analysis. Key contemporary thinkers.* Cambridge: Polity Press.

Spitz, R. (1945). Hospitalism: genesis of psychiatric conditions in early childhood, *Psychoanalytic Study of the Child, 1, 53-74.*

Steiner, C. M. (1966). Script and counterscript. *Transactional Analysis Bulletin 5.18 pp.133-135.*

Steiner, C. M. (1971). The stroke economy. *Transactional Analysis Journal, 1. 9-15.*

Steiner, C. M. (1974). Healing alcoholism, New York: Grove Press.

Steiner, C. M. (1979). *Scripts people live,* New York: Grove Press.

Steiner, C. M. (1987). The seven sources of power: an alternative to authority. *Transactional Analysis Journal 17 102-104.*

Steiner, C. M. (2000). Radical psychiatry. In: Corsini, R.J. (Ed.) *Handbook of innovative therapy.pp.578-586.* Chichester: Wiley.

Steiner, C. M. (2003). Core concepts of a stroke centred transactional analysis. *Transactional Analysis Journal 33 178-181*

Steiner, C. M. Campos, L. Drego, P. Joines, V. Ligabue, S. Noriega, G. Roberts, D. Said, E.(1999). A compilation of core concepts. *Report of the Task Force on Core Concepts of the Development Committee of the International Transactional Analysis Association. San Francisco CA.*

Steinfeld, G. J. (1998)Personal responsibility in human relationships: A cognitive-constructivist approach. *Transactional Analysis Journal, 28, 188- 198.*

Steinfeld, G. J. (2004). On beliefs systems, research, cure, and the newer energy therapies. *The Script, 34.9, 8.*

Stern, D. N. (1985). The interpersonal world of the infant. New York: Basic Books.

Stewart, I. and Joines, V. (1987). *Transactional analysis today: A new introduction to transactional analysis.* Nottingham: Lifespace.

Stewart, I. (1992). *Eric Berne.* London: Sage.

Stewart, I. (1996). *Developing transactional analysis counselling,* London: Sage.

Stewart, I. (1996). History *of* transactional analysis – in Dryden, W. (Ed.*) Developments in psychotherapy: Historical perspectives.* London: Sage.

Stewart, I. (2001). Ego states and the theory of theory: The strange case of the Little Professor. *Transactional Analysis Journal, 31, 133-147.*

Summers, G. and Tudor, K. (2000) Co creative transactional analysis. *Transactional Analysis Journal. 30, 23-40.*

Symington, J. and Symington, N. (1996). The clinical thinking of Wilfred Bion. London: Routledge.

Tarthang, (1977).*Time, space and knowledge: A new vision of reality.* Oakland, CA: Dharma Publishing.

Temple, S. (1999). Functional fluency for educational transactional analysts *Transactional Analysis Journal 29.3 pp.164-174.*

Thomas, L. and Harri-Augstein, S. (1985). *Self-Organised Learning: foundations of a conversational science for psychology* London: Routledge and Kegan Paul.

Thorne, B. (1991). *Person-centred counselling: Therapeutic and spiritual dimensions.* London: Whurr Publishers.

Tiller, W.A. (1997). Science and human transformation: Subtle energies, intentionality and consciousness. Walnut Creek, CA: Pavior Publishing.

Tilney, T. (1998). *Dictionary of transactional analysis.* Whurr Publishers: London.

Tomkins, S. S. (1962-63). *Affect, imagery, consciousness Volumes I and II* New York: Springer Publishing.

Toomela, A. (1996a). How culture transforms minds; a process of internalisation. *Culture and Psychology 2, 285-305.*

Toomela, A. (1996b). What characterises language: A reply to Tomasello. *Culture and Psychology 2, 319-322.*

Tschudi, F. (1990). *Flexigrid.* University of Oslo.

Tuckman, B. W. and Jensen, M. A. C. (1977). Developmental sequence in small groups. *Journal of Group and Organisational Studies, 2, 419-427.*

Tudor, K. (1999). *Group counselling.* London: Sage.

Tudor, K. (2003). The neopsyche: the integrating adult ego state. In: Sills, C. and Hargaden, H. (Eds.) *Key concepts in transactional analysis, Contemporary views: Ego states.* London: Worth Publishing.

Tudor, K. and Hobbes, R. (2002). Transactional analysis. In: Dryden, W. (Ed.) *Handbook of individual therapy, 239-265.* London: Sage.

van Beekum, S. and Krijgsman, B. (2000). From autonomy to contact. *Transactional Analysis Journal, 30, 52-57.*

van Beekum, S. and Lammers, W. (1990). Over the border: Script theory and beyond. *Transactional Analysis Journal, 20, 47-55.*

van Deurzen-Smith, E. (1988). *Existential counselling in practice.* London: Sage

Vick, P. (2002). *Psycho-spiritual body psychotherapy.* in Staunton, T. (Ed.) *Body psychotherapy.* Hove: Bruner-Routledge.

Visser, F. (2003). *Ken Wilber: Thought as passion.* Albany: State University of New York.

von Bertalanffy, L. (1968). *General systems theory: Foundations, development, applications.* New York: George Braziller.

Vygotsky, L. S. (1937 - English translation 1962). *Thought and language.* Cambridge: Massachusetts.

Wade, J. (1996). *Changes of mind: A holonomic theory of the evolution of consciousness.* Albany, NY: SUNY Press.

Wadsworth, D. and DiVincenti, A. (2003). Core concepts of transactional analysis: An opportunity born of struggle. *Transactional Analysis Journal. 33, 158-177.*

Walsh, R. and Vaughan, F. E. (1996). Comparative models of the person and psychotherapy. In: Boorstein, S. (Ed.) *Transpersonal psychotherapy.* Albany: State University of New York Press.

Wangyal, T. (1999) *The Tibetan yogas of dream and sleep.* Ithaca, New York: Snow Lion Publications.

Ware, P. (1983). Personality adaptations. *Transactional Analysis Journal, 13, 11-19.*

Watkins, J. G. and Watkins, H. H. (1997). *Ego states: Theory and therapy.* New York: Norton.

Weiss, E. (1950). *Principles of psychodynamics.* New York: Grune and Stratton.

White, A. (1994). Life positions. *Transactional Analysis Journal, 24, 269-276*

White, A. (1995a) "I'm OK, You're OK": Further considerations *Transactional Analysis Journal, 25, 234-236.*

White, A. (1995b). Response to Erskine's, English's and Hine's commentaries. *Transactional Analysis Journal. 25, 241-244.*

White, A. (2001). The contact contract *Transactional Analysis Journal, 31.3 194-198.*

371

Wilber, K. (1977). *The spectrum of consciousness.* Wheaton: Quest Books.

Wilber, K. (1979, 1981) *No boundary. Eastern and western approaches to growth.* Boulder: Shambhala.

Wilber, K. (1980). *The atman project: A transpersonal view of human development.* Wheaton: Quest Books.

Wilber, K. (1983). *Eye to eye: The quest for a new paradigm.* New York: Anchor Books.

Wilber, K. (1986). The spectrum of development - in Wilber, K. Engler, J. & Brown, D. (1986) *Transformations of consciousness; Conventional and contemplative perspectives on development.* Boston: New Science Library.

Wilber, K. (1991). *Grace and Grit: Spiritual healing in the life and death of Treya Killam Wilber.* Boston: Shambhala.

Wilber, K. (1995). *Sex, ecology, spirituality: The spirit of evolution.* Boston: Shambhala.

Wilber, K. (1996). *A brief history of everything.* Dublin: Gill & Macmillan.

Wilber, K. (1997). *The eye of spirit: An integral vision for a world gone slightly mad.* Shambhala: Boston.

Wilber, K. (1998). *Essential Ken Wilber: An introductory reader.* Shambhala: Boston.

Wilber, K. (1998). *The marriage of sense and soul: Integrating science and religion.* Dublin: Newleaf.

Wilber, K. (1999). *One Taste: Daily Reflections on Integral Spirituality.* Boston: Shambhala.

Wilber, K. (2000). *Integral Psychology: Consciousness, spirit, psychology, therapy.* Boston: Shambhala.

Wilber, K. (2001). *A theory of everything: An integral vision for business, politics, science and spirituality.* Dublin: Gateway.

Wilber, K. (2004). *The simple feeling of being: Embracing your true nature.* Boston: Shambhala Publications.

Windes, K. L. (1977). *The three "C's" of corrections: cops-cons-counsellors.* In: Barnes, G. (ed.) *Transactional analysis after Eric Berne, 138-145.* New York: Harper's College Press.

Winter, D. A. (1992). *Personal construct psychology in clinical practice: Theory, research and applications.* London: Routledge.

Winter, D. A. (2003). Repertory grid technique as a psychotherapy research measure. *Psychotherapy Research 13, 23-42.*

Wolinsky, S. (1993). *Quantum consciousness: The guide to experiencing quantum psychology.* Connecticut: The Bramble Company.

Wolinsky, S. (in collaboration with Ryan, M. O.) (1991). *Trances people live: Healing approaches in quantum psychology.* Connecticut: The Bramble Company.

Wood, J. D. and Petriglieri, G. (2005). Transcending polarization: Beyond binary thinking. *Transactional Analysis Journal, 35, 31-39.*

Woollams, S. and Brown, M. (1978). *Transactional Analysis.* Dexter: Huron Valley Press.

Wyckoff, H. (1976) (Ed.) *Love, therapy and politics: Issues in radical therapy – the first year.* New York: Grove Press.

Zalcman, M. J. (1990). Game analysis and racket analysis: Overview, critique and future developments. *Transactional Analysis Journal, 20, 4-19.*

Zinker, J. (1994). *In search of good form.* San Francisco: Jossey-Bass.

Author Index

Adler, 38, 359
Agazarian, 2, 62, 71, 72, 141, 149, 165, 166, 167, 168, 169, 173, 175, 228, 359
Agel, 18, 359
Allen, 9, 11, 18, 273, 287, 359
Allen and Allen, 9, 18, 273, 359
Almaas, 277, 278, 282, 294, 296, 359
American Psychiatric Association, 68, 311, 359
Andreas, 229, 231, 295, 359
Anthony, 62, 165, 363
Atherton, 265, 359
Atwater, 278, 285, 359
Avary, 273, 287, 359

Bakhtin, 359
Bales, 168, 359
Bannister, 68, 359
Barkham, 253, 359
Barnes, 5, 7, 8, 9, 38, 47, 50, 68, 71, 115, 119, 120, 123, 143, 177, 182-186, 189, 267, 275, 298, 303, 359, 360
Basch, 62, 360
Bateson, 265, 360
Beck, 48, 98, 330, 342, 344-347, 360
Beisser, 298, 360
Benjamin, 67, 69, 70, 136, 187, 215, 264, 270, 298, 360
Bennett, 10, 360
Bennis, 149, 168, 173, 360
Berger, 264, 360
Bergman, 140, 367
Berne, 2, 5-11, 14, 15, 18, 19, 21, 22, 25, 26, 29, 36-39, 41, 47, 49-51, 54-56, 61-63, 65, 67, 68, 70-74, 77, 98-100, 103, 110, 112, 119-121, 136, 140-145, 147, 149, 150, 156, 162, 163, 167-170, 173-177, 181, 182, 186-189, 194-200, 203-207, 212, 219, 221, 224, 226, 228, 229, 235, 267, 272-278, 284-293, 296, 298, 300-302, 305, 312, 333, 334, 338, 340, 347, 350-352, 359, 360, 362-365, 370
Bion, 62, 149, 165, 173, 272, 360, 370
Boholst, 9, 360
Boorstein, 302, 371
Bower, 71, 140, 360

Bowlby, 69, 98, 360, 361
Boyd, 100, 181, 362
Brandt, 277, 361
Broadbent, 368
Brown, M. 115, 273, 289, 366, 372
Brown, D. 362, 372
Buber, 16, 272, 361
Budgell, 272, 361

Callahan, 313, 361
Caloff, 287, 288, 361
Campbell, 38, 361
Campos, 11, 361, 370
Canetti, 80, 361
Capace, 9, 114, 365
Caplan, 326, 361
Carrington, 313, 361
Cartwright, 62, 165, 361, 363
Cassius, 312, 361
Childs-Gowell, 312, 361
Choy, 67, 68, 76, 78, 114, 177, 361
Clarke, J., 77, 78, 86, 88, 126, 328, 361,
Clarke, S., 252, 368
Clarkson, 7, 9, 16, 18, 68, 76, 79, 80, 82, 140, 150, 168, 169, 173, 177, 273, 276, 278, 361
Clyde, 365
Conway, 273, 361
Corbin, 272, 361
Cornell, 301, 312, 361, 362
Cowan, 48, 330, 342, 344-347, 360, 362
Cowles Boyd, 362
Craig, 313, 314, 361, 362
Crittenden, 131, 362
Crossman, 86, 126, 362

Dalton, 68, 363
Damasio, 362
Darley, 80, 366
Davis, 19, 362
de Shazer, 115, 362
DiVincenti, 11, 12, 371
Dorrian, 368
Drego, 10, 293, 294, 362, 370
Dusay, 96, 208, 362

Engler, 277, 294, 362, 372

English, 22, 59, 61, 64, 68, 76, 79, 80, 82, 111, 112, 120, 146, 150, 151, 177, 181, 188, 205, 248, 278, 312, 353, 354, 355, 362
Erickson, 285, 286, 288, 362, 368
Erikson, 300
Erskine, 8, 9, 18, 63, 73, 83, 98, 101, 114, 116, 119, 120, 123-126, 182, 194, 233, 287, 304, 312, 363, 363
Erskine, Moursund and Trautmann, 63, 73, 98, 101, 114, 116, 119, 123, 124, 125, 194, 312, 363
Etherington, 4, 134, 180, 337, 363

Fairbairn, 98, 300, 363
Federn, 8, 300, 363
Fenton, 27, 121, 364
Field, 272, 363, 366
Fishman, 369
Flavell, 120, 363
Foulkes, 62, 165, 363
Fox, 221, 363
Fransella, 68, 359, 363
French, 151, 155, 248, 363
Freud, 27, 28, 38, 276, 289, 300, 302, 363

Gallo, 312, 363
Gendlin, 100, 363
Gilbert, 70, 177, 178, 363
Gildebrand, 10, 364
Goffman,, 155, 364
Goldberg, 131, 362, 364
Goldwyn, 131, 367
Goleman, 337, 364
Goodman, 98, 368
Goulding, 15, 18, 126, 192, 328, 364
Graves, 48, 342, 345, 347, 362, 364
Grégoire, 7, 70, 363, 364
Groder, 38, 364
Grudermeyer, 313, 364
Guntrip, 98, 277, 364

Handy, 151, 364
Hare, 168, 364
Hargaden, 9, 15, 16, 18, 25, 27, 55, 121, 169, 171, 276, 278, 296, 300, 329, 362, 363, 364, 371
Harri-Augstein, 265, 370

Harris, 38, 364
Hefferline, 98, 368
Hendrix, 120, 121, 136, 364
Heron, 170, 171, 364
Heylighen, 268, 364
Hillman, 272, 364
Hine, 9, 50, 120, 177, 186, 188, 189, 196, 208-210, 222, 293, 294, 364, 365
Hobbes, 17, 18, 371
Horowitz, 68, 365
Hudson, 287, 365
Hyams, 365
Hycner, 295, 365

Jacobs, A., 9, 10, 15, 16, 38, 68, 76, 79, 80, 98, 111, 112, 115, 116, 120, 150, 177, 180, 365
Jacobs, M., 15, 16, 98, 272, 311, 328, 330, 365, 367, 369
James, 276, 345, 365
Jayyusi, 61, 365
Jefferson, 61, 365, 369
Jensen, 167, 168, 371
Joines, 2, 9, 14-16, 19, 25, 36, 37, 39, 61, 63, 77, 82, 83, 114, 132, 133, 135, 136, 191, 275, 284, 287, 289, 296, 301, 365, 370
Joslyn, 268, 364
Jung, 38, 302, 365, 369

Kadis, 369
Kahler, 9, 15, 76, 89, 133, 135, 136, 137, 138, 177, 207, 365
Kaplan, G., 9, 114, 136, 365
Kaplan, K., 9, 114, 365
Kapur, 149, 173, 365
Karol, 287, 366
Karpman, 37, 39-41, 46, 67, 68, 70, 76, 119, 120, 123, 186, 303, 338, 339, 366
Kelly, 10, 68, 220, 229, 230, 231, 366
King, 165, 369
Kinnaman, 312, 361
Kirchner, 313, 364, 366
Klein, 27, 38, 366
Kohlberg, 282, 283, 366
Kornfield, 323, 326, 366
Kovel, 6, 366
Krijgsman, 371

LaBerge, 297, 366
Lammers, 273, 313, 364, 366, 371
Lankton, 115, 273, 308, 366
Lapworth, 276, 278, 361
Latane, 80, 366
Laurillard, 265, 359, 366
Law, iii, 50, 70, 98, 115, 123, 126, 160, 174, 177, 178, 182, 194, 215, 260, 261, 366
Le Guernic, 67, 68, 76, 78, 177, 366
LeDoux, 97, 366
Leiman, 10, 366
Lepper, 61, 366
Levin, 282, 289, 328, 366
Lewin, 62, 141, 165, 366
Ligabue, 370
Linehan, 115, 294, 367
Linton, 61, 62, 147, 148, 219, 367
Lister-Ford, 9, 367
Loevinger, 283, 367
Loria, 12, 367
Luborsky, 258, 311, 367
Luckman, 264, 360
Luft, 159, 367

Mackewn, 295, 367
Mahler, 71, 119, 140, 367
Mahrer, 272, 367
Main, 131, 136, 365, 367
Margison, 359
Marrone, 131, 367
Maslow, 33, 283, 285, 324, 367
Massey, 67, 71, 72, 140, 141, 150, 151, 152, 228, 367
Masterson, 2, 367
May, 45, 58, 116, 150, 174, 367
McCormick, 274, 369
McFarlane, 33, 367
McGrath, 359
McKenna, 154, 180, 208, 218, 367
McLeod, 4, 367
Mead, 61, 62, 367
Mearns, 272, 367
Mellor, 61, 123, 177, 230, 231, 260, 317, 323, 326, 327, 367, 368
Mellor-Clark, 252, 359
Merton, 87, 215, 367, 368
Milhollon, 273, 287, 359
Miller, 365
Milnes, 359

Moiso, 18, 55, 368
Mollon, 313, 368
Momb, 369
Morgan, 278, 285, 359
Mothersole, 18, 368
Moursund, 18, 63, 73, 98, 101, 114, 116, 119, 123, 124, 125, 194, 312
Muir, 131

Nadel, 62, 368
Noriega, 370
Novellino, 18, 55, 368
Novey, 9, 368

O'Connell, 115, 368
O'Reilly-Knapp, 12, 180, 368
O'Reilly-Knapp and Erskine, 12, 180, 368
Ohlsson, 9, 368
Oller-Vallego, 12, 70, 368

Parry, 10, 360
Pask, 264, 265, 359, 368
Perls, 18, 98, 99, 368
Pert, 313, 368
Peters, 2, 62, 71, 72, 141, 149, 165, 166, 167, 168, 169, 173, 175, 228, 359
Petriglieri, v, 23, 372
Piaget, 71, 120, 140, 281, 282, 289, 291, 302, 368
Pine, 71, 119, 140, 367
Pollock, 253, 368
Polster, 67, 70, 229, 231, 368
Poston, 341, 368
Porter-Steele, 273, 276, 277, 279, 317, 368
Price, 273, 287, 368, 369
Pulleyblank, 274, 369

Rank, 38, 369
Raven, 151, 155, 363
Reynolds, 302, 369
Richman, 369
Richo, 326, 369
Roberts, 370
Rogers, 100, 369
Rosch, 267, 369
Rossi, 285, 286, 288, 362
Rowan, v, viii, ix, 15, 16, 98, 233, 253, 272, 286, 288, 302, 311, 323, 328, 330, 369

Ruben, 165, 369
Ryle, 10, 67, 68, 69, 70, 122, 123, 178, 182, 185, 197, 204, 208, 227, 253, 272, 312, 369, See also Anthony Ryle
Ryle and Kerr, 10, 67, 182, 208, 253

Sacks, 61, 369, 370
Said, 370
Salters, 14, 369
Samuels, v, 272, 301, 369
Savary, 276, 365
Schiff, 8, 18, 68, 77, 82, 89, 105, 112, 123, 124, 188, 289, 318, 351, 359, 369
Schiff et. al., 8, 68, 77, 82, 89, 112, 124, 188, 289, 351
Schwartz-Salant, 272, 369
Schwock,, 177, 369
Segal, 294, 369
Shapiro, 313, 370
Shepard, 149, 168, 173, 360
Shepherd, 360
Sills, 9, 10, 17, 18, 25, 169, 171, 278, 362, 363, 364, 369, 370, 371
Silverman, 61, 370
Spitz, 98, 370
Steiner, 12, 18, 38, 68, 86-90, 126, 150, 215, 333, 370
Steinfeld, 294, 314, 317, 370
Stern, 15, 285, 370
Stewart, 2, 6, 9, 18, 36, 37, 39, 61, 63, 70, 77, 82, 83, 115, 132, 133, 135, 136, 191, 274-276, 284, 287, 289, 296, 301, 365, 370
Summers, 9, 17, 18, 32, 370
Symington, 272, 370

Tarthang, 325, 370
Teesdale, 369
Temple, 9, 135, 136, 180, 334, 370
Thomas, 63, 265, 370
Thorne, 272, 371
Tiller, 313, 371
Tilney, 63, 122, 277, 371
Todorovic, 48, 362
Tomkins, 62, 371

Toomela, 68, 371
Trautmann, 83, 98, 101, 114, 116, 123, 125, 312, 363
Tschudi, 227, 371
Tuckman, 371
Tudor, 9, 17, 18, 25, 140, 169, 173, 293, 294, 370, 371
Tulku, 325, 371

van Beekum, 9, 273, 371
van Deurzen-Smith, 272, 371
Vaughan, 30, 31, 56, 274, 326, 330, 371
Vick, 16, 371
Visser, 302, 325, 371
von Bertalanffy, 165, 371
Vygotsky, 68, 303, 371

Wade, 16, 371
Wadsworth, 11, 12, 371
Walsh, 30, 31, 56, 274, 326, 330, 371
Wangyal, 297, 371
Ware, 9, 14, 15, 371
Watkins, 285, 288, 371
Weiss, 8, 371
White, 38, 120, 185, 363, 371
Wilber, 16, 26-35, 55, 103, 120, 135, 138, 260, 266, 272, 273, 276, 277, 279, 281-284, 288-294, 296, 301, 302, 314, 319, 321, 324-326, 344, 346, 347, 362, 371, 372
Williams, 369
Windes, 115, 372
Winter, 10, 220, 372
Wolinsky, 55, 56, 284-286, 292, 293, 294, 325, 335, 372
Wolz, 369
Wood, 23, 372
Woollams, 289, 372
Wyckoff, 18, 372

Zalcman, 8, 9, 40, 120, 186, 194, 196, 204, 233, 300, 304, 363, 372
Zander, 62, 165
Zinker, 99, 372

Subject Index

3Cs, 49, 50, 186, 191, 193, 195, 199, 200, 204, 209, 211, 347, 355, 356, 357
3Rs (Significant Incidents) 234
3Rs (Significant Learning Logs) 254, 263

Active Acceptor, 45, 96, 113-116, 123, 124, 127-130, 136, 250
active role network, 52, 215, 253
adaptation, 154
Adult ego state, 7, 37, 223, 274, 321, 327
alienation, 154
all quadrants – all levels, 31, 35; see also AQAL
Announcer, 45, 46, 113, 115, 116, 127, 129, 130, 133, 136, 137, 143, 158, 234, 235, 250
AQAL, 31, 135, 138, 266, 283, 290
archetypal roles, 302
assertion, 127
attachment, 130
attunement, 124
authentic (style of relating), vi, 17, 271, 285, 328
authority, 24, 45, 48, 94, 115, 138, 140, 145, 149, 150-152, 157-163, 172, 174
autonomy, 5, 54, 56, 102, 115, 124, 149, 151, 271, 273-276, 278, 283, 285, 333, 343
availability of roles, 147
awareness, 32–34

Basic Role Imago Template, 51; see also BRIT
Beholder, 44, 45, 46, 85, 96, 97, 100, 101, 103, 104, 106, 107, 109, 112, 115-117, 123-125, 127-131, 133, 136, 137, 142, 143, 146, 147, 158-160, 169, 178, 210, 229, 232, 242, 250, 294, 304-307, 309, 318, 326
bioenergetics, 294, 336
bodywork, 316–18, 336
brief therapy, 304–311
BRIT, 51-53, 214, 215, 217-223, 225, 232, 239, 249, 259, 260, 261, 262, 332, 333
Bystander, 44-47, 49, 50, 68, 79-83, 85, 95, 96, 100, 101, 103-107, 109-112, 115-117, 121, 123, 124, 128-131, 147, 159, 160, 174, 178, 183, 184, 195, 200, 202, 204, 205, 209-211, 221, 223, 234, 237, 248, 254, 255, 258, 260, 302, 304, 305, 307, 308, 319, 339, 347, 348-352, 354-357, 359

centring, 46, 56, 259, 297, 309, 320, 322, 323, 325-327, 329, 330, 335
challenge, 126
Child ego state, 7, 37, 44, 55, 69, 76, 87, 89, 114, 134, 157, 257, 261, 274, 275, 283, 284, 286, 287, 291, 293, 323, 327, 334, 337, 339, 343, 365, 371
co-existent contact, 46, 99, 101, 107, 146, 159, 160, 230, 231
Cognitive Analytic Therapy, 10, 47, 51, 68, 121, 181, 184, 196, 197, 200, 203, 207, 226, 258, 302, 310, 331, 332
collaborative contact, 46, 99, 101, 107, 146, 159, 160, 230, 231, 263
Communication, 186
compelling contact, 46, 99, 101, 107, 146, 159, 160, 230, 231
Confirmation, 186
consciousness, iv, v, vi, 3, 16, 30-33, 35, 55, 56, 60, 62, 75, 102, 108, 119, 169, 269, 271-274, 277, 278, 280-282, 284, 285, 287-291, 293-301, 310, 318-320, 323, 325, 326, 329, 330, 333-335, 342, 364, 372, 373
contact, iii, iv, vi, 1, 2, 12, 15, 43, 46, 47, 51, 54, 57, 58, 61, 63-65, 67, 72, 73, 83, 86, 87, 93, 95-104, 106-108, 113, 118, 122-124, 127-129, 132-138, 142, 146, 153, 155, 159-161, 168, 174, 175, 181, 186-189, 191, 193, 194, 201, 208, 210, 212, 214, 217-219, 227, 228, 230-232, 240, 252, 253, 256, 257, 259, 260, 262, 263, 271, 272, 294, 295, 304, 318, 320-324, 326-331, 335, 365, 367, 372, 373
Contact Cube, iii, iv, vi, 44-49, 51, 57, 75-79, 98-106, 108, 109, 113, 114, 116, 117, 118, 122, 123, 125, 127-130, 133-138, 141, 143, 147, 149-151, 154, 158, 160, 161, 164, 168, 169, 173-176,

180, 196, 197, 214, 220, 221, 226, 229, 230, 232, 248, 250, 251, 253, 257-260, 262, 263, 293, 302, 304, 305, 309, 310, 320, 325, 326, 329, 330, 331, 333, 335, 337, 339, 340

Contact Cube -as a research tool, 134

Contact Cube - limitations, 134

Contact Cube - parameters, 103–106

Contact Plane, 46, 102, 106, 108, 174, 327, 340

Contact, Communication and Confirmation, 49, 53, 185-188, 195, 198, 221, 332; see also 3Cs

Contextual Role Imago Template, 52, 219, 225, 332; see also cRIT

Conversation Theory, 264

co-operative contact, 46, 99, 101, 107, 146, 159, 160, 230, 231

countertransference, 16, 121, 184, 268, 270, 299, 310

cRIT, 52, 53, 219, 220, 225, 332

Critical Point, 102; see also Contact Plane

current role set, 51, 52, 214, 215, 217, 219, 223, 253

development of ego states, 287-290

Developmental Transactional Analysis, 20

Dialectical Behaviour Therapy, 293

dissociation, 55, 56, 280, 285-287, 291-294, 297, 323-325, 327, 329, 330, 334, 335, 363, 364

distal self, 55, 282, 287, 290, 291, 334

diversity, 6, 11, 13-19, 24-26, 64, 174, 299, 345

diversity/competitive labelling divide, 6, 10, 11, 14

divides, iii, v, vi, 1, 5, 7, 23, 24, 26, 32, 75, 138, 152, 169, 176, 199, 232, 271, 331, 333, see also diversity/competitive labelling, health/pathology, practice/research

Drama Triangle, 37, 39, 41, 47, 67-69, 74, 76-79, 81, 82, 105, 119, 131, 167, 174, 185, 302, 319, 337, 339, 352

dRIT, 53, 54, 220, 221, 225, 227, 232, 253, 256-258, 260-262, 268, 332, 333

Dynamic Role Imago Template, 53, 220, 225; see also dRIT

EFT, 312-316, 319, 322, 335, 370

ego states, 7, 8, 11, 12, 15, 32, 36-38, 41, 48, 55, 69, 70, 71, 72, 74, 76, 89, 109, 128, 131-134, 136, 137, 139, 157, 189, 206, 223, 228, 271, 273, 275, 276, 278, 279, 283, 286-291, 293, 295, 299-301, 323, 329, 333, 334, 337, 339, 346, 352, 354, 359, 362, 364, 366

emotional freedom technique. See EFT

epistemology, 26–30, 266

empowerment, 125

ERICA, iii, iv, 1-3, 30, 32, 33, 35-37, 40, 41, 43, 46, 47, 50-58, 64, 65, 72, 73, 95, 105, 110, 111, 128, 131, 132, 136, 144, 164, 166, 167, 175, 185, 200, 203, 206, 207-210, 228, 230, 232, 252, 257-259, 262-265, 267-270, 293, 297, 298, 300, 302, 304, 309-313, 316, 318-320, 327, 329, 334, 335, 349, 354

executive power, 44, 52, 76, 300, 327

expectations, 141–147

expertise, 157

formalised roles, 43, 48, 65, 141, 150, 154, 160, 167, 174, 218

Formula G, 37-39, 41, 49, 51, 67, 72, 77, 119, 185, 186, 188, 198, 199, 204, 205, 207, 211, 332, 351

frame of reference, 77–78

Functional Fluency Index, 179

grounding, 29, 46, 259, 297, 306, 309, 320, 322, 324-327, 330

group dynamics, 164

group imago, 2, 63, 71, 120, 139-142, 148, 149, 155, 162, 166, 172

group process, 147–149

group therapy, 164–168

group-as-a-whole, 140, 143, 144, 146-149, 162, 165-167, 170

health/pathology divide, 6, 15, 75, 138, 180, 232, 251, 252, 263, 331, 332

historical role set, 51, 91, 215, 218, 219, 221

hypnotherapy, 294

identification, 15, 38, 55, 121, 132, 136, 151, 157, 181, 187, 188, 256, 260, 261, 272, 277, 279, 281, 282-285, 287, 288, 292, 294, 313, 324, 327, 332

imago images, iv, vi, 2, 46, 54, 72, 73, 98, 108, 134, 135, 137, 160, 161, 169, 174, 181, 193, 201, 209, 210, 212, 227-232, 253, 257, 259, 262, 263, 271, 304, 306, 307, 313, 320, 331, 353
imagos, 43, 58, 65, 71, 74, 227, 230
inactive behaviour, 75
indeterminate outcome role sequences, 49, 51, 178, 193, 194, 318, 354; see also IORS
influence, 150, 267-268
inquiry, 123
Institute of Transactional Analysis, 20
instrumental (style of relating) vi, 15, 16, 27, 98, 252, 285, 310, 328, 329
intentionality, 326
internalisation, 157
involvement, 124
IORS, 49, 51, 178, 180, 193, 195, 196, 197, 199, 201, 254, 255, 318, 354
ITAA, 11, 20, 22, 23, 24, 36, 138

Key Points, vi, 4, 24, 34, 65, 73, 106, 116, 135, 162, 174, 197, 210, 225, 230, 261, 269, 278, 290, 297, 318, 329

levels of contact, 122
life position, 41, 49, 63, 72, 86, 110, 119, 121, 123, 124, 142, 181, 193, 201, 227, 230, 295, 304
linking, 273

memes, vi, 48, 337, 342-347
mixed outcome role sequences, 49, 51, 177, 194, 197, 209, 210, 212, 259, 318; see also MORS
MORS, 49, 51, 177, 180, 193, 194-197, 199, 201, 210, 212, 213, 254, 255, 318
mutual OK-ness, 49, 50, 51, 70, 87, 90, 93, 96, 101, 177-179, 188, 190, 193, 194, 197, 206, 266, 331, 332
myths, 76

negative outcome roles sequences, 49-51; see also NORS
networking, 156
neuro-linguistic programming, 294
NORS, 49-51, 177, 180, 183, 185, 188-199, 201, 203-205, 207, 209-213, 254, 255, 300, 302, 305, 318, 347-359

Observer role, iv, 46, 47, 56, 102, 108, 115, 123, 132, 151, 174, 259, 274, 277-279, 282, 285, 287, 294, 299, 318, 320, 323, 325-331, 333, 335, 340, 368
Observer self, iv, 46, 47, 56, 174, 274, 282, 285, 291, 292, 294-296, 322, 327, 329, 334
overall self, 55, 282, 287, 289

paradox of change, 297
Parent ego state, 7, 37, 44, 55, 69, 76, 87, 89, 114, 134, 157, 274, 275, 283, 284, 286, 287, 289, 291, 293, 323, 327, 334, 337, 339
Passive Acceptor, 79, 80, 109-111, 113, 115, 116, 128, 129
Persecutor, 39, 40, 41, 44-46, 49, 50, 68, 70, 76, 79, 82, 83, 85, 93, 94, 95, 100-107, 109-111, 115, 121-123, 127, 131, 133, 159, 160, 177, 181-184, 188, 200, 202, 204, 211, 223, 234, 237, 248, 250, 258, 260, 285, 302, 304, 305, 307, 308, 338, 339, 348-354, 356, 359
Personal Construct theory, 219
personalised roles, 43, 44, 46, 48, 49, 52, 53, 62-65, 70, 71, 74-78, 80, 89, 98, 102, 106, 107, 111-116, 118, 120, 123, 124, 133, 134, 136-141, 144, 146, 147, 149-168, 174-176, 189, 193, 196, 197, 214, 215, 220, 221, 225, 271, 303, 331
PORS, 49, 51, 177, 178, 180, 188, 189-193, 195-199, 209, 210, 212, 254, 255, 302, 318
position (in organisations), 155
positive outcome role sequences, 49, 51, 177, 190, 197, 198, 206, 209, 212, 260, 318; see also PORS
power, 149–151
practice/research divide, 10, 24, 75, 133, 138, 179, 192, 193, 232, 251, 332
proactive behaviour/contact/roles, 43, 46, 60, 65, 71, 73, 75, 99-101, 147, 148, 152, 160, 161, 172, 204, 213, 334
Promoter, 44-46, 79, 86-96, 100-103, 105, 106, 109, 113, 115, 116, 123, 125-127, 129, 130, 136, 137, 159, 160, 173, 192, 229, 234-236, 250, 307, 310
Protester, 45, 46, 80, 109, 110, 113, 115, 116, 129
Provocateur, 45, 46, 96, 113-116,

126-129, 136, 242, 250

proximate self, 55, 282, 287, 291, 295, 334

psychosynthesis, 294

quality of contact, vi, 46, 58, 65, 85, 95-96, 100-102, 120, 137, 146, 155, 159-161, 167, 186-191, 194, 210, 212, 252, 276,-277, 304

Qigong, 311, 337

racketeering, 39, 46, 50, 79, 82, 83, 100, 131, 180, 181, 187, 194, 195, 197, 204, 211, 352, 353, 354, 359

reactive behaviour/contact/roles, 43, 46, 60, 65, 71, 73, 75, 99-101, 107, 160, 161, 170, 204, 303, 380

reciprocal roles, 2, 47, 70, 177, 221, 252, 304, 331

reciprocals, 49, 50, 51, 176-179, 183, 184, 189, 195, 197, 199, 200, 202, 205, 207, 208, 210, 211-214, 226, 227, 229, 238, 252, 257, 260, 262, 263, 268, 271, 304, 309, 318, 320, 331, 332, 347-349, 351-355, 358, 359

reciprocity, 122

relational (style of relating), vi, 17, 32, 97, 120, 232, 271, 285, 310, 328, 344

relationships, iii-vii, 1-5, 11-13, 20-28, 35, 39, 43, 47-51, 58-64, 67-75, 84-90, 95-104, 107, 120, 133-141, 146-147, 154-167, 174-178, 181, 193-197, 200-207, 210, 212-218, 225, 227, 229, 232, 252, 256, 258-264, 268-271, 271, 295, 311, 320, 326, 329-335, 338, 342-345, 354, 360

research, iii-vii, 1-5, 7, 10, 15, 17, 24, 25, 30, 47, 53, 73-75,118, 131-140, 146, 161-163, 167, 172-174, 178-180, 193, 195-197,200-206,210-218,225-232, 251-260, 263, 269, 301-303, 312-314, 318, 319, 331-335, 340, 347, 352, 361

Rescuer, 39, 40, 41, 44-46, 49, 68, 70, 76, 78, 79, 82-86, 95, 100, 101, 103, 106, 107, 109, 111, 115, 116, 121, 123, 125, 127, 129-136, 159, 160, 177, 178, 181-184, 187, 188, 200, 202, 204, 211, 223, 234, 237, 242, 248, 258, 260, 285, 302, 304, 305, 308, 338, 339, 348-354, 356, 359

Resister, 45, 46, 80, 109, 110, 113-115

resources, 150, 152–153

Responder, 44, 45, 46, 79, 83, 84, 85, 86, 95, 100, 101, 103, 106, 107, 109, 113, 115, 116, 122-125, 127-130, 136, 137, 142, 143, 159, 160, 178, 229, 234, 235, 250, 307, 318

role functions, 48, 63, 65, 147, 149, 164, 167, 170, 257, 263, 267, 270, 331

role imago, 2, 51, 53, 54, 63, 125, 132, 138, 142, 176, 197, 207-210, 212, 214, 216, 225, 227, 232, 248, 249, 252, 257, 258, 262, 263, 305, 307, 309, 310, 332

Role Imago Templates, vi, 134, 214, 219, 220, 221, 232, 263, 269, 331

role networks, 51, 52, 87, 214, 215, 225

role profile, 49, 51, 52, 75, 106, 122, 123, 125-127, 132, 133, 135-137, 176, 183, 184, 187, 192-194, 197, 200-202, 214, 219, 229, 237, 248, 250, 253, 258, 260, 305, 306, 310, 318, 331, 356, 359

role sequences, iii, iv, vi, 49, 51, 176-180, 195-198, 201-204, 214, 221, 232, 238, 261-263, 301-309, 320, 326, 331, 333, 347-359

role set, 51, 52, 87, 88, 91, 92, 127, 132, 214, 215, 217-219, 221, 223, 225, 253

role theory, 61–63

roles, 2, 43, 58, 63, 67–71

roles - identificaion, 130–34

rules and procedures, 155

scripts, 36-38, 40, 41, 70, 71, 134, 188, 278, 302, 311, 319, 329

second divide, 9–10

self, 55, 275–278

self as a process, 56, 275, 294-295

Self Supervision Suggestions, vi, 4, 35, 66, 74, 94, 108, 117, 130, 137, 163, 175, 199, 212, 225, 231, 262

Servant, 45, 96, 113-116, 124, 127, 129, 136

Significant Incident, 2, 47, 52-54, 63, 111, 138, 144, 146, 149, 161, 162, 210, 214, 215, 217-221, 225, 228, 229, 232, 238, 239, 241-245, 247-253, 257, 259- 261, 269, 308, 332, 333

Situational Role Profile, 173, 175

situational roles, 43, 65, 167-169, 174, 175

Slave, 45, 80, 109, 110, 113, 115-117
social interaction, 138
social mobility, 156
social organisation, 140
spectrum of consciousness, 32, 55, 280, 280–282, 290, 329, 333
Spiral Dynamics, vi, 163, 341-343

third divide, 10–23
time structuring, 180
trance, 55, 273, 280, 283-287, 291, 292, 294, 306, 307, 310, 329, 334, 364
transactional analysis proper, 36, 41
transference, 15, 19, 37, 57, 121, 165, 184, 268, 270, 299, 304, 310, 361
transpersonal, iv-vi, 1, 26, 27, 30, 33-36, 54-56, 73, 74, 96, 122, 263, 271-274, 277-280, 285, 287, 295, 299, 300-302, 310, 318, 323, 325, 327-330, 333, 335, 368
transpersonal (style of relating), vi, 17, 32, 97, 120, 232, 271, 285, 310, 328, 344

Type One sets, 190
Type Three sets, 191, 210, 212
Type Two sets, 191

United Kingdom Council for Psychotherapy, 7, 20

Valuer, 44-46, 97, 98, 100, 101, 103, 106, 115, 117, 123-125, 127, 129, 130, 133, 136, 137, 142, 143, 159, 160, 228, 229, 234, 235, 242, 250, 318
Victim, 39-41, 44-46, 49, 50, 68, 70, 76, 78, 79, 81-83, 85, 95, 97, 100, 101, 103, 105-107, 111, 115, 117, 121-123, 130-133, 159, 160, 177, 181-184, 187, 188, 200, 202, 204, 211, 223, 229, 234, 235, 237, 248, 250, 258, 260, 285, 302, 304, 305, 338, 339, 347-350, 352-354

witnessing, 39, 46, 55, 56, 131, 133, 137, 259, 278, 289, 292-297, 320, 323-327, 329, 330, 334, 335

"The soul, as I am using the term, is a sort of halfway house, halfway between the personal ego-mind and the impersonal or transpersonal Spirit. The soul is the Witness in you as it shines forth in you and nobody else. The soul is the home of the Witness in that sense. Once you are established on the soul level, then you are established as the Witness, as the real Self. Once you push through the soul level, then the Witness itself collapses into everything witnessed, or you become one with everything you are aware of. You don't witness the clouds, you are the clouds. That's Spirit. …..

In a sense the soul or Witness in you is the highest pointer towards Spirit and the last barrier to Spirit. It is only from the position of the Witness that you can jump into Spirit, so to speak. But the Witness itself eventually has to dissolve or die. Even your own soul has to be sacrificed and released to let go of, or died to, in order for your ultimate identity with Spirit to radiate forth. Because ultimately the soul is just the final contraction in awareness, the subtlest knot restricting universal Spirit, the last and subtlest form of separate-self sense, and that final knot has to be undone. That's the last death as it were. First we die to the material self – that is, disidentify with it – then we die to an exclusive identity with the bodily self, then to the mental self and then finally to the soul. The last one is what Zen calls the Great Death. We make steppingstones out of all our dead selves. Each death to a lower level is a rebirth on a higher level, until the ultimate rebirth, liberation, or enlightenment ….

It is true that the Witness is not identified with the ego or any other mental object, it just impartially witnesses all that it witnesses. But that's just it: the Witness is still separate from all the objects it witnesses. In other words, there is still a very subtle form of the subject/object dualism. The Witness is a huge step forward, and it is a necessary and important step in meditation, but it is not ultimate. When the Witness or the soul is finally undone, the Witness dissolves into everything that is witnessed. The subject/object duality collapses and there is only nondual awareness, which is very simple, very obvious. Like a famous Zen master said when he got his enlightenment, "When I heard the bell ring, suddenly there was no "I" and no "bell", just the ringing". Everything continues to arise, moment by moment, but there's nobody divorced or alienated from it. What you are looking out of is what you are looking at. There is no separation between subject and object, there is just the ongoing stream of experience, perfectly clear and luminous and open. What I am now is what is arising. Remember that great quote from Dogen: "To study mysticism is to study self; to study the self is to forget the self; to forget the self is to be one with, and enlightened by, all things". (Wilber, 1991, pp. 102 -103)

There is a looker-on who sits behind my eyes. It seems he has seen things in ages and worlds beyond memory's shore, and those forgotten sights glisten on the grass and shiver on the leaves. He has seen under new veils the face of the one beloved, in twilight hours of many a nameless star. Therefore his sky seems to ache with the pain of countless meetings and partings, and a longing pervades this spring breeze – the longing that is full of the whisper of ages without beginning.

I will meet one day the Life within me, the joy that hides in my life, though the days perplex my path with their idle dust.

I have known it in glimpses, and its fitful breath has come upon me making my thoughts fragrant for a while.

I will meet one day the Joy without me that dwells behind the screen of light – and will stand in the overflowing solitude where all things are seen by their creator.

Rabindranath Tagore